GANGS

A GUIDE TO UNDERSTANDING STREET GANGS

5th Edition

Al Valdez, PhD

Law Tech Publishing

Law Tech Publishing

Tel: (800) 498-0911

Fax: (949) 498-4858

email: Gangs@LawTechPublishing.com

www.LawTechPublishing.com

Comments and suggestions are welcome.

v.5e. 062609

pp 528

(4th Ed. published under ISBN's: **1-563250-78-0** & **978-1-563-078-1**)

ISBN: **978-1-56325-147-4**

About The Author

Al Valdez is currently a professor at the University of California, Irvine and adjunct professor at California State University, Long Beach and for Argosy University. He retired from the Orange County (California) District Attorney's Office in 2006. He has over 28 years law enforcement experience with special emphasis on narcotic and gang investigations, undercover field operations, multi-agency task forces and prosecutions.

Al is a nationally recognized trainer and consultant in the areas of youth violence, gang sociology and behaviors, gang investigations/prosecutions, parent/teacher awareness issues, prevention/intervention models and occult/ritual crimes. He is on staff at several local community colleges where he designs and teaches advanced officer/supervisor training programs. Al is also a consultant to the California and U.S. Departments of Justice, as well as the U.S. Military and the Bureau of Alcohol, Tobacco, Firearms and Explosives and for the Customs Border Patrol agency. He has instructed nationwide for criminal justice professionals at the local, state and federal levels.

Al has written over 89 articles and 6 books on gang histories, customs and practices and related issues. He also authored the *Community Response to Gangs* monograph for the California Attorney General's office.

Al has also earned Bachelor of Science degrees in Biology and Chemistry, a Master's degree in Law and Criminal Justice and his Ph.D. in Psychology. Al was also selected the 2001 District Attorney Investigator of the Year for the state of California and was the 2005 Award recipient for Educational Achievement from the Asian Gang Investigators Association of California. In 2009 Al was selected as the Professor of the Year by the Greek Society at the University of California, Irvine.

Acknowledgments

There are so many people that have contributed to this book that to list them all would be another book. So to all of you who have contributed in anyway "thank you." However, special thanks is needed to all the gang investigators, probation/parole officers, prosecutors, community outreach workers, parents and teachers who deal with gang members. The community will benefit from your commitment and sadly you may not be recognized for your work, so thank you. A special thank all military service personnel who have served our country, whether retired or active duty you sacrifices are not forgotten and appreciated.

A special thank you to Joanna Do who edited portions of this book. You are a great friend and colleague.

This book also contains material from interviews of gang members who wished to remain anonymous and from specialized training seminars I have attended.

To Margaret
and for those who serve their family, the public, the government.

Foreword

My personal library contains every book I could find about gangs and no other author provides the detail and personal touch that Dr. Al Valdez does. Al has a passion for sharing his experience from many years of investigating gangs, and a knack for sharing this knowledge in an unbiased, very readable way. This most recent edition promises to be even more comprehensive than the last. I am confident that it will complement many a library — not only for those who work with gangs on a daily basis and those who study them, but also for parents, teachers, and community leaders who want to figure out what is happening in their community. This book should be required reading for all criminal justice majors and minors. Al's work continues to impress me. I know where he got the experience — I'm not sure where he gets the energy!

Carter F. Smith, J.D., Author, Criminal Justice Professor, US Army CID Special Agent (Ret)

Preface

As you begin your study of gangs you will ultimately determine it is the behaviors, customs and practices that characterize all types of gangs. You will quickly note that all gangs share many of the same behaviors even though they may be expressed uniquely. This book attempts to give you the genesis and history of a few of the larger better-known gangs to be illustrations of these unique but shared behaviors. They are not mentioned to glorify gang activity, but rather to better understand the affect that culture and history has had on gang development in the United States and the world.

Street gangs tend to form as a result of bias, racism and class distinction. These three social factors appear to be root causes that facilitate gang formation. Whether perceived or real these social factors exerted and continue to exert an influence on people who live is this country. There are many reasons why youth join gangs; but basically they begin with an excluded group. That is why there is no "one size fits all" solution. Gangs are a complex issue that includes recruitment, culture and criminal behaviors motivated by membership. To combat street gangs effectively suppression, intervention and prevention programs are needed. To be successful intervention and prevention models should also be gender, age, culturally sensitive.

By 2009 the color of all gangs has become green. Money appears to motivate much of the gang related crime encountered in the world. What appears to be at the center of much of this gang related violence is drug, arms and human trafficking along with the trafficking of pirated materials and money laundering. Street gangs are a ready-made trafficking network for criminal groups involved in these activities.

Street gangs are function of demographics, geography and community dynamics. Therefore it becomes easier to understand why communities should not compare their gang issues with other communities. Every community is different yet there appears to be a common thread that links all gangs together and makes them similar. That common thread is the behaviors, customs and practices shared by all gangs.

There are a number of different types of gangs, but as you will learn American gang behaviors have become the template for worldwide gang behaviors. There are a number of mechanisms that have contributed to the globalization of American gang behaviors. These can include music, movies written media, migration, deportation, criminal activities and news reports. Technology has facilitated globalization, especially the Internet and cellular telephones. Gangs can also be involved in non-violent crime such as check fraud, identity theft, mail theft, counterfeit identification and insurance fraud. To truly understand the gang phenomenon you have look at gang histories and impact of world events that helped shaped the gangs we encounter today.

Contents

Contents

Contents

Contents

Contents

Contents

Contents

Contents

Chapter 1

Overview

This chapter will talk about gang behaviors and sociology that is common among all street, prison and outlaw motorcycle gangs. It is ultimately the behaviors that can be used to diagnose whether or not a n individual is a gang member or an incident is gang related.

American Street Gangs

American street gang behavior has been documented since the colonial America developed. Modern day street gangs first formed in the New York during the 1800s. Gangs of yesteryear share many behaviors with the gangs of the 21st century. History helped formed modern day gang behaviors.

Street Gangs

If you think about it, originally the word gang had no bad connotations. In Old English, the word simply meant a number of people who went around together. Today, the word takes on a totally different meaning. As you have probably already concluded, gangs form, grow, migrate and change for a number of different reasons.

The term gang has also been given many definitions including a group with an organized leader; a group whose members show unity through clothing and language and a group whose activities are criminal or threatening to society. These definitions have been based on what the gang does and how the members look. No definition will include information on the origin or development of a street or prison gang. A look at American history will help us understand why today's street and prison gangs operate the way they do. The history of U.S. street gangs really contains answers to questions that are seldom asked and may also give clues that identify youth at risk for gang membership. For example, how do you think you would answer the following question? Do you think today's gang violence is based on behaviors that began in the early 1900s?

Historically, the earliest form of gangs in the United States developed because of class distinction, bias and racism. During the early 1800s gang members tended to come from the lower socio-economic strata and from the same ethnic and/or race background. Class distinction caused bias and prejudice to develop and allowed a group-solidarity to form. Bias and prejudice also tended to act as a catalyst to organize those it was directed at. The end result was that the targeted group of people developed a dislike, distrust and hatred toward the other group. In other words, a rivalry formed between the two groups. These attitudes only solidified the bond between the members and potential members of both groups. As these feelings intensified, so did the rivalry. Ultimately, this led to violence between the groups.

Class distinction, bias and racism also helped to cultivate an "us verses them" attitude between those groups. Whether real or perceived this attitude becomes a mechanism that contributes to the formation of street gangs. A retired sergeant from the Los Angeles County Sheriff's Department stated that: *The breeding ground for all gangs begins with an excluded group, who feel victimized by poverty, or the establishment, or some other type of injustice, whether real or imagined. It is fed by an anti-establishment culture of drugs, crime, hate and racial separatism"* (Valdemar, 1996).

In late 1999, I was being helped at a local law enforcement agency front counter. I was picking up some crime scene photographs. A man walked up behind me, interrupted my conversation with the police clerk and said, *"I am Captain ____ from the ____ Sheriff's Department, how much longer do I have to wait out here with the common folk before I get escorted to the meeting?"* His tone was bit demanding and condescending. The receptionist replied that the meeting attendees were being escorted one at a time and he would have just a short wait. The Captain walked away in a huff, without even saying pardon for the interruption. Subtle forms of class distinction can been found everywhere today.

Historically, some of the earliest identified groups with gang-like behaviors surprisingly formed after the Revolutionary war in 1793. The Smiths Vly Gang, the Bowery Boys and the Broadway Boys all had White members. The first African-American gangs were known as the Long Bridge Boys and the Fly Boys. Remember this was colonial America during the late 1700s (Osman, 1992).

At that time, all members of these groups were not criminals and age-wise, the majority of members were in their early teens and twenties. Another unique fact about these gangs was that all the members were not from the same economic class.

However, the majority of the membership was from the poorer classes. Most, but not all members were from the same race or ethnic background, a phenomenon still seen today in some street gangs. These early proto-street gangs became the first in a long gang lineage that ended up establishing customs, practices and behavior expectations for the next generation of street gangs. Customs and practices that society attempts to deal with currently.

Criminal Street Gangs

The first modern day street gangs appeared in the early 19th century. The most famous were the Irish street gangs that formed in New York and membership was comprised of Irish immigrants. Even during this early segment of U.S. gang history you can identify indicia of membership that is still used today to aid in the identification of gang members. For example, the Irish gangs had developed a particular dress code; they used monikers (nicknames) and most associated in one area of New York known as Five Points (turf).

Some early street gangs even had formal leadership. For example, in 1826, the Forty Thieves was the first Irish street gang to have a recognized leader. It was Edward Coleman. He also organized the gang. Initially the gang formed to rebel against the low social status and prejudice shown toward the Irish immigrants. In the end, the gang members turned to crime for profit to relieve their frustration. The younger Irish immigrant members also formed a sub-set or clique of the gang, called the Little Forty Thieves. This was based on the on the age of the member. Clique or set formation is still encountered and can be based on age or the geographical location of the sub-set.

During this time additional street gangs also developed in the Bowery section of New York. The Bowery area gangs and the Forty Thieves became bitter rivals and routinely fought over turf and ethnic differences. This behavior should sound familiar because it still occurs between street gangs and has been the cause of countless gang related deaths and injuries.

Another Irish gang formed in the Five Points area during this time. Membership in the Kerryonians was limited to those who could who trace their ancestry back to County Kerry, Ireland, the original home of the Irish immigrants who established the gang (Osman, 1992). We encounter the same kind of membership philosophy today in many of the Skinhead gangs and white supremacist groups. Members must be able to trace their White heritage and keep it pure as a gang requirement. The development of some Mexican street gangs in the Los Angeles area also followed this membership philosophy. No mixed-race Mexicans were allowed to join certain gangs. Prejudice and bias within a particular ethnic group is not a new phenomenon.

By the mid 1800s Chinese gangs appeared in California. Remember how the Chinese railroad workers were abused? Class distinction was again the motivation for the formation of the first Chinese gangs. Another example of how gangs form for protection and out of frustration formed from bias and racism.

The development of early street gangs dates back as far as a decade before the civil war of 1861. During this time street gang membership swelled in New York. New York street gangs were literally out of control, partially due to corruption in the city government. At one time, the street gangs robbed stores and businesses, burned ballot boxes and even attacked and robbed citizens in their homes. Home invasion style robberies were born a lot earlier than we all thought. This was all done without fear of police interference.

The City of Brotherly Love, Philadelphia reported gang activity as early as 1840. Between that time and 1870, Philadelphia was the home to over 100 street gangs. Murder had become a test of toughness for these gang members and drug use became part of street gang life. Cocaine, morphine and laudanum were the main drugs of abuse. Laudanum was a liquid containing alcohol and opium, or a solid preparation containing opium. With the introduction of drug use, gang violence escalated. Gang drug trafficking and use is still a major problem.

In 1998, The National Drug Intelligence Center, Pennsylvania, published a report showing the results they compiled after surveying 500 law enforcement agencies. The executive summary stated: "...*of the 1,250 gangs identified as significant by the respondents, 78 % were involved in local drug transactions, 77 % were involved in assaults and 57 % were involved in street crimes.*" When asked what drugs were mentioned the most, the respondents indicated cocaine and heroin. Sadly, there is nothing new about the connection between gangs, drugs and violence.

After the Civil War ended in 1865, historical records indicated the presence of Jewish, Italian, African-American and Irish street gangs in New York. As immigrant populations increased, so did the gang populations. At one time or another, New York became the operations center for many gangs, including the forerunners of some La Cosa Nostra type organized crime families. Something else was noted after the Civil War. The Whyos of Five Points became the first street gang suspected of using murder as a membership requirement (Osman, 1992).

It should be no surprise that major cities have become the home bases for some gangs. In fact, street gangs now have a presence in all 50 states, Canada, Mexico, Japan, England and Europe. American type gang activity has also been reported in Europe, Africa, and the Middle East and in Australia. The American gang culture has been exported world wide. The globalization of some gangs is now a reality.

There were several identified ways to join a street or prison gang. Committing a violent crime or murder to fulfill membership requirements is not uncommon. Today, many prison gangs have the same requirement for membership. By this time many street gangs had also started to develop distinctive styles of clothing to show membership. For example, some gangs identified with special jackets.

Modern Day Gangs

During the early 1900s, major cities on the east and west coasts experienced a rapid population growth. At the same time the rich got richer and the poor got poorer. Another type of class distinction had formed, this time based on the amount of money you had, rather than heritage. As the U.S. headed into the Great Depression era, the economy worsened and street gangs developed in many poor neighborhoods. To complicate matters further, there was a wide spread use of firearms. The country also experienced a migration to cities from rural areas. The big cities offered limited employment opportunities, but at least there was a chance to find a job.

Mexican street gangs were already established in the Los Angeles area by this time. In the mid 1920s the city of Chicago reportedly had over 1300 street gangs and more than 25,000 gang members. Although there is no way to verify this data, anecdotal evidence suggests that there were many active street gangs in Chicago during this time period. In fact, some Chicago street gangs had an all White membership. Increasingly, gang warfare was based along racial, ethnic and cultural lines. Some parts of Chicago literally became a gang war zone. New York continued to experience the appearance of new street gangs and new levels of violence. During the 1920s African-American populations migrated to the north and west. This migration partially aided in the formation of early L.A. based African-American street gangs during the 1920s.

New immigrant populations had a continual effect on the development of street gangs during this period. A good example of this effect can be found during World War II. Between 1941 and 1945 during the war, over a half a million Puerto Rican immigrates entered the United States. Most settled in New York, which was their port of entry. Currently, The Latin Kings is one of the largest street gangs that still operate in the New York area and gang membership is based from the Puerto Rican population. In the last 20 years, the U.S. has received immigrant and refugee populations from countries like, Southeast Asia, Russia, Cuba, Mexico and Central America. In many instances these populations were treated the same way the Irish were when they arrived. Therefore, it should be of no surprise to note that within those immigrant populations ethnic youth street gangs developed.

World War II marked another milestone for street gang activity. In 1943 during the war, the now famous Zoot Suit Wars between the Mexican street gangs and military personnel occurred in Los Angeles. The conflict with U.S. military personnel actually helped to establish new standards for gang behaviors. Street gang members began to develop certain guidelines or street rules to follow. Basically, a gang ethic was forming, especially for Mexican street gangs. This is another factor that influenced gang development. A gang rivalry had formed between the Mexican street gangs and a common enemy. The enemy was the U.S. military personnel in Los Angeles county waiting to be sent overseas. The police were also disliked. When the war ended the country experienced the greatest era of gang growth and activity ever seen.

For the Los Angeles based street gangs the military presence was gone. With no common enemy, the Mexican gangs turned on themselves, but still distrusted and hated the police. Gang fighting rose to an all time high in cities like New York, Philadelphia, Boston, Chicago, Los Angeles, Detroit and Cleveland. Many of these gang members were in their early teens. By this time street gangs had also developed well-defined dress codes, expected and anticipated behaviors, a gang slang and rules of conduct. Part of the rules of conduct was based on respect and revenge. Gang members were and still are compelled to get even with the gang or gang member that disrespected them or their gang. Usually, this pay back was done in an escalated manner. This behavior is now a standard for retaliatory responses to disrespect.

Remember the term rumbling? It was used when gangs fought each other. Other terms used to describe a gang fight were bopping and jitterbugging. Today, you might hear terms like "taking care of business", "playing" or "gang banging" that are used to describe gang conflict. Gang members at one time used homemade weapons like baseball bats, knives and guns as tools of the trade. Unfortunately, today guns have become the weapons of choice for street gangs. Because of this concept of an escalated retaliation, many people die as a result of gun violence. As gang members say now, "we are strapped," which means they are carrying a gun. Sadly, it has been estimated that nationally, 50 percent of the people who die in gang related gun violence are innocent bystanders.

During the late 1940s and 1950s, most gang violence was motivated over turf battles and girls. Many gang members thought it was important to protect the honor of their girlfriends and well as their gang's reputation. Many gang members commonly used drugs like alcohol, marijuana and heroin. Currently, alcohol and marijuana continue to be the most popular drugs of abuse for gang members. Today, gang members also worry about their personal and gang respect.

The post war era also brought forth a couple of new type of gangs. Between 1956 and 1957 California's first prison gang formed and developed within the state prison system. Prison gangs had been identified in other states since the early 1930s. Prison gangs recruited their members from the ranks of street gangs. Prison gang membership was and still is racially polarized. In another post war phenomenon, some U.S. military personnel who could not adapt to the post war civilian life and started a new lifestyle. As a result, the west coast saw the appearance of the first motorcycle gang. Today, there are over 1200 different outlaw motorcycle gangs in the United States and Canada.

The East Coast in the 1950s saw the formation of fighting gangs in New York, Boston, Chicago, Detroit and Cleveland. These gangs had unique names like the Mau Maus, Dragons, Enchanters and Tigers. The gangs roamed the streets of the city and fought each other and committed crimes. Teenagers usually made up the membership. Surprisingly the gangs were formally organized and leaders had titles such as president, captain and warlord. Fighting was the primary activity and black leather jackets were the uniform of the day (Osman, 1992).

The first American female street gangs can be traced back to the 1860s, but by the late 1950s female gangs appeared to be well established. Early on, these female gangs were closely associated with a particular male gang. They acted in a manner that made them more like assistants, rather than independent gangs. The 1950s presence of females in street gangs was not a brand new phenomenon, but simply an expansion of one. In New York, by 1961, the New York City Youth Board reported approximately 6000 female gang members (Osman, 1992).

Street gang evolution can be a reaction to social pressures, national and international events. The 1960s brought a new influence on street gangs. During this time the U.S. entered the Vietnam conflict, experienced the new drug culture and witnessed the civil rights movement. This led to an over all decrease in gang growth and gang related violence.

Nevertheless, some new gangs did form. Some of the Folk Nation gangs were beginning to establish themselves in Chicago, The Black Panthers was established in Oakland, California in 1968 and the Young Lords, a Puerto Rican gang formed in New York during the early 1970s. In the late 1960s and early 1970s, the occult movement started to gain momentum and the now well-known Crip and Blood gangs started to form in Los Angeles County. At the same time, the Jamaican street gangs appeared in the southeast and eastern portion of the country. Some of the early academic studies around 1960 suggested that gangs were present in only 58 cities across the country. Ironically, 10 years later, only 101 cities nationally reported the presence of street gangs (Klein, 1995).

By 1972 gang violence started to increase again. Street gangs were growing in number and membership size. These gangs also had a tendency to be increasingly more violent. Firearms became the weapon of choice for many street gang members. Guns give a person instant and absolute power and control over others. Juvenile gang members were sometimes used to commit violent crimes because they would be sentenced differently from adults. The United States then experienced another wave of Mexican immigrants and in the mid 1970s started to receive the first wave of Southeast Asian immigrants.

By the mid 1970s to early 1980s law enforcement agencies across the country responded to this wave of violence by forming specialized gang suppression units. Other criminal justice agencies also followed suit. Parole, Probation, Corrections and District Attorneys Offices started to develop gang units. There was also a concerted effort between communities, law enforcement and the judicial system to curb gang violence. As a result many gang leaders went to prison.

The Skinhead gangs made their appearance during this time. Originally, the skinhead dress style was only associated with a certain type of music. However, by the late 1970s the white supremacist philosophy and a particular type of punk rock-heavy metal music were clearly associated with the skinhead movement. Simultaneously, the People Nation gangs made their presence known in the streets of Chicago. These gangs were the rivals of Folk Nation gangs.

By 1980, even with the high level of gang violence and massive criminal justice response, only 197 cities nationally reported the presence of street gangs (Klein, 1995). Nobody wanted to admit the presence of street gangs in their community. Denial and under-reporting of the gang problem by some politicians, law enforcement, policy forming, school and public officials, was overwhelming. Gangs developed new street tactics to assault each other. Drive-by shootings became commonplace. A new drug also appeared on the streets, methamphetamine. It rapidly gained in popularity and competed with the new way to use cocaine, crack. The mid 1980s gave birth to the crack wars between rival drug dealing Blood and Crip gangs. The drug market also helped establish some unique relationships between rival gang members. Crack addiction spread like a flu virus throughout the country.

Our country's drug appetite still continues to influence unique alliances between street gangs that were once bitter rivals with other. The business of drug trafficking means these groups can expand their sales turf, move more products and ultimately make more money. Drug trafficking tends to become the primary source of income for gang members who become involved in the business (HIDTA, 2005).

The first Indo-Chinese street gangs were forming in the west coast by the late 1970s to early 1980s. At first, our communities did not acknowledge the Indo-Chinese street gangs because the membership did not share many if any of the characteristics of known west coast street gangs. Within a few years, Indo-Chinese street gangs started to be influenced by their Western counterparts and started to use unique membership indicia. Female Southeast Asian gangs appeared shortly after that. Sometimes Indo-Chinese gangs are referred to as Southeast Asian.

The mid to late 1980s brought the arrival of many undocumented El Salvadorian, Haitian and Honduran immigrants into America. This only added to the gang populations and the formation of new gangs. Undocumented immigrants found it difficult, if not impossible to find consistent work, which made them prime candidates to be victimized by the local gangs or for street gang membership. In fact, some undocumented immigrants formed gangs to protect themselves against the established street gangs. The first Stoner gangs were formed in Southern California around this time (Valdemar, 1996).

The late 1980s brought the birth of the Tagger and Party Crews to the west coast. The tagging phenomenon actually can be traced back to World War II. It developed in the New York area around 1970 and by the late 1980s spread throughout the country. Today, tagging has now become an international problem.

By this time, street gangs were no longer only a big city problem. They had spread to smaller cities, suburbs and to rural America. Many street gangs compromised school security and safety because gang members no longer considered school campuses neutral turf. Between 1985 and early 1990 crack cocaine sales and use reaches an all time high within the Unites States. The homicide rate in the United States reached 440 per 100,000 persons between 1974 and 1997. Between 1924 and 1974 it was only 110 per 100,000 persons (US Department of Justice, 1999).

By 1990, gang migration started to play a bigger role in the formation of gangs outside California. Members from the Los Angeles based Hispanic gang; 18th Street migrated out of California. They were actively trying to recruit new members to try and set up drug franchise operations for their gang. Sureno street gangs were starting to form in many states. These Sureno gangs claimed a Southern California origin. In 1992, surprisingly, only 796 cities in America reported the presence of street gangs (Klein, 1995).

Also by mid 1990, Sureno gangs could be found in the Southwest, Northwest, South, Native-American lands and in the Midwest. Hybrid gangs were formally recognized. These gangs had broken the race and gender membership barriers. This allowed for quick growth in membership and unique relationships to form with other gangs. Tagging and Party crew membership started to decline, but these gangs still exist today. A few street gangs started to recruit new members from these alternative gang groups. For example, the 18th Street gang was known to jump in members from tagging crews. This not only allowed 18th Street to increase its' membership, but gave the tagging crew access to a large number of gang member back ups. In 1996, only 1,100 cities in the country reported the presence of street gangs (Howell and Decker, 1998).

To try and help control the increasing violence and criminal activity associated with the growing gang problem; in the mid to late 1990s undocumented immigrant gang members were deported back to their country of origin, after completion of their local or state prison sentences. This practice helped local law enforcement, but only introduced versions of L.A. based street gangs into Central America and Mexico. For example, 18th Street and Mara Salvatrucha became this nation's first international Hispanic street gangs. Both gangs are now established in Canada, Mexico, El Salvador, Guatemala, Costa Rica and the Honduras. Don't forget American type street gang behaviors and activity has been reported in England, Australia, New Zealand, Africa and Japan. The gang culture has clearly been exported throughout the world.

By 1997, a few Los Angeles based street gangs had also established themselves nationally. For example, the 18th Street gang could be found in Alaska, Colorado, Texas, Oklahoma, Florida, Ohio, Iowa, Nevada, Oregon, Washington, New Mexico, Idaho and California, a total of 13 states and four countries. Even with the growing awareness, only 2,100 cities in the nation reported the presence of street gangs in 1997.

By late 1998, no one could deny the impact of the modern street gangs. Gangs were now reported in every state of the union, in the military, in law enforcement, in private business and on Native American lands. Some believed that gang migration from California caused this gang culture to spread within the country. This is simply not true. Even though there are a number of identified gang migration mechanisms, gang migration accounted and still accounts for a small percentage of new gang formation.

What was exported throughout the country and world between 1989 and 1999 was the gang culture. This was done with the help of the music and movie industries, through the written and video media and the Internet. With instant communication across the country, citizens could watch TV and see violent crime or police pursuits, in real time. The concepts of what a gang member does, how one should be dressed, and how one should act were spread nationally and internationally. In essence, the gang culture was electronically spread to every state and throughout the world. Add to this, the other factors of urban decay, the drug trade, bias, prejudice, boredom, the use of guns and poverty and it should be no surprise to anyone by the year 2005, the United States would be home to an estimated 2 million gang members (Valdez, 2003).

The street gang sub-culture continues to be very dynamic and changes constantly. For example, some gang members currently use the World Wide Web to communicate and challenge rival gang members. All street gangs share common, but unique characteristics with each other. The following chapters attempt to give an examination of youth violence in our country and then a closer look at the characteristics, behaviors, customs and practices of street and prison gangs. A brief history of the country's major gangs is then presented; to demonstrate the unique relationships between bias, class distinction and racial membership barriers.

Gangs can also set street trends, so what will street gangs be like in 2010? School safety and gang violence have become important issues for our children and educators. What can schools; parents and students do to combat the gang influence? Are Goths believers in Witchcraft or Satanism? The gang-drug connection has been around for a long time, but what kind of drugs are being used and sold? The T.A.R.G.E.T. model is a nationally recognized suppression program, why does it work? As more gang members go to prison, what kind of impact will be placed on corrections?

I have attempted to give you some answers to these questions in this book. More importantly, you will quickly appreciate the complexity and violent nature of the gang culture and the unique behaviors that are associated with it. Street gangs are not a recent or new phenomenon, just the evolution of one that has been around for more than two centuries. After reading this book, you will determine that gang membership is really demonstrated through behavior. It is not necessarily what a person wears or what tattoos are worn and it is not the age, race or even baggy clothes that make a person a gang member. Gang activity and membership is motivated by a particular code of street ethics. One of the main codes is based on respect. Unfortunately, in today's world respect for gang members is based on fear.

It is the voluntary acceptance of these street codes that becomes the basis for behavior rules and practices that encourages violent acts and then rewards them with respect. It is easy to conclude why this country has experienced the street gang phenomenon for such a long time. It is also logical to conclude that street gangs may impact the quality of life for many Americans.

Summary

In order to understand American street gangs you have to have a good understanding of the history of American street gangs and the social factors that affect the formation of gangs. Every street gang in the country began from an immigrant or excluded group and initially formed for protection against existing living conditions. As the gang matured some members resorted to violence to settle disputes.

Gang Violence

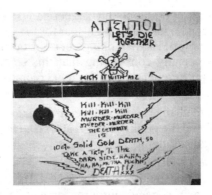

You will find that gang violence is unpredictable and most likely a result of random or chance encounters between rival gangs. There are many factors which affect the level of gang related violence in America. Gang violence may be cyclic in nature and may be impacted by factors normally not associated with gang activity and membership.

There are many theories why the nation encounters varying levels of gang related violence. Generally, the country experiences cycles of violence naturally, therefore gang related violence maybe related to these cycles. However, academic research and anecdotal law enforcement evidence tend to support the hypothesis that gang crime is also related to a number of other sociological conditions. So, let's look at some of these other suspected factors.

Youth Crime

Youth crime and violence are two topics that have become national concerns. During the 1990s the nation experienced a tremendous increase in crime, violence and death, especially within our juvenile population. Frankly, America's youth were dying at an alarming rate. The Center for Disease Control (CDC) even listed violence as a leading cause of death for the nation's youth. Throughout the country, cities of all sizes were seeing youth bringing loaded guns to school, and using deadly violence to settle disputes.

Between 1999 and 2001 the nation experienced a slight decrease and then leveling off of violent crimes committed by youth. This decrease is most likely the result of natural cycles, demographic changes, poverty levels and the number juveniles in America. There is no way to totally predict crime rates or changes accurately because of the complexity of our society. A slight decrease or increase in crime rates may influence how resources are utilized, however the rate changes may not be indicative of a developing shift or trend.

Part of the wave of violence that is still encountered is associated with gang sub-culture. Gang violence has become a national and international issue. The fear of being victimized by a gang has even dictated how many people live, what they wear or where they socialize. Gang violence and crime have now become a primary concern for the majority of us who live in the United States.

Every year it seems the nation is setting new records for the number of people killed or injured by gang gun violence. This includes innocent children, adults, students, criminal justice professionals and gang members who all can become victims of gang-gun violence. Since the early 1990s, the gun has been the instrument of choice for gang members to use in violent confrontations. Many law enforcement experts assert there are an unprecedented number of firearms available on the street and they are so easy to get that anyone can buy them. This includes elementary and high school age children. Guns have been confiscated from students on college campuses. In December, 2005 the San Bernardino County Sheriff's department reported that guns were used in more than 85 percent of the gang related homicides in California (Cruz, 2005).

In many cities and towns all over the country street gangs seem to control specific areas. Many of the residents who live and visit these areas fear for their safety. Ad hoc studies suggest that gang membership accounts for less than one percent of our total population. This unique fact is startling and ironic, especially considering that this small percentage of the nation's population directs the distribution of such a large percentage of our law enforcement, educational, judicial, medical, prevention, intervention resources and how many people live.

Gang trends will continue to change and it will be difficult to predict exactly what is in store for the criminal justice system and the public in the year 2010. However, there are some general trends that may be indicators helpful to assess future gang activities. One trend is gang migration.

The street gangs have now appeared in small towns and rural America. Some gang experts have quarreled over whether or not gang migration or gang imitation is at the root of the increased national and international gang activity. Early, academic research suggested that gang migration had little if any influence on the formation of street gangs within the United States (Klein, 1989). This observation may have been accurate during the 1980's but does not seem to be the current trend. The globalization and nationalization of street gangs has impacted gang migration. The use of technology seems to be driving this phenomenon (Valdez, 2006).

Media Influence

Some experts argue that the entertainment industry has glorified the gang lifestyle with movies and through music. About a year after the movie *Colors* was released, law enforcement in southern California noted the existence of Hybrid type gangs, similar to those depicted in the movie. Was the movie the cause? No one will ever be able to argue that case successfully. However, interviews with hundreds of gang members suggest one thing, these gang members identified with the movie characters, and some believed that the gang life style shown in the movie really represented their lives.

What is important is that these gang members said they identified with the violence displayed in the movies. What these gang members have suggested is that the ruthlessness of the violent acts displayed in the movies becomes the standard for their actions. For some gang members the movies feed a hunger or curiosity to experience violence vicariously. A few gang members have even confided to me that the movies also seem to justify their own personal use of violence. To them, the fictional movies are a reflection of their lives, a sort of unauthorized biography.

Gang members who listen to violent gangster rap music have commented the lyrics represent their lifestyle and how they feel about society, women and the police. Often, these lyrics speak of violent police confrontations, murder and physical abuse of women. The gangster mentality and ideal lifestyles are represented in the song lyrics for many gang members, whether or not the artist is involved in the sub-culture. And like gang members who identify with the characters in gangster movies, some gang members identify with gangster rap artists, whether they are real gang members or not.

Music can have a tremendous impact on a person. Remember the movie *Top Gun*? In many of the scenes the music enhanced the action and viewer participation. The flying scenes with the music motivated many viewers. The final air combat scene would not have had the impact without the music. Everyone remembers the theme song to *Jaws*. Whenever you hear that music, what images immediately come to mind?

Music can affect attitude and behavior. Tom Metzger, a well-known white supremacist once said that music is the greatest propaganda tool for young people. He had a belief that song lyrics in the racist music helped influence and spread the belief in white supremacy, especially to young people. Music might be used as a recruitment tool, spread the culture medium and for motivational purposes. The effect of gangster rap music has even been used as a defense in the murder of a Texas state trooper. The accused stated that the gangster rap music he was listening to caused him not to act normally.

How far has gangster rap influenced life? Some foreign music artists have adopted the gangster rap style and put racist lyrics in the music. These artists present the first skinhead-white supremacists gangster rap (U.S. News and World Report, 2006).

Demographics

Another factor that may influence the levels of gang violence we see in the future is demographics. The country's population demographics have and will continue to change. Predictions indicate that by the year 2014, Whites will comprise about 60% of the U.S. population, down from 80% in 1980 (U.S. News and World Report, 1996). The major demographic changes will obviously be within the Asian, Black and Hispanic populations. As population demographics shift within the United States so will the street gang membership and gang related criminal activity. Gang membership and the type of gangs that form are a function of demographics and geography (Valdez, 2002).

For example, a November, 2005 newspaper reported that by 2020 California will be more crowded, the state's population older and demographically Hispanics would be the majority. By 2020, "one in seven Californians will be 65 years or older; the state will add 10 million residents and Hispanics will account for 43 percent of the population with Whites accounting for about 34 percent" (Inland Valley News, 2005).

Hybrid gangs have now been documented in many parts of the country. These gangs have broken the race and gender membership barriers and for some of these gangs the concept of turf can be fluid. For example, fighting gangs whose membership is comprised from upper middle class youth have made their appearance. Hybrid gangs are probably some of the fastest growing gangs in the country and will continue to be popular among the younger population. The growth of these gangs maybe related to changing demographics.

Another demographic trend we expect to see is the presence of a larger teenage population. Research suggests that there will be an increase in the 14-24 year-old age bracket. In fact, by the year 2006 this age group is predicated to reach 30 million plus. This is the same age bracket where a large percentage of substance abusers and victims of gun violence come from. This research conclusion also suggests that gang violence could also increase because gang membership itself will increase. In addition the general U.S. population reached 300 million in October, 2006.

Family

Some experts feel that the decline of traditional two parent families may also have an impact on street gang growth. In 1960, 53 percent of American families were two parent families. By 1995 that figure was down to 36 percent according to a published report (U.S. News and World Report, 1996). Another report estimated that 18 million children, 27 percent of America's kids, are growing up in a single parent home. This is twice as many as in 1970 (U.S. News and World Report, 1994).

The implications were that this trend was driven by more births to teenage moms, to older women who tire of waiting for a mate, as well as persistent high divorce rates within the United States. It was noted that youth from single-parent homes are much more likely than dual-parent children to grow up poor, to fail in school and to become single parents themselves.

There are many good, single parent homes in America. We know gang members come from all walks of life and many social and economic backgrounds. However, failing in school is a primary risk factor associated with juvenile delinquency, which includes gang membership.

Education and English

Schools are unique places these days. There has been a 50 percent increase in children entering school knowing little or no English. Some estimates suggest there are at least 3 million students in America who speak little or no English. Spanish and the Asian languages are the native tongues to these students. For example, during the mid to late 1990s California had 40 percent of the nation's limited English speaking students and Texas ranked second.

According to a report in 1995, 46 percent of the students in Los Angeles had limited English-speaking abilities. In New York the figure was 15 percent; Chicago 14 percent; Houston 25 percent; Dade County, Florida 13 percent; and in one city, Santa Ana, (Orange County) California 69 percent of the students had trouble with the English language (Time Magazine, 1995).

How can we teach youth and motivate them to stay in school if they do not understand the language? Failing in school has been shown as a primary risk factor for youth to join gangs and become involved in juvenile delinquent behavior (Hill, Lui and Hawkins, 2001). Language and culture may be a silent and subtle factor that helps bind kids together in a street gang. It may be ignored or not noticed.

School Violence

A newspaper article depicted a bad case scenario. A Frankfort, Kentucky teacher had to get a civil restraining order and sue the parents to get a student to behave in class. School officials did all they could to control the behavior, but it continued and the teacher went to court. As sad as it sounds, the civil proceedings were needed to get the child to behave (Register, 1995). Many of our educators, the people we entrust our children to for 6-8 hours a day, have been forced to become surrogate parents as well as teachers.

At a teachers training conference where I was a presenter, a young mother walked up to a teacher I was talking with and begged her to call her house that evening. The parent wanted the teacher to try to talk her son (the teacher's student) into taking his medication because he would not take it when she asked him to. What is wrong with this picture?

In some places in America, estimates are that one in five students brings a weapon to school. If these estimates are accurate, then 20% of our student population is armed. How many more school shootings have to happen before we all take responsibility for our youth? School safety has become paramount especially since gang violence often occurs on school grounds. Surveys of students suggest that at least one-half worry about their personal safety while at school.

The trip to and from school can be perilous for some. Nationally many youth injured or killed on the way to or from school as a result of gang violence. Even though the violence did not occur on campus, often the school is included in media reports. This may give a false indication that the violent acts are associated with the school, when fact they are not.

Juvenile Crime

Juvenile crime in America had outpaced adult crime for a long time. Juvenile crime was skyrocketing in the 1990s. Street gang members can commit all types of crimes. In 1999 violent crime rates were at an all time high for the 14-24 year-old age group. The same was true for the under 18 year-old age group as well. During that time period according to the FBI, a murder occurs every 21 minutes, every day, and all year around. That equates to approximately 3 per hour. If the United States had the same homicide rate as Canada, the nation would only see about 5,600 murders annually, rather than 25,000. Violence is used a tool by many gang members. The cycle of violence we associate with street and prison gang violence originated with colonial Americans. Sadly, violence is part of the American culture (Valdez, 2006).

The critical age group is comprised of 14-24 year olds. It is not surprising to find that in many parts of the country, this age category accounts for up to 65-70% of the street gang membership (Valdez, 2005). Should suppression, intervention and prevention programs be age and cultural specific? The U.S. Department of Justice estimates that teenagers commit 1 of every 3 violent crimes. Since 1980 we have noted two things. The big rise in juvenile gang homicides decreased and that the average age of the person arrested for murder also began to decrease. Violent acts committed by gang members across the United States have help fuel these increases.

Custodial Time

During the mid 1990s the average time served by adults convicted of murder in the United States was 41 months. The average time a juvenile served who was convicted of murder was 60 months (U.S. News and World Report, 1996). In many parts of the country, the public still debates the issue of whether or not the death penalty should be applied to juveniles. A southern California newspaper reported that the number of teenagers sentenced to death has remained constant and small (Register, 1994). Nationally, a small number of teenagers are sentenced to death each year. As of the writing of this text no juvenile who has been sentenced to death has been executed as a juvenile. Several have been executed as adults after their appeals process and options had terminated.

A look at the statistics will reveal that although as a nation we have more than two million people in custody we still experience crime.

Many people feel that incarceration is a good deterrent to crime. The numbers tell a different story. As we put more people in jail, the crime rate continued to climb until the mid to late 1990s. The United States, the most advanced and powerful country in the world, ranks number one for putting people in jail. A focus on individual rights, rather than societal rights, continues to impact the number of people incarcerated. The United States has more people behind bars than we have in the entire active U.S. military (Valdez, 2000).

Substance Abuse

Substance abuse is yet another issue that affects the gang sub-culture. Not all gang members are drug addicts. However, using, possessing and selling drugs are part of the gang lifestyle. For many, casual and social substance abuse is also part of the gang culture. When drugs are sold, they are not sold in the highly organized fashion with a vertical command structure like a few Crip and Blood sets or some of the Folk and People Nations street gangs have. There are many independent street dealers that collectively account for the majority of drug sales. The lure of instant money is a temptation that is hard to refuse, for anyone.

Some media reports in the mid 1990s suggest that drug usage among high school students had increased not decreased (U.S. News World Report, 1995). The National Parents Resource Institute for Drug Education reported that the number of students using cocaine and hallucinogenic drugs has risen and that marijuana usage in this group has increased by one third. The potency of some of the drugs has also increased. For example, the marijuana of today can be 10-30 times more potent than the marijuana grown 25 years ago.

The usage of the so-called soft drugs, alcohol and cigarettes has also increased especially within the street gang population. The presence of methamphetamine, a cheap stimulant, known as crank or crystal has allowed some youth a new way to get a cheap high and make a buck. Drug abuse, sales and manufacture by juveniles also contributes to the rising violent crime rate. There is no harm reduction with this type of substance abuse and trafficking.

GHB and ecstasy have also become popular drugs of choice for many young Americans. Where there is a market, dealers develop. This trend has also become so popular that currently some gang members use and sell these drugs. Ecstasy or E has become one of the most popular drugs of choice used at rave parties. The first sentence of the Executive Summary in the 2005 National Gang Threat Assessment suggested that the primary source of income for street gangs comes from drug trafficking (National Alliance of Gang Investigator Associations, 2005).

Juvenile Arrest Trends

Since juveniles were committing a lot more crime in the mid 1990s, there was an effect on arrest rates as well. If arrest rates continued to climb at the 1995 rate, by the year 2010 juvenile arrests will have doubled. If the rates stay the same juvenile arrests will still increase by 20 percent (U.S. News and World Report, 1995). The juvenile detention facilities around the country are already overcrowded and over booked. Any increase, no matter how small will have a profound impact on the already taxed system.

You have to be asking yourself a question right now. Where are we going to house these juveniles? Some boot camp programs have had limited success. These programs are targeted at juveniles as an alternative to custodial status. Some have been successful at changing attitudes and lifestyles. The juveniles are forced to learn self-discipline and self esteem. Fundamental tools needed to survive legally.

Here is some food for thought. What happens to juvenile criminals at the federal level? At one time the Federal criminal justice system was not set up to deal with juvenile criminals effectively. If the Federal criminal justice system cannot handle juvenile cases and they are not handled at the state level, potentially juveniles could get away with serious criminal behavior. Recently, levels of juvenile crime have decreased and leveled-off. However, they are still higher than they were in 1964.

Societal Apathy

Apathy in society is yet another factor that has affected the response to the gang issues. The event that highlighted this issued occurred in 1965. Kitty Genovese became the symbol of urban apathy that still haunts the nation today. While walking down a street in Queens, New York, Kitty was attacked by a stalker. Thirty-eight neighbors watched and listened. The killer fled twice when the neighbors turned their lights on, but returned when the lights went out. Thirty-eight neighbors heard Kitty's screams, and did nothing to help. No one even called the police.

This kind of apathy has led to attitudes like it can't happen in my neighborhood or that only happens in that part of the city. This kind of thinking also inhibits people from getting involved as cooperative witnesses in criminal cases. Sadly, even victims of gang related crimes sometimes do not want to get involved. This attitude also helps justify denial. Combined they prevent an effective and rapid community response to issues that fuel the gang problem.

Some experts suggest that America is losing its middle class. As Americans become more affluent, middle class America is disappearing. The disparity between the nation's poor and upper class is getting greater. Some feel that this trend also contributes to societal apathy because those in the financially affluent class ignore, do not acknowledge and do not care about issues that do not directly affect them. This was highlighted in 2005. During a Channel 11, FOX News story about drug trafficking and the Hell's Angels motorcycle club in Ventura County, California the investigative reporter was interviewing local high school students. The reporter was asking about the allegation that the Hells Angels were using high school students to sell drugs. One male student told the reporter that he didn't care because it did not involve him.

Risk Factors

Risk factors for gang membership come from the community, family, school and the individual or peers. Many factors exert an influence that helps cause substance abuse, delinquency, teenage pregnancy, school dropout rates and youth violence. The next chapter will discuss these in detail. Some risk factors may include age, ethnicity and poverty levels.

Singly, these risk factors may not have a major impact on someone's life. Collectively, they can have a profound impact. It may only take two or four to dictate life changing events, effect attitudes, help form anti-social behaviors and ultimately lead to violent criminal behavior.

Poverty Rates in America

Poverty levels for many Blacks, Native American, Hispanic, Asian and Whites since 1980 to now have increased. By 1990, the number of people with incomes below the poverty level had increased so much that figures show the poverty levels for Blacks at 29.5 percent, Native Americans 30.9 percent, Hispanic 25.3 percent, Asian 14.1 percent and White at 9.8 percent (Time, 1995). For many Americans, life has not gotten better. Research has suggested that as poverty rates increase so does the chance for criminal victimization.

Time magazine also reported another number one position for the United States. When comparing the major industrialized countries of the world, the United States has the greatest gap between the income of the poorest people and the income of the richest (Time, 1995). Even though unemployment is down for the general population, the rate is still high for gang members. There is some anecdotal evidence that suggests gang members who are gainfully employed tend not to have the legal issues their unemployed counter parts have.

Cycle of Violence

Sometimes it helps to see the big picture (national) and then our own community status is put into perspective. National trends reveal that more and younger people are getting involved in violent crime, specifically, the young people in the 14-24 year-old age category. This is not gender specific, females are involved as well, but not at the same level as males.

There are many ways to discuss the issue of gang violence. Sometimes diagrams and special terms are used to describe the cycle of gang violence. I suggest we examine the American cycle of violence to help understand the gang cycle of violence. America has been a violent country since Columbus discovered the land. The cycle of violence we experience today with street gangs has been around Americans since the big discovery in 1492.

Our nation has used violence to settle disputes for a long time. The first disputes in the new land were with the Native American Indians. The initial cycle of violence America experienced is well documented here. Violence is a learned behavior. All the social factors we discussed can have a direct impact on this behavior. Along with those factors and the cycle of violence, it becomes easy to understand why the gun has become a symbol of power and authority.

According to the FBI, guns are used in 72 percent of all the homicides committed in America. If you examined gang related homicides, guns can be used as much as 93 percent of the time. Guns have taken on a traditional importance to gang members. They bring instant power and control. For gang members guns have become a symbol of power and authority. They hold the same significance as they did during the settling of the West. As one 17-year-old gang member stated to me, *"he who has the gun has the power and control."*

So why look at this little bit of history and the current societal issues? Combined, they provide a possible explanation of the past, current and future gang trends. For gangs, violence has become an acceptable way of dealing with conflict. This attitude has become foundational in understanding the gang mentality because violence helps create fear. Unfortunately, for gang members fear is often equated to respect.

Violence can be projected toward anyone, including non-gang members, gang associates, family, students, teachers, and criminal justice professionals, at any time. The violence we experience today within the gang sub-culture is really deeply rooted in American culture, including the use of guns. Current social conditions for many youth who live in and out of the United States may help explain the violent behavior and the use of guns for the gang members.

As Martin Luther King, Jr. said, *"The ultimate measure of a man is not where he stands in moments of comfort and convenience, but where he stands at times of challenge and controversy."* The challenge is trying to understand the causes of gang behaviors and trends. The solutions to minimize the impact of gang violence will be found in the innovative techniques that combine suppression, intervention and prevention models.

Summary

American street gangs are constantly changing as a result of variety of factors. Although there are subtle rules of conduct that are both expected and challenged that all street gangs share; each street gang is unique. Street gangs will mirror the communities they develop in. Although there are a number of factors that affect gang violence; apathy continues to affect the community's response to gang violence. Apathy also facilitates the denial that gangs do not exist.

Can Gang Membership Be Predicted?

The answer to the question about predicting gang membership cannot be answered with certainty. Research has been able to identify risk factors that seem to influence the likelihood of youth joining a gang. However, these factors do not take into account generational gang membership. Hispanic generational gangs present a unique issue and do not follow current models of gang membership.

Seattle School Study

Although the proliferation of youth street gangs has been well documented during the past 20 years, a well-defined mechanism that can predict gang membership has not. Hill, Lui and Hawkins (2001) studied over 800 youth from 1985 to 2001 and were able to identify a number of gang membership risk factor categories that increase the potential to join a street gang.

Their findings also support other research conducted by Pettit (2000), Kokko and Pulkkinen (2000) that suggested the more risk factors present, the greater likelihood of membership in a gang. To suggest that gang membership increases incarceration rates implies that gang members engage in more criminal behavior than non-gang members. It has been well established that gang members tend to be involved in more crime than non-gang members.

Hill, Lui and Hawkins (2001) research supports this correlation. Their research suggests that gang members engage in more delinquent behaviors than their peers who are not in gangs. Hill, Lui and Hawkins (2001) also found that compared with youth who are not gang members, those who are gang members more often commit assault, robbery, and burglary and felony theft.

Gang members also use and sell drugs and are arrested more often. Studies conducted by Spergel (1995) and Thornberry (1998) also suggest that gang members are more likely to commit violent crimes, property crimes and abuse drugs. Gang members are more than twice as likely to carry guns and three times as likely to sell drugs according to research conducted by Bjerregaard and Lizotte (1995).

It follows that the earlier gang membership starts, the earlier delinquent and criminal behavior begins. This would increase the likelihood of earlier police contact, arrest and more frequent incarceration. This becomes important when discussing generational street gangs because it suggests that in generational gangs, delinquent behaviors may start at an earlier age. Significant family members early on in life can model gang behaviors.

Albeit, that the progression into the actual formal status of membership may be subtle and progress over a number of months or years, gang behaviors are demonstrated long before actual membership is earned, granted or acknowledged (Valdez, 2005). Based on some research there are some identifiable risk factors that can be used as predictors for gang membership. Hill, Lui and Hawkins (2001) suggest that the prime age to join a street gang is 15 based on their research findings. However, it is also clear that gang membership can occur at any age. In California, gang membership has been documented with children as young as 9 years old and as old as 69 years. Analysis of data in the California Cal-Gangs system indicates that approximately 60 percent of gang members are between 14-24 years old.

Hill, Lui and Hawkins (2001) did not examine generational street gangs in their study. Their research included over 800 youth from several different parts of Seattle. They were followed in a longitudinal study and were monitored between the ages of 13 and 18. The youth lived in high crime neighborhoods and the data was used to enhance the understanding of predictors for gang membership.

The research began in 1985 with 5th grade age students from 18 Seattle, Washington area public schools that served "high crime" neighborhoods. However, the study did not define what constituted "high crime." Approximately half the student participants were female, 49 percent. The sample was ethnically diverse and included European Americans (46%), African American (24%), Asian American (21%), Native American (6%) and 3% of other ethnicity.

In this study 46 percent of the families reported an income of less than $20,000 per year. Well below the established poverty level in the United States. However, this level of income is commonly encountered in many social-economic deprived communities. This includes communities where street gangs have formed, but is not a critical requirement for the formation of a gang. Being poor in it self does not translate to automatic gang membership. If it was, then all youth from a socially-economic deprived area would be gang members. This is not observed. Gang membership is a choice, albeit some youth have more choices than others.

The data was collected annually from age 10 through age 18 by using a questionnaire that required responses to a variety of questions about family, community, peers, gangs, substance abuse, drug selling, violence, weapon use and victimization. The researchers also collected data from the participant's parents, teachers, school, police and court records. The longitudinal data identified risk categories that were precursors for gang membership.

Hill, Lui and Hawkins (2001) reported that 124 of the 808 children studied joined a gang between the ages of 13 and 18. This represented only 15.3 percent of the sample. Of those children who joined a gang, the vast majority were male, 72.5 percent. Over 25 percent of the gang members were female.

The percentage of male gang members seems low when compared to statistics published by the California Attorney General's office. Male gang members comprise approximately 90 percent of the state's gang population. In California female gang member populations have varied between 6 and 10 percent. This has also been the trend in the rest of the country. There will be exceptions to this reported observation based on unique regional characteristics.

In the Seattle study, 26.2 percent of the African American students joined a gang, verses 12.4 percent of the Asian American and 10.2 percent of the European American students. There is also no information comparing the studied student population with the community demographics. One has to assume the study's demographics also reflect the general population demographics. If this assumption is accurate, there was not an influential amount of Hispanic students in the schools that were used for the study.

According to the study, the risk of joining a street gang rose sharply for children who were 15 years of age, even though there was risk of membership at every age. Notably, most children start high school near or at the age of 15 and it is a time when secondary sexual characteristics are developing. However, it is obvious that gang behaviors can exist prior to formal gang membership recognition. Usually, gang membership is not granted quickly. There is a courting process involved. Field interviews give anecdotal evidence that suggest this process can last for months (Valdez, 2000).

The majority of children who joined a gang were active members for one year or less. Only 16.9% were active for two years or less and 10.5 % for three years or less. Only 2.4 percent remained in the gang for four years. Of the 124 children who joined the gang this represents only three children. Only one child of the 124 studied remained in his or her gang for five years (Hill, Lui and Hawkins 2001).

This is good news. Hill, Lui and Hawkins findings suggest that for the majority of youth who get involved in street gangs are only part of the sub-culture for one year or less. According to their research approximately 27 percent of the involved youth are part of a gang for three years or less. What is suggested is that only a very small percent of the youth who get involved in a street gang, stay in for a longer period of time.

Now, here is the not so good news. This model is not consistent with findings for generational gangs, in particular generational Hispanic street gangs (GHSG), where it has been common to identify 10 to 20 year veterans of gang membership. In fact, GHSG members tend to remain and live within the areas of the communities where they grew up in (gang turf) and remain members of their gang for life. GHSG members tend to pass on street gang membership to their siblings and close family relatives (Jankowski, 1991).

Risk Factors and Characteristics

What the Seattle study and generational gangs have in common are the risk factors that are used as predictors of and associated with gang membership. The study identified risk factors and conditions that can predict gang membership in general. These risk factors can also be used to define a mechanism for predicting gang membership in generational street gangs like GHSGs.

Not surprisingly, the Seattle study researchers concluded the more risk factors that are present, the greater the chance of joining a street gang. Other researchers and criminal justice professionals support this position like Pettit (2000), Kokko and Pulkkinen, (2000). The risk factors tend to have a cumulative effect on the child's propensity to join a gang. The identified risk factors were classified into five distinct areas: neighborhood, family, school, peer and individual and were categorized as:

Neighborhood

- Availability of marijuana
- Neighborhood youth in trouble
- Low neighborhood attachment

Family Structure

- One parent only
- One parent plus other adults
- Parental attitudes favoring violence
- Low bonding with parents
- Low household income
- Sibling antisocial behavior
- Poor family management

School

- Learning disabled
- Low academic achievement
- Low school attachment

- Low school commitment
- Low academic aspirations

Peer Group
- Association with friends who engage in problem behaviors

Individual
- Low religious service attendance
- Early marijuana use
- Early violence
- Antisocial beliefs
- Early drinking
- Externalized behaviors
- Poor refusal skills

(Hill, Lui and Hawkins, 2001)

These risk factors that were identified specifically increase the likelihood of gang membership and are considered by many criminal justice professionals as the primary risk factors that can be used to predict gang membership. These risk factors are the most common predictors for membership in any type of gang.

Hill, Lui and Hawkins (2001), also suggested youth joined gangs as a result of antisocial influences in neighborhoods, antisocial tendencies in families and peers, failure to perform well in school and early initiation of individual problem behaviors. Gang membership also appears to be symptomatic of dysfunctional familial, social and individual conditions. This is a reported observation only and not meant as an apology for the criminal actions and violence that is associated with gang membership.

The study also suggested youth who remained in gangs for longer than one year were the most behaviorally and socially maladjusted in childhood. In particular, youth who exhibited early signs of violent and externalized behavior were twice as likely to remain in a gang for more than a year. The identified behaviors included aggression, oppositional behavior, inattentiveness and hyperactivity (Hill, Lui and Hawkins, 2001).

The researchers in the Seattle study divided the children into four groups depending on the number of risk factors children at ages 10-12 were exposed to. "No risk" youth experienced only no risk factors or only one. "Low risk" youth experienced two to three risk factors. "Medium risk" youth experienced four to six risk factors. "High risk" youth experienced seven or more risk factors during the evaluation period. Compared with no risk youth, low risk youth were 3 times more likely to join a gang; medium risk youth were 5 times more likely to join a gang and high risk youth were 13 times more likely to join (Hill, Lui and Hawkins (2001). In areas where generational gangs like GHSGs develop often there are more than six risk factors present (Valdez, 2002).

Based on studies, early childhood aggression and a high-risk status suggest the greatest likelihood of long term (more than five years) gang membership (Hill, Lui and Hawkins, 2001). This is supported by the observation that these youths are exposed to six or more risk factors. Cultural issues may also play a part in generational gang membership. Culturally based customs, sometimes labeled as tradition, may become the vehicle to transfer gang membership within families who live in social-economic deprived neighborhoods (Jankowski, 1991).

Childhood aggression is fostered in some homes and is also encountered in homes where generational street gangs have developed. Aggression becomes the method of choice to solve all problems for many people, including gang members. Academic research has shown that childhood aggression is a powerful determinant of subsequent poor educational attainment (Brook and Newcome, 1995). Childhood aggression can also be a predictor for drinking problems (Brook and Newcome, 1995). Both behaviors are encouraged, approved and expected in the gang sub-culture. In the gang sub-culture aggression is used as tool to create fear and to solve problems.

Generational Street Gangs

At issue is the identification of variables that distinguish membership in generational gangs like GHSGs from gangs studied in the Seattle research. What makes generational gangs like GHSGs unique is tradition. In these types of street gangs tradition based on cultural attitudes becomes the vehicle for the transfer of gang behaviors and customs within a family. For example, culturally and as a group, Hispanics tend to identify with the community they live in. As a group, Hispanics have identified their rung on the social ladder and it has also been acknowledged. In these communities, the bonding between the community and the gang partly originates with the adults' identification with the gang and their encouragement to their own siblings and close family members to be active in the gang (Jankowski, 1991. pages 180-181).

It has been asserted that tradition plays a crucial role in parents encouraging gang involvement and membership, especially in Los Angeles based Hispanic gangs. There was a reported sense of tradition in which the gang and family were intertwined (Jankowski, 1991, page 182). Jankowski (1991) also identified that 32 percent of the Hispanic fathers interviewed had been in the same gang as their children. It was also demonstrated that 11 percent of the fathers reported four generations of men in their family had been in the same gang (Jankowski, 1991. pages 180-181). However, this figure may be higher if larger samples of Los Angles based Hispanic street gangs are studied.

Indoctrination into the gang life for GHSGs begins at home at an early age, with the parent(s), siblings and /or close family members. Young children are exposed to traditional gang behaviors and attitudes that are modeled by the adults. A child receives positive reinforcement for antisocial attitudes and behaviors because it continues the tradition. An examination of the family structure, neighborhood, peers, academic performance and individual generational gang members indicates that a plethora of predictors were and continue to be present at a greater rate than in non-generational gang communities. These observations follow the prediction model of Hill, Lui and Hawkins, (2001).

Three other psychosocial reasons may impact why gangs get adult support. First, a significant number of adults from low-income areas identify with the resistance component of street gangs. This attitude can be observed in impoverished communities, like those where GHSGs are formed. These adults empathize with the desires, frustrations and resentments that the youth of low-income neighborhoods experience because they have experienced them too. Thus, these adults identify with the gang because they are sympathetic to the gang members attempts to resist their poor social-economic position (Jankowski, 1991, pages 182-183).

The second psychosocial reason relates more directly to the personal experience of the adult sympathizers. Some of the adults in a study implied they had failed in life and were frustrated about this. The respondents also implied they found some comfort that their children were also having the similar difficulties (Jankowski, 1991 page 181). These parents responded to their children's gang involvement with an absence of discouragement. This lack of action, acted as a form of informal encouragement. These parents knew that gang involvement would eventually result in difficulty with the law and incarceration, but their encouragement was based on ambivalence about wanting a better life for their children (Jankowski, 1991. pages 182 to 183).

The third psychosocial factor comes from the community where generational gang members live. Some generational gangs like GHSGs are turf oriented. They claim a geographical area of the community they live in as theirs. The "neighborhood" becomes the area where GHSG members feel safe from rival gang attack. The neighborhood becomes their turf and the boundaries are well defined. Rival gang members, friendly gang members and non-gang members become street savvy and are aware of the gang's boundaries.

This behavior can be taken to an extreme as demonstrated by the Avenues, a generational Hispanic street gang operating in Highland Park, Los Angeles. In July 2006 several members were federally prosecuted for assaulting and murdering Blacks who invaded their turf. The basis for the prosecution was that members of this gang specifically targeted Blacks because of their ethnicity and therefore committed hate crimes (Los Angeles Times, 2006).

Despite the fact that typically more police personnel are deployed in these areas, the gang has more of a presence. Non-gang community members who also share the poor social economic status can also derive a sense of safety from the gang. GHSG members tended not to victimize the people who live in the neighborhood they claim, therefore many of those community members may have felt the gang protected them (Jankowski, 1991. pages 182-183). There is some evidence to suggest that currently this community "Robin Hood" mentality has changed.

Many community residents report that they are controlled by fear of the gang rather than having the freedom to live unmolested by the gang. Anecdotal law enforcement evidence also suggests that during the late 1990s and early 2000s many victims of GHSG violence lived in the neighborhood the gang claimed.

GHSG members consider themselves the policemen of their neighborhood. They are acutely aware of all street activity that happens within their neighborhood. They can be strategically located to alert the gang if a stranger, rival gang member or the police enter their neighborhood. Some community members feel that the gang is able to deter crime better than the police (Jankowski, 1991. page 185). This may happen because as a group GHSG members tend to stay in the neighborhood they claim, thus giving the gang a 24-hour, seven day a week presence and influence in the neighborhood.

In generational gangs like GHSGs, behaviors and customs associated with gang life are introduced to children at an early age. Adults give positive reinforcement to the children when they display antisocial behaviors. Many of the behaviors are modeled by youth after observing them displayed by adults or other youth.

As you can see, a number of factors influence gang membership and participation. Factors like culture, poor social and economic status, attitudes toward drug use, family structure, a lack of hope a sense of being at the bottom of the social ladder, community anger and many more play a role in determining how the risk factors impact a particular youth. Unfortunately, as we have all seen gang membership can become a vehicle to help deal with living conditions and frustrations.

In generational gangs like GHSGs, gang membership becomes a lifestyle that is passed on within a family. This would suggest that culture and unique family attitudes are partly responsible for the generational aspect of gang membership. It appears that gang membership is passed on through tradition to the next generation gang member (Jankowski, 1991). Membership in any type of street gang, including GHSGs may become predicable based on academic investigations completed by Hill, Lui and Hawkins (2001). Uniquely, generational gang membership can last a lifetime.

The answer to the question about being able to predict gang membership cannot be answered with certainty. The Hill, Lui and Hawkins risk factors can be great predictors that support theories on what contributes to youth gang membership. These factors do not take into account generational gang membership. Further studies will be needed to determine the link if any to the Hill, Lui and Hawkins risk factors and generational gang membership.

Summary

Gang membership is hard to predict. Hill, Lui and Hawkins (2001) identify membership risk factors that may be helpful in assessing the potential for youth to join a gang. The research suggests that for the majority of youth who join a gang their tenure is short. The vast majority of youth who get involved in a gang remain involved for about a year. Generational Hispanic street gangs may have added risk factors that facilitate generational gang membership because membership and affiliation appears to be lifelong. These factors may be culturally based and impact membership.

Being On The Same Page

Developing a standard definition for what a gang becomes essential to triage the current impact that street gangs have on our communities. This section will help you understand a standard definition; examine leadership structures and membership initiation rituals for street gangs.

Gang Definition

Just what do people mean when they talk about street gangs? How do we define the term? Much depends on your perspective as you examine the issue. From our sociological perspective, let's define a gang by using this general definition:

1. Any group of three or more

2. That has some type of association,

3. With a common identifier,

4. And they commit crime.

This is a good four part definition to work with because it is simple and direct. Please note that territory or turf has not been included with this definition because not all gangs are turf oriented. In fact, some gangs are transient and claim no particular area as their neighborhood. The type of crime can be infractions, misdemeanor or felony in nature. Gang members do not have to commit a drive-by shooting to be considered as a gang member. Usually there are no qualifying crimes that have to be committed to be a gang member. Virtually any crime could be committed as part of an initiation ritual.

The caveat here is we are not discussing the definition of a gang for the purposes of criminal prosecution. In states where legal enhancements exist there may be a specific legal definition of a gang member or gang that qualifies a defendant for a harsher sentence if convicted. I am not using that kind of definition here.

There are many ways to examine the myriad of gang issues. Parents look at gangs in a unique way, especially if they or one of their children were or are involved. Teachers have their perspectives when dealing with at-risk youths and potential gang members. Mental health professionals examine the gang phenomenon from yet another point of view. Of course, we cannot forget the law enforcement, prevention and intervention perspectives.

Perspectives

Perspectives come from the different goals that parents, teachers, mental health and law enforcement professionals have when dealing with gang-related issues. Parents want to protect their children while teachers want to educate and train them. Mental health professionals want to assist children in becoming emotionally and psychologically healthy. Law enforcement just wants gang members to obey the law. Intervention programs are designed to facilitate a successful escape from gang life. Prevention programs focus on awareness and preventing at-risk youth from joining a gang. Depending on what perspective you have, you may be inclined to use or design another definition of a gang. We should not do that because in doing so only aids in strengthening denial. I suggest we use the simple definition already mentioned.

Age

Gang members can be any age. Frequently, gang members who are contacted by the police are between the ages of 11 and 24 years old. In youngest reported gang member was eight and the oldest was 69. There have been a few reports by law enforcement of gang members as young as 7 years old. By far the majority of gang members fall between the ages of 14 and 30. Anecdotal evidence suggests that 60 to 75 percent of the gang membership falls within this age category. The majority of gang members are male. Age is not used as a profile for gang membership because gang members can be of any age.

Gender

The latest studies, based on law enforcement surveys indicate that males comprise pretty close to 90 % of the gang membership. Most studies suggest that females constitute between 8 and 15 percent of documented gang population. Female gang populations may fluctuate depending on what part of the country they are located in. Therefore, do not be surprised if your female gang population is higher that 15 percent. Do not forget, female gang members can have the same propensity for violence as their male counterparts.

A popular theory of why we saw an increase of female gang members was based on the development of Hybrid gangs. These types of street gangs broke the gender and race membership barriers. So, female members assumed an equal partner status.

Leadership Models

Most gangs are without formal organization and the leaders tend to be the strongest or boldest members. Age can also be a factor in determining who will lead a gang. Sometimes, the oldest surviving gang-member is called upon for advice and leadership. In gang sub-culture, actions speak louder than words. As one 14-year-old Latino gang member told me, *"The crazier you are, the more respect you get."*

This is a sobering reality of gang life. Some street gangs have fluid structures. Membership will grow and decrease as people join and leave. Some street and prison gangs maintain somewhat of a permanent core membership with little if any influx of new members. Some street gangs may have an informal leadership structure, others have a semi-formal chain of command, and others have a changing leadership structure.

As you read this book you will find out a few gangs have a formal leadership structure. Sometimes there are specific titles that are associated with rank and responsibility. However, the majority of street gangs do not operate in this fashion. Do not be surprised if some street gangs start to organize. The impact of drug trafficking will cause some gangs to organize and develop relationships with rival street gangs (Valdez, 2005)

Membership

People have always grouped together since the beginning of humankind. Most gangs initially formed for protection. Once a gang is formed, behaviors and activities change due to economics, power struggles, respect and from responding to challenges. Behaviors can also be a function of the individual members who can exert an influence on other members. The gang can become the "family" that provides essential elements for survival. Gang life offers many of the same benefits that a traditional family life offers. The gang in many respects can become a surrogate family to its membership. However, there is one big difference. Gangs use violence, fear, criminal activity and intimidation to obtain the benefits of their membership.

Because of these behaviors and influences, gang membership is not a static phenomenon. In fact, it is just the opposite. Street gang membership is constantly changing in response to the street environment and internal change. Due to this factor, assume that the gangs themselves evolve or change. The gang may start out as a social group, or form for protection, but over a period of time, the gang can mature and become prone to violence.

Because the membership is dynamic, the direct and indirect influences if acute can cause a rapid change within a gang. There are no completed academic studies that indicate how long these transitions take. Some street gangs that initially started as a social group tried to avoid these change. But the influences of the street life prevent that. For example in Southern California, several tagger crews lost members and then split into different groups based on the issue of whether or not to use violence. A majority of the crew wanted to only create graffiti. The minority wanted to start to carry and use firearms and started to compare themselves to traditional street gangs.

There can be formal initiation rites that formalize membership. A person may have to be an associate member first, before being formally accepted into a street gang. Then, after several tests, this person will be initiated into the gang as a full member, with all membership rights. The initiation rituals can also take the form of committing a felony crime, or simply fighting three to six fellow gang members simultaneously to show how much heart you have. Fighting like this is known as a jump in.

The jumping in is a symbolic ceremony used as a declaration of commitment and loyalty by the new gang member to his new gang family. It is the final step in formalizing gang membership. The jumping in is the end of the membership process. However, you can be a gang member and not have been jumped in.

There are many reasons why young people join gangs. Gang experts, at times, may disagree on the numbers and reasons but many experts feel that sociology and economics can play an important role in understanding the causative factors. The reasons that are discussed here are not the only valid reasons. There are many direct and indirect causes for gang membership and association.

Why?

Probably the most-asked question about gangs is, "Why do gangs continue to exist?" By now, you can understand that gang membership and the formation of street gangs is a complicated and unique process that is affected by many factors. It is also a very dynamic process, which means gangs can change over time, sometimes quickly. To truly understand why gangs exist in our country is difficult because there is no single answer to that question. The answer becomes complicated because of history, the cycle of American violence, drug use; drug trafficking, the family environment, the community, the individual, poverty and culture. Just to name a few.

Understanding the dynamics of gang sub-culture like the customs, traditions, cultural differences, the non-verbal, written, oral language and the behaviors which are the underlying basis for gang behaviors and membership becomes the key to answer the question why.

To complicate this issue further is the motivation for gang membership. Youth join gangs for a number of reasons. Some of the most common reasons come from gang members themselves. Gang members I have spoken to have stated they joined a gang for economic reasons, safety, friendship, status, recognition, curiosity, excitement, to hide from authorities, out of a sense of tradition (generational), drug abuse, and peer pressure. While there are probably many other reasons why our children join gangs, these are the ones most often mentioned by the gang members.

I have asked thousands of gang members, what does the gang give you? Frequently, the response indicates they get something from the gang that is missing in their lives, whether real or perceived. Many have a very strong sense of loyalty to their gang. It appears that belonging to a gang gives members many positive feelings including a strong sense of belonging, a sense of being wanted, a sense of contributing, a sense of honor and pride, and status among both gang and non-gang members. Gang members also receive guidance, shelter and money from the gang. The gang becomes the source of survival and positive and powerful feelings for the gang member.

Belonging to a gang can give the member a sense of power and control over a certain area, or over certain groups of people, or over oneself. The gang members I have spoken to almost always mention love. All the gang members said they give and receive love from the gang. Almost all of the gang members refer to the gang as their family. The gang becomes the surrogate or replacement family for many of the gang members. Unfortunately, gang members get positive reinforcement for joining the group and that only reinforces their loyalty and commitment to the gang.

The positive reinforcement can also take the form of giving the gang member a sense of direction and focus, a sense of purpose. Along with an increased sense of commitment and loyalty comes status. A profound feeling of power over non-gang members and with peers also increases providing a false sense of security. This may tend to fuel a need to protect the gang's reputation.

Life experience dictates that you don't get something for nothing. There is a cost for everything. The cost for the positive reinforcement obtained through membership is commitment to gang lifestyle. This includes acceptance all of the gangs philosophies, expected behaviors and the willingness to take part in violent crimes. In essence, the members develop a blind loyalty to the gang. Which in turn allows them to hurt someone else or be hurt themselves for the gang.

Some gang members call it, backing up the gang or being down for the gang. To the gang member, he or she is simply protecting their family. Don't forget, to the member the gang is the source of everything that is good in his life. By using violence and fear a gang member is ensuring his survival by protecting his gang.

In our quest to answer the why question we also have to examine another area. I have spoken to thousands of gang members all over the United States and have noted three unique characteristics that are common among all those interviewed. First, all the gang members had an immediate need for gratification. For most, there was no work ethic apparent. If they wanted something, they wanted it now and simply would take it from a person or location. If resistance was encountered it was countered with violence. *"Take what you want, when you want it,"* explained a 13-year-old female gang member from Portland, Oregon.

Secondly, all interviewed gang members had a distorted view of reality. They think that cartoons and movies are representations of normal, everyday life. There also seemed to be a general sense of fatalism among many interviewed gang members. Many believed they would not live past the age of 24. Violence was used as a tool, with no thought of the consequences. So they would as a 16-year-old gang member from Los Angeles, California, stated, *"Live for the now."*

Some gang members also had a unique perspective against society or some part of it. Some gang members believe that minorities where the cause of all societal problems. Others believe that the criminal justice system was designed to destroy them because they are members of a minority group. Some gang members believe that all law enforcement officers should be the enemy, not other gangs. The point is that all have a skewed perspective of life that is influenced by a particular gang's mentality.

The last unique characteristic that was observed was all had a tremendous survival instinct. All the gang members were resigned to do whatever was needed to live. For example, if their survival depended on hurting or killing someone. They would attempt to do it. With this attitude it is easy to see how attacks against police officers, are justified or how criminal behavior is justified. It also becomes easy to understand the *liaise fair* attitude that is given when an innocent victim, like a child is killed.

Some gang members I have spoken to indicated they would like to leave their gang if they could. Still, most of these gang members believed it is impossible. Many have dropped out of school and have limited job skills. A few said they were too old and set in their ways to leave. As one Latino gang member told me, "... *maybe if I was younger and still in school I could have made it out... I am too old now and can't change.*" He was only 16 years old.

The reality of this statement forces one to think, was gang membership needed to survive? It has to be affirmed again that gang membership is voluntary. Membership is a choice, granted some kids have a limited number of choices and others have many options. Nevertheless, joining a gang becomes a conscious decision. It is not a forced membership. In a gang neighborhood, youth have the option of limiting the time they spend with a gang. In addition some academic research suggests that all youth who reside within a gang controlled neighborhood do not join a gang. This implies that many youth make the choice not to join a gang.

Violence

Many types of street and prison gangs are in existence today. Gang trends can change, sometimes overnight. However, one thing is constant. Gangs use violence to intimidate, maintain control, influence others, and gain respect, to commit crime and to have status. Even though gangs may have formed to protect turf or commit crime for profit, or under certain political or religious philosophies, or have formed a hybrid under a non-traditional basis all commit crimes using violence or respond to a real or perceived transgression with violent acts. Violence is always used, sometimes as the last resort and sometimes as the first option.

Street and prison gangs are without a doubt some of the most violent groups in America today. What makes them so scary is that their violence is often deadly, unpredictable and indiscriminate. Today, the violence creates fear. For street gangs, fear is equated to respect.

Please, do not forget this: gang-related homicides are the only statistics kept when counting acts of gang violence. Think for a moment about how many gang-related crimes occur and go unreported and are not monitored for one reason or another.

To date, there are no statistics that track gang-related serious and minor injuries. There are many cases where the victims are injured for life, completely or partially blinded, or lost the use of a limb. Not to mention the emotional stress caused by these incidents, which not only affects the victims, but also the parents, siblings and friends.

There is a hidden cost to some of the violence. The Orange County Register newspaper (1993) reported that our culture of American violence is expensive. The annual cost to taxpayers is around four billion dollars. That is in 1993 dollars. Most of the money goes to gunshot victims with no medical insurance.

In the mid 1990s according to some estimates, a firearm injury costs approximately $53,831. The taxpayers pay about 85% of that. On average, a firearm fatality costs $373,520 and the taxpayers pay $317,500 of that. It is believed that these costs are ultimately passed on to the privately insured patient.

In one attempted homicide I interviewed the victim, a gang member, who was shot in the face with a 12 gauge shot gun at close range. Miraculously, he survived. The medical bills for the victim exceeded $500,000. The victim had no medical insurance and paid nothing for his care. He had to be covered under indigent medical care services, which meant the county taxpayers paid for his medical care.

With many different perspectives and limited understanding of the gang sub-culture, there is some confusion about the actual effect gang-related violence has on our lives. There may never be a truly accurate accounting of all the expenses and resources that are being used in an attempt to deal with these issues.

Traditional Latino street gangs protect their turf. Black street gangs sell crack cocaine and fight over sales turf. Asian-American street gangs work as mobile criminal enterprises and commit crime for a profit. White Supremacists, including skinheads, have formed, under the guise of White Pride, ostensibly to protect the so-called Aryan race from sub humans and race traitors. Tagging crews account for millions of dollars spent removing tag graffiti, which now appears worldwide.

Add to this America's insatiable hunger for illegal substances, alcohol and a societal tolerance for violence and it is not hard to begin to understand why street gangs became so violent. Many consider Los Angeles County the gang capital of the United States. The truth is that today street and prison-gang activity can be found in every state of the nation. Still, many people feel that the street gangs they see are a direct result of migrating gang activity from Los Angeles. Gangs are a function of demographics, geography and the export of the gang culture through movies, music, magazines and the Internet.

Prison Gang Influence

Prison gangs can have a direct influence on street-gang activity. For example, in 1994, La Eme a West Coast Latino prison-gang actively made an effort to curb the violence between Latino street gangs in Southern California. In Chicago, Larry Hoover, who is in prison, controls one of the larger gangs, Black Gangster Disciples. He directs the daily operations of the street and prison gang from jail.

For some gang members joining a prison becomes a goal. It is almost like getting that Fortune 500 company job after going to college. Once in prison, the prison gangs educate many street gang members. Although this is not the design of incarceration, there is a knowledge transfer and an opportunity to join a prison gang.

Symptoms of Membership

Even though the gang sub-culture can be examined from many perspectives, most share many, if not all of the following characteristics: stylized dress; tattoos; graffiti; use of hand signs; spoken and written languages; stylized haircuts; stylized jewelry; use of certain colors; stylized music; monikers; burns; scars; body piercing; branding; substance abuse; business cards; special writings and drawings; gang photographs; gang mementos; weapons; association with known gang members; use of pagers; cellular telephones; scanners; and self-claiming membership.

Street and prison gangs also present with unique philosophies such as a code of silence, payback, and no insult goes unanswered - no matter how small; initiation rituals, some gangs have distinct levels of gang membership; some specialize in drug manufacture or sales; and an anti-social mentality. Some gang members have a few symptoms of membership, others have many and others may have none of these symptoms.

The symptoms are indicative of a life style, gang behaviors and mentality. Some gang members are very successful in hiding their membership because they present no symptoms; yet they are gang members. Some gang members literally lead double lives because they can camouflage the gang mentality successfully and blend well within general society.

Gang Lifestyle

Understanding gang mentality may seem difficult for some and even harder to accept. The gang mentality requires subscribers to honor a unique set of rules and for lack of a better word a set of gang ethics. This lifestyle is centered on violence, rigid rules and the use of guns. The gang mentality allows one to believe that life has little or no value, especially for the gang members themselves.

There are a number of factors to consider when making a diagnosis that a person is a gang member or an incident is gang related. This diagnosis should be done on a case-by-case basis.

Initially, most street and prison gangs were formed for protection. Today, street and prison gangs exist for protection of turf, drug sales, and crime for profit, or to sustain a political or religious philosophy. Some groups claim not to be a gang, like clubs, clicks, posses, tagging and party crews. They may make a real effort not to be violent like street gangs. Nevertheless, these groups are predisposed to react to a real or perceived insult, loss of respect or threat just like a violent street gang.

All gangs share these characteristics. When dealing with these characteristics understand there are going to be exceptions. Recently, some street gang members have been contacted who share none of the classical street-gang profiling indicators. Other street-gang members refuse to claim their gang affiliation to law enforcement officials.

Many street gang members have no tattoos. Some street gang members literally have led double lives; one as a part time active member and the other as a good student with a part-time job. In these cases gang members were able to fool parents, teachers, employers and even siblings. Others may hold down full-time jobs, go to college, be parents, volunteer time to the community and go the church.

Unfortunately having a stable two-parent family, college education and financial stability does not exempt youth from gang membership, leadership and commitment.

Gang activity really affects many parts of our community. Gang crime and violence has not only had an impact on the law enforcement, judicial and probation systems, but also has had an impact on our medical facilities, schools, shopping centers and personal lives. Gangs affect everyone, directly or indirectly. The American gang phenomenon has even exerted its influence internationally. Street gangs are reported in major cities across the globe. Street gangs can now be found in Canada, England, New Zealand, Australia, Russia, Africa and Japan.

The Community Response

As a group, witnesses should want to help the police. Many times in gang cases these witnesses are scared and concerned about gang retaliation. Unfortunately, some witnesses are targeted for intimidation by gang members or by family members. Often, witnesses are non-trusting of the judicial system, or sometimes they may even be rival gang members.

Responding to a subpoena requires a civilian witness to take time off work and spend a day in court. Being a witness may not be an easy role, but without witnesses criminal cases may not be filed or prosecuted. A good witness liaison program can help save the prosecution of criminal cases as well as make the experience easier to cope with for the witness.

Many educators have become surrogate parents for too many students. Strict dress-codes and even voluntary school uniforms have been adopted in many school districts around the country to help stop the gang influence at school. Think about the tremendous responsibilities we have given our educators. Often students stay at school for six to eight hours daily. Many educators have expressed an all-too-real concern for their safety on school campuses. The main reason for many is gang violence. Teachers have become witnesses and victims in gang cases because the violence happened on school grounds.

How about the children? Do you know what your child's fears are concerning the gangs at their school? What about the trip to and from school? I have spoken to many children who worry about becoming a victim of gang violence going to, while at or leaving their school. These same children often are the victims and witnesses in gang cases. Frightened and concerned about testifying, these witnesses need support.

This issue may even go further than you think. Some students report they fear for their safety while at school. A few 5th grade elementary school students reported that they were afraid to use the restroom at school because 6th grade gang members were charging a quarter to use the bathroom. The 5th grade students were threatened with a physical assault if they reported the activity. This means there are no witnesses to the extortion. Another example of how a gang can control with fear and intimidation.

Mental Health

Mental health professionals can anticipate some unique problems when dealing with gang members as patients. Gang members are sometimes placed voluntarily in mental-health programs as an alternative to going to jail. Their gang mentality accompanies them. These patients are able to disrupt program routines. A special triage at entry may eliminate or minimize potential problems. When two rival gang members recently entered the same substance-abuse program and were housed in the same facility, the staff was unaware of the potential conflict between the two patients.

At first, the two patients would just stare at each other during meals. Then, as one staff member said, "They made some type of sign with their hands whenever they saw each other." About a week after they entered the program, a fistfight ensued between them. Neither was seriously injured, but the commotion, and the incidents, both reported and unreported, caused setbacks for many of the other patients. The gang rivalry and gang mentality were present, just not recognized. Gang crime can occur anywhere.

Mental health professionals could also be needed as expert witnesses and to help victims, gang members and their families attempt to deal with all the psychological and emotional stresses of gang life. Especially when surviving victims, families and witnesses have to deal with such emotional and psychological atrocities as the deaths of innocent children or loved ones.

Mental health professionals can also be a great resource as providers of parent education and conflict resolution curriculum. Understanding child development and guidance issues may aid in the design of intervention and prevention programs.

The saying, today's victim is tomorrows suspect, is commonly used because of the pay back concept. This gang philosophy is a generic way of describing the continual cycle of gang violence. Gang investigations can include interviewing gang witnesses, gang victims and gang sympathizers. As one Orange County, California, gang prosecutor told the jury, "... *when a crime is committed in hell the witnesses are not angels.*"

Gang Myths

Even with all the awareness concerning the activities of street gangs some people still are in denial or have biased information on street gangs. For whatever reason, several myths about street gangs are still encountered today. These include the belief that the majority of street gang members are juveniles. Juveniles (younger than 18 years) actually comprise only about 20 percent of the total gang membership.

Secondly, people still believe that gang members only harm themselves. The reverse is actually true. More often than not gang members usually hurt innocent bystanders. Sadly, according to data published by the U.S. Department of Justice, 50 percent of the victims of deadly gang violence are innocent bystanders.

Many people still believe that gangs have to be turf oriented. Turf is not a criteria used to establish the existence of a street gangs. Remember our definition? Many street gangs do not claim any turf. Some street gangs act as mobile criminal enterprises and have no turf.

Another common myth about street gangs is that females are not allowed to join. The reality is that females are joining gangs at a record pace. Many female gang members are just as violent as their male counter parts.

Some people still think the only weapons that gang members use are chains, knives and baseball bats. Unfortunately, guns have become the primary weapon of choice for street gang members (Cruz, 2005). Handguns as well as high-powered semi- automatic and automatic assault rifles such as the Uzi, AK-47 and Mac 10 are commonly used in gang confrontations. A gun has even been concealed in the handle of a knife and in a cellular telephone.

At one time it was thought that street gangs have only one leader and are tightly structured. The reality is most street gangs are loosely knit groups. Leadership roles are not formalized in many street gangs. The shot callers may include a group of the most active gang members, rather than just one individual.

Contrary to popular belief, graffiti is not just an art form. Graffiti is the written language for the street gang. Graffiti is used to give death threats, mark off turf, show gang alliances, list gang members, list fallen comrades and to shoe dominance. Graffiti has many purposes in the gang sub-culture and it is simply not an art form.

Many people want to believe the way to solve the gang problem is to lock up all the gang members. A candid look at prison shows that for many street gang members, state prison is like going to college. Many street gang members aspire to become prison gang members. Putting young gang members in prison is like sending them to criminal college. Rehabilitation of hard-core gang members has proved to be ineffective. Changing criminal behavior is a difficult job at best.

Lastly, many citizens feel that gangs are only a law enforcement problem. Gangs are a problem for everyone. They are a societal issue. Collaborative programs involving law enforcement, probation, schools, churches, private business, parks and recreation and parents are the most successful at curbing the gang problem.

With all the awareness, all the media coverage and all the violence, gangs have become a pandemic issue for society.

Summary

Understanding gang sociology is not difficult, but can be a little confusing. Gang members can join a gang in a number of ways. Once a formal member that person freely accepts a set of rules and customs that are for the most part unwritten. Most gangs have no formal leadership structure, but that is changing for a few gangs. Prison gangs can exert an influence on street gangs. There are still many myths about American street gangs that many Americans still hold as truth. Belief in these myths only helps increase denial.

Gang Sociology

Graffiti artists and critic.
Circa early 1970's.

In this section the four organizational characteristics of gang types will be discussed from three perspectives. They are sociological, law enforcement and levels of membership within the gang, including some leadership structures of street gangs. There are many factors that affect the formation, operation and changes that occur within street gangs. There may be several internal and/or external factors acting together which cause a change in gang operations or philosophy.

Social Gangs

Early academic studies by sociologists Larry J. Siegal and Joseph J. Senna categorized street gangs as social gangs, delinquent gangs and violent gangs.

These researchers see the social gang as a relatively permanent group that may hang out at a specific location such as a store or a street corner. Members develop a sense of comradeship and often participate with in-group activities. The group would typically stay together because of the mutual attraction among its membership, rather than the need for protection (Siegal and Senna, 1989). This may be seen in some turf-oriented gangs and can be viewed as part of a process in the early stages of development for both Hispanic and African-American street gangs.

This has also been observed as a mechanism for some Indo-Chinese gangs that have formed in Southern California. The gang members had known each since elementary and junior high school days. They were a group that started out as friends because of extended family relationships, school mates or neighbors. The group participated in minor delinquent behavior at first. Over a period of just a few years they were committing residential burglaries and drug trafficking. The group also became involved in gang related violence. The members acknowledge that even thought they referred to themselves as a party crew, they were really a gang.

However, this may not be true for all Hispanic and African-American street gangs. In the early 1990s Central- American local L.A. based street gangs victimized immigrants and refugees. It was this victimization that became the catalyst for some Central-American immigrants to join the 18th Street gang. This was specifically done to prevent them from being victimized. It appears that joining a gang was done for protection. The formation of the first Blood gang in Southern California was done in an effort to protect themselves from the Crip gangs.

Siegal and Senna also believed the social gang will not normally participate in serious delinquent activities and will try not to engage in violence unless they are attacked (Siegal and Senna, 1989). Some skateboard groups can be classified as social gangs. Currently, a few of the tagger crews, posses, clubs, clicks and party crews might be characterized as social gangs. It should be noted that these groups could react violently if confronted or challenged in some manner.

Delinquent Gangs

According to Siegal and Senna delinquent gangs are groups of minors who function as an organized gang with the goal of obtaining monetary gain from illegal activities. Members depend on one another to carry out planned activities and to provide help if necessary to complete the current activity. Leaders who emerge from these groups are usually excellent organizers and planners (Siegal and Senna, 1989).

Members of this type of gang are usually stable and are able to organize their time and efforts for criminal activity. They view gang activity as a way of getting ahead in the world. Delinquent gang members accept some of society's goals such as wealth, success and power, but reject the legitimate way of obtaining them. This may lead the way to adult criminal behavior if this lifestyle and attitude is continued. This also fuels the immediate need for gratification and helps form a distorted sense of reality.

American-Asian gangs function in this manner. These groups are usually not territorial in nature and operate as a unit to commit crimes for profit. They may be more sophisticated in the planning and execution of crime than the average African-American or Latino gang member. These groups may be involved in violent behavior if needed or use violence as a tool to achieve their goals. This type of behavior can be seen within Southeast Asian, Chinese, Korean and Pacific Island; out law motorcycle and some prison gangs.

Violent Gangs

The third Siegal and Senna category is the violent gang. This gang is organized so that the violent activities it is involved in will bring some kind of emotional gratification to its members. Members spend their time building arsenals and planning their activities. The general membership tends to over-estimate the importance of size and power for the gang. The leaders may be emotionally unstable (Siegal and Senna, 1989).

Structure for this type of gang is always changing. One day its allies are enemies and vice versa. Intra-group violence is commonly reported, perhaps the result of a constant jockeying for status within the general membership. Sometimes this conflict is verbal and other times it takes a more physical form.

According to these researchers violent gangs seem to emerge spontaneously. They provide a vehicle for violent, hostile youths to act out their aggressions and personal problems. Membership within these types of gangs seems to be changing constantly (Siegal and Senna, 1989).

Sub-groups can develop within the main gang. These sub-groups, often called cliques or sets are regularly seen with Black and Latino street gangs. The groups can be divided by age or geographical location. Skinhead gangs can also operate in the same fashion, utilizing violence as a tool for their cause. Mara Salvatrucha cliques also appears to follow this mechanism.

Street gangs have been generally categorized into these three sociological types of groups. In real-life situations, out in the streets, in the housing projects and the neighborhoods, a gang could contain members from all three social categories. The membership may not be evenly distributed between classifications. For example, you may not find one-third belonging to the social gang class. A group as whole may mature into the different Siegal and Senna gang models.

Having different types of gang personalities from a sociological point of view will complicate the development of the street gang. I suggest that individual gang members themselves share all the Siegal and Senna sociological traits and they are transitory in nature. This adaptive behavior allows for gang members to function within the sub-culture.

Law Enforcement Perspective

Although working with the same groups, law enforcement officers tend to classify gangs a little differently from a sociologist. Yet, law enforcement definitions share the some of the same descriptors and global views.

Gangs can be classified in a variety of categories depending whether or not you are examining history, activity, function or membership. As an active member of the law enforcement community, I have discovered that street and prison gang personalities are comprised of many different factors that include history, activity, function, and membership. To classify a gang with any single category could potentially exclude or include groups. From a law enforcement perspective there are four gang classifications that can include all types of groups. The individual categories are based on many factors.

Turf Gangs

Turf gangs have also been called traditional street gangs. These gangs obviously claim a turf or neighborhood as theirs. The turf or neighborhood may be a specific geographical area of a city. It could be a park, or several city blocks. In a few instances, it can be the entire city. The motivation to join these types of gang is usually generational in nature. Some members of traditional street gangs consider themselves the policemen of their neighborhoods. For example, Latino, some African-American and Tag Banger gangs all have claimed turf.

In generational gangs previous or current immediate family members were or are members of a street gang. This has led to the appearance of generational gang members. Gang membership is based on as tradition or as a normal part of growing-up. In some instances, you can trace gang membership back three or four past generations. The gang's activity can be motivated by the desire to protect the neighborhood. Everything that happens in the neighborhood is their responsibility.

In generational gangs the gang's perspective and mentality is passed on to the next generation from within the family. Gang indoctrination can begin at an early age. In these environments youth as young as 7 or 8 years old can present with gang behaviors, including a dislike for authority.

It is easy to see how these types of gangs can literally take control of certain parts of a city. Imagine if you live in this type of neighborhood and you are not part of the gang. As stated before, even though gang membership is a choice some may have limited choices.

Crime for Profit Gangs

These gangs are usually mobile and commit crime for profit. Therefore, they will not claim any specific turf. Committing crime for profit appears to be the main motivation for membership and activity. The best examples are the Indo Chinese or Southeast Asian street gangs. Members will travel long distances to commit a crime and make a buck.

It is not a requirement for these types of gangs to be mobile, but many gangs are. Prison gangs make a profit and they never leave the institution where they are housed. However, being mobile is certainly an advantage to have.

The crime for profit gangs may specialize in a particular type or types of crimes. For example, some street gangs specialized in home invasion robberies, residential burglaries, credit card and check frauds, drug sales, extortion, identity theft and murder for hire. Not all crime committed by these groups has to be violent.

Sometimes gangs in this category have been referred to as mobile criminal enterprises, or nomadic gangs. Members of these types of gangs may have a few or all the traditional gang classifiers, including, scars and burns, tattoos and stylized clothing. They also may be computer literate and be able to access and navigate the Internet.

Generally, when these gang members get into the 18-24 year-old age group their clothing style may change and they may work with members from a rival gang. The motive is to make money. Therefore older gang members may form new gang and they may resemble organized crime groups in activity, sophistication and type of crime.

Philosophical Gangs

The third category of gang membership is based on a belief system. The belief system may be political or religious in nature. Membership and activity would be motivated solely by the belief system. This would include the use of violent crime committed in the support of the belief system. Membership does not have to claim a turf nor does it necessarily have to commit crime for profit. Motivation for committing crime is solely based on the philosophy of the group. Classic examples are the skinhead gangs. Activity and membership are based on their belief of the white pride and can include a white supremacy conviction.

As one 17-year-old skinhead claimed, *"He is my brother because of belief and the cause,"* referring to another skinhead he had just met. The cause was saving and purifying the white race.

Occult groups are small when compared to the over all gang membership, nevertheless their membership and activity are based from an occult religious perspective. People who involve themselves in these groups do so based on religion. These religions are not mainstream Christian based belief systems. The major religions encountered in street gangs are Witchcraft, Satanism, Santeria and Palo Mayombe. Religious affiliation alone is of no legal concern. However, sometimes members of these groups become involved in criminal activity. That is when the legal system steps in.

Crime motivated by these belief systems can include ritual animal sacrifices, murder, assaults, fraud, graffiti, grave desecration, substance abuse and drive by shootings. As you can see, a powerful belief system can compel the believer to commit a variety of crimes.

I must add an observation here. The majority of occult religion practitioners are law-abiding citizens. They are no more likely to commit a crime than members of the general population. Youth introduce themselves to these religions and use the religion to justify their actions. The media reports these activities and there is a tendency for the general public to stereotype all practitioners with the reported behavior.

Hybrid Gangs

The last category is referred to as Hybrid or Semi-Traditional gangs. Street gangs in this category often mimic traditional street gangs in dress, tattoos, hairstyle, graffiti, attitudes and sociology. However, they may also claim not to fight over turf and try not to commit violent crimes.

Membership can be mixed-raced and include females. Hybrid gangs can include groups like party crews, rebels, clubs, posses, clicks and some tagger crews. All have attempted to steer away from the violence that normally accompanies street gang life. An earnest attempt is made not to be violent. However, for all street gangs including Hybrid gangs, the issue of respect is important. When respect is lost or taken away, the response for these groups is always the same. Sooner or later they react with violence to perceived or real threats, insults and loss of respect.

The original tagger crews of the 1980s are another example of a Hybrid gang. Membership and activity for the traditional tagger crews are based on fame or respect. There is a certain amount of respect that is earned and given for the amount of graffiti a particular person or crew can complete. As one L. A. based tagger told me, "*... to get up and be seen is what it's all about...*"

Some Hybrid gangs have broken the race and gender barriers when it comes to membership, so you may encounter a co-ed gang.

A few Hybrid gangs claim affiliation with other gangs like the Blood, Crip, Folk or People Nation gangs. Some Hybrid gangs may claim the entire city as their turf and may mimic traditional turf gang in their activities. Often, graffiti will be present and the gang members will identify with a specific color or hand sign. A few Hybrid gangs can also be fighting gangs, whose main goal is to earn respect through violence. They share membership indicia with traditional street gangs, but often do not claim turf.

Gang Leadership Models

There are a number of leadership models that have been identified in street and prison gangs. Like membership, leadership models can change with time and with direct and indirect influences on the gang. The FBI's leadership theory is based on gang criminal operations. As gangs get more involved in criminal operations they must develop an organizational structure if they are to function efficiently. The model becomes dependant on this assumption.

The assumption is correct for some gangs, not all. There is a tendency for street and prison gangs to become vertically organized and develop a well defined leadership as the gang becomes more involved in criminal activities. The Federal RICO prosecutions against the Lil Cycos clique of 18th Street, Nuestra Familia, Mexican Mafia and in 2006 against the Aryan Brotherhood bear this out.

There is also the belief that most gangs are loosely knit coalitions of small autonomous cliques. The model is based on the assumption that apart from a general commitment to their gang and the gang life style, the only unifying force is combat with outsiders. The Fighting gangs are a good example of this. Gang leadership is usually decentralized, non-hierarchal and even situational. Gang leadership is more a function of individual prowess and reputation (respect) than a formalized structure for making collective decisions. Leadership can change rapidly and may vary by activity. As with most gangs leadership is "age-graded" and older members may be powerful role models. The type of gang leadership varies from gang to gang and by geographical area (Weisel, 2002).

Gang leadership is a complex behavior and practice area to examine. For example, gang leadership is not always a function of age. In other words there are no rules that require the gang leader(s) to be the oldest most experience gang members. The most criminally active gang member(s) can assume leadership roles. Some gangs can have multiple leaders and both male and female gang members can assume leadership roles.

The FBI is correct in that leadership changes from gang to gang and geographical area. However the model is probably not valid for the myriad types of gang encountered today. There have been three distinct gang leadership models I have encountered in my experience. But for the vast majority of street gangs this is not encountered.

Nuclear Model

The first gang leadership model can be described as the group leadership model. Imagine a small circle within a larger one. The center circle represents the membership who leads the gang. This inner circle or nucleus of the gang may consist of anywhere from one to multiple members. These leaders seem to be the most feared or influential members of the gang. Females can also assume this type of leadership role. Often, this type of leader is called a shot caller, in Asian street gangs they also known as a dai-low (older brother). Some street gangs receive their direction and focus from a few of the older more experience gang members also known as OG's or veteranos.

Most street gangs do not follow an official organizational chart. Leadership is often an assumed role and can change, especially if the gang gets involved in drugs sales, fraud or identity theft. In the nuclear leadership model there are no formal leadership rankings such as president, vice-president or treasurer. Leadership tends to be fluid because as one gang member becomes more active his influence over the other members may increase while another member's influence decreases.

This nucleus or cadre assumes the responsibility of leadership by offering advice, consultations, protection, and acceptance of other gang members. Most families offer some type of guidance, usually by an older, more experienced family member. The same holds true for gangs who use this type of leadership model. Many times, the leadership roles are more like that of a parent raising a family or playing the big brother role. In essence, the gang's leadership is controlled by a small group of its most active membership. Age may not be a factor and the most active gang members set the pace for the rest of the gang.

It becomes easy to understand why the gang becomes the surrogate or extended family for the member and why some gang leaders may be young or female members.

If a gang is large enough, small cells or cliques form. The cliques may form based on age or geographical area. The one usually leads these sub groups or two gang members who are the most active or charismatic. These gang leaders become shot callers or event leaders. They tend to be the most respected and have the most authority within the clique. Failure to obey the gang rules could result in disciplinary actions ordered by the shot callers. This process is sometimes referred to as *"courting"* or *"check courting."*

A nationally established gang like 18th Street or Mara Salvatrucha could have hundreds of cliques; all claiming to part of the whole gang and yet never in contact with all the membership. These cliques are led by small groups of gang members within the gang. The younger members tend to follow the directions and orders of the shot callers. I use the term younger in two ways here: younger as in year age and younger as with membership tenure.

Generally, Latino street gangs use this type of leadership. The gang is considered to be the family of the gang member. Often, the leadership comes from the older or more experienced gang members. Almost always, the role is assumed, there is no voting. Sometimes, these cadres of gang members are called veteranos. They may have been incarcerated in county jail or state prison. Certainly, they are experienced with all aspects of the gang lifestyle. They are often viewed with honor and esteem. They become the cliques shot callers. They run the show.

Musical Chair Leadership

Since the environment within gang sub-culture is very dynamic, some street gangs do not require a territory to function or exist. As a result, these street gangs may use a fluid type of leadership model to operate. For example, some Indo-Chinese gangs have developed a unique style of leadership based on function rather than tradition. These nomadic gangs are motivated to make a profit, so committing crime is really an efficiently run mobile criminal business.

Leadership within these types of street gangs can be an interim assignment. Each member is still part of the gang family but would have a specific function when the gang is conducting business. Usually, a single person directs the group's activity during a specific crime or at a particular location. This may happen because that person has unique knowledge of the location and/or targeted victim.

When the location changes for the next operation, a different member of the street gang may take over and direct the criminal activity. Most of the time leadership roles are freely interchanged between gang members in order to run the business more efficiently. The business of course is committing crime for profit.

Sometimes, due to internal conflict, a single member or small group splits off from the parent gang and forms a sibling gang. The disgruntled member(s) of the parent gang could lead the sibling gang. The sibling gang may or may not be rivals with the parent gang.

However, the sibling gang may become the new competition in the area where they formed. They can develop rivalries quickly because of the respect issues. The end result can be the rapid appearance and disappearance of nomadic gangs within certain communities. The level of gang violence also may vary as gangs form new alliances, change operation locations, or by adding or dropping members.

Loyalty to the gang can also be fluid, especially in Indo-Chinese gangs and tagging crews. Gang members may change gangs with little or no repercussions.

A single individual may have been a member of several different street gangs. It is not uncommon to find childhood friends or siblings who were in the same gang together and are now bitter rivals because one person joined a different gang. The gang members consider this a normal part of the gang life. Another factor that might fuel inter-gang membership is drug trafficking. The business of drug trafficking has help rival gangs become business partners and individual gang members to become part of different gangs or drug trafficking organizations.

This can be seen as street gang level drug suppliers work with prison gang and drug cartel members to purchase drugs.

Another example might be with some Indo-Chinese street gangs who specialize in certain types of criminal behavior. It may be auto thefts, auto or home burglaries, home-invasion robberies or commercial take over robberies. With each type of criminal specialization one member normally assumes the leadership role. This person would plan or direct the criminal action. He may have help from the other members, but many times he or she will assume the leadership role. As victims, criminal specialty or operation locations change, it is also possible for the leadership to change.

Organized Leadership

The third type of leadership is really two variants of the same leadership model. The leadership model is structured and there is a vertical organization component to it. But, there may be an informal and formal version of this leadership model. Certain street gangs run successful drug-dealing and criminal operations that rival traditional organized crime groups. To be successful in business requires some type of order and organization. Someone has to be in charge, make decisions, and a support staff is needed to augment the changes.

Sometimes these street gangs have an informal organizational set-up for members and a formal chain of command to follow. Many times small groups within the organization have specific tasks such as money collection and protection, drug sales, drug transportation and accounting. It is not uncommon to find out these street gangs are run by one person, with a best friend or relative designated second-in-command to run the day to day operations, and have sections or small groups to conduct the business. The entire organization is really a street gang whose members run the business at all levels.

Good examples are some of West Coast Blood, Crip and Black Gangster Disciple gang sets from Chicago. These gangs have become so efficient in the sales of crack and cocaine that now some sets deal directly with the Colombian suppliers. These gangs have spread their operations throughout the United States. In Southern California Blood and Crip gang members are terminally bitter rivals. Yet, out-of-state, often they will cooperate together to set up and run crack or cocaine operations.

The Black street gangs who run these types of operations conduct the retail sale of drugs with order and organization. Missing are official organizational charts, production reports or budgets; nevertheless, the operation is conducted in such a manner that it mimics the way legitimate successful business is run.

A few prison gangs actually have organizational charts and official titles and ranks. Specific are assigned duties Along with a specific rank comes specific duties. Written documentation that defines rank roles has been seized. The ranks within the prison parallel military organization. Not surprisingly some street gangs also have a prison counterpart. Therefore, the gang operates in prison and on the street. Good examples are the United Blood Nation, Black Gangster Disciples, Nazi Low Riders and Public Enemy Number One gangs.

As a particular gang evolves, membership and the type of leadership may change. This implies that a gang may be changing as members are incarcerated, new members enter, as members leave the gang, as law enforcement suppression programs are started, a demographic change in population, parolee demographics, the introduction of drug trafficking, gang migration, unemployment and the presence of a military base. These are just a few of the factors that can affect gang leadership and membership.

By 2005 some law enforcement officials were reporting that some cliques of the MS-13 gang had become more organized. Some cliques were holding monthly meetings for its members and requiring them to pay dues. There were also reports of regional meetings where clique leaders would meet to discuss regional operations. The third type of law enforcement report concerned the observation that in some MS-13 cliques formal titles and responsibilities were being assigned to the leadership. All are anecdotal evidence of a vertical leadership model being developed.

It is interesting to note that these types of behaviors were seen within the Whyos gang during the mid 1800s in New York. Some Whyos gang members later became the first members of the La Cosa Nostra type organized crime families.

Gang Membership Levels

There are arguments that suggest that several levels of gang membership exist. The easiest way to categorize or measure the level of commitment would be to sub-group gang members into four categories. However, there are membership level models that suggest there are many more categories of membership.

The least involved are the target group. Often, they are a section of the population who form the potential core of new gang members or associates. These can be youth who become enchanted with the gang lifestyle and attempt to associate with gang members or the gang. As young as eight to 11 years, these youngsters find gang life exciting and intriguing. For youth who are exposed to many risk factors, this can easily become an entry-level position leading to full gang membership.

However, there is no age specific requirement to be in this group (Hill, Lui and Hawkins, 2001). Youth at this level may imitate real gang members by wearing stylized clothing, using gang slang or gang hand signs. As Tiny a 9-year-old Hispanic child said, *"We just hang around the guys, we just watch them... we try to be like them."*

The second level of gang membership consists of peripheral or associate gang members, sometimes referred to as the gang dabblers. Some will openly claim gang affiliation to non-gang members, school authorities, peers and law enforcement. Other members will deny any association with the gang, but frequent contacts by the police, photographs and videotapes, and behavior, indicate otherwise. Associate gang members may be able to successfully hide their alternative lifestyle from parents and other family members. Often, associate gang members will have no formal arrest or contact records with the police.

An associate gang member will frequent the areas where the gang hangs out. It would not be uncommon to have an associate gang member photographed with and by other gang members. Many times, they will be able to participate in criminal activity with other gang members. Alternatively, some are bonefide gang members but will claim only associate status to law enforcement officials in an attempt to conceal their membership or leadership status.

Another term that is used to describe associate membership is "*wanna be.*" It is often used to describe youth who act like gang members but are not considered gang members by law enforcement. I feel this term is misleading and misused. A gang member at this level is more like an apprentice. This is sort of a part-time gang membership. The associate can simulate the way the regular gang members dress, talk and act. Sometimes, the associate may even sport a tattoo. A person acting in this manner is a serious candidate for regular full-time gang membership. There is no particular length of duration a person remains at this level. Certainly the more time the person spends associating with the gang the quicker the transition to full-time gang member status. Using the term wanna be only allows for denial to be used to justify the claim that "*we do not have gangs in our city, only wanna bes*".

Sometimes gang membership is like having a part time job. Many young people are really successful at having a school personality and a gangster personality. Many Asian gang members have told me that if they do well in school their parents will not bother them in any way. This provides an opportunity to participate in a gang without family or parents knowledge.

The third level of membership contains regular gang members. The people in this group are committed to the gang lifestyle. Membership at this level comes with increased recognition and responsibilities. The recognition comes from two groups. Peer gang members who now welcome the new full-time gang member into their group and the former associates who now envy his or her status. Non-gang members validate the uniqueness of being a gang member by responding with fear or intimidation when confronted.

For many gang members a false feeling of power and importance is felt because so many educational, legal, law enforcement, judicial and medical resources have been employed to fight gang violence. Thus, gang membership becomes a status symbol. In addition, the war against gang violence only further legitimizes the status of being a member of a gang for some gang members.

For others it is a continuation of a cultural battle against the system that began long before their birth. For these gang members the battle becomes a tradition and is passed on through each generation. This is done even though a knowledge and awareness exists that continuing with the gang tradition can result in death or long-term incarceration. There is a tacit approval of this behavior by many parents and family members.

Some young women also find it exciting and in vogue to have a gang member as a boyfriend. Sometimes, these girls are not gang members but gang groupies. Gang members are quick to notice some of the perks that come with full or part-time membership. This type of recognition can have an intoxicating effect.

Gang members at this level have responsibilities. Members of turf gangs are responsible for helping to protect the area claimed by the gangs, or assist in gang operations. Blind loyalty to the gang is expected and given. Gang members assist in retaliatory actions, drug sales, transport and usage. At this level, some gang members may even have some minor leadership responsibilities. The gang lifestyle may demand dedicating life and all resources to the gang. Gang members in this group can be of any age, but typically range from 10 to 25 years old. Within this group, the newest members are often referred to as "*youngsters.*" Older members with more gang experience can act as mentors and leaders.

Hard core gang members comprise the fourth category of membership. Often, these types of gang members have been incarcerated in local or state facilities. They also may have had numerous arrests and contacts with the local police. As veterans of gang life, they have a certain notoriety attached to them. They have survived. Hard core gang members know gang violence intimately. Many have been arrested for attempted murders, murders and assaults with deadly weapons. Many have been injured in gang-related violence.

Sometimes the shot callers emerge from this inner-core of gang members. Often, younger gang members will look up to these veteranos (veterans) or OGs (original gangsters) for advice and help with personal and gang related matters. The younger gang members normally have a tremendous amount of respect for the hard-core gang member.

Hard-core gang member status does not necessarily require a lot of time in as a gang member. The hard-core status can be attained easily by involving oneself in repeated acts of gang violence. Unfortunately, hard-core gang members may be as young as 11 years old. Age is no longer a good indicator to assess gang membership level or leadership status.

Gang members at this level are so committed to this lifestyle that some describe it as, "*To eat, sleep, and think of nothing but the gang.*" All too often, their families have no role in their lives. These types of gang members, as well as the other types may still live at home or with relatives. They tend to minimize interaction with family members. School is not important for some and others do well in school or college. These gang members may be highly motivated street criminals and some are very adept at hiding that fact.

The hard-core gang members comprise the nucleus of the gang. As such, they can be well insulated by the rest of the gang membership and may hold a leadership role within the gang. Often, it is very difficult to gain their confidence or communicate. Hard-core gang members can carry so much influence that sometimes their actions alone direct and control the activity of the entire gang.

These four classifications of gang membership can be used as a guide to further understand the gang sub-culture. As with any diagnostic system, there are going to exceptions. Police find gang members who have never been contacted by law enforcement, who have not been arrested, and who have no tattoos, and who lack any of the traditional gang membership indicia. In my experience, this type of gang member is the exception rather than the rule and they account for a small percentage of the total gang population. Nevertheless, these gang members can be gang leaders. Some may appear to be very insulated from the gang.

Also I have interviewed a number of gang members who routinely deny any gang affiliation or membership. This trend is popular now. Gang members realize the impact their self-admitted membership can have when used against them in criminal proceedings. Being arrested is not a criteria for gang membership, neither is school or employment status.

Some gang trainers believe that there are three to six levels of gang membership. They could many more levels of gang membership depending on what perspective you are using. The point here is to understand that gang membership can be examined by looking at the level of commitment to the gang. Knowing and understanding the commitment level can aid in determining the type of intervention program the youth or young adult will do well in. It may also help develop the direction for suppression and prevention strategies.

Gang Crime

Gang members can be involved in a variety of criminal activity. Some gangs specialize in certain types of crimes for particular reasons. Some gangs are run with a business-like efficiency. Many gangs are quite organized when committing crime. Frequently, gang members, in their attempt to protect the gangs honor, save face, gain respect or protect their turf, are involved in homicides; robberies; drug sales, usage and transport; burglaries; rape; assault; arson; trespass; witness intimidation; kidnapping; extortion; weapons violations; threats against police officers, probation officers and court officers, including judges; hate crimes; cemetery desecration; animal killings; malicious mischief; thefts; credit card fraud, identity theft and the list could continue.

The point is that gang members can, and do, commit all types of crimes. Some gang members can also be employed and graduate from high school and/or college.

Some street gangs are following a trend regarding gang shootings. In the past, an older more experienced gangster would be the only one allowed to shoot. That may have changed for some gangs. Younger gang members under the age of 16 have become the triggermen. Being a shooter in a drive by attack can be the initiation one has to complete to join the gang. If caught, the gang member as a juvenile is exposed to less jail time, than an adult gang member who commits the same crime. All veteran gang members know and are aware of this fact.

Summary

Remember gang life today is constantly changing. There are many unspoken and unwritten rules that govern gang behaviors, membership, leadership and criminal activity. This diagnostic system can be used to help classify what type of gang(s) you may be dealing with and help assess levels of membership.

Understanding gang histories, customs, practices and behaviors will help you to make an accurate diagnosis. Having a good understanding of these will also help to identify the gang mentality. The symptoms (membership indicia) that are used for a diagnosis are really an extension of a certain mentality. It is this mentality that really qualifies a person to be a gang member. It is this mentality that allows a person to commit a gang related crime.

Gang Growth and Migration Studies

Now we will examine the problems and issues of not having a nationally accepted definition for a street gang. We will also examine mechanisms that influence gang migration and growth. After reading this section you will also understand that there are sub-populations within the general gang population.

Two of the most frequently asked questions about the gang sub-culture are: Why do gangs grow? Why do gangs migrate? Some law enforcement officials, politicians, educators and parents might suggest and believe that youth in their city are only "imitating" tougher L.A. street gangs or that the gang problem in their jurisdiction is result of migrating gang members from Los Angeles or Chicago. You will hear the terms "wanna be" or "street corner groups" or "misguided youth" used to describe the groups and you can be given a number of reasons why the groups in these areas are not gangs. You might also hear comments suggesting that gang imitation and migration are the reasons why street gangs have now been reported in all 50 states.

Gang Definition

There is another issue here that has to be addressed before the questions can be asked. It is accepting a standard to measure gang growth and migration. That standard is the definition of a street gang. Developing and then using a nationally accepted definition for a street gang becomes the fundamental basis to build examination of growth and migration. Having a standard definition becomes the fundamental building block to answer the two questions.

Studying gang growth is a little more complicated than just surveying cities for data. Without a standard gang definition to identify a gang, any official findings could be biased and misleading. Any responding jurisdiction could potentially use a different definition to identify the gangs in their area. Often, law enforcers, the public, educators and politicians use a penal code gang based definitions of a criminal street gang as a general working definition for a street gang. If the gang does fit within this legal definition used for penalty enhancement only, then the group is not reported as a gang according to this philosophy. The jurisdiction has no gangs. You can clearly see the issue here.

This will certainly lead to under reporting the number and types of street gangs present. Using a legal based definition of a street gang is appropriate from a prosecutor's point of view. Unfortunately, too many communities, politicians, educators, parents and law enforcement officials use this philosophy. This way of thinking will only reinforce denial and delay the identification and treatment of the gang-community issue.

Many states now have gang enhancement laws similar to California Penal Code Section 186.22. In California this law is commonly known as the STEP Act. It outlines a legal definition for a violent criminal street gang. That definition is used to qualify a defendant(s) for sentencing enhancement, after being convicted for any number of specific crimes listed in the legal text. The crimes that qualify are felony grade and are commonly committed by street gang members.

The California code defines a criminal street gang as:

Any on-going organization, association or group of three or more persons, whether formal or informal, having as one of its primary activities, the commission of one or more of the criminal acts enumerated...

The enumerated section refers to a long list of serious crimes ranging from murder and carjacking to money laundering and extortion. If a gang member is convicted of an alleged crime, and the crime is proven to benefit the gang, the enhancement will be applied when sentenced by the court. In 2006, the California legislature added ID theft and a few other fraud type crimes to the list. Enhancements like PC 186.22 are used as a deterrent to gang violence. If you get convicted of a gang related crime that fits the legal definition you can be sentenced to a longer term in jail.

All gangs have the willingness, readiness and capability to use violence. But, much of the street gang life entails delinquent-type behavior and misdemeanor law violations. Often, the community over looks this behavior and they will become alarmed until a serious violent crime occurs. Many people, including law enforcement officials, politicians and parents believe that a group has to be involved in a drive-by shooting or murder for the group to be called a gang. And when this happens, the behavior is referred to as an "isolated incident" or a "spike in activity." This way it is easier to say, "We do not have a gang problem."

Not all gang activity qualifies for prosecution under STEP Act type laws. Therefore, a Step Act type or legal definition of a street gang should not be used to define a gang or its activity. In fact, many street gangs do not fit this very special legal definition. As I suggested earlier, we need to use a simple more direct approach. A good working definition for a street gang is:

1. Three or more individuals

2. in association

3. with a common identifier (like a name, graffiti, hand sign)

4. committing crime (infractions, misdemeanors, felony)

All gang members have the potential to commit violent acts. Some of the more violent gangs commit and tend to have a history of continual involvement in felony conduct. In fact, many gang members commit delinquent acts and misdemeanor crimes to benefit themselves and/or their gang. What I am suggesting is that a gang is a gang, not a street corner group or misguided youth. In other words, a group does not have to meet a legal enhancement standard based on a penal code law to qualify as a gang.

Still, there is no nationally accepted definition of a gang, even between law enforcement agencies. Some other definitions claim turf is an essential component. Others have self-admission as a critical factor and another one requires that the group must commit major felony level crimes before it should be considered as a gang. State by state, there are literally dozens of definitions. The academic professionals and social scientists tend to use an academic based definition. Many schools use an administrative based definition. Even the U.S. military has developed their definition of what a street gang is. Sometimes, the definition of a gang can literally change city-by-city and county-by-county.

With so many definitions, it becomes virtually impossible to accurately determine how many gang members and street gangs exist in America. They are not measured in the same way. Without accurate data, there is also no way to monitor the growth and activity of street gangs. More importantly without accurate data, it becomes difficult to use and place valuable resources.

To complicate this issue a little more. Consider that it is possible for a gang's criminal activity to be dormant for a while. It will appear as if the gang has gone away or it is no longer involved in crime. Then, there is a sudden spurt of reported criminal activity. As conflicts arise and develop gang members will take part in retaliatory actions until the problem is settled. Gangs that were dormant can become active again. The cause of the sudden activity can be just about anything from bad drug deals, insults to a stolen girl friend. Just because there has not been a law enforcement response to the neighborhood does not mean the gang has disbanded, it has just been inactive.

Commonly, gangs tend to retaliate as the opportunity presents itself. The majority of gang crime appears to be opportunistic in nature. Most violent acts between gangs also appear to the result of a chance encounter. Today, since so many gang members are armed, especially when traveling outside their home base, violent confrontation should be anticipated. But there have been cases where a gang will wait for a year or more before retaliating and where they have planned an attack.

No wonder it is so difficult to get an accurate picture of what is going on. This is why a standard definition needs to be used. It will provide a vehicle for us to get an accurate pulse on the number of gang members and street gangs in the country. It will also become the basis to track this data. And it will help to distribute the appropriate resources to minimize the impact of gangs in our communities.

Growth

The information that helps explain the national situation is limited. Let's take a look at some data collected by the U.S. Department of Justice. A 1997, Office of Juvenile Justice and Delinquency Prevention (OJJDP) report was based on information collected in a 1995 survey of police and sheriff departments. When the data was analyzed, some surprising findings were reported on the number and size of U.S. street gangs.

According to the National Youth Gang Center gangs are not reported in all 50 states. Trend wise, there was a large increase in the number of identified and reported gangs in the mid to late 1990's. The number of gangs being reported actually decreased staring 1999 and remained that way until 2004. Beginning in 2005 the number of gang being reported in the country again started to increase. The same trend could be seen with the actual number of gang members being reported. This is all based on law enforcement data (IIR, 2009)

What causes findings like this to be reported? During the 1995 survey, the country as a whole was becoming aware of the street gang phenomenon. One factor was the reported growth in the number of street gangs in the country. Malcolm Klein, a well-known University of Southern California sociologist, confirmed the growth of street gangs, by studying the number of cities across the country that reported the presence of street gangs.

Amazingly, Klein's studies revealed only 58 cities across the country reporting street gang activity in 1960. That number grew to 101 cities in 1970. In 1980, 179 cities across the country reported gang activity. Not surprising, most of the reported gangs were on the west coast in California. By 1992, 769 cities reported the presence of street gangs (Klein, 1995). By late 1998, street gangs were reported in all 50 states, with over 1200 cities reporting the presence of street gangs. There is abundant evidence of the growth of street gangs.

One Percent Rule

As the number of street gangs increased, the nation also experienced a growth in the number of gang members. Basically, the gang population exploded during this time. In early 1980 there was thought to be only about 300,000 gang members in the United States. At that time, California alone reported almost 150,000 gang members in the state. Because of denial, inaccurate reporting and non-reporting, there is no accurate estimate for the country's gang population. Many of my peers and I suspect there were more gang members than reported.

Other reports from government agencies estimate the national gang population between 650,000 and 850,000 members (National Drug Intelligence Center and U.S. Department of Justice). The number of different gangs also varies depending on what study is used. The estimates vary between 25,000 and 35,000 gangs. In April, 2008 the U.S. department of Justice submitted a report that suggested there were 1 million gang members in the country (US DOJ, 2008). It is logical to see how the findings are dependent on the survey responses. The responses become the critical variable in determining an accurate picture. With a tendency to under report or not report gang activity, it is easy to see how official findings may be inaccurate.

The findings of informal studies I conducted in several cities in California, Washington, Nevada, Arizona and Georgia suggest a different outcome. I used the definition of a street gang mentioned in this text and spoke with gang investigators. I believe a more accurate estimation of the U.S. gang population comes from what I call the "one percent rule." This theory states that gang populations will run about one percent or less of the general population. The ad hoc studies conducted suggest this, whether a single city or an entire county is examined. The findings suggest that the total gang population accounts for less than one percent of the general population. They tend to be between .6 and .7 percent.

There were a few exceptions. In locations where gangs originally developed, a slightly higher percentage was calculated. In these cities the data suggested that gang populations on average ran between .7 and .9 percent, but not greater than 1.1 percent based on 2004 data. The data from ICE deportations also suggests that illegal immigrant gang populations run about 1 percent of the total deported population (Valdez, 2009). The U.S. military also suggests that active duty military personnel who are involved in gangs runs around 1 percent or less of the entire active duty population (Smith, 2008).

For example, in 2005 the general Los Angeles County population was estimated at 9.935 million people (U.S. Census Bureau, 2006). Los Angeles is also considered to be the birthplace of Hispanic gangs. In March 2006, the Cal-Gang intelligence system reported an estimated 89,000 street gang members in the county. The one percent theory predicts that .89 percent of the L.A. population were gang members. The same analysis in Orange and San Diego counties (California) suggested a .85 percent gang population. In other cities that I have been able to get statistical data on gang populations, gang populations are well under one percent.

Reported gang populations change for many reasons. Anecdotal law enforcement evidence from 1993-2006 tends to support that theory. The latest data from Los Angeles County suggests that the gang population is less than 1 percent of the general population that is a change from 1998. This is a great example of the value of using a standard definition for a gang member and street gang. You can track, compare and develop a history of the number of gang members, types of street gangs and gang related activity accurately.

Based on these ad hoc studies and using this theory let's examine the U.S. population. The last census (2000) estimated the national population close to 285 million people. The one percent theory suggests that the U.S. gang population should be closer to 2 million. This is more than double the highest Department of Justice estimate. If this is true the gang problem is more severe than we want to believe or previously thought. Under estimation of gang populations and activity can hinder or prevent the implementation of suppression, intervention and prevention programs. The inaccurate data can cause a false sense of security to develop.

If you also take into account the fact that the U.S. population reached a benchmark size in October, 2006 the gang populations could be higher. By October, 2006 there were over 300 million people living in the country. This would predict that the gang population should be closer to 2.5 million, triple the highest academic based estimate.

Age and Activity

In California the number of street gang members was estimated at 300,000 (California Department of Justice, 2003. If that estimate is accurate, in that state, gang members outnumber the police three to one. Nationally, the majority of street gang members are adults. Juvenile gang members only comprise 20-25 % of the total street gang population. What gang population is the most criminally active? Media reports help suggest that the juvenile population is the most active. Other surveys suggest the adult gang population is the most active. In reality, it is neither population. It is both.

We should look at the 14-24 year-old age group. The crime rates within this age group have been very dynamic and continue to rise. In fact, the homicide rate in this age group was estimated to be five times higher than just the adult or juvenile age group. This suggests that this combination age group might become a key in developing models about street gangs.

Ad hoc studies suggest that the 14-24 year-old age group becomes a critical factor when studying street gangs. By examining this age group, I have found that it contains approximately 65-70% of the total street gang population. Like the one percent theory, there are a few exceptions. In a few areas of the country the percentage may be a bit lower.

Knowing that the majority of street gang members fall into this combination age group, examining this age group will help give a clearer picture of street gang activity. One issue becomes to try to establish the size of this group. Again, not using a standard definition will lead to a biases finding. This issue becomes a little more complicated because of the non-and under reporting of gang activity, number of gangs and number of gang members. However, the U.S. Department of Justice predicted that by 2006 the overall 14-24 age population will reach 30 million. It did by November of that year. That is the largest this population has ever been.

In those areas of the country where street gangs originated, the 14-24 year –old age group represents about 50-55 percent of the population. This may occur in these areas because the gang population is a lot older and more established verses locations where the gangs were recently established. You should recognize that gang membership spans a complete age spectrum. For example, using December 1998 Cal-Gang data for Orange County, California, the youngest gang member reported was an 8-year-old Hispanic male and the oldest was a 59 year old Hispanic female. Shockingly, across the country children as young as 7 years old have been reported to be gang members.

In rural parts of America, the 14-24 year-old-age group may comprise the entire gang population. This may be true especially if the gang is newly established. This tends to occur in smaller towns and rural America because of the demographics of the youth population. In these adolescent gangs, there are no old timers, age wise around. The gang itself has not been around long enough to have older gang members. The gang members who refer to themselves as OG's or veteranos (veterans) may be in their early teens. Today, gang membership covers a complete age spectrum and shows no gender or racial boundaries.

However, for the greatest potential impact of any strategy this is the age group that should be targeted for suppression, intervention and prevention programs. This is the age group were the greatest dollar return can be realized. This issue may also be true for street gangs that develop outside America, especially in under developed countries where poverty and unemployment is high.

Migration

It has been suggested that California based gangs migrated to other parts of the country and then started new gangs or sets of their own gang. This may have been concluded partly because gangs in other parts of the country displayed many characteristics and behaviors that were consistently encountered with L.A. based street gangs. The challenge becomes to identify what mechanisms and/or societal factors really accounted for this national gang growth; and to determine whether or not a gang brand name was adopted.

Klein's population studies in the early 1990s also suggested that most gangs were home grown. Believe it or not, most street gangs are a function of local geography and demographics.

During the late 1980's and early 1990s law enforcement did not report many Los Angeles or Chicago based gangs in new areas. There were a few cases, but nothing indicative of a developing national trend. Prior to and during the period when Klein conducted his studies, there was little if any documented street gang movement between states.

But don't forget, it is during this time period the gangster rap music industry was developing, movies started to have gang themes, the media was making the public aware of increasing gang violence, there were numerous newspaper and magazine articles about street gangs and the use of the Internet was increasing. Society was changing and still continues to. What these communication medias did was help export the gang culture to other states and worldwide. By the mid to late 1990s it was apparent that the gang culture had literally saturated the country and was entering mainstream society.

Consistent with Klein's studies, many law enforcement officials, including myself also concluded that migrating gang members had a minimal influence on the formation of street gangs outside California between the early 1990s. But one thing was noted by law enforcement. When the occasional move did happen, transplanted gang member(s) had a profound effect on the local community where they resettled. Law enforcement observed that when the move happened, other street gangs had a tendency to form.

However, this may not be the case now. Since the mid 1990s west coast and Chicago based gangs have been reported in many states. Currently, it appears that gang migration is on the rise and having a greater impact than before. Some of the newly arrived gangs tend to be a bit more organized than their parent groups.

Something also happens after the arrival of a west coast or Chicago based gang member. That transplanted gang member assumes an immediate degree of street stature simply because he or she is from California or Chicago. In the gang culture, there is an automatic street status given to any gang member who claims to hail from California, especially southern California or Chicago.

Gang migration can also be intra and interstate. Gangs can move from city to city within a state and from state to state for a variety of reasons. The intrastate migration of gang members can account for the presence of new sets or cliques of a particular gang in new areas of the state. For example, a gang that is known to be active in one particular state may now be active in another state. A question still exists, what mechanisms account for these migrations?

Immigration

In addition, the constant influx of new immigrants adds to the gang equation. Some gangs specifically recruit from these populations or form new gangs themselves. 18th Street and Mara Salvatrucha are good examples of this. When a new Latino based gang forms, it will often use a west coast gang name. There may even be a southern California based street gang with the same name. Many times there is no direct or formal connection to the California based street gang. But, there is an assumption made by mid-west and east coast based gangs. If you claim membership to a gang that appears to be a southern California gang, all of the members have to be from California. This gives members of the gang instant recognition.

This also occurs when a transplanted Los Angeles based gang member gets relocated he receives instant street respect from the local gang. Using the name of a southern California based gang tends to enhance the new gang's reputation. This phenomenon has been well documented with Hispanic and African-American types of gangs that have formed in the mid-west and east coast. Even though this is not a true form of gang migration, it tends to be a leading cause for the formation of new cliques that claim a southern California affiliation in the mid-west and east coast.

By the late 1990s Southern California based street gangs have established themselves in the Mid-west and East Coast through other mechanisms which tended to support the theory that there had been an increasing level of gang migration. There can be a number of mechanisms that contribute to gang migration. Individually they might impact the number of migrating gang members. However, collectively then have a larger impact than most people would like to believe.

We need a word of caution here. There is a tendency for the public to define all or the majority of immigrant population based on the actions of a very small number of immigrants. Experience and anecdotal evidence suggest just the opposite. A small percentage of immigrants get involved in street gangs; remember around 1 percent. Sadly, this small percentage is able to dictate how a large percentage of us live. You must also consider two basic types of migration processes; transnational and national immigration and migration. One focuses on movement within a country and the other on movement between countries.

Quality of Life

Family moving could be another factor that influences migration and immigration. When a family moves to a new community to get their children out of an unsafe environment many times these families already have a child absorbed in the gang life. All too often, this environmental issue is the only one addressed. Many parents have told me, "*I thought moving would get my child out of the gang.*" In essence, the gang mentality and behaviors that were within a child were never dealt with and they were taken to the new home.

If there is an existing street gang in the new area, these youth tend to migrate toward them. It is almost as if they are on autopilot. Regardless of how the parents try to prevent this, the same problems appear and again the family unit is compromised.

Under the same circumstances if there are no gangs in these areas, the transplanted families inadvertently can potentially bring a gang seed with them. The child now becomes a big fish in a little pond. These children sometimes start up new gangs or factions of the gang they belonged to. In the mid- west and east coast, these gangs tend to take on a distinct west coast style. They may even use names like Sureno, Sureno-13, Crips, Bloods, MS-13, or 18th Street.

I would like you to try and remember a concept we all learned in high school biology. Osmosis is a simple concept; between a cell membrane water seeks to be in equal concentrations. So water will cross the membrane until it is in equal concentrations. I want you to consider our southern border as an economic membrane. There is migration across the membrane by people in search of work and opportunity. Criminals take advantage of this behavior and blend in with those coming across the border. Based on the actions of those few criminals entire populations are labeled. This is known as stereotyping.

Employment

There are many minimum wage paying jobs in the mid-west and east coast. These types of jobs are an ideal form of employment for immigrant and migrant working families. The search for employment has driven west coast and newly arrived families to move to where the work is. When the family makes the transition they bring along their children. Some youth are members or associates of southern California based street gangs, others can be become part of a new victim or recruitment pool.

Once relocated, these youth have instant notoriety with the local youth because they are gang members from southern California. In turn some form a clique of their L.A. based gang, recruiting from the local youth pool and establish a southern California based street gang in the mid-west or east coast. The local youth pool can also include immigrant youth.

There are a number of seasonal agriculture working families that make a living by traveling to where the work is. As the agricultural seasons change, the families move to the next area in search of employment. Sometimes the children attend local schools. The new children become the target of local gangs. They may form a gang initially for protection and the cycle starts again. These types of relocations can be frequent or semi-permanent.

Klein, Maxson and Miller (2001) suggest that families searching for employment are one mechanism that aids in gang migration. Families will relocate to get a better paying job or to increase job opportunities. In an attempt to increase the family's quality of life the move often also transplants gang members from one are to another. They are correct the economic membrane is crossed everyday for this very reason.

Probation / Parole

Another mechanism for intrastate migration is the parole and probation system. When a gangster is released from prison or local jail, he or she may be paroled or place on a probation grant in a different county or a different part of the state. The relocated parolee or probationer will have to stay within the jurisdictional area and could establish a new set or clique of his gang. When this happens, the newly formed gang tends to be the rival of any existing gang, especially if the gang is turf oriented.

Forced Moves

Sometimes moves may be forced. Factors that have forced the move have included when a family member is relocated through a victim/witness program. Or a family member is injured and the family relocates near the treatment center. Sometimes a family is evicted from a rented residence. In some cases, the family moves near the prison where a husband, son, daughter is incarcerated. Regardless of the reason, younger siblings who are involved in gangs are brought with the family. The gang again can be transplanted.

Siblings who have a dysfunctional family life may be forced to move. They may relocate to a relative or friend's home. Often here are only temporary accommodations. Sometimes these youth will live on the street because they have no money to afford rent.

Gang Alliances

Another mechanism that helps inter and intra state gang migration is the establishing of gang alliances for national criminal activities. Gangs from the west coast can establish working relationships with gangs from the mid-west or east coast. These relationships can assist to establish national drug routes or money laundering operations.

Recent law enforcement observations have confirmed some unusual alliances between west coast gangs and gangs from the mid-west. Normally these gangs are rivals with each other. A few business relationships have been documented and it is theorized that the reason for the cooperation between the gangs is for making money through the drug trade.

Because of the advent of trans-national gangs cliques of the same gang may have contacts in other countries. These alliances may be difficult to track and monitor. In addition, trans-national contacts can facilitate gang related criminal activities and present prosecution issues.

Crime

Some gangs operate as mobile criminal enterprises as commonly seen with some of the Asian gangs, especially with some Indo-Chinese gangs. When traveling from city to city, county to county and from state to state occasionally a gang member or two will remain behind. It may be because of a disagreement between gang members or simply because they like the area. When this happens only a short period passes before these gang members start recruiting members to form a new gang or they join an existing street gang.

Indo-Chinese gangs are not the only street gangs to do this. Some Hispanic, African-American, White and Skinhead gangs have traveled within different parts of a state to commit crime for profit. The Indo-Chinese gangs are not the only street gang to travel to commit crime. As a group, they attempt that type of crime more often than other street gangs. Traveling to commit criminal activity becomes another type of migration mechanism.

Based on the findings of current research drug trafficking appears to be a major factor in gangs migrating between states, within states and out of the country (National Alliance of Gang investigators, 2005).

Military

Another migration mechanism involves an unwilling participant, our U.S. military. The armed forces need to keep our military in a ready state. This necessitates transfers and re-assignments. This movement becomes a built-in mechanism that has been used by enlisted gang members. These gang members use the military as a resource. Transfers and re-assignments can also facilitate the gang recruitment process. It is easy to understand why all types of gangs are represented in our national military installations, overseas and aboard Navy surface vessels.

The longer an unnoticed enlisted gang member can stay in the military, the more transfers and relocations he can get. An active gang recruiter can recruit and spread his gang all over the world. The key is to be a good soldier, marine, airman or seaman. The enlisted person that brings the least attention to himself is never noticed. In the military, this can be easily accomplished by doing your job.

As enlisted/officer transfers occur, family moves are inevitable. If a dependant belongs to a local street gang off base before the move, when the family relocates to new base, so does the gang member and gang. Just as in the civilian population, the dependant gang member(s) can become a big fish on a base with little or no gang problem. This can be particularly perplexing for any military police or investigative service. To compound the issue the military is generally not allowed to keep gang intelligence files. As a result the military police and investigative service units assigned to one base often do not pass on information to sibling units at other bases. Intra and inter communications between other branches of the service id non-existent when it comes to sharing intelligence on gang activity.

Divorce

A divorce or separation is not thought of as a gang migration mechanism. But a family break up can be just that. Unfortunately, the United States has seen a decline in the traditional two-parent family. One early 1990s estimate indicated that 18 million American children (27 percent of the nation's children) are growing up in single parent homes. As divorce and separation rates continue to climb we see the un-anticipated impact on gang migration.

Youth are more likely to have problems when parents divorce or separate. This makes them prime targets for the gang association and membership. If a child is already part of gang to escape an emotional or physically abusive home, the subsequent court ordered custody to one parent and subsequent move become the mechanism that allows that gang member to move. This can happen whether the re-location and parent assignment is voluntary or court ordered.

These divorces and custody battles can be very emotional and ultimately the children bear the blunt. No matter what is done or said many times the children feel they are responsible for the divorce. As the children are tugged between households, they yearn for a consistent family life. The gang family can offer that. As one 16 year-old gangster told me, *"My homies, my family is always there for me."* The sad fact is the replacement or gang family demands unquestioned loyalty and with that loyalty comes a commitment and willingness to employ violence.

Schools

Sometimes, gang migrations may be caused by a school expulsion. If a child is expelled from school, often the student gang member relocates to a relative or friends home in a new school district. This type of student then registers in the new school district; enters the student population and brings his gang mentality with him. All too often, the new school experiences the presence of the gang member transplant very quickly. Teachers have commented they first notice the new gang member's presence through written schoolwork or through classroom behavior.

Some students do make an attempt to turn their lives around. However, as new students sometimes the existing students immediately single them out. If the new school already has an existing gang influence, the new student's entry can be difficult. This is especially true if the new student has gang tattoos, because the tattoos would advertise his gang membership to a foreign gang.

Do not forget that some gang members go to college. When they enroll they also can enroll their gang life style. This can be seen in college dorm life. Although somewhat more subtle than living in the neighborhood, the gang presence is almost always noticed.

Drug/Human Trafficking

The previously mention factors in themselves may not be considered as migration influences by other professionals. Individually, they may not impact gang migration much. Collectively they do. Of all the migration factors the next one is probably the most influential. Probably because money is involved and gang members tend to make illegal activities the primary way to develop income.

The trafficking of illegal drugs and human beings has become a common enterprise that some street gangs have engaged in. Research also suggests that younger street gang members are selling drugs. The Office of Juvenile Justice and Delinquency Prevention reported in the executive summary for the 1998 National Gang survey that one third of the youth gangs were drug selling gangs (OJJDP, 1998).

Not at the organized level associated with major drug cartels or prison gangs. But at the street level and the dealers tend to be younger local street gang members (National Drug Intelligence Center, 1998). And why not? The country as a whole contains about 1/21st of the world's population. As a nation we consume over 50 percent of the world's illegal drugs (DEA, 1999).

Evidence to support this theory may have some anecdotal origin, but it is strong. For example, in 2006 a 2400 foot long tunnel was found leading from a home in Mexico to another home across the border in the San Diego area. DEA officials were able to show that the tunnel complete with lighting and ventilation was used to transport drugs into the United States. A drug dealer can make enormous amounts of unreported income selling drugs. A sales territory can become very important, especially to those who use and are addicted to drugs.

This candid observation becomes important when discussing gang migration. Drug dealers need product to sell. The drugs that are sold locally come from drug suppliers who often operate out of the country. Sometimes the suppliers are often trusted members of the gang, extended family members or trusted dealers. If you relocate to another part of the country there is a tendency to maintain your relationships with your drug connections back home.

This implies that if you are a west coast transplant your drug supply comes from the west coast. This in turn facilitates the interstate transport of illegal drugs. And in turn, spawns a new tentacle within the gang sub-culture to develop a specialty crime; drug trafficking. Gang members and associates are used for the interstate transport of drugs for their street gangs. This includes using public transportation like buses and trains, personal cars and commercial airlines.

An academic study (Goldstein and Huff, 1993) tends to support three mechanisms that influence this type of gang migration. Moving into smaller cities means that competition between drug dealers and suppliers tends to be less intense because there are fewer gang members. This makes it easier for migration gang members to establish narcotic trafficking. The first street gang into a specific location is able to designate its own boundaries. This can allow a gang to develop a monopoly. This type of scenario can also allow members of this gang to claim they own the entire town. Of course the gang will have to defend this drug sales turf from other gangs.

Secondly, illegal drugs are often more scarce in smaller cities and rural towns. This will provide a mechanism to make a greater profit. Remember the law of supply and demand. A low supply of product will result in higher prices. All we have to do is remember what happened during the gas shortages. This factor will continue to be important because the majority of drug supply lines bypass rural towns and small cities.

Last, in rural towns and small cities the local law enforcement may be less experienced at dealing with gang members, and or gang members who traffic illegal drugs (Jensen and Yerington, 1997). It should be no surprise to note the executive summary of the 1998 National Youth Gang survey also suggested that rural America was seeing the largest increase of gang that sell drugs (OJJDP, 2000).

Gang Studies

The street gang phenomenon had relatively little scientific inquiry until the 1970s. Prior to that time, only a few academic studies on the dynamics, profiles, types or the customs and practices of street gangs where conducted. It has been generally accepted that a study completed by Thrasher (1927) was the first gang research project in the country. However, the majority of research on street and prison gangs is less than 50 years old and much of that, less than 15 years old. Even though gang behaviors can be traced back to colonial America only a few studies done in 1960 sparked the interest in street gang research.

There were a couple of societal influences that sparked a 1970s academic interest in street gangs. One was certainly media coverage. The entertainment and music industry took advantage of the gang sub-culture. Movies gave fictional accounts of what street gang life should be while glorifying street gang violence. Hardcore rap music today still continues to express a great anger with the system. Hard core rap song lyrics promote the idea of a conspiracy by White America to systematically eradicate the Black man. The use violence against women and the police was and still is a popular theme. These themes are also carried in Hispanic gang and White Supremacist rap music.

The advent of watching live police shootings and pursuits on national television also aided in the spread of what I call vicarious violence. People watched TV, saw the movie or listened to the rap music, then walked away, as if nothing has happened. There was no consequence, because what was experienced was entertainment. Without realizing it, many young people experienced violence and nothing physically happened to them, or so it was thought. Many criminal justice professionals have known about this phenomenon that mental health professionals have observed and commented about.

Two things can happen. First, the viewer or listener has a tendency to become desensitized. Secondly, for some people, the movie characters are not fictional, but real life people. The rap music lyrics are not only representative and just verbal frustrations of a small segment of the African-American population. For some gang members they actually represent their real struggles against the police and the establishment. Some gang members identify with the rap music artist or movie character.

The result, of course, is that for some young people, fiction becomes reality. Some street gangsters began, have and continue to aspire to be like the character they saw in the movie. In fact, for some gang members there is a direct connection between the movies and their own lives. In 1999 Jokey, a female gang member from the Drifters street gang, in Los Angeles said, "*... people spend seven dollars to go to a movie and see what I live everyday for free.*" An astonishing remark for a pregnant female gang member who was smoking marijuana laced with crack. She also chose to be homeless and was only 18 years old.

Ironically, only a few major news networks produce specials about life in the gang sub-culture. When they are aired, some criminal justice experts claim these specials only glorify the gang life. Investigative reporters have told me they believe the public has a right to know about street life. Chris Blatchford, investigative reporter, FOX News, Channel 11, Los Angeles told me in an interview, *"that some reporters might have a tendency to push because of the intense competition between news agencies."* Blatchford was also quick to point out that reporters have a job to do and that job is to get the news out.

Formal academic studies tend to show that the street gang life for the majority of street gang members is nothing like what is portrayed in the news specials. This is true. The reality is that street gang life is mixture of both perspectives. The academic studies may show what the majority of street gang members do. The news specials document what the violent minority does. From a criminal justice perspective, we deal with the violent minority most of our time. Research suggests that the violent minority gang membership is thought to be somewhere between 8-10 percent of the total gang population and appears to be responsible for about 52 percent of the violent gang crime (Smith and Kent, 1995).

Another factor that prompted formal studies was the growth of violent gang crime in the late 70s and early 80s. These changes in crime trends also caused academic professionals, social scientists and criminal justice professionals to look at specific age groups. As foretold, the mid 1990s became the crime peak that many professionals predicted in the late 1970s and early 1980s. But something odd happened, instead of a rising through the mid to late 1990s, the crime rates took a slight downward trend and then leveled off, during 1997 and 1998.

The violent crime rates still continued to drop slightly into the year 2000. Some crime categories stayed static during 2003 and 2004 and a few tended to rise. Although violent gang homicides seem to be stable, violent assaults that do not include murder are on the increase. Drug trafficking by gang members was also on the rise during 2003 and 2004.

A national attitude soon developed. We are safer now because the crime rate has dropped. The media was the tool used to spread the good news by citing U.S. Department of Justice reports based on crime rate data for juveniles and adults. This has helped promote an attitude that there is no longer a problem. Well, I don't completely agree with this interpretation of the crime rate data. Yes, if we look at just adult and juvenile crime rates separately, there has been a decrease and stabilization of the crime rates.

However, the level at which crime rates have stabilized it is still 3 to 5 times higher than they were in the 1960s. Just because the crime rates have decreased and leveled off, are we really safer? Besides, the crime rate indexes show that violent juvenile crime committed with a gun is still rising and offers no explanation of why juvenile homicide rates increased 150 percent before stabilizing. Nor does this change offer any explanation why juvenile crime has out-paced adult crime between 1990 and 2000 and why it appears to continue to do so.

10-10-80 Theory

There is really no accurate way to determine the number of gang members in the country because of the definition issue. Only gross estimates can be made based on available data from surveys on street gangs and gang populations. The gang population has a minority membership that is involved in the majority of violent crime. It is estimated to be somewhere between 8 and 10 percent. The majority of the time gang life involves around, legal, delinquent and misdemeanor behavior. All gangs have a willingness and potential to use violence. Some street gangs violence randomly, as they feel it is needed and some use violence consistently. Trend-wise, it appears that more gang members are getting involved in drug sales. If this increases, drug sales could fuel gang migration within and without of a state.

I want to present the 10-10-80 theory here. I am suggesting that many formal academic studies work with about 80 percent of the gang population. Most academic research does not target the most active gang members in the country. The behavior models that are developed and suggested may be accurate for 80 percent of the gang population.

Research completed by the Westminster Police Department suggests that the majority of violent gang crime (over 50 percent) is committed by 8 to 10 percent of the gang members (Smith and Kent, 1995). This implies that there may a sub-group of gang members within the general gang population. I concur because anecdotal law enforcement evidence suggests that this 8 to 10 percent group accounts for a disproportional amount of gang crime. Therefore, behavior models for this group may not fit published academic models because they describe two different groups of gang members. Basically we are comparing lemons and oranges, both are citrus fruits but distinctly different, yet both share many of the same characteristics.

In my theory I am also suggesting that the criminal justice profession never contacts a small percentage of the gang population. These gang members successfully conceal their gang membership and activities much like many drug traffickers. The actual percentages may be smaller a comprehensive research project would ultimately be able to determine that.

However, what my theory suggests is that the majority of gang members do not commit the majority of the violent gang crime. I suggest that a ratio exists between three sub-groups within the general gang population and the relationships within these groups affect suppression, intervention and prevention program design and implementation. Criminal justice professionals and the media often deal with the 10 percent group that commits the majority of crime. Academic professionals deal with a majority of the gang population. A small percentage, roughly 10 percent are not contacted at all, hence the 10-10-80 name. These three sub groups comprise the entire gang population (Valdez, 2000).

Summary

Even though a number of gang migration mechanisms have been identified in this text there are probably more. In the early 1990's migrating gang members accounted for a limited number of new gangs that formed across the country. When a migrating gang member forms a new gang the impact may be felt immediately. The exported gang culture and local societal factors have had the greatest influence on the formation of street gangs across the country. Most gangs form within the geographical boundaries of their city or town and draw their membership from the local population. However, migrating gang members are having an increasing effect on this phenomenon. A small percentage of gang members account for a disproportionate amount of the violent gang related crime.

Gang Behaviors

What exactly does gang membership mean? Can a person be a gang member 24 hours a day or is he just a member when the group is present? Gang membership could be based in attitudes and a certain mentality that manifest itself in behavior. It is likely that stylized clothes, tattoos, slang, hand signs, drawings and other membership indicia are really symptoms of that mentality. Group behaviors are learned, expected and anticipated. Some gang will also punish members for deviation of expected conduct.

Respect and Reputation

There are many behaviors that have been associated with the gang sub-culture. One such behavior is the use of violence to settle problems, especially between rival street gangs. Gang violence can and has been directed at rival gang members, innocent civilians, at criminal justice professionals, at military personnel and at members of the same gang. U. S. statistics show that at least one half of the victims of gang violence are innocent civilian bystanders. But how does violence and gang crime help the gang and why is it done?

When a person begins to associate with a gang or with gang members, a learning process starts. It is part of the courting process, indoctrination to the gang sub-culture. The gang code, ethics and morals are shared. Early on in the education process the person may start to change his behaviors. Often, what is first seen is a change in dress style and language, the presence of tattoos, delinquent behavior and changes in attitude, especially toward family and school.

The gang offers positive re-enforcement for this change. It takes the form of friendship, love, direction, status and guidance. As the person becomes more familiar with the gang code, the changes can become more pronounced. A transformation can be seen. It's like when a person enters boot camp and graduates. At graduation that person is familiar with the military codes of conduct, and looks and acts differently.

Essential to the process of learning the gang codes of behaviors is the fact that respect and reputation for the individual gang member and the gang is earned through the use of violence in criminal actions. For example, this mentality can be demonstrated by showing a willingness to always back up your peer gang members.

Gang members and affiliates learn that some of their respect and reputation depends on their support to the gang. The support is often some participation in criminal behavior. The more support that is given, the more respect and reputation are gained for the individual and gang. Criminal behavior only enhances the gang member's status within the gang and is expected, since it is part of the gang code. Not following the gang code leads to a loss of respect, and damages the reputation for the gang member and the gang.

When a gang is involved in a crime, the members participate willingly because it offers them an opportunity to increase respect and enhance reputation for the gang and themselves. Often the gang leader or those who are involved do not direct or request this behavior.

Here is a good metaphor to help explain this behavior. During a baseball game if a batter gets hit by a pitch sometimes there is a brawl. The batter will run toward the pitcher with the catcher in chase. All of a sudden the batter's bench empties and the other players run out to assist the batter. No single baseball player or manager gave the order or requested the other team members to participate. The other ball players joined the fracas because they are loyal to each other. They wanted to support their fellow team member and to protect their personal and team reputation.

This is accurate when comparing a gang's behavior to the baseball team response to a violent act (getting hit by a pitch). For street gangs, there maybe no shot caller or gang leader directing the participation of the other gang members, yet all present will take part in the assault or other crime, just as all the baseball players got involved in the fight. To a gang member it is understood that getting involved usually means involvement in criminal activity. Unfortunately, gang members exhibit a willingness to get involved.

Showing a willingness to use violence enhances one's reputation and includes committing violent criminal actions. This can impress younger members and associates. These acts will cause the younger members and associates to give more respect to the violent gang member. This respect enhances their status and reputation within and outside the gang. So creating fear becomes a vehicle to get respect.

Generating fear-based respect a member(s) can be transported into a leadership position; also known as a "shot caller." The gang code dictates that criminal activity enhances individual and the gang's reputation. For many people both violent and non-violent gang related criminal activity creates and instills fear in the community. These actions are also noted by the gang and rival gangs. This fear within the gang sub-culture is equated to respect and allows a gang to gain control of a community. Community residents fear and expect gang retaliation and intimidation. The attitude develops that the more you fear me the more you respect me.

Respect and reputation are the cornerstones for the creation, growth and behavior of a gang. The gang code, a perverse gang ethic and moral are based on respect and reputation. Respect and reputation of the individual gang member and collectively for the gang allows the gangs influence to increase. This allows the gang to grow and become more powerful. This in turn, makes many citizens fearful and reluctant to help the police in criminal investigations and prosecutions. Witnesses want to remain anonymous.

Sadly, without the help of the community the police cannot investigate gang related crime or any crime. This community response to fear promotes an increase the gang's reputation. Partly because it creates the false impression that the gang and its members are above the law. Secondly, it allows the gang to feel a false sense of power over the community, peer gang members and rival gangs. The gang will tend to flourish because the continued unchecked criminal activity acts as a vehicle to enhance the gangs' reputation.

Once a person becomes a member or is involved in a gang, they realize and know that the gang is criminally oriented. They know this because criminal activity is the fundamental way to gain respect and reputation. Members are willing to participate because they get positive reinforcement, increased respect and enhancing reputation. A member who participates in a gang related crime tends to demonstrate:

1. A willingness to support the gang.
2. A willingness to use violence.
3. That the gang in turn trusts the participant.
4. The participant understands the gang code, ethics and morals.
5. The behavior will increase individual and gang respect and enhance reputation.

These behaviors effectively make that involved person an active participant in a gang related activity and also holding a kind of acute membership. The gang member fully understands that the gang sub-culture functions around respect and reputation. Members are motivated to protect and enhance individual and gang respect and reputation. This is part of the gang code, ethics and morals.

Defense of the respect and reputation is therefore logical and an expected gang behavior. In fact, it becomes a primary function of gang membership. Any disrespect or challenge to the gang or one of its members will force an action. The challenge must be answered to save the respect and reputation of the gang. The disrespect has to be dealt with in order gain back lost respect and keep the gangs reputation from being damaged. The action is usually violent and criminal. Gang members tend to willingly and excitedly seize this opportunity to increase individual and gang respect and reputation.

This participation in violent crime only continues to motivate other gang members. Gang members will protect respect and reputation so zealously, that they will kill and die for it.

This presents two major scenarios for the gang member:

1. Gang members get involved in gang crime because is shows their support of the gang. Participation in crime can be undirected by involved members or gang leaders. Participation will gain and enhance individual and gang respect and reputation.

2. Gang members may participate in criminal activity at the direction of a gang shot caller (leader). A specific event whether planned or a result of a chance encounter will motivate the gang to protect or enhance respect and reputation. A gang member can assume temporary leadership and direct specific gang behavior(s).

In either scenario, participation is voluntary and only trusted members of the gang can participate and be present.

Shot Caller

Don't forget, there may be no formal assigned leadership in many street gangs. So the leadership may come from those gang members who are the most criminally active at the time, or have a history of being very criminally active within the gang. This allows these gang members to lead by action, as well as by motivation. Sometimes these gang leaders are very charismatic and are good communicators. There is also some law enforcement anecdotal evidence that suggests gang leaders tend to enjoy the authority they have over other gang members.

In some gangs with formal leadership structure, the leader might delegate assignments to trusted members who assume subordinate leadership roles. This can also insulate the gang leader from direct criminal liability because he or she may be shielded with several layers of management. This behavior is seen within prison and motorcycle gangs, as well as some street gangs.

A gang leader may also be called shot caller or event leader. In Asian street gangs the leader(s) are called Dai Low(s). This type of gang leadership may be transient and fluid in nature. A gang might not always have the same leader. If the leader goes to jail or is taken out of the picture usually another gang member steps up into that role. During times of conflict with rival groups, the most feared gang member or the most criminally active gang member may assume leadership by directing the activity of other gang members. This is because he has the most respect.

A gang may have a small cadre of leaders, two or three members that lead indirectly or subtly at different times. It has been my experience when interviewing gang members that the thought of not following directions was seldom, if ever considered because participation in crime was a way to gain more respect and enhance their reputation. Following orders or putting in work would give the gang member an opportunity to get more individual and gang respect, and enhance his and the gangs reputation.

Gang members welcome the opportunity to prove themselves to the rest of the gang, because of the positive reinforcement they receive. There is also the misguided loyalty aimed at protect the gang's reputation, respect, interests and peer gang members. This becomes a fundamental part of the gang code, ethics and morals and directs gang member behavior.

Behavior Dynamics

During times of conflict between rival groups, gangs become aggressive as a group. The most aggressive group wins. The metaphor that can be used here is of two football teams battling it out in a close game. The team that wins, executes the plays better than the other team, and often has superior players and a good quarterback. Quarterbacks are sometimes switched during the game and between games. Certain members are counted on to play well, to help win the game.

However, the game cannot be won, without the help of all the players on the field and off, because this is a team sport. Those players who are not playing support their team members from the sidelines and during practice. All team members will encourage the team emotionally. Some will assist in helping a fellow teammate get up after a play and will be willing to substitute for them. All the players want to play to win, not because they are afraid the coach will discipline them, but because their individual and team respect and reputation is at stake. There is a genuine desire and willingness to play for keeps, and to win. Sometimes one or two players excel and also motivate the team to win.

Gang members will sometimes mimic this mentality and behavior. A gang member will have a desire and willingness to help save or enhance the gangs respect and reputation, so he will willingly participate in criminal behavior fully understanding the possible consequences. This crime may be a theft, car jacking, and assault, attempted murder, marking graffiti, or challenging and fighting rival groups. Sometimes, another involved gang member may direct and /or assist in the activity.

During the game the quarterback will lead the team by calling plays, essentially directing the players. Other times the coach will call the plays and send them in (insulated leader). Sometimes the quarterback plays especially hard himself, leading the team by his actions, much like the shot caller or event leader would do during the commission of a crime or during a conflict with a rival group if he was leading the action. This may occur whether the meeting is planned or the result of a chance encounter. Often, the gang is prepared for this chance encounter, having armed themselves and done some formal or informal pre-planning.

Other times the encounters can be planned. The gang members may meet at a pre-determined location. The plan may involve a simple fistfight, but the participating parties may also bring a weapon(s) in preparation. This can present a problem because gang members tend to react to both real and perceived threats. Deadly violence has result between rival gangs that scheduled themselves for a physical showdown. A member from one or both gangs brings a handgun(s) and the outcome is a shooting.

Social Behaviors

Gang members will socialize together just sports team members will often socialize together. Socializing can occur when not playing a game and some players will maintain close contact with each other during the off-season. They may even train together off-season and between games, practice. Of course, football teams are not gangs, and I am only using the football team metaphor as a metaphor to help explain transient gang behaviors.

As with many professional football teams, the players have a variety of personalities. Some players are very well known because of their eccentric behaviors on and off the field, just as some gang members are well known for their violent reputations and behaviors. Remember, this activity increases respect and enhances reputation. These gang members might become known as Trigger, Mad Dog, Blaster, Psycho, or as gangs known as the Crips, Shower Posse, Hells Angels and Mara Salvatrucha, 18th Street or the Black Gangster Disciples. All the names connote a certain willingness to use violence and participate in crime.

Therefore the action a few gang members may influence the entire gang's status. Just like a few sports players influence the reputation of an entire team. The gang as a whole enjoys status within the gang community based on the gang's reputation of being tough and in some cases a history of being involved in violent crime. A sort of gang tradition can develop and is carried on by newer members.

This commitment or willingness to be violent can earn respect for the gang member. An 18 year-old gang member said, "... *if you are a gang member you can not get respect without using violence.*" Unfortunately, this mentality is true for many gang members. If you fear me, you will respect me. This is also true for some gang leaders.

Many gang members socialize together. They will share personal triumphs and problems with each other. So gang members do not "gang bang" 24 hour day. The off season for gang members may be when the gang is not in conflict with another gang. The gang mentality is always present and gang members are opportunistic. So just because there is no confirm gang war does not mean the gang will not use violence.

The Gang Gun

Let's use the football metaphor again. During a game, those players who are on the sideline know whether or not their team is on defense or offense. They know who has the ball and where the ball is. Within a gang clique or set members who are not actively involved in a crime, but present, know who is participating in the crime and know who is armed. If their participation is necessary, it will be done willingly. It is common for larger gangs to form sets or cliques, which are small cells of the same gang. Sometimes geography or age decides which clique or set you are assigned to.

If a car with four or five gang members is involved in a drive-by shooting, it is my opinion that all the members in the car knew which one of their peer members was armed with a gun. Knowing who has the gun is an expected behavior and is common knowledge among gang members. It's just like how the offensive team members know where the football is, even though they may not see it. All participants believe they will get more respect and enhance their and gangs reputation for participating or backing up their gang.

Commonly, in multiple defendant criminal cases, the individual gang members will deny having any knowledge that a weapon was in the car in an attempt to minimize their criminal liability. In candid conversations after cases were adjudicated and appellate windows gone, gang members have confided that they knew who carried the gang's weapon, or who was armed. Ultimately some said they either saw and/or talked about the weapon prior to the attack.

They admitted that respect and reputation were the root cause for their involvement in the crime they were convicted of.

Out of custody gang members have made similar comments. Although not armed 100% of the time, some gang members have indicated they can get a shared gang gun, use their own gun or buy a gun easily. In some instances, guns are hidden in easily accessible areas only known to gang members. It is also a common practice to hide guns with individual gang members in order to prevent them from being seized by law enforcement. The point is that for many gangs there is a weapon that is accessible by any member when needed. It is a community weapon.

The same scenario may also confirm that gang guns may be hidden at a public park or in a house where gang members meet and socialize. Sometimes, multiple weapons are hidden in these areas. All gang members who frequent the location know where the weapons are hidden. I have personally found weapons hidden in public park garbage cans, under the plastic bag full of garbage. The gang's gun was stored there for a couple of reasons. Any gang member could retrieve it at any time, but if seized by the police, no gang member could be held liable for possessing it.

It becomes logical to understand that if a gun is hidden in a car, that all persons occupying the car knew where the gun was by conversation, observation or handling it. However, this may be difficult to prove in court. Understanding and effective explaining gang behaviors may help overcome the proof hurdle. There have been instances where gang members have hid contraband in locations normally not frequented by them. A gun used in a murder may be hidden in mother's closet, especially if the gang member is on probation. Obviously, the mother never knew the gun was in the closet. Girlfriends may also hide or buy weapons or other contraband for their gang member boyfriend. Just as drug dealing mothers hide contraband inside their baby's diapers.

Transient Gang Behavior

The gang set or clique may also be dynamic, with members floating in and out of the clicks for a variety of reasons. Some gang members may be incarcerated, while others may be busy with work and school. Some gang members may move out of the immediate area and only hang out with the gang when they visit. Whether or not they are physically with the gang, often they still claim membership, just as the football players are still part of a team, whether or not the season is active.

Transient participation is sort of like being a part time gang member. The gang member may be living and working outside of the gang neighborhood's geographical turf. These types of gang members may visit the gang, on the weekends, once a month or once every couple of months. When they are gone, they might associate or align themselves with another street gang, or have no gang contacts at all. They may be full-time students or gainfully employed or have a family. However, upon their return to the neighborhood, they are welcomed and accepted by the gang as if they never left. They maintain their respect and reputation.

These part time gang members may even participate in crime when they are visiting. Being a member of a gang includes responsibilities to protect the gang's reputation and respect within its operating area. A visiting member would not hesitate to participate in this endeavor, especially if their reputation was built on active gang support. This is an example of transient gang behavior. There is no time qualification either. A gang member may be returning back after a lengthy incarceration term or a short local jail stint or coming home after a semester of college and still be welcomed by the gang.

Criminal justice professionals have encountered groups of young men and women who belong to groups they call Posses, Clicks, and Party Crews. They profess their groups are not a gang because they don't have a history of violent behavior. These groups will have a common name with more than three members and frequently as a group, have minimal police contact. Often, these youth are doing well in school and come from middle to upper middle class two parent families. The race and gender barriers for membership have been broken for these gangs. Yes, they are street gangs; because these groups fit the previously mentioned model of a street gang.

Granted these groups may not have a recorded history of violent crime, but a closer examination will reveal that the group has been involved in sporadic misdemeanor and delinquent behavior. Often the participating members will not have been prosecuted for it. Drinking under age, minor assaults, vandalism, substance abuse and petty theft are the most common forms of criminal behavior. Frequently, individual members become very aggressive as their confidence is built up because of the lack of prior police contacts and also because the group is building its street reputation and respect.

Within the street culture there is a motivation to be known as strong and aggressive Remember, *"the more you fear me the more you respect me."* No gang wants or enjoys a bad reputation. This would only cause rival gangs to disrespect and victimize them. When an established street gang insults, attacks or challenges this group, this is considered a disrespect or insult. The natural and anticipated response is to use violence against the attacker or insulting individual or group. This is done to get back group's respect and reputation. Add alcohol use and the encouragement of peer members, and this relatively unknown group can get involved in a murder or serious assault. The so called non-gang group is really gang.

A violent act maybe out-of-character behavior for these types of gangs, but for that moment in time, the group acted just like a violent criminal street gang. The majority of past behaviors may never have qualified the gang or its participating members to fit this legal gang enhancement definition. An incident like this becomes an example of transient violent gang behavior. Just as the frequent non-felony crimes are examples of transient gang behavior.

This concept demonstrates a commonly overlooked fact. All gang are involved in transient behaviors. Even though some gangs have a documented history of being involved in felony conduct often members are involved in non-felony criminal and non-criminal conduct.

Intra-Gang Violence

Intra-gang violence can be directed at peer members for disciplinary reasons. For example, if a gang member breaks one the gang's codes, there will be a possibility of some type of disciplinary action. In speaking with gang members who have been disciplined, one of the punishable violations has been for ranking or ranking out.

This term refers to a gang member not backing up another gang member or not claiming his gang affiliation to a rival gang member, law enforcement or another person. The term is generically used to describe that an expected behavior was not done. That lack of action has been interpreted as a form of disrespect to the gang, harming its reputation. The lack of action may indicate the gang member is weak. The member therefore, has to be disciplined in some form.

This shows the other peer members that the gang is not weak and allows the offending member an opportunity to gain back the lost respect, returning him to good membership status.

For some street gangs the discipline takes the form of a ritual beating called "courting" or "check courting." It is similar to the jumping-in process, except this time it is preformed for a disciplinary purpose. Sometimes, a gang member may be lured into the area for another reason, for example, to help with a jump in. This gang member may not even know that other gang members have judged him.

Sometimes, the gang member realizes that he violated the gang code and is aware that he will be disciplined. He may be present during discussions concerning his error. Sometimes, the severity of the beatings depends on the type of infraction. A minor infraction would demand a minor punishment, while a major rule breaking could require a severe beating. Some prison gangs have disciplined their members by killing them.

Gang members will attack each for other reasons as well. Sometimes attacks are between sets or cliques of the same gang because of problems. Some of the more common reasons for this type of intra-gang violence have been disrespecting another gang member, stealing the girl friend of another gang member, committing crime in the gang neighborhood or not completing an expected or assigned task.

Even though gang members of the same gang consider themselves family, some gang members just don't like each other and sometimes fight amongst themselves. As one Hispanic gang member told me, "...*personality conflicts man... they never get along...*" referring to two peer gang members.

Violence is also sometimes used when a gang member wants to leave his gang. There can be a ceremonial beating when one leaves a gang. This is known as a "jump out." This beating is usually worse than the jumping in initiation. In a few instances, an accidental death has resulted from a jump out. Many gang members have told me, they believe jumping out is a way to leave the gang with respect. This is another example of intra-gang violence.

Many times gang rules are not written down anywhere. There is normally no gang behavior code book. The rules are usually passed on to the gang members by word of mouth. These rules are the basis for traditional expected gang behaviors, which are learned and expected by the group. For example, the code of silence, paybacks and answering insults. There are a few reported exceptions. For example in 2005 several cliques of the MS-13 gang produced sets of 13 written rules for their members. The rules were hand written and were somewhat different for each clique. There also a tendency for prison gangs to have written charters and rules of conduct. This are formalized and each member is expected to understand and follow the rules. For a few street and prison gangs basic rules have to be memorized before membership admission.

Summary

You could say that the gang members are anxious to prove themselves and are willing to do just about anything to show that. This action would give a gang member additional respect and status in the gang. It will also enhance the personal and gang reputation, a form of positive reinforcement for negative behavior. Violation of rules can lead to punishments, even minor infractions. Intra-gang violence is part of the gang sub-culture, just as some parents would discipline their children. These behaviors are expected and done to enhance the personal and gang respect and reputation. These actions and beliefs have become a fundamental impetus for gang related crime to continue.

Membership Psychology

Gang membership means having a specific life style and way of thinking. This would include having rules to follow, responsibilities and behaviors. Much like some military professionals become "lifers" and become highly decorated and earn tenure hash marks and rank, some gang members earn a status by being a lifer. Nevertheless, with any membership, short medium or long the gang life style causes the member to act and behave in an identifiable and somewhat predictable way. Generic gang indicia or membership characteristics and mentality will be discussed in this chapter. The concepts presented will aid in identifying gang membership.

Gang Life

The research suggests that for most gang members membership is temporary and will last around a year (Hill, Lui and Hawkins, 2001). Remember, the particular gang member you are examining may not acknowledge that they think in the same ways mentioned in this chapter. Sometimes it is difficult for gang members to personally identify and verbalize the specific mentalities discussed here. Although talk about a specific scenario and the gang member will tell you how he would react clearly demonstrating the gang psychology. The amount of gang indicia present may be helpful, but is not necessary because the diagnosis of membership is really based on behavior and psychology.

Don't forget as gang trends change some membership indicia can become outdated or no longer used by a gang's general membership. Since street gangs as a group can change very quickly, they have the ability to adapt and make the best of a terrible situation and they have become master opportunists. These behaviors are based in the gang's mentality or psychology.

Today, it is common for gang members to deny gang affiliation and membership. It seems that many gang members know of the consequences, special probation conditions and enhanced sentencing when membership in a criminal street gang is proven in a criminal trial. Gang indicia or symptoms of membership have three functions within the gang sub-culture. For gang members and the savvy public they can act as a form of greeting, challenge and intimidation.

Contrary to what the general public believes, age, ethnicity and baggy clothes are NOT membership characteristics used by the police to determine gang affiliation. The police do not stop and detain people because they are young, wear baggy clothing, or because they are minorities. These are not criteria used to determine gang membership. But remember, gang indicia are all too often a demonstrative extension of a life style. Gang indicia can act as silent advertisement showing a gang affiliation and membership. This is why membership indicia can become evidence to support membership. Some gang members have a lot of indicia others few symptoms. A few gang members will display no membership indicia yet will be a bonefide member of the gang or gang leader.

It is the behavior that is motivated by the gang psychology that makes a gang member. Understanding gang psychology becomes paramount in understanding the sub culture and the membership symptoms that is associated with it. Membership behaviors can also be transient and appear to be associated with a group gang psychology. Unfortunately, this way of thinking can lead a few gang members to get involved in felonious conduct including murder and attempted murder.

The gang psychology also justifies a member's actions such as supporting fellow member in criminal activity. This mind set will also allow the members of a gang to consider their peer members as family. Therefore to protect family ANY behaviors are allowed and expected. From the gang member's point of view, they are protecting loved ones. Much like when a parent protects his or her child. These are powerful forces that motivate the continual traditional gang psychology to prevail and control gang members. Let's examine a few of these behaviors to demonstrate this concept.

Payback

Simply put, the payback is a justifiable way to get even. The payback concept is one of the first behavior practices a gang member learns and it is easily identifiable. The payback concept includes avenging a real or perceived insult and is usually accompanied by total disregard for human life. This attitude can be aimed towards rival gang members, peers, and sometimes at the public in general. Recently, law enforcement has also become a target of this type of gang violence.

Many gang members also have a dismissive attitude towards authority, and the never say die ethic. These two attitudes also help mold the gang mentality and aid in the perpetuation of the cycle of gang violence. The gang payback usually also includes an escalated or more intense retaliation. A 17-year-old Hispanic gang member makes this point clear by claiming, "Take one of us out and well take three of you out... that's payback." It is easy to see how a gang war can start and continue with this way of thinking.

The retaliation does not have to occur immediately after a violation. Most gangs operate in a sort of state of readiness. They are primed to respond to a real or perceived threat. If a score needs to be settled, a gang will seize any opportunity to get even. There have reported law enforcement cases where this process has taken a year or more. In one case, the retaliation was done on the year anniversary of a deadly assault between rival gangs.

Code of Silence

Another part of the gang mentality also includes following the code of silence. It is a practice where gang members use this unwritten code to justify their non-cooperation with police officials when victimized. The gang life requires that the gang to take care of problem by themselves. The gang mentality is a learned behavior. It can be passed on through generation and sometimes it can be adapted to fit into a particular gang lifestyle. Many times this code is referred to as tradition. The behavior can also be directed toward the family, teachers and siblings.

Not cooperating with the police also justifies a gang to retaliate themselves. This behavior can become an opportunity to increase the gang's respect because the violence that will be associated with the payback.

Respect

Respect is also very important to gang members. To "dis" or disrespect a gang member or a gang is forbidden. Any disrespect is taken as an insult whether it is real or perceived. Disrespecting gang members can be in the form of a derogatory stare or glaring. This is called "mad dogging" or "dogging." It can also take the form of crossing out rival gang graffiti or purposely drawing a rival's graffiti incorrectly; for example drawing the symbol or graffiti upside down or in the wrong color.

Disrespect can also take another non-verbal form as expressed through the use of hand signs. A verbal challenge to fight may be as simple as asking a suspected gang member where he is from. This is known as a "call out." Asking another youth "where are you from?" or "who do you claim?" are very serious questions to a gang member. Answering either of these questions incorrectly (to the asking gang member) can become the basis for an assault.

For many gang members, the level of respect also includes a willingness to commit violent acts. Fear is often used synonymously with the term respect. This mentality was discussed in detail in Chapter 7.

Insults

The general rule gang members follow is that no insult ever goes unanswered, no matter how small. This is important because with the gang concept of respect an insult can become the trigger for a violent reaction. Many conflicts between street gangs have begun this way. Then each gang uses this way of thinking to justify further attacks.

It is easy to see how this behavior can disrupt the quality of life, especially for those who live in a socio-economic depressed area that is controlled by a street gang. The issue is compounded further if the community has an undocumented alien population because these immigrants are often afraid to make contact with police for fear of deportation. This fear allows a gang to victimize immigrant population with virtual immunity.

There has been some research that suggests for gang members who live in these types of neighborhoods an ugly cycle of violence develops because the youth rather become aggressors than victims. In fact, the late Stanley "Tookie" Williams stated that in the neighborhood he grew up in he had to make the same choice. Becoming a gang member and or associating with a gang is a way of dealing with poverty, a socially-economically deprived life style and lack of opportunities for some of America's youth.

Survival Instinct

Another part of the gang life includes the basic need to survive, and survive at any cost. This leads to the development of a tremendous survival instinct. This in turn allows a gang member to commit violent acts with little or no remorse. Sometimes, defense attorneys try to explain away the commission of violent gang crime through the use of gang experts. These experts may attempt to justify the behavior because in their opinion the behavior is related to a drug addiction or long-term drug use and not the gang psychology.

In one trial a gang member robbed a pizza store in the morning, knowing that only single person was present. The store manager was a young single mother of two children. The gang member was an ex-employee and used a rouse of wanting a job application to trick the single mother into opening the store's door. Feeling sorry for the ex-employee, the young mother opened the store and allowed the gang member in.

Once inside, the gang member forced the woman to open the safe and he took the money. Before leaving the store the gang member tried to force a blue bandana down the victim's mouth. She felt that he was trying to kill her. So she fought back.

The gang member then slammed the victim's head on the floor several times knocking her out. He then dragged her to another part of the store and stabbed her in the head 15 to 20 times with a screwdriver as she was drifting in and out of consciousness. The gang brought the screwdriver with him. Before leaving the severally injured victim for dead, the gang member dropped a 100-pound helium tank onto the victim.

The gang member was enraged and committed a violent attack. The victim was cooperative until the gang member tried to force the bandana down her mouth. The suspect in this case was caught a short time later and had a history of drug abuse and addiction. The victim almost died from her head wounds. In fact, during the trial the emergency room doctor stated that the victim's head and neck wounds were "life threatening."

A defense expert, a medical doctor who specialized in dealing with addiction testified. He justified the defendant's brutal actions by saying the gang member had a rage reaction because of his drug use. The doctor implied that it was the victim's fault she was so severely hurt because she fought back during the attack. The expert's testimony suggested that the victim caused the defendant's rage reaction "by fighting back and the rage reaction was part of the addictive behavior that is associated with methamphetamine addiction." In essence, the doctor stated the violent behavior was not part of the gang culture and mentality. It was an effect it was the result of the prolonged drug use.

However, the survival instinct and gang psychology that gang members voluntarily accept, prescribe to and practice allow this type of behavior. In fact, they encourage this type of behavior. Gang membership had an impact on this defendant. Violent attacks are part of the culture and way of thinking and acting. Drug addiction may make it easier for a gang member to be violent. Drug addiction may lower the inhibitions and allow a person to commit more violent actions, but it is gang membership that is based in violence and fear. This life style allows gang members to get accustomed to violent brutal encounters. Drug use, weather prolonged or acute only tends to facilitate these actions.

Committing crime and murder are justified because those behaviors are done in order to survive. Compound this issue with a distorted sense of reality, blind loyalty to the gang, a willingness to hurt someone else and immediate need for gratification, and the results are young killers with no worry about the consequences of their actions. Certainly, drug addiction may play a part in the process, but the gang psychology is foundational to all types of gang related criminal behaviors.

Not Responsible For My Actions

Part of the gang psychology includes a careless and un-empathetic attitude towards victims of crime. This attitude allows a person to be violent because the victims are less than human. Some experts believe that as humans we are hard wired not kill. In order to do so humans have to be re-programmed somehow (Grossman, 1996). For gang members part of this reprogramming may be this concept of their victims being less than human. That way a gang member can blame the victim for their injuries or demise even though he was the cause.

For example, on Christmas Eve, 1989, three gangs members drove into their rival gang's neighborhood with a backup vehicle full of gang members. They quickly found their target, a group of five or six rival gang members drinking in front of a garage. A loaded 20-gauge shotgun was aimed out the car window and at the last second the triggerman pointed the gun up above the heads of the rival gang members, and then fired.

While being interviewed, the triggerman, a 17-year-old Hispanic gang member, learned that an innocent 4-year-old girl was shot and seriously injured instead of rival gang members. The shooter told me at the last second he decided to just scare the rival gang members, rather than shoot them. What he didn't know was that above the garage, where the rival gang members were standing, was the balcony for the adjacent apartment. Playing on the balcony, waiting for

Santa Clause to arrive, was a little 4-year-old girl. She was at her friend's house enjoying the evening anxiously waiting for Christmas to arrive.

A full discharge of pellets hit the child in the head, neck and abdomen. When the triggerman learned what he had done, his first comment was, "She shouldn't have gotten in the way of the bullets. It was her fault." I cite this interview because it demonstrates an example of the gang psychology and how gang members feel about their victims. The little girl survived, but suffers from painful headaches. Christmas will never be the same for her and her family.

Violence

Part of the gang psychology allows gang members to use violence as a tool. Gang violence can be indiscriminate and for the most part is unpredictable. As is often the case, the public finds out the victim was an innocent bystander.

In 1991 there were 771 gang-related deaths in Los Angeles County. About 25 percent of those killed were innocent bystanders, people who had nothing to do with gangs (Guzman, 1992). Some might say these victims were simply in the wrong place at the wrong time... or were they? In 2004, sadly about 50 percent of the victims of deadly gang violence are innocent by-standers.

In 2004, two researchers from the University of California, Irvine published their findings concerning a study of homicides in California. The researchers studied 10,000 youth gang homicides that occurred in California between 1981 and 2001. The study showed that 75 percent of those homicides occurred in Los Angeles County. Surprisingly, 2001 almost 50 percent of Los Angeles homicides were gang related compared to 14 percent for the rest of the state (Tita and Abrahamse, 2004). Violence is used as a tool by many gang members.

In 2006 the Office of Juvenile Justice and delinquency Prevention published their findings for the *2004 National Gang Survey*. The findings suggested that within areas that serve larger cities 82 percent of the police agencies reported experiencing gang problems.

One hundred seventy-three cities with populations of 100,000 or more responded and reported gang problems and homicide data for the 2004 survey. In the cities of Los Angeles and Chicago more than half of the combined homicides were considered gang related. In the remaining 171 cities that responded approximately one fourth of the homicides were considered gang related (Office of Juvenile Justice and Delinquency Prevention, 2006).

The gang psychology often precludes gang members from seeing what the consequences of their actions are. Often, gang members act in groups, but individual gang members can act on their own. Sometimes gang members socialize by going parties, funerals, restaurants, or kick back together. These behaviors do not preclude these seemingly harmless groups from killing.

The Collective

During my 28 plus years as a law enforcement officer I have talked to thousands of people. I would either be directing a lost citizen, giving citations or arresting suspects and there was always the sense of dealing one-to-one with these people.

However, sometimes when talking to individual gang members, it seemed as if I was addressing the entire membership. This is especially true with the hard-core veteran gang members. As gang members increase their levels of commitment to the gang, usually with tenure, so does the difficulty in communicating. This characteristic may play a key role in the failure of conventional rehabilitation programs to sustain rehabilitation.

Often parents, teachers, medical, law enforcement and mental health professionals are dealing with the entire membership's psychology and philosophies when talking with individual gang members. Without realizing it the professional may be addressing the gang's philosophies, desires, fears and social attitudes. A gang member can adopt the collective gang personality as his own during these times. This will probably give an individual gang member the confidence to act defiant and remain uncooperative. This also becomes a major hurdle for the professional to over come if he wants to communicate.

Breaking this collective gang personality can be very difficult, but not impossible. Some police officers, probation officers, parole agents, parents and teachers, are successful in penetrating the gang's hard shell. It may take a combination of patience and techniques. Understanding the history and culture will allow a professional the ability to recognize individual trigger words or gestures that open successful communication.

Your own experience, knowledge, and training are the keys here. You have to approach gang members in a way that makes you feel comfortable and yet remain safe and at the same time honor some gang codes. Understanding the concept of respect can become critical because giving or showing a gang member respect may be the key in talking with that person. Respect is a trigger for every gang member.

Back Up

Gang members also gain a certain degree of confidence from the fact that they have "back up." This concept implies that the entire gang membership will back up an individual member. It is almost like a one for all and all for one attitude. Knowing that you have peers who are willing to avenge any wrong done to you, maybe even die for you can boost anyone's confidence. That is why the common answer to the question who shot you is "Don't worry about it, my homeboys will take of it for me."

Knowing about and understanding gang back up creates strong and powerful cohesive forces that bind an individual member to the entire gang. This also helps and increases the force of the collective personality.

The gang lifestyle involves a series of commitments and changes. Part of the change involves the development of loyalty. The changes are not only with the way a person dresses, but includes a mental attitude change as well. As gang membership tenure increases so does the commitment to the gang. As commitment increases so does loyalty to the membership and the strength of the gang psychology. Strict adherence to gang rules follows and the result is a gang member who is totally committed to the gang.

This misplaced loyalty is the result from accepting the unwritten rules like the code of silence, insults, payback and respect; and from understanding that your gang will back you up under any circumstances. For a gang member, these rules should never be violated and become a code of conduct to live by. They are understood and freely accepted and adopted as part of the life style. They also provide well-defined boundaries that hold together a social framework for the gang member and they become a foundational structure for the gang psychology.

Gang members who have been injured and know who their assailants are often will not talk to the police. No need to get the police involved, the peer gang members will take of it. They will back you up. This code helps perpetuates the cycle of violence and affords the gang member a false sense of security.

When a gang member has been insulted, it can become an insult to the entire gang and someone from the gang must deal with it. Today, the most common solution is the use of violence. Often because of the backup behavior more than one gang member is involved in the retaliation.

This mind-set also allows the gang member to feel she or he is important but expendable. As one 14-year-old gang member commented, *"If I die, I die. That's that! My homeboys love me and I love them."* This blind loyalty also aids in the ability to commit violent acts and to sacrifice your life for the gang. When a member dies in gang related violence, he also becomes a hero and martyr to the rest of the gang. Most gang members surprisingly seem ready and willing to make this ultimate sacrifice. Part of this mentality is founded in the belief that you have to back up a peer member and that may require you to become injured or die.

Sometimes, gang members have little self-esteem. For many, a genuine sense of hopelessness is present, even after they join a gang. Most have joined the gang because membership gives them the feeling of belonging to a family, sense of direction and adds focus to their lives. A strong sense of camaraderie also develops. For some gang members this acts as a powerful motivator to keep returning to the gang life; the membership fulfills a need.

For a few gang members, even though many psychological and emotional needs are being met, there still is a sense of hopelessness. A few gang members understanding the gang life and know it will ultimately lead them to incarceration, injury or death. They sometimes will acknowledge that they do not want any of those things; yet they freely and willingly accept their destiny.

Sadly because they believe there is no way out and no good future for them. The gang's hold may seen too strong to break. This distorted outlook on life can cause a person to be stuck in a cycle of street life they do not want.

Distorted Sense of Reality

For other gang members there is also a real distorted sense of reality. For example, a major relocation for many gang members simply means moving a mile or two away. The short move to these gang members is the equivalent to relocating a thousand miles away. This problem with reality causes gang members to view their world differently and also aids with justifying using violence as a way to settle disputes. Many gang members know no other lifestyle.

This way of viewing the world also allows a gang member think that violent acts are good because they increase respect and reputation. It allows a gang member to blame an innocent victim for getting in the way of the bullets. It allows a gang member to view the police and the enemy and co-operating with a criminal investigation as bad.

It allows a gang member no have a brutal survival behavior. Do whatever it takes to get what you want. Use trickery, theft and violence as the tools to survive. Be so loyal to your gang that you would kill a family member, friend or peer gang member. This distorted sense of reality will also allow a gang member not to be afraid of death or injury.

The public and victims are viewed differently. Sometimes they may be viewed as different or bad. So if you were a gang member you could do anything to them.

Quid Pro Quo

The answer to the question, "What does gang membership give you?" provided some surprising answers. After interviewing thousands of gang members and asking that question I found a unique perspective from the membership. To a gang member the gang gives a lot of positive reinforcement to its membership. All the gang members answered the gang gives them a strong sense of belonging, direction and a degree of self-confidence. The gang also becomes the source of everything good in life for these gang members. The gang provides acceptance, love, food, shelter, money, excitement and a sense of worth, status, power and control. Many gang members say, "*...the gang becomes my family.*"

Just as any person would protect their family, gang members tend to do the same. A distorted sense of reality allows a gang member do whatever they deem is necessary to protect the gang's respect and reputation. In doing so, they also have a chance to enhance their respect within the gang. Protecting the gang family becomes a primary concern for each member.

Being Down

One accepted universal street law is, "*you don't get something for nothing...there is a cost to everything in life and nothing is free.*" Frankly, there is a cost for all the good things the gang gives its membership. The blind loyalty for the gang allows members to zealously commit themselves to protect their gang family. Gang members call this commitment being down for your gang. Generally, this requires a willingness to hurt someone else or be hurt yourself in the defense of your gang. Members are compelled not to let their gang down and are rewarded for being loyal.

The mental and behavior patterns previously discussed are reflective of a collective sum of many changes. Social life, school life, family life, economic life, peer pressure, law enforcement pressure and self-esteem are just a few of the factors that contribute to the development of the gang psychology. Often symptoms of accepting the gang psychology can be seen in changes in personal appearance, academic achievement, changes in friends, withdrawing from the family, substance abuse and secret behaviors.

Summary

The gang psychology helps form the unwritten codes of conduct that gang members live and die by. This psychology can and will influence individual as well as group gang behaviors. This way of thinking and behavior can motivate gang violence by forcing individual actions through a type of gang peer pressure. These behaviors in turn allow gang members to form close emotional and psychological bonds to the gang collective personality. These bonds will also act as a strong cohesive factor that strengthens unity within the gang. These are very powerful forces at work here. There is a tendency for these forces to increase in strength with gang tenure.

Membership Indicia

Let's now examine some of common forms of gang indicia that are often associated with membership. Most gang members will display some of the indicia and some will display none, yet be an active member of a street gang. The membership indicia are really an extension of way of thinking that is based in the gang psychology. It is this psychology that influences gang behaviors. Think of indicia as symptoms of membership.

No Indicia

You might assume that without the presence of any gang indicia one cannot be a gang member. This is not true. It is the gang mentality and behavior, the gang psychology that really makes a person a gang member. It is the behaviors of the group that qualify it for becoming a gang. Remember membership indicia can be an extension of that mentality. The absence or presence of indicia is not the sole standard or indicator that is used to determine gang membership. Behavior becomes that standard. So it is the questioned behavior that needs to be compared with consistent known gang behaviors?

This makes it difficult to tangibly identify what exactly is gang psychology and behavior because they can be well hidden or camouflaged. Some gang members and leaders have been active duty U.S. military, high school and college honor students, parents or full time employed. These actions have not been traditionally associated with gang membership. For the majority of gang members, indicia is often the first objective symptoms of gang membership seen and therefore are commonly used to diagnose gang membership or status. This is because the majority of gang members display some of them.

At one time, the presence of gang indicia was the only way used to make a reliable determination of gang membership. As a general trend the more indicia that are identified the greater tendency for membership. However, this is not always true.

Law enforcement observations and anecdotal evidence now show the existence of non-profile gang members or gang members that display none of the traditional forms of membership indicia. These youth have successfully joined and actively participate in street gang activities. They freely adopt the gang psychology and behaviors, yet do not present with gang indicia.

It is common for these gang members to deny gang membership or affiliation. They often support their position with the fact that they are good students, employed and have no prior police contacts or arrests and sometimes they may also claim to be members of non-gang groups such as party crews or posses. They may even be parents or public volunteers. Yet they are active part-time gang members.

Nevertheless, these gang members associate with other gang members, may or may not be seen in gang photographs and even have a leadership role in the gang. Understanding the gang customs and practices can aid in determining gang membership and affiliation for these unique gang members. Remember the 10-10-80 theory? This type of gang member can easily fall into the 10 percent category that is seldom if ever contacted by law enforcement or the 10 percent category that commits violent crime. Examining personal behavior is a key that might help determine if a gang psychology is present.

Sometimes peers may consider a few of these types of gang members as part time gang members. This implies that some non-profile gang members may only be with their gang on a limited basis. These gang members may live out of the area where the majority of members live, like another city or county. They may be separated geographically or financially. Some gang members come from very financially affluent families. Some gang members are literally from families that are worth millions of dollars.

What was surprising in many of these cases is that parents, teachers and clergy were convinced the police had made an error. The person they knew was not a gang member. Unfortunately, the police had made no error. The percentage of non-profile gang members is relatively small when compared to the total gang membership. However, the non-profile gang member can be involved in lethal violence just as any gang member can be. Currently, there have been no reported academic studies on this aspect of gang life. Speaking from practical experience, the non-profile gang member has been seen in all types of street gangs and they successfully are able to hide their gang affiliation and/or membership from their parents, family and teachers.

Examining membership indicia is just one tool used to identify symptoms of gang membership. And remember this is an extension of the gang psychology. Just to make sure some gang members will have none, some will only have a few and other will have or use many of the indicia. This diagnostic system may also help determine the level of gang membership. The more gang members you talk to, watch and listen to, the easier it will be to distinguish between non-gang and gang members. The most common symptoms of membership include, but are limited to:

Graffiti

Probably one of the first signs of gang activity and most commonly seen is gang graffiti. Graffiti is the gangland's newspaper (Bustamante, 1997). Graffiti in the gang sub-culture is one of the most commonly used methods to communicate among peer gang members and with rival gangs. Graffiti can be characterized as the written language of the gang. Gang graffiti has been called an extension of gang type tattoos or the gang mentality.

Graffiti can be written on anything. Sometimes, it almost seems like a contest is ongoing to see which gang can put their graffiti in the most inaccessible locations. This could include moving vehicles like buses or trains. A quick look at the graffiti can tell a lot about a gang's recent activity and its membership and affiliation. Common terms used by gang members when talking about graffiti are writing, plaquing (gang term for writing graffiti) or tagging.

Graffiti can be written with Old English, Box, New Wave, Square and Balloon styles of writing or displayed with the use of symbols, like a 6-point star, a 5-point crown or top hat. Sometimes the style of lettering can help determine the type of street gang represented. Graffiti is not created by any particular ethnic group and can appear anywhere within a community. Graffiti can also identify a gang's name. Local law enforcement can always tell if the gang is

Latino, White, Asian American, Black or Tagger in origin by examining the graffiti. Graffiti will sometimes list the entire gang's nicknames. More often it will list the monikers of a clique or set that hangs out, socializes and commits crime together. It may also list the county the gang is from or a general statement about a gang's affiliation.

For law enforcement personnel sometimes field interview records of suspected gang members can be used to help identify a gang member. Gang investigators can link individual gang members to the nicknames or monikers used in the graffiti. This information can be important in the prosecution of gang crimes, especially when trying to prove gang affiliation. Teachers may see graffiti in schoolwork or displayed in student artwork. Too many times I have heard from parents after showing them graffiti in their son's room, "*... my son is not a gang member, some of his friends are, but not my son.*"

Sometimes the color of the graffiti has a symbolic importance. Obviously, if we are talking about some of the west coast African-American gangs, the colors red and blue are important. The color red means association with a Blood gang, while, blue means association with a Crip gang. Bloods and Crips are the two most powerful African-American gangs. The color of graffiti can also be important to gangs based in Chicago and New York, like the Gangster Disciples and the Latin Kings.

Outside the state of California, many Latino gangs identify with the colors red and blue. Latino gang graffiti written with red paint signifies that the gang is claiming affiliation with Northern California. Using the blue color would indicate that the gang is from Southern California. Latino gangs from Northern California are bitter rivals with gang members from Southern California. For example, Mara Salvatrucha or MS-13 gang identifies with the color blue. This announces that they are Sureno or southern California based Hispanic street gang.

For gangs where colors are important they can also be displayed on shoelaces, pants, shirts, handkerchiefs, belts and any article of clothing that is worn.

Graffiti can be found on schoolbooks, school papers, drawings, personal papers, stereo cassette tapes and holders, bedroom furniture, mirrors, inside vehicles, letters, magazines and bedroom walls. Gang graffiti has even been etched on glasses used for drinking. Graffiti can be put anywhere. Currently gangs can also post pictures of their graffiti on gang Web sites.

Why the use of graffiti? There have been many explanations by professionals. Gang members belonging to, Latino, African-American, Asian American, White, Hybrid and Occult gangs including new members and those who were multi-generational, gave the same basic reasons why they use graffiti.

Traditional street gangs, who claim territory, including most Latino gangs, say graffiti has several functions. The primary function of the graffiti is to establish territorial boundaries. The graffiti is displayed in the neighborhood the gang controls. It is used as a warning to rival gang members and to the people who live in the neighborhood. The graffiti translates to, "you are entering my turf, beware." Other terms used instead of turf are neighborhood, barrio, or hood. Remember, these gangs have no legal right to the turf they claim.

Graffiti can also define the area where gang members live or where they hang out. This could be a housing project, a street, an alley or a park. The graffiti advertises and marks the territory as home for the gang.

A second reason graffiti is used is to communicate with other peer gang members. Graffiti announce the names of the gang members in their own gang, new members and returning members. Graffiti can communicate threats or insults. A death threat can be given by writing the numbers 187 next to a gang's name or individual gang member. In the California Penal Code, this is the Homicide Section. Gang members throughout the United States use these numbers to give death threats and to intimidate other gang members, citizens and law enforcement.

Graffiti is also used to give a warning or challenge. For example, to drive home an insult to a rival gang all you do is puto-out (cross out) another gang's graffiti. Crossing out graffiti is considered an insult or disrespect that must be answered back. In investigating thousands of gang related crimes I have discovered that the motive for several homicides could be traced back to this type of gang insult. It was simply the crossing out or writing over the graffiti of a rival gang. Depending on what part of the country you are from, writing rival gang graffiti upside down is another way to insult a gang.

Graffiti can also announce what has happened and who did it. I noticed gang graffiti that was crossed-out and the numerals 187 written next to it. The next day, as if announcing who the shooters would be, someone had spray-painted Trigger and Blaster next to the crossed-out graffiti. During the night there was a drive-by shooting between the two rival gangs.

The initial crossing out of the graffiti was the insult. The 187 sign gave the threat and a warning that someone was going to die from the rival gang. To an experienced person the graffiti can offer clues or indicators of what is currently happening in a particular gang.

Graffiti written by gang members and street artists (taggers) can become a serious city problem. Most cities now have graffiti hot lines where citizens can call to report graffiti. City crews normally respond within a very short time to paint over the graffiti. For tagger crew members, graffiti is not viewed as a bad thing. For these gang members there is a certain excitement and thrill that accompanies the act of getting up (writing graffiti). The more graffiti they write, the more people see it and the more respect they have. Many taggers consider their kind of graffiti artwork and feel no laws are broken for expressing themselves.

When these important clues and indicators of gang activity are removed too quickly, local police may lose a chance to document the graffiti. This can happen when a city attempts to remove the graffiti rapidly.

Graffiti can also show alliances between different gangs. Graffiti can be a form of silent advertisement for the gang because it announces their presence in new turf or the presence of a new gang within a territory. Graffiti can also be written as a memorial for a fallen comrade. Often, one can find RIP (rest in peace), as a final tribute to a deceased gang member. Usually the name of the gang member who gave up his life for the gang will be next to the RIP.

Unfortunately, graffiti can be the prelude to gang violence. Monitoring graffiti in the schools, neighborhoods and homes can be a good indicator to show rising tensions between individual gang members and rival gangs. Remember some gangs do use graffiti or use it in a limited fashion.

Stylized Clothing

Another indicator or symptom of gang membership is special clothing or stylized dress. Gang members wear certain types of clothing as if the clothing was a uniform. Gang attire can be considered a uniform. There are uniforms for battle, for kicking back (relaxing) and formal uniforms for funerals and weddings. Each gang usually has their own set of uniforms.

Some of the more popular generic types of gang clothing worn includes hats, jackets, jerseys, pants and tee shirts with professional athletic team logos on them. Today, most gangs use black, tan and white as neutral dressing colors. These colors alone do not announce anything specifically, except that the wearer may be gang affiliated.

Clothing color and style may be important for both female and male gang members, because female gang members identify with the clothing worn by their male counterparts. Some female gang members claim that lady gang member fashions can even include a particular hairstyle and color. Some female gang members related they all wear the same color and style of face makeup as part of their gang uniform.

If a gang member who claims Blood affiliation wears red clothing in known or unknown Crip territory, he or she is asking for trouble. This is considered an insult and will be answered with violence. There have been several homicides of non-gang members who unknowingly wore the wrong colored clothing in a particular neighborhood. Youth who grow up in a gang neighborhood develop savvy or street smarts on what color of clothing is acceptable.

Parents should be aware of this. Many parents allow their children to dress like gang members even though they are not. What the parents do not realize is that they children are actual wearing a type of gang uniform that could invite a real gang member to ask them the hit up question. The gang member is compelled to determine whether or not the wearer of the uniform is friend or foe. Wearing this type of clothing draws attention to gang members. So here is the question: Why would parents knowingly place their children in harm's way by letting them wear a gang uniform?

Baseball caps can show gang affiliation. The cap may have the name or insignia of a professional baseball or football team and the moniker or initials of the owner. Examine the cap carefully. Sometimes the gang names and monikers are hidden under the bill or inside the cap lining.

Current gang trends suggest that many gang members favor wearing professional sport team clothing, including jackets, tee shirts as well as baseball caps. In Southern California, ice hockey team emblems, such as the Los Angeles Kings, have been adopted for this purpose as well as the all black or blue Los Angeles Dodgers baseball cap. Clothing with the L.A. Raiders football team emblem is commonly worn. Some gangs use these clothing items because they have identified themselves with a particular team's reputation. These professional sports teams do not endorse any aspect of gang life.

Another aspect of sports team clothing also includes wearing team colors and uniforms for well-known colleges. The gangs will chose this style of dress because the letters that are used to abbreviate the college name also can be used to represent the gang name. In addition, the college colors are representative of the gang's colors. Although the wearer will deny gang membership and claim they are just team fans, there is seldom truth to this. The colors and team uniforms are chosen in an effort to camouflage gang membership. There is further discussion of the use of professional and college sports wear at the end of this chapter.

Baggy clothing has generally become popular with the younger generation. During the 1970s and 1980s only people who associated with the gangs once wore this style of clothing. Non-gang members are now wearing the oversized baggy pants, three quarter length baggie shorts, jackets and shirts as well. For some reason this style of clothing has become very popular in the general 14-24 year-old age group.

Unfortunately, gang members often assume that anyone wearing their type or color of clothing (gang uniform) has to be another gang member. Sometimes a particular gang or gangs of a particular race wear certain brand of clothing. For example, many Hispanic gangs favor the Ben Davis brand of clothing. An emblem of a small monkey signifies the brand. Other common clothing brand names used by gangs have been Frisco, Nike, Fila and British Knights. This is just a partial list. There are more. None of these companies support or endorse gang membership or gang violence. The gangs have adopted the use of their clothing brand as part of their street uniform.

When gang members are involved in acts of violence against rival gangsters they do not stop to confirm the intended victim's identity. Often the target can simply be someone who lives in rival-gang territory. By dressing like a gang member youth increase the chance of becoming a target of gang violence. To the real gang member you appear to look like a member of a rival gang because you are dressed like one.

The clothing issue has become so important, that some public schools have, or are adopting a uniform dress program. The uniform program along with a strict dress code is an effort to keep gang fashions out of the schools because the stylized clothing presents a silent advertisement of gang affiliation. Gang clothing can offer greetings to peer gang members, challenges to rival gang members, and can be a form of intimidation for both the non-gang member student and educator. Don't forget that gang clothing styles can change. The fashion industry has helped popularize gang-style clothing, expect gang fashions to evolve as well.

Gang Tattoos

Tattoos are another type of indicia that can show a gang member's the level of commitment to the gang life. While some people consider tattooing a form of body mutilation, others consider it body art. In the gang sub-culture there are several tattoos that are significant and are only found on people who were or are involved in the gang sub-culture. These types of tattoos are only indigenous to the gang sub-culture.

For example, in gang nomenclature and geography, California is divided into North and South for Hispanic gangs. Gang members living south of Bakersfield, California, are considered to be from Southern California. Gang members north of Bakersfield are considered from Northern California. The north and south geographical barrier may be changing because of Sureno gang migration.

The tattoos used to represent the northern and southern divisions are Sur (South) or Sureno (southerner). Gang members from the north will be branded with Norteno (northerner) or Norte (north).

Other tattoos that separate north from south are the numbers 13 and 14. The numbers may be written in a variety of ways including, but not limited to, Roman numerals. North or south affiliation is especially important for Latino gang members who are sentenced to state prison as well as outside the state of California. The number 13 represents0 the thirteenth letter of the alphabet, the letter "M." The way you say the letter "M" in Spanish is "eme." Eme is also a moniker for the Mexican Mafia Hispanic prison gang. So using the number 13 infers that the wearer is aligned with the Mexican Mafia and accepts the southern California style of Hispanic behaviors.

The number 14 represents the fourteenth letter of the alphabet, which of course is the letter "N." The way this is written in Spanish is "ene." This is a number that infers the wearer is aligned with the Nuestra Familia prison gang and accepts he northern California style of Hispanic gang behaviors. The Mexican Mafia and Nuestra Family prison gangs are rivals just as the norteno and sureno street gangs are.

Many gang members will wear certain tattoos. Some tattoos are specific to a particular gang; others are generic signifying a style of gang. For example one of the most common gang tattoos is the three small dot tattoo that forms a triangle. The three dots represent three Spanish words, "Mi Vida Loca," meaning "my crazy life." This tattoo can be found anywhere on the body, but often is found on the hands and arms of gang members. I have never seen this particular tattoo on non-gang members or on people who have never associated with gangs.

This tattoo is not a military tattoo nor does it fall into the category of body art. It is a form of a generic gang tattoo. No membership to a particular gang can be inferred from this tattoo. It is certainly one worn by someone who understands it meaning and significance and it not seen in non-gang members.

Some gang members will also use the numbers 13 or 14 to show a generic form of gang alliance.

History and tradition play a significant part here. Post World War II the first subsidized housing project in Los Angeles for Latino immigrants was named Maravilla (marvelous). The origin of today's Latino turf wars can be traced back to this housing project. The turf concept has stimulated the growth of many Latino street gangs. As other housing projects were built, rivalries between the projects grew and intensified. The people within one project would ban together to solve problems they had with other housing projects. In this way turf rivalries were born.

In the mid to late 1940s, the letter M represented the Maravilla gang, for the first project, The Maravilla gang was considered the mother of all Hispanic gangs (Guzman, 1992). A few gang members have even told me that the number 13, the letter M represented the first letter in marijuana. However, currently almost all Sureno based gangs today use the number 13 to show a general allegiance to the Mexican Mafia. California. The origin of gang membership is important to many gang members. So important, that gang members have lost their lives simply because they were from a certain area.

In Southern California, a geographical tattoo is often seen. It is the combination of OC and/or a 5-point star. The star is point up. Gang members have claimed it represents being from Orange County, (located south of Los Angeles). The star may also mean its owner has spent up to one year in the county jail. However, the 5-point star is used by many types of gangs in the Midwest and East and will have many different meanings. Gang tattoos tend to have regionalized meanings.

A teardrop tattoo has also been used to represent that the wearer sent a year in county jail. Sometimes the teardrop is worn near the inner or outer portions of the eye. Another meaning for each teardrop is that it represents every person killed by the wearer. If the teardrop is worn near the nose under the eye it could represent a lost boyfriend or fellow gang member.

Other experts debate the use of the teardrop tattoo. Some believe it means that you have been incarcerated and you cry for your loved ones. The more teardrops you have the more time you spent in custody. Another meaning is related to whether or not the tattoo is filled in. The outline of a teardrop could represent the death of a peer gang member. If it is not filled in the death has not been avenged. Sometimes if the teardrop is worn next to the nose it could indicate that the wearer has no more real tears to cry. The teardrop could in this case represent the lifestyle of a gang member (Bondell, 2005).

Often, gang members will tattoo their gang name somewhere on their body. This can include 6-inch high letters spelling out the gang name on stomachs, across their chests and backs or even on foreheads. Some gang members will also attempt to conceal their gang tattoos between figures and on the ankles or feet.

Sometimes gang members will tattoo their moniker (gang nick name) or last name on their necks, top part of their back, arms, chest or hands. Some law enforcement experts believe this is done in an effort to conceal gang membership. Several gang members I have spoken to indicate this type of tattoo helps not only to conceal membership from the police, but also their parents. Tattooing in this manner is form of generic tattoo. It is a type of tattoo that is indigenous only to the gang culture but does not relate a specific relation to a particular gang.

Spider-web tattoos are also common among gang members who have spent time in a state prison. A fly tattooed in the spider web may represent a person that was murdered by the wearer. Some gang members even tattoo their genitals or scalp with the name of their gang. Female gangsters may also decorate themselves with similar tattoos.

Another very common tattoo used by all types of gang members are the happy and sad theatrical faces. This tattoo represents a unique perspective of the gang psychology, "happy now and cry later." As an 18-year-old skinhead told me, "...*the tattoo really refers to the gang life style, happy one minute and sad the next.*" He was referring to the unpredictability of the gang life. The theatrical happy and sad mask tattoo is another form of a generic tattoo.

Tattoos alone are not sole indicators of gang membership. In fact, some gang members have no tattoos at all. However for those who wear tattoos, they may be an indicator of gang membership and commitment. The longer a person is with his gang the more tattoos he will sport. Being incarcerated in state prison is also another way to increase the number and type of tattoos. Tattoos in combination with other membership characteristics may indicate whether or not you are dealing with a hard-core gang member. Remember, many non-gang members also have tattoos. Body art tattoos are normally non-gang related tattoos.

In some parts of the country, gang symbols are tattooed to show affiliation and membership. Tattooing a rival gang's symbol upside down relays a powerful message. Symbols can range from five and six point stars to pitchforks, hearts, crowns, top hats, carton type characters, animals, pictures of fences clocks, guard towers, people and triangles. Remember, like graffiti tattoos can also have a regionalize meaning.

Burns and Brands

In early 1980, Southern California law enforcement professionals began to notice a peculiar thing among the newly emerging Indo-Chinese street gangs. Many of the gang members that were contacted by the police had what appeared to be cigarette type burns on the top portion of the hands, the arms and at the top of the wrist. At first, it was suspected that these burns were the result of some type of child abuse.

It quickly became apparent that the burns were self-inflicted. The gang members in order to gain more respect and to show how brave they were for their gang would burn themselves, usually in front of other gang members. One young female Vietnamese street gang member told me, "*...to be down is to burn...*" The new Indo-Chinese street gangs began a unique way to show that the wearer was down for his or her gang. For the first time west coast law enforcement professionals encountered a new form of body modification that demonstrated so sort of gang commitment.

Today, multiple cigarette burns are commonly encountered on all types of street gang members; not only on Indo-Chinese gang members. The number of cigarette burns is not important. At one time, law enforcement officers entertained the idea that an even number of burns meant you were an active gang member, while an odd number meant you were out of the gang.

Burning is often done with cigarettes, coins or wire. In some cases, for example, motorcycle gang members that leave the club in disgrace may have the club tattoo burnt off with a hot spoon, leaving a painful burn scar. Gang members who burn themselves today normally do it to show their bravado and to gain respect from their fellow gang members.

Mid-west street gangs have used a crude form of branding to show gang affiliation. A coat hanger would be shaped into a symbol of the gang. The homemade-branding iron would be heated over a stove, then pressed to the right or left shoulder. Branding has also been used by non-gang members so affiliation to a particular group. For example, fraternity members have branded themselves to show membership.

Scarring

Along with burning another common practice started by the Vietnamese street gangs was body scarring. These are self-inflicted knife wounds that when healed leave a long rectangular shaped scar. In the Indo-Chinese community this type of body modification is normally not done. Those who have this type of scarring are intimidating to others. Some Vietnamese gang members will scar themselves in this fashion to scare and intimidate non-gang members. As far as body modification goes, scarring is not new.

These practices are gaining popularity within the street gang sub-culture. Like tattoos they represent a form of rebelliousness against traditional societal norms. Many young people across the nation are experimenting with all types of body modification. The 14-30 year-old-age group seems to be the most interested in these forms of body modification. Remember, the majority of gang members also fall within this age category. You can expect gang members to also be involved in these body modification techniques.

Body Piercing

Fads come and go within the gang sub-culture and one of the newest fads is body piercing. I have met gang members from every type of street gang who have pierced their bodies in some fashion. However, the actual number of street gang members who have pierced bodies is relatively small when compared to the total gang population.

Today, the most common areas of piercing include the eyebrows, nose, lips, nipples, navel, and ears and in a few cases the genitals. The piercing can be done at special studios that cater to this type of body modification. However, the number of gang members who have body piercing seems to be increasing. Some of the gang members I have spoken to have admitted that they have pierced themselves, or with the help of a friend. Piercing by itself is not indicia of gang membership and appears to be a popular form of body modification that is also popular with some gang members.

Stylized Hair Cuts

Today, it seems the haircut of choice for most gang members is the shaved head. Unfortunately, like many other types of gang indicia the shaven head hair cut is also very popular with many young people, not just gang members. All males who have a shaved head are not gang members.

Along with the shaved head hair cut another popular hairstyle is to have the sides of the head shaved and the top hair long. The hair is normally combed straight back, sometimes gang members will also have a pony tail. Haircut styles change just like clothing styles. I have noted that gang members can wear any style of hair cut, even though some styles are more common than others.

Some gangs will identify with a certain hairstyle. For example, skinheads identify with the shaven head, punk rockers with the spiked hairstyle and the Jamaican gangs with dreadlocks. Currently, many skinheads do not have shaven heads, but instead have very short haircuts. Another trend that may be encountered is using the haircut to write the symbol or name of the gang.

Sometimes when a shaved head is used as a canvass for tattoos the hair will be grown out to cover the tattoos.

Cellular Telephones

With the advent of instant communication and modern communication tools, gang members have joined the mobile communication group. Cellular telephones afford easy and mobile communications. The cost of operation has dropped significantly allowing more cellular telephone operation. This technology has helped in the globalization of street gangs.

During the mid 1990s the cloned cellular telephone made its debut into the gang sub-culture. Cloned analog cellular telephones were inexpensive and easy to get if you have the right connections. These cloned telephones could be bought for as little as $50.00 to $100.00.

Basically, the cloned telephone is a cellular telephone that has someone's cellular identification and telephone numbers programmed into it. These numbers at one time were easy to steal off the airwaves using a special reading device. Then they were re-programmed into a legitimately purchased or stolen cellular telephone and sold.

Gang members were quick to take advantage of this technology. This allowed unlimited cellular telephone use until the account was closed due to the excessive activity. It was common for law enforcement to come across street gang members possessing and using cloned cellular telephones. With the advent of digital cellular telephone service the use of cloned analog cellular telephones ceased.

The current use of digital cellular telephones can aid in the commission of crimes. Gang members use cellular telephones in all types of criminal activity, ranging from drug sales, murder, attempted murder, to home invasion robberies.

Pagers

At one time personal text pagers made life easier for many of us. Street gangs also commonly used this form of communication technology. Pagers were used to give instant requests and messages to gang members. Pagers also warned of pending police contact by sending a code like 911 or a text message. Even though pagers are a great way to communicate, it is safe to say they are old technology.

At one time gang members that I interviewed acknowledged they used pagers to communicate with each other by using special codes. Each gang member would have their individual code to identify themselves. Some gangs even developed their own digital codes to send standard messages. They used the codes much like the police use radio codes to communicate for clarity and brevity. This behavior becomes important because those gang members who sold drugs also used pagers to facilitate trafficking. With the advent of instant cell phone text messaging and devices like the Blackberry pagers are not used. The use of the cell phone by gang members is another example how technology aids the general public and those involved in criminal activities.

Scanners

Police scanners are used for one thing, to monitor police radio activity. Police radio codes are not classified nor are they top secret. Electronic stores legally sell scanners, lists of police radio codes as well as federal, state and local police radio frequencies. Anyone can listen to a scanner and with a little practice determine what the police are doing and where they are responding.

Like any police buff, gang members can also use scanners to monitor police activity in their areas. I have met gang members who have escaped arrest because they were listening to their scanner and knew of the pending police arrival. Gang members who traffic drugs commonly use scanners. Knowing when the police are coming can help in hiding or destroying the contraband.

For example, some home invasion robbery teams sometimes use scanners to test and time police responses to emergency calls. This aids in the final planning of a commercial and home invasion type robberies. During the robbery a scanner has been used to monitor radio traffic to see if police are dispatched to the robbery location. If the police are dispatched to the robbery, the gang members are afforded a chance to escape just by listening to the scanner. It is not illegal to possess a scanner and gang members have used to aid in escaping police contact and to plan criminal activity.

Gang Association

Some gang membership indicia may center on certain behaviors. These behaviors may be ignored because some parents were themselves active gang members and feel that being a part of a gang is just a normal part of growing up. For others, denial will not allow them to understand or deal with the situation. Association with known gang members often leads to gang affiliation and eventually membership for many youth.

Behavioral changes may also mean something more serious is involved, such as emotional problems, physical or sexual abuse. Obviously, to diagnose emotional problems that are accompanied by physical, emotional, psychological and/or sexual abuse takes an expert to analyze the symptoms and offer appropriate treatment. After careful examination any underlying psychopathology can be treated with therapy and or a closely monitored prescription treatment program.

Students who become interested in gangs may ignore their studies and the result will be failing or struggling in school. Unexcused absences with no explanation or help from the parent(s) are another indicator. These kids may withdraw and fail to participate in class activities. They will become more difficult to communicate with. They also may have a change of friends or may start to associate with other gang members. They will be involved in atypical behaviors.

Lifestyle changes such as staying out late; developing a substance abuse or addiction, being involved in drug sales and/or transport can also be symptomatic of gang association or membership. Criminal behavior can start with minor violations, like underage drinking and or smoking. The student may become more difficult to work with at home or at school. These behavioral changes may be noticed first by teachers, law enforcement professionals, mental health or allied health professionals.

There may also be a noticeable change in appearance. Hairstyles and color may change. Females may wear certain types and colors of makeup. Gang fashions may be worn. There may be a tendency toward secrecy, a lack of interest in family activities, as well as difficulty with parent-sibling relations.

Some parents never see these changes. Sometimes it is difficult for parents or family to recognize these particular behavior changes. This may happen in a dysfunctional family setting. By the time the parent(s) recognize the issue, there may be police and court involvement. This may also occur in a family were generational gang life has become the norm.

The young person may start to use gang language, street slang and hand signs. The appearance of gang graffiti might be found on personal papers such as address and phone books, or in bedrooms. Students sometimes start to tattoo themselves. There may be a problem with local law enforcement in the form of frequent contacts, and even arrests. Gang membership and/or association could be the root cause for all these behavior changes. These behavioral changes are all too often the result of gang association.

Photographs

Street and prison gangs can often become a surrogate family to their membership. Like all families when celebrating a special day, a family gathering, or birthday, pictures are taken to memorialize the occasion. This holds true for the gang family as well. Some gang members keep complete photo albums memorializing their gang affiliation and related activity.

It has been my experience that gang members normally will not let a non-gang member pose with them for a picture. Many gang members have told me that when a person has his picture taken with other gang members it is only because that particular person was a member of the gang and could be trusted. The trust and respect allows the person to have his or her picture taken with the gang and thus shows acceptance as a member of the gang.

Many times gang members will take special photographs of themselves. Often, they will display their gang hand signs and the background may be covered with their gang's graffiti. The photographs can show a few of the members or the entire clique or set membership. These photographs are like team photographs taken in high school or college except they may show gang members holding and or shooting all types of weapons or displaying gang hand signs.

The individuals who possess these photographs sometimes will alter some of them. Gang monikers and gang names may be written in or scratched into the photograph. The gang members do not have to take all the photographs. For example, gang members sometimes cross out their rival's picture in a high school yearbook. This is sort of a private insult to a particular rival gang member. The yearbook may be shared with a few of the gang members peers and then kept in his bedroom.

I have investigated many cases where the parents never looked at their son's yearbook. The youth was doing well in school so the parents assumed their son was doing well because of his academic achievement. In reality the youth was a member or leader of a street gang. The student did not display any of the traditional indicia associated with gang affiliation. In all cases the youth had no prior contact with the criminal justice system. The high school yearbook held the key to unravel the riddle of this youth's involvement in gang related crime. In the yearbooks were notes, cross outs and graffiti and gang names of rivals and the name of the gang the youth belonged to.

With the arrival of the hand-held video camera, gang members have taken video footage of some of their activities. Video footage can show weapons and live fire gun practice, gang parties, and shown youth and adults claiming gang membership and loyalty. The photographs and video footage are good evidence proving gang affiliation and may be hidden from unsuspecting parents. Sometimes, gang initiation rituals like a jump in or a sex in are videotaped by the participating gang members.

Hand Signs

To the gang member, communication with hand signs is just as important as written or verbal forms of communication. Hand signs have become another non-verbal form of communication for and between gang members. Flashing or the throwing of hand signs has resulted in deadly gang violence. Throwing or flashing hand signs is another way to announce your gang's presence or offer a greeting, a challenge or to intimidate. Some gang members view the flashing of hand signs from rival gang members as a disrespect and challenge. Remember in the gang sub-culture every challenge or insult demands a response.

Hand signs are simply forming letters of the alphabet with the hand and fingers. Usually the letters are an abbreviated way to represent the gang name or affiliation. Standing in groups, a few gang members can form several letters to send a message. For example, the letters W P are sometimes formed and they translate to white power. Like graffiti, hand signs can be used between gangs or to individual gang members and are considered a form of gang advertisement. Hands can form symbols of the gang like pitchforks or hearts and can be used to form specific numbers as well.

Midwest based street gang members can also use hand signs to tell a story. This is referred as "stacking" and is usually accompanied with rap music. Remember how the Hawaiian hula dancers tell a story with their hands. It is the same concept. Stacking can also be used in a jump in ritual. After the new members is beaten in sometimes, he will kneel down on one knee and the gang member brothers will stack over the new member. This part of the jumping ritual resembles the knighting ceremony by a king.

Slang

Some street gangs have developed their own spoken code or gang slang. This slang is also known as an argot. An argot is a specialized language that a sub-culture develops. This language distinguishes the sub-culture from the rest of society. Depending on which gang you are dealing with, the language may change. Gang members from different types of gang find many ways to say the same thing.

Common terms used by gang members are: *homie* or *homeboy*, meaning fellow gang member; *blasting, bustin* or *capping*, meaning shooting. *Plaque* or *plac* is an individual's nickname or signature in graffiti. *Gauge* refers to a shotgun. A *gat* or *quete* or *strap* refers to a handgun. For example, "being strapped" is gang slang that someone is carrying some type of gun.

Specific vocabulary used by each type of gang will be discussed in their respective chapters. The vocabulary can be extensive and confusing. Remember, there are three ways gang members can communicate, written (graffiti), verbal (slang) and visual (hand signs).

What is being said here? *"Say cuz I was kicking in the hood when this slob dissed me with red. He starting capping from his bucket so we ghosted and the strawberry across the street dropped a dime on one time."* Not all gang members talk this way but understanding gang slang will help you understand that the person who said this was a victim in a drive by shooting. He is telling you the street version of what happened. The victim was relaxing in his neighborhood when a raggedy beat up old car came by and a blood gang member disrespected him by showing him the color red. The blood gang member starting shooting at him, so he ran away and a white cocaine prostitute across the street saw the shooting so she called the police.

A rule of thumb is that if you do not understand what the gang slang means it is probably best not to use in conversation. You may inadvertently use the term incorrectly and insult the gang member you are talking to.

Monikers

The gang culture has another parallel trait with traditional family life. Think for a moment of how you grew up, and how your family functioned. Most of us were part of what sociologists might term a traditional family. As a child perhaps our parents, brothers or sisters gave us nicknames. The name was based on some personality or physical trait that our parents thought was cute or unique. For example I nicknamed my youngest son "Pepperoni" which was shortened to "pep" by his older brothers. I did this because of all the sons I was blessed to have the youngest would share with me the strangest views of life I ever heard. I always said I love the way he allows me to see the world through his eyes. He is the spice of my life, hence pepperoni.

In the surrogate gang-family, members are often, but not always given nicknames. These nicknames are called monikers and are usually based on a physical or personality trait of the particular gang member. Gang peers normally give the name. Usually only one person can use a given name. For example, if a particular gang member is always quiet, he may be called "Silent." If a gang member is physically large, he may be called "Oso", the Spanish word for bear.

If another gang member of the same gang wants to use the same name, he or she has to use a derivation of the original name. For example, a gang member is known as Flaco (skinny); a second gang member is also very thin and he wants to be called Flaco. He may be called, Flaco 1 or Lil Flaco. The same name is used but changed slightly so that each gang member can retain his individuality.

Gang members within the same gang follow this general rule. Problems sometimes arise when gang members from different gangs use the same gang name. Theoretically, we could find ten Flacos in one city all from ten different gangs.

Substance Abuse

Substance abuse is a major issue for many gang members. Anyone can be at risk to use or become addicted to drugs, but gang members increase their risk through membership and association. Drugs are commonly used in social settings like parties or special events. The most common substances of abuse are alcohol, marijuana, cocaine, LSD, methamphetamine, inhalants and heroin. Not all gang members are abusers, but a vast majority are.

Drugs may also be manufactured, transported and sold by gangs or individual members. Current research suggests that many gang members are getting involved in drug sales. Not at the organized cartel level, but at the street level. With America's appetite for drug consumption, it is easy to understand why this may be occurring. America has a tremendous drug appetite which only fuels the continual importation of drugs from other countries.

To compound this issue, some of the drugs sold on the streets today are more powerful than the drugs sold 20 years ago. For example, the marijuana sold today can be 10 to 30 times more powerful than the marijuana sold 30 years ago. Many of the nation's drug experts feel that a

1960s attitude is being developed towards the use and abuse of the controlled substances. Some research has suggested substance abuse among the nation's high school age students has increased during the mid to late 1990s; during this same time period it was suggested that drug use has doubled in the 12-17 year-old age category. Later research in the early 2000s suggested that high school age drug use may have decreased slightly. Drug use and abuse within the gang population does not follow models for the general public because it is sometimes an expected part of the social process.

There is a type of gang that does not use drugs or alcohol. They are known as the Edgers or members from Straight Edge gangs. These gang members believe in keeping their bodies pure. So they refrain from drugs, smoking, alcohol and premarital sex. Some Straight Edgers affiliate with Skinhead gangs.

Stylized Jewelry

Gang membership can also display subtle forms of gang indicia. Sometimes a certain style of jewelry will be worn to show gang affiliation. The jewelry can be a ring or unique necklace. It is worn as a subtle marker. Other times gang members use the jewelry to show specific gang affiliation. For example, a female skinhead gang member can wear a swastika necklace. The jewelry would show a belief in white supremacy and possible skinhead affiliation. Some tagger crew gang members wear what looks like a broad tip marker as a necklace. Often, these are hollow in the middle and are used to conceal can spray paint tips. Some gang members wear a lot of gold jewelry showing off their financial success. Either male or female gang members can wear this jewelry.

There has even been some extreme use of jewelry. For example, some gang members may put gold letters or number on their teeth to demonstrate their gang dedication. Some youth are now using subcutaneous jewelry. Some youth have gone so far as to have horns implanted on the front portion of their skulls.

Sub-Culture Magazines

Sub-culture magazines may also be a good indicator of gang affiliation. There are a variety of specialized magazines that cater to every type of street gang. They included Latino, Tagger Crews, Skinheads, Party Crews, Occult, marijuana growers or users, body art enthusiasts and Motorcycle gangs. The magazines are catered to people who are active in these sub-cultures. The articles give relevant information about what is currently happening within a specific group or rival gangs.

These magazines have the same function as gardening, car, or computer magazines... to show what is current. Magazines like *Teen Angel*, *Can Control*, *Prison Life*, *Street Beat* and *Blood and Honor* are a few examples of the magazines available. Possessing the magazine does not by itself make the owner a gang member. Nor is it illegal to publish them. But a light bulb should go on here. One issue here is that non-gang members tend not to subscribe and posses these types of magazines.

Music

Stylized music has been associated with gang sub-culture for a while. Some of the common styles of music associated with street gangs are Hip Hop and Gangster Rap. A few hardcore rap artists are self proclaimed gang or ex-gang members. The lyrics of this type of music often allude to and glorify gang life by referring to killing, domestic violence, drug use or sales and fatal law enforcement contacts.

Some experts believe this music exerts a strong influence over youth at risk. Gangster rap music is all about attitude (Stallworth, 1999). It is an attitude of I don't care, I'm going to get mine now, which seems to dominate youth culture of today, especially those involved in gangs. It appears to be a musical version of the gang psychology.

In a few cases, gang members have written special rap lyrics about their gang and the types of crime they were involved in. The song lyrics can contain threats against the rival gangs or particular rival gang members. These are customized songs that are gang specific. The music may also be specific to the type of gang.

Currently, there is special Hispanic gangster rap. The music lyrics talk about the rivalry between the Sureno and Norteno Hispanic gangs that are based in California. Some gangs are even producing and publishing their music on their own music label. The rap style of music is so popular that in Europe, white supremacist skinheads have developed Aryan rap (Boser, 2006).

Mementos

Many gang members keep mementos of gang events they or their gang was involved in just like traditional families practice. Most often these personal mementos are kept in order to memorialize an event. This could be as obvious as keeping the newspaper articles of a shooting you or your gang was involved in. Other gang members may keep extensive photo albums, giving a photographic history of his or her activities with the gang. Other types of mementos have included hood ornaments from cars that were stolen, expended bullet casings from bullets fired in a crime, letters, funeral announcements and recruitment flyers. These mementos are sort of a trophy for the gang member.

There may be other types of mementos like balloons that were received for a birthday, cards and clothing that may hold a significant meaning. Because of technology advances mementos in the form of pictures and movies can now be posted on the Internet on popular social networking sites like Myspace and Facebook. They may be stored on personal computers and cellular telephones.

Drawings

The gang psychology is easily identifiable by looking at the drawings youth make. These drawings can depict scenes of shootings or jail scenes. The happy and sad theatrical faces are often included in artwork. Prison guard towers or jail bars are also very popular when one is in custody. Many times you will find some reference to the type of gang affiliation the drawer is affiliated with.

Often, the drawing will contain the actual gang name or symbol. Drawings may be kept in personal journals or even completed as school assignments. Gang drawings can reveal what a person is thinking about. They can be a symptom of a specific mentality. Gang drawings may also be used to send a message to others.

Letters

Gang members write letters to others, especially when in custody. Often, these letters contain references to gang activity and/or retaliatory plans. Many times, the writer will sign his gang affiliation and moniker on the letter. There could also be references to the location of stolen property or the location of a fugitive gang member.

The letters may contain requests or orders to peer gang members. Many times, the letter will contain the gang member's explanation of what happened. Often gang members who receive them keep these letters. A large collection of letters could be a potential gold mine as far as historically documenting gang activity.

Letters can also confirm gang affiliation and status by what the author writes; the choice of words, the way he writes and how the name is signed.

Some communications can be in code or written with a substance that cannot be seen. For example, human urine is sometimes used as an ink. The reader has to apply an external heat source to develop the writing. This was highlighted in expert testimony during the 2006 Federal prosecution of several Aryan Brotherhood prison gang members in Santa Ana, California.

Self-Admission

Many gang members freely admit to their gang membership to a particular gang. However, it is now common for some street gang members to deny gang membership and affiliation. Many gang members try to conceal their membership because they are aware of special punitive enhancements for criminal actions that are done in associated with a street gangs.

There are still gang members from all types of street and prison gangs that are proud to claim their membership and gang affiliation. It is almost like these gang members get a special recognition from their peers when admitting gang membership to another person. Gang members tend to claim their membership to subordinate gang members, peer members, students, teachers, to those they wish to intimidate and often to their siblings and parents.

Many times immediate family members who have knowledge of gang membership tend to deny it to criminal justice professionals. As 15-year-old Smokey told me, "... *I'm not afraid to tell anyone who I am and where I'm from... it's not against the law to be a gang member*." He is correct. It is not against the law to be a gang member in the United States. This may not be true in other countries. For example in some Central American countries it is illegal to be a member of a street gang.

Generational Gang Membership

For some youth it is expected that you join a street gang. In some families gang membership is considered a normal part of growing up. These youths may have one or both parents who themselves were gang members. In some instances the parents are still active gang members, especially when their children are not school age. Families that continual to have grand parent(s), parent(s) and sibling(s) in street gangs are known as generational gang members.

Generational gang membership is encountered in all ethnic groups. Today, there are third and fourth generation Latino gang members. There are second and third generation African-American gang members and we are now encountering the first generation of Southeast Asian gang members. It is difficult at best to count just how many generations of white supremacists the nation has because many families keep this belief well hidden. Children in generational gang families are indoctrinated to the gang psychology after birth. The children watch and listen to their parents. Children tend to mimic parental behaviors.

At the young age of 8 or 9 years old a generational gang member can already have an advanced understanding of gang customs, practices and well versed in accepted and expected gang behaviors. They may not be able to articulate it, but they have a fundamental understanding of the gang psychology.

Internet Use

Today many gang members use the Internet to communicate, recruit, and advertise and sometimes to plan crime. In fact some gangs now have their own Web page. The Internet allows for instant communication between gang members and it becomes almost a non-traceable way to communicate. In one criminal case I was involved in a subordinate gang member was instant messaged by his gang leader to help with a fight that ended up in a multiple shooting with one death.

The Internet also allows for the rapid worldwide spread of the gang culture. In the past gang photographs could only shared with local membership, now gang photographs can be seen worldwide anytime. The Internet has become one technological tool that has helped globalize the American street gang culture. The Internet helps create an international cyber neighborhood for street gangs.

College and Professional Sports Wear

Although there are many indicia of gang membership one of the most pronounced is gang style clothing. Remember, normally clothing style alone cannot be the only evidence used to suggest gang membership. The most obvious reason for this is the popularity of "gang style" clothing. Many non-gang members wear this style of clothing. A great example is the three quarter length cut off baggie shorts. This style of shorts was once only associated with Hispanic street gangs. Today, it is one of the most popular styles of shorts worn by gang members and non-gang members across the country.

For many street gangs, professional and college team sportswear has become extremely popular. Numerous gangs across the country have adopted professional or college sport team's apparel for a couple of reasons: because the team's colors match the gang's colors and or the team's symbol can be used to represent a symbol of the gang.

A well-known professional or college team or a team that has changed its color scheme to match a gang tends to be chosen by many East Coast and Midwest based street gangs. For example, the red and black color combination of the Chicago Bulls is popular with the Latin Counts, Black P Stone Nation and the Vice Lords. All are mid-western based street gangs that identify with those colors.

Other street gangs may have focused on a team insignia or name. For example, the L.A. Kings hockey team baseball caps are popular with the Latin Kings because the word "Kings" appears on the cap. A professional or college team's nickname can also be adopted to represent a certain street gang. The California State University at Fresno is a good example. The University's mascot and nickname is the bulldog. The Fresno Bulldogs is a well known Hispanic street and prison gang.

The sport team's name or initials can be used by a street gang. The University of Nevada, Las Vegas is abbreviated as "UNLV." When read backwards has been used to represent the Vice Lord Nation, another Midwestern based street gang.The gang may choose a professional or college sport team simply based on the colors used by the sports team. The Gangster Disciples have affiliated themselves with the Universities of Georgetown and Duke because their school colors are Black and Blue.

The Kansas City Star newspaper recently reported that the street gang called "Simon City Royals" has adopted the new Kansas City Royals uniform to represent their gang. The Royals updated their uniforms and added the color black to the traditional blue and white uniforms. The Simon City Royals colors have been blue and black. The street gang adopted the basketball team's new color scheme (Kansas City Star, 2003).

The Simon City Royals are located mostly in Chicago, with sets in Milwaukee and Mississippi (www.gangsorus.com). This gang has been described as a "drug-dealing, gun peddling, white supremacist gang" in a Milwaukee Journal-Sentinel newspaper article (Doege, 1998).

Right about now you probably are asking yourself the why question. Why do street gangs do this? I have spoken to gang investigators across the country and several reasons become readily apparent. The anecdotal evidence suggests that gangs have been using a college or pro team's color scheme or emblems as a way to disguise gang affiliation or membership. Gang members across the country are well aware of the importance of wearing the appropriate colors and clothing. Don't forget the team's colors and clothing are easily recognizable uniforms for gang members.

Non-gang members may not realize this. By wearing a particular sport team's colors it could be advertising that the wearer is a member of street gang to other gang members. Sports apparel has become a way to disguise gang membership because it is also a popular form of dress for bonafide team fans. Nationally, some gangs have gone "low pro." It is an effort to wear non- traditional gang attire in an effort to avoid police contact. Wearing sports apparel is one way to accomplish this.

There is also some thought that some professional and college teams have a national reputation of being tough and ruthless. For example, Oakland Raiders football team has a well-known national reputation of being one of the most physically punishing football teams in the country. The team colors are black and silver. Many street gang members identify with the teams reputation of being physically tough and the color scheme is somewhat neutral for street gangs. As a result gang members have indicated that they identify with the team's character and use the colors to show it.

For example, Hispanic, Blood and Crip gang members have and continue to wear Raiders football jerseys. It tells the rest of the gang sub-culture members, "I am tough." Professional and college sports attire can also help advertise a gang or gang member's mentality and be representative of the gang psychology.

This is not to say that some gang members cannot be sports fans. They can and some are. However, common sense and experience dictates that many, if not most of the gang members who wear professional or college sport team wear do it as a way to identify their gang affiliation or identify a gang or help exhibit the gang psychology.

A third reason a gang member might wear sports attire is the fact that team name, nickname or symbol can be used to identify a particular gang or a gang's mentality. Let's use the Raiders football team example again. For some Folk Nation gangs, the letters in the name stand for "Ruthless Ass Insane Disciples Everywhere Running Shit." For Blood gang members it may stand for "Run After I Die Erickette." The team's name becomes an acronym to identify a particular gang mentality or affiliation.

This association is not limited to sports attire. It can also be used with nationally known clothing or shoe brand names. Many gang members also commonly wear the Addias brand shoe. At one time for Crip gangs, the brand name stood for "All Day I Disrespect All Slobs." The Dallas Cowboys sportswear worn by some Chicago based and West Coast based street gangs is another example. The People Nation gangs identify with the five-point star which is the team's symbol. The five point star is also a common symbol of People Nation gangs. For the west coast based Crip gangs, the letters of the Cowboys team name represent, "Crips Out West Bangin On You Slobs."

Nike brand shoes are very popular with many types of African-American street gangs. The letters of the brand name indicate, "Niggas Insane Killing Everybody." The Gangster Disciples, a Folk Nation gang has adopted the "Fila" brand. The letters of the brand name represent "Folks in Love Always" for the gang. British Knight brand sports shoes are also popular with Crip gang members. The letters BK for them represent "Blood Killers." A person in theory could wear no distinguishing color of clothing or sports attire and be able to support his gang affiliation just by wearing a brand name pair of shoes.

Sometimes the number on a sports jersey will have a specific meaning. For example, many southern California gang members will wear a blue and white colored sports jersey with the number 13 on it. If you remember the number 13 represents the 13th letter of the alphabet, the letter "M". For Hispanic gang members it also represents an alliance with the Mexican Mafia prison gang. It is also another way to advertise that the wearer is from southern California.

Crime

This can also be a form of membership behavior that might be used to help with the diagnosis of membership, affiliation or activity. Criminal behaviors can also be a form of gang indicia. The gang culture offers a complex and changing lifestyle to study, with its own unique behaviors and sociology. All combined help form a unique lifestyle that defines the gang psychology.

The ultimate tests to diagnose gang membership are behaviors. Remember, membership indicia are symptoms or an extension of the gang psychology. The indicia can show a mind set and suggest an affiliation a particular group or a way of life. Combined with criminal behavior, they can be a good indicator of gang membership. Committing crime in small groups of two or three, or with known gang members can be another indicator. The type of crime may also help determine if it is gang related, for example, a drive-by shooting, walk-up shooting, or an execution style shooting.

Some gang members can also commit sex crimes as part of their gang criminal life. Unfortunately sexual assaults have been used as a form of or part of gang initiation rituals. These criminal acts bring the gang member and the gang respect, and help build the reputation of both. Gang members are therefore motivated to commit crime for the gang because they get rewarded. The reward is additional status within the gang and with rival gangs. In a few instances individual gang members can commit a crime by themselves and their actions can still benefit their gang.

I have also encountered gang members who have very successfully hidden their gang affiliation or membership from their parents. Doing very well in school and not wearing traditional gang attire can accomplish this. Young people can be very flexible. The style of clothing, haircut, gang type tattoos, use of gang slang, hand signs, graffiti, etc., are not necessarily required to be a gang member or to participate in gang related crime.

Remember many gang members are unemployed and many are juveniles. Only about 25 percent of the nation's gang population is comprised of juveniles. Between the hours of 2:00 PM and 8:00 PM most of nation's juvenile crime is committed. Juvenile gang members will be very active during these hours.

Gangs can also fight amongst themselves, usually over girls or personal dislikes. If a gang member fails to obey a rule, members of their own gang may also discipline him or her. This is in itself, another form of criminal behavior. Gang members can also be opportunistic, not really looking for trouble, but ready to react violently over a chance encounter with a rival gang. Gang violence, when it happens, may be explosive in nature. Research suggests that for most gang members, the day-to-day life can be quite boring (Klein, 1995).

Don't forget, committing a crime may also be a way for a prospective gang member to gain formal acceptance into the gang. When caught by law enforcement that person may have no prior record or gang history because it was his first criminal act with and for the gang. Nevertheless, the criminal act is gang motivated and gang related. Also, the person committing the crime should be considered part of the gang because normally gang members will not allow a non-member or non-trusted person to commit a crime with them. The crime could be as simple as a beer run. Gang related crime does not have to always be felonious conduct.

Gang members can be members of their gang 100 percent of the time, but only be present on a part time basis. Some gang members live far away or are in custody nevertheless they are still part of the gang. Only when they return or visit can they be involved in crime. Living out of the area does not take gang membership or loyalty to the gang away.

Remember that gang indicia can also have three functions. To peer gang members, it can be a form of greeting. To rival gang members, it can be a form of challenge or threat. To non-gang members, it can be a form of intimidation. Some gang members have several forms of indicia associated with their membership, others have only a few and others can have none. The lack of membership indicia does not disqualify a person from being a gang member. A trend that started in the west coast in the early part of 2000 was sometimes referred as being "low pro." This meant that a gang member went low profile and did not use traditional gang indicia, nevertheless was a bonefide gang member.

Summary

Since gang life is a lifestyle and not a transitional stage for many youths, the lifestyle is taken with the individual wherever he or she goes. The displayed indicia can become an integral part of this street culture and are an extension of the gang psychology. With any culture, the sociology is understood by understanding the language, ethics, behaviors and traditions of the group. Understanding the gang culture requires understanding several forms of communication, mentality, history, behaviors and trends of the particular type of gang you are studying. One must not forget the functions of membership indicia. Besides being symptomatic of a specific psychology membership indicia can also function as a form of greeting, challenge or intimidation to both gang and non-gang members. With the advent of the non-profile gangster, some gang members will attempt to conceal their affiliation and membership by not displaying any traditional indicia.

Chapter 2

Ethnic & Gender Based Gangs

This chapter will discuss the histories some of the major ethnic based street gangs. After the general histories there sections giving examples of specific ethnic based street gangs and the common and unique behaviors of these gangs.

West Coast Latino Gangs

Even though Southern California Latino gangs are not the oldest street gangs in the United States, they are probably one of the most emulated. Many other gangs have used traditional Latino street gang behaviors and membership indicia for years. Their sense of stylized dress, tattoos, graffiti, mentality and hairstyle are just a few of the many characteristics associated with Latino gangs that have been used by many other types of street gangs. The California Latino street gang behaviors have also had a major influence in the development and evolution of many other street gangs throughout the United States; that is why a brief look at the history of West Coast Latino gangs is most appropriate. An understanding of the early development of these street gangs will help to understand how the customs and practices of West Coast Latino street gangs today are used by many other national and international gangs.

(Early) History

Latino gangs today are in many parts of the country. A look at history reveals the real origin of these gangs started a lot earlier. Some formed as the result of gang migration and some mimic LA-based Latino gangs. Others were formed by undocumented immigrants for protection against the existing street gangs and still others formed from first generation Latinos born in the United States. Most experts believe that Mexican street gangs started in Los Angeles in the early 1900s. These first generation gangs developed as a result of events that happened more than 50 years earlier.

In 1718 the Mission of San Antonio Balero was established on the banks of the San Antonio River in south central Texas. It was located in the city we now know as San Antonio. This mission later became known as the Alamo. Remember, during 1718, what is now the southwestern part of the United States was the northwest part of Mexico. The redistribution of national boundaries was in full swing by 1835 with the revolt against Mexican control by US citizens.

In February of 1836, Colonel William Travis and 189 men took control of the Alamo from the Mexicans. In late February, Mexican President Santa Ana and approximately 3,000 Mexican soldiers attacked the Alamo in an effort to regain control. On March 6, 1836, thirteen days after his arrival President Santa Ana and his troops re-took control of the Alamo. In that battle, the valiant U.S. resistance fighters had killed more than 400 Mexican soldiers.

Although the Mexicans prevailed, a myth was born, creating the strong antagonism between Latinos and Whites to which gang life propagates. The history books report all the U.S. fighters were lost in battle. What is not always reported is there were in fact, a few U.S. survivors. They surrendered to President Santa Ana, who, to their surprise, ordered their immediate executions. The orders were carried out. Word of these executions quickly spread throughout the resistance movement and became the rallying cry for the Texas forces, *"Remember the Alamo."* This saying may have been a motivator to fight hard against the Mexicans from a sociological point, but also it was the genesis of U.S. anti-Mexican sentiment.

The anti-Mexican sentiment continued to grow during the conflict and continued to spread throughout the country afterwards.

The Treaty of Guadalupe Hidalgo in 1848 formally marked the end of the war between the United States and Mexico. A forgotten fact is that the United States paid Mexico 15 million dollars plus 3 million in compensation for the northwest part of their country. Basically the Mexican government sold the territory to the Americans. Today we know that area as Nevada, California, Arizona, New Mexico, Utah, Texas and half of Colorado.

Many Mexican street gang members felt and still feel that the U.S. stole this part of their country from their ancestors. They are angry and hostile, passing on this biased version of history down to family members and the community. This not only aids in the development of anti-social behaviors but for some also tends to justify gang membership and activity because it enhances the "us verses them" mentality.

In reality, the country of Mexico lost less than one percent of its population. The United States offered a naturalization program to those Mexican citizens to help them become US citizens. All but about 2,000 Mexican nationals became naturalized citizens. Nevertheless, there was still a high degree of resentment by U.S. citizens against any Mexican, because of what happen at the Alamo twelve years earlier. Like the bias, this resentment was also passed down through generations and still continues.

Imagine how it must have felt to be Mexican back then. You might feel displaced and without a country. One day you are a Mexican citizen, the next day you are not and introduced to a whole new culture and way of thinking. You might not feel accepted because a day earlier you were the enemy and the public often reminds you of this.

The great California gold rush started in 1849. This fueled a migration of many settlers to the West. These events affected gang development by setting the attitude and social and economic conditions for Los Angeles during the early 1900s. Those conditions, along with the rapid growth of Los Angeles and other historical events, helped shape and direct the initial behaviors of street gangs nationwide. California became the 31st state in 1850.

The First Mexican Gangs

In the early 1900s, Los Angeles experiences the birth of the first Mexican street gangs. The Mexicans that were in the pueblo of Los Angeles still felt displaced, even as naturalized citizens. Many of the new citizens were often treated as second-class citizens and told to go back to their home, Mexico.

In their mind, they were home, but now annexed and part of the United States. They were in a country where they were not wanted, but unable to return to Mexico due to their new citizenship status with the United States.

The Mexican immigrants tended to live in the same areas, with family or with other Mexicans whom migrated from the same geographical areas of Mexico. These were also some of the poorest neighborhood areas in the rapidly growing City of Angeles. These conditions aided in the development of rivalries between various immigrant groups.

A modern form of class distinction was also developing. Mexican street gangs formed in part due to economic conditions, prejudice and racism (Guzman, 1992). Do you recall Irish street gangs in New York during the 1800s? The Irish and Mexicans formed gangs for similar reason. Gangs tend to form because of bias, racism and class distinction. In the early 1900s similar attitudes, social and economic conditions were present in Los Angeles, the same as they were in New York over 80 years earlier.

The growth of the city corresponded with the development of an underground drug and prostitution market that evolved between Los Angeles and El Paso, Texas. Early L.A. some gang members started to mimic the dress style, mannerisms and language of the Mexican drug and vice dealers that operated in these areas. During this time some Mexican and non-Mexican youths became interested in swing music and started to use the "Calo" language, a blending of Spanish and English words. This was sort of pig Latin type street slang spoken by many youth, including gang members.

For example, by 1909 the Alpine Street gang had formed in Los Angeles. The membership of the gang was based in local and immigrant populations The Mexican revolution began in 1910 and continued until the 1940. The revolution started an influx of undocumented immigrants north into California and Texas. Following the previously established trend, the new immigrants usually tried to relocate where family members or friends had previously settled. The majority re-settled in the Los Angeles, San Diego and El Paso, Texas areas.

This immigration only helped fuel the growth of the anti-Mexican sentiment in California and Texas. That in turn helped to develop an "us verses them" attitude to develop between Mexicans and non-Mexicans. This again emphasized the class distinction, racism and bias aimed at the Mexicans, especially in the L.A. area.

The White Fence gang formed in 1911 near the railroad tracks in downtown L.A., where Belvedere was a section of the city occupied by the Russians and Jews. And a second part was occupied by Mexicans. These tracks really separated two sections of the community. Poor Mexican immigrants lived on one side of the tracks. Mexican youths who lived in this area would cross this set of railroad tracks to enter the part of the city where the rich people lived (Russians and Jews) to go to a local store. In doing so, the Mexicans would travel through the very affluent neighborhood on the other side of the tracks. This upset some of the people who lived in this part of the wealthy community.

Some of the local residents complained and used their political influence with the railroad, to keep the Mexicans from passing through the affluent neighborhood. The railroad company built a fence one side of the tracks. The fence was painted white; hence the gang is really named after the white colored fence, because it was a man-made boundary where the members lived, (Valdemar, 1995).

Los Angeles was growing rapidly and became the center for growth in the West. Originally settled by the Spanish and later expanded by the Mexicans, Los Angeles had a diverse Latino population. Los Angeles also saw immigrants from Arizona, New Mexico, Texas and Mexico. Immigrants from all over the world heavily influenced the city's demographics. The pueblo of the 19th century evolved into the dynamic and ever changing multi-cultural city that is known today. As the city grew in size so did the number and type of street gangs.

El Paso Influence

El Paso became a center for many immigrant Mexicans much like Los Angeles. During the 1920s and later, Mexicans who went prison in Texas were sent to a prison in Huntsville, near El Paso. While in the Huntsville prison, the Mexicans formed a prison gang called the El Paso Tip. It got its name from the area of Texas where the prison was located. Fellow gang members would greet each other by saying, are you tipped up? Or are you tipped? Meaning, are you from the El Paso area where the prison was located (Valdemar, 1995). This was one way to determine whether or not the peer inmate was an enemy or friend. The prison gang continued to function well into the 1930s.

An informal underground travel route developed between the two cities. This route allowed for a direct influence of El Paso gang trends to be introduced to L.A. street gangs.

The 1920s also brought the beginning of the depression era. Most young Americans today will not identify with Black Thursday, the name given to October 24th, 1929, the day the stock market crashed.

1930s

The Great Depression dominated this decade although the recovery from the crash started in the early 1930s, many people still suffered and struggled for many years. By 1931, about 25 percent of the population or eight million people in the United States were out of work which included the immigrant populations and the poor, who were hit the hardest.

President Roosevelt's New Deal started the nation on the road to financial recovery. The Al Capone and Babyface Nelson type gangsters of the 1930s, while despised as thieves paradoxically projected an image of a businessman because of the suits they wore. They did not choose typical business colors and styles, but took every detail to extreme. Their suits featured wider stripes, more colorful ties, pronounced shoulders, narrower waists and wider trouser bottoms. They topped their extreme look with felt hats. This style of dress became the predecessor to the Zoot suit was later developed.

The Zoot suit fashion was really born during this time period. Cab Calloway and other entertainers popularized the dress style in the nightclubs of Harlem in the early 1930s. Originally, Zoot suits were an exaggerated look comprised of an oversized jacket, wide lapels and shoulders, with baggie low-crotched pants that narrowed dramatically at the ankle. The Zoot suit style of dress remained an influence on young people throughout the 1930s and 1940s. The Zoot suits were quite popular on the east coast during this time. The suit under went some minor modifications as the style traveled west and south into Mexico, but basically stayed the same.

By the late 1930s, Mexican gang members in southern California began to formally induct members by test of a ritual fight to earn membership. The fisticuffs were used to show how tough the prospective member was and whether he had the heart to take a beating for his gang. The test was known as the "jump in" and became an initiation ritual to formalize and confirm gang membership. This type of initiation ritual was not new. The New York Irish street gangs of the early 1800s utilized a similar initiation ritual. The art of hand-to-hand combat was considered a sign of strength and leadership for gangs during this time.

Adolph Hitler announced his presence to the world in 1939, by leading German forces in the invasion of Poland. England and France responded by declaring war on Germany. On September 3, 1939, World War II started. But Mexican street gangs continued to develop and were temporarily unaffected by world events.

1940s

As recovery from the great depression continued, the aircraft and support industries grew in the Los Angeles and southern California area. As a result of this industry growth, work was available and many people were drawn to Southern California, especially Mexican immigrants. Employment and quality of life issues drove migration then as it still does today (Maxson,1998).

Some anecdotal evidence suggests that in early 1940, a young boy Mickey Garcia from Pachuca, Hidalgo, Mexico migrated north and relocated in El Paso, Texas. He immediately joined a local Mexican street gang from the Segundo Barrio. The Segundo Barrio was a name given to three different Latino gangs in the area. Garcia also brought with him a unique style of dress initially thought to have been born in Mexico. Garcia's dress style became an instant hit with all the local young people, especially the local gang members (Guzman, 1992).

His fashion included a felt hat with a long feather in it, called a *tapa* or *tanda*. The pants had pleats in them and were baggie fitting, they were known as *tramas*. The shirt was creased and called a *lisa*. A *carlango* or long, loose fitting coat was used. The shoes were French toe style or Stacey Adams brand and were always shined. They were called *calcos*. To complete the outfit, one had to have a long chain attached to a belt loop that hung past the knee and into the side pocket of the pants (Guzman, 1992).

This outfit became known, as you have probably already guessed, the Zoot suit. Garcia was not the first to wear the Zoot suit. However, he may have been one of the first Mexican street gang members to adopt this popular style of dress. In the past, many angry parents would use the term, *pachuco*, in a derogatory manner to describe this popular dress style. It is thought that the term pachuco was derived from the name of the Mexican town that Mickey Garcia came from, Pachuca (Guzman, 1992). This style of dress later became known as the pachuco look and it became very popular in Mexican street gang culture. Mexican street gang members were sometimes called "pachucos."

Garcia's actions certainly helped spread the popularity of the Zoot suit within the El Paso Mexican street gang population. Don't forget, it was the Italian mobsters in the 1920s that invented the original Zoot suit not Mexican street gangs.

Remember the underground route that developed between Los Angeles and El Paso? Via that route, the pachuco style of dress was most likely introduced to the Los Angeles based Mexican street gangs. The travel route was also used by migrating people who were coming to southern California in search of employment. It did not take a long time for the pachuco style of dress to become popular with some Los Angeles Mexican gang members. There is some anecdotal evidence that suggests the Zoot suit was already present in the L.A. area in the late 1930s however the local street gangs did not adopt it as part of their clothing style until the early to mid 1940s.

Another term that was commonly used in the Texas street gang sub-culture was "chuco." If you were chuco, that meant you were from El Paso, Texas. El Chuco was also a term used as slang to describe El Paso. Both words have their base in the now well-known term pachuco.

The Maravilla housing projects started after World War II ended and became the first Federal housing projects in Los Angeles. The Maravilla gangs started to form during the mid to late 1940s and continued to grow well into the 1950s. The concept of protecting turf was expanded within the housing projects known as Maravilla. The Maravilla gang took its name after the project since many members lived there. The immigrants shared something else in common as they migrated from the same state or area within Mexico and thus, often lived as neighbors within the housing project.

As other housing projects developed, competition also grew between the occupants. Competition for jobs, women and turf became issues for the Mexican youth who lived in this area. Eventually rivalries began between the people who lived in the different projects. If there were problems between the groups they would be handled by themselves, and outsiders, like the police were not allowed (Guzman, 1992).

This mentality developed into an early behavior of claiming turf. When you claim turf, protecting it naturally follows. These behavioral concepts were then adopted and used by the other Mexican street gangs and were rapidly accepted and put into practice. This gang psychology for Mexican street gangs continued to develop. Today, there still some street gangs that claim "turf."

As the social dynamics continued these housing projects evolved into some of the neighborhoods or barrios we know of today. Historically speaking you can trace the origin of turf wars for Mexican street gangs back to these housing projects. These behaviors also led to the formation of behaviors that eventually influenced current gang customs and practices now seen worldwide.

Some gang members currently pronounce the gang term for neighborhood with a "v" or "b". Somehow during the growth of L.A. based Mexican street gangs the "v" and "b" became interchangeable. You may see the Spanish words *varrio* or *barrio* used to describe a neighborhood.

While this was going on, the U.S. entered into World War II which had been underway for over two years for the English and French. The attack on Pearl Harbor by the Japanese on December 7, 1941, forced the United States to join the war on December 8th. The country became galvanized after the attack. Every American wanted to contribute something to the war effort. President Roosevelt signed the War Rationing Act into law. All Americans willingly contributed to the effort. These sacrifices became a symbol of American patriotism and support to our GIs.

Sleepy Lagoon Murder

As U.S. war involvement escalated, Mexican gangs continued to evolve. Protecting turf and answering insults became an essential part of gang life. On August 2, 1942, a young Mexican was beaten up and subsequently died from a skull fracture received in the assault. The killing of Jose Diaz was near a popular swimming hole known as Sleepy Lagoon. Sleepy Lagoon was located on the Williams Ranch, which is now the city of Montebello, California. The police blamed Diaz's death on a gang fight (Guzman, 1992).

LAPD literally rounded up the usual suspects and ultimately arrested 24 members of the 38th Street gang. Later on in the month the L.A. Grand Jury indicted 22 of the 38th Street gang members for the murder of Jose Diaz. One of the arrested gang members was a youth named Henry Levays. He was well known gang member to, LAPD because of his frequent encounters with the police.

The subsequent criminal trial resembled a kangaroo court. On January 13, 1943, three gang members were convicted of first degree murder, nine members were convicted of second degree murder, five members were convicted of assault with a deadly weapon charge and five members were found not guilty. The 17 convicted 38th Street gang members were sent to state prison. The Mexican community responded with outrage. They felt the trial was fixed and the convictions were based on race. Many in the community did not trust the police.

Mexican street gang behaviors changed forever because of these convictions. The jail sentences also acted as a glue to unite the Mexican community in a common cause; a fight against class distinction based on prejudice and racism, a fight against the establishment. It also helped establish a common enemy, the System.

While in prison, the convicted 38th Street gang members never complained even though they were given the worst jobs and treated unfairly. The prison population at this time was mostly White. The 38th Street inmates kept themselves clean and shined their shoes. They cleaned and pressed their clothes even though they were issued garments that were too big for them. The 38th Street gang members kept tough and maintained their dignity while in prison.

These prison behaviors set a new standard for Mexican gang members who were subsequently sent to jail. They demonstrated a type of gang pride and resolve never seen before. These behaviors also elevated the incarcerated 38th Street gang members to folk hero status within the Mexican community. The street gang members especially held them in high esteem.

The trial also caused the Mexican community to develop an anti-White sentiment and distrust for the establishment, especially the police. Anti-Mexican sentiment also grew because of this community response. The class distinction only became more prevalent because racially motivated abuse continued to be directed at Mexicans for many years. It did not matter whether they were U.S. citizens or undocumented immigrants; they were Mexican. "Remember the Alamo."

You can easily understand why this mentality develops within immigrant populations and is strengthen by racism, bias and class distinction. The breeding ground for all gangs begins with an excluded group, who feel victimized by poverty, or the establishment, or some other type of injustice, whether real or imagined. It is fed by an anti-establishment culture of drugs, crime, hate and racial separatism (Valdemar, 1995).These beliefs only act to further polarize communities. This community response was also encountered in the 1800's except it included the Irish immigrants in Five Points, New York.

Zoot Suit Riots

1943 becomes an important year in the evolution of Mexican street gangs in Los Angeles. The Sleepy Lagoon murder convictions only helped set the stage for additional changes in the customs and practices of the street gangs that are still encountered today. The gang psychology continues to develop as these new behaviors are adopted by street gangs.

As the nation got more involved in the war effort, Los Angeles and San Diego became major deployment points for the U.S. military involved in the Pacific campaign. As a result the military population in both cities increased dramatically, almost overnight.

In April 1943 the Japanese Americans were subject to internment. Basically, this a politically correct term used to describe the seizing of property, money and freedoms from the Japanese Americans living on the West coast. A prevailing mentality was present. Americans were looking for the enemy everywhere because we were at a state of war. Many west coast Americans were afraid of an attack by the Japanese. This xenophobic fear aided in increasing anti-Mexican sentiment.

By this time, the "us versus them" attitude was increasing between Mexican- Americans and the residents in the southern California area. In addition, some undocumented Mexicans never registered for the draft, nor did they enlist in the military. The actions of a few youths stereotyped an entire community.

Therefore, many in the surrounding community felt all Mexican-Americans were just like the few angry Mexican youth who did not volunteer for the draft. Most of the L.A. based Mexican community was looked down upon and considered second class citizens, branding Mexican-Americans as lacking patriotism. Mexicans were told to go home, back to their country.

Lastly, the visiting military were dating and socializing with the local women, including the Mexican women. The local Mexican men and gang members felt this competition for the women, further fueling the growing rivalry between the two groups. These conditions only allowed the anti-White sentiment and anti-Mexican sentiment and polarized Southern California.

This biased attitude developed even though thousands of U.S. born Mexicans, some first and second generation, volunteered for service in the military. Many saw front line action and many sacrificed their lives for the people back home. In fact, one of the first U.S. servicemen to die in action during the attack of Peril Harbor was a Mexican-American aviator. Nevertheless, many of the general public still harbored feelings of distrust and dislike towards the Mexicans.

These prejudicial attitudes became catalyst sparking conflicts between the military personnel and Mexican street gang members. There were major assaults on the Mexican gang members by the military personnel and then retaliatory assaults by the Mexicans. The involved military personnel were almost never arrested. The police would routinely arrest only gang members. These conflicts only galvanized the Mexican street gang members to unite against a common enemy and to develop a uniform of their own.

In June 1943 the Zoot Suit riots of Los Angeles started. The non-Mexican community, especially the military personnel felt the Mexican-Americans were not contributing to the war effort. Their dissatisfaction was directed specifically at the young Mexican-Americans and Mexican street gang members who wore the Zoot suit. The large over sized Zoot suit simply appeared to waste valuable fabric that could otherwise be used toward the war effort. In fact, many southern Californians and the military considered the Zoot suit as a form of contraband.

The public's perception was people who wore this garment obviously did not support the war effort and thus, had to be anti-American. This attitude stereotyped the Mexican community (Guzman, 1992).

A story published in a newspaper solidified southern Californians belief the Mexican-American population was linked to the Japanese attack on America. The article suggested Mexicans were related to the Japanese via a connection with Native-Americans. Even though this sounds ludicrous now, in 1943 the article was taken seriously (Dunn, 2007).

These attitudes and biases culminated in the Zoot suit. There are several versions of how the riots started. Regardless, the root cause was the animosity between the U.S. military personnel station in the Los Angeles area and the young Mexican-American population which erupted in violence.

On June 3, 1943 the riots began with some Navy personnel claiming Mexican gang members attacked them. The Mexican gang members claim the Navy personnel were going to attack them. One of the sailors had his jaw broken in the fight. When the sailors returned back to the base and reported what happen about 200 sailors commandeered taxis and return back to the area of the fight. Any Mexican wearing a Zoot suit was attacked. Only after were the police were called. But it was the Mexicans who were taken into custody.

Another version of the riots suggests that they started June 4, 1943 after two assaults by pachucos were reported. In one assault pachuco were allegedly involved in the near fatal beating of a sailor and the second involved the molestation of two Navy wives during a robbery by a pachuco (Dunn, 2007).

On the evening of day two approximately 1,000 sailors and military personnel took to the streets of Los Angeles and beat up Mexicans. Again, the police took the victims into custody. Mexican youth became galvanized as the military and police were seen as a common enemy.

On night three almost 2,000 military personnel were on the streets of L.A. Some were even driven by civilian citizens in their private vehicles. Any Mexican seen was beaten up. If they were wearing a Zoot suit, they were stripped in public; the Zoot suit was then burned and the wearers of the Zoot suit were assaulted during the process. By this time the police were following the taxis and private vehicles and continuing to arrest the assaulted victims. Local newspaper headlines stated *"Let Military Clean Up Our Streets"* (Guzman, 1992).

It was seven days before the riots are quelled. Assumptions to the longevity of the riots are because either the police could not stop the riots or they chose not to. Nevertheless, the conflict concluded when military personnel were ordered not to return to the city. No one was killed, but imagine the impact this event had the Mexican-American community living in the Los Angeles area. Imagine how you would feel if this happened to you or family or friends. As a group you would be angry at the military and police and at the system.

Sleepy Lagoon Appeal

One other event occurred in 1943 that still has a profound impact on Mexican gang behaviors. On October 4th, the California Appeals Court overturned the all the convictions of the 38th Street gang members from the Sleepy Lagoon case Remember they were found guilty of the murder of Jose Diaz. The appellate court found that the criminal trial was flawed because the defense attorneys were not allowed to bring up a defense for the accused. The appellate court also found that some evidence presented in court had been falsified by the police. There was also some evidence to suggest that some police officer witnesses had perjured themselves. There was also some evidence to suggest that the judge may not have been as impartial as he should have.

The incarcerated 38th Street gang members were released from prison and welcomed back into the Mexican community as heroes. The appellate court findings only validated the Mexican-American beliefs about the system and the police. This successful appeal also allowed the Mexican street gangs to be convinced that the enemy was the police. In addition, this belief acted as a catalyst facilitating the unification of Mexican gangs based in Los Angeles. The gangs had a common enemy.

In addition, the appellate court's findings served to confirm suspicions that the 38th Street convictions were based on prejudice, bias and racism. Meanwhile, the 38th Street gang members had set a new standard of behavior for Mexican gang members while in jail. Prison style clothing also started to become popular with gang members because of this incident. Especially, the use of oversized prison type clothing.

During the late 1940s the number of Mexican street gangs and gang membership increased in the L.A. area. Mexican youth found certain solidarity in street gangs, believing their cause was just. Why not? The Appellate Court proved it. During this time, some gang members identified with heroes of the Mexican revolution, like Emilio Zapata. They identified with the phrase, "... *it is better to die on my feet, than to live on my knees.*" The gangs were fighting against the military and the establishment. Therefore, there were very few fights between Mexican street gangs (Guzman, 1992).

1950s

The post war era brought even more change to Mexican street gangs in Los Angeles. After the war, with no common enemy, the frustrations and aggression amongst the gangs was re-focused at themselves. The Maravilla gangs formed in east L.A. also developed a notorious reputation for being violent and ruthless. Don't forget a number of other street gangs were growing and developing. Simultaneously, White Fence, Big Hazard, Temple Street and 38th Street were just a few. The competition for turf between gangs also began to grow. There was exponential gang proliferation.

As the number of street gangs grew, so did the tendency to claim turf, and to settle problems with violent fights. Insults against a gang or a member were not tolerated and intense rivalries between gangs formed. Any insult was answered with retaliation. By the late 1950s more guns were used by gang members. The violence increased and a new word was introduced in the gang vocabulary, the drive-by.

Another post war change further impacted Mexican street gangs. The 1950s proved to be a decade of rapid urban sprawl for Los Angeles. Man-made structures, like freeways and major highways defined new geographical turf boundaries for many gangs. The new man-made boundaries also sub-divided existing gang turfs and made new gang cliques or subsets of same gang.

To compound the growth issue, the suburb became a popular place to live from many Angelinos and many families were moving away from L.A. to the smaller surrounding cities to avoid the ever-increasing inner city gang violence. Newly arrived immigrants would in turn move into the City of Angles. The 1950s urbanization and suburbanization also added to the street gang growth (Valdemar, 1995).

This family flight from inner city gang violence also turned out to be one of the first identified mechanisms for gang migration. Families would move out of the inner city to try and prevent their children from joining street gangs or to stop further involvement or for work. For some families, it was too late. The relocated families and their children moved away physically, but the move still brought the gang philosophy and psychology with them. Transplanted gang members joined local gangs or formed new cliques of the gang they associated with in Los Angeles. Southern California gang proliferation started.

To honor their gang heritage and what was considered the mother of all gangs, Maravilla, it was suggested to newly transplanted gang members started to tattoo themselves with special symbols. The number 13 was tattooed on gang members. The number signified the 13th letter of the alphabet, the letter M. The letter represented Maravilla, one of the oldest and most violent

L.A. street gangs. This tattoo gained immediate popularity with many Mexican street gang members (Guzman, 1992).

As a result, some gang members used the tattoo. Surprisingly, some young Latino gang members who used this tattoo claimed it was code for the letter M that represented marijuana. Don't forget, the Mexican Mafia was not formed yet. This particular tattoo practice was short lived.

Throughout the 1950s the number of gang related violent crimes increases dramatically, as does the number and size of Mexican street gangs. Because of the violence, law enforcement increased their measure of response. As a result, many Mexican gang members were sent to prison. This caused the racial demographics within the prison population to change as more Latino gang members are sent to prison.

During this period, Mexican street gangs also developed ethnic pride. The term "chicano" was introduced to help describe a racial pureness. Chicano is an Aztec word meaning Mexican (Guzman, 1992). Another street gang term was introduced, "puro." This is a Spanish word meaning pure. Street gang members began using these words to describe their pure ethnic heritage. They were 100% Mexican; they were "puro Chicano." Some gangs would only allow new members to join their gang provided they could prove that they were "puro".

Along with the name or nickname of gang, some members also began to tattoo themselves with the words puro and or Chicano. Tattoos quickly became a form of silent advertisement of the type gang you belonged to. Tattoos could transform your body into a billboard, silently advertising a gang affiliation.

Between 1956 and 1957, 13 Eslos (gang term for East Los Angeles) gang members were doing time at the Duel Vocational Institute located in Tracy, California. They banded together to form the gang of gangs in prison. They modeled their gang after the Italian Mafia. They started the first prison gang in California corrections. This Latino prison gang became known as the Mexican Mafia. The gang later became known as La Eme. "Eme" is the Spanish word for the letter M. Initially, the gang was formed for protection against the other inmates and the prison staff and as a way to unite all Latino street gang members while incarcerated in state prison.

However, very quickly it was obvious that the gang had gained power base within the institutions. The Mexican Mafia attempted to take control of the prison narcotics trade, prostitution and criminal activity. The formation of this gang set the stage for major changes in street and prison gang behaviors. Any Latino gang could potentially become part of a power base for this prison gang.

The Texas prison gang the El Paso Tip eventually evolved into the Texas Syndicato between 1950 and 1960. Gang members would great each other with the term "Ese." "Ese" is the Spanish word for the letter S. This letter represented Syndicato, an abbreviation for the Texas Syndicato. Some Mexican gang parolees released from the prison at Huntsville traveled west to California or "Califa". The travel between El Paso and Los Angeles enhanced the exchange of gang culture between the two states. One result was that southern California Mexican street gang members now started to also greet each other by using the word "ese". Ese became a reference to the letter "S", which was an abbreviation for sureno or southerner. This became a welcome and greeting between Latino gang members (Valdemar, 1995).

1960s

The street rivalries, which began after the war, only intensified. The rivalries fueling the Mexican gang turf wars started in the late 1950s, continued to the mid 1960s. Gun violence between gangs escalated to a degree never experienced before in southern California. This was also the start of the baby boomer era.

The 1960s heralded another factor that heavily influenced the street gang culture, drugs. Although gang members used drugs before the 1960s, the country's growing drug appetite and curiosity motivated many gang members to start selling and using drugs. Some refer to this period as the "sixties drug culture." The lure of instant money enticed street gangs to get involved in the sales, manufacture, transport and abuse of drugs. Some of the first formal academic studies of street gangs were started in the mid to late 1960s. Ironically, only 58 cities nationally reported the presence of gangs during this time (Klein, 1995). The mid 1960s brought the United States into the Vietnam conflict. The draft was taking many young Americans off the streets and into the military. Gang related activity deceased and leveled off nationally, but especially in southern California.

The identity with Mexican racial purity also caused a kind of racism and bias within the Latino community. Mix-race youth would not be allowed to join certain gangs because of their racial impurity. These biases eventually lead to the formation of a new type of street gang in the mid 1960s. This new type of gang would allow anyone from any race to join.

By 1966 the attitude toward mixed-race Mexicans had reached a breaking point. The now infamous 18th Street gang formed because of this cultural bias. The 18th Street was started by mix-raced youth who were not allowed to join the traditional Latino street gangs. Initially the gang of "throw away" youth called themselves the Baby Aranas (spiders). Then were known as the Latin Kings (not associated with the East Coast Latin Kings). This gang would eventually become one the largest Latino street gangs in the nation because of its non-discriminatory membership policy. Anyone could join the 18th Street gang (Cantu, 2003).

By 1967, the Mexican Mafia was trying to unite all Mexican gang members who were in state prison. Some informal rivalries developed between Mexicans from Northern California and those from Southern California. The Mexicans from the north were thought of as less sophisticated because they were farm workers or from the farm working community. While in-custody they would be taken advantage of by the Surenos, the southern California Latino street gang members.

If the north/ south unification were completed, the Mexican Mafia would have become the largest and strongest prison gang in California. Many young Latino street gang members aspired to become professional gang members by joining the Mexican Mafia. At the same time, La Eme began to recruit new members from the ranks of Southern California street gangs.

In 1968, the stabbing of a northern California Mexican gang member over a pair of shoes at the hand of Mexican Mafia prison gang member ignited the California state prison Shoe Wars and forever bifurcated the north and south Mexican prison populations forever. A formal rivalry resulted. The Mexican prison gang, Nuestra Familia was established to protect "nortenos", the northern California Mexican street gang members from members of the Mexican Mafia and the "surenos" the southern California street gang members. The Mexican Mafia and Nuestra Familia became bitter rivals.

Mexican gang members from Northern California started to identify with the color red. They chose the red color because when Nuestra Familia was formed, most the Mexican Mafia gang members had the blue colored state issued handkerchiefs. As this rivalry continued to develop the nortenos started to identify with the number 14. This represented the 14th letter of the alphabet, the letter N (North). The term Norte was used and the city of Bakersfield, California set geographical boundary separating the two gangs.

As a result of this norteno/sureno division, individual street rivalries between Latino gang members were to be set aside while in prison. All Southern California Latino street gang members inherited a common enemy, any Latino gang member from northern California. This prison gang rivalry acted as a glue to unite all street gangs from the north against all street gangs from the south. This polarization also allowed the Nortenos to be rivals of the Surenos became the power bases for the Mexican Mafia and Nuestra Familia prison gangs.

By this time the street code of conduct for Latino street gang members had become:

1. Do not cooperate with the police.

2. Take care of business yourself (handle your own problems).

3. Never snitch or inform on gang activity (be a rata).

4. No insult no matter how small goes unanswered (Guzman, 1992).

This inferred that Latino gang members would protect their neighborhoods at all costs, even if they had to kill someone, go to jail or sacrifice their lives. The gang members displayed "a fighter pilot" type cockiness. They were extremely confident of their control and power. This caused the local communities to fear street gangs and allowed these gangs to control entire neighborhoods.

Latino gang members also developed a set of customs and practices that became the rules of engagement for the street. They became like a set of gang ethics:

1. Never commit crimes in your own neighborhood.

2. Never involve innocent people, like women and children.

3. Schools are considered neutral grounds, as well as churches, stores and movie theaters (Valdemar, 1995 and Guzman, 1992).

The penalty for violating these rules would have turned all gangs against the violating gang. Although, the rules were strict for street gangs, they were basically followed. The older gang members or veteranos enforced these rules. These older, more experienced gang members were the informal leaders of their gangs. They tended to tutor the younger gang members and taught them the street behaviors and ethics of gang membership. In fact, some acted as surrogate parents and mentors to younger gang members (Valdez, 1999).

1970s

By late 1970s, firearms became the weapon of choice for many Latino gang members. Latino street gangs continued to increase in size and in number in southern California. Many gangs recruited new members to become stronger and more formidable. The traditional jump in ritual started to become more violent. A few gangs also required a prospective member to commit a crime to earn membership (Valdemar, 1995).

Many Latino street gang members by now considered themselves the policemen of their neighborhoods. They felt, and some still feel, they have a duty and obligation to protect their neighborhood. Most Latino gangs battled over turf violations. During this time incarceration became a status symbol for many young Latino gang members.

Joe Morgan was of Slavic decent and enamored with the Mexican culture. Joe Morgan was asked to join the Mexican Mafia. He was invited and became a member of the Mexican Mafia. He was later considered the god-father of the prison gang and eventually became the figure head leader. He also developed strong ties with the Italian Mafia and the drug traffickers from Mexico (Valdemar, 1996).

In the 1970s the prison life mentality was taken to the streets by the parolees, who in turn, schooled younger street gang members with this "*only the strong survive and prey on the weak*" philosophy. These parolees were considered "veteranos" or veterans. They were given the utmost respect and held in a highest degree of honor by the street gang members. Street gang members were required to learn this new way of thinking and behaving. Ultimately, this code standardized the expected behaviors for Latino street and prison gang members. This included the proper way to dress, talk, act and conduct business. The veteranos also punished those who violated of these rules. The rules and codes were part of the street gang psychology.

In the early 1970s, the United States also experienced another major influx of undocumented Mexican nationals. The economy in Mexico had deteriorated. The immigrants mainly relocated to the southwestern portion of the country in search of work and a better quality of life. Unfortunately, this functioned as a new recruitment pool for the Latino gang populations in California. As the street gangs proliferated, the violence also increased. This trend is still generally true.

Specialized law enforcement units were established to help fight the growing gang problems. The police, Probation departments, Corrections, District Attorney offices, the community and courts united to try and curb the gang violence. The concerted effort paid off. As the gang violence started to decrease during this time the number of gang members that went to prison increased. There was a focus on sending the gang leaders and the most active gang members to prison.

This coordinated attack on gang violence had an unforeseen result and impact on the street gangs.

The gang leaders, the veteranos were the mentors and enforced the gang rules and psychology. Because so many gang leaders were jailed in the late 1970s, the traditional gang ethic was not passed down or enforced. The young gang members matured with no rules and developed a new model of gang behaviors and also affected the gang psychology. As a result gang violence started to escalate again in southern California.

The Island Gang

The Fresno Bulldogs formed in the early 1970s. What made this Latino gang so unique is that it is physically located in Central northern part of California. Theoretically, the gang should have aligned itself with La Nuestra Familia, in which the gang's membership would be part of the nortenos, the northern power base of the Nuestra Familia (the northern Latino prison gang). The Bulldogs did not and still do not align themselves with any northern or southern prison gang. They are independent, something not seen before with Latino street gangs.

The gang uses the color red and the number 14 to identify with, yet it's rivals are both norteno and sureno Latino street gangs.

By 1975, law enforcement was still focused on violent street gang members. Determinate sentencing in California impacted violent gang members that were in prison. This protocol allowed for their early release from prison and return to the street. A new wave of prison gang influence impacted Latino street gang culture.

1980s

By this time, some of the traditional codes and rules of the Mexican street gangs had all but been abandoned. Latino street gang members had begun to commit crimes in their own neighborhoods. Non-gang members and undocumented immigrants became a new class of victim for these Latino street gangs. Some of the immigrant youth started to form their own gangs for protection against the established street gangs. This only helped increase inter-gang conflicts between these two types of Latino gangs. Gang violence was well established on school grounds, malls, theaters and churches. Innocent women and children had begun to be victimized by Latino gangs. There were no rules, except only the strong survived. The concept of respect for Latino street gangs was now based on fear, respect, control and power. The gang mantra becomes the *"more you fear me, the more you respect me"* (DeCastillo, 2000).

By now some Latino gangs were in their second and third generation. The Latino gangs of the 1980s actually believed the turf they claimed was really theirs. Because of this, many shop and homeowners were targeted for crime and extortion. Some Latino street gangs started to take over entire communities through the use of fear and intimidation. Many citizens became reluctant to assist law enforcement with gang related investigations because they feared retaliation. There was a real and constant fear for those who lived in gang controlled neighborhoods.

Cocaine had become a very popular drug of abuse across the country. The crack formulation of cocaine became so popular that crack addiction nearly became epidemic. Drug use once again became prevalent among the young population, especially gang members and many gang members started to get involved in drug trafficking.

In 1984, a new type of Latino gang developed as an alternative to street gangs. They became known as Stoner gangs. The majority of the members were Latino youths. These gangs based their activity and membership on heavy metal music and drug use. The gangs formed as an alternative to joining a traditional Latino street gang. However, Stoner gangs shared many behaviors of the more traditional Latino street gangs (specifically the second and fourth rules of engagement). Therefore, Stoner gangs were not immune to the violence associated with gang life. They just directed it toward other Stoner gangs and amongst themselves. Most Stoner gangs were short lived (Valdemar, 1995).

By mid 1980, it was clear gangs chose guns as their favorite tool. Guns were used to create fear and to intimidate rival gang members, peer gang members and the community. The number of juvenile gang murders was increasing nationally. Latino street gangs had established strongholds in several areas of Los Angeles County. Assaults on innocent by-standers, law enforcement and corrections officials had also increased.

By the late 1980s, several Latino gangs were also heavily involved in drug sales. Gangs like 18th Street, 38th Street and Big Hazard started to sell drugs for profit. Trafficking narcotics became a specialty crime that some gang members perfected. Some Latino prison and street gang members also begin to form relationships with drug suppliers in Mexico. Gang globalization had started as drug trafficking required networking with foreign drug suppliers.

By 1988, Los Angeles County reported 452 gang related murders and approximately 50,000 gang members in 450 different gangs. In a little more than 88 years L.A. based street gangs had grown tremendously and impacted the quality of life for many Californians.

Street gang violence was so bad that another type of street group formed as an alternative to conventional street gangs. In the late 1980s southern California experienced the rapid growth of Tagger Crews. The majority of members were young Latinos who did not want to join a street gang or those who had left a street gang. The members of these crews known as taggers focused on graffiti vandalism. Initially, most crew members were against the use of violence. They would settle any problems with a tagging battle. The tagging crew that placed the most graffiti up within a certain time and geographical area won.

The tagger crews grew in size so quickly they started to infringe into the turfs claimed by Latino street gangs. This violated street gang law and made taggers targets for gang retaliation. After being assaulted, many taggers started to arm themselves with guns for protection against further gang attacks. Being heavily influenced by the street gang culture, Tagger crews sought revenge for their assaults. This attitude put them in an offensive posture and some crews became increasingly more violent.

Rivalries between some tagging crews grew so intense that crews started to assault other each other with guns. A sub-set of Tagger crews evolved into what was called Tag Banging. Because of their propensity for violence, tag bangers became yet another type of street gang. Some tag banger crews were just as violent prone as many of the older Latino street gang counterparts.

By the mid 1980s the incidents of juvenile gang gun violence was also skyrocketing across the country. Juvenile gang members became involved in an unprecedented number of gun assaults as the number of gang members grew across the country. The gun had become the weapon of choice for most gang members.

We are all painfully aware of the 1980's violent and deadly civil war that lasted 12 years in El Salvador. Over 70,000 people were killed in this conflict (Washington Times, 2003). The constant, elevated levels of violence and lack of employment opportunities forced the mass migration of over one million El Salvadorian nationals. Most of the refugees and immigrants settled in Los Angeles and Washington, D.C. in 1984 and 1992. Some of these refugees and immigrants had ties with La Mara, a street gang in El Salvador. However, not all new comers had criminal ties. As with every immigrant population, most just want to start a new life free of oppression and violence (Valdez, 2003).

As the immigrants arrived it was realized that some also had ties to and were ex-members of the Farabundo Marti National Liberation (FMNL), a paramilitary group made up of peasants trained in guerilla warfare. This association in El Salvador provided these immigrants with some special training and organizational skills. To date, there are approximately 1 million El Salvadorian immigrants who have resettled in the United States (Americas.org, 2003).

By early 2000s, it is nationally estimated that there are 8,000 to 10,000 Mara Salvatrucha (MS or MS-13) gang members in 137 cliques and reported presence in 33 states (NDIC, 2003). MS-13 is not only a nationally recognized street gang, is has gained international status. MS-13 gangs have been operating in Canada, Mexico, El Salvador, Honduras, Guatemala and Nicaragua. There are an estimated 17,000 MS-13 gang members in El Salvador alone (Homieunidos.org, 2003). A 2004 report estimated that there are between 70,000 and 100,000 gang members across Central America and Mexico (New York Times, 2004). Gangs are often referred to as "maras" in Central America.

In Los Angeles, most of the newly arrived immigrants settled in the Rampart area. One of the largest and most active street gangs present in this area at the time was 18th Street. As a result of this influence, El Salvadorians, who initially got involved in street gangs, joined 18th Street. Unfortunately, many El Salvadorians suffered from a type of culture shock. Even though they were of Hispanic ethnicity, they were not fully accepted into the existing Los Angeles Latino culture. Yet, another subtle form of class distinction and bias focused on a new immigrant group. This status allowed some of the local gangs to view the immigrants as prey. Street gangs and unscrupulous business owners victimized El Salvadorian immigrants, taking advantage of the undocumented resident status of the immigrants and refugees.

Because of this undocumented resident status, much of the victimization and crime experienced went unreported to the police. This dynamic becomes the vehicle that allows the first El Salvadorian based street gangs to form in the Los Angeles area and for El Salvadorians who had joined the 18th street to leave. The first Mara Salvatrucha (MS) cliques formed in Los Angeles between 1988 and 1989. Stoner groups were popular during this time period in Los Angeles (Nguyen,2001).It has been reported the actual founding members of the gang were first members of a L.A. based heavy metal stoner group. The gang was first known as MSS or Mara Salvatrucha Stoners.

The gang later changes its name to MS or Mara Salvatrucha. The number 13 was not used yet. When MS was first formed, membership started to increase rapidly because membership provided a haven for newly arriving immigrants and for those immigrants who are having problems adjusting. Initially, the gang provided a source of protection, assistance, associations and a vehicle for connections for the immigrants. By the early 1990's the Mara Salvatrucha gang has grown enough in size to influence street gang activity in the Los Angeles area.

The main rival of MS became the 18th Street gang. The two gangs battled for control of the Rampart area of Los Angeles and this only increased the tension between these two gangs and the surrounding neighborhoods. Violence between the gangs escalated and drew other Latino gangs into the conflict. By 1992, there was no clear winner, but the Mara Salvatrucha gang gained a foothold in some of the Rampart area.

1990s

The 1990s brought a lot of change for Latino street gangs. By the early part of 1990 gang violence had escalated to an all time high. Many considered Los Angeles to be the gang capital of the country. By now there were two major ethnic gangs prevalent in Los Angeles county, Latino and African-American gangs. The two gangs had co-existed for years tolerating each other's presence. Most gang battles were confined within each ethnic based gang.

The 1990s also brought another alternative street group into the scene. Party crews also broke racial and gender barriers for membership. However, the majority of members remained young Latino males and females. Just like Tagger crews, the Party crews tried to steer away from the violent nature of street gangs. The proximity and heavy influence of gang culture eventually caused violent conflicts between Party crews and local street gangs. Most Party crew members did not want or expect the violence, but the membership required response to any disrespect and insults to be handled in the same manner that street gangs would. Party crews had adopted the street gang psychology without being able to acknowledge it.

Sometimes violence occurred when a sponsored party drew gang members as well as rival party crew members to the party. The visiting gang members could be from the local area or may have traveled out of their neighborhood to attend the party. Occasionally, a party crew member invited a gang member friend to attend, but often that person also brought many fellow gang members with him.

It was and still is a common practice for gang members not to travel by themselves when they leave their turf or area they associate in. Gang members can travel by themselves, but usually do not when socializing. The group travel rule is not universally applied. If a rival gang catches a solo gang member by himself, he is caught "slipping". Slipping makes a gang member easy prey for rival gangs. This situation is avoided and probably part of the reason for group travel. There is safety in numbers for gang members.

In 1992 the California based Mexican Mafia prison gang sent an edict to the local southern California Latino street gangs. They were to pay a tribute, a percentage of money based on the illegal activities the street gang was involved in. Because of their well-known reputation for violence and their gang status, many gangs paid the tribute. However, some Latino gangs did not, including many MS cliques. This caused further conflict between MS, the Mexican Mafia and the Hispanic gangs that were paying the tribute.

By 1993, MS becomes formally involved in the trafficking of illegal drugs, extortion, robbery and murder. The Mara Salvatrucha gang also aligned itself with other southern California street gangs and the Mexican Mafia after settling the tribute issue. MS cliques started using the number "13" along with their gang name to signify the Sureno alliance. A short time later, probation and law enforcement encountered MS or MS-13 tattoos and graffiti. Because of the southern California alignment, MS-13 similar to other Latino street gangs may use the common "sur" or "surneo" tattoo or graffiti to further emphasize the alignment. If these terms are used, they are referencing a general alliance to the Mexican Mafia and the sureno style of gangsterism encountered in southern California (Nguyen, 2001).

By 1996, Mara Salvatrucha gang members had been contacted in 14 states and by 2002 the gang's presence was noted in 28 states. Along the West Coast, Oregon, Washington, Alaska, Hawaii, Mexico, Central America and Canada also reported the presence of Mara Salvatrucha gangs. Don't forget, a large population of El Salvadorian refugees and immigrants also settled in Washington, D.C., and some relocated to New York.

What makes the MS gang unique is that unlike traditional U.S. street gangs, some members maintain active ties with MS factions in Central America. Like 18th Street, Mara Salvatrucha has also become an internationally known street gang. Some east coast MS members also have family ties to west coast MS members.

There is some law enforcement anecdotal evidence to suggest that some MS gang members who maintain contact between each other within the United States and El Salvador, do so for one reason. It is suspected that MS members have a business type relationship with other criminal organizations in Central America to establish illegal firearms, drugs and human smuggling networks.

America's appetite for illegal drugs drives an underground import and transport business, much of which is controlled by street gangs. Law enforcement evidence also suggests that some

MS gang cliques are also involved in human trafficking, the transport of illegal drugs and firearm trafficking.

The crackdowns by U.S. Immigration in the early 1990's are an identified gang migration mechanism. At the peak of the program in the mid 1990's, 40,000 criminal illegal immigrants were being sent back to Central America each year. Some were US trained and experienced MS and 18th Street gang members. As the process continued Central American countries experienced an unprecedented growth of street gangs and violence. The two main gangs to develop unchecked were MS-13 and 18th Street, also known as Mara 18. It has been estimated that up to 70 percent of the Central American youth who joined a gang are either members of MS-13 or Mara 18.

There are a number of MS-13 cliques in southern California and Southwest and Northwest that do not appear to be highly organized even though a number of members are involved in drug trafficking. Most cliques do not have formal titles in the gang's organizational structure and do not hold regular meetings.

In Southern California a few gangs have evolved out of the party crews that were very popular in the late 1980s and 1990's. These party crews provided pre-recorded music at private parties for a fee. Flyers would be distributed and entertainment was advertised. One of the 1990's term used to identify these groups was Rebels. The number of Party crews decreased dramatically by the late 1990s; due to the many conflicts arising between the gang members and party members, which often ended in deadly violence. However, a limited number of Party crews are still present and continued to sponsor flyer dances. These dances were still attended by gang members and conflicts continued to occur.

Party crews, like Tagger crews tried to stay away from the violence, but being so close to the gang sub-culture the violence continued to follow them. For example, in early 1999, a party crew sponsored dance ended in the tragic death of the DJ and the wounding of two party crew members when two invited gang members settled a dispute with gunfire. Unfortunately, incidents like these were and are still not uncommon.

In 1990, it was rumored La Eme chose the 18th Street gang to be its counterpart on the street because it was involved in the drug business and at the time had become the largest Latino street gang in Los Angeles. 18th Street had also developed a reputation for being extremely violent and ruthless. By this time some 18th Street gang members had begun to migrate out of California in an effort to start up new drug enterprises under the guise of looking for work. The gang could easily accomplish this by recruiting new members from the area they wanted to target.

The end of 1990 established the 18th Street gang nationally and internationally. The Mexican Mafia really didn't choose the 18th Street gang as a street partner. Research suggests that La Eme was putting pressure on 18th Street gangs to purge its members of non-Latinos. 18th Street had gotten out of control because of its size and involvement in drug trafficking (Valdemar, 1996).

At this time there was also an attempt to educate the public on gang awareness. Latino gangs continued to proliferate. In 1990, Los Angeles County reported approximately 690 gangs operating within the county. By 1991 there were estimated to be 100,000 gang members and 750 different street gangs in the county. Latino gangs continued to account for a majority of the street gangs present and a proportional amount of the violence.

In 1992, after the Eme Edict was made. Joe Morgan, the figure head leader of the Mexican Mafia issued street orders to the Southern California Latino gangs to stop the drive-by shootings. The order was issued to stop the gang violence and the media publicized this. This was a community service made by a prison gang to decrease Latino street gang violence according to several Mexican Mafia members and associates. This Mexican Mafia order resulted in a so-called gang truce between Latino street gangs in Southern California. At least it was presented and appeared that way.

To give you an idea of how powerful and influential the Mexican Mafia was, between April and September of 1992, there were no drive-by shootings in the east L.A. area of Los Angeles (Guzman, 1992). This part of L.A. was traditionally very active with gang violence and very deadly. The edict did not take effect right away because the county experienced 803 gang related homicides that year, up from 771 the year before (McBride, 1993). The majority of gang murders still involved Latino street gangs.

History now tells us there was also a hidden motive for the so-called gang truce. It appeared the Mexican Mafia attempted to extend its controlling influence on Southern California Latino street gangs. This was really an effort to coordinate the control drug trafficking in Los Angeles and surrounding counties. This motive was secretly hidden within the public cry to stop the gang violence.

The Mexican Mafia exertion of power went beyond the subsiding violence. In the early 1990s before Joe Morgan died, the Mexican Mafia also started to require Latino street gangs to pay them a tax or tribute on the drugs sold and from any other money making operation. The imposed tax was supposed to help their comrades when they were sent to prison. The tax was not paid by some Latino gangs and by some individual gang members. This attitude developed because the non-paying gangs and gang members felt that the drug money they earned was theirs and would not be shared with the Mexican Mafia. In order to maintain status, the Mexican Mafia in turn put the non-tax paying gangs and gang members on a green light list. Being on the list simply meant that it was open season to attack or kill any non-tax paying gang or gang member. This action was taken even though publicly the Mexican Mafia was advocating the Latino street gang to stop the violence.

Some street gang members were also being used as muscle for the Mexican Mafia. There were cases where a gang member would kill another member of his own gang on orders from La Eme. The opposition to paying the Mexican Mafia tax grew so much that some Latino gangs started to call themselves "green lighters." They became proud of the fact that they were tax-free and they would advertise it. In fact, some of these gangs started to use tattoos that said tax-free and green light. Occasionally, the gang graffiti also included the words, "tax free neighborhood" (Valdemar, 1996).

In 1992, the Rodney King verdicts were released and Los Angeles experienced the now famous riots. The media focused on the African-American community's frustration with the verdicts as the source of the riots. The riot also had an unexpected impacted on local Latino and African-American street gangs. The normal tolerance between Latino and African-American gangs seemed to disappear. The Latino and African-American street gangs began to have major conflicts on the streets, local jails and state prison. It appeared that the gangs started to become racially polarized at the street level.

By 1993, the Fresno Bulldogs had become the largest and most violent Latino street gang in Northern California. So many gang members went to prison that a prison gang branch of the gang was established. Street activities for this gang included murders, robbery, takeover robberies and drug sales. Rivals of the Bulldogs would be any Latino gang or gang member from Northern or Southern California.

In the later part of 1994, Sureno street gangs were established outside the state of California. Some of these Latino gangs were mix-race and had broken the gender membership barrier. Many were not directly connected or related to Southern California based street gangs. Nevertheless they claimed that status (sureno). Methamphetamine became very popular within the 14-24 year-old age group and for many Latino gang members. Some gang members, including Latino gang members became so brazen that assaults on law enforcement officials also began to rise. Gun battles between some gang members and police became increasingly more common.

By late 1995, the concept of gang respect had changed completely. Respect was no longer based on age, experience and knowledge. As mentioned before, respect was based on fear, "the more you feared me, the more you respected me". But the concept of gang respect had been changing subtly for years, partly because of the lack of control of the younger gang members, gun violence had become the predominate way to settle disputes, gangs had grown in number and size, and drug use and trafficking had increased within the gang population. By now the gang ethic of the 1950s and 1960s was completely gone. New rules prevailed for street gangs. The new rules meant there were no rules for many gang members. The gang psychology had permanently changed.

The mid-1990s also brought another trend for Latino gangs. Many gangs had established access to a "gang gun." The entire membership or gang clique could share these weapons. Gang members could use any type of weapon and used machine guns like the AK-47, when accessible. Assault rifles were very popular, because they provided superior firepower but were harder to hide. Often the gang gun would be some type of handgun because of the ease of concealment. Anyone who was member of the gang could use the weapon and then return it to the location where it was hidden.

Also by this time, some Latino gang members were involved in arson and bombings. Pipe bombs and Molotov cocktails were the commonly used explosive devices. The Internet offered instant access to direction and plans on how to build these improvised explosive devices. A few gang members specialized in arsons and would fire bomb rival gang members' homes and cars instead of participating in a drive by shooting.

For most Latino gang members guns were and are still used to settle any dispute. The gun had become the favorite instrument used to get respect. Respect can be obtained by using guns to commit violent crimes and assaults. This behavior intimidated the victims, the surrounding community and other gang populations. The most violent prone gang members received the most respect from their peers and rival gang members. The gangs which were the most violent prone were the most feared and therefore the most respected. This part of the gang psychology fuels much of the gang related violence we still encounter today.

The statistics in early 1995 for Los Angeles clearly revealed gang violence was still increasing. Between 1993 and 1994 there were a reported 1,507 gang related murders in the county. There were approximately 140,000-gang members in some 1,100 different street gangs with the majority still being Latino street gangs (McBride, 1996).

Some Latino gang members had also begun not to claim their gang membership or affiliation openly to the police. This was probably due to an increased awareness of the California gang law that provided for additional prison time if convicted of gang related violent crime. By 1995, it became apparent some Latino gangs had developed criminal specialties. Some gang cliques focused on car thefts and drug sales while others specialized in counterfeit identification and extortion. Some Latino street gangs had even become experienced at committing home invasion and take over style robberies.

Central American gang members and Mexican nationals were involved in the manufacture, transport and trafficking of millions of dollars worth of methamphetamine. A number of Southern California Latino street gangs had also gotten involved in the manufacture and trafficking of methamphetamine. One Santa Ana, California based Latino street gang was involved in a million dollar-a-month methamphetamine business. Not bad for street gang members.

1995 was a peak year for gang related murders in L.A. County, 807 people died. Gang populations reached an all time high with some estimates indicating that there were over 1,500 different street gangs within the county. The 18th Street gang was activity recruiting tag bangers to join their gang. The 18th Street gang had also become the largest Latino gang in California with an estimated 20,000 plus members. At the time based on anecdotal law enforcement evidence it was estimated that there were at least 30,000 18th Street nationally.

Specialized corrections, law enforcement and judicial units were working overtime to curb the gang violence. Latino gangs had also emerged in the rural parts of the country. The Mexican drug cartels started using Latino gang members to assist them in their drug trafficking operations. Some street gang members were trained to help with gang hits, money collection and for extortion. Some Latino gang members even helped with the smuggling of undocumented Mexicans into California is evidence suggesting the involvement of Latino street gangs in human trafficking operations.

1996 brought an unexpected decline in the amount of gang related murders. For the first time in several years, gang violence seemed to be decreasing. Nationally, it is well established that violent crime had started on a downward trend.

In 1997, Southern California experienced another decrease in gang related murders. Los Angeles County only had 452 gang related deaths. Overall gang murders declined in the entire state. Violence between Latino gangs was also decreasing. Gang membership in Los Angeles County had also decreased slightly. Although there are still many active Party, Tagger and Tag Banging crews into the late 1990 and early 2000s. If any new trend was well established, it was the activity of female gang members that accompanied a slight increase in the number of female gangs.

The number of Latino female gangs was and remains relatively small. During the 1990s, females only accounted for about six percent of the total L.A. gang population. Besides being jumped into a gang, west coast female Latino gang members had the option of being sexed in. The first sexing-in rituals dictated that dice would be rolled and whatever number came up, that is the number of sexual partners the prospective female gang member must be with in order to formalize membership. Currently, sexing in can involve any number of male gang members.

Female gang membership had increased to about ten percent in some parts of the country. The majority of female gang members continued to be Latino in California. For some Latino street gangs, the gender barrier was broken. Females could be members in co-ed street gangs. In some cases females had even been co-leaders of their gang. Female gang members were becoming increasingly more violent. It was like an informal competition had developed between some female gang members and their male counterparts. Female Latino gang members by now had been involved in drive-by shootings, robbery, carjacking and murder. Some female Latino gang members shared equal responsibility to protect gang turf and fellow gang members.

By 1998, street gangs were reported in every state and on Native-American lands. Street gangs also had established a hold in rural America and in small to mid-sized towns across the country. Latino gangs could be found in 48 states. The California north-south rivalry still continued to be a major cause for violence between Latino gangs throughout the country. Across the country Latino and African-American gangs continued to draw the majority of new gang members. Sureno type gangs were now considered prison gangs in some states. In general, Latino gangs continued to be loosely structured. A cadre of shot callers still had a major impact on what the gang would do. These gang leaders could have a strong hold over the subordinate gang members. Shot callers were now as young as 15 or 16 years old. It appeared as if the most criminally active and/or the most prone to violence assumed gang leadership in an informal manner. Latino street gangs now operated in cliques or small sub-sets of the gang they belonged to.

However, as 1999 came to an end there were still Latino gangs that continued to pay the Eme tribute. This only added strength to the Mexican Mafia influence on southern California based Latino street gangs. By 1999, the 18th Street gang was also reported in 17 states and Canada and Mexico. This L.A. based Latino street gang now had international status. In addition, the a few cliques of the 18th Street gang had developed and solidified strong ties with Mexican drug traffickers that operated in the Tijuana area of Mexico.

By 1999 Latino street gangs had become the fastest growing type of gang in the country. Many Latino gangs had established a mix-race membership. Traditional Latino turf oriented gangs can still be located across the country, but the concept of turf for some gangs had changed. For some Latino gangs the concept of turf has become fluid. This suggests that for some gangs the location where they are could become their temporary turf. These gangs could claim an entire city as their turf, not just one part of it. These gangs also may not have used graffiti in the same manner of traditional Latino gangs. There was no need to, since there were no turf boundaries to identify.

By the late 1990s, some Latino gang members of the same gang lived in different cities and some in different counties. These gang members would travel to the gang turf to meet their peers. Traveling gang members that belonged to Latino gangs are not uncommon. These gang members became a sort of part-time gang member. When not with the gang they might be full-time students, gainfully employed and even married sometimes with small children. When not with the gang these members would have a fairly normal life style. When visiting their gang they would revert back to the gang psychology.

Traditional Latino gang members also remain loyal to the same gang no matter where they moved to, or whether or not they were incarcerated. Not true for some Latino gang members in 1999. This type of gang member might belong to one gang in the city of residence, belong to another gang where he socialized and if in prison may even belong to a third gang.

Current Trends

As the millennium ended, a national trend for Latino street gangs was well established. Although not organized, many Latino gangs were getting involved in the drug trafficking. Younger Latino gang members were becoming involved in drug trafficking and carrying guns. For some Latino gang members making money had become the motivating factor for membership and participation.

A few Latino gangs were also getting involved in non-violent crime, following in the footsteps of some Southeast Asian street gang members; such as the manufacture of counterfeit bus passes, payroll checks, credit cards, social security cards, driver licenses, alien registration cards and birth certificates.

The Mexican drug cartels continued to recruit assistance from Latino street gangs as the cartels paid extremely well. This turned out to be a golden opportunity, especially since there was a focus on money for some gang members. The Mexican drug cartels recruited street gang members to deliver drugs, collect money, and act as enforcers. A few Latino transnational gangs operate in Mexico and Central America. There is some evidence to suggest that Latino street gang members are also involved in human trafficking between the borders of Mexico and the United States, and between the countries of El Salvador, Honduras and Guatemala and Mexico (Breve, 2007).

Some younger Latino street gang members continued to aspire to join the Mexican Mafia and become the professional gang member. Latino gang violence, when it happened could be brutal. Gang shootings by late 1999 had occurred in churches, aboard public buses, at movie theaters and on and near school campuses. Younger Latino gang members tended to be very violent. Gang members when socializing and kicking back were almost always armed and continued to travel in small groups. They were prepared for a chance encounter with a rival gang member or gang. Latino gang members have repeatedly stated they were not afraid to go to jail. Some Latino gang members have even displayed a willingness to go to jail or prison.

Latino street gang members have been involved in witness intimidation, the death of witnesses, ambushes of on and off duty police officers and rape. Some Latino gangs had earned such a reputation for retaliation and violence that some jurors in criminal trials have expressed their fear of gang members. By late 1999, another unique phenomenon was seen with Latino street gangs. Some gang members and associates had been able to get and hold down jobs as court clerks, police cadets, police officers, state and county employees, military enlisted personnel and in Fortune 500 type companies. Many of these Latino gang members did and still do not display gang type tattoos or clothes.

Nevertheless, while legitimately employed these gang members are obliged to back up their peer members in order to still maintain their membership. This type of Latino gang member can straddle two worlds successfully. Leading a double life is more common than you would think.

Today, many Latino gangs still guard the turf they believe belongs to their neighborhood. This hostile and misplaced reactive need to protect continues to be the cause of violence between Latino gangs. In the Latino street gang culture, losing a life in defense of the neighborhood is valued. It is an honor to the gang and to the individual gang member who has paid the highest price. The gang member's ultimate sacrifice will never be forgotten and his surrogate family, his gang will avenge his death.

A gang member's death is often memorialized in a well-attended funeral. Peer gang members will dress in special black colored gang clothing. Many times at the burial site peer gang members will lay their gang's colors down on the coffin, as a last gesture of respect. Some gang members say farewell by pledging to avenge the death. It is almost as if the deceased gang member becomes a martyr for the cause. This feeling intensifies the rivalry between gangs. A gang funeral can be a very emotional and potentially volatile situation.

If a gang member is wounded while defending his turf or a peer member he will receive instant recognition for his deeds. The wounded gang member will also enjoy an increased status with his gang. If the gang member is married and in the hospital, his peers will sometimes help take care of his family finances until he has a chance to get back on his feet.

Getting even for the loss of a comrade is called "payback" or retaliation. This concept still motivates a gang to strike back at the gang that initiated the first attack. Payback for an insult is most often in the form of violence. If a gang member was killed, the payback could be a multiple counter-killing. There is a tendency for a pay back or retaliation to be in an escalated manner for all gangs, especially Latino street gangs.

Motives for gang-related homicides have been as simple as the crossing out of gang graffiti by a rival gang. Gang members have been killed for a mad dog stare or for seemingly no reason at all. In the gang culture, an insult never goes unanswered, no matter how small. In the case of an insult the entire rival gang including individual gang members is held responsible. No matter how minor the transgression was it shall be answered in an escalated way.

Some turf wars are literally generational, stretching back 20, 30 or 40 years. Gang members who are currently fighting with another gang often do not really know why. When asked, the answer is their family has always been fighting that gang one 17-year-old Latino gang member proudly claimed, "*it is a tradition.*" California has experienced over 100 years of Latino street gang activity.

This tradition is so irrational that today some gang members are fighting battles that began long before they were born. Certain gang rivalries have been traced back through two or three generations, starting with a great-grandfather. An infringement of turf was made years ago and in some cases the battle still rages today. The sad reality of this unique behavior is that Latino gang members are being injured and dying for something that does not even belong to them or their neighborhood. For turf oriented street gangs there is a strong sense of community identity. These gang members feel a strong tie to their neighborhood, hence the desire to defend it against any outside intrusion.

More tragically, innocent people, as well as small children are dying because of this attitude. Sadly, it is estimated that 50 percent of the victims of deadly gang violence are innocent by-standers. There is no gang ethic and the gang psychology justifies the use of violence. Innocent victims are often considered collateral damage. Gang members often do not feel responsible for the results of their life style.

The non-documented Latino immigrant population continues to be victimized by the established street gangs. Recently, in some areas in the southwest groups of immigrants have banded together, forming their gangs to protect themselves from the existing local Latino street gangs. For many immigrants there appears to be a limited number of choices to make; either be the victim or the aggressor. This is part of the effect that local street gangs have on newly arrived immigrant groups.

There is a tendency for the newly formed immigrant gang to use the dress and language (manner of speaking and writing) commonly used in local street gang culture. Sometimes, a new symbol or unique name is adopted as the new gang is formed. These new gang members also consider themselves the policemen of their neighborhood, and the cycle of violence between rival gangs continues.

Since these gang members have most likely recently entered the United States some will still have close ties with their country of origin. Frequently, after committing a major crime, these immigrant gang members flee back to their country, leaving the jurisdiction of the state they fled from and contributing to further gang migration. Many times a suspect is identified however but because of international issues, law enforcement officials are not allowed to apprehend the suspect in a foreign country. This is especially true if the suspect gang member is under 18 years of age.

Generational Gangs

For some Black, Latino, and American-Asian families, gang membership is an accepted way of life. In some cases, one or both parents were, or still are gang members. Gang ideals and ethics are modeled for the children. This begins the indoctrination to the gang psychology. This cycle of gang membership may have begun three or four generations before the child was born. For these youth belonging to a street gang is considered a normal part of growing up. In these types of families, gang membership may be expected or considered a family tradition.

Clothing

Clothing can be another indicator of Latino gang membership. This unique style of dress becomes a uniform and developed when the barrio rivalries were escalating in the 1940s (Guzman, 1992). Gang attire is a recognizable street uniform to gang members. When dressing like a gang member real gang members will assume that the person who looks like a gang member is one.

During World War II there was competition between local southern California Latino gang population and the U.S. military for the limited number of women in the L.A. area. Uniforms separated military people from the civilian population and accented their presence. To compete with the servicemen at the same level, the Mexican gang members had to develop their own uniform. The solution was both logical and economical.

The Southern California Mexicans were not well off financially. A uniform was needed to accent and separate the local young men from their competition. Their uniforms had to be practical and durable. It appears that for economic reasons khaki pants were chosen. They were bought several sizes larger than needed that way the owner could grow into them and would be worn on or below the waist. If cared for properly, the pants would last a long time. The owners would wash and press them regularly. The treatment of the 38th Street gang members in prison and their responses helped develop these behaviors.

Pendleton woolen shirts were chosen later because they were both practical and unique. In winter, they could be worn buttoned all the way up to the neck to keep the wearer warm. In summertime, it could be draped over the arm and used at night if it became chilly. Pendleton style shirts served a dual role. It distinguished the wearer and identified him as a gang member and at the same time was useful in cool or cold weather (Guzman, 1992).

The somewhat oversized clothing also tended to intimidate other non-gang members by making the wearer appear to be larger than he was. Also, one could easily hide a weapon within the clothing and it would not be noticed.

During this time period in the L.A. area Latino gang members wear black leather shoes as part of their street uniform. The black colored pointed French-toe leather shoe was popular. Similar to the clothing, if the footwear was taken care of, it would last a long time. Latino gang members would keep them clean and polished at all times.

With time, the style of dress changed slightly. The excessive oversized pants are still commonly worn by many Latino gang members, but today many other types of gang members and young people wear this style of dress. The baggie style of clothes can no longer strictly be associated with the gang sub-culture or membership. However, to a gang member the style of clothing still signifies a gang uniform and the person wearing it is assumed to be a gang member. This is an important part of the gang psychology. If a person dresses and looks like a gang member a real gang member will assume that person is a member as well.

Sometimes brand name clothing such as Ben Davis, Nike or Friscos are chosen by a gang as part of their street uniform. Don't forget, brand name clothing is also popular with the non-gang member population. Today, Latino street gang members can sport many different dress style looks. For example, there is a prison gang look, where oversized prison style clothing is worn, or the old pachuco style look, where a dark colored wool watch cap is worn with oversized pants and a sleeveless under shirt.

Currently some Latino gang members wear pants that have been cut off at the knee and knee-high white socks, usually with some type of brand-name athletic shoe. This type of baggie shorts are also a very popular dress style with Americans of all ages. However, the style is still used by many types of gang members, not just Latino. It would also be safe to say that the local weather also influences the style of clothing worn by gang members. If a tee shirt is worn it can be oversized or the sleeveless undershirt type (also known as the wife beater).

When asked why they choose that particular style of dress, most Latino gang members answer with, "*that is what everyone else wears*." The three-quarter-length shorts style probably originated in the California prison system. There, if a Latino inmate showed any part of his leg to fellow inmate it was interpreted as a homosexual advance and was a forbidden gesture. Prisoners who wanted to cool off during hot spells would cut off their pants at the knee. To avoid the perception of homosexuality the knee high white socks were used to cover up the exposed portion of the leg. Today, this style of dress is now commonly seen on the street and is popular with many types of street gangs. This style of baggie shorts is also very popular with the general public.

Many Latino gang members use metal belt buckles with a letter of the alphabet cut out representing the gang name and are worn with a military-style web belts. Today, some gang members will use a belt with a combination of buckles each with a letter to represent their gang affiliation. There are a number of ways belt buckles can be combined to send a cryptic message of gang affiliation.

Baseball caps are also frequently worn by gang members. The gang name or the member's nickname may be embroidered or written somewhere on the baseball cap. Sometimes, professional sport team baseball caps are worn because the gang identifies with that teams reputation, color, and symbol or name abbreviation.

Clothing color for some Latino gangs can be a major issue and like the Bloods and Crips. Latino gang members may be confined to wearing only certain colors and styles of clothes. For example, within California Sureno gang members tend to wear blue colored clothing while Norteno gang members tend to wear red colored clothing.

Outside California, especially in the Northwest, Latino gang members use the colors red and blue to signify allegiance to either Northern or Southern California. Commonly, the red or blue railroad handkerchief is worn or displayed to signify this. The most common neutral colored clothing combination is black or tan and white.

Since clothing style and color have become significant indicators for gang membership or affiliation, many entertainment parks have adopted rigid dress codes in an attempt to control gang confrontations. The dress codes were adopted to decrease the noticeable presence of the gang members, to try stop gang conflict and the intimidation to the non-gang attendees. Remember, stylized clothing can act as an unspoken form of advertising; the wearer belongs to a gang or the wearer belongs to certain gang. Some schools have also adopted similar dress codes for students while on campus.

Another clothing item for Latino gang member is the moco rag. This is an old-fashioned railroad bandanna. The color of the moco rag can be an important part of the gang uniform. For example, some Latino gangs in the Los Angeles area might denote their individuality by wearing khaki pants and a blue or brown or colored moco rag. Another gang will wear khaki pants and a black colored moco rag. The moco rag can also be worn on the head as a skullcap. Another type of headdress is the dark colored watch cap, usually worn over the ears.

Tattoos

A word of caution here — a lot of people have tattoos. In fact, there are groups who consider the tattoo an art form, something beautiful. However, within gang subculture there are tattoos that are commonly worn by gang members and are only associated with the gang sub-culture. These are the ones we should focus on.

I have mentioned the tattoo of three dots. If connected, the dots would form a triangle. The three dots represent three Spanish words, "Mi Vida Loca." Translated they mean "my crazy life." This refers to the crazy life style of a gang member. It is a generic gang tattoo and by itself cannot be used to conclude gang membership to a particular gang. However, it only encountered in the gang culture.

Anyone who has this particular type of tattoo currently is or was in the past connected to the gang sub-culture. Don't be fooled when the person tells you the three dots are the beginning of a cross or the front face of a die. This is a type of generic gang tattoo. The three dot tattoo was once only associated with Latino gang members. Today, many different types of gang members can display this particular tattoo, including skinheads, tagger and party crew members, Asian and African-American gang members.

There are hundreds of types and shapes of tattoos. Some of the more common tattoos worn by Latino street gang members are: the gang name, the nickname of the gang member, In memory of..., spiders, women or men depicted in barrio life, a picture of a male gang member, a smoking gun, good times, sad times (the happy and sad theatrical faces), a five point star, OC, the number 13, a tear drop, a cross, SUR, NOR, the number 14, a low-rider type car, the Virgin Mary, animals, RIP with the name of a dead gang member, the name of a girlfriend or mother, or a tattoo of the last name of the person wearing them.

These are just a small sample of the tattoos worn by Latino gang members. The tattoos can be applied to any part of the body. The arms, neck, chest, stomach, forearms, biceps, face, hands, fingers and back are some of the most common areas where tattoos can be found. Members may be tattooed on the lower leg, feet, penis, breasts and buttock areas. Some Latino gang members have even placed tattoos of their gangs name on their foreheads. This bold and brazen practice makes a firm statement about the total commitment to this lifestyle. In general, the more gang style tattoos there are on a person, the greater chance that the wearer is affiliated with a gang.

Tattoos can also have a regionalized meaning. A particular tattoo in California might mean something different to the wearer in Chicago or New York. As previously mentioned tattoos also are a permanent form of gang advertisement. The tattoo can also silently announce gang affiliation to rival gang members. The tattoo can also intimidate non-gang members by denoting the wearer as a gang member. Tattoos like graffiti are a form of silent communication indicating gang membership and affiliation.

Tattoos are rarely removed and therefore present an unforeseen problem for some gang members. If a member wants to leave gang life, the presence of tattoos can be a hindrance. These tattoos continue to act as a silent form of communication, announcing that the wearer is a gang member even though they may have completely dropped out of the gang. Via tattoos, the gang life can still follow the ex-gang member. In addition, gang tattoos help the public stereotype gang members.

Some people make the conclusion that those wearing gang tattoos are always going to be gang members. An individual's attitude may change, but gang tattoos may prevent a reformed gang member from getting a fair chance at success. As a result of this stereotypical attitude, many gang members are having their tattoos removed by laser. Some of the lucky ones get this done for free because of special programs. The goal is to remove the silent messages the tattoos declare about gang membership and affiliation.

Trends change with law enforcement pressure. By the mid 2000s some Latino gang members no longer sport the traditional tattoos. The behavior is sometimes referred to as 'going low pro' short for low profile. This has been encountered with many American and Central American street gangs.

Hair Styles

Personal appearance is important for Latino gang members. The male Latino gang member has and likes to show a lot of machismo. If the hair is worn long it may be combed straight back to expose the face. Currently, many gang members sport the shaved head look. There are some Latino gang members who shave the sides of their head, leaving the top of the hair long. A particular hairstyle in itself may not signify gang affiliation, however a few street gangs will identify with a particular hairstyle.

Some female Latino gangs have used a particular brand and shade of hair color to identify their gang membership. Makeup for some Latino female gangs has also become an indicator of membership or affiliation. Some Latino female gang members might feather their hair and apply their makeup in a particular fashion to show membership.

Body Branding and Piercing

Body branding and piercing are trends that have gained momentum in the gang sub-culture. Latino gangs are not immune from in vogue youth fads. On occasion, I have spoken to gang members who have branded themselves with their gang name or symbol. The brands were burnt on arms, legs and on the top of the back. Sometimes the gang's initials were branded on the arms. The branding can be done with homemade branding irons made from coat hangers or wire. A few of these gang members claimed to have used red-hot wire to brand themselves.

As body piercing becomes more popular with the 14-24 year old age group, it will also become more popular within the gang sub-culture. It appears that body piercing has become more popular for some male and female Latino gang members. Body piercing can now be found on the ears, nipples, eyebrows, tongues, backs, noses, belly buttons and genitals.

Graffiti

Graffiti has become the newspaper of the streets for all gang members. As I mentioned before, graffiti mars territorial boundaries, act as a warning to rival gang members and advise that they are entering a danger zone. Latino street gang graffiti can be written using a variety of letter types such as the old English or block style lettering. Graffiti can be written anywhere. It has shown up on school books, wallets, mirrors, tables, trees, police vehicles, walls, houses, streets, abandoned buildings and anywhere you can write. The graffiti can be written with anything from pencils and markers to spray paint.

Taking the time to examine gang graffiti can help determine a substantial amount of information about the gang and its membership. Typically, after the gang's name you will find a list of gang members. The names will be the gang member's monikers (nicknames), and the person who wrote the graffiti will put his or her name first or last. The remaining names are a list of the other gang members that may associate with a particular clique of the gang. All the gang members do not have to present when the graffiti is written.

Sometimes you may find a county or city designation in the graffiti. Due to the north-south split in California Latino gangs in southern California (Sureno) might use the number 13, SUR or SURENO in the graffiti. In Northern California, you could expect to find the number 14, NORTE or NORTENO with the graffiti. The number 14 is another way to represent NORTE (north) just as the number 13 signifies the Southern California.

Outside California you will also find these graffiti peculiarities. Don't be surprised if you find the norteno gangs using red colored spray paint to write their graffiti and sureno using blue colored paint, especially outside California.

Graffiti can also be used to send messages to rival gang members or to a gang member who has fallen out of favor. In California, Penal Code section 187 is the homicide section. The number 187 is used in graffiti to give a death threat to a specific person or to the entire gang or to the police or to a particular police officer.

The marking-out of graffiti by a rival gang member is taken as an insult by the gang membership. This marking out of a gang's placa (name or mark) is considered disrespectful and can be interpreted as a challenge to fight. The crossing-out or "puto-out" of graffiti is like the traditional face-slapping challenge the French used prior to a duel. Many times, this behavior ultimately leads to a fatal confrontation between gangs.

For all Latino gangs this is a challenge or insult never goes unanswered and normally the response is escalated. All this is surrounded with the belief that the insult or challenge is an act of disrespect to the entire gang. Retaliation for graffiti mark outs becomes another way to save face and increase gang respect.

Ranking out is another disrespectful act can occur when an individual gang member or associate fails to claim his gang affiliation when challenged. This gang member or associate becomes a "buster" or "ranker" for failing to claim his gang association. When a gang member fails to get involved in an incident like a fight, he fails to back up his gang. Both behaviors are considered to be actions that can get a gang member the "leyva" a Spanish word for the cold shoulder. Both behaviors are not tolerated well by Latino gangs.

These gang members must earn back the gang's trust and respect. Sometimes, this can be accomplished through a test of strength and courage. The gang member must prove his worth. As you can see respect is very important to all gang members. Sometimes the gang can hold a meeting and the offending gang member(s) are check courted or courted. This means their peer members punish them usually with a physical assault for violating gang rules.

Hand Signs

Hand signs are another form of non-verbal communication used by Latino gang members. This form of communication has the same impact as graffiti and tattoos to peer and rival gang members. The hand sign announces what gang is present. If the hand signs are shown to a rival gang member this exhibition is taken as a form of challenge. I have personally investigated several cases where a homicide was committed as an answer to the hand sign insult.

Hand signs can also be used as a form of intimidation to rival gangs or non-gang members. Displaying hand signs is also known as "flashing" or "throwin down" and it announces that the signer is a gang member. Witnesses to gang crimes are often rival gang members, family members of the rival gang members or non-gang members who live in the rival gang's neighborhood. A good way to intimidate reluctant witnesses is to display a hand sign at them while in court or just prior to testifying.

The results are excellent: no one testifies. The flashing of hand signs has successfully intimidated and scared witnesses. A few times it has been so successful that criminal cases have had to be dismissed because the witnesses are so intimidated they hide or leave the jurisdiction.

Normally, the hand sign is displayed by forming a specific letter of the alphabet with the fingers and hand. This is a form of sign language for the gang member. Several letters can be shown in rapid succession to give a message, warning, or announcement to other gang members. The hand sign is also used as a form of greeting. Gang members from the same gang often greet each other by flashing their gang's hand sign to themselves.

Mad Dog

Another type of non-verbal communication is called mad dogging. This term is used to explain the stare down between two gang members. When a harsh look is received it is perceived as a challenge to fight, threat and a sign of disrespect. In the animal kingdom, a dominant male may stare down a challenging male until the challenging male looks away in order to avoid the confrontation. A gang member may also look away in an attempt to avoid the fight. This is seldom successful in the gang sub-culture. During a mad-dog gang members are expected not to look away because if they do it will reveal a weakness.

Unfortunately, the gang psychology usually does not allow the option of a non-aggressive solution. This is because the disrespect to the individual gang member is taken as an insult to the entire gang. The membership as a whole is perceived as having been disrespected therefore retaliation is required in order to save respect (face). This response behavior is sometimes taken so seriously that it often leads to gang shootings and death.

Slang

When the California Latino gangs were proliferating during the 1940s the spoken gang language was "Calo"; a pidgin version of English and Spanish blended together. The term Pachuco was used to describe gang members who understood the new language (Guzman, 1992).

Although the Calo language is not used much today, it had become the foundation for the development of gang slang terms that are currently used. The gang slang used today is sort of a verbal code between gang members because they tend to be the only people understand it. Just a reminder, please remember if you do understand what the slang term means it is probably better not to use it in conversations with gang members.

Recruitment

Recruitment into Latino gangs can begin as early as age eight or nine years old especially if you are not born into a generational gang family. There is normally a courting process that can include substance abuse, peer pressure and spending a lot of time with the gang. At one time it was believed that you could just say no to gang membership. However, that has proven to be incorrect.

Unfortunately, it is currently believed that refusing to join a gang can end up with threats against the individual or his family. Although this is rare, there have instances where this has happened. This is most likely to occur in a gang controlled neighborhood. Frankly, on occasions youth will be compelled to join a gang in order to protect themselves. Unfortunately some youth have very limited number of choices; either become the aggressor or victim. Let's be candid here, none of us would want to be a victim. Ultimately, for many gang membership becomes the choice.

Sometimes membership is sought to protect the barrio, the family, or the peer homeboys (fellow gang members). Some youth join out of a sense of duty, or simply because they identify with the lifestyle. Nevertheless, membership is a voluntary decision.

Most Latino gangs still have a jumping-in ritual or ceremony. In the past, sometimes the new member was invited to drink or use narcotics before the ceremony. Commonly, most new members will be sober for the ceremony. The ceremony can last from a few seconds to several minutes and is a test of the new member's courage, strength and commitment to the gang. In this ritual, the prospective new member has to fight several of the regular gang members simultaneously.

The jumping-in ritual is a symbolic ceremony. It is the last step in the membership courting process. This ceremony is a formal recognition of membership status. I have never spoken with a Latino street gang member who failed his jumping-in ritual. I have spoken to hundreds of gang members who confided something about membership status. They felt they were already a member of their gang before they were actually jumped-in.

Sometimes to test the new member's loyalty, the individual gang member is invited to help commit a drive-by shooting or an assault on a police officer or school official. The criminal act is sometimes bold and may be considered another form of jumping-in. Any type of criminal act could be part of a gang initiation ritual. These acts not only confirm the member's loyalty, but also help establish a gang member's reputation within the gang as well as for the rival gangs.

I have also spoken to many Latino gang members who were never jumped into their gang. Most often, these gang members walked in. These youth may have also been in the nucleus of youth who started the gang or were one of the first members of a gang, or simply a friend or family member who wants to join and were sponsored into the gang.

Crime

Unfortunately many acts of gang violence are done with guns. Semi-automatic handguns as well as semi-automatic and automatic assault rifles are the weapons of choice for many gang members. The AK-47, AR-15, Uzi and Mac-10 are some of the assault rifle weapons encountered by law enforcement officials during criminal investigations.

Every conceivable type of weapon has been confiscated by law enforcement, including but not limited to all calibers of handguns, shotguns, homemade and altered weapons, explosives, all types of daggers, knives, armor piercing ammunition, hand grenades and military ordinance. Handguns are seized most often and are probably the most popular because they are easily concealed.

The advent of the drive-by shooting has lead to a number of variant crimes such as walk-by shootings, bicycle-by shootings, run-by shootings and dance-by shootings (a shooting that occurred on a dance floor). Times have changed for the gang member. The battle over turf or responding to disrespect is no longer handled as an individual or group fist fight. The earlier exception to the rule has now become the rule. Shoot! There has been some research which suggests that nationally younger Latino gang members are arming themselves with handguns. This theory is based on survey reports from a limited number of law enforcement agencies. However, from a practitioner's perspective the theory is proven to be accurate.

Vehicles

While some Latino gang members still drive the stereotypical Cheech and Chong lowered Chevy; the majority of the Latino gang members today drive many types and styles of vehicles. In other words, today's Latino gang-member may drive any type of vehicle, including Toyota or Isuzu Mini-Trucks and other clean cars like Buicks, Pontiacs, Volkswagens, BMWs, or Mazda RX-7s.

Sometimes gang members will steal or borrow a car in which to commit a crime. Often, the person who lends the vehicle has no idea what the car is used for. Latino gang members have also been involved in car-jacking crimes. In Westminster, California, a teacher's aid was shot in the head and killed when she did not stop for four Latino street gang members who wanted to steal her car. They wanted her car to complete a retaliatory drive-by shooting on their rival gang.

Cliques

Latino gangs can be divided into small groups known as cliques. They can be separated by age groups, or geographical boundaries. The word clique is pronounced "klee ka." Some gang members have also spelled this term as "clicke". The cliques are parts of the main gang. If the division is by age group, the cliques might be named with terms such as Pee Wees or the Tiny (ages 10-13). If the division occurs due to geographical boundaries, the gang will use the primary gang name and a landmark to denote the location. For example, F-Troop gang might use F-Troop El Salvador Park, or South Side F-Troop. The cliques may also be comprised of a small cadre of friends who all are in the same gang. A single gang may have hundreds of cliques nationally. For example, Mara Salvatrucha or MS-13 has many cliques based on geographical location.

Hard-core or the most active gang members can be any age but are often between the ages of 14 to 24. The oldest living gang members in a particular gang or cliques may be considered veteranos. As a veterano usually these gang members will have the ability to influence and guide younger members. In some parts of the country, the veterano has lost standing with the younger gang members. In a few cases younger gang members have even challenged established veteranos. This in turn has caused a power struggle to develop within a gang. In a few instances members of a clique will break away from the main gang and start a new one.

Veteranos are usually veterans of local or state prison and may have had many encounters with law enforcement. Another term used to describe a veterano is OG, meaning original gangster and may also imply that this particular gang member has been around for a while. This status is usually applied to a gang member who can assume the role of an older brother or father; or acts as a role model for the younger gang members. Some Latino gangs can have many veteranos. Sometimes the veteranos become the ex-officio leaders of the gang.

The term younger gang member includes two groups; those with shorter little gang tenure as well as the younger age-wise members. At one time veteranos could be identified by age. However, today veterano status may be given for the amount and frequency of gang activity; therefore a veterano can be 13 or 14 years old.

Normally, veteranos are given the utmost respect and honor by younger less experienced gangsters. I have spoken to gang members as young as 16 and 17 who were considered veteranos by their peers.

Female Gang Members

Traditionally, Latino gangs were comprised solely of males. The role of the female member or associate was that of an auxiliary member. As gang philosophies changed so did the activities of female associates and members. Young Latinas have formed their own all-female gangs. Sometimes the female gang associated with a particular male gang. In these cases the female gang name would normally be a female gender version of the male gang name.

All female Latina gangs can also develop the same type of rivalries as their male counterparts. Female gang members may battle over turf and have adopted the same membership indicia as their male counterparts. Some Latina gangs can travel between the gang territories of all male Latino gangs without incident. At times a gang rivalry may compel a female gang to back-up their male counterparts.

Today, female Latina gang members can be just as brazen and criminally active as some male gang members. Early on, Latina gang members played a minor role in gang related crime; currently, their role has assumed a much more importance. Now female Latino gang members can commit major criminal acts. There have been several reported crimes where Latina gang members have assaulted both non-gang and gang members with guns. There have been attempted and completed carjackings where the main criminal players were armed Latina street gang members.

For example, in Orange County, California, 1990 two juvenile Latina gang members were charged as principles in a drive-by shooting which resulted in a fatality of a rival male Latino gang member. One female Latin gang member was 16 and pregnant. The other juvenile was only 17. Both were sent to the California Youth Authority after adult convictions for murder in 1991.

These two young girls were minors at the time of the incident. The 16-year-old delivered her child in prison. Females can be just as violent and ruthless as the males. As one 17-year-old female gang member told me, "*We can do everything they (males) can and better.*" For some female gang members there is an informal rivalry that motivates the females to be more competitive.

With the increased popularity of sexing in, some female gang members are motivated to try and improve their status within the gang. For some gangs sexing in does not bring the same amount of respect as a jumping in.

Allegiance and Loyalty

Generally speaking Latino gang members will remain loyal to the gang they join for life. Beyond that most Latino gang members are loyal to the neighborhood (varrio) they belong to even if they move out of the area. Sometimes, parents move their family to a new community in an effort to leave a gang neighborhood and improve the family's' quality of life. Or the move may be an attempt to rid their youth of the gang influence. Sometimes these moves are not always successful. This behavior may also account for the reason why deported gang members still claim allegiance to their southern California based street gang even though they are in another country.

At times the youth simply establishes a new clique of the gang in the new neighborhood or will go back to visit the old neighborhood. Gang contact is maintained, even if it is minimal. This misguided loyalty fosters a strong sense of commitment for the gang member for his or her neighborhood.

This strong sense of loyalty, along with the identity, recognition, fellowship, and protection that the gang-life offers, have help facilitate the proliferation of Latino street gangs. "*The gang is more important than the individual,*" one 16-year-old told me. This one-for-all philosophy contributes to the cycle of gang violence even though the gang member knows that they may forfeit their life. These attitudes are part of the gang psychology and influence membership behavior.

Contrary to street myth, Latino gang members can leave their gangs by being "jumped out." This ritual is the same ceremony as the jumping in but done as a symbol of a formal resignation from active gang status. A person who is jumped out still maintains the respect of the gang members and will normally be left alone. The jumping out is akin to an honorable discharge from military service.

Other street gang members have told me they have simply walked away from their gangs without any repercussions. Other gang members who have successfully left their gang have joined the military or gotten married and started a family.

Understanding Latino Gang Graffiti

Placa, as we have learned refers to graffiti used by Latino gangs. It is written in Spanish or a combination of Spanish and English. There also may be differences in the graffiti meaning between gangs from different cities. Latino gang graffiti also can use codes that have common meaning throughout gang sub-culture. The main body of the placa is normally the name of the gang. You will rarely if ever find the street gang members names without the gang's name next to it. Graffiti is also used to mark off turf boundaries for Latino street gangs, to announce street alliances, to give warnings, to threaten or announce the death of a peer or rival gang member.

While graffiti is an eyesore, it allows police an opportunity to track gang activity. Graffiti can also serve as a membership roster and often indicates pending conflicts between gangs. When reading Latino gang graffiti, look for some or all of the following elements incorporated with the gang name and names of the gang members:

Puro Pure or 100%

P/V For life, an abbreviation for Por Vida

Rifa Controls, Rules or Reigns

R Abbreviation for Rifa, we rule

C/S Abbreviation for con safos, back to you

Y Que So What, a challenge

Rata(s) Rat(s), as in informer

Trucha Watch Out

Puto Male prostitute, homosexual, fag, (an insult)

Controla Control, as in: we are in control

Somos We are (abbreviated SMS)

Sur South or southern California

Surenos Southerner, being from southern Califonia

Norte North, Northern California

Nortenos Northerner or being from northern California

XIII The 13th letter of the alphabet, allegiance to La Eme

13 Sureno style, allegiance to La Eme

XIV Norteno style, allegiance to Nuestra Familia

14 The 14th letter of the alphabet, allegiance to Nuestra Familia

O.G. Original Gangster

O.C. Orange County (a county in Southern California)

V.L Vato Loco, crazy dude (male gangster)

V.L. Vata Loca, crazy dudette (female gangster)

V Refers to Varrio, the neighborhood

Barrio The same as Varrio, the neighborhood

Tax-Free The gang doesn't pay tax to La Eme

Summary

A history of the development of west coast Latino street and prison gangs was presented to give you an idea of how social and world events impacted the proliferation of street gangs in southern California. The Mexican culture also played a role in the development of generational gangs. Understanding the gang psychology allows one to understand why we observe gang behaviors and why there is an unwritten gang code of conduct. It should be obvious now why street gang membership can act as a powerful cohesive force that binds the membership together and why a gang can become a surrogate family. A major part of the gang psychology revolves around the concept of respect. Gang respect is almost always at the center of violent confrontations.

Latino street gangs also use a slang language. These are words or terms that have special meanings to gang members. Use infers an understanding of the gang culture. Historically Latino street gangs changed some behaviors and continue to use old school behaviors. Marginalization of immigrant groups also plays a role in why gangs form (Vigil, 1993). It should be noted that culturally Latino families tend to be very close. Extended family members can exert an influence over younger family members. Often, families will live geographically close to each other and socialize together on a regular basis. This aids with family unity, but can become part of the mechanism that transfers gang association and membership.

Decker and Van Winkle (1996) demonstrated that violence is part of everyday life in gang neighborhoods and families. Decker (1996) uses Loftin's (1995) "contagion" concept and the notion that gang cohesion grows in proportion to the perceived threat represented by rival gangs (Klein, 1971). In Latino street gangs this perceived threat of rival gang(s) is passed on through tradition with the family (Jankowski, 1991).

Sureno and Norteno Gangs

Since the presence of Sureno gangs has been documented in several areas of the country the logical question to ask is, "Where did the Sureno gangs originate?" The next question then becomes, "What does the Sureno name really mean?" A look for the answers to these questions shows us that they come from a pair of shoes, and a Mexican prisoner in state prison and the Mexican Mafia. To answer the questions completely you also have to examine Hispanic street gangs today. Research suggests that Hispanic street gangs among the fastest growing gangs in the country today. Law enforcement personnel have also made another observation: There may be prejudice and racism within ethnic based street gangs. Together the history and social factors account for the presence of Sureno street gangs outside California.

History

During 1956 and 1957, Huero Buff Flores and other East Los Angeles gang members were doing hard time at Duel Vocational Institute, California. Together, they formed what they called the gang of gangs or La Eme, California's first prison gang. Surprisingly, some of the original members were Mexican, mixed-race Mexicans and one was Korean.

La Eme originally formed in part for protection; protection from the other prison populations. Having its membership based on race, it was logical to start recruiting new members from the Los Angeles based Hispanic street gangs. As the Mexican Mafia prison gang membership grew a rivalry started to develop between the Mexicans from the northern part of California and those from the southern part of the state.

Mexicans from the northern part of California were considered unsophisticated because they still spoke Spanish and worked in the rural and farming areas. As the internal rivalry developed, the northern gang members considered Mexicans from the south as hamburger eating Mexicans (Valdemar, 1996). Because many of northern California Hispanic gang members only spoke Spanish, almost all were agricultural workers and still deeply entrenched in the Mexican culture. The southern California gang members made fun of them because of this. The northern California gang members were considered the "Juan Gumps" of Mexican street gangs.

This attitude resulted in some northern California gang members being taken advantage of while in prison. Some northern gang members were being taxed, robbed and victimized by Eme prison gang members.

By 1967, hierarchy in La Eme was trying to unite all the Mexicans within the state prison system. There was a concerted effort to put down the minor rivalries and unite the northern and southern California Hispanic gang members under the control of the Mexican Mafia. The goal was to form the strongest and largest prison gang in the state.

In 1968 at San Quentin, a state prison in Northern California, something happened that would change prison and street gangs forever. An Eme gang member named Pieface was the

San Quentin cellmate of, Hector "Mad Dog" Padilla, a Mexican gang member from northern California. Mad Dog had a pair of black leather shoes that were his prized possession. In fact, Padilla would shine and care for the shoes every day. One day while he was out of the cell, Pieface stole the shoes.

Pieface quickly discovered the shoes were too small for him and in an effort to win some points with La Eme, he decided to give the shoes as a gift to another member of the Mexican Mafia. Pieface gave the stolen shoes to an Eme gang member named Robert "Robot" Salas.

The shoes fit Robot and he walked back into the cell area only to find Mad Dog frantically looking for his shoes. Mad Dog immediately recognized that Robot was wearing his shoes. An argument ensued because the real owner of the shoes accused Robot of stealing them. This of course was an insult to the Eme gang member and the fight started. Sometime during the argument and fight, Mad Dog got stabbed several times and died. Word of Mad Dog's demise quickly spread throughout the prison system, especially among all the Mexican inmates.

In the second version of the incident Robot Salas was the cellmate of Mad Dog Padilla rather than Pieface. Pieface still steals Mad Dog's shoes. Robot still gets the shoes as a gift and returns to the cell, which of course is shared by Mad Dog and that is where the fight starts.

North-South Division

Mad Dog's murder sparked the solidification of the rivalry between northern and southern Mexicans, both in the prisons and on the streets. The Mexicans from the north responded to Mad Dog's murder by forming Nuestra Familia (NF), a second Mexican prison gang. It formed to protect the northern Mexicans from members of La Eme; the southern California based Mexican prison gang.

Nuestra Familia prison gang members started to identify with the number 14. It represented the 14th letter of the alphabet, the letter N. The letter stood as an abbreviation for the word Norteno, the Spanish word for northerner. The Spanish word for the letter N is "ene." The word norte was also used to show that a person was from northern California. Anybody from southern California was automatically considered a rival, in or out of prison.

Southern California gang members started to identify with the number 13. The 13th letter of the alphabet is the letter M. The word for this letter in Spanish is "eme." Southern California gang members in and out of prison started using words like Sureno, meaning southerner to identify their allegiance, much like the participants of the U.S. civil war did. Sometimes Sureno was abbreviated as Sur, meaning the south. Gang members also started to tattoo themselves with the number 13 and with the words Sureno or Sur to signify their allegiance.

Mexican street and prison gangs from Northern California also claimed the color red, based on the fact that most of the original members had the red colored railroad issued handkerchief when the Nuestra Familia gang was formed. The only color left was blue, so it was assigned as the color for the Sureno based gangs. The Bloods and Crips were not the first to use these colors, it was the California Mexican prison gangs that did. Remember the Crips as we know them today did not form until the later part of 1969 and Blood gangs were not around until the middle to later part of 1970.

Even though this polarization started in prison, it quickly spread to the street. It helped establish a gang style that was particular to northern and southern California street and prison gang members. California was essentially split in two. The Sureno and Norteneo style of gangstership has now also spread to many other states and even other countries.

Rival southern California Hispanic street gangs now had one thing in common; they all were enemies with any gang members from northern California and vice versa. This rivalry united southern and northern California rival Hispanic gang members while they were incarcerated. Somewhere, while the dust was settling between these groups, an imaginary geographical line was made. It was suppose to mark the boundary between northern and southern California. But this geographical boundary really turned out to be a gray area in central California. It was usually agreed that the division was located somewhere between the cities of Bakersfield and Delano. North of the boundary rival Hispanic street gangs would affiliate with the northern California prison gang Nuestra Familia. Hispanic street gang members from southern California would align themselves with the Mexican Mafia.

Non-California Based Surenos

Outside the state of California, this north-south rivalry intensified. Mexican street gangs even started to write graffiti with red and blue colored paint to signify what part of California they were from. In the late 1980s, states to the north of California started to see the appearance of Sureno and Norteno gangs and of course the related violence associated with the rivalry.

By the late 1980s to early 1990s, the southwestern states started to note the presence of street gangs calling themselves Sureno or Sureno-13. Outside the state of California sometimes members of Sureno gangs were not from California or they were different rival gang members from southern California now associating as one gang. Sometimes, these types of Sureno street gangs claimed Southern California allegiance by adding the number 13 to the Sureno name. This could happen even though there were no formal connections to traditional Hispanic street gangs from Southern California. The same mechanism could also occur with Hispanic street gangs that formed outside California that claimed Norteno affiliation.

These kinds of Sureno and Norteno street gangs can be localized in one part of a city or they can travel all over a city. In some cases, these kinds of Sureno gang members live in different cities or counties and meet to socialize and/or to commit crime. Females can also be members in these types of Sureno gangs. With the gender membership barrier gone the gang can grow rapidly. Sometimes the females may be the girlfriends of a participating gang member. This makes them a gang sympathizer and or a gang associate willing to help with gang business. The most common form of business appears to be drug trafficking. Sureno and Norteno female associates have been used as drug couriers and or to gather intelligence on rival gangs.

I have mentioned before, that the majority of street gangs usually develop in the geographical location where they are located. This seems to be supported by the academic literature. Gang migration has accounted for a small percent of gang growth (Klein, 1995). However, there is plenty of law enforcement anecdotal evidence to suggest that some California Hispanic based street and prison gang members have formed new gang cliques in other countries and states. These types of gang members could act as catalysts that can cause the rapid, seemingly overnight appearance of Sureno or Norteno type gangs outside the state of California.

Some Sureno or Sureno-13 gangs will have roots that can be traced back to Southern California. Enough time has past to see first or second generation Sureno gangs outside the state of California. Some of these Sureno gangs mimic the attitudes and activities of the traditional California Hispanic street gangs. This has included the claiming of turf, wearing gang related clothing and tattoos even though they are geographically located outside California. This appears why some believe members are from or maintain contact with their southern California based parent gang. Often, there is no connection between the gangs except the use of the name.

The term Sureno now has three definitions. The first refers to the southern California style of gangstership that was developed by Hispanic street gangs. Sureno style behaviors also suggest an allegiance that southern California Hispanic street gangs have with the Mexican Mafia. This is why many Sureno gang members use the number 13 in tattoos or graffiti. In Southern California Sureno based gangs have become the power based for the Mexican Mafia. The same concept will also be true for those gang members that claim Norteno status.

The second and more recent definition refers to Hispanic based street gangs, outside the California that have southern California gang members from different and/or rival gangs associating as a Sureno or Sureno-13 street gang. In California these individual gang members may attack each other because they are rivals, but out of state Sureno or sureno-13 street gang members are peer gang members.

For example, in early 1993, rival Hispanic street gang members from Los Angeles formed a Sureno-13 gang in New Mexico. Being turf oriented in California they battled whenever they saw each other because they were southern California rivals. In New Mexico these rival Hispanic gang members began to work together to traffic illegal drugs. Cooperating together, they attempted to take over drug markets from the less experienced and less violent groups in an Albuquerque area known as the "war zone." These rival gang members banded together under a common name, Sureno-13 (Blatchford, 1996). Again, rival gang members from northern California could band together and call themselves Norteno or Norteno-14.

This tactic was successfully used by the Crips and Blood gangs in the late 1980s, when they expanded their cocaine market outside California.

The third definition of Sureno is applied to non-native California gang members who claim membership in a gang that uses a name of a southern California based street gang. Members in these types of street gangs tend to be immigrants from Mexico and Central America. Often these types of Sureno gangs are encountered in the mid-west and eastern parts of the country. There are many 18th Street, Mara Salvatrucha and Sureno-13 gangs whose members have never been to California. Yet, all three gangs use a sureno style of gangstership. This implies they have a formal connection to southern California. More often than not, they do not. They only tend to only have the southern California gang name in common. The same concept will also be true for Norteno based gangs in other countries or states.

Law enforcement has encountered all three types of Sureno and Norteno gangs. They are the Sureno and Norteno gangs that have family ties to or were formed by migrating California gang members, Sureno and Norteno gangs that adopted the name and have no formal ties to California. There are also Sureno and Norteno gangs that have members from different California Hispanic street gangs working together as one gang.

Sureno Prison Gangs

Sureno and Norteno street gang members who go to state prison or county jail outside the state of California can start Sureno and Norteno prison gangs. They will probably solicit new members from the existing prison population and street gang members who are incarcerated. In some states, inmate Sureno and Norteno street gang members are also classified as being part of a prison gang. Another phenomenon can be seen with Sureno and Norteno prison gangs. Youth who belong to a non-Sureno and Norteno Hispanic gangs in their city when incarcerated, can claim Sureno or Norteno affiliation. It is probably very similar as when rival California Hispanic street gang members get incarcerated. They all align themselves with La Eme or la Nuestra Familia and put their personal gang rivalries set aside while in custody. When released back to the community, these youth may resume loyalty to their original street gangs.

Some states have reported the presence of both street and prison Sureno and Norteno gangs. The Sureno and Norteno prison gangs tend to operate much like the Hispanic prison gangs of California. There also may be some confusion here because there is no way to confirm if the Sureno or Norteno street gang is really a version of the California street gang or a classification given to incarcerated gang members. Another factor can have an influence here. What if an incarcerated gang member who claims Sureno or Norteno prison gang affiliation gets released and starts a street version of his prison gang?

This mechanism was first seen in the 1920s. It was observed when parolees from the Illinois state prison system were released. They belonged to a prison gang while incarcerated and extended their gang's influence onto the streets when they were released. Eventually, these parolees became the forerunners of some Folk and People Nation based gangs that are encountered today.

Characteristics

If tattoos are present you may find the number 13 or 14, Sur, Sur-13, Sureno or Sureno-13 or Norteno or Northern Warrior anywhere on the body. There may also be the name of another Hispanic gang, especially if the person was a member in a Los Angeles based gang who has joined a non-California street gang. I have interviewed Sureno gang members from the southwest part of the country that have no tattoos at all and where part of co-ed Sur-13 street gang.

I have even encountered Sureno gang members that all belong to a single family. They battled with another gang whose members were also all related. This is sort of a new version of the Hatfields and McCoys. I have also encountered some Native-American gang members who claim Sureno and Norteno status. These Native Americans were members of gangs that were based on reservation lands and yet frequented non-reservation locations. There are also all female Norteno street gangs reported on Native American reservations (Mountain Lion, 2008).

Graffiti may also be unique depending on the type of Sureno or Norteno gang present. Some Sureno and Norteno street gangs will use graffiti just as traditional California Hispanic gangs do. They will mark turf boundaries and issue insults with it. Other Sureno and Norteno street gangs will rarely use graffiti; in fact it is possible for some gangs not to use graffiti at all. The presence or lack of graffiti does not necessarily mean a non-California based Sureno or Norteno street gang is present.

Sometimes there may be no particular color or style of dress associated with Sureno or Norteno street gang membership. If a particular color is worn, for Sureno gangs you should expect a shade of blue, black, or khaki color. Norteno gang members usually wear some clothing that is red colored. Some Sureno and Norteno gang members still wear the traditional baggie pants, but not all. Some Sureno and Norteno gang members, like the majority of gang members across the country will wear some type of athletic shoe. It would also be consistent to encounter Sureno and Norteno gang members wearing some type of baseball caps.

Sureno and Norteno street gangs have been involved in all types of crime. There does not seem to be any focus on a particular type of crime. Sureno and Norteno gang members have been convicted of multiple murders, extortion, drug trafficking, attempted murder and vandalism. This chapter would not be complete without a short parallel discussion on Norteno gangs.

Norteno Influence

In general Hispanic street gangs from northern California consider the Hispanic street gangs from the southern California as their rivals. This rivalry became formalized after the 1968 stabbing assault of Hector "Mad Dog" Padilla in a California state prison. The rivalry seems to intensify between the gangs while members were incarcerated until the late 1980s when the rivalry spilled out into the streets of California.

The appearance of Norteno type street gangs in California can be traced back to the mid to late 1960s. Sacramento, California encountered the first Sureno gang in early 1990 and was called the 47th Street Surenos. The original gang members from this gang migrated from the Los Angeles and relocated on 47th Street in Sacramento. Simultaneously, the schools experienced an influx of Hispanic youths. These youths were placed into English-as-a-Second-Language (ESL) classes. They were also picked on by the local Hispanic gang members (Nortenos) who thought that they were all undocumented immigrants from Mexico. The established Sacramento Hispanic street gangs considered them Surenos.

Even though the new arrivals were not truly from the south, they eventually adopted the Sureno title and formed into the 47th Street Sureno gang to protect themselves from the established northern Hispanic street gangs. There is anecdotal evidence to suggest that the majority of the Sureno gangs in Northern California started this way and a small minority started from migrating southern California gang members (Delgadillo, 1994).

A law enforcement theory suggests pressure from existing Norteno street gangs was one factor that helped influence the development of several types of Sureno street gangs in northern California. One type of northern California Sureno gang can be formed from migrating Southern California gang members. A second type of Sureno street gang was formed from undocumented immigrant farm workers from Mexico, who initially formed into a Sureno gang for protection. A third type of Sureno gang has a membership comprised from local youths who live in Northern California. These gang members have no formal ties to the south but claimed Sureno affiliation.

The appearance and growth of Sureno gangs in northern California fueled the formation of Hispanic street gangs that do not claim a specific turf or gang, but claim a general Norteno status. Of course these gangs, as well as established traditional northern Hispanic street gangs became the rivals of any Sureno type gang (Delgadillo, 1994).

Two factors probably influence the spread of Sureno gangs in northern California. The first is age. Sureno gangs have been active since the 1900s. Many of today's Norteno type street gangs weren't seen until late 1968. There is a 50 plus year difference in age for these gangs. Northern California Hispanic street gangs started to form in the 1940's, however the intense north/south rivalry did not start until 1968.

Second, there is a demographic difference between the two types gangs. The Sureno gangs outnumber the Norteno gangs. Although, no formal studies have been completed some law enforcement experts feel the difference may be as high as four or five to one. This could explain why southern California law enforcement has not encountered Norteno gang members who migrated into southern California and why southern California youth do not openly claim Norteno affiliation.

The appearance of Sureno gangs in northern California has also fueled unique confrontations between Norteno and Sureno street gangs. The concept of turf has become fluid for some of these gangs. Unlike traditional Hispanic street gangs some Norteno and Sureno gangs claim an entire city as their turf rather than a specific area of a city. Since there is no specific geographical area of the city that is claimed as gang turf, the members of the gang tend to meet and socialize in locations that appear to be convenient. Gang members may even live in other cities or counties and travel into a specific meeting to socialize. A good example of this phenomenon is the Hell Park Surenos. Members live in Yolo, Placer and Sacramento counties, yet meet at a specific park in Sacramento (Delgadillo, 1994).

Because of the increasing presence of all types of Sureno street gangs in northern California the north-south geographical barrier appears to have been moved north to the city of San Jose, California (Valdemar, 1996). Some unique graffiti and tattoos have also appeared in northern California uniting all types of Sureno gangs. Commonly seen is BST, which references Barrio Sur Trece (South 13 Neighborhood). No one can predict if the Sureno gang influence will continue to migrate north within the state. One thing is for sure; Sureno and Norteno gangs have made their appearance outside the state of California and in other countries. Sureno and Norteno type gangs have been encountered in the Midwest, south, northwest, and east coast and northeast parts of the country.

Slang

Gang slang that Sureno gang members use may also have regionalized meanings. Like all gang slang is most likely subject to constant change. Sureno gang members that have been debriefed tend to shared many terms that are commonly used by Hispanic gang members from Southern California. Believe or not the geographical location where the Sureno gang is located will also influence the specific type of clothing that the gang members will wear. For example, on the east coast where winter temperatures drop you would expect Sureno gang members to wear heavy outer coats. This would not be encountered in Phoenix, Arizona. A couple of unique terms are used between traditional Sureno and Norteno gangs.

Norteno = Derogatory Terms for Surenos

SCRAPS = Trash

SCRAPA = Trash

Sureno = Derogatory Terms for Nortenos

CHAPS = Dirty complexion, skin color

CHAPETA = Pussy

BUSTER = Used By Both Gangs; Not claiming gang membership when you are one

18th Street Gang

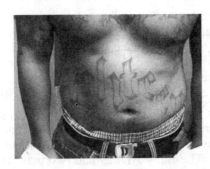

By now it is quite clear that many factors influence the formation and growth of street gangs across the country and worldwide. Anyone who is familiar with Hispanic street gangs should also be familiar with the diversity of these street gangs. Some gang histories can be traced back to a specific reason why the gang formed, other evolved from car clubs and others from groups of schoolmates hanging around together.

Today, the 18th Street gang is probably one of the largest Hispanic street gangs in the country. It is now also considered a transnational gang. The 18th Street gang has a unique history, and a closer look at the reason why the 18th Street gang formed indicates a clear and precise cause. The 18th Street gang formed because of racism and bias on the part of Mexican street gang members against mixed-race Mexicans and non-Mexicans who wanted to join the neighborhood gang. A sort of class distinction and racial bias developed within the Clanton Street gang and the mix-raced neighborhood youth who wanted to join that gang could not.

The Gang's History

Today, 18th Street gang members have been encountered in many states and a few countries including Mexico, El Salvador, Guatemala, Honduras and Canada. 18th Street gang members have also been contacted in Alaska, Washington, Oregon, Idaho, Nebraska, Arizona, New Mexico, Colorado, Illinois, Utah, California, Nevada, Virginia, North Carolina, Florida, Texas, and on Native American lands. Some estimates have reported that the 18th Street gang has between 8,000 and 20,000 members, just in the southern California area alone (www.rapdict.org). The tremendous membership size appears to be the result of a massive 18th Street gang recruitment program and the expansion of 18th Street to other states during the early 1990's.

The 18th Street gang was formed in the late 1960s, largely as a result of Mexican prejudice. There was an established Mexican street gang in Los Angeles known as the Clanton Street gang. The gang originally formed in the area during the 1920's. The first members were Caucasian youths. By the 1960's, the gang's membership was comprised of all Hispanic males. In fact the gang was in its second generation. It was truly an all-Mexican gang. Because of urban flight, the neighborhood changed demographically and by the 1960's it was comprised of mainly Hispanics, mixed race youth and Koreans (Valdemar, 1996).

Many youth who lived in the Clanton Street neighborhood wanted to join the gang, but were denied membership. During this time membership to Clanton Street was limited to only to those who prove their 100% Mexican ancestry. Undocumented immigrant youths, non-Mexican Hispanics and Mexicans of mixed ancestry were not allowed to join the gang (Valdemar, 1996).

Turned away by Clanton Street, some of these potential juvenile members still participated in criminal activities. Like many young juvenile offenders they were arrested by the police and ultimately sent to juvenile detention facilities. While in these facilities, their membership to Clanton Street was still denied. As a result, the youth from the Clanton Street neighborhood, who were denied membership because of their tainted ancestry, eventually formed their own gang. They became the original members of what now is known as the 18th Street gang.

There is a little more to the history according to one of the original members of 18t Street. Before 18th Street got its name, a gang of these youth had already formed. They initially called themselves the "Black Wrist" gang and they use to hang around a house of a prostitute named Sade. She later died of a drug overdose. The house was located near the corner of Magnolia and Pico, Los Angeles. The members of Clanton Street hung around another prostitute's house near the intersection of Pico and Venice, Los Angeles. The Clanton Street gang members knew the lady of the house as "Mama China."

The initial Black Wrist gang members had monikers like Chapo, Chocolate and Mr. Chino, Duke and Creo. Later the Black Wrist gang changed its name to the Latin Kings, then to the Baby Aranas (Baby Spiders). The Baby Aranas had two main rivals, the Clanton Street and Hazard gangs. The initial members eventually decided that the individual gang members should not have a moniker, but rather the gang should take on a name that could represent the diverse membership.

They decided on naming their gang 18th Street because 18th Street is a small street that was between Magnolia and Venice near Pico Blvd. The street was a natural selection because it was in the middle of the area where the Baby Aranas were drawing new members. The year was 1966 (Cantu, 2003).

The Baby Arana gang member who actually thought of the idea of forming a gang using all the Clanton Street throw-away youth lived on 18th Street, just four blocks away from the Clanton Street gang. Some members of Clanton Street left their gang and joined the 18th Street gang. The new gang adopted the name of the street that was in the middle of the area where the founding members lived, 18th Street. This area is now in the Rampart area of Los Angeles (Valdemar, 1996, Cantu, 2003).

The 18th Street gang grew quickly because it did not have a racial barrier that limited membership. 18th Street membership was largely composed of immigrant youths and those youths of mixed racial backgrounds. This is because the 18th Street gang recruited heavily from the populations of undocumented immigrants entering the United States from Mexico and South America, especially in the LA area.

By the later part of the 1960's a pair of brothers join the 18th Street gang. They are Rocky and Mark Glover, mixed race Native-American and German. The pair became the most ruthless and violent 18th Street gang members during their tenure. Rocky developed the reputation of being the most violent 18th Street gang member during this time. He was known to shoot and or kill anyone who had a conflict with the 18th Street gang. By 1975 all the original 18th Street gang members were gone (Cantu, 2003). However, the gang continued to grow membership wise and established new cliques through the country.

The 18th Street gang became the first Hispanic street gang to officially break the racial membership barrier. This allowed for a rapid and unchecked membership growth. Predominately composed of Hispanics some cliques of the 18th Street gang have even recruited African-Americans, Asians, undocumented Mexicans, Caucasians and Native Americans for membership. Some Tagger crews and Tag Banger crews that were located within 18th Street territory were also actively recruited. Only those Tagger or Tag Banger crews with reputations for violence were recruited. For example, West Side 18th Street jumped in 50 members of a tagger crew known as KWS, or Kings With Style. KWS members were known by law enforcement to be involved in robbery, burglary, assaults, drive-by shootings and murder. Currently, 18th Street continues to be heavily populated with undocumented immigrants and Central Americans, but not as many Asian, Caucasian, African, Native-Americans members.

Migration

Another unique characteristic about the 18th Street gang was that although it was primarily turf oriented, some gang members traveled to other areas and states to establish new cliques and to start illegal activities. This may suggest a mechanism that helps explain why there is 18th Street gang presence in several other states. Nationally, the gang's membership is estimated between30, 000 and 50,000. The gang has been reported active in 44 cities in 20 U.S. states (DOJ, 2009). Other research suggests that 18th Street cliques have been reported in 37 states and the District of Columbia and 10 foreign countries (www.rapdict.org). A few of the foreign countries where the 18th Street gang has been reported are: Canada, Mexico, Guatemala, El Salvador, Honduras, Peru, Spain and Lebanon. The 18th Street gang has qualified to be classified as a transnational gang.

Worldwide the 18th Street gang has many names such as 'deseocho' (Spanish word for 18); '666' three sixes are equal to 18, Mara 18 or Mara deseocho (mara is the Central American Spanish word for gang). The gang will be known by several names due to its transnational nature.

Remember, there are a number of mechanisms that account for gang migration, but they account for a small percentage of gang growth within and outside a state during this time period. The academic research at the time tended to support the model that most gangs were indigenous to their areas (Klein, 1995). However quality of life issues still appear to be the main reason why people move (Maxson, 1998).

Very few gangs will deploy members out of state or to another country to specifically recruit new members or to establish new gang cliques or sets. However, there is some law enforcement anecdotal evidence to suggest that this is exactly what happened with a few 18th Street cliques. In doing so, the 18th Street becomes one of the first Hispanic gangs to establish non-California based cliques. Law enforcement intelligence and anecdotal evidence has supported the theory that some gang migrations and recruitments had specific purposes.

The 18t street gang's influence grew quickly. At one time it was believed that local Tagger crews would be assimilated into the 18th Street gang to become tax collectors, enforcers and distributors of illegal drugs. Drug trafficking became a major factor in the migration of west coast based street gangs into the Northwest, Midwest and east coast. This includes some members of the 18th Street gang who go where the drug market takes them.

The heavy law enforcement response to 18th Street gang violence in the late 1980s to mid 1990s may have been an aggravating factor that influenced gang movement. Some 18th Street gang members who were contacted outside the state of California confided they left the state to avoid local law enforcement contact, to avoid prosecution and to avoid being subpoenaed as a witness in a criminal case. This may be one of the reasons why undocumented immigrant 18th Street gang members return back to their country of origin.

Similar to some non-California Sureno gangs, 18th street made its appearance on the East Coast in the mid 1990's. Unlike, the original west coast 18th Street gang members, East Coast members were mainly undocumented Mexican immigrants. However, it appears that some East Coast 18th gang members have direct ties to their West Coast counterparts even though they may have never lived in California. The connection may be based on extended family members or friends. Technology may facilitate communications and exchange of information and intelligence between 18th Street gang members. The use of the Internet and cellular telephones has certainly impacted the way the gang can conduct business.

Criminal Activity

Like most gangs, 18th Street is involved in many types of criminal activities including auto theft, carjacking, drive-by shootings, drug sales, arms trafficking, extortion, rape, murder and murder for hire. Although national and international drug trafficking seems to be the main criminal activity that 18th Street is involved in, it is helpful to know that 18th Street has also established ties with the Mexican and Columbian drug cartels. Because of the amount of drugs being distributed and sold, 18th Street also has connections with the Mexican Mafia prison gang and many African-American street gangs.

The drug-gang connection is strong. Don't forget, recent surveys completed by the National Drug Intelligence Center (NDIC), support the premise that about 78 percent of all street gangs are involved with some type of drug transactions. The 18th Street gang is no different, drug transport and trafficking has become a primary source of income for the gang. The 1998 NDIC report also strengthen an existing belief that street gangs as a whole are becoming more involved in the drug market and are concealing their membership status. The 18th Street gang has been known to market rock cocaine, marijuana, tar heroin and methamphetamine. As the methamphetamine market continues to expand across the country you can expect the presence of 18th Street gang members to increase if the gang continues to follow their current money making strategies.

Tax collection is another area where 18th Street is well established. Typically, in occurs in the area that 18th Street claims as turf. Gang members will collect a tax from any other person involved in a criminal activity or operating a legitimate business. This would include street vendors, shop owners, prostitutes and drug dealers. 18th Street gang members have threatened non-tax payers with death. This appears to be one of the gang's most profitable businesses (California Department of Justice, 2004).

However to enforce the collections the gang must sometimes resort to violence and have the reputation of being violent. In one year alone, 1994, the Los Angeles County District Attorney's Office handled 30 murders that were a result of hits made by 18th Street gang members for lack of tax payment. On clique of the gang the Columbia Little Cycos (CLCS) were so efficient at collecting taxes they were able to collect as much as $250,000 a month from local drug dealers. In 2002, members of the CLCS were arrested and charged under Federal RICO laws for their criminal enterprise (California Department of Justice, 2004).

In 2007, members of the 18th street gang were trying to extort a man and his wife for selling pirated DVDs. The man did not pay the tax and on the third attempt to collect members of the gang shot the man and his wife; when shot the man was carrying his 23 day old baby who was also killed (www.worldnetdaily.com).

As law enforcement puts pressure on the drug and violent criminal activities, some 18th Street gang members have become involved in non-violent criminal enterprises, such as fraudulent INS identification cards, immigration papers, credit cards, bus passes and even food stamps. The gang was once active in the cellular telephone cloning market. This activity decreased because of the introduction of digital cellular telephone service.

There is some law enforcement anecdotal evidence that suggests due to the injunction efforts in the Los Angeles some 18th Street gang members no longer carry weapons. The gang injunction effort also may carry a collateral effect. Juvenile age 18th Street gang members may attempt more felony level crimes and the use of females to transport and hide contraband may increase (California Department of Justice, 2004).

Of all the criminal activity the 18th Street gang is involved in drug trafficking is a growing business. The gang has transnational status and the FBI has confirmed some Hispanic gangs have a working relationship with Mexican drug cartels (www.worldnetdaily.com). This could provide a direct connection to import illegal drug into the U.S. from Mexico.

Membership Indicia

Often, 18th Street gang members will adorn their bodies with tattoos. Most common tattoo is some form of the number 18. Gang tattoos can be located anywhere on the body. Some members will cover their entire body with 18th Street tattoos. Other 18th Street gang members have been known to tattoo the number 18 on their foreheads, or above their eyebrows. Some gang members have used the number 666 to represent 18th Street. The tattoos might also indicate what clique of the 18th Street gang the member is from. Individual 18th Street cliques can have specific names that will normally end in the number 18.

18th Street gang members wear many types of clothing. The colors most often seen are brown or black colored pants and a white t-shirts. Some 18th gang members will also wear professional sports type clothing. 18th Street gang presence is probably first noticed when graffiti appears. 18th Street uses graffiti to mark turf just as many traditional Hispanic street gangs have done. The presence or lack of graffiti is not necessarily the best indicator of 18th Street activity.

Central America

In El Salvador the some cliques of the 18th Street gang appear to be developing a vertical type leadership structure and some degree of sophistication in their criminal operations. 18th Street gang cliques are called 'canchas' in El Salvador. One cancha in particular, the Tiny Locos (TLS) in La Libertad stands out as a prime example of this process. The leader is known on the street as 'Trece.' He orchestrated his escape form a court detention area with the help of members from several different 18th Street gang canchas.

Although Trece was in custody for a while he order and developed extortion schemes, sold drugs and ran his clique all from jail. He even sent Salvadorian TLS members to the United States to start cancha franchises. Interestingly, Trece ordered four U.S. based Salvadorian TLS cancha members to attempt a gang style hit. The four members were caught by U.S. authorities and federally indicted for the crime. Here is the interesting part; Trece was also indicted for the crime even though he has never set foot in America (Ponce, 2009).

The 18th Street gang in El Salvador is still rivals with the MS-13 gang. Brutal attacks designed to intimidate still continue to occur and the gang appears to expanding its level of violence though out the region.

Trends

Some cliques of the 18th Street gang have access to their own arsenal of weapons. Therefore, many in law enforcement consider 18th Street gang members to be armed and dangerous. Some 18th Street gang members have been encountered with Tech-9s, Mac 10s, Mac 11s and AK-47 assault rifles. Like all street gangs, many 18th Street gang members have access to all calibers of handguns. The 18th Street gang as whole has a reputation for being extremely violent and ruthless, with the possession and use of firearms only adding to this reputation.

Some cliques of 18th Street are evolving into a more sophisticated organized crime type group. This is probably due to the connections maintained with the Mexican Mafia and the Mexican drug cartels. The 18th Street gang membership will continue to grow, especially outside the state of California as new drug markets are taken over. The gang's propensity for violence will continue as it continues to grow in size. Some 18th Street cliques continue not to pay the Mexican Mafia tax and they have fallen out of favor with La Eme, while a few other cliques pay the tribute.

There is one caveat here. The 18th Street gang also recruits children to join their gang. They have known to target 8 to 15 year olds who are promised all the typical glorifications of the gang life such as money, recognition, status, women and a special identity. Because of this practice, 18th Street has also been called the "children's army" (Heim, 2003). A mother of a 14 year old 18th Street gang member told me, "the gang has total control over my son, he goes whenever they call, the gang gives him money, he has dropped out of school and I think he sells drugs… he is going to end up dead or in prison."

Generally speaking 18th Street gang does not have a solid organizational structure, therefore no direct leadership. Historically 18th Street cliques have been loosely connected and have operated in well-defined areas. On the West Coast a few 18th Street cliques have appeared to be more organized and have developed direct connections to the Mexican Mafia and Mexican drug cartels. For the most part currently 18th Street cliques operate independently and not as one cohesive unit. In southern California

At one time 18th Street is divided up into four major groups, Southside, Eastside, Northside and Westside (Blatchford, 1995). Los Angeles gang researcher Alex Alonso suggests that 18th Street gang is divided up into five groups. His research suggests there is a Central L.A. subset (www.streetgangs.com). The gang is then divided up into a number of smaller groups called cliques within these five geographical areas. The 18th street gang operates as a loose conglomerate of mini-gangs focused on criminal activity in areas where they claim turf.

Traditional rivals nationally have been the Mara Salvatrucha and Florencia-13 gangs. It would be consistent to find regionalized rivals of 18th Street, rivals that are specific to particular geographical areas. 18th Street has a general allegiance to west coast based Sureno gangs.

Like many gangs 18th Street utilizes the Internet. Use of the World Wide Web allows the gang to "cyber bang" against their rivals, chat with their homeboys, show off their pictures (flikas), flaunt their tattoos (ink) and graffiti (placasos), to make special greeting (shout outs), issue challenges (dis) and boast about their gang affiliation. The Internet can also be used to enhance their criminal activities and instantly connect east and west coast members to members in Mexico or Central America. What was once only seen in local areas can now be viewed worldwide. The Internet now becomes a cyber vehicle to spread the gang culture.

Summary

The 18th Street gang has grown into a diverse group of autonomous cliques that share the general name of 18th Street. Many individual cliques and clique members will not have any direct contact with other cliques or members; their only connection is probably the name of 18th Street. However, a few cliques have grown in sophistication and have become involved in national and transnational criminal activities.

Some of the larger clique names for this gang in Los Angeles are North side 18th Street. 54th, King Blvd G's,106th Street, Columbia Little Cycos, Pico Locos, Kdubs, Diablos, Tiny Winos, Bebitos, Shatto Park Locos, South Central, Smiley Drive, Alsace Locos, Ranch Park, 7th and Broadway, Wall Street, and Rimpau. Currently, 18th Street as a cohort t is a well established gang involved in a variety of violent and no-violent criminal activity. It is common to find cliques of the gang throughout and outside the U.S. using the same names as Los Angeles based cliques. This should not automatically imply the cliques are directly connected.

Mara Salvatrucha or MS-13

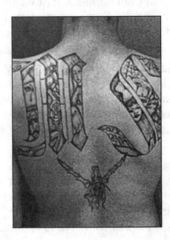

The Mara Salvatrucha gang had its birth in the City of Angels. Then gang initially formed as a social group to assist other Salvadorian immigrants in the areas. Very quickly the group evolved into a street gang and resorted to violence in order to compete with the existing L.A. based street gangs. Some unique social issues may account for some of the extreme forms of violence associated with this gang.

Social Issues

The United States has experienced the growth of many types of street and prison gangs within the past 50 years. The East and West Coasts have both been impacted with foreign-based street gangs. One identified mechanisms that aids in the formation of these new street gangs has been the influx of legal and undocumented refugees and immigrants from other countries. People flee their country of origin for many reasons. The two most common have been extreme poverty and internal conflict. However, physical abuse and extreme poverty go hand in hand with internal conflict. Just look at the situation in Yugoslavia with the mass exodus of Albanians and remember what happened in Southeast Asia during the communist takeover or the dynamics of the Mexican revolution. Therefore, it is not surprising to see an exodus of refugees from war torn countries or countries that have a recent history of internal conflict, like a civil war.

For example, it has been suggested by the American media that American type street gangs were a new phenomenon in Central America just a few years ago. The media has often reported that these gangs have become the key part of a new wave of organized violence after a decade of peace and the accords that brought an end to the guerilla wars in Central America.

In 2008 and 2009 U.S. foreign aid will most likely give the Mexicans close to a billion dollars to help combat drug trafficking and the related gang violence associated with it. Central American countries are scheduled to receive approximately 150 million dollars to help combat the same social issues. But don't forget quality of life issues motivate migration. Anecdotal evidence suggests it is the effects of poverty and violence that appear to be the most common reasons why people leave their countries.

History

We all are painfully aware of the 1980's violent and deadly civil war that lasted 12 years in El Salvador. Over 70,000 people were killed in this conflict (Washington Times, 2003). The constant, elevated levels of violence and lack of employment opportunities forced the mass migration of over one million El Salvadorian nationals. Most of the refugees and immigrants settled in Los Angeles and Washington, D.C. in 1984 and 1992. Some of these refugees and immigrants had ties with La Mara, a street gang in El Salvador. However, not all new comers had criminal ties. As with every immigrant population most just wanted to start a new life free of oppression and violence (Valdez, 2003). Some estimates suggest that as many as 300,000 Salvadorian immigrants have settled in Los Angeles (Johnson, 2006).

As the immigrants arrived it was recognized that some also had ties to and were ex-members of the Farabundo Marti National Liberation (FMNL), a paramilitary group made up of peasants trained in guerilla warfare. The association in El Salvador provided these immigrants with some special training and organizational skills. The early membership was reported to have some former guerillas and Salvadorian soldiers whose training and combat experience enhanced the brutality that is now associated with the gang worldwide (The Economist, 2006).

To date, there are approximately 1 million El Salvadorian immigrants who have resettled in the United States (Americas.org, 2003) and countless other who have relocated in Mexico, Canada, Europe and other parts of Central America. The current population in El Salvador is estimated to be 5.2 million. Research suggests that street gangs in this country account for 60 to 70 percent of all criminal activity. This has contributed to the 2009 per capita homicide rate of 55/100,000 (Ponce, 2009).

This suggests that approximately 1/5 of all Salvadorians have left their country. You have to ask yourself; why would approximately 1/5 of a country's population leave? Could the answer be in the amount of violence and opportunities for education and employment? Quality of life issues can drive migration.

In the early 2000s, it is estimated that there are between 8000 and 10,000 Mara Salvatrucha (MS or MS-13) gang members in 137 cliques and they have been reported to have a presence in 33 U.S. states (NDIC, 2003). However, in 2008 the FBI suggested that American law enforcement reported MS cliques in 42 U.S. states. Law enforcement anecdotal evidence also suggests that the total U.S. MS-13 population may be closer to 15,000 to 20,000 members (Valdez, 2008). In 2008, the Center for Immigrations Studies released a report that suggested the presence of MS-13 cliques in 48 states (Vaughan and Feere, 2008).

MS-13 is not only a nationally recognized street gang, is has gained international status. MS –13 cliques have been reported operating in Canada, Mexico, El Salvador, Honduras, Guatemala and Nicaragua, Spain and Italy. There are an estimated 17,000 MS-13 gang members in El Salvador alone (Homieunidos.org, 2003). A 2004 report estimated that there are between 70,000 and 100,000 gang members across Central America and Mexico (New York Times, 2004). Gangs are often referred to as maras in Central America. At issue here is the fact that there are no clear estimates of MS-13 gang populations, nationally or internationally.

West Coast

In Los Angeles, most of the newly arrived Salvadorian immigrants settled in the Rampart area. One of the largest and most active street gangs present in this area during this time was the 18th Street gang. As a result of this influence, initially those few Salvadorians, who got involved in street gangs, a few joined the 18th Street gang. Unfortunately, many Salvadorians suffered from a type of culture shock. Even though they were of Latino ethnicity, they were not fully accepted into the existing Los Angeles Hispanic culture. Yet, another subtle form of class distinction and bias focused on a new immigrant group. This status allowed some of the local gangs to view the immigrants as prey. As a result, street gangs and unscrupulous business owners victimized Salvadorian immigrants. These groups took advantage of the undocumented resident status of the immigrants and refugees.

Because of their resident status much of the victimization and crime went unreported to the police; due to the fear of deportation. This dynamic becomes the vehicle that allows the first

Salvadorian based street gang to form in the Los Angeles area and for Salvadorians who had joined the 18th Street gang to leave that gang. The first Mara Salvatrucha (MS) cliques formed in Los Angeles between 1985 and 1989. It has been reported that the actual founding members of the gang were first members of a L.A. based heavy metal stoner group. The gang was called MSS or Mara Salvatrucha Stoners. Stoner gangs were popular during this time period in Los Angeles as an alternative life style to street gangs (Nguyen, 2004 and Sanchez, 2008).

When MSS was first formed, membership started to increase rapidly because membership also provided a haven for newly arriving immigrants and for those immigrants who are having problems. Initially, the gang provided a source of protection, assistance, associations and a vehicle for connections for the immigrants. By the late 1980s to early 1990's the Mara Salvatrucha gang has grown enough in size to influence street gang activity in the Los Angeles area. According to one of the original members of the gang the name changed from MSS to MS in the early 1990s to mid 1990s. The Stoner name was dropped and the gang became known as Mara Salvatrucha or MS (Sanchez, 2008).

The main rival of MS became the local cliques of the 18th Street gang. The two gangs battled for turf control of the Rampart area of Los Angeles and this only tended to increase the tension between these two gangs. Violence between the gangs escalated and drew other Hispanic gangs into the conflict. By 1992, there was no clear winner, but the Mara Salvatrucha gang gained control of some the Rampart area and any 18th Street clique became the rival of all MS members.

Some anecdotal law enforcement evidence suggests that sometime during 1992 the California based Hispanic prison gang, the Mexican Mafia, sent an edict to the local southern California Hispanic street gangs (Surenos). The Sureno street gangs in California were to pay the Mexican Mafia a tribute, a percentage of money that was earned in the illegal activities the street gang was involved in. Because of their well-known reputation for violence and their prison gang status, many Latino street gangs paid the tribute. However, some Hispanic gangs did not, including some MS cliques. This caused further conflict between MS cliques, the Mexican Mafia and the other Hispanic gangs that were paying the tribute.

By late 1992 to early 1993, the L.A. based MS cliques became formally and firmly involved in the trafficking of illegal drugs, extortion, robbery and murder. The Mara Salvatrucha gang also aligned itself with other southern California Hispanic street gangs and the Mexican Mafia after settling the tribute issue. During the same time period southern California based MS cliques started using the number "13" along with their gang name to signify the Sureno alliance.

This implied that MS cliques were formally accepted as a Sureno gang and the gang adopted the associated Sureno gang behaviors. MS or MS-13 tattoos and graffiti were encountered by probation and law enforcement officers a short time after. Because of the southern California alignment, MS-13 like other Hispanic street gangs used and continues to use the "sur" or "sureno" tattoos or graffiti to further emphasize the gang alignment. When these terms are used they are referencing a general alliance to the Mexican Mafia and the Sureno style of gang behaviors encountered in southern California.

Migration

In 1996, Mara Salvatrucha gang members had been contacted in 14 U.S. states and by 2002 the gang's presence was reported in 28 states. Along the West Coast, Oregon, Washington, Alaska, Hawaii, Mexico, Central America and Canada also reported the presence of Mara Salvatrucha cliques. Don't forget, a large population of Salvadorian refugees and immigrants also settled in Washington, D.C., and some relocated to New York during the 1990s.

What makes the MS gang unique is that unlike traditional U.S. street gangs, some members maintain active ties with family members and MS factions in Central America and Mexico (Franco, 2008). Like 18th Street, Mara Salvatrucha has also become a national and internationally known street gang. Anecdotal law enforcement evidence suggests some East

Coast MS-13 members had family and gang ties to West Coast based MS members. There are a few theories that attempt to explain the transnational issue with some M-13 cliques. Refer to the last chapter for more information on gang globalization.

There is also some law enforcement anecdotal evidence that suggest a few MS gang members maintain contact between each other within the United States and El Salvador. They do so for one reason. It was suspected that these MS members had a business type relationship with some members of the Salvadorian army and other MS cliques and gang members. After the civil war anecdotal law enforcement evidence suggested that the Salvadorian army became a source of automatic weapons, hand grenades and explosives. At one time, a hand grenade sold for $1.00-$2.00 (U.S. currency) in El Salvador. An M-16 rifle will sell for approximately $200-$220 U.S. dollars. However, this is currently not true.

These communications and alliances could provide a mechanism for MS and other gang members to have access to surplus military munitions and also can help in establishing a network to traffic illegal firearms or other types of contraband in Central America and Mexico.

Drug trafficking appears to have also influenced some gang migration of MS gang members. America's appetite for the consumption of illegal drugs drives an underground import, transport machine, much of which is controlled by street gangs. The East Coast MS gang cliques that are involved tend to sell the drugs at higher price than those in the West Coast. The United Nations estimates the world drug market between 341 and 400 billion dollars per year (Niam, 2005). This is approximately 8 to 10 percent of the world's economy. It is easy to understand why so many gangs are involved in the drug business.

There is also another identified migration mechanism. The U.S. Immigration began a crack down on street gangs in the early 1990's. At the peak of the program in the mid 1990's, 40,000 criminal illegal immigrants were being sent back to Central America each year. This included U.S. trained and experienced MS gang members who were being sent back to Central America. However, in academic literature the MS-13 and 18th Street gang were reported present in El Salvador as early as 1990 (Cruz, 2007).

As the deportation process continued Central American countries experienced an unprecedented growth of street gangs and violence. The two main gangs to develop unchecked were MS-13 and 18th Street, also known as Mara 18. It has been estimated that up to 70 percent of the Central American youth who join a gang are either members of MS-13 or Mara 18 (Franco, 2008). This may have also been influence by the fact that some Central American youth adopted the brand names of MS-13 and 18th Street because it was in vogue. Latino street gangs had been present in Central America since the late 1950s (Cruz, 2007).

In Central America entire neighborhoods were plundered by violent turf wars waged by young MS-13 and Mara 18. During the 1990s gang members would arm themselves with machetes and home-made shot guns called "chimbas." As a result, gang violence soared and so did the homicide rate, especially for men under 30 years of age. To help control the gang violence some Central American governments enacted what a few consider extraordinary measures. The 'Mano Dura" and "Super Mano Dura" suppression programs were started and the police arrested thousands of gang members in Honduras and El Salvador.

In Central America gang membership suddenly became a criminal offense punishable with prison time. Gang related tattoos were used to help prove membership. A few experts referred to the Central American anti-gang laws as "draconian measures." In Central America gang members and victims of gang violence could be and still are found beheaded sometimes with messages carved onto their bodies (Casa Aliancia, 2006). To avoid the aggressive enforcement and stiff penalties for gang membership, some Central American gang members tended to flee back to the United States, especially in the Midwest and East Coast and to Mexico. A number of MS-13 and 18th Street (Mara 18) gang members have even fled to Canada (Teran, 2006).

There a number of MS-13 cliques in southern California, the Southwest and Northwest. In the early 2000s they did not appear to be vertically organized even though a number of members were involved in drug trafficking. Most clique leaders did not have formal titles and the cliques did not hold regular meetings.

Things have changed for some West Coast MS cliques. As early as 2006 law enforcement anecdotal evidence suggested that some MS-13 cliques were developing a vertical command structure. Gang leaders now had formal titles and the membership was required to attend weekly meetings. Some cliques even collected dues from their membership. If a member missed a meeting he or she would receive a fine or a physical punishment. Although relatively very small in numbers there are a few female MS-13 gang members. The majority of members remain Salvadorian, but there are Mexican, Honduran and Guatemalan members (Franco, 2008).

East Coast

Mara Salvatrucha gangs are reported to have appeared in New York between 1992 and 1995 (Daily, 2002). In Fairfax County, Virginia MS-13 gang members were contacted by law enforcement as early as 1992. The MS gangs in the East Coast formed for the same reasons as they did in Los Angeles, except there is one caveat. Initially, most all East Coast MS gang members were from the East Coast, not from southern California. During this time there were most likely no formal ties to link any East Coast MS gang members to their West Coast MS counterparts except maybe for family for a limited number of members. The media helped to suggest the gangs on both coasts were highly organized and connected.

Salvadorian immigrants that formed gangs in the East Coast often adopted West Coast street gang names and behaviors to compete with existing street gangs. The East Coast received another influx of immigrants and refugees from El Salvador around 1995. Many of the new arrivals were ex-military. Some joined cliques of the MS-13 street gang. Soon after, some MS-13 cliques in the East Coast seemed to become more organized and sophisticated. Sometimes special meetings would be held and facilitated by the ex-military gang members and they presented discussions about organizing the gang and developing Salvadorian Pride. During this time, some gang members tattooed themselves with "SWP" which really was an abbreviation for Salvadorians With Pride, not Supreme White Power as used by some Skinhead gang members.

To compete with the established East Coast gangs, MS-13 gang members turned to violence. Fear becomes a tool to establish respect and a street reputation within the gang community. Guns become part of the arsenal that is commonly used to enhance this reputation. The main focus of the Mara Salvatrucha gang cliques became to unify and to be respected by the other East Coast street gangs. As a result, MS-13 violence starts to increase. Fear, intimidation and violence were used against any MS rival, the local immigrant population and law enforcement. Although guns are easy to get sometimes MS 13 gang members would use a machete in an assault. The use of a machete is an effective tool to help establish a reputation of being brutal and ruthless. This tended to enhance the publics and rival gangs perceptions that MS-13 was extremely violent.

By the mid 2000s the MS-13 street gang developed a national reputation for being very violent and organized. MS criminal activities in the East Coast seem to parallel the criminal activities of West Coast MS cliques. However, a few East Coast MS cliques appeared to be more organized and mobile than their West Coast counterparts. Law enforcement criminal investigations also revealed that some MS-13 gang members travelled from coast to coast, often stopping in cities in the Midwest and south. Criminal case evidence also suggested the use of cellular telephones facilitated some criminal activity.

Crime

As a way to make money, MS gang members on both coasts turned to illegal activities such as drug and human trafficking, extortion, robbery, auto theft, intimidation, assaults and murder in the United States and a few cliques in other countries like Mexico, Canada and Central America. A few MS-13 cliques are also involved in check fraud operations.

There is some law enforcement evidence to support the theory that some West Coast MS-13 members have relocated in the mid-west and East Coast. One of the major factors appears to be employment. Migrant workers and their families go where the jobs are. When the move is made, members of the family that are gang members bring the gang with them. The meatpacking, poultry processing and construction industries have been a popular source of employment opportunities for migrant workers, especially in the mid-west and East Coast.

It is easy to understand why some MS-13 gang members can lead a double life. Hey tend to work in a local or mobile industry. These members are excellent employees in the day and active gang members off duty. Imagine how easy it is to move with the business to various parts of the country and at the same time camouflage the gang's movement and criminal activities. There is no evidence to suggest that there was or currently is a mass migration of MS 13 gang members travelling from coast to coast.

There is also some law enforcement anecdotal evidence to suggest that drug trafficking opportunities may account for the migration activities of a few individual members (Valdez, 2003). This may also be true for members of other types of gangs. Some law enforcement officials believe that some MS-13 gang members from southern California liaison with MS-13 gang members on the East Coast. This seems logical and consistent with current trends within the general gang population, but to determine to what extent is MS-13 is involved is difficult to analyze (National Youth Gang Survey, 1998).

If you think about it, the U.S. drug trafficking industry can also fuel gang migration and the formation of unique alliances between different gangs. This theory can explain some East and West Coast gang migration and movement in general, not just MS 13. On reported unique alliance has been the apparent connection of some MS-13 members with Mexican drug trafficking organizations such as Los Zetas.

Don't forget there can be inter and intra state gang migration. It is a well- established fact that where there is a market for illegal drugs, someone will bring the drugs to the consumer. Rural parts of the country, small towns and cities seem especially vulnerable and often it is a gang that provides the illegal drug(s). These areas would be ideal for any street gang to attempt to start a drug trafficking business.

MS-13 gang members have been known to use small elementary school aged children to transport drugs in school backpacks in order to avoid police detection. The children are forced to comply under the threat of physical harm to themselves or family members. Being refugees or immigrants themselves they comply and do not report the activity to the police (Valdez, 2003).

MS-13 gang members have also been involved in assaults and murder of police officers. The gang members can be extremely violent. For example, in Central America, MS-13 gang members have been known to behead their victims with an ax (Washington Post, 2003). The force of illegal immigration and re-immigration has made MS and 18th Street two of the fastest growing gangs in the United States (New York Times, 2004).

The gangs also bring their reputations for extreme violence with them. In a northern Virginia suburb during August 2004 members of a MS clique were blamed for almost hacking off the hands of their 16-year-old victim with a machete. The East Coast has also been the location for MS gang members to rape a disabled female, extort civilian immigrants and to stab a pregnant 17 year old who was assisting the police with a murder investigation.

What makes the MS-13 gang appear to be unique is the willingness for some members to use extreme forms of violence at the slightest provocation. This behavior has helped enhance the street reputation and respect within the gang sub-culture. It also has presented itself as a problem to non-gang member immigrants and refugees. The fear of being victimized has lead to intimidated and forced compliance to the gang. The more you fear me the more you respect me. The behaviors of a few MS gang members have also helped the public stereotype and conclude the entire gang membership is violent and ruthless.

MS-13 gang members have also been involved in gun running, prostitution, computer theft, chop shop and counterfeit identification operations. In June 2003, one MS-13 gang member while in custody bit the face of a Blood gang member while waiting in a holding cell, despite being outnumbered 10 to 1 (New York Post, 2003).

The Name

What exactly does the name Mara Salvatrucha mean? No one knows for sure, however there are four popular translations. The first one translates to "Long Live El Salvador". It is based from the La Mara street gang and the Salvatrucha guerilla fighters in El Salvador. The second translation, "Watch out Maravilla, El Salvador is here." This is not the most common, but apparently derived from a reference to the Maravilla (Mara) street gangs of Los Angeles, "salva" for El Salvador and the Hispanic gang slang term "trucha" for watch out. The third translation encountered is "Watch out the El Salvador gang is here." In El Salvador, "mara" is a word used to describe a group of juveniles or gang. Trucha is the gang slang for watch out and salva is used to represent El Salvador.

There is a fourth translation comes from an immigrant who was born in El Salvador. Mara is the Central American Spanish word for group and it is often used to describe a gang. Salvatrucha is a Central American Spanish word that is derogatory term for El Salvadorians. Mara Salvatrucha then simply translates to the El Salvadorian gang (Arriaga, 2004). This is probably the correct translation.

Membership Indicia

Typically Hispanic gangs share many of the same symptoms of membership, sometimes referred to as indicia. This is true for the MS-13 gang. Of course the indicia maybe regionalized or take on certain meaning depending on what part of the country or the world the gang is from. In general, the MS-13 gang shares graffiti, hand signs, color identification, name, moniker use, tattoo, rivals, similar crime involvement, photographs, slang, drawings, writings, Internet use and clothing style.

MS-13 gang members may display some, all or none of the traditional gang indicia. Commonly, MS graffiti will display the gang name in an abbreviated form or spelled out. The number 13 may be present as "13" or "XIII" or "Trece (Spanish word for 13)" or "X3." Often the graffiti will also display a letter abbreviation for the specific clique the gang represents. Sometimes the members will shave part of their eyebrows off or scare themselves with lines to display the number 13 on their face.

In the mid-west and East Coast some MS members use "eme" and "ese" as tattoos. These are the Spanish words for the letters "M" and "S". This is not an indicator that the member is a member or associate of the Mexican Mafia (La Eme) prison gang. He tattoo can be used by any bonefide MS-13 gang member. Don't forget the Mara Salvatrucha gang is a sureno based gang and as such have an indirect tie to the Mexican Mafia.

Mara Salvatrucha gang members will also identify with the color blue because of the southern California or Sureno alignment. Because of this alignment MS-13 gang members may also use the words "sur" or "sureno" in tattoos, writings or graffiti. In addition, any MS-13 gang member can use the common three dots, happy and sad theatrical faces, pachuco cross and teardrops tattoos. These tattoos can be worn anywhere on the body or on the face. Many Latino street gangs commonly use these tattoos. A few MS13 members will also display "SWP" (Salvadorians With Pride) or "SP" (Salvadorian Pride) tattoos.

MS gangs can to also display their clique name. So in addition to the generic graffiti or tattoos you may encounter clique names abbreviated like:

PVLS- Park View Loco Salvatrucos; CLCA- Coronado Latino Cyco Style; HLS-Hollywood Locos Salvatrucos; PLS-Pino Locos Salvatrucos; GLS-Gangster Locos Salvatrucos; WLS- Western Locos Salvatrucos; NSLS-Northside Locos Salvatrucos; ULS-United Locos Salvatrucos; NLS- Normandy Locos Salvatrucos;

FLS- Florencia Locos Salvatrucos; PVLS-Park View Locos Salvatrucos; BGLS- Big Gangster Locos Salvatrucos; VLS- Virginia Locos Salvatrucos; Centrales Locos Salvatrucos; RLS- Roosevelt Locotes Salvatrucha; LLS-Leeward Locos Salvatrucha; MGLS-Midnight Gangster Locos Salva; VLS-Venice Locos Salvatrucha; NCLS-North Carolina Locos Salvatrucha and the SLS-Silva Locos Salvatrucha.

Each name denotes a specific clique of the Mara Salvatrucha gang. There can be more than one clique of the gang, for example Florencia Locos Salvatrucos might be found in Fairfax County, Virginia, Pedro San Sula, Honduras, San Salvador, El Salvador, Madrid, Spain and in Salt Lake City, Utah. It is possible that members of these cliques do not know each other and may not have any direct contact with members from the same clique located in different countries. The gang cliques may have simply adopted a popular clique name. But make no mistake, each clique will conduct criminal activities and be involved in violence because they are gang members.

The MS hand sign can also be displayed in graffiti and is a popular form of tattoo. At first glance the hand sign may appear to look like a set of horns displayed because the index and pinky fingers are drawn in an exaggerated manner. The two middle fingers are held against the palm and the thumb is placed on top of them. Logically MS-13 gang tattoos can contain many if not all the symbols and words used in MS graffiti. The tattoos can be displayed on any part of the body, including the inner lips and genital areas.

Clothing styles for the gang members will vary depending on what part of the country or the world the gang clique is from. However, members will typically wear blue and black colored Nike brand clothing. Any style of footwear can be worn but commonly MS-13 members have been encountered wearing black and white colored Nike Cortez brand shoes. Members have been known to wear blue and black bandanas, Nike brand baseball caps and blue or black colored canvas belts. The Nike® brand has apparently been adopted by many MS-13 gang cliques as part of uniform. Remember for gang members this style of clothing becomes sort of a recognizable street uniform that helps identify peer members, allies, unknowns and rivals. But also note that clothing styles can change quickly and many non-gang members will wear the same style and brand of clothing that a street has adopted.

Central America

There is some evidence that suggests MS-13 gang members are organizing while in and out of custody (Ponce, 2009). Due to the violence between the 18th Street and MS-13 gangs Salvadorian criminal justice professionals were forced house gang members from each gang in different prisons. Salvadorian prison officials had to deal with extreme forms of violence between the gangs including the dissection of rival gang members. While this has decreased the violence within the prisons it has also given each the opportunity to develop a power base with the prisons. This has also afforded the opportunity for the gangs to develop a vertical command structure and take this reorganization into the streets.

For example, in Salvadorian prisons MS-13 gangs have formed a "ranfla." This is a committee of gang members that collect money and make decisions for the gang while in custody. Each committee member is called a "ranflero." The main ranfla for the gang is located in Zacatecoluca prison, El Salvador. This is unique because the prison is home to civilian, 18th Street and MS-13 gang members.

Outside of prison there is further organization. Each local gang clique is run by a member called a "shot caller." Cliques within a Salvadorian state belong to an overall organization called a "program." The purpose of the program is to link the local cliques together to spread resources or man power. Each state has a "program leader," he is contact for all the shot callers (Ponce, 2009). The MS-13 and 18th Street gangs both have this type of organization in and out of prison in El Salvador.

Trends

As more information about MS-13 gang activity has become known it has been suggested that MS gangs are involved in drug trafficking operations where ever a clique has been established. MS-13 gang members were at one time almost exclusively comprised of Salvadorian immigrants. Not true today. Although, the majority of MS-13 members are of Salvadorian decent, there are also many members from other Central American countries and Mexico. Law enforcement evidence also suggests there are a limited number of female members in Central America and the United States.

MS-13 street gangs will continue to use fear, intimidation and extreme forms of violence as a tool to maintain control over rival gangs, law enforcement and the communities where they have established turf. MS-13 gangs fit the traditional model of turf oriented gangs, however many MS-13 cliques are very mobile and members have been known to travel intra and interstate to facilitate criminal activities. MS cliques across the country will also continue to evolve and adjust their criminal operations. Some of the cliques seem to be evolving or morphing into more sophisticated organized gang cliques.

Some MS-13 gang members have become technically advanced as it appears they produce and maintain Internet web sites within the United States and in Central America. Like other street gangs MS cliques will continue to use the Internet for many reasons. For example, gangs use the Internet to communicate, recruit and plan crime and to socialize. The Internet also provides the perfect vehicle to spread and globalize the gang culture.

One unique characteristic about MS gang members is in general they show no fear of law enforcement. Some members are not easily intimidated and will act defiantly. Mara Salvatrucha gang members were reported to have been responsible for the execution of three federal agents and numerous shootings of law enforcement officers across the country (Kiser, 1999).

Barras

Honduras is home to a several major soccer teams. The fans for these teams form into large groups called 'barras.' In the beginning the barras normally were not involved with local street gangs. However, during the mid 2000s some MS-13 and 18th Street gang members have infiltrated and joined the barras (fan base). This behavior has lead to some of the barras acting more like the English Hooligan soccer groups. One researcher suggested that the gang members are joining the barras in an effort to recruit the most violent members for their gangs.

The barras initially formed around 1995-1996 in Honduras. By 2002-2003 rivalries between the barras started to escalate and so did the violence. Nationally the total barra membership is estimated to be between 12,000 and 13,000. As the number of street gang members join there appears to be an escalation of violence. There has been an estimated 12-13 deaths while people are travelling to the local soccer games that have been attributed to the barras.

There are four major barras in Honduras as of 2009. The "Ultra Fiel" (Extreme Faithful) has a membership that is estimated between 5,000 and 6,000. This barra is associated with the Olympia soccer team. Like many American based street gangs, the barra is divided up into smaller groups or cliques that are called penas. In the capital city of Tegucigalpa there are a reported 16 penas, each having at least 100 members (Ruiz, 2009 and Casco, 2009).

The "Revos" (for revolutionary) is affiliated with the Motagua soccer team. The barra membership is estimated at 3,000 and it too is divided into smaller cliques. The Revos refer to these cliques as bandas or commandas. Each Banda or commanda is divided further into smaller units called micro-bandas or micro-commandas.

The "Mega Locos" (super crazies) is affiliated with the Espana soccer team based in the Pedro San Sula area. The membership is estimated in the thousands and the cliques are called bandas or commandas.

The fourth barra is relatively new and is comprised of all females. They are known as the "Vampiras" (vampires). The total membership is unknown (Ruiz, 2009).

What is of particular concern are the behaviors of the barras. Many cliques have started to use graffiti to mark off turf and announce the barra's presence. Graffiti has also been used to issue challenges between barras. One particular popular form of graffiti has been the skeleton face.

The membership is drawn from then youth population and can include rockers, youth and gang members. The barras focus appears to be on physical aggression and vandalism on or near soccer stadiums. The barras tend to travel in large groups and cause fights at soccer games. Some barra members have been known to travel where ever their affiliated soccer team plays (Ruiz, 2009).

Summary

The MS-13 gang will continue to expand and get more involved in narcotic trafficking and distribution in the United States, Mexico and Central America. Drug trafficking in the region will allow some gang to form alliances in an effort to maximize profits. This may explain why the MS-13 and 18th Street gangs are working together in Honduras, yet remain bitter rivals in other countries. In Honduras the MS-13 and its rival 18th Street gangs have apparently changed recruitment tactics as they are currently linked up with the barras.

A few MS-13 gang members are currently members of the California based Mexican Mafia prison gang. This may help insure connections to the international drug trafficking cartels and could expand the influence of the Mexican Mafia into Central America. Based on behaviors it appears that some MS-13 and 18th Street cliques and individual members are developing an organized vertical leadership structure, expanding globally and may be getting involved in the local politics.

Asian Gangs

A historical look at the formation and proliferation of Asian street gangs will uncover how Occidental gangs influence the behaviors of these gangs. And how certain practices of Asian street gangs influence west coast based American gang behaviors. Culture shock played a key role in the marginalization of Asian youth; which in turn impacted gang membership. Examine the differences and the relationship between Asian organize crime groups and street gangs. This chapter will also demonstrate the common and distinct gang behaviors between Asian and Western street gangs. One more comment. The term "Asian" really refers to a number of different ethnic groups which can include Japanese, Chinese, Korean, Indo-Chinese (Southeast Asian) and Pacific Islanders. Indo Chinese groups can include Vietnamese, Cambodian, Laotian (Hmong and Minh) ethnic groups.

History

Asian immigrants and refugees have flowed steadily into the United States for many years. Immigrants from Southeast Asia, Korea, Japan, China and the Pacific Islands have settled in all parts of the country. In California, Asian immigrants and refugees have clustered in San Francisco, in the Los Angeles basin, and in Orange County. In the Midwest, immigrants tended to settle in the Houston, Texas area. In the East Coast, New York became a haven for many refugees and immigrants especially those who entered the country through Canada.

First generation and immigrant youth within these groups have had to adapt to Western styles of living many times while parents and older family members tried to survive maintaining traditional ways. As a result, conflicts tended to arise between some Asian youth and their families. This was partially due to the intimidating nature of Western culture, language barriers and traditional values. This culture shock helped to distance these immigrant youth from their families. These youth became social outcasts (excluded groups) within their own communities.

Asian immigrants also had several barriers to hurdle. Besides the ethnic and cultural barrier, there were also problems with language, mode of transportation, the monetary system, law enforcement and judicial systems, education and the unexpected peer-influence and personal experience in the educational system. As with most groups, the new Asian immigrants tended to settle where fellow countrymen lived and worked. This banding together was based on many reasons, but the primary factor was and still is culture and language. This mechanism holds true for all immigrant groups.

Because the local gangs considered Asian immigrants and refugees different some youth immediately became the object of criticism and bias. Asian youth were stereotyped by Westerners. This behavior helped Asians to stereotype Westerners and caused many immigrants and refugees to withdraw from Occidental society and become more dependent on each other. Remember the "us verses them" attitude that developed with the Irish immigrants and Mexicans after the Treaty of Guadalupe Hidalgo? This is the attitude that polarized immigrant groups and subsequently helped form our nation's first street gangs.

This same social force also acted as a catalyst that helped form the first Asian street gangs in the United States. Add a reluctance to learn English, and a general mistrust for the Western way of life, including a distrust of the police, victimization by existing street gangs and it becomes clear to see why Asian street gangs formed in the country.

The diversity of ethnic backgrounds explains the corresponding numbers and types of Asian gangs. It is beyond the scope of this book to give a complete history of the formation of all types of Asian gangs in America. The gangs discussed here will be categorized by ethnicity and be limited to larger street gangs. Although Asians gang members tend to group together while in state prisons there has been no report of an Asian prison gang forming in the country. Asian street gangs can form rivalries between other Asian street gangs, but the rivalries tend to be shelved when members are in custody.

The general characteristics and membership indicia discussed in previous chapters can also be used as a template to help identify membership in Asian street gangs. Initially, most Asian gangs were ethnically based and open only to Asians; however a few gangs have adopted different membership rules and now allow members from any ethnic background. Many Asian gangs unlike the traditional Latino street gangs are not bound together by a geographical based turf. These Asian street gangs tend to be nomadic and group together to make money. Asian street gangs tend to remain in a city but usually do not claim it as their turf. Being non-turf oriented, mobile and flexible tends to be a unique characteristic of some Asian street gangs.

Some gangs use an informal network of contacts throughout the United States, Canada, and Southeast Asia that facilitates gang mobility and globalization. Asian gang members can literally be in Los Angeles, California, in the morning and Houston, Texas the next day. The use of commercial air travel, buses, trains and personal vehicles are common modes of transportation. Asian street gang members tend only to victimize members of their same ethnic group, but will fight with other ethnic based street gangs. This is also another unique characteristic of Asian street gangs.

A few Asian gang law-enforcement experts predicted these gangs would eventually victimize the general population when they run out of Asian targets (Frank, 1990). Time has suggested this prediction did not come true. Currently, the majority of victims of Asian street gang activity still tend to be other Asians. The non-Asians targets have been law enforcement professionals and those engaged in illegal activities such as narcotic trafficking. In general, most Asian street gangs are more organized and efficient when planning and executing crimes. Crime committed by these gang members can involve youth as young as 13 or 14 years old (Frank, 1990). This degree of sophistication is another unique factor that can make Asian gangs different from their western counterparts.

As Asian street gangs evolved it was apparent that Western street gang psychology and behaviors influenced and eventually become part of Asian street gang life. This would predict and rightfully so that some Asian street gangs could share indicia of membership with their Occidental counter parts. As the gangs gained tenure law enforcement officials started to observe graffiti, use of hand signs, stylized clothing, gang nicknames, the use of tattoos and the use of gang slang. In the late 1990s some Asian gangs have been involved in drive-by shootings and car-to-car moving shootings a behavior once observed with Hispanic and African-American street gangs.

The reverse is also true. For example cigarette burning was once thought to a behavior practiced only by Indo-Chinese (Southeast Asian) street gangs. In the early 1980s this was true, however currently some Hispanic, Skinhead and African-American street gangs also use cigarette burning.

As you have already discovered street gang formation and activity are impacted by a variety of social conditions and Asian street gangs are no exception. Although relatively new age-wise when compared with the other Western style street gangs Asian gangs are still affected by societal changes and pressures. One result has been the appearance of non-Asian gang members in Asian street gangs. In some instances, Caucasian youth have been the leaders of Asian street gangs that normally were only of Asian membership. Male and females can also join some Asian street gangs.

Another trend was the involvement of American-Asian street gangs in credit card and check fraud schemes, identity theft, computer chip theft and the counterfeiting of video compact discs. Asian street gangs can also use the Internet to communicate, socialize and advertise their culture. In a few instances Asian street gang members have used "instant messaging" to plan criminal activity. These gangs were some of the first street gangs to get involved in and specialize in this type of non-violent crime.

Korean Gangs

When federal immigration laws were changed in 1965, over 30,000 Koreans immigrated to the United States (Kim, 2003). As expected, almost all the families experienced some kind of culture shock. The demands of assimilation into Western life style caused severe problems for some Korean families. Out of necessity both parents worked long hours, often, at two menial jobs, just to make ends meet. This in turn left some Korean youth alone for many hours.

Cross-cultural problems intensified when the children learned English as a second language. At the same time their parents spoke little or no English at all. The children adapted to American culture at a rapid pace, while their parents were trying to cope, using the traditional ways. The same conditions have affected many immigrant families as well.

For some immigrants, internal conflicts within the family increased. Ostracized from their families, some youth were simultaneously victimized by the local street gangs. Some Korean youth naturally started to band together to protect themselves and because they had common issues. Along with speaking the same language and having similar customs these groups began setting the stage for the formation of the first Korean gangs in the United States.

In forming first-generation Korean street gangs, Korean youth further separated from their families by intensifying the bond between the gang and themselves. The gang quickly became the new street-family. Gangs offered increased sense of security, but also a need for money, housing, transportation and food. To fulfill their needs the gang turned to illegal activities. The birth of the Korean street gang was formalized in southern California in late 1968 about three years after the first wave of immigration. This is about a year after the Mexican Mafia formed in San Quentin, California.

During and after the mid 1970s, Korean gangs committed residential robberies, burglaries, auto thefts and a variety of other crimes. The most notorious of the early Korean gangs were the KK, Korean Killers; BK, Burger King; and the AB, American Burger. These gangs were localized in the central Los Angeles area. The Korean Killers were the most organized and continued their criminal activity into the 1980s (Sully, 1990).

A female counterpart to this group also developed, calling themselves KGK Korean Girl Killers. The members of this gender exclusive gang were led by and associated with the members of the Korean Killers. The same dynamic existed for some Chicago based street gangs that had female gang counterparts that affiliated with a single male gang. Female auxiliary gangs are not a new phenomenon.

Current activity by Korean street gangs has kept pace with all gang activity. Korean street gangs still continue with profit-oriented crimes, working together as a coordinated unit to commit burglaries and residential or business robberies. Korean gangs can be sophisticated and well organized when it comes to committing crime. Usually, the gang knows their victims. Often, the intended victim is followed before the crime is committed in order to collect intelligence on the victim's routine and habits. Once the information has been obtained, the robbery plan is designed, sometimes with an escape or alternate plan in case something goes wrong.

Primary robbery targets for the Korean street gangs have been jewelry stores, but burglary, extortion and auto thefts are also committed to supplement the gang's lifestyle. Korean street gangs have even started to sell the drug Ice (a smokeable form of methamphetamine). Some Korean gangs have also committed a number of home-invasion robberies.

Gang crimes against persons occurred with frequency in the Korean population. At one time common gang crimes included sexual assaults with teenage girls as victims. As in most Asian societies, this type of crime is seldom reported to the police, most likely due to a strong sense of shame the victim and family feel. Many Asian victims feel the victimization is their fault. They have done something to cause their victimization. Gang rape is the most frequent sexual assault and sometimes is used to initiate females who wish to associate with a particular gang.

In general there is little reporting of crime among the Korean population in part because of gang intimidation. This is also true with many Asian populations. Many victims fear that the gang will return if the initial crime is reported to the police. That belief combined with a general distrust in the legal system and the perception that many law enforcement personnel cannot be trusted are the major reasons why crimes are not reported. This is why understanding culture plays a key role in dealing with ethnic based communities.

Many Korean gang members like nightlife. They frequent cafes, Korean nightclubs and billiard halls. Most Korean street gang members avoided the stylized dress of Latino street gangs. Tattooing and body scaring are rare, but still encountered. When Occidental gang behaviors are adopted some Asian street gang members tend to copy indicia used by traditional Hispanic gangs. As a result, some Korean gang members may sport gang related tattoos and stylized clothing.

Korean gangs also have their own style of graffiti showing the gang name, and city of origin. Korean gang members will often deny gang membership and make an attempt to conceal all gang indices. Sometimes Korean gang members come from very affluent families with white collar professional parents. Many Korean gang members successfully complete high school with excellent grades. Some will even have part time employment. Some gang members go to and successfully complete college.

Korean gang members tend to follow traditional initiation rituals. Formal initiation into a Korean gang may include a jump in, commission of crime or being sponsored into a gang. There have been a few reported incidents where a sexual assault has been used as part of the gang initiation. As with other gangs, the Korean street-gang members should never be underestimated. The use of weapons during the commission of a crime is frequent. Korean gang members could be violent toward law enforcement and the community at anytime. In the United States, Korean street gang activity is only limited due to the relatively small Korean population. Korean street gangs represent a small percentage of the total Asian gang population.

Filipino Gangs

Gang activity in the Philippines originally began in the country's prison system around 1940. Prison gang members, upon release, banded together in an attempt to take control of the streets. Within 10 years, young Filipinos were being heavily recruited into these street gangs. Many contemporary U.S. Filipino street gangs originated with these first Filipino street gangs. Some of the same gang names are still used today, such as Bahala Na and Sige Sige.

During the late 1970s and early 1980s, there was a major immigration of Filipinos into the United States. Political unrest in the Philippines was a leading factor for this migration. Like Korean immigrants the majority settled in the southern California area. There were an estimated 1.2 million Filipinos in California during the late 1990s. Political unrest continues to play a role in the mass migration of refugees and immigrants into the United States.

The Philippines are a group of approximately 2,000 islands in the South Pacific. Eight main languages are spoken in 89 different dialects, and a great diversity of culture exists within the Filipino communities themselves. With increased immigration into the United States there was a blending of social elements between the new arrivals and the existing Filipino society. This cultural blending resulted in ongoing problems between some of the younger Filipinos and their families. Culture shock can affect any immigrant family.

Some newly arrived Filipino youths who attend high school immediately became targets for the existing Black and Latino street gangs. A similar mechanism occurred with some immigrant Korean youth. Young Filipinos often banded together for social reasons, using a traditional custom called Barkada, which is a social-grouping system.

This system allowed young Filipinos to meet in groups of 10 or 20. These groups had names and gave each member a nickname. Some law enforcement experts feel this tradition may have lead to the development of the first Filipino street gang in the United States (Sully, 1990).

Currently, it is estimated that there are over 50 Filipino gangs in southern California. Gangs that are commonly encountered are the Satanas, Pinoy, Pinoy Real, Red Dragons and the Troupang Hudas (Troop of Devils). Filipino street gangs are somewhat territorial but do not fight over turf like Hispanic gangs. Filipino gangs may favor a particular park, store or other predetermined location where they meet and socialize. Some Filipino street gangs have been known to change their favorite meeting location in order to avoid a confrontation with the police.

Some Filipino gang members modeled their lifestyles after the Latino and Black street gangs. Gang members dress fashionably, wearing baggy pants and oversized shirts. Three-quarter-length black trench coats were once common for some members, while others wore white tee shirts and baggy pants. The term Ninja was used to refer to wearing all black colored clothing as a sign of respect while attending a funeral, or while committing a crime. At one time the "disco dress" referred to a gang member's dance or party clothes. Overall, the Filipino gang member will appear neat, clean and dresses fashionably.

As with other gangs, some Filipino gang members have family members who are also gang members. In these cases, sibling gang members may belong to a rival gang. This unique gang diversity surprisingly causes no conflict within the Filipino household. This behavior is also encountered with all types of ethnic based street gangs.

Like traditional Hispanic street gangs, Filipino street gangs can form different cliques based on age or geographical location. These cliques will still identify with the parent gang, but will operate independently of each other. Filipino gangs tend mark their favorite meeting locations with graffiti and use monikers similar to those commonly used by Hispanic gang members. By the 2000s graffiti was not a requirement for Filipino street gang participation. Many gangs are trying to keep a low profile in an attempt to conceal membership and activity.

If gang graffiti is used often it will list the monikers of peer gang members and may also show some type of cartoon character. Some Filipino gang members tend to use the name of fantasy figures such as Aladdin or Sinbad or a well-known 1920s era gangster's name such as Pretty Boy or Capone.

New gang members are initiated into the group by the traditional jumping-in ceremony. With Filipino gangs this beating ritual became so brutal that in a few cases the new gang member was stabbed. Many Filipino gang members reported that death is the only way to permanently leave the gang. As it turns out this is a common belief and myth among almost all street gang members. The reality is not so. There have many documented instances where gang members, including Filipino gang members have successfully left their gang without being killed.

Some Filipino gang members will scar themselves, using cigarettes or red-hot quarters in order to show their hardcore gangster mentality and willingness to endure pain for the gang. The scars can be found on arms, legs and hands. Female Filipino gang members may also scar themselves in this manner to show their gang association. The burn scars are a form of generic gang tattoo. By themselves cannot indicate a particular gang membership. However, this form of body modification is commonly seen within the gang culture and not within the body modification culture.

In the gang culture burning oneself with a cigarette is a demonstration of courage and a test of pain. The more cigarette burn marks present, the crazier the person is. At one time it was believed that as a general rule an odd number of marks indicated an active gang member and an even number indicated a retired gang member in good standing. This conclusion was false. There is no rule concerning the number of burns. Filipino gang members are not the only gang members to use the cigarette burn marks. Currently many types of gangs use the burn marks, including some party crews, other Asian gangs, Hispanic gangs and a few African-American gangs.

Filipino gang members can have a variety of tattoos that can include, but not limited to monikers, initials, three dots, the happy and sad theatrical faces or the gang name. Some members will also tattoo their initials or a complete gang logo on one side of their body. Older gang members may tattoo a tear-drop on the inside corner of their eye next to their nose, as opposed to the Hispanic gang practice of putting the tear drop tattoo on the outside corner of the eye.

Most Filipino families are very closely knit. Sometimes parents tend to help a family member hide from the police. This practice is not limited only to Filipino families. It is encountered within every ethnic group. For Filipinos because of family connections in the islands helping a gang member son or daughter could include sending the gang member son or daughter back to the Philippines in order to hide from authorities. A similar practice is also encountered with Hispanic, Vietnamese and Chinese families.

Filipino gangs seem to prefer victimizing their own ethnic group. Very few crimes are reported to the police from this community. A few Filipino gangs are somewhat mobile. Law enforcement anecdotal evidence suggests that some of these gangs drove 20 or 30 miles to commit crimes. Most Filipino gangs will form friendly associations with gangs of different ethnicity. Rivals can vary depending on the geographical location the gang clique (Sully, 1990).

Crime wise Filipino gangs are involved in extortion, auto theft and drive-by shootings. In the past, one of the most popular weapons used was the sawed-off shotgun. Like many gangs any weapon can be used in a violent crime. Interestingly a Filipino gang member told a Garden Grove, California, gang investigator, *"We may be small, but a Colt equalizes everything"* (Martin, 1990).

Many Filipino gang members believe life has little meaning. In many street gangs there is an attitude that it is O.K. to die for the gang. This belief is centered on the concept that dying for your gang makes you a respected and honored member who will never be forgotten. Unfortunately this is not necessarily true. There may also be a cultural influence here as well. In many Asian cultures dying is not death, but rather another step in the life journey. Passing away means nothing is lost. This may help explain why many Asian street gang members speak of not being afraid to die.

Samoan Gangs

With growth of the Samoan community in the United States during the past years, there has been a commensurate increase in Samoan street gang activity. Samoa, a territory of the United States, had established small colonies of expatriates in Hawaii and California during the early 1970s. That was about the time southern California law enforcement began to notice a significant increase of gang activity involving Samoan youth.

At one time Samoan gangs in California adopted traditional Latino street gang characteristics as their own. This included combing the hair straight back and wearing khaki baggy pants, white colored sleeveless tee-shirts, bandannas, Pendleton, baseball caps, athletic wear and professional sports emblems. Some Samoan gang members still display this type of membership indicia.

In Californian the Samoan gangs differ from Latino gangs because they have aligned themselves with one of two competing African-American gangs. Samoan street gangs aligned themselves with the Crips or Bloods. Most of the L.A. based Samoan gangs have aligned themselves with the L.A. based Crips. Samoan gangs can also form a number of sets. In turn each set would claim Blood or Crip affiliation.

Like African-American street gangs, the Blood and Crip affiliated Samoan gangs are bitter rivals with each other. Samoan gangs also place an importance on the colors red and blue, just as the Bloods and Crips do. Samoans who are involved in street gangs can and will fight over set affiliation, like their African-American counterparts.

Samoan gangs may also use graffiti as a form of non-verbal communication. The graffiti can be blue in color and use terms such as cuzz, SCAT (Samoan Crips Are Tough) boys, BK (Blood killers) and slob (a derogatory term for Bloods used by Crips). BK and slob are insulting terms to a Blood affiliated gang member.

Red colored graffiti usually indicates that the Samoan gang associates with Blood gangs. Gangs slang such as Blood, Piru, CK (Crip Killer) and E-Rick are commonly used. CK and E-Rick, insulting terms that refer to a Crip affiliated gangster. Gang graffiti can be written anywhere and can also be found on personal items such as schoolbooks, personal papers and drawings. The same behaviors first encountered with the California based Mexican street gangs.

Samoan street gangs have been known to claim a specific geographical location rather than a neighborhood as their turf. The area could be a specific park, a school that a member attends or any single location where gang members frequently meet. Normally, gang graffiti will be present at these locations. The meeting area can also change and it tends not to be defended as traditional Hispanic gangs would defend their neighborhood.

Samoan gang members also use nicknames, or monikers. They tend to follow name the name patterns of African-American gangs. Samoan gangs are influenced by traditional Samoan familial-tribal culture in their leadership and member status structure. Culture can influence gang behaviors. For example, older male members tend to be the shot callers and the groups can have some strong social bonds. Another unique characteristic seen with this Pacific Islander gang is that membership can be racially inter-mixed with Whites, African- Americans and Latinos. Therefore, some Samoan gangs may actually be a Hybrid gang because of mixed race membership. Females have been able to associate with Samoan gang as well.

During the 1980s and early 1990s Samoan gangs were known for their auto-theft abilities and willingness to commit assaults and weapons violations. To a gang member, a stolen vehicle is known as a G-Ride. Some common names used by West Coast Samoan gangs are the Royal Samoan Posse (RSP), Sons of Samoa (SOS), Samoan Krook Style (SKS), Bounty Slob Killers (BSK), Hoodlum Crips (HCG), Park Village Crip (PVK), all which claim Crip affiliation.

Krook City Bloods (KCB) is an example of a Samoan street gang that claimed Blood affiliation. However, most of the Samoan gangs claim affiliation with the Crips, probably since the Crips have the reputation of being one of the most violent and ruthless street gangs. This affiliation with the Crips gang also serves to further enhance the reputation of the Samoan gang. On the street it is assumed that any gang associated with the Crips is also just as violent and ruthless. In other words, more peers and rivals may be intimidated and fear the gang because of the gang's name. This is another way to increase and command respect from non-gang members and within the gang community. Currently, other types of street gangs will use this behavior, including some Folk Nation and other Asian gangs.

Samoan gang members can use tattoos that resemble their gang graffiti. Words like cuzz or crip may be seen on the top portion of the hand or along the arms. The set affiliation will also determine the types of tattoos a Samoan gang member will sport.

Samoan gangs have been known to fight with other ethnically based gangs including Southeast Asian and Latino gangs. However, most Samoan street gang members tend to be sociable and are very family-oriented. Samoan street gangs, as well as Filipino and Korean street gangs, can be located throughout the United States.

Indo-Chinese Gangs

Understanding Indo-Chinese street gangs requires an understanding of the history of Southeast Asia, especially Vietnam. Formerly French Indo-China, Vietnam, occupies the Southeast Asian Peninsula and is surrounded by the countries of China, Laos and Cambodia, and the South China Sea. Vietnam has a population of approximately 76.3 million people (Wikipedia, 1999). Thailand comprises the remainder of the geography and lies in the west coast of the peninsula.

Vietnam's history provides the picture of a country in conflict for thousands of years. The culture of Vietnam has been shaped by the strong influence of China and France. France, as a colonial power played a major role controlling Vietnam from 1800 to 1954.

While the French were in control, Vietnam's society was also being influenced in the areas of language, education, and religion and by the migration of people out of the villages and coastal towns into larger cities. This movement tended to have lasting effects on the family unit and traditional lifestyle of the Vietnamese family. Vietnam's language developed into several dialects as a result of French influence.

Even though the majority of the Vietnamese are Buddhist, there are many Catholics, Taoists, Mormons, Lutherans and Confucians, when combined these religions also make a great social impact on the Vietnamese. Religious diversity adds to cultural shock that immigrant and refugee populations experience during transition and resettlement. In addition, these religions were also re-established in the areas where refugees and immigrants settle.

As a group the Vietnamese tend to be very family oriented and take great pride in their family units. This tradition is thousands of years old, probably the result of the small village lifestyle. Even when families move to large cities, individual family members will choose to live close to each other. We still find this true today in the United States. Often, family members are next-door neighbors or live within a block of each other. This type of behavior is also encountered within the Hispanic, African-American and some Caucasian populations.

During the time the United States entered the Vietnam conflict some Vietnamese government officials were corrupt. In Vietnam, to oppose the government was extremely dangerous. Where corruption existed, it also extended into all branches of the government, including law enforcement. As a result, and rightfully so, many Vietnamese developed a fear of the police. Bribery was a common way to get family members released once in police custody. Total disappearance of a family member after police custody was all too common. This corruption was intermittent and did not affect all government officials. However, corruption continues to play a role in many developing countries.

The influx of Indo-Chinese into the United States began after 1965, with the establishment of the Immigration and Nationality Act. As the conflict in Vietnam and the rest of Southeast Asia decreased, a steady stream of wealthy and educated Southeast Asian immigrants arrived in the United States.

The Relocation

There is a distinct difference between immigrant and refugee status. An immigrant has time to plan before leaving his country and moving is voluntary. The immigrant may take personal belongings and may travel as a family. On the other hand, refugee status means the person left as a life threatening emergency, often leaving family members behind. This is a forced exodus made under great peril and many times all personal belongings were left behind. Often, refugee families were split up because the children may have been sent ahead of the parents.

There are four major ethnic groups that comprise Indo-Chinese refugees and immigrants. The Vietnamese, Cambodian, Laotian and Hmong initially all relocated to various specific areas on the West Coast. Today these groups can be found anywhere in the United States, Peru and Canada, however the majority of the Indochinese can still be located in southern California.

Saigon's fall in April 1975 initiated a mass exodus of people from Vietnam, Laos and Cambodia. Since then, three additional waves of refugees left Southeast Asia and resettled in America. The first wave of Vietnamese immigrants arrived in the United States in 1975. This group of approximately two hundred thousand refugees included high-ranking military officials and educated middle-class professionals. They were, as a whole, well educated and most spoke English. These characteristics made the matriculation into a western life style less traumatic.

The second wave of refugees fled Vietnam in over-crowded boats and then fell victim to Thai pirates. These refugees commonly experienced rape, pillage, torture and death when assaulted by the pirates. This group of refugees became known as the Boat People. Many upon arrival to the Unites States had no legal papers showing age or birth date. It was not uncommon for children to arrive without their parents or other family members. To migrate to the United States in this fashion had to be a horrible ordeal.

This group of Vietnamese immigrants arrived throughout the 1980s and they had varied educational levels. Most did not speak English and approximately 40 percent were ethnic Chinese. This second wave of immigrants came from the rural and coastal areas of Vietnam.

A third wave of refugees started to enter the United States in 1987. Passage was guaranteed when Congress approved the Amer-Asian Homecoming Act that year. As a result, thousands of Amer-Asian children, offspring of Vietnamese mothers and American GI fathers, entered the United States.

A fourth wave of refugees began to arrive in the United States in 1990. Since that time approximately 50,000 political prisoners and their families have resettled in the U.S. as a result of an agreement with the Hanoi government. The agreement expired in 1995, and by that time officials believe that 100,000 additional refugees had resettled in the United States.

The four waves of refugees and immigrants were from five different ethnic groups and came from three different countries in Southeast Asia. They were Vietnamese and ethnic Chinese born in Vietnam, Cambodians from Cambodia, the Hmong and Laotian from Laos.

Young refugees from these Southeast Asian ethnic groups formed the first Southeast Asian street gangs in the United States. When these gangs initially formed in southern California, they were based solely on their ethnic origin, but as the gang members matriculated into the American gang culture, this barrier disappeared for some gangs.

First Vietnamese Gangs

Many gang experts believe that Southeast Asian street gangs made their first California appearance in 1978, about three years after the fall of Saigon (Frank, 1990). They were comprised primarily of Vietnamese youths. Initially it was generally accepted by law enforcement that these gangs formed for the purpose of committing crime for economic gain (Nye, 1992). Other experts believed that the first street gangs formed because the youth had similar issues and problems; and that protection and survival initially were the reasons the youth groups gelled in to a gang. Some of these youth were homeless and as the group's survival needs increased they resorted to criminal activities.

These gangs initially had no names, were loose-knit and normally did not associate on a continual basis. As their criminal activity increased, so did their association. A natural bonding between the members of these groups occurred, and they developed into today's Vietnamese and Cambodian street gangs.

The attitude of many of the initial gang members was based on the belief that anything they could do to better their financial situation was acceptable, including criminal activity (Nye, 1992). These refugees grew up during a very violent portion of their country's history. The violence they must have experienced while traveling at a young age to the refugee camps surely had a profound effect on their lives. Brutal violence was such a daily occurrence it may have come to seem like a normal part of everyday refugee life.

In Vietnam, at least 10 percent of the population became war casualties. In Cambodia, 25 percent of the population, nearly two million people, were exterminated in just three years. Those experiences, combined with the violence experienced while traveling to the United States, probably lead some refugees into accepting violence as a way of life. Violence became a tool to use with little regard to the consequences of its use. This exposure and use of violence by no way justifies the brutality these gangs use against their victims. This information is presented to help understand why these gangs use the violence. It also tends to show that violence is a learned behavior.

In the early to mid 1980s it was once thought Southeast Asian street gangs developed a unique behavior for a street gang. Many of these gang members developed an ability to involve intelligent, school-attending juveniles in criminal activity. Some Southeast Asian street gang members literally lead a double life. Excellent students and good family members; yet they are involved in gang activity. As one 16-year-old Southeast Asian street gang member told me, "... *if I do good in school my parents don't hassle me... I get to do whatever I want as long as I get good grades."* It is not surprising to find that as a whole that Southeast Asian gang members go to school and often maintain excellent grades.

In the early 1990s, at a southern California college, four Vietnamese engineering students were arrested for committing home invasion robberies. These gang members actually represent a small percentage of the total Southeast Asian street gang population. For this example, the uniqueness is that they were college students in good standing at school. They were involved in home invasion robberies to earn extra money and for the thrill of the crime. This is not a unique behavior; many gang members led double lives and have effectively hidden their gang membership and activity.

It is not uncommon to find Asian street gang members enrolled in local colleges and universities. Formal education is important to some Asian gang members. These gang members tend to be good students and successfully earn college degrees. In one case a Vietnamese student who was active with his gang paid his way through college by using profits he made selling drugs.

At one time Southeast Asian street gangs were considered to be somewhat disorganized by American standards for street gangs. Nevertheless, in regard to the ability to initiate and conduct illegal activity, they surpass the traditional Western street gangs in terms of methods and sophistication of criminal activity.

Some anecdotal law enforcement evidence suggested that leadership within these gangs may change depending on the type of criminal activity the gang is involved in. In fact, some Southeast Asian street gangs have been known to allow a leadership change depending on the location of the crime or if a member has particular knowledge of the potential victim(s).

The weapon of choice for Southeast Asian gang members is usually an automatic or semi-automatic firearm. During the mid 1990s some Southeast Asian gang members admitted they felt outclassed in size and weight when fighting other gang members and semi-automatic or automatic weapons would even up the odds. Southeast gangs tend to prefer weapons of a larger caliber and/or a weapon with a large magazine capacity. But remember gang members can use any type of weapon.

Unlike most traditional western street gangs, the Southeast Asian gang members usually will not go to great lengths to defend their gang's name. However, as a group Southeast Asian gang members tend to be quick to respond to an individual insult that causes the gang member to lose face, honor or respect. Personal respect is important to any gang member. Southeast Asian gang members tend to react more rapidly and quickly to salvage their personal respect and reputation. This behavior may in part be culturally based.

The California Department of Justice estimates that there could be as many as 15,000 Asian gang members in the state. The majority is representative of Vietnamese, Laotian and Cambodian gangs; and their members vary in age from 13-35 years old. Gangs have names like the Natoma Boys, Tiny Rascals Gang, Black Dragons, Triad Boyz, and the Street Killer Boys (www.cgiaonline.org/gangs2000/asian90s.html). The Wah Ching gang affiliates with Blood gangs and identifies with the red color. Their arch rival the Asian Boyz aligns with Crip gangs and identifies with the blue color.

Based on ethnicity Cambodian, Hmong and Laotian street gangs developed and have spread throughout the United States. The Tiny Rascal Gang (TRG) is probably the most well known of these ethnic based gangs. TRG initially formed in Long Beach, California. There was a female counterpart gang that associated with TRG. It was known as LRG, the Lady Rascal Gang. However in the mid 1990's LRG was disbanded and the female members were able to join the once all male gang. TRG effectively became a co-ed Asian street gang.

Membership

Asian youth who belong to a street gang that is structured like this have additional responsibilities. Members from one clique will back up members from another clique even if they are based in another county. Who is ever is a rival of one clique is a rival with all the cliques, as long as the cliques belong to the same gang.

Some gang membership can be based in extended family or neighborhood and school friends. Some Southeast Asian gangs evolved from a small group of students or friends that grew up in the same neighborhood and went to the same schools. The genesis of the gang seems cloudy because the members will often explain that they never considered themselves as a gang. Some groups referred to themselves as party crews or "just a bunch of guys."

A closer examination of the group's behavior will indicate otherwise. The matriculation into gang status can be slow. At first the group members might just smoke cigarettes and ditch school together. Parents would be unaware because often both work and during school hours assume their children are at school. As a group, Asian youth tend to be successful at school. Parents assume if the student is doing well in school, then all is well with their child. This attitude is partly based in cultural norms about the educational process.

Delinquent behaviors can transition into fistfights, petty thefts and some drug abuse. As the group matures usually one of three things can happen.

The group can form into a street gang. They will formally adopt a gang name (if they already haven't) and can ally itself with other street gangs, as well as develop rivals.

A second change might provide a vehicle so that the group becomes part of an existing street gang. Its membership is recruited into another larger gang and becomes part of that organization.

Lastly, the group maintains the belief that it is not a street gang and the members will continue to get involved in more serious criminal activity.

The caveat is that with any choice the members adopt behaviors and psychology that are consistent with street gangs. In fact, even at the stage where the group is involved in delinquent behavior it acts as a gang. The fact that the group denies having a name does not disqualify them from being considered as a street gang, especially for the purposes of prosecution.

When law enforcement makes contact with school officials or the parents they are usually met with the impossibility of gang involvement because the student in question is doing well at school, works part time and/or is involved in school activities. In addition, the student has never been arrested and some of the parents are both white-collar professionals living in an affluent area. Therefore, the attitude of the parents and many teaching professionals is that the police are mistaken.

Social-economic status, GPA and arrest records are not criteria for gang membership. Remember a gang member can come from any part of your community, from any social-economic strata, from duel parent homes and from any ethnic background. There is a more detail examination of membership in this chapter under "I Am Not a Gang Member."

Some Indo-Chinese street gangs are forming business relationships with organized criminal groups like Triads and Tongs. For example in Chicago Vietnamese gangs tend to work for the better organized Chinese gangs like the North Side Sings and Hung Mun Tong. The Vietnamese street gangs serve as the "muscle" for these groups. The Red Door (Hung Mun) and its satellite gang, the Hung Ching is composed of underage children who are involved in drug tracking and home invasion robberies (www.ispn.org/asg08107.html)

Turf

For Southeast Asian street gangs the name of the gang does not necessarily imply the gang is from a particular area of the community. For example, the Santa Ana Boys gang has members in Los Angeles, Orange and Riverside counties (California). Probably one of the largest Southeast Asian gang the Tiny Rascal Gang (TRG) draws its membership from Fresno (California) to San Diego. This is a distance of over 400 miles (Frank, 1990). This does not imply that it is also one of the most geographically diverse gangs.

However, TRG gang members have been contacted in Washington, Oregon, Alaska, Idaho, Massachusetts and Texas. Unlike, some Hispanic gangs TRG gang members tend to keep in contact with one another through an informal network. TRG gang members will provide assistance to visiting out of state gang members.

Some Southeast Asian street gangs stay localized and many travel only between cities or counties to commit crime and socialize. Los Angeles based gangs have been known to frequent cafes and clubs in other counties. Although all the members of a particular gang may go to the same high school and live in the same general area, there may be other cliques or sets of the same gang based in another city, county or state. For example, the Wah Ching street gang has several cliques known as "sides." These can include such sets as the East Bay Side, Ken Side, Paul Side, Sonny Side, MP Side, PSS Side, A Side and the Frisco Side (www.wikipedia.or/wiki/List_of_California _street_gangs). All are based in California, but members have been contacted in other states and in Canada.

The non-territorial nature of Southeast Asian street gangs can led to a mobile and nomadic style of crime. Some Southeast Asian gangs can roam between the United States, Mexico and Canada. One time I tracked a Vietnamese gang involved in home invasion robberies in Orange County, California, to San Jose near San Francisco. The gang traveled from there, to Portland, Oregon, Seattle, Washington, Ontario, Canada, and finally to Houston, Texas. These five gang members traveled by car and completed the trip within 30 days. A total of eight home-invasion robberies were reported to law enforcement. Some law enforcement experts believe that only 30% of the home invasion robberies are reported to the authorities. There is a trend for immigrant communities not to report crime to the local police.

When a Southeast Asian gang becomes nomadic; the gang can travel and live in inexpensive motels as a group. The gang members refer to the motel room as the "mo." The room can be used as a temporary headquarters for the gang. The room also becomes a crash pad (safe house) and it is common to find runaways or parolees in these areas. Gang members that travel together are usually a very close-knit group who eat, sleep and commit crimes together.

This group can be the entire gang or a clique of a lager gang. A safe house can be established in cities where the gang decides to commit crime. Crash pads have been located in hotel/motel rooms, apartments and rented residential houses.

Burning

When Southeast Asian street gangs first appeared in California during the late 1970s to early 1980s, law enforcement officers noticed what appeared to be cigarette burn scars on the hands and arms of some suspected gang members. At first, some gang experts believed the youth were victims of some type of parental physical abuse. Gang investigators quickly learned that was not the case. The cigarette burns were self-inflicted. Burning in this fashion was considered an act of bravery and proved commitment and loyalty to the gang. "The *cigarette burn was a sign of being down*," as one 15-year-old female Southeast Asian gang member explained to me.

Although the Southeast Asian gangs started the burning behavior many other types of street gangs also practice cigarette burning. This is an example of how behaviors in the Asian gang culture influenced Occidental street gangs. Normally, the gang member who scars him or herself in this manner is sober, not drunk and not using drugs. The more cigarette burn marks you as unique. It implies that you are the braver and crazier gang member.

Scars

Along with burning some Southeast Asian gang members also cut themselves to form scars. The scarification process is obviously painful but the scars themselves have the same significance as burns and tattoos. They represent that an individual is committed to the gang lifestyle and is violent. A non-gang member seeing scars on a person will almost always assume that the person is a gang member, especially within the Asian community.

The presence of scars, burns and tattoos are very intimidating to non-gang members. This may be due to the cultural attitudes about the body. The general public will shy away from and youth who have these types of body modifications.

Tattoos

As a group Southeast Asian gang members prior to 1990 tended not use tattoos. Since then some Asian gang members have adopted the use of this particular Western street gang membership indicium. Tattoo use by Asian gang members is currently more commonly practiced and encountered. Some Southeast Asian street gang members may use tattoos and also continue the practice of burning and scarring.

If tattoos are used you may find the name or initials of the gang. Tattoos of panthers, dragons, eagles with out-stretched talons, three and or five dot tattoos, gang names and monikers are commonly seen. Youth who are part of gang can also wear a tattoo of four or five T's. Each of the T's represents a Vietnamese word that begins with the letter T. The words are: Tinh for love; Tien for money; Tu for prison; Toi for crime, and Thu for revenge. The T's tattoo can also be found on Southeast Asian gang members who have done state prison or California Youth Authority (CYA) time. However, incarceration is not required to sport the T tattoo. The T tattoo is an example of a generic gang tattoo. This tattoo is not part of normal body art and is used solely within the street gang culture. However having the tattoo is not evidence in itself of gang membership.

The Ts can be located on the back, stomach, neck and arms. Recently, Vietnamese gang members have been using tattoos that are common at the county jail level. Some gang experts feel that tattoos can be an indicator of gang commitment. For example at one time in Orange County, California, the five-pointed star was also being used to indicate a veteran of county jail. This is an example of Asian gangs adopting and using Occidental gang indicia.

I mentioned two other commonly seen tattoos used by Asian gang members. They are generic tattoos and do not confirm membership to a specific gang however, they are only seen on gang members. The three dots tattoo is usually in the shape of a triangle. It is the same tattoo used by Latino gang members and now seen within Southeast Asian gang circles. For Southeast Asian gang members the three dots represent the Vietnamese phrase "Toi O Can Gica" which means "I care for nothing." It is the Southeast Asian gang member's way of saying "mi vida loca," the Spanish phrase for my crazy life. The saying refers to the unpredictable life style of a gang member.

There is a second tattoo that is only found on youth who are members or associates of a Southeast Asian street gang. Remember this is a generic tattoo and cannot confirm membership to a particular gang. It is an arrangement of five dots forming a square, with one dot in the middle, like the face of a die. Each dot represents a Vietnamese word and the phrase is "Tu Hai Giai Huynh De" which translates to "a group of good friends."

The five and three-dot tattoo are also sometimes seen in youth who do not belong to a particular street gang, but who identify themselves with the criminal aspect of gang life. This tattoo will aid gang members to hire them as part time help for criminal activity. Gang members will look for youth who have this tattoo. Some youth who wear this tattoo are sort of mercenary gang members. They'll help any gang for one reason, because their participation in criminal activity nets them money. For example, these mercenary gang members may help with a home invasion robbery when there are not enough gang's members to complete the crime. These in essence become gang members for hire because while they are assisting a particular gang they become part of that gang. This behavior is not encountered in Hispanic or African-American street gangs.

While on an extradition during the mid 1990s the Southeast Asian gang member that I was bringing back to California indicated the five-dot tattoo he was wearing was another way to wear the five T tattoo. According to this gang member each dot represented one of the letters in the five T tattoo. This version of the five-dot definition has gained some popularity with some Vietnamese gang members.

Another type of tattoo commonly seen on Southeast Asian gang members is the word Vietnam or a map of Vietnam. Southeast Asian gang members have suggested these two tattoos can represent Yellow Pride, pride in the Southeast Asian race. It is also a generic type of tattoo only seen on Asian gang members. It has also been my experience that non-gang members do not wear the three or five dot or the five T tattoos. I have never encountered a non-gang member sporting the three or five dot tattoo. And conversely, I have encountered many Asian gang members who do have these tattoos.

Regardless of the number and type of tattoos most Southeast Asian gang members will deny gang membership. This is especially true for many Asian youth who get involved in street gang life. During the late 1990s and 2000s it was increasingly more common to arrest Asian gang members that had no tattoos.

When Cambodians refugees initially arrived in Southern California they settled in less advantaged neighborhoods. As a result, they associated and were influenced by the existing street gangs. Many Cambodian gang members emulated the stylized dress of the Hispanic and Samoan street gangs. Some Cambodian gang members tend to dress like traditional Latino gang members.

Cambodian gang members were quick to adopt and use Western street gangs membership behaviors. This included the use of gang tattoos, gang nicknames and the gang attire of Western street gangs. Cambodian gang members are somewhat proud of their membership, and tend to acknowledge it when asked. Interestingly, Cambodian gangs were the first of the Southeast Asian street gangs to exclude the issue of race as a factor for membership. You could and still can be of any ethnicity and belong to a Cambodian street gang.

The Laotian and Hmong refugee youth formed street gangs much like the Vietnamese and Cambodians. There is a significantly lower population of this Laotian and Hmong refugees and as a result the gangs that are active today tend to be of mixed ethnicity. Laotian-Hmong gangs have also generally allied themselves with the Cambodian street gangs.

The majority of Laotian-Hmong refugees settled in small cities in the central valley area of California, north of Los Angeles. The largest Cambodian population seems to be concentrated in the Long Beach, California area. However, these gang members have been contacted throughout California and the West and can found almost anywhere in the United States. For example, Cambodian gang members from the Tiny Rascal Gang (TRG) have been contacted in Anchorage, Alaska and Chicago, Illinois.

Criminal Activity

As a group Southeast Asian street gangs have become experts in extortion, burglary and auto theft. At one time they were the specialists in computer store take-over robberies and computer chip thefts. Some Southeast Asian gangs also traffic illegal drugs like cocaine, marijuana, heroin and ecstasy. Since many Southeast Asian gang members frequent expensive nightclubs and after hour parties there is a market for ecstasy and other drugs. Successful Southeast Asian gang members tend to drive expensive import cars that are customized. Some gang members also get actively involved in the street-racing scene. It is not uncommon to find out that expensive modifications were made to the cars.

Other characteristics that make Asian gangs a little different from Occidental street gangs is an informal pledge of secrecy; the ability to adapt and overcome law enforcement efforts against them and a sheer determination to succeed. History may have played a part in the development of these characteristics (Nye, 2004).

However, home invasion robberies were one crime that made Southeast Asian street gangs well known. Home invasion robberies were once a specialty crime of these gangs. However, home invasion takeover robberies are now committed by different gangs.

Home Invasion Robbery

Home-invasion robbery at one time was thought to be the specialty crime of only Asian street gangs, especially the Southeast Asian gangs. The characteristic that makes the Asian street gang method of home invasion robbery unique is the amount of planning and the execution of the robbery. All Southeast Asian street gangs seem to ethnically target their home invasion robbery victims. In other words, they prey on their own people. However, all types of gangs including Hispanic, African-American, Jamaican, Motorcycle, prison and Skinhead gangs have committed home invasion style robberies.

Once a target is picked, information is collected on the family. How many people are in the family? Where do they hide the valuables? Is there an alarm system? What time do they leave for work or school? It is not uncommon to find out that a thorough background check was completed before the robbery took place. Or that the victim and family were under surveillance for 5-10 days before the home invasion was attempted. With the advent of the Internet do not be surprised to determine that an online search was completed on the victims before the robbery was committed.

It is also common for Asian gang members to follow their targeted victim(s) to and from home and work. One Vietnamese gang member told me that his gang followed the targeted family for three days before committing the robbery. Sometimes female gang members or associates can be used to help collect intelligence on the victim's family many times from the victim's school age children. Female associates or gang members would befriend these students in order to gain information on the family's routines.

Often a rouse is used to gain entry into a house and a female associate or gang member will be used. The rouse is a trick that is used to gain access to the house. One gang member or associate goes to the door and asks for some kind of help, directions, a friend, use of the telephone, or medical help. Or a female who claims to be a school friend needs to return a music CD, video game or video. Once the door is opened, male gang members force entry into the house usually at gunpoint. All the occupants are herded into one room where they are bound with duct tape, electrical or telephone cord, rope or even articles of clothing.

Sometimes, stolen and/or borrowed cars are used for the actual robbery and the getaway. A few times a second car is used for blocking potential police interference or a second car is used as the real get a way vehicle. This type of practice has been documented by several law enforcement agencies in Southern California. This is also a common practice used by other street gangs. For example, gang members from different L.A. based Crip sets go in to another county to commit a bank robbery. They drive away from the scene in an unreported stolen car, then within a few blocks of the crime scene the robbers switch to second vehicle, a cold car to make their escape.

Asian youth have started participating in home invasion robberies as young as 14 or 15 years old and can be heavily involved by the time they are 15 or 16 years old. Asian youth as young 13 years old have reportedly been involved in home invasion robberies (Frank, 1990). This would be consistent with reported gang activity in Chicago where underage youth participate in home invasion robberies.

Once inside the victim's home many questions are asked. Answers are demanded. Where are the valuables? Where is the cash money? Are there any precious stones? Do you have gold or silver? Since many Asian refugees and immigrants had distrust for the American banking system, most Asian refugee and immigrant families tended to keep valuables and cash at home. Cash can also be converted into gold, silver, or precious stones. Asian gang members know and understand this culturally based practice and take advantage of this knowledge.

What characterizes the home invasion robbery is that if there is any delay or resistance by the victim-family members to give up their cash and valuables it results in an immediate physical assault. Some assaults are so severe that they qualify for torture under penal code definitions.

Here are a few examples of the type of violence I am attempting to describe. These reports come from victims of home invasion robberies. One victim reported that a toddler was hung upside down over a toilet and continually dunked head first in the water until the parents provided the requested information.

Another described how a loaded .45 caliber semi-automatic pistol was inserted into a child's mouth, in front of the parents. The child's life was threatened if the information is not given. Other forms of torture include having a mother's throat slowly cut with a knife until the information is given, or shooting a victim in the leg. In a few reported cases young female family members were sexually assaulted.

Sometimes young children are separated from their parents and scared. The parents are blindfolded and hear their children scream in terror. Many times no physical harm befalls the children; the tactic is used as psychological torture, compelling and forcing the parents into submission and cooperation because they believe their children are being tortured.

In a 1995 case in San Bernardino County, California, an entire family of five was shot. The father watched in what had to be absolute horror as his three children were shot. Two died and miraculously his 3-year-old son survived. Then he had to endure his wife being tortured by having her teeth pulled out, before being shot execution style. The man was then also executed, shot in the head.

Home invasion robberies can be brutal and last hours. This means the victim-family members are under siege. It is not uncommon to find out the robbers, while in the house, cleaned out the refrigerator.

Once the cash and valuables are collected, the victims are threatened with the loss of their lives if the police are called. In addition, some adult victims commonly say their children's lives are the ones that will be lost if they cooperate with the police, not theirs. With that kind of threat, any parent or sibling would be reluctant to assist the police especially when a gang member threatens to kill the younger family members.

It appears that the Southeast Asian culture inadvertently exerts a tremendous amount of pressure based on fear, intimidation and shame not to report this type of violent crime to the police. As a result, law enforcement has a very limited database to track and prosecute some Southeast Asian gang members. To compound the problem even more, sexual assaults are almost never reported to the authorities, even when the robbery is.

The victims of sexual assault tend to lose face with their family and within the Asian community. Seen in these cultural terms, reporting a sexual assault would be disastrous for the victim and her family by Asian cultural-social standards. Again, the victim often feels the assault is the result of something they did wrong. So in addition to the cultural pressures, the victims tend to blame themselves for the crime. This attitude is sometimes encountered with assault victims from other ethnic groups. It is not just an Asian cultural phenomenon it has to do more with victimology.

The perpetrators may leave the location in the same stolen car they arrived in or they may steal the victim's vehicle to complete their getaway. The switch may be made to confuse the police who may have received a suspect vehicle description from a non-victim witness.

Southeast Asian gang members tend to use violence as a tool. This may help explain why some home invasion robberies became so brutal. The experience of being victimized in a home invasion robbery has lasting traumatic effects on the victims. Many times small children or elderly family members become the focus of the torture. Enduring this event is traumatic enough and because of cultural taboos is often kept within the family. Therefore, all too often victims tend not to seek appropriate psychological assistance. This can have long term psychological effects on the surviving victims and their family.

There are groups of Southeast Asian criminals who claim no gang membership at all. The financial incentive becomes so alluring that a non-member will help a gang with a home invasion robbery for a cut of the profit. When a gang home invasion robbery team is short a member, one is hired. These for hire robbery team members can be found at billiard halls and cafes that are frequented by local gangs. These for hire team members become part of the gang on a temporary basis.

In fact, rival Southeast Asian gang members have at times been known to assist each other in attempting and completing home invasions, just as some of the Blood and Crip gang members have worked together to sell crack in another state. A well-planned home invasion robbery has netted the robbery team 50,000 to over 100,000 dollars in cash, jewelry and gold.

A few times victims have been able to get a 911 call out to the police as the robbery began. Frequently these calls were received as incomplete 911 calls and field officers were dispatched to investigate. After arriving, police attempted to make contact with the residents. Sometimes the robbers would answer the door as if they were the homeowners. They would tell the police the call was placed by accident because a child was playing with the telephone. The robbers acted as the homeowner.

In a few cases, responding officers met armed suspects at the door. The point is many times these Asian gang members acted as if they had nothing to lose. This attitude potentially makes these types of dispatched calls extremely dangerous. Unfortunately, police reports indicate that responding police officers have been shot at and ended up in vehicle pursuits with guns being tossed out onto the street by the suspects.

Southeast Asian gangs can be violent and gang motivated homicides are not uncommon. Southeast Asian street gang members have killed to save face or respect. Killing means gaining respect from other gang members and the community. Unfortunately for many gang members assaulting and killing a law enforcement officer brings them a greater degree of respect from their peers.

Residential burglary is another favorite crime of Southeast Asian gang members.

Southeast Asian gang members seem to be more organized than their Occidental counterparts when committing residential burglaries. In Southern California, a group of Vietnamese gang members were stopped by police who found a local phone book with Southeast Asian entries highlighted. The suspects also had a map to the highlighted addresses. It appeared that this daytime burglary team had targeted the Southeast Asian population within this community. Residential burglaries can turn into home invasion robberies if the occupants show up or happen to be in a residence that was thought to be unoccupied.

Another common crime committed by Southeast Asian gangs is strong-arm robberies. Purses or jewelry are literally grabbed off the victim while in a mall or while to their car. Sometimes the theft happens so quick the victim cannot describe the suspect. If the victim struggles the suspect tends to become physical and can assault the victim.

There is a strange business-like attitude about the use of deadly force. It is as if deadly force was just a part of everyday life. Some Southeast Asian gang members seem to have little or no remorse for their use of violence; even if the use of force results in a death during the commission of a crime. If an innocent person is injured or killed often it is considered destiny. A 16-year-old Vietnamese gang member once told me, "...*they (victims) would have gotten hurt or killed anyway.*" In Southern California there have been several incidents where male gang members have helped female gang members assault rival female gangs. Sometimes there can be a working alliance between male and female gangs.

Non-violent Crime

Cellular Telephone Cloning

This type of theft applied to the old analog cellular telephones and was a great example of how gangs can get involved in non-violent crime. Many cellular telephone owners did not realize that when an analog cellular telephone was on it emitted its telephone number, mobile identification number, (MIN) and its electronic serial number (ESN) every ten or fifteen minutes. These codes help the telephone track itself within the cellular communication system.

Some gang members obtained a special device that read and captured these electronic signals. It was known as a MIN-ESN reader. This is an electronic device that captured and stored MIN-ESN combinations while they are being transmitted by the cellular telephone. The MIN-ESN reader stores this information and then it could be retrieved by reading the numbers and writing them down or by down loading the MIN-ESN combinations into a lap or desktop computer. The MIN-ESN combination is specific to each cellular telephone. There is only one set per telephone subscriber.

These combinations were then re-programmed into several other cellular telephones. These telephones could be stolen or legitimately purchased. The cloned cellular telephones were then sold on the street for about $75.00 to $100.00. Ten to twenty people might simultaneously have unlimited use of the same cellular telephone number.

Southeast Asian street gang members did not own the market in this area. Anyone with a computer, the right software, hardware and access to the MIN-ESN combination sets could clone analog cellular telephones. However, law enforcement professionals frequently contacted

Southeast Asian gang members with cloned cellular telephones. With the advent and popularity of digital mobile telephone service old school cloning practices have stopped. However, this was not until the telephone companies and legitimate service prescribers were victimized for major losses.

This is no longer the case as digital telephone technology currently prevents this from happening. Gangs are Darwinistic in nature. They as a cohort are not a static phenomenon. As technology changes so do some gangs. Currently, gang members have access to instant messaging, telephones with Internet capability, lap top computers that can use programs like Skype and other Internet telephony software. Some gangs have become very sophisticated in the use of technology.

Fraud

Non-violent white-collar crime continues to be a criminal specialty for Southeast Asian gangs. It was common for Southeast Asian gangs to be involved in all types of check and credit card fraud. However, currently many other types of street gangs are involved in this type of crime. Counterfeit check fraud is easy to complete with a computer. A "borrowed" payroll check(s)are scanned into a computer. A computer program is then used to modify the information that was scanned in. The fraudulent payroll checks are then printed out with the names of gang associates. The checks are cashed at local businesses and banks.

One commonly employed West Coast trick is to cash checks that are drawn from a company in the East Coast and vice versa. A legitimate company could easily lose up to $90,000 to $100,000 in a month and would not find out until the bank statement arrives. Southeast Asian gangs have also been involved in the manufacture of fraudulent travelers' checks. All these are good examples of paper fraud operations a non-violent gang crime. This has become as easy way to make money with little or no criminal exposure.

Credit cards can also be altered or fraudulently manufactured using easily obtainable computer software. A lap top computer and a magnetic strip reader are needed. Both are easily obtainable and routinely used. Credit card fraud is a million dollar business and can ruin legitimate consumer credit ratings. Credit card companies have responded by changing procedures and adding more security features to the cards.

Currently, ID theft is a popular crime that some gangs get involved in. Fraudulently obtaining credit profiles and credit information like social security number are part of this type of crime. These are examples of credit fraud. Identity theft has become a major issue and is a commonly committed crime.

Even more lucrative are high end-technical counterfeit operations that include the illegal duplication of movies, music and computer software. These types of operations have become the operation of choice for some Asian street gangs. The success of the counterfeit operations has hinged on advanced computer technology, Gray and Black-market cash, local and international connections. It has generated millions of dollars of non-recorded income and has generated millions of dollars of lost income for the victims.

CD duplication machines are commonly used in legitimate business practices. However, some unscrupulous business owners sometimes use their machines to illegally duplicate thousands of copies of copyrighted material that includes music, movies and computer software. The automated duplication processes can produce thousands of CD's in just a few hours.

The replicator machines that actually produce the printed CD can cost up to $1 million dollars each and automated printing machines can cost up to $80,000 each. It seems like the expense to start a business out weights the potential profit, but it does not. The Gray and Black markets provide start up cash and a vehicle for distribution. Unfortunately a common practice is to run counterfeit operations in the middle of legitimate manufacturing processes. This effectively hides the counterfeit operation and makes it extremely difficult to uncover.

The process is not complicated, a legitimate music CD, movie DVD or VHS tape is purchased. A special master computer tape is made from the original legal copy. The tape is known as a DLT tape. It is taken to another location where a circular metal device called a stamper is made from the DLT tape. The stamper becomes the CD master because the information that was on the DLT tape is transferred to the stamper. All copies are imprinted with the information that is on the stamper through a process in the replicator machine. Stampers can cost about $400 to $500 to make.

Once the stamper is made it is place in an automated replicator machine and thousands of copies can be made. A good stamper will provide 50,000 copies or more. Once the CD's are made, they have to be labeled. This can be done with a silkscreen or photo etching operation or with an automated printed machine. Using automation helps produce more copies and helps keep containments out of the duplication process.

So those specials you see advertised on the Internet like the 2006 XP Windows Operating System for $99 or the 2006 Norton's Utilities System for $29 are probably cloned versions of those software systems. Easy and quick non-reportable income can be generated by selling cloned CD's at swamp meets and at small retail shops or via mail order (Valdez, 2006).

Another business that street gangs can be involved in the counterfeit production of identification which can include birth certificates, green cards, driver licenses and passports.

Although not always highlighted as gang related crime, but many times involves street gang members in the formula is the crime of human trafficking. In 2006, the U.S. Department of Justice estimated that there were over 12 million undocumented immigrants in the United States. Even thought the majority may be of Latino ethnicity there are still a number of Canadians, Europeans and Asian undocumented immigrants and refugees living in the country. Street gang members can be involved as the facilitators and transporters once illegal immigrants are in the country.

Threats

Non-verbal threats in the form of intimidation can be given with a mere look within the Southeast Asian community. This look sometimes called a "mad dog" and often results in the intimidation of a victim or witness. The majority of the Southeast Asian community fears the revenge capabilities of these street gangs because of their violent reputation and when intimidated witnesses and victims often cease to cooperate with law enforcement and prosecution. Since the Southeast Asian community tends to be so close knit, like home invasion robberies, witness intimidation tends to be seldom reported.

I have arrested Vietnamese gang members in court, during witness testimony for this look. Some Southeast gang members can be brazen and will openly defy law enforcement. The display of gang related tattoos; burns and scars to non-gang member can also have the same effect as the mad dog stare. All are a form of silent non-verbal intimidation that is effectively used within the Southeast Asian community. Therefore understanding culture and being able to identify these behaviors becomes an important part in dealing with minority groups.

Female Gangs

Young Southeast Asian women female youth have also formed all-female street gangs. In Asian society, the woman's role has traditionally been one of subservience. This cultural tradition was continued in the initial development and activity of these all-female gangs. Initially, females were delegated to support roles in activity conducted by the male gang members. Over time this secondary role must have led to a high degree of frustration for these women, especially after being exposed to the modern western way of life for women.

Female Southeast Asian gangs usually allied themselves to one Southeast Asian male gang. The girl gang members normally fought with females who associated with rival male gangs. In the early 1980s the existence of all female Southeast Asian gangs was confirmed. Currently, some Southeast Asian female gangs still exist today. Many are now independent of any particular male gang affiliation. Southeast Asian female gang members now can carry concealed firearms; they can also be involved in assaults and traffic narcotics. Refer the chapter on female gangs for more details.

Female gang members have been recruited by some Asian gangs to carry weapons for male members and to help male members in criminal activity. Some female gang members assist with home invasion and jewelry store robberies. Female Asian gangs can use names like Wally Girls, Pomona Girls, Lady Rascals, Innocent Bitch Killers and the Dirty Punks. Female gangs can have 20 to 50 members between 13 and 20 years-old (www.cgiaonline.org/gangs2000/asian90s.html).

I Am Not In A Gang

I have mentioned the proverbial phrase, "I am not in a gang" a few times in this chapter. Understanding that some Asian gang members do not have to go through an initiation ritual to belong to a gang is a helpful start in understanding that statement. In fact, for many Asian gang members there might not be a formal recognition that the group they belong to is a street gang, at least until they get arrested for a gang related crime.

The genesis of some Asian street gangs can initially develop from a small group of friends. Sometimes, they are schoolmates or neighbors who basically grow up together. They may be bound together as friends because they live close to one another, they may be extended family or they may simply be friends at school. Family or friendship can act as culturally based glue that binds the youth together as a gang. Some Asian gang members have confided to me that they have known each other since first or second grade. They were in their early to late teens before they realized they were members of a street gang.

Being friends does not qualify the group as a gang. It is the gang behavior that is introduced into the group that changes it. This influence does not have to be the formal introduction of a gang member into the group, although this has happened. The motivation for change may be as simple as the group members see other young people their age with money, cars, nice clothes, status and girls and they want the same. Street savvy youth know that gang related criminal activity is a good way to gain a reputation and to earn money, tax free money. Drug sales, auto burglaries, residential burglaries, counterfeit identification, credit cards and checks offer a way to earn a lot of money for a high school age youth.

The group's initial criminal activity may start out as simple petty thefts, or a sale of single marijuana cigarette. A few members may commit a petty theft together or they may simply get into a fight together. Something happens and the line that separates the group of friends to a gang is crossed. That line is criminal activity. Once that is done, the group of friends has become a street gang. Often, the group may simply dabble in criminal activity that goes unnoticed or un-investigated. It can start with cigarette smoking, drinking and ditching school. These delinquent behaviors are many times viewed as transient behaviors or "part of growing up" by members of society and tend to be easily concealable from parents, teachers and employers.

The key becomes that for most youth those behaviors are transitory in nature. Doing those things does not become a way of life. That seems to be a difference between non-gang and gang groups. Candidly speaking, I think it is safe to say that some delinquent behavior is a normal part of maturation.

We have all participated in those types of delinquent behaviors, but stopped. For youth groups that evolve into a gang these behaviors become a part of normal life and tend to escalate with time. Early on, by themselves they are non-violent, delinquent behaviors that many teachers, parents and law enforcement would not think twice about.

The issue is that the delinquent behaviors act like a glue just as the friendship did. The glue becomes stronger for those who remain in the group. Dabbling in delinquent type behavior for an extended period can lead to more serious criminal behavior over time. The group may also become smaller as members move, grow out of the group or get arrested. The cadre remains bound by common experiences and common goals make money, save face, gain respect and have fun.

Sometimes rivalries can start between similar groups when the small groups get into competition for the same women, music, parties or the sales of drugs. The turning event may occur when a bully at school picks on one of the members. The event may even occur when a known gang recognizes the group as a rival gang and challenges or attacks the membership. This causes the group of friends to unify further because now they have a common enemy or rival. As the rivalry escalates, violence is used and the membership becomes more united.

Usually by the time these youth reach high school the behaviors have not changed. Now older and a little more street wise, these groups may have interacted with the neighborhood street gangs. Maybe some of the members "hangout" with a street gang or are friends of street gang members. Sometimes older street gang members will solicit members of this group to help with drug sales or non-violent crime.

The introduction into the street gang life can be subtle. There may be no jumping in rituals. The members may not use monikers and or tattoos. But the street gang mentality seed is planted through contacts with street gang members and is shown through related behaviors. The gang psychology is well developed. At the same time these youth will have excellent academic grades and performance and may even work part time.

For example, an Asian Boyz gang member got straight A's in school, volunteered at a hospital and delivered jewelry while he was involved in a five crime spree in 1995 that left seven people dead. This gang member was eventually convicted after he was arrested. Asian gang members don't necessarily hail from broken homes or live in poverty. Many Asian gang members come from affluent families and live double lives (www.lang.pasadenastarnews .com).

As these Asian youth get older they in turn may solicit the help of yet younger Asian youth. A kind of hierarchy develops. The older youth may even distance themselves from the primary group. Divisions of the street gang may develop based on age or geographical location. Yet all the members would most likely tell you they do not belong to a gang. I have heard *"we are just a group of friends"* used by Asian youth who belong to a gang.

In debriefing such Asian gang members they have confided they grew up with a small group of friends, either from school or where they lived. Ditching school, drinking and smoking tied the group together. Besides for many of these youth both parents worked or a single parent worked long hours to make ends meet. The long work hours provided the opportunity for the youth to escape school. Their parent(s) would never know. The work schedule of parents seemed to offer some unique advantages to these youth, not whether or not they had two parents or one.

These Asian gang members went on to further describe that as a group they got away with a lot of crime. Burglary and drug sales were often mentioned. Most of the crime was committed to get money to "play" with. Money for these Asian youth brought girls, guns, cars and status. As more and more money was desired the frequency of criminal behavior increased. As one Asian gang member told me, *"I did not realize I was in a gang until it was too late."* Many Asian gang members do not realize they are in a gang because of long term friendship based relationships they have with other members. Frankly, denial also plays an important role here.

For some Asian youth criminal behavior is an accepted and welcomed part of a life style. The life style is not recognized as the Asian gang life style until the members get arrested for a crime or they grow out of the street gang. Unfortunately, some members do not ever leave.

Sadly, most of the younger members do not recognize or associate their behavior with the street gang culture until they get involved in a criminal case.

The older gang members can become role models for younger gang members who will put in work for their mentors or Dai Lo (older brother) who are the gang's leaders. Sometimes, Dia-los attempt to insulate themselves from the gang's membership by limiting their direct involvement. This can prevent them from being involved in a criminal case.

Reasons for attempting to justify non-gang membership have been, *"we have no tattoos"*, *"we are in school"* or *"we have never been arrested."* The general denial of gang membership is based on these characteristics and consistent with modern day membership in Asian street gangs. The use of traditional gang indicia does not have be a part of Asian street gang membership. It is the behavior that becomes the major indicator.

Sometimes the leadership in Asian street gangs will not have formal names and remain informal in operation. Other times there are formal operating procedures along with specific ranks for the members. Gang members may have a Dai Lo (older brother) who is a section leader or the Dai Lo may report to an inner circle of older gang members.

It is common to find out that some Asian gang members literally lead double lives. They may be young successful high school or college students, businessmen, even married with children and still maintain active membership and participation with an Asian street gang. This phenomenon is also encountered in other types of street gangs.

Cliques or sets of the same Asian gang may develop when a member moves out of the area. The gang member may take the gang name with them and establish a new clique of the gang. There can be informal or formal ties to the original gang. As Asian gang members continue to move so does the gang and it can continue to grow in size. Two very common reasons why a gang member moves are the family is relocating because of employment or the parents move into a more affluent community.

Do we have street gang operating here? The answer is yes. Many parents and gang members would deny it. However, the behaviors of the group's members would tend to support the diagnosis that a gang is operating and members are gang members.

Trends

Since the appearance of Southeast Asian street gangs in the early 1980s many changes have been observed with behaviors, practices and criminal activities. First and second generation Southeast Asian street gang members can be found throughout the country but at the same frequency generational Hispanic gang members are found. These gang members tend to be much more accustomed to western ways than their predecessors of the 1980s. Because of their American birth these gang members also more savvy about police practices and will deny gang membership. Many display none of the traditional membership indicia associated with the Western gang sub-culture.

Southeast Asian gangs can be found in many parts of the country, but they are still concentrated along the west coast, especially in California and in the Northeast, especially in New York. Drug and gun trafficking have provided the vehicle for west coast based Asian gangs to establish business partnerships with east coast based Asian street gangs.

Some older gang members like those who are 19-28 years old still maintain limited contact with street gangs and tend to focus more on non-violent white-collar type crime. Specialties in the production and sales of counterfeit CDs, video tapes, computer software, travelers' checks, remarked computer CPUs, fraudulent identification and drug sales have become sources of income for some older Asian street gang members.

These older gang members can be very mobile and may have been rivals with each other when younger. It is not uncommon to find older gang members from different gangs working together committing non-violent crime or being used as muscle for an Asian organized crime groups.

With the advent of computers, the easy access to stock papers and the use of the World Wide Web, a new class of street gang crime has emerged, non-violent financial crime. Asian gangs use the Internet very effectively and some gangs have followed the lead of other gangs in posting gang Web pages, gang photos and history. Some Asian street gangs have also begun to get involved in the sale of counterfeit cigarettes and other counterfeit products in the gray markets.

Organized Crime Groups

Triads

When discussing Asian gang life some of us wonder about the more sophisticated criminal groups that tend to recruit street gang members into organized criminal activity. As with other types of organized groups, Asian career criminals also have unique indicia and behavior characteristics. The oldest known Asian associations are the Chinese Triad groups. The Triads are related historically to secret societies, whose primary aim was originally patriotic, the re-establishment of the Chinese as the rulers of China.

The term Triad is an English term used to describe the symbol used by these Chinese secret groups, a triangle representing the powers of heaven, earth and man. Triad members were bound by secret oaths to a blood brotherhood, whose aim was overthrowing the foreign conquerors in order to restore of the House of Ming to the throne of China. The oaths were partially based in religion (Taoism or Buddhism) that emphasized the family. The religions had aspects of ancestor worship and combined shamanism and alchemy. So they were almost tailor made for use by secret societies. Term has also been used to name a few local Asian street gangs. These gangs are not connected to the Triads as discussed here. They simply use the same name.

The first reference to a secret society that may have been a precursor to modern day Triads was the Red Eyebrows around 9 AD. Members of this group rouged their eyebrows and originated in the Shantung province. Modern day Triad societies are generally believed to have started in the seventeenth century. Secrecy played an important part for the Triad member because if membership was discovered it meant almost certain torture and death. Therefore, all members adhered to a strict code of secrecy and believed that silence is paramount towards the success of their operations. Triad societies used secret hand signs to describe ones membership and position within the group (Badley, 1988 and Booth, 1990). The use of hand signs by modern day gang members is a practice that is almost 2000 years old.

Fear was the tool used to hinder public and government actions, by making it known that death was near for anyone who opposed the membership. This secrecy and fear coupled with mystic initiation rites made the Triad Societies a powerful force within the Chinese community. Triads were directly responsible for certain rulers attaining positions of power. As a result, the Triads received special rewards and grew even more influential. It appears the Triad Societies had become the first political action groups. However, over time some Triad societies were persecuted by the very same rulers they help put into power.

Many historians believe the Triad Societies had seized control of the Chinese labor market by the mid 1850s. China's ruler responded by sending his imperial troops to arrest all Triad members in an effort to bring an end to these societies. Many Triad members fled to Hong Kong where they remained. Between 1857 and 1912, new branches of the Triad Societies were set up just as quickly as the fleeing Triad members would arrive.

Today, Triad Societies remain criminally active in Hong Kong. No one society has a monopoly on any particular criminal enterprise. Unlike Italian organized crime syndicates, there is no Godfather type leader for the organizations. Triad Societies have extended their operations internationally, according to some experts (Badley, 1988).

Currently, initiation into a Triad is still entrenched with ritual and ceremonies. Numerology plays an active role in these rituals and ceremonies, as well as secret handshakes and the use of passwords. Remember all members to further the success of the group practiced secrecy. All the rituals, ceremonies have religious overtones and help form a strong bond of loyalty to the group. The formal initiation rituals that street gangs use serve the same function; to form a strong bond of loyalty to the gang or surrogate family.

By the 1900s, some Triads had changed from political action based groups to criminal cartels involved in opium smuggling, prostitution, protection rackets and many other types of crime. Almost all of the heroin production in Southeast Asia is controlled by these secret societies. This would include the Golden Triangle area (Badley, 1988).

There are a few experts who believe there are two levels of membership in Triad societies. One level involves Chinese street gangs and youth street gangs in the United States. Even though these gang members do not formally claim Triad membership, they model their traditions, operations and gang structure after the Triads, including the use of the Triad name. The second level is formal acceptance and membership in a Triad group (Bresler, Fenton, 1981). In some cases street gangs will act as muscle for the organized criminal group.

It has been estimated that there are more than 57 Triads groups in Hong Kong, some are highly organized and others are street gangs. Triads have also been reported in Taiwan, Macau, Europe, South Africa, and Australia and in North America. Triads that do not mimic street gang behaviors tend to follow a vertical hierarchical leadership. Although it is believed that no central command structure unifies the different factions within a Triad society. Most Triads tend to operate independent of each other (www.pbs.org/wnet/wideangel/shows/elsalvador/handbook.html).

Tongs

There is a second organized group that is part of Asian organized crime culture. These organizations are known as the Tongs. The word Tong comes from the Chinese word Tang, meaning party. Tongs in America were merely Chinese working groups that formed based on the type of work done. Immigrant Chinese workers joined these groups for support and guidance in the new world. Tong membership was also sometimes based on place of birth. In the United States laundry and medicine Tongs are two examples of the types of Tongs formed.

By the 1880s Tongs had developed into formal organizations some with a structured leadership. To avoid the onus of bad publicity when Tongs warred among themselves, the groups changed their names to Benevolent Associations. Membership was limited to only those persons of Chinese descent. The Tongs started out with truly worthwhile objectives but over the years some Tongs changed, especially when criminals began to join them.

Some Tongs have exhibited control by criminals with ties to the Triad groups. The general membership has been tainted with the criminal element in the community. Some Triad and Tong members have been identified as active members of Chinese street gangs such as the Wah Ching, Ghost Shadows and United Bamboo. This becomes anecdotal evidence to support the theory that these organized crime groups have ties to Asian street gangs since it appears the street gangs have become recruitment pools.

In 1997, pursuant to a mandate by Great Britain, Hong Kong was released from British authority. The mainland Chinese communist government will resume all care-taking responsibilities for the city. Some law enforcement officials anticipated a mass exodus of Chinese criminals into the United States. This would include members from Chinese Triad and Tongs.

The impact of the release of Hong Kong by Great Britain has not been fully understood yet. There continues to be an influx of Chinese immigrants and refugees into the United States. Some Tongs located in the United States have attempted to take control of some Asian street gangs. Under the influence and control of a Tong a street gang may become the muscle for this organized crime group. A good example of this mechanism is what happened to the San Francisco faction of the Wah Ching street gang and in Chicago with Hip Sing and On Leong tongs (http://www.ispn.org/asg 08107.html).

Yakuza

The third major group involved in Asian organized crime is of Japanese origin. Japan has the lowest murder rate of any developed country. Handguns are illegal there and a person would usually get his wallet back if lost (www3.tky.3web.ne.jp/~edjacob/ bloodbaths.htm). However, Japan still has its fair share of gang violence. The Japanese National Police call these groups Boryokudan (violent ones). They are more commonly known as Yakuza. Estimates identify about 2,500 groups worldwide with a membership that exceeds 100,000. Historically, the Japanese public with a sort of Robin Hood type image once accepted the Yakuza even though the Yakuza were involved in gambling and prostitution.

The general attitude toward the Yakuza changed when ordinary citizens became targets of their criminal activity. Today, Yakuza groups are typically organized like Italian organized crime families. Members openly claim their association to other Yakuza groups. Each Yakuza group or family has its own distinctive insignia and flag, which are openly displayed at their meeting locations (Badley, 1988).

A large percentage of the Yakuza membership will tattoo themselves with snakes, dragons and mythical figures. These tattoos symbolize the history of the group to which they belong. They also may show the level of membership commitment to a particular organization. The tattoos can cover a significant portion of a member's body, and are seen as a mark of respect in the underworld. Tattoos are sometimes obtained to show ones courage and strength by enduring pain, especially when elaborate designs are placed all over the body.

There are a small number of famous Japanese tattoo artist who still use bamboo needles to apply tattoo designs. Using bamboo needles to apply tattoos is a very painful process and some designs can take days to apply. Enduring this type of pain for such a long time can become a symbolic sign of commitment to the Yakuza.

When a member of the Yakuza makes an error he atones for it by ceremonially cutting off the top digit of his little finger. The member then wraps the severed digit in a white cloth and presents it to his superior. If the apology is accepted, the boss would take the offering and place it in a jar next to the severed digits of other errant followers. The individual, by cutting off his finger, acknowledges his error and is asking for forgiveness. Called Yubisume, this ritual is still practiced (Badley, 1988).

Yakuza activity in the United States has been on the increase since about 1974 for three reasons. The United States has served as 1) a source of weapons, 2) as a place to make investments with excess capital, and 3) as a significant financial base due to the tourist industry, which is heavily influenced by the Yakuza.

Japanese Gang Syndicates

An estimated 40 percent of the 96,000 Japanese street gangsters belong to one of the Big Three gangs, Yamaguchi-Gumi, the Sumiyoshi-Kai or the Inagawa-Kai. There are many other gangs in Japan, but these three seem to dominate most of the activity among the street gangs. Rivalries can develop into bloody wars and because the general crime rate is low the activity can appear overwhelming.

Like other parts of the world, criminal gang activity can include all types of crime. In 1990, the Yumaguchi-Gumi gang was responsible for the fatal shooting of two police officers. According to a 1992 police report, about one in five people sent to prison in Japan is a gang member. Generally speaking gang related street crime mimics the type of crimes committed by their Occidental counterparts.

The Yumaguchi-Gumi is probably the biggest of the street gang syndicates in Japan and one of the largest in the world. The membership is estimated to range from 23,000 to 30,000 people. The gang is based out of western Japan. Historically Harukichi Yamaguchi founded the gang in 1915. Recently the gang has been able to increase in size and strength because of police suppression. The smaller gangs unable to withstand the police pressure have joined the Yumaguchi-Gumi or have yielded their turf.

The second largest gang, Sumiyoshi-Kai has a reported membership of approximately 8,000 to 10,000. The gang is centered in and around Tokyo. Jusaku Abe founded the gang around 1918. Under the current leader, Shigeo Nishigushi, gang operations have expanded into northeast Japan.

The Inagawa-Kai gang syndicate is probably one of the most well known gangs in Japan because of a political-organized crime scandal. The membership is estimated to be only around 7,400 making it the smallest of the Big Three. The political scandal occurred in 1991, when Susumu Ishii, the leader, was linked to top well-known businessmen, conservative politicians and the former Prime Minister Norboru Takeshita. Susumu Iishii died later in 1991 but was believed to have used his underworld influence to help Takeshita win the office in 1987.

Like other countries in the world Japan has enacted special laws to help curb the gang growth and activity. Many proactive steps have been taken to stop gang violence. As in many other countries, the gang violence still continues.

Probably one of the most spectacular gang battles of all times took place in Japan between the Aoyama-kai gang and about 30 or more street gangs under the leadership of Mitani-kumi. It lasted over six hours and involved 1400 to 2000 gang members. The fight began on December 22, 1925 in Kanagawa, Japan. The fight started over a construction contract. The battle erupted over an insult and was fought with pistols, rifles, swords, farm implements and with bare fists. The local police were unable to stop the fight and called the Tokyo police and the Kempei-Tai (the Japanese secret police) and had to declare a state of martial law before the fighting subsided (www3.tky.3web.ne.jp/~edjacob/bloodbaths.htm).

In 1985 a war was raging between the Yamaguchi-gumi and the Ichiwa-kai gangs. The Yamguchi-gumi gang members were looking to retaliate against the Ichiwa-kai gang for the death of one of their leaders. Two Yamaguchi gang members who are still unidentified today located their target at a local bar. The two began casing the bar and planned their attack. Their plan was to have one of them dress up as a woman in order to get close to their target, Susumu Akasada who was lone of the Ichiwa-kai leaders. On October 26, 1985 the normally well protected Akasada was caught with only two body guards next to him. While the cross-dressing gang member was entertaining the patrons the second Yumaguchi-gumi gang member attacked. Akasada was shot five times and the sixth bullet went to one of his body guards. The second body guard was stabbed to death by the cross dressing gang member (www3. tky.3web.ne.jp/~edjacob/ bloodbaths.htm).

Summary

To briefly summarize this chapter you should remember the term Asian is really an umbrella term describing many types of street gangs. Many writers have used the term "Asian" to describe Japanese, Chinese, Korean, South Pacific Island, Indo-Chinese street gangs and organized crime groups. There are Asian street gangs in Southeast Asia, Japan, China, Korea and the Pacific Islands, as well as within the United States. Asian street gangs have been reported operating in Canada,, Australia and New Zealand.

Generally Asian street gangs are nomadic. They will not claim turf like their traditional Latino street gang counterparts. All Asian street gangs and organized crime groups are criminal enterprises. They banded together with one goal in mind, to make money. Asian organized crime groups tend to have a formal leadership structure while most Asian street gangs have no formal leadership structure. There are exceptions to this rule. A few Asian street gangs follow a well-defined and organized leadership. Some leaders try to insulate themselves from the street soldiers.

Some American based Asian gang members can have very affluent backgrounds and will have family ties back to Asia and other countries. Tattoos, self-mutilations and burning have become an important custom for some Asian street gangs and organized crime groups. These body modifications are displayed to show ones loyalty to the group, as a form of association advertisement to rival and peer gang members and to intimidate non-gang members and victims. These gang membership indicia tend to give the wearer status.

Some Asian gangs relate to a stylized dress that is unique to their particular group or is modeled after traditional Latino or African-American street gangs. Asian street gangs may claim an association to an African-American street gang. Although there may be no formal connections the Asian gang will use the reputation of violent sets of Crips or Bloods to enhance their street status.

Many Asian street gang members, especially the Southeast Asians, have a propensity to use violence as a tool. Torture of uncooperative victims is common as well as assaults on responding law enforcement officers. Witness intimidation is used against many victims and their families and is usually not reported.

As the Asian community matriculates into the changing western life, so will so Asian street gangs. You should expect the race barrier for membership to be broken by some Asian street gangs. Do not be surprised if you encounter non-Asian gang members in a normally all-Asian street gang. Gang behaviors that were once only encountered with Asian street gangs can now be observed with some Occidental based street gangs. The reverse is also true. Some Asian street gangs have adopted Western gang customs and behaviors.

All Asian street gangs and organized crime groups tend to victimize citizens from within their own ethnic groups. As a whole, Asian gangs seem to operate with some degree of criminal sophistication when compared to Western street gangs. Often, there will be surveillance and planning before these groups commit a crime.

Trends suggest that some gangs are becoming involved in non-violent crime. The idea of crime for profit has lead some groups into credit card and payroll check fraud. The manufacture of fraudulent travelers checks, pirate videos and cloned music, movie and computer software CDs are a few of the non-violent criminal activities.

Language barriers and ethnic based customs have hindered the general reporting of crime from these communities. There is still distrust within some Asian communities for the law enforcement and judicial systems. Victims of Asian street gang crime are often intimidated by the gang's presence and threats. Issues regarding Asian street gangs and organized crime groups are growing, especially with the recent growth into white-collar criminal activity. These issues potentially could have a major impact on entire communities in the near future.

Social customs and cultural based biases can affect gang membership. For example, many if not most Asian parents are reluctant to share their feelings with their children (Nguyen, 1996).

Kim, Annie (2003)South Korea and Korean-Americans in the United States also see:

http://www2.bc.edu/~brisk/korea.htm#Immigrants_in_the_United_States

www.ispn.org/asg08107.html

www.wikipedia.or/wiki/List_of_California_street_gangs

www3.tky.3web.ne.jp/~edjacob/bloodbaths.htm

www.cgiaonline.org/gangs2000/asian90s.html
www.pbs.org/wnet/wideangel/shows/elsalvador/handbook.html

Tiny Rascal Gang

Law enforcement can anticipate changing gang trends because of the evolving dynamics of the country's street gang population. Asian street gangs have been part of this sub-culture for a number of years, and been evolving like other gangs, but there are number of types of Asian street gangs. Like other gangs, Asian gangs have grown and shrunk in membership size, number and complexity. No street gang is immune from demographics or societal changes. Partly due to their mobility, U.S. Asian street gangs have had an impact internationally and nationwide, especially within the Chinese, Korean, Taiwanese, Japanese, Vietnamese, Laotian and Cambodian communities. Some Asian street gangs have matured into semi-organized crime groups and a few have even established ties with local and international Asian organized crime groups.

An argument could be made that suggests street gangs can become more criminally sophisticated and expand their criminal operations over time (Sullivan and Bunker, 2003). The research describes a maturating process that some street gangs can go through. The behavior template can be applied to different type of street gangs, including some Asian street gangs.

What this all means is street gangs that exhibit the most flexibility seem to grow the quickest, migrate and establish themselves on a national and international basis. This adaptation has been well documented and demonstrated by the 18th Street, Mara Salvatrucha, Black gangster Disciples, Latin Kings, Jamaican and other street gangs. I will also suggest that there is plenty of anecdotal evidence to suggest that more street gangs will use this adaptability. Let's look at a particular Asian gang as another example of the flexible nature of some street gangs.

One of the nation's largest Asian street gang is probably the Tiny Rascal Gang, otherwise known across the country as TRG. However, an interesting question arises. How did this relatively new American street gang get so large in such a short time, especially considering that street gangs have been in the United States since the early 1800s?

History

To understand how and why the Tiny Rascal Gang grew so rapidly, one has to first look at the history of the gang. Within 5 years after the fall of Saigon in 1975, the first Cambodian refugees arrived in California and many settled in the Long Beach area. As with many refugee groups, ethnicity and limited English speaking ability helped create a barrier that isolated the Cambodian people from the existing mainstream society. That barrier was a form of class distinction based on bias, directed at the new immigrant groups. The general community often viewed these immigrant groups as social outcasts. This was especially true when the

Cambodians were looked at by other ethnic based groups like the Indo-Chinese (Southeast Asian) and local Hispanics.

If you remember similar circumstances led to the formation of the Irish street gangs during the 1800s. There appears to be a cycle that involves newly arrived immigrant groups. Newly arrived immigrant groups are often socially separated even with their own race. This dynamic can lead to many processes that affect the immigrant family. Gangs begin with an excluded group and the exclusion can be real or perceived (Valdemar, 1996).

For example, a familiar struggle developed within the some Cambodian refugee families. Many Cambodian youths wanted to become westernized, so they could be accepted into the general youth population. This pressure tended to be the strongest at the junior and high school levels. Sometimes, the conversion process was in direct conflict with many of traditional Cambodian customs and family philosophies. Some Cambodian youth ended up feeling resentment towards their families and certain aspects of their culture. This resentment was only increased as the western influence became stronger and the families put more pressure on the young to adhere to the traditional customs. This is sometimes referred to as culture shock. Add to this equation a slender build, fear of authority and unfamiliarity with a new country and it becomes easy to understand why some Cambodian youth joined a street gang.

This cultural conflict between the Cambodian youth and their families resulted in some Cambodian youth running away to live on the streets, only to be exposed to the criminal elements and the street gangs operating in the location. These young Cambodians survived in the street by banding together and committing crime thus helped each other. The street youth started to form loose bonds between themselves because of common status. In addition these youth were simultaneously exposed to the local street gang sub-culture.

Seeing the activities of African-American, Hispanic and the newly formed Vietnamese street gangs of the 1980s all influenced these Cambodian youths. The cities of Long Beach and Fresno, California became relocation focal points for these refugees. So if you had to predict where Cambodian street gangs might develop what areas would most likely see the first Cambodian street gangs?

By the mid 1980s these Cambodian street youths banded together for protection against local street gangs. Initially, these youth banded together for protection against being victimized, because they had similar problems, they spoke the same language and similar cultural and social needs. These youth also realized that as a group, they could be stronger and more formidable. In addition, this gave the newly forming gang a chance to become the aggressor not the victim, and presented an opportunity to make more money.

By this time the Cambodian street youths had formed into several small street gangs. It was out of these small gangs that that eventually the Tiny Rascal Gang (TRG) evolved. However, the formal acknowledgment of the gang began in 1985 when an alleged Hispanic gang member hit a newly arrived Cambodian youth in the face with his fist (Manzer, 2004).

This assault became a catalyst that sparked years of attacks and murders between the TRG and other gangs. A philosophy also developed that allowed TRG members to get involved in auto-burglary, residential burglary, commercial burglary, auto-theft, drug sales, assaults, firearm violations and murder.

In October, 1989 the local police formally recognized TRG as a viable street gang after a car load of TRG gang members pulled a long side a car of Hispanics, many who were East Side Longos. The contact was made near Anaheim and Cherry Streets in Long Beach. Both groups claim turf in this area and exchanged insults between each other. The rude gestures that followed culminated with the TRG gang members pulled out hand guns and started shooting at their rivals. TRG claimed another victim as 16 year-old Oswaldo Carbajal was killed (Manzar, 2004).

One Long Beach, California Hispanic gang, the East Side Longos, heavily influenced TRG in a couple of ways. Tiny Rascal Gang members tended to emulate the dress styles, graffiti writing and more important, the, gang behaviors of this Hispanic gang. TRG gang members tended to mimic other gang behaviors they observed from the East Side Longos. TRG gang members also tended to use Hispanic gang relate, slang, tattoos and graffiti more than other Asian street gangs. These Asian gang members would also shave their heads like their Hispanic counter parts. Sometimes TRG members would be mistaken identified as Hispanic gang members because of this.

In essence the Cambodian gang adopted the traits of their assailants. The Cambodians were often targeted for assaults while on the way to and from to school by this Hispanic gang. It is not surprising to determine why the East Side Longos also became the rivals of the Tiny Rascal Gang. One TRG gang member actually wrote a nine-page instruction booklet, complete with photographs, on how to be a TRG gang member and complete a drive by shooting, while in the California Youth Authority.

The East Side Longos are not the only rivals TRG has. In Providence, Rhode Island and Bridgeport, Connecticut the Exotic Foreign Cambodian Crips are rivals with TRG. 18th Street and the Latin Kings are enemies in the Boston area. In Long Beach, California the Asian Boyz Crips are also rivals (www.wikipedia.org).

This philosophy has also helped some unique relationships to develop between the TRG and other street gangs. One such relationship evolved into an intense rivalry with the group that influenced TRG the most, the East Side Longos. The TRG and Eastside Longos became and still are enemies. This rivalry has resulted in over 45 gang related deaths over the years and countless assaults and attempt murders. Like many other American street gangs, the TRG has also adopted the use of guns and violence to protect their turf and reputation. TRG gang members also have a history of assaults and attempted assaults on criminal justice professionals.

Turf

As you would predict, TRG gang members were and still are very mobile. TRG gang members have been located and identified all over the country. TRG presence has been reported in Vermont, Maine, Massachusetts, New Hampshire (state prison system), Rhode Island, Connecticut, California, Alaska, North Carolina, Tennessee, Philadelphia, Washington, Nevada, Kansas, Missouri, Colorado, Hawaii, Oregon, Georgia, New York, Virginia, Florida, Texas, Minnesota, North Carolina, Canada and Cambodia (www.gripe4kids.org ; www.wkikpedia.org). This is a total of 25 states and three countries.

However, the TRG is unique in a couple of ways. First, where TRG develops a strong presence, the gang tends to claim a turf. Secondly, on the other hand, the TRG will continue to be very nomadic and travel in small groups across a state, or across several states. TRG is a gang that claims turf, but is mobile. This particular behavior was something not seen before with street gangs. Normally the gang would be mobile or turf oriented, but not both. In California, TRG gang members have been contacted north of Sacramento and San Francisco and as far south as San Diego. However, TRG presence seems to be concentrated in Long Beach and Fresno. This makes the TRG influence extend over 800 miles, just in one state (Frank, 1998).

The Tiny Rascal Gang has also focused in a crime for profit operating philosophy. A 1998 report from the National Drug Information Center indicated a total of 33 states reported the presence of Asian street gangs that were involved in drug sales. Many of the TRG gangs are also involved in drug sale operations, although they have not involved into an organized drug trafficking businesses.

Membership

Early on, TRG membership was limited only to Cambodians. However, in the early 1990s, TRG broke the membership rules concerning the race and gender barriers, a behavior several other street gangs have exhibited before. TRG now allows mixed-race Cambodians, other races and females into their gang. This philosophy allowed the TRG membership to grow rapidly and subsequently make it easier to establish itself across the country. Because of the adaptable and changing membership rules, this growth and expansion was accomplished in a short period of time. As of 2008 TRG presence has been reported in at least 25 states and two countries.

At one time, the TRG had an all female associate gang aligned with it. It was known as LRG, or the Lady Rascal Gang. In early 1990, LRG was disbanded and all female members were assimilated into the TRG. The Tiny Rascal Gang became one of the first co-e street gangs in the west coast and certainly the first co-ed Asian street gang.

The female gang members share the same work, and responsibilities as their male counterparts did. Female gang members take an active role in the commission of crime, protection of fellow gang members and drug sales. TRG female gang members tend to treated as sisters, with the respect and dignity afforded any male gang member. At the end of 1990s the female portion of the gang remained at less than 10% of the total TRG membership. By the early 2000s female TRG membership had dwindled and currently the majority of the membership is still male.

Characteristics

Tattoos are commonly seen on TRG members, as well as the most popular gang hairstyle. Commonly it has been the shaved head. Those gang members that have tattoos will sport the letters TRG, rascal or raskal. Being a type of Asian gang also accounts for the three and five dot tattoos that are sometimes seen on TRG gang members. The clothing styles vary, depending on where the TRG gang is located, but commonly seen are Hispanic styles of gang dress. Most of the TRG gang members are between 14-24 years old.

Because of the heavy Hispanic gang influence TRG gang members will use graffiti at times to announce their presence and to mark turf boundaries. To the untrained eye, some Cambodians may physically look very similar to Hispanic people with facial features and skin color tones allowing for the confusion. A gang tactic that has been used by TRG is to have all the members shave their heads before a crime is committed. Because of this, TRG gang members have been misidentified as Hispanic gang members by witnesses, especially when they wear Hispanic style gang clothing.

Like many other street gang members, TRG members will use hand signs as non-verbal gang communication. TRG gang members are often well armed and are not afraid to engage rival gang members in gun battles.

Currently, gang membership identifies with the color grey and/or red. If the professional sports attire is worn it may be a football jersey from the Oakland Raiders team. The team has no formal connection to the gang, but the gang has adopted the colors and for them the team name is a moniker for "Remember As I Die Every Raskal Survives. TRG gang members have also been known to wear the White Sox baseball hat because the letters SOX on the hat represents "X Out Slobs" to them. A numeric code for TRG is the number 7126 and rascal is often spelled "rascal (http://gangsacross america.com; www.wikipedia.org)

At one time Asian street gangs had no formal ritual to establish membership. Another sign of the Hispanic gang influence on this gang is the method that TRG uses to formally establish gang membership. Adapted to fit their needs, the membership ritual may vary from individual to individual. For example, if you are well liked and have a history of supporting the gang, especially by participating in criminal activity with other gang members you can be walked in. In other words, the gang simply formally recognizes you as an official member. It would not be uncommon for one or more TRG gang members to act as sponsors, especially if they were crime partners.

The other common method used to confirm membership is the jump in. A prospective member has to fight two or three gang members for a specified time. The fight is symbolic, as it is suppose to show whether or not the prospective member has the heart, attitude and guts to back up the gang. The performance during the assault determines this level of fortitude or courage. Many street gangs use this membership ritual.

Females can join the gang in the same way, or be sexed in. The prospective female has to have sex with a number of gang members in order to be recognized as a member. Many times, females will choose this form of gang initiation because it is the least violent. Sometimes, rolling dice or a die determines the number of sexual partners. Sexing in a female gang member has become more popular in the last couple of years for many street gangs. Sexual assaults have unfortunately become common place as rituals prospective females will endure to join a gang.

In 1996, national TRG gang membership was estimated to be over 2000. That figure is sure to be low, especially when African-American, Caucasian, Filipino, Hispanic, Hmong, Korean, Laotian, Samoan, Cambodian and Vietnamese TRG gang members have been contacted. Inaccurate and under reporting of gang contacts has also played a role in the under estimation of the general gang and the TRG population. Unofficial estimates in the late 1990s reported the national TRG membership somewhere between 4,000 to 7,000 members. By the 2000s anecdotal law enforcement evidence suggest the national TRG gang membership is now closer to 7,000 and 9,000 members. The gang may also be considered as transnational as its presence and activity have been reported in Canada and Cambodia.

Criminal Activity

As mentioned before, the Tiny Rascal Gang can also be monetarily motivated. Any criminal actions that will bring money to a gang member are committed. Therefore, the TRG has been involved in extortions, home invasion robberies, robbery, burglary, auto theft, assault, drug sales, attempted murder and murder. There is a certain unique characteristic behavior that TRG engages in when selecting crime partners. TRG members from a different part of a state or from outside the state will work together as a team to commit a crime. These unions seem to happen with some spontaneity. TRG gang members tend to be connected informally across the United States as their Vietnamese counterparts.

For example, in Sacramento, California, during a July, 1995 home invasion robbery two members of a Vietnamese family were murdered and third wounded. Sacramento area law enforcement was able to identify the four suspects. They were all TRG gang members and one was from Portland, Oregon. The other three TRG gang members were from the cities of Pomona, Sacramento and San Bernardino, California. This demonstrates an interstate cooperation and the national informal gang network between TRG cliques.

According to an 18 year-old Orange County, California, TRG gang member Michael "Mini Mike" Vu, gang rivals look for other rivals at local churches and Buddhist temples. "Mini Mike" was a prosecution witness in a gang related shooting. As with other types of gangs TRG gang members can come from conservative middle class families and be straight A students. As of 2006 "Mini Mike" was free and living in the Little Saigon area, Westminster, California. "Mini Mike once claimed he assaults people to gain respect from fellow gang members and whose goal is to lead the TRG someday. He also bragged to the police "I don't care about anybody... I don't have any mercy" (Moxley, 2006).

The TRG gang has also been known to issue death threats toward police officers, gang investigators, witnesses and victims. At one time it was believed that TRG gang members had access to military C-4 explosives and grenades. These concerns suggest some kind of connection to those who have access to or dealers in military munitions and weapons.

In late 1990 there was anecdotal evidence that suggested TRG members maintained an alliance with the Asian Boyz, a Vietnamese street gang based in California. These two gangs were believed to have had connections to the Ghost Shadows; a New York based Chinese gang operating on the West Coast. At one time it was also suggested that the TRG and Asian Boys were receiving weapons from the Ghost Shadows in exchange for protection services at prostitution and illegal gambling locations. However, due the growth of both gangs and the subsequent Asian Boyz alliance to the west coast Crips this relationship may no longer exist.

Narcotics sales, prostitution and illegal gambling will continue to draw Asian street gang members to a more sophisticated criminal life. Street gang members are involved in cocaine, marijuana and heroin distribution at the wholesale and retail levels in the New England HIDTA area. These include but are not limited to the Latin Kings, Mara Salvatrucha, 18th Street, Latin Gangster Disciples, Asian Boyz and the Tiny Rascal Gangsters (National Drug Intelligence Center, 2007).

In the west coast the situation may be a little different. As the northern and eastern California HIDTA districts report in the Sacramento area the Varrio Gardens, Elm Street Gangsters, Tiny Rascal Gangsters and the Tiny Little Rascals are involved in the distribution of heroin, cocaine methamphetamine and marijuana. Methamphetamine tablets are a popular form of the drug that is sold at rave parties (National Drug Intelligence Center, 2001).

In the Boston area, TRG has become rivals of the Latin Kings fighting over drug sales turf (Murphy, 2006). In Providence, Rhode Island Dara 'Little Sniper' Som was shot after being asked "what's up?" by another Asian man. 'Little Sniper' is a member of TRG and the shooter is suspected of belonging to Laos Pride, a rival gang. The shooter was accompanied with approximately 15 other suspected gang members (Malinowski, 2008).

It now can become clear why in the middle and later part of July, 2005 U.S. Immigration and Customs Enforcement (ICE) arrested more than 1, 057 immigrants in operation "Community Shield." What is not commonly known is that the operation targeted more than 54 violent street gangs including Mara Salvatrucha (MS-13), Surenos, 18th Street, Latin Kings, Vatos Locos, Mexican Mafia, La Raza, Border Brothers, Brown Pride, Norteno, Florencia 13 Asian Boyz, Jamaican Posse and the Tiny Racal Gang. 582 gang members and associates, including 11 gang leaders were arrested in this operation (ICE, 2005).

Like many other gangs TRG has introduced the gang on the Internet. All you have to is go to You Tube and then in the search box type in Tiny Rascal Gang, over 40 sites containing TRG videos and pictures accompanied by gangster rap music are displayed. One site even claims to have a movie about TRG (www.youtube.com/watchg?v= 042SIQFAz8w&feature=related). The videos demonstrate the how the gang has grown and just how far they have developed since the mid 1980s. Another Internet site is MySpace a popular social networking program. Many gangs use both.

Summary

The TRG gang is a prime example of the type of gang diversity that has become more common. The ability to adapt to a changing sub-culture environment will continue to allow some street gangs to grow quickly, migrate, expand and establish themselves in criminal markets. The TRG has changed since its inception and now members can be involved in any type of criminal activity including drug. The multi-ethnic membership base will allow the gang to continue to grow and allow continual gang expansion.

Asian Boyz

Understanding that some gang trends are regionalized and others are nationally based might help to understand how gang migration affects the growth of street gangs. Gang migration is becoming more prevalent in certain areas of the country. A few national research projects indicate that some street gangs are migrating from larger cities to smaller cities and into rural America. Some families move to where work is available, bringing along a sibling who is involved in the gang life. A few gangs have migrated to get involved in a drug trafficking. Could these migration mechanisms partly fuel the growth of Southeast Asian street gangs?

History

In the late 1980's a small gang surfaced in the Los Angeles China Town area. The gang was unique because the members dressed like traditional Hispanic street gangs of the time, yet they were Cambodian. These gang members were easy to spot because they did not dress like the Chinese street gang members in the same area. In fact, they stood out because of the way they dressed and they were the only other Asian gang in a predominately Chinese area (Nguyen, 2001).

When the police contacted these youth, they claimed to belong to the "Oriental Lazy Boys" (OLB) street gang. Los Angeles at the time had a very small Cambodian population. Quickly, the Oriental Lazy Boys found out that their gang was nestled in the middle of a four square block area of L.A. that contained four to five established Hispanic gangs. The Oriental Lazy Boy gang members would frequent China Town and only to be out numbered and out gunned by the existing Chinese street gangs, the Wah Ching, Kool Boys, Black Dragons and the Home Boys. Anywhere Oriental Lazy Boy gang members went they encountered rival gangs and trouble.

The Oriental Lazy Boy gang remained very small in size. The reason for this was simple at the time only Cambodians could join the gang. This limited the size of the gang because over all Cambodian population in the L.A. area at the time was very small. The membership rules never changed for the California based Oriental Lazy Boys. To try and neutralize the potential problems with the existing Hispanic and Chinese street gangs some members of the Oriental Lazy Boys decide to form a sibling gang. They called this gang "Asian Boy Insane or ABI." The ABI gang appeared in China town near the end of 1989.

The membership for this gang was drawn from Cambodian, Laotian, Vietnamese, Viet-Ching (ethnic Chinese born in Vietnam), Chinese youths or any other group they could draw a member from. The gang was able to grow quickly because of the non-biased membership rules. Practically anyone could join ABI. The leader of this new gang was a young man named Piv Tang and he used the moniker of "King Cobra" (Nguyen, 2001).

The Asian Boy Insane gang would back up the Oriental Lazy Boy gang and would associate with OLB gang members. However, because of the social status of Cambodians with other Southeast Asian groups the Asian Boy Insane gang members were not allowed to participate in criminal activities with the Oriental Lazy Boys. There was a unique but distinct class bias against Cambodians by the Vietnamese, Chinese, Viet-Ching and Laotians. It was almost like the Cambodians gang members were like second-class citizens within the Southeast Asian gang community.

During a LAPD police investigation in the later part of 1990, a LAPD gang detective contacted Piv Tang. Tang told this detective that the ABI gang had stopped using the "Insane" part of the gang name because "no one was noticing them." Tang told the detective the gang was now called the "Asian Boyz" and it was abbreviated as "ABZ or AB." Later, this gang set also became known as the China Town Asian Boyz. As members of the original Asian Boyz gang began to relocate in Los Angeles and Orange counties, they established new gang sets of the Asian Boyz.

There were a number of reasons why some of the Asian Boyz gang members relocated. A few left to find work, others left when their parents relocated because a new job. A few Asian Boyz gang members left because they were fleeing law enforcement. Others went to live with extended family or friends and took the Asian Boyz gang life style with them.

During the early to mid 1990s Asian Boyz sets were established in Long Beach, California, which is south of Los Angeles, and in the Vallerio Projects, in the Van Nuys, California area. In a short period of time, by around 1995 other Asian Boyz sets were forming, especially along the west coast and Midwest and a few sets in the east coast. Meanwhile, the original L.A. parent gang, the Oriental Lazy Boys remained small because of the exclusive Cambodian membership.

Other literature review suggests that gang started in Long Beach, California in the early 1990s by several Long Beach area Asian youths. This gang eventually developed into a multi-ethnic gang that specialized in crimes such as extortion, home-invasion robbery, assault, car theft and murder (California Department of Justice, 2000).

The Asian Boyz gang is a relative new comer in the gang culture considering that modern day street gangs have been around since the 1850's. In California, street gangs have existed since the early part of 1900; as of 2005 the Asian Boyz gang is only 15 years old in "gang years." Even though relatively young for a street gang, the Asian Boyz have become one of the more violent gangs criminal justice professionals have encountered throughout the country.

By the mid-1990 the Oriental Lazy Boys and Asian Boyz had become rivals. The OLB had aligned themselves with the African-American Blood gangs and started to use and identify with the color red. Naturally, when this happened the Asian Boys aligned themselves with the Crips and used and identified with the blue color. It is funny to note that these associations were made by the Asian Boyz and are not formally recognized by the African-American street gangs. It is like the OLB and AB chose sides to enhance their gang's reputation. An Asian Boyz gang member probably could not recognize a real Crip gangster and would most likely shoot them (Nguyen, 2001).

This could explain why many Asian Boyz gang members use the blue colored railroad handkerchief as part of their gangster attire. This tends to suggest that inter- gang assaults may occur over the issue of color with the Asian Boyz sets that claim Crip association. This is consistent because the Asian Boyz gang considers all other ethnic based street gangs as enemies; this includes other Asian street gangs.

The Asian Boyz gang is like many other street gangs. They make money by committing crimes and love to enhance their reputation within the gang sub-culture through the use of violence. Although no crime is beneath the gang, the majority of Asian Boyz gang crime has centered on murder, home invasion robbery, extortion, witness intimidation, attempted murder, robbery and assaults.

Many Asian Boyz gang crimes are crimes of opportunity. Although, generally not involved in drug trafficking, some Asian Boyz gang members have sold drugs to make a quick dollar. Some Asian Boyz gang members have also been involved in the sales of marijuana, ecstasy and guns. The Asian Boyz gang continues to be well adjusted to the street gang culture. Very few if any ABZ members have graduated into more sophisticated criminal activities (Nguyen, 2004).

Asian Boyz gang leadership is fluid, unlike the Wah Ching gang that appears to be more organized. As opportunities for criminal activity present themselves, whoever has the most information, an inside contact or knows the target seems to assume the leadership role. This behavior is consistent for an Asian street gang. Each set of Asian Boyz seems to operate independently of other sets, even though they share the same name.

The Asian Boyz gang sets may also have an affiliate female gang. Known as the "Asian Chicks," these female gang members tend to have a support role to their male counterparts. Often, these female gang members will have no outward indications of gang membership. Nevertheless, they will carry contraband for their male counterparts. Asian Chicks gang members are not used for sex; they are considered as "little sisters" and treated with some respect by male gang members.

Debriefings with several Asian Boyz gang members revealed that Asian Chicks members often carry, conceal and transport Asian Boyz gang guns. Asian Boyz gang members seem to have a knack to hide weapons in their cars. Air conditioning ducts, behind door speakers and in backs of the car seats have been used to conceal contraband. Asian Boyz gang members have also learned a shooting tactic that involves multiple vehicles and multiple shooters.

Indicia

Asian Boyz gang members can dress in any style of clothing. However, many wear clothing similar to Hispanic street gangs. Some Asian Boyz gang members tend to wear blue colored clothing, including baseball caps. Many Asian Boyz gang members will tattoo themselves with "ABZ" or "AB" to signify their gang membership. AB gang members will also use tattoos that ate commonly used by other street gangs. This includes and is not limited to the three and five dot tattoo and tattoos of power animals.

The Asian Boyz gang has established itself throughout California and has an estimated 700 members statewide. The Asian Boyz gang has also been reported in Alaska, Florida, Kansas, Massachusetts, New York and Texas (California Department of Justice, 2000).

In 1995 California experienced the "Summer of Madness" when several Asian Boyz gang members from the city of Van Nuys went on a murder and assault spree. Eight Asian Boyz gang members were ultimately arrested and convicted. Examine how eight gang members caused so much fear and how the violence enhanced their reputation within the gang culture. The crimes included:

On April 14, 1995 as part of an ongoing turf war with a Van Nuys Hispanic gang Asian Boyz gang members shot and killed two Vilerio Street gang members. The shooting could be overheard on the 911 calls that the police received. This ambush assault resulted in the execution style murder of two Vilerio Street gang members.

On July 6, 1995 Asian Boyz gang members were at a nearby bowling alley when they saw another small group of Asian youth who they believed to be rival Wah Ching gang members. Other Asian Boyz gang members were called and told to respond to the bowling alley and bring weapons. They did. When the Asian youth left the bowling alley they were confronted and two were eventually shot. The victims were not gang members and were unarmed.

On July 23, 1995 A carload of Asian Boyz gang members became involved in an early morning shootout with another car containing two 18th Street gang members. After a high speed chase the car with the 18th Street gang members crashed into a parked car. The passenger was able to get out and escape, the driver was injured and trapped in the car. Asian Boyz gang members shot multiple times and killed the driver of the car.

On August 1, 1995 several Asian Boyz gang members entered a café and noticed some rival gang graffiti. Assuming the Asian youth in the café were responsible for the graffiti they called other Asian Boyz gang members and told them to respond and bring weapons. As the Asian youth left they drove onto the freeway only to be followed by three carloads of armed Asian Boyz gang members. The result was an unprovoked attack on the four youth. All were shot and three died.

In March 1966 an Asian Boyz gang member who agreed to testify was shot in the back of his as he was walking to his house. On October 23, 1998 the father of one of the witnesses answered the door to his San Jose home and was killed by gun fire. Both incidents were associated with the Asian Boyz gang crime spree.

By 2000 all eight Asian Boyz gang members were arrested, seven were convicted and sent to prison. The eight was pending trial. Activity like this can also enhance the false feeling of control and power with the involved gang members. This Asian Boyz clique was so sophisticated that gang members practiced their drive-by shooting skills on a ranch in northern California that was owned by the parents of one of the members.

Some Asian gangs will continue to use violence as a calling card, while other Asian gangs may specialize in financially based fraud crime.

Summary

David Evangelista was an Asian Boyz gang member. He got straight A's in school, volunteered at a hospital and even delivered jewelry while he was involved in a five month crime spree that left seven people dead in the L.A. area. This is an example of how some Asian gang members can successfully lead a double life. Gang members like Evangelista can come home and be respectful to their parents and on first glance appear to me normal high school or college age youth who earn excellent grades and contribute back to the community (Gonzales, 2004). This type of behavior is consistent with modern day gang behaviors.

Currently, many gang members, including Asian Boyz tend not to claim membership to law enforcement authorities. There is a general reluctance to openly admit membership in a street or prison gang. Asian Boyz gang members can also be involved in a variety of criminal activities including prostitution, extortion, credit card fraud and drug trafficking.

Wah Ching

The Wah Ching is a Chinese street gang that first formed in San Francisco, California. Again the processes of bias, class distinction and racism play a part in the initial formation of the gang. From the streets of San Francisco to across the United States this gang has now become transnational and has been implicated in the trafficking of drugs, humans and arms.

History

The Wah Ching street gang was formed in San Francisco during 1964 by Hong Kong-born youth. Anton Wong is credited as being the founder of the gang (Yee, 2005). This first generation gang had approximately 15 members and was a very close-knit group. The gang initially formed for protection from against American-born Chinese and African-American gangs (www.crosswinds.net). The gang name Wah Ching translates to Chinese youth or Chinese young men. The gang's initial members were in their late teens, young men.

The genesis of the gang started in several places with Chinese youth who migrated from Hong Kong and settled in large metropolitan cities like Los Angles, New York and San Francisco. San Francisco at one time had the largest Cantonese Chinese population in the country. In San Francisco eventually the Hop Sing Tong took this gang under control and showed them how to survive in America. The Hop Sing Tong at the time was comprised of Chinese elders. The Hop Sing Tong dates back to the 1500s. At the time the Wah Ching was taken under its wing the Tong was involved in drug trafficking and other illegal businesses. Initially the Wah Ching became the muscle on the street for Hop Sing Tong.

Local law enforcement provided the name "Look See Boys" because they would encounter Wah Ching gang members acting as look outs at underground houses of prostitution or gambling locations. In reality the gang members were working for the Hop Sing Tong. Look See Boys is an American nickname for Wah Ching gang members (Yee, 2005).

The Wah Ching started to develop a well-known reputation within the gang community based on their criminal activity, at the time mainly for extortions and robberies. In the early 1970s the Wah Ching gang broke away from the control of the Hop Sing Tong. The gang kept its original name.

In 1971 another gang the Yau Lay (half profit) formed in San Francisco. Initially the Yau Lay and Wah Ching gangs were allies. One of Yau Lay's gang's lieutenants was a young man named Joe Fong. Joe Fong had three brothers, two younger and one older. A faction of the Yau Lay gang led by Joe Fong broke away to get away of the Hop Sing Tong control. Fong relocated the headquarters of his new gang outside Chinatown into the Ingleside district of San Francisco in 1972 (www.crosswinds.net). All of the Fong brothers also joined the new gang.

The new gang was initially called the Cheung Ching Yee. Fong nicknamed his gang the "Joe Fong Gang" that was later changed to the "Joe Boys" (Yee, 2005). The local press is also credited with calling the gang the Joe Boys (www.crosswinds.net). The Joe Boys would allow Cantonese Chinese youth as members as well as "ABC's", American born Chinese youth. Very quickly the Joe Boys also became involved in the same criminal activities the Wah Ching was committing. This only further intensified the gang rivalry as both gangs competed for control of the criminal activity.

The two gangs battled sometimes in school resulting in fistfights. Between 1972 and 1977 the Wah Ching and Joe Boys were engaged in a bloody war resulting in many murders, including those of innocent people. Surprisingly during this time a few Joe Boys gang members would leave their gang and join the Wah Ching gang and a few Wah Ching gang members would leave their gang and join the Joe Boys gang. Gang loyalty was fluid for these gangs not true for Hispanic street gangs. The Wah Ching gang was allegedly responsible for the murder of Joe Fong's older brother and that helped solidify and escalated the already intense rivalry between the gangs (Yee, 2005).

The pressure of this rivalry erupted on September 4, 1977 at 2:40 AM at the Golden Dragon restaurant (www.mistersf.com). The Joe Boys attacked Wah Ching gang members in the restaurant after they vandalized the graves of several Joe Boys gang members. This assault became known as the Golden Dragon Massacre. Five innocent bystanders, including two tourists were killed and 11 others injured in a hail of gunfire that came from enraged Joe Boys gang members (www.mistersf.com). Tony Young and six or seven other Wah Ching gang members were present and escaped with their lives. Tony Young was hit by the gunfire and survived (Yee, 2005).

This incident became the catalyst that helped the police form a gang task force that focused on the Joe Boys gang. Eventually four Joe Boys gang members were sent to prison for their roles in the murders (www.mistersf.com). Because of the law enforcement focus on the Joe Boys the Wah Ching gang assumed control of the streets in San Francisco. Due to desire to organize the Wah Ching in Los Angeles in the late 1970s approximately 10 members of the San Francisco Wah Ching moved to Los Angeles where another faction of the Wah Ching had already begun. This included San Francisco Wah Ching gang members Tony Young, Vincent Jew and Kenneth Fong (Yee, 2005).

Fong, Jew and Young met with the founding members of the Los Angeles based Wah Ching gang. During the late 1970s there were approximately 300 Wah Ching gang members in Los Angeles. The Wah Ching's reputation for violence increased during the late 1970s to mid 1980s. Some Joe Boys gang members were in the Los Angeles area and were still considered rivals of the Wah Ching. So the conflict between the gangs continued. In addition the L.A. based Wah Ching gang was involved in extortion of Chinese business and restaurant owners (Yee, 2005).

From as early as 1965 there were reports of L.A based Wah Ching activity in Los Angeles County. The L.A. Chinatown area was under control of the L.A. faction of the Hop Sing Tong. In 1969 an older faction of the Wah Ching broke off naming themselves the Yau Lay after the San Francisco gang. The Los Angeles based factions of the Wah Ching and Yau Lay were involved in a bloody struggle between 1969 and 1973 for control of Chinatown. The Yau Lay gang was pushed out of Chinatown leaving the Wah Ching in control (www.crosswinds.net).

During this time the China Town Homeboys gang also formed. The gang was basically involved in gambling and fighting. Their attacks on Chinese youth motivated many of the victims to join the Wah Ching gang for protection. As a result the Wah Ching gang membership grew and the gang gained more power in Chinatown, Los Angeles. The China Town

Homeboys, Joe Boys and Wah Ching were the three largest Asian street gangs in Los Angeles during this time (Yee, 2005).

California received many Southeast Asian refugees and immigrants during the late 1970s after the fall of Saigon. Even though the majority relocated in Orange County, California many relocated in Los Angeles. The newly arrived immigrants became a recruitment pool for the existing gangs. As a result initially about half of the Vietnamese males who joined a street gang joined the Wah Ching and the other half joined the Joe Boys gang. Many of these newly arrived immigrants were known as Viet-Ching, ethnic Chinese born in Vietnam. Quickly the Viet-Ching gang members left both gangs and formed a gang themselves.

The first Viet-Ching gang became known as the "Kool Boys" because they all smoked the Kool brand of cigarette. Later the gang changed their name to the Viet-Ching gang. This Vietnamese gang focused on making money and not fighting like their counterparts. The Viet-Ching gang also started to compete with the Joe Boys and Wah Ching gangs in criminal activity. This only fueled the rivalry and the violence between the gangs. By 1980 the L.A. based Wah Ching was led by Tony Young. At this time Vincent Jew controlled the San Francisco Wah Ching faction. Also during this time anecdotal law enforcement evidence suggested there were 600 to 800 Wah Ching gang members in California (www.crosswinds.net).

By late 1985 many of the Joe Boys gang membership had left Los Angeles and returned to the San Francisco area. Those Joe Boys gang members that remained in Los Angeles joined the Wah Ching gang. A flying eagle tattoo became the symbol associated with the Wah Ching gang (Yee, 2005).

In the early to mid 1980s the Wah Ching gang usually did not use the jumping ritual for new members. Membership was allowed if you were Cantonese or Taiwanese. Graffiti if used usually displayed the letters "WC." Eventually many of the Joe Boys gang members in San Francisco changed the gang's name to the Jackson Street Boyz. Other Joe Fong Boyz gang members realigned with the Hop Sing Tong and became known as the Hop Sing Boyz (Yee, 2005).

By the late 1980s a younger set Taiwanese immigrants had joined the L.A. based Wah Ching gang. A young immigrant youth named Sonny Ting was one of these gang members. Two distinct populations of members within the Wah Ching gang developed during the early 1990s. A group of older and young new members emerged within the same gang. This was not a new phenomenon, age based membership sub sets like this form in other street gangs.

Many of the older Wah Ching gang members became addicted to heroin and other went underground to avoid law enforcement contact. This left the younger Wah Ching gang members to run the gang. As the Wah Ching gang activity slowed down, the Viet Ching gang became a predominate power with the Asian gang culture. A sibling gang from the Viet Ching gang also formed during this time. The Black Dragon gang formed causing further pressure on the Wah Ching gang.

Another incident resulted in the formal separation of the San Francisco and Los Angeles based Wah Ching gangs. Until 1992 the Wah Ching gang was considered as one with factions in San Francisco and Los Angeles. In 1992 the Taiwanese organized crime group Wo Hop To formally arrived in San Francisco. The presence of the Wo Hop To forced the San Francisco based Wah Ching faction to merge with it. The gang for all purposes was taken over by the Wo Hop To, but still operated as the Wah Ching gang. This in turn left the L.A. based faction by itself. A formal separation was acknowledged between the gangs (www.crosswinds.net). However, the presence of Wo Hop To gang members was noted as early as 1989 (www.cgia.org/gangs2000).

It is clear that the Wah Ching developed into a formidable organized group from a street gang. From its genesis the gang has demonstrated remarkable organizational and communication abilities. The non-turf nature of the gang gave it a flexibility that most likely contributed to the rapid growth and expansion. Between the 1970s and 1980s the Wah Ching gang was the gang that controlled most of the criminal vices in the San Francisco Chinatown and the L.A. Chinese communities (www.cgia.org/gangs2000).

The typical criminal activities of the gang include extortion, burglary, gambling, prostitution, loan sharking, narcotics trafficking, robbery and murder. Wah Ching operations include the operation of legitimate businesses including real estate investments, jewelry stores, restaurants, nightclubs, travel agencies and the entertainment industry (www.cgia.org/gangs2000).

The Wah Ching gang has factions in Los Angeles and San Francisco. There is law enforcement anecdotal evidence that suggests as a group the gang has developed strong associations with other Asian organized crime groups and gang members in Los Angeles; Seattle; Vancouver and Toronto, Canada; Boston, Massachusetts; New York and with the Sun Yee On and 14K Triads in Hong Kong (www.cgia.org/gangs2000).

The L.A. based Wah Ching gang also had a number of young Taiwanese members who became shot callers within the gang. The gang was now located throughout Los Angeles County. Cliques or sets of the Wah Ching evolved and they were named after the Dai lo of the gang. These gang sub sets became known as sides. Sonny-Side, Ken-Side, T-Side and Paul-Side became well known in the Asian gang culture.

The Wah Ching gang continued to grow. The L.A. based Wah Ching gang under the leadership of Tony Young became a dominate force in he southern California organized crime base. By 1993 a faction of the Wah Ching called the Hung Mun led by Paul Liu broke away. This split resulted in several gang related murders. More factions split away from the mother gang as it continued to grow. At one time there were over 12 different Wah Ching sides in southern California. All could be traced back to the original gang led by Tony Young (Yee, 2005; www.crosswinds.net).

Many of the sides were exclusively Cantonese Chinese however some sides recruited ethnic Taiwanese and Vietnamese members. By 1995 the California Department of Justice reported approximately 1,800 Wah Ching gang members (www.crosswinds.net).

On January 23, 2002 the federal grand jury in Los Angeles indicted 11 Wah Ching gang leaders and members for racketeering violations that included murders, robberies, extortion and narcotic trafficking and other violent crimes that aided the racketeering activities. The indictment outlined the organizational structure of the Wah Ching gang. A Dai-lo or Big Brother headed each side. Under each Dai-lo there were associates and lieutenants, who in turn controlled crew chiefs. The lowest raking Wah Ching gang member was called a Sai-lo, little brothers or youngsters. Sometimes the Sai-los would be called soldiers (www.usdoj.gov/usao).

The Wah Ching gang had evolved from street gang to a type of organized crime group. The gang existed for the purpose of making money for its members and expanding the power of the gang through intimidation and the use of violence. These goals were accomplished through regular meetings of the membership, sharing firearms that were used in criminal activities such as murder and robberies, extortion of local businesses and trafficking narcotics (www.usdoj.gov/usao).

This criminal case involved the Ken–Side, T-Side, Paul-Side and Sonny-Side cliques of the Wah Ching gang. The Dai-los of each were between 30 and 40 years old. They had effectively distanced themselves from the criminal street activities yet benefited from them through the gang's organizational structure. It is the nature of older gang members and/or gang leaders to get less involved in the criminal street activity. Usually newer and younger gang members commit the crimes for the gang and the leaders benefit. With time and good performance younger gang members have the opportunity to get promoted. The history of the Wah Ching gang becomes a great example of how some immigrant youth organized into a street gang and how quickly the use of violence and organizational skills facilitates the growth and spread of the gang.

Summary

All gangs can change and evolve with time. As of 2009 for some Wah Ching gang members there are no longer any sub groups or sides to the gang. Members just refer to themselves and "dubs." As members get older attitudes change and there may be a change in the type of criminal activity the gang is involved in. As with many gangs the Wah Ching criminal activity is based on making money. Some members of the gang have now branched out into human smuggling and many members continue to be involved in the primary activity of the gang: drug sales.

African-American Gangs

African-American gangs have been established in southern California since the 1920s. Early "negro" street gangs were nothing like the Bloods and Crips that are nationally known today. Street gangs interact with each other and the African -American street gangs are no different. Black gang history is not documented well and there are several proposed theories of how the Crip and Blood gangs developed in southern California. However, the violence between the two gangs is well documented. As a group African-Americans have some unique characteristics that may have facilitate and motivate gang membership. Social and world events also influence African-American gang behaviors.

1920's

African-American street gangs have existed in South Central Los Angeles since the 1920s. Early "Negro" or "colored" gangs were usually composed of family members and close friends who involved themselves in limited criminal activity. This activity was done to enhance a gangster image, and it was also way to establish or enhance an income. African-Americans on the west coast were experiencing similar biases as early Mexican settlers.

Between the 1920s and 1950s African-Americans in the west coast endured the depression and World War II. The classic mechanisms that influenced the formation of the nation's first street gangs in New York were also present in southern California. The youth groups that formed during time tended to be in a state of constant change.

During the 1920s and 30's gangs like the Goodlows, Kellys, Driver Brothers, Magnificents, Bloodgetts, and the Boozies were active around the area of the Imperial Freeway, Los Angeles. The Boozies membership was comprised of a family of brothers and friends that were involved in prostitution, robbery and forgery. During this time period many of the African-American youth who became involved in gang life did not do so until they were around 20 years old. This became a unique phenomenon that made African-American gangs distinctly different from Mexican street gangs. Youth under the age of 20 usually were not part of an African-American street gang during this time (http://davadnai.users.omniglobal.net/crips.html).

One factor that impacted change started when African-Americans moved from the Lynwood, Watts, Slauson and Manchester/Firestone areas into the southern area of Los Angeles. The southern part of Los Angeles at the time was demographically comprised of mostly White families. As the African-Americans continued to move into the area, the Whites moved away. This movement became known as the modern day urban phenomenon of "white flight." South Los Angeles has become hot bed of street gang activity.

White flight from a behavior perspective refers to an avoidance mechanism that develops from dismay at changing demographics within a community. In this case, the changing demographics included an influx of African-American, Mexican nationals and Mexican-Americans into a predominately White area of Los Angeles. When these groups moved into this southern area of L.A. crimes rates started to change. For the original residents, the quality of life began to change. Personal safety issues, the lack of understanding of different culture and stereotyping added to the citizen "dismay" that developed.

1940s

During the 1940's African-American street gangs began to grow in numbers and size. Many African-American street gangs were involved in prostitution, forgery, gambling, extortion and robbery. These gangs were very effective at forcing local merchants into paying them for protection. Just as many Indo-Chinese gangs did to Vietnamese merchants in southern California and Chinese street gangs to Chinese merchants in the bay area northern California. Some of the well-known gangs in the LA area during this time period were the Purple Hearts, 31st Street and the 28thStreet gangs (http://davadnai.users.omniglobal.net/crips.html). Even though conflict between African-American gangs did occur, it was very limited. Conflicts were usually settled with a fistfight.

Alonso in his work suggests there are two major periods of African-American gang growth in Los Angeles. One is post World War II to 1965 and the second from 1970 to 1972. Alonso refers to the time frame between 1965 and 1970 as a sociopolitical period. His work crystallizes prior academic research and includes the factor of geography as part of the African-American gang development equation (www.streetgangs.com/ history). According to Alonso the first major Black gang formation started in the late 1940s. This was the result of thousands of African-Americans migrating from the South to fill World War II jobs in southern California, especially the L.A. area.

Here is where his geography factors play a key role in the development of African-American gangs in Los Angeles. At the time there were very restrictive regulations legalized in the 1920s that maintained social and racial homogeneity of neighborhoods by denying non-Whites the ability to own property. This in effect forced African-Americans into living and residing in particular areas of the city. By the 1940s this practice made much of Los Angeles off limits to all minorities.

As a result chronic overcrowding became a major issue and created congested, substandard housing conditions exacerbated by the artificially created boundaries. Geographically this was the Central Avenue neighborhood. As African-American went to court to challenge this regulations animosity grew between many African-Americans and Whites. Throughout the 1940s resentment toward the African-Americans increased. As African-Americans attempted to integrate into public schools while legally challenging the housing discrimination laws some White Angelinos reacted violently.

In the near communities of Huntington Park, Bell and South Gate some White teenagers formed "clubs" during the 1940s to terrorize African-American youth. One of most infamous was the "Spook Hunters" that often attacked African-American youth, especially when they were outside "their" neighborhoods. The 'Spook Hunters" and other White street "clubs" focused their efforts on spatially confining African-Americans to their neighborhoods through instigating fights and intimidation (www.streetgangs.com/history).

You would anticipate that some African-American youth would form gang to protect themselves as a result of the assaults, serious overcrowded living conditions and social segregation. The Businessmen were one of the first African-American street gangs to form in the late 1940s.

This type of social confrontation was not limited to Los Angeles. Thrasher identified a White gang in Chicago that formed in the 1920's. The "Dirty Dozens" gang attacked often African-American youth with knives, blackjacks and guns because of racial differences (Thrasher, 1927, p37). Gregory noted the same type of activity in the Corona neighborhood in Queens, New York. The "Dukes" a White gang were intimidating African-American residents and exacerbating racial conflict (Gregory, 1998, p.63). In Chicago a 1919 race riot contributed to the formation of African-American gangs to protect themselves from hostile White hoodlums that were terrorizing the African-American community (Spear, 1967, p.210; Perkins, 1987,p.40).

It appears that fear of attack by another group acted as a gel that unified African-American youth and helped form the first Black street gangs. I suggest that social polarization creates fear and mistrust within any minority group that it is aimed at. In fact, I suggest that all minority groups have been targeted at one time with this polarization. The social conditions of class distinction, racism and bias create a psychological and geographical social segregation that in turn facilitate youth involvement in street gangs.

1950s

By the middle to late 1950s, a new generation of African-American neighborhood youth groups had developed within South Central, Los Angeles, California. Many of the 1930 and 1940s gangs evolved and were now active social organizations involving young African-Americans. These youths were involved with house parties and car clubs. Friday night school dances or socializing at a particular roller skating location became a primary activity. There was only one requirement. To be able to be a member and participate, you had to be from the same neighborhood as other members of the group.

Popular car clubs included the Coasters, Highwaymen, Road Devils, Gladiators, Slausons, Watts Farmers, Blood Alley, Huns and Businessmen (http://davadnai. users. omniglobal.net/crips.html). The clubs tended to be territorial and were not organized. Membership was small. Gang rivalries intensified and fights between car clubs were common. However Black on Black murder was rare. Most conflicts were resolved with a fight. The car club that had the most standing members at the end of the fight was declared the winner. Many of the car club members were still involved in criminal activity such as extortion, robbery, gambling and assaults.

Smaller neighborhoods started to band together or joined larger ones for protection. These groups became the forerunners that eventually evolved into the West Coast African-American street gangs we know today. This gang evolution also became the catalyst for significant growth in gang membership and increase the degree of criminal sophistication. Another change occurred during this time. Gang members became younger and younger. Teenage youth now were joining street gangs.

1960s

By the early 1960s African-American street gangs had adopted names like the Slausons, Gladiators, Huns, Watts, Avenue Boys, 135s and the Valliant's. The Avenues were offshoots of the Slausons. The Avenues were sometimes referred to as the Kitchen Crips according to some law enforcement authorities. The Avenues did not co-exist well with the other gangs. In fact, most of these gangs started to become territorial in nature and all were rivals with each other. Individual gangs in separate territories were referred to as sets. The set name signified the neighborhood where the gang was formed, but the set still affiliated themselves with a particular gang. Often, man-made geographical boundaries like major streets, freeways or urban development projects would dictate the boundaries for different gang sets.

During this time period there was a significant growth in gang membership and a little decrease in gang related activity. This was also a time when "Black Awareness" was its height. Many African-Americans were involved in political movements and social change; this also included some street gang members. For some African-Americans this meant joining the Black Panthers, a violent militant group.

African American gangs started to develop strategies to combat the White intimidation and efforts against integration. From the African-American point of view the formation of youth gangs for some was justified because they provided a legitimate defense and voice against the system. White Americans in L.A. probably felt just the opposite; the burgeoning minority population was a threat. White flight in the City of Angels led to a change for African-Americans (www.streetgangs.com/history).

As Alonso (1999) points out White flight left the central district of L.A. as a "Black enclave" that represented 71 percent of the inner-city population (Brunn et al., 1993 p.53 and www.streetgangs.com/history). By 1960 the African-American communities of Watts, Central Avenue and west Adams had consolidated into one large continuous Black with low, middle and upper class districts. Prior to the White Flight these were islands of African-American residents (Alonso, 1999; Robinson, 2000, p.158).

A rule in physics" is that for every action there is a reaction. The same holds true in the social dynamics of street gangs. As White flight continued so did the presence of White gangs. With a common enemy gone, African-American street gangs turned to conflict amongst themselves. In fact during this time period African-American gang activity represented a significant amount of the gang related incidents (Los Angeles County Probation Department and Youth Study Center, 1962, p. 1). By 1960 gang rivalry caused six murders according to the LAPD. This was very high for the time (Los Angeles Police Department, 1961, p. 28). Black-on-Black gang violence was staring to become a concern.

Initially, most gang leaders were selected on their popularity, ability to fight and their material assets. Members would refer to other members as homeboy or homie. Hand signs, copied from elder uncles and fathers who belonged to African-American fraternal societies or Masonic groups, were used to identify specific sets (Valdemar, 1996). The hand sign was also a way to determine if any outsider was present within a specific set. As gangs proliferated conflict began to increase and violence between African-American street gangs also started to increase.

Gang fights would often take place at prearranged locations. The weapons used were bumper-jack handles, baseball bats, chains and occasionally knives. Firearms were almost never used.

During this time, some African-American street gang members still committed strong-arm robberies, burglaries and assaults. These gangs were also were involved in illegal dice games and limited narcotic sales. The favorite drugs of use at this time were uppers (amphetamines), downers (barbiturates) and marijuana. As whole, African-American street gangs started to develop a reputation based on the behaviors of certain members; however the group enjoyed the reputation.

The gang psychology that was well developed in Hispanic street gangs was also well on its developmental cycle within African-American street gangs. A certain behavioral sophistication was developing. But as mentioned in the Hispanic gang chapter world and social events can impact street gang evolution.

From the mid-to-late 1960s there was a substantial decrease in African-American street gang activity and growth in membership. Sociologists believe there are a number of reasons why this happened. First, the Vietnam War and the ensuing draft which appeared to disproportionately select African-American youth.

Secondly, an increased Black awareness brought about by the interest in civil rights issues initiated by Martin Luther King Jr. and H. Rap Brown. Third, there was a highly visible presence of Black militant organizations stressing the need for all African-Americans to unite. As a result these three social factors impacted the involvement of African-Americans in local street gangs. This is why some sociologists believe there was a decrease in the African-American street gang activity.

One cannot discuss these vents without including the Watts Riots in 1965. After the "Watts Rebellion" and in combination with the Black Awareness movement and the Vietnam conflict most of the gang rivalries ended under the leadership of several socially conscious organizations. There was a tendency for Black youths to become politically mobilized and many turned their attention toward the social problems that plagued their communities (www.streetgangs.com/history).

1969-1970

Crips

The history is a bit cloudy here. There are number of different histories on how the Crips actually got their name. The first, and most obvious, is Raymond Washington's use of his cane when he walked or his confinement to a wheel chair led to the nickname of Crip, short for crippled. His nickname was applied to his gang and hence we have the birth of the Crips.

The second and least believable hypothesis is that the name came from a popular television show at the time entitled Tales from the Crypt. However, a small number of older African-American gang members that I have debriefed believe this is really how the Crips got their name.

The third and once popular theory is that the Crip gang is really an offshoot of the Slauson Street gang. However, there is no anecdotal evidence to suggest that the people credited with the formation of the Crips were members of the Slauson Street gang.

A fourth version of Crip history suggests that the Crips were originally called the Avenue Cribs. Allegedly, Raymond Washington in the mid 1960's was a student at Fremont High School in Los Angeles. He initially founded the Baby Avenues. It is believed that the gang name was taken from the established African-American Avenues street gang. Initially, the gang was established as a political organization and during the late 1960s was used to provide protection from the other African-American street gangs and to profit from criminal activities. The gang became known as the Baby Avenues or Avenue Cribs.

In this version of Crip history, it is believed that Washington modeled the Cribs after the Black Panther Party and one of the older African-American street gangs, the Avenues. Original members of this gang are also reported to include Washington, Michael Conception, Raymond Cook, Melvin Hardy, Bennie Simpson, Mack Thomas and Angelo White. The name Crip was adopted by the Cribs in February 1972 when a newspaper article published in the Los Angeles Sentinel referred to some Crib gang members as "crips", a slang abbreviation for cripple because some of the gang members carried canes (Virginia Gang Investigators Association, 2004). However, other historians believe that Washington was not the greatest speller and the term Crips started because Washington misspelled cribs (http://davadnai. users.omniglobal.net/crips.html).

In yet another version of this story; a local newspaper published an article about the Cribs. The newspaper made a typographical error and referred to the Cribs as the Crips in the middle of the article. A street version of history suggests this is how the Crips adopted their name.

A caveat to the 1972 newspaper story is if the information is accurate 1972 is the time period when the Crip name was applied to the gang. This seems to be different because of African-American gang activity at the time. It has been well established that the Blood formation occurred in mid to late 1972 and the term crip was well known in the later part of 1969.

A more recent fifth version and less believable history is that the gang originally wanted a name that would infer the toughest men imaginable. The gang members thought of the superhero Superman and the only thing that could hurt Superman was Kryptonite. Phonetically spelled and abbreviated, the term Crip was developed.

A sixth version of Crip history suggests that Stanley Williams or Raymond Washington had a cousin who was injured in a drive-by shooting. This cousin was confined to a wheel chair because he lost the use of legs. According to the story, Williams or Washington use to call their cousin with a phrase similar to "come on my cripple cousin." In time that phrase was abbreviated to, "come on my crip cuzz." Allegedly, this is where the name Crip developed from and that is why Crip gang members refer to each other as cuzz.

In a seventh perspective, Black gang historian Akil S. Batani-Khalfani offers a different and at least partially accurate developmental history for the Crips and Bloods. Khalfani believes the Crips formed right after the Watts Riots of 1969. Khalfani accurately recalled that bigotry; racism, prejudice and discrimination were present. The riots were a social rebellion against those factors, and the formation of the Crips was a continuation of that rebellion (Khalfani, 1996).

Washington High School is often mistakenly mentioned as the birthplace of the Crips. Khalfani believes this confusion arises from the name of one of the founding members of the Crips, Raymond Washington. Washington was from 76th Street off Central Avenue in South Los Angeles. However, Raymond Washington and his gang did go around Washington High School to recruit, fight and do business.

While lecturing at a conference in Las Vegas, a police officer from Phoenix, Arizona approached me and related the following story on how the Crips got their name. While growing up in the Phoenix area African-American gang members would rob and assault their victims. The street savvy person knew that the attacking African-American gang members would stomp on the victim's legs to break them, making them crippled. The term Crip was applied to these African-American gang members (Dunn, 2004).

Alonso suggests that's as a 15 year–old student at Fremont High School, Raymond Washington started the gang that became known as the Crips. According to Alonso Washington was influenced by the 1960s Black Panther Movement. Washington was too young to join, but was heavily attracted to the philosophies and ideologies of the movement. Washington's gang was initially a "mini-me" version of the Black Panther Party; which included dressing like Black Panther members (www.streetgangs.com/ history).

Washington also admired an older gang known as the Avenues that was active during the 1960's. The Avenues were led by Craig and Robert Munsen. Washington decided to name his gang the Baby Avenues, also known as the Avenue Cribs. The gang was supposed to represent a new generation of African-American youth (www. streetgangs.com/history).

Another unknown writer suggests that Washington, Stanley (Tookie) Williams and friends founded the Baby Avenues in 1969. The gang became known as the Avenue Cribs due to the age of the members. According to this source the name Crips was first introduced in the Los Angeles Sentinel newspaper in an article where victims were describing their attackers as young men with canes, as if they were crippled. There is also some evidence to suggest that the word Crib was misspelled as Crip in the article. The name Crip struck with the gang. There is one additional piece of information presented by this unknown writer. Stanley Williams allegedly also founded his own gang; the Westside Crips in 1971 (http://en.wikipedia.org/wiki/Crips).

No one can tell exactly when, but the name Crip was applied to the group that was allegedly controlled by Stanley Williams, Raymond Washington and Michael Conception in late 1969 to early 1970. By that time the Crips had grown in number and size and blue color was associated with anyone who belonged to the gang.

In a spirited 2006 FOX channel news interview an early member of the L.A. based Crip gang stated Stanley Williams was not a co-founder of the Crip gang even though he is generally believed to be. Jamal Barnes an original member of the Crips claimed that he and Williams were body builders. Stanly "Tookie" Williams even an appearance on the "Gong Show" in 1978. According the Barnes, Williams got his nickname for his propensity to take things. Interestingly, Raymond Washington who many believe is one of the Crip founders was gunned down and murdered in 1979 (Williams, 1998).

Tookie Williams was convicted and sentenced to death Aril 20, 1981 for 4 murders that were committed in 1979. While on death row, Williams with Barbara Bicnel co-authored a series of children's books focusing on anti-gang, violence and drug themes. For his work Williams was nominated for the 2001 Nobel Peace Prize, even though he was convicted of the 4 murders. Williams did not receive the Nobel Peace Prize and was executed in 2006 (Blatchford, 2006).

Some of the first Crip gang activity started in Southwest Los Angeles near Fremont High School around the later part of 1969. The gang committed robberies and assaults, along with extorting money. These crimes usually took place on or near the high school campus. The Crips would also travel to other neighborhoods and victimized the youth groups or gangs residing there. The Crips quickly developed the reputation of being very dangerous and violent. Their reputation was quickly based in fear.

As a result of the Crip attacks on other neighborhoods, youth groups banded together for protection and formed their own gangs. However, the Crips weren't the only gang that was active. Don't forget, all the African-American street gangs at the time attacked each other and this included the Crip gang.

Stanley "Tookie" Williams who was credited as being one of the co-founders of the Crip gang explained it this way in a 1997 TV interview. In his neighborhood you could either the victim or the aggressor. Stanley said he chose to be the aggressor. As the number of African-American street gangs increased unique set names developed. Many Crip sets were established using the street name where the members lived or the name of a local park they frequented, then added Crip at the end to name of the gang name. This mechanism allowed the non-Crip gang to be formally affiliated as a Crip set. For example, the Main Street Gangsters became the Main Street Crips. According to the U.S. department of Justice being young, a minority and poor are risk factors that increase the chance of being violently victimized. William's comments highlight the fact that many of America's youth have very limited choices.

Even though some gangs adopted the Crip affiliation they remained independent and maintained their own leadership. Gangs like the Kitchen Crips, Five Deuce Crips and the Rollin 20s Crip formed. This individuality may explain why so much Crip verses Crip violence occurred. By the early to mid 1970s the African-American street gang violence had made its way onto school campuses.

1970s

Piru Gangs and the Bloods

There are many reported historical perspectives that suggest how the development of the Blood and Crip gangs occurred. One of the most popular perspectives presented has been the Washington High School history. By late 1969 and the early 1970s the most popular gang in South L.A., California, was the Avenue Boys. A sibling gang, the baby Avenues was led by Craig Munson, Stanley "Tookie" Williams and Raymond Washington. They developed a unique style of dress that was just as intimidating as their reputations. The Avenue Boys wore

Al Capone style hats, leather coats, Levis or sharkskin pants. They also wore an earring in the left ear and used walking sticks or closed umbrellas when walking.

At this time African-American students were being bused from the inner city areas of Los Angeles to White schools in the valley. Williams, Washington and a third youth, Michael Conception began to victimize students that were attending Centennial High School, Compton, California. They would steal the leather-sleeved varsity jackets and within a short period of time gathered a significant following.

During this time Williams, Washington and a small group of followers attacked Sylvester Scott and Benson Owens students at Centennial High school. Washington was reportedly confined to a wheelchair, due to an injury he received in an earlier gang-related incident. In another version it was another member who was in the wheel chair not Raymond Washington. Benson and Scott refused to be victimized and fought off the attack. Both men lived on Piru Street in Compton, California. As the confrontation ended words were exchanged between the two groups. Allegedly, as Raymond Washington's group was leaving, someone said, "don't mess with anyone from Piru Street and take that crip nigger with you." Crip was referring to the disabled attacking gang member.

Scott later became the founder of the first African- American based Piru gang as an original gangster because he lived on Piru Street. Benson started the Westside Pirus. The two gangs initially were started for protection against the Crip gangs. Initially the Piru gang used the blue colored handkerchief to identify with and used the name Piru Crips. This practiced ended within a short time (http://en.wikipedia.org/wiki/Bloods). Then the gang identified themselves by wearing red colored clothing; ultimately they joined and became part of what we now know as the Blood gangs.

Before the late 1960's early 1970's the families that lived on Piru Street were mainly of Mexican descent. In the mid to late 1950's there was a Mexican street gang that was based out of Piru Street. Due to a change in demographics by the time the assault on Owens and Scott occurred most of the neighborhood was ethnically African-American.

By the early 1970s the Piru gang was established and became another rival to all other African-American street gangs. During this time period all African-American street gangs fought each other. There were no alliances between any gangs, however, the largest and most violent gang were those who belonged to the gang that later became known as the Crip gang. The Crip gang was really an alliance between many different sets that aligned themselves with the blue color.

By late 1971 the Avalon Garden Crips and the Inglewood Crips had joined forces with other Crip sets in battling all non-Crip African American street gangs. This included expanding into the Brim territory. The Brims were targeted because they were not part of the Crips. Other non-Crip gangs like the Bishops, Athens Park Boys and the Denver Lanes were also being victimized by the Crip sets.

During the summer of 1972 the Crip and Piru gangs had a major conflict. The Pirus lost and sought the assistance of the Lueders Park Hustlers as back up. The Piru gang set up a meeting between themselves and the Lueders Park Hustlers and invited all other non-Crip associated gangs. The Denver Lanes, Bishops and Brims were a few of the gangs who attended. A strategy was developed at the meeting on how to combat the Crip gangs. It was also decided to stop using the blue colored handkerchiefs and instead use the red colored ones. Up until this time many of the rival Crip gangs still used the blue colored railroad handkerchief. These gangs formed the united organization that became known as the Blood gangs (http://en.wikipedia.org/wiki/Bloods). The rule of thumb became that any gang that was against the Crips could join the Blood gangs as an ally.

In yet another version of how the Blood gang began. It is believed in 1972 the Crips from Compton and newly formed Piru Street Boys were in the middle of a gang war. The Crips end up murdering a member of the L.A. Brims. As a result of this attack the L.A. Brims, Denver

Lanes, Piru Street Boys, the Bishops and other gangs met on West Piru Street and forms the Blood alliance. According to this source the Bloods choose the color red to identify with because there were only two colors of the handkerchief available at the time. The Crips had chosen the blue colored ones, so the Bloods chose the red colored ones (Gangs Across America, 2009).

Remember until 1972 all the African-American street gangs had two things in common with each other. All were rivals and were being constantly attacked by the Crip gang sets and fighting each other. All the non-Crip African-American gangs were outnumbered by more than three to one by the Crips. The 110 or Harbor Freeway became a geographical boundary that divided L.A. into east and west. Eastside and Westside Crip sets formed. As a result all west coast Black street gang members affiliate themselves with either the Bloods or Crips. The Pirus made Centennial High School in Compton the predominant school for the Blood associated gangs just as many Crip sets did with Washington High School in Los Angeles.

Blood gangs also began to develop in housing projects such as the Bounty Hunters from Nickerson Gardens and the Pueblo Bishops. During the mid to late 1970s the Blood and Crip gang populations exploded throughout Los Angeles County. Essentially equal in their level of resources, the Blood and Crip gangs were the same except for the colors they chose and the number of members.

For many African-American youth the only other alternative was to be continually victimized, run away, or join the neighborhood gang. African-Americans as a group have the highest levels of single-family homes and are considered one of the poorest ethnic groups in the country. With statistics like that, it is clear to see that most families could not afford the luxury of relocation. To survive many African-American youth joined street gangs. As the number of African-American gang members and gangs increased, so did the violence. The gang activity and violence received a lot of media attention and helped stereotype the entire African-American population.

The 1970s brought in another trend; Crip on Crip violence. Allied gang sets started to fight each other as well as rival Blood sets. Crip on Crip violence started to escalate in southern California.

1980s

Between 1980 and 1990 Crip and Blood gang violence escalated. Both gangs expanded into narcotics trafficking which facilitated migration. Sometimes, Blood and Crip gang members would leave southern California in an attempt to escape the violence. They would visit family or extended family members outside the state only to find an emerging and often undeveloped drug market. Being opportunistic in nature, these gang members seized the opportunity to establish new drug trafficking operations in these neighborhoods.

There is some anecdotal evidence which suggests the Crips developed a new form of cocaine. Crack was introduced to America. It was and still is an inexpensive and highly addicting form of cocaine. African-American gangs, especially some Crip sets made an enormous profit from trafficking crack and used the capital to advance into other drug markets. Throughout the 1980s and 1990s a few Crip and Blood sets developed intricate local and nationwide networks, sometimes involving family or extended family to facilitate their drug trafficking operations. In doing so the Crips and Blood gangs established a national reputation and respect (http://en.wikipedia.org/ wiki/Bloods).

Naturally, the drug suppliers were gang members and associates located in southern California. Since drugs were generally scarce in the new neighborhoods prices became inflated. As a result street gang members were able to generate tremendous amounts of money through drug sales. It was been estimated that by the 1980s there were approximately 30,000 African-American gang members in the Los Angeles area (http://davadnai.users.omniglobal .net/crips.html).

There are 88 incorporated cities and dozens of other unincorporated sections within L.A. County. By 1972 there were 8 known Crip gangs that grew into 45 gangs in 1978. There were 109 Crip gangs by 1982 within the county. This is not including the Blood sets, Hispanic or Asian gangs all which were present and proliferating. In the late 1990s there were a known 199 individual Crip gangs active in Los Angeles County (www.streetgangs.com/history).

1990s

The later part of the 1990s was a tumultuous time for both gangs and the public. Local law enforcement responded and formed a task force. There was limited success and the violence between the two gangs decreased. It certainly appeared that racial hate was part of the violence formula used by both gangs. Historically, Black and Latino street gangs in L.A. held a shaky truce between them. At times a Latino gang may even back up African-American gang. In the mid 1990s Lueders Park Piru nicknamed the Latino gang they were buying drugs from as Lueders Park 70. Due to the business relationship the Latino gang backed up the African-American gang.

Don't forget during the early 1990s Blood gangs were also forming on the East Coast. The United Blood Nation gang formed in 1993 within the New York City jail system on Riker's Island. The onus for the gang's formation was the constant victimization by the Latin Kings and the Netas, Hispanic prison gangs that controlled much of the New York Jail System at the time (Gangs Across America, 2009).

In L.A. the gang feuds have historically been Black-Black and Latino-Latino. In the 1990s as Latino immigrants moved into Compton and South Los Angeles. As a result of that movement a type of Black Flight occurred. As more Latinos moved in more African-Americans moved out and resentment built between the two races, especially those youth who were involved in gangs. In 1980 the area was 80 percent African-American and 20 percent Latino. By 2000 Latinos represented 60 percent of the neighborhood and African-Americans only comprised 40 percent (Glazer, 2006).

Based on law enforcement anecdotal evidence the mid to late 1990s brought some change to the demographics in Compton and South Los Angeles. Along with the changing demographics street gangs moved into money making crimes like ID theft, credit card theft and more drug trafficking. Gangs that were rivals sometimes became business associates. When a dope deal goes sour, it can go really sour especially when it involves violent street gang members.

2000s

In late July, 2006 four members of the Avenues gang, an older well known Latino gang were convicted of federal hate crimes; crimes that are usually charged against white supremacists. In 1999, the four were joy-riding in a van when they saw a Black man parking his car and decided to kill him. Alejandro "Bird" Martinez and two other gang members popped out of the van and shot Kenneth Kurry Wilson. The three riddled Wilson and his car with bullets from a .357 revolver, a 9mm semi-automatic and a 12 gauge shotgun (Glazer, 2006).

The murder and conviction highlighted community and media speculation that a race war had started between some Crip sets and Latino street gangs. There was a flurry of Black-Latino assaults, especially between some East Coast Crip sets and the Florencia 13 Latino gang. Within a 3 square mile area which was turf occupied by both gangs; assaults between the two gangs fueled media reports of a Black-Latino gang race war.

A closer look at the motive for the crimes was drug trafficking dispute between the East Coast Crip and the Florence 13 gangs. As the feud escalated so did the shootings and killings. At one time gang members from both side simply stated that people from each others' races were targets. Derogatory remarks made by the Latinos against the Blacks and the Blacks against the Latinos only further escalated the violence.

As far as race wars between African-American and Latino gangs we'll probably not see a lot of activity. Occasionally as seen with the July, 2006 L.A. case street gangs can and will resort to committing hate crimes as part of their solution to a problem. Remember gang respect is all too often equated to violent attacks and fear.

Indicia

African-American street gangs adopted membership indicia commonly used by Latino street gangs. For example, African-American gangs used graffiti to mark their territory and like Latino street gangs would and would often list the names of the members of their set in the graffiti. The geographical area the Crip gang originated from became known as the hood or neighborhood. Gang leaders would also recruit new members from within the local neighborhood.

The larger the set, the more powerful and fearful it was. Don't forget this follows a law enforcement observation that the larger the gang is the more violent it tends to be. A popular saying spread throughout Los Angeles County, "Crips don't die, they multiply." Crip gangs became so popular that sometimes the gang name was taken from a particular housing project that originated from. Gangs like the Park Village Crips, Grape Street Crips, and Avalon Garden Crips. The name Crip inferred a violent ruthless and cunning gang member.

As the conflicts between gangs increased, so did the level of violence. Fistfights became a thing of the past. The Crip gangs began to arm themselves with small caliber handguns, rifles, and sawed-off shotguns. Therefore, the Blood gangs followed suit and armed themselves. Soon all African-American gangs had access to all type of high-powered large caliber weapons. The gun became the weapon of choice used to settle all disputes. Gun Violence escalated in Los Angeles County.

When a homeboy was killed in the violence, the payback or retaliations started. The concept was to hurt them worse than they hurt you. This attitude only fueled the violence. The pay back became an excuse to inflict violence on rival gang members because you were avenging the prior assault and protecting your reputation and respect. The violence also increased because in order to accomplish this gang members became bolder. This included retaliatory shootings at gang funerals. Crip gang violence escalated to the point where drive by shootings became a common occurrence. By the late 1970s, the Crip gangs were an established violent street gang.

Unfortunately many African-American youth had limited choices. Some choose to be the aggressor and not the victim. Membership in African-American street gangs increased. As drug trafficking became a major source of income for these gangs violence increased.

Gang rivalries had existed between Los Angeles and Compton gangs for a long time. The formation of the African-American version of the Piru Street gang only rekindled this rivalry. This rivalry became another vehicle used to increase gang violence within the Black community. As other African-American street gangs formed new alliances were developed for protection from the Crips. Logically these gangs align themselves with the Blood gangs. Soon all the anti-Crip gangs were referred to as the Bloods. The Bloods including the Piru gangs would engage the Crip gangs in mutual violence whenever possible. Gang violence was sometimes planned, but often opportunistic, as result of a chance encounter.

Since the Crips outnumbered the Blood gangs almost three-to-one, they became increasingly more violent. Of the Blood aligned gangs, the Pirus developed the reputation of being the most violent. You can see how violence becomes the vehicle to establish a street respect and reputation for gang members and their gang.

Graffiti

Crip and Blood gangs share graffiti writing behaviors with Latino and Asian gangs. Crip and Blood gang graffiti normally contains the gang name and set, along with a list of the set members. As with many other types of street gangs African-American street gangs tend to operate in small sub sets of the gang they belonged to. Usually this cell of gang members contained only 3-12 members.

Sometimes the gang graffiti roster may only list the names of some of the set membership. Like Hispanic street gangs the members named on the graffiti roster do not have to be present when the list is made. The color of the graffiti was and still is important. Therefore, Crip gangs tend to use black and blue colored paint. Blood gangs tend to use black and red colored paint for graffiti whenever possible. I have seen Blood gang graffiti written with blue paint. Under the graffiti was a note that read: This paint is red.

Sometimes, Blood gang members try to avoid using the letter C in their graffiti because of its connotation with Crips. Likewise, some Crip gang members attempted to avoid using the letter B in their graffiti. When the letters have to be used they are crossed out with an X. Both the Crip and the Blood gang members tattoo themselves with their gang names or slogans.

Tattoos

The tattoos can be evidence of membership to a specific set and/or to a gang. Tattoos however, at one time were not common to a majority of this gang population. Trends suggest that tattoos are now more commonly used among many African-American gang members. Tattoos have the same function as stylized clothing, graffiti and hand signs they can offer a greeting, issue a challenge, or intimidate, peer and rival gang members, as well as the non-gang population.

In keeping up with trends African-American gang members have know to brand, burn and pierce themselves as part of the gang life style. You should not be surprised to encounter Blood or Crip gang members with these body modifications.

Hand Signs

Crip and Blood gangs have also perfected the use of hand signs as a form of silent communication. The hand signs were a form of stylized greeting displayed between gang members. The hand signs could be "flashed" or "thrown" to show disrespect or to challenge rival gang members. Flashed and thrown are gang terms that mean the hand sign was formed and shown to another person. A Crip gang member could form the letter C using his fingers and hand. Blood gang members might form the letter B as their hand sign. Hand signs can also be formed making several letters consecutively announcing a gang and a specific set.

Hand Signs can have an intimidating affect on non-gang members. Flashing hand signs has been the precipitating event that very quickly escalated into assaults and murder. Remember no insult goes unanswered to matter how small. Leon Bing writes, "Gang members identify themselves by signing with their hands in gestures similar to the alphabet for the deaf" (Bing, 1991).

Clothing

The Blood gangs still continue to identify with the red and white colors. Blood gangs have been known to use other lighter colors to identify specific sets. For example, a light green color is used by the Lime Hood Pirus, a Blood gang. The clothing styles for African-American gang members have changed three or four times over the last 40 years. At one time bib overalls were popular. Next, brand name sports gear. No matter what the fashionable style worn, the color of red or blue can be seen in some manner. It may be the blue or red shoelaces, just a blue baseball cap or a special belt buckle with a blue or red colored canvas belt; all can signify a gang affiliation.

It follows that the clothing colors for Crip gang members tends to be blue and white. If professional sports wear is worn the team that is chosen will most likely have the same color the gang identifies with or the team logo, initials or name has a specific meaning to the gang. Many African-American gang members also identify with neutral colors such as black or khaki.

Sometimes a gang chooses to wear a particular brand of athletic shoe or baseball cap as part of their attire. Gang attire is important to gang members. It is sort of a street uniform that is easily recognizable by peer and rival gang members. When gang members recognize specific clothing it triggers a response if they do recognize the individual who is wearing it. Don't forget that gang attire is a gang street uniform that is easily recognizable to gang members.

Because of color or specific style of clothing gang members assume the person wearing the gang attire is also affiliated with a street gang. This belief compels gang members to make contact with other youth who are dressed like gang members. There is a potential problem here. Often, gang attire becomes a popular clothing style with the general youth population. Parents who are unaware of this gang behavior can unwittingly place their children in harm's way by buying or allowing them to wear gang attire.

Psychology

Some experts believe the word "blood" is an old African-American slang term meaning brother. Today, Blood gang members often greet themselves by calling each other Blood. The initials CK are used often to refer to being a Crip Killer, enhancing the reputation of the Blood gangster. CK can be used in gang graffiti or tattoos. CK can also refer to Cop Killer or "Cerial" Killer. Blood gang members will also try not to use the letter B when speaking or writing. For example, Blood gang members will say "Bompton" instead of "Compton."

Crip gang members continue to use the color blue to identify their Crip gang in general. Crip gangs also use other dark colors such as brown, black and purple to identify individual sets. For example, the Grape Street Crips in Watts, California uses the color purple to identify their Crip set. Crip gang members will identify with and greet each other with the word Cuzz. This African-American slang word is short for cousin and refers to one being of the same race or gang family.

Crip gang members also sometimes avoid using the letter B when speaking or writing. To the gang member the letter B refers to the term Blood. The initials BK might refer to the gang or gang member being a Blood Killer. These are also the initials for British Knight, a brand name athletic shoe that is popular with many African-American street gang members.

The initials OG refer to a gang member being an Original Gangster for both gangs. Normally, this term was used to describe an older gang member, some who may have been in prison, or one with considerable gang experience. However, today you can find gang members as young as 14 using this term to describe themselves. The term OG is similar in meaning as the Latino gang word Veterano. Another term commonly used is BG, an abbreviation for Baby Gangster, which refers to a young gang member.

At one time both gangs used the term "cluck head," or "base head," which refers to a person who smokes crack cocaine. The word "mission" refers to a drive by shooting. Both gangs will use the term "gang banging" to refer to fighting other gangs.

Insults can be exchanged using verbal challenges, through graffiti, with hand signs or even displaying a certain color. A verbal form of insult for African-American gangs can be made with a couple of words. If a Blood gang member wants to insult a rival Crip gang member he will call out "Crab" or "E-Rickette" (pronounced E-rick or E- rickete). If a Crip gang member wants to insult a rival Blood gang member he will call out using the term "Slob." Both types of verbal insults are accepted as challenges. Any challenge is always answered, usually ending up with a fight. These fights have ended with knife attacks and shootings.

African-American gang members are more likely to use a gun rather than fists to resolve any problem. With the ease of obtaining weapons nowadays almost all gang members have access to some type of gun. Blood gangs are always ready to fight Crip gangs because they are bitter rivals. However, Crip on Crip violence at one time was common. It is unusual for Blood sets to fight each other.

There is some evidence to suggest that after the now famous Rodney King incident African-American gangs in the Los Angeles area either made an informal truce with each other and/or developed a common enemy. Post Rodney King many Crip and Blood sets fought with Hispanic gangs, especially in local in-custody situations. These groups had been polarized by race within the California correction system for years and now it appears that the bias is now expressed on the streets.

There is also some anecdotal law enforcement evidence that tends to suggest many west coast African-American gang members are uniting under the black rag. This may be occurring at least in part to drug trafficking. As the drug business gets larger some gangs will have to associate with rival gang members to facilitate their operations.

There may be a second reason why this is happening. As race started to become a big issue for these street gangs the common enemy appeared to unit gangs that were once the bitterest of rivals. There has been a notable decrease in Crip versus Blood violence. Sometimes Crip and Blood gang members would signify this behavior by claiming to "fly the Black rag." This is a great example of how a social event influenced gang behaviors.

Crip gang sets can be unstructured or structured and have literally been reported all over the country. The majority of Crip sets tend to be located along the west coast, Texas and in the southern states. It was estimated that in 2002 there were approximately 800 sets and between 30,000 and 35,000 Crip gang members nationally. Only the states of West Virginia and Vermont reported no Crip gang activity during this time period.

These behaviors are an extension of the gang psychology. As with all types of gangs African-American street gangs have developed subtle behaviors that announce gang affiliation. As with other street and prison gangs the use of violence is at the center of this psychology.

Drug Sales

By the mid-1970s, a general interest in drug trafficking began to flourish. The most common drugs on the market during this time were phencyclidine (PCP), marijuana, barbiturates and amphetamines. Drug networks were established and African-American gang members found out just how profitable the drug business was. By late 1981 African-American street gangs became involved with the sale of cocaine. Initially, most of the cocaine sales were confined to the Los Angeles County, California, in areas that were occupied by the Crips and Bloods. Almost immediately, gang members found out that power, influence, exclusive homes, nice cars, expensive clothes and jewelry, and women of their choice, could now be bought with the proceeds from drug trafficking.

The crack salesperson now could be as young as 12, and as old as 35. As gang drug sale operations became a business, money became the motivation to join the gang. Gang members as young as 14 years-old could make $100,000 a year, selling drugs (Simpson, 2005).

This was an easy and attractive lifestyle to fall into. Drug trafficking became the easiest way to get what one wanted. The basic form of cocaine being sold was rock and crack cocaine. Gang members would convert ordinary powder cocaine into crack because they could double or triple their investments.

Soon, drug operations spread throughout California and the surrounding western states. Today, crack cocaine can be found throughout the United States. Some African-American gang drug sale operations have become so sophisticated they parallel those of the traditional Italian organized crime syndicates. As the volume of crack sales increased, security problems associated with large sums of cash and drugs were encountered. Some African-American street gangs stopped fighting over colors, substituting cocaine, cash investments and sales territory.

As the gang drug business expanded, so did the gang's influence. In Los Angeles County, Blood and Crip gang members were rivals. In Seattle, Portland, Denver, Cleveland, or anywhere else outside Southern California, these same gang members would work together selling crack. Their rivalry would be set aside in order to take care of business. Because of that business attitude many Crip gang sets now have a business relationship with the Black Gangster Disciple gangs based in Chicago.

When a gang member travels, he may attempt to conceal his gang identity. Nevertheless, wherever they move they would tend to still pursue the gang lifestyle. This way new gang sets could be established anywhere in or out of the country. A new word entered the gang vocabulary: rock house. The term usually described a rented house where crack cocaine was manufactured, sold, and sometimes used. This was a place of business.

Specific jobs developed as this drug business grew. There are the mules, which transport the drugs. Street peddlers sell the drugs on the street. Lookouts watch out for the police and warn the street peddlers. Enforcers use threats and violence to make collections on unpaid debts. There are also the intelligence gatherers who collect all the information they can regarding other drug dealers and law enforcement operations.

There are now second-generation Crip and Blood gang members. Traditions are being established within these gang families. The African-American street-gang lifestyle has become an acceptable way of living for some families. Within a set there can be up to four sub-sets or sub divisions: the OG, the Gangster, the BG (Baby Gangster), and sometimes the TG (Tiny Gangster). These gang sub-sets are divided up by age.

As with other ethnic street gangs, there are levels of membership or commitment to the gang, including hard-core members, regular members, associate members and those in the recruitment pool. Each level demands more and more commitment and loyalty. As a group, the main source of income for Crip gang members continues to be from trafficking powdered cocaine, crack, marijuana and PCP. It should not shock anyone to determine that the lager sets can collect millions of dollars from retail and wholesale sales of these drugs.

Rivals

It is common knowledge and well accepted that the primary rivals of all Crip sets are Blood affiliated street gangs. Other Crip rivals now include any gang that is affiliated with the People Nation alliance, specifically the Latin Kings. Other People Nation alliance gangs include the Black P Stones, Bloods, Cobra Stones, Vice Lord Nation and the El Rukins. Most of these gangs are based out of the Chicago area (Virginia Gang Investigators Association, 2004).

By the early 2000s some Crip sets had form an alliance with the Chicago based Gangster Disciples. This alliance is unusual due to the fact that normally these two gangs were rivals. As previously mentioned the purpose of such an association is well known; make money. The association was most likely made in order to expand drug trafficking operations.

The same would also hold true for some Blood sets. Normally there rivals would be the People Nation gangs based in the mid-west. But alliances between some Blood sets and the mid west gangs have formed.

Female Gangs

While some female gang members portray themselves as playing major roles in the gang they claim, in reality the majority of young women play a very minor role in the life of the African-American street gang. However, a few African-American women actually take part in gang activities. It was not unusual for female gang members to hide narcotics or weapons for their male counterparts. Women were rarely jumped-in, but they will dress down with either red or blue, depending on what neighborhood they belong to. Most of the time females acted as auxiliary members for the male gangs with which they associated.

On occasion, female gang members have actually participated in violence against a rival gang. However, females have historically had a very limited part in the daily gang operations. Today, female African-American gangs exist and the ladies can be just as violent as their male counterparts. In 2002 an all female gang emerged in the Compton area and were known as the Rainbow Crips. This gang's female members were allegedly lesbian and hence the word rainbow in the name. Anecdotal evidence suggested that gang operates like a party crew.

Summary

Sanyika Shakur also known as "Monster" Kody Scott stated in his book that he had to learn that there were three stages of reputation [respect] to go through before the title of Original Gangster (OG) could be bestowed upon an African-American gang member.

"1. You must build the reputation of your name, i.e., you as an individual;

2. You must build your name in association with your particular set, so that when you name is spoken your set is also spoken of in the same breath, for it is synonymous; and

3. You must establish yourself as promoter of Crip or Blood, depending of course, on which side of the color bar you live" (Scott, 1993).

These tenants are part of the gang psychology. Although stated uniquely for African American gang members per Scott they are commonly believed by any gang member. Respect and reputation become the focus of gang life. The more work fore the gang you put in the greater the status you have with the gang.

African-American street gangs have help spread the use of cocaine and the problems associated with those who become addicted. The inherent intrigue and excitement of the street-gang lifestyle continues to attract those who are least able to resist. The use of fear and violence has become the main stay for these gangs.

Unfortunately, the majority membership and recruitment pool for the gang continues to come from the disadvantaged and under-educated portion of the African American population. The influence of these street gangs has been so strong in Los Angeles County, California, that high school football games have been canceled to protect the spectators and players.

United Blood Nation

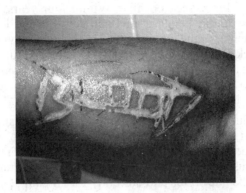

Almost everyone is familiar with African-American gangs like the Bloods and Crips. Nationally and internationally, they enjoy a reputation that is commonly associated with the Los Angeles based Crip and Blood gangs. However, there are a number of other African-American street and prison gangs in the eastern part of the United States that share some of the same behaviors and characteristics of their west coast counterparts, yet at the same time are unique to west coast based African-American street gangs.

History

A good example of this phenomenon is the east coast Blood gang now known as the United Blood Nation (UBN). The gang is sometimes called East Coast Bloods or Bloods. The UBN is really comprised of a number of different gang sets based in the east coast. The gang was initially formed within the New York Department of Corrections at the George Motchan Detention Center, Rikers Island in 1993 by Omar "Mack" Portee and Leonard "Dead Eye" McKenzie. They are credited as being founders of the gang. UBN was originally formed to protect African-American inmates who were not members of any gang from attacks by members of the Netas and Latin King gangs. Historically, protection has been a mechanism and a major reason why many street and almost all prison gangs form.

The Netas prison gang was originally formed within the Puerto Rican prison system. Puerto Rican youth who migrated to the United States banded together when assaulted by New York based street gangs. These youth formed a clique of Netas in New York and competed with another Latin based gang, the Latin Kings. Today, the Netas gang now operates in east coast prisons and streets.

In the beginning, Portee and McKenzie adopted the anti-oppression ideology of the Black Panther Party for the gang but they also promoted the gangster lifestyle. Within a year of its formation, the UBN membership had grown so much that multiple sets started to develop. Leonard McKenzie formed the Nine Trey Gangsters and Omar Portee formed the One Eight Trey gang. Initially, six other sets were formed. They included Sex, Money Murder (SMM), Hit Squad Brims, Valentine Bloods, Mad Stone Villains, Blood Stone Villains and the Gangster Killer Bloods. It is assumed that these are the original sets of the UBN gang.

Like many other street gangs, these gang sets rapidly spread into the surrounding communities as members were released from the correctional facilities. This mechanism of growth is not encountered with west coast based African-American street and prison gangs. In fact, this mechanism is uncommon with street gangs that form in the west coast. West coast based street gangs tend to form on the street, within certain geographical parts of a community, not in prison. However, there is possibly one exception, the Nazi Low Riders street gang originally formed in the California Youth Authority and yet operates as both a street and prison gang. You can refer the Chapter on Nazi Low Riders for more details.

As the UBN membership on the street grew quickly; the primary source of income for UBN members became the trafficking crack cocaine. Within four years, by 1997, UBN sets were established in upstate New York, Pennsylvania and New Jersey. Like the Crip gangs, UBN gang became known for their extreme violence. The UBN brand of violence became "slashing," a razor blade or knife attack. There is some anecdotal evidence to suggest that some West Coast and East Coast Blood gangs had a series of meetings in 1999. It was after these meetings that the name United Blood Nation was used to describe the Blood gangs on the east and west coasts of the United States (www.gripeforkids.org).

By 2000 the UBN influence had also spread to the southeast part of the country. The main mechanism for this spread appeared to be the UBN members who were released from prison that returned to their homes in the southeast; or migrating New York based UBN members expanding drug connections or fleeing law enforcement. Gang migration becomes increasingly more important between the late 1990s and currently for all gangs.

Academic research suggests that a growing narcotic trafficking trade is commonly encountered with all street gangs. This theory is also verified through some law enforcement observations and experiences (NAGIA, 2005). This anecdotal evidence and academic research suggests that involvement in drug trafficking operations appears to be one of the driving forces behind gang migration. This observation appears to be one of the driving forces that assisted in the spread of UBN influence along the eastern seaboard (www.gripeforfids.org).

The formation of the UBN gang within the east coast correctional facilities also caused a reaction. Prior to the formation of the UBN few African-American inmates in the Northeast and East claimed membership to any well-known street gang. In fact, these inmates tended to group together based on where they were from. After World War II, many Mexican immigrants did the same thing in southern California. They tended to group together based on what part of Mexico they migrated from and while in custody. This common geographical connection can act as a very strong cohesive factor that binds people together, especially those who have similar issues.

Once the UBN gang was established, many African-American inmates incarcerated in east coast prisons tended to join the gang or a gang that aligned itself with UBN. The opposite also occurred. Those African-Americans who did not like the UBN gang tended to join any UBN rival gang. This dynamic has fueled additional security issues within the affected institutions and on the streets. It seems logical that the larger the UBN gang became, the more violent members tended to be. The anecdotal evidence suggests that the larger a street gang is the more violent it tends to be. This phenomenon has been observed in all street gangs, not just the UBN gang.

Currently, there are a number of UBN sets that tend to be dominant. They include the original eight and the Five Nine Brims, Mad Dog Bloods and the Mad Stone Bloods. However, there are a number of smaller sets that have formed in the east coast and in correctional institutions. UBN sets have been reported in at least 10 states. It is thought that this has happened due to the migration of UBN behaviors motivated by gang activity and by gang members returning to their homes after being released from incarceration.

Because of their Blood affiliation UBN sets to align themselves with other Blood gangs, including west coast Blood sets and other gangs that are part of the People Nation alliance. There is some anecdotal evidence that suggests some UBN sets have also struck an alliance with a few MS-13 gang cliques in the east coast. This may have been motivated with drug trafficking.

Unique to some UBN sets is the fact that on occasions they have even aligned themselves to rival gangs like the Latin Kings and some Crip sets. These associations benefited the financial status of both gangs and commonly the main criminal activity has been drug trafficking. Narcotics' trafficking appears to be one of main income generators for many street gangs. As gangs become more involved in drug trafficking there is a tendency to become more vertically organized. This implies that a formal leadership structure develops.

These types of gang alliances are not new. In 1995, members from rival Sureno gangs based in California formed an alliance in New Mexico to traffic drugs. They called themselves the Sureno-13 gang. In the mid 1980's Blood and Crip gang members formed the same type of associations outside California, again the association benefited their drug tracking operations. In fact, drug trafficking has become the vehicle that continues to bring rival gangs and gang members together to form unique business relationships and alliances throughout the country.

Some Blood gang members refer to themselves as "dawgs." This is not a bad thing. The term can also be used as a greeting or as a general reference to a peer gang member. Some gang members will use cigarettes to burn what appears to be an upside down triangle on their arms. The symbol that forms looks similar to a dog paw print. This is another reference to the term dawg and most likely is a symptom of membership as non-gang members do not normally use this type of body modification (www. gripeforkids.org).

The main UBN rivals continue to be all the Folk Nation gangs, Crips, as well as the Latin Kings and Neta gangs. The UBN gang as a cohort also tends to be more organized that than their west coast counterparts. For example, the UBN gang has a formal oath of allegiance, a prayer, a concept of war, motto and pledge. All are formalized in writing and members are expected to memorize them.

Membership

Some UBN members tend to share some of the membership indicia of their west coast counterparts. However, since the UBN gang formed in the east coast you could also expect to note some unique membership indicia as well. For example, some UBN members will use the code "031" in tattoos, personal writings and graffiti. This code translates to "much love to another member." West coast based Blood sets do not use this code. At one time some UBN gang members wore green and red bead necklaces to show their gang affiliation. The necklace trend never caught on with west coast based Blood sets. By 2009, the use of beaded necklaces by UBN members appears to be no longer popular.

The UBN gang has initiation rituals just as West Coast Blood gangs. Besides slashing another commonly reported initiation process for UBN sets includes: committing acts of violence, especially on rival gang members, on witnesses in criminal cases, other in custody gang members and law enforcement. The slashing assault is sometimes referred to as "spilling blood." A potential member may also be required to "put in work." This is gang slang for committing any type of crime for the gang. Putting in work has the same meaning for all west coast based African-American street gangs. As with other gangs, in some UBN sets all members must approve membership of a prospective member. This characteristic is also observed with outlaw motorcycle gangs and some prison gangs.

Another part of the initiation process can include a jumping in. Remember that is when a prospective gang member is beat up by several members of the gang he wants to belong to. This ceremony is also known as a beat-in. It is a commonly initiation ritual used by many street gangs. For a potential UBN member he or she would be assaulted for a period of 31 seconds. Don't forget 031 in the form of a tattoo, graffiti or writing sends a message of brotherly love to another UBN member. The 18th Street gang will assault a new member for 18 seconds.

For females who wish to be members of a UBN set, they also may have to be sexed-in as an initiation. This would require the prospective female member to have sexual intercourse with some or all the male members of the set.

At the end of the initiation process the new member recites the UBN oath or pledge and receives the dog-paw mark. It appears to look like the three dot tattoo that is commonly used by Hispanic gang members. However, normally the dog-paw is burnt into the skin with a cigarette.

West coast Blood set initiation rituals are much less formalized and normally do not require the recital of an oath or pledge and the burning of a gang specific mark.

The three-dot tattoo is a generic gang tattoo for west coast street gangs. For the east coast based UBN gang member the three dot burn or tattoo is gang specific. As of 2008 some east coast Latino youth also refer to the three dot tattoo as "party dots." These youth claim the tattoo refers to the wild party life of young people. This reinforces the fact that tattoos can take on regional meanings and how some gang characteristics/behaviors are being adopted by youth in the general population.

The UBN gang has one exemption to the traditional initiation processes. An individual born to UBN parents is considered a member by birth. This is sometimes referred to as being "born-in." The born in status might suggest a generational aspect to UBN membership.

Indicia

Since the UBN gang is aligned with the People Nation gangs, UBN members may also display a five-pointed star as a symbol of this affiliation. Other common symbols used by UBN members include a bulldog, a bull, the three dots, CK (Crip Killer), B (Blood) and 031. Naturally UBN members identify with the color red, as do their west coast counterparts.

Clothing colors tend to be red, but many UBN members will wear professional sports jerseys and baseball caps. The Chicago Bulls basketball team and Boston Red Sox baseball team professional sports wear is often worn by UBN members. The clothing is also worn in a manner that is consistent with People Nation gang practices. Therefore, baseball caps will be tilted to the left; red shoelaces are only worn on the left shoe. There is general orientation to the left side of the body. This behavior is referred to as representing. It is commonly encountered with many other Folk and People Nation street gangs. Some UBN members have displayed no membership indicia, but are still members of the gang. Trend wise as of 2009 some gang members around the country and internationally some gang members are doing the same thing. This has been done in order to avoid identification by law enforcement.

One other point must be made here. Even though the UBN gang shares many of same behaviors and customs of west coast Blood sets and street gangs in general, the gang also has a unique practice for written communication. Many UBN sets use written codes for communicating to the membership. The codes could be a simple as letter substitution of the alphabet or using numbers to represent the letters of the alphabet. Some codes are more complicated and based on ciphers. West coast based Blood sets have not used coded writings.

Here are a few example of how slang can be used as verbal or written codes. A UBN member may say, "Nothing but nigga" which really means, "I got 100% love for you." "Splish, Splash" really refers to a razor. A reference to "Mr. Window" refers to murder, death or killer.

Numbers can be used in the same fashion. For example, "000" really means, I am a blood. "009" translates to what's up blood. 013 is a reference to tear a person up, hit that person. West coast street gangs sometimes use 24/7 to mean 24 hours a day, seven days a week, slang for all the time. UBN gang members sometimes used the number 435 to mean all day.

Since the UBN gang aligns itself with the People Nation alliance. You could anticipate that some UBN writings, graffiti, tattoos or slang may contain symbols or words that are generally used by People Nation gangs. A debrief with a Virginia UBN gang member indicated that the dog paw tattoo is significant to show legitimate membership. According to the UBN gang members all Blood gang members are united across the country (Grizzard, 2004).

Summary

The UBN gang is a good example of how gangs across the country share similar characteristics and yet develop regionalized characteristics that make them unique. The gang's activity in drug trafficking allows for expansion and sophistication of some sets. Although the practice of being born into the gang is unusual it may become a mechanism for fathers/ mothers to pass down the illegal gang related criminal enterprises down to their siblings. This also may open the door for female leadership in the gang.

The Lanes

This chapter will examine the history of the Denver Lane Bloods (DLB) and Pasadena Denver Lanes (PDL) and how these gangs have spread throughout the country. The term "Lanes" has been used to describe any Blood gang that is part of the Denver Lane Blood or the Pasadena Denver Lane gang. It is possible that DLB and PDL members migrated from the Los Angeles area and started new sets of the gang in other states and cities.

One of the most common reasons for most gang movement has been quality of life issues, including eluding peer and rival gang members, fleeing from police investigation or simply trying to leave the local gang culture and start over. Anecdotal law enforcement evidence also suggests that some Blood gang members leave the Los Angeles area to other parts of the country in order to build up gang membership and presence. A local gang member may also be sent to leave with uncle, aunt or grandparents in another state. Once there the L.A. based gang member quickly realizes that he or she has instant street credentials because they are from Los Angeles. These recruiters bring the L.A. style of Blood behaviors and southern California gang connections to the east coast and establish new sets of the gang (Ross, 2009 and Nunn, 2009).

It is likely that there are other mechanisms besides migration that could explain why the 'Lanes" and other Los Angeles based gangs are encountered in other states. The persona of Denver Lane Bloods or the Pasadena Denver Lane Bloods could have been adopted by gangs in other regions of the United States through use of the Internet on sites like My Space or You Tube or through email connections. Written media such as magazines could also help spread the culture or 'brand name' of these Blood gangs.

History

The Denver Lane Bloods originated in the city of Los Angeles. The actual genesis of the gang is most likely traced back to two different L.A. based street gangs. In 1970, two individuals, Sam Bell and Pea Body allegedly founded the Denver Lane Boys (Mac, 2008). The gang was designed for those youth who did not want to join the predominate Crip or Blood gangs in Los Angeles. Some of the Denver Lane Boys membership most likely came from the ranks of the Figueroa Boys gang. The gang's name is most likely derived from the street that ran north and south through the gang neighborhood. The Denver Lane Boys gang became popular and immediately grew in membership.

The local high school in this area was Locke High School. In late 1971, Locke High School had a large membership of two different gangs at the school; the Denver Lane Boys and the Athens Park Boys. Due to the large gang population the high school became known as a "blood school" in the street gang culture (Mac, 2008). During the early 1970s the Figueroa Boys gang became defunct as its membership shrank and ultimately disappeared, probably because the members joined the Devil Lane Boys. Approximately at the same time the Denver Lane Boys change their gang name to the Denver Lane Bloods.

In the 1970s, the DLB gang grew in size so much that it became the largest African-American gang in Los Angeles. The gang's size posed a threat to the local Crip gangs. At onetime the Denver Lane Bloods controlled activity in over 20 city blocks. The size of the DLB gang was so predominate that many Crip gangs consolidated. For example, the 102nd Street Crips and 118th Street Lil James sets joined the East Coast Crips and battled their main rival, the Denver Lane Bloods. This is a common dynamic that can be the onus for gang alliances and rivalries to form. Gang consolidation is a way to increase in size and become a more formable force. This behavior also increased the rivalry between the Bloods and Crips (Mac, 2008).

The major concentration of the Denver Lane Bloods was the west side of the Harbor Freeway also known as the 110 Freeway and in south Los Angeles. This area of L.A. was known for the presence of cheap motels and prostitutes. Right in the middle of the DLB territory was a major street known as Imperial Highway. Imperial Highway was and still is a major thorough fare for Los Angeles area commuters. At the time rival Crip gang members would drive on Imperial Highway to get to different parts of their territory. This made these Crip gang members ideal targets for the DLB gang since parts of Imperial Highway were in DLB turf. As a result, numerous shootings involving DLB gang members against Crips passing through on Imperial Highway were reported and unreported.

As suggested earlier, as cities grow in population, rural areas tend to become suburban areas and infra-structure changes occur. These infra-structure changes include the building of freeways, major streets, businesses and homes. This also happened in Los Angeles during the 1960s and 1970s as the county's population grew. When the construction of the new Los Angeles 105 Freeway began, it also cut right through existing gang turfs including the Denver Lane Blood gang. These man-made boundaries effectively isolated the Denver Lane Bloods and left them surrounded by rival gangs.

To the north were the Hoover Crips; to the east were the 112th Broadway Crips and the 118th East Coast Crips; to the west were 107th Street Hoovers and to the south were the 120th Raymond Avenue Crips (Mac, 2008).

All Blood gangs do not necessarily get along with other. There is Blood/ Blood violence as rivalries develop within a gang set or between Blood gangs. For example, during the 1980s a well known Blood gang known as the Van Ness Gangsters (VNG) developed a sibling gang known as the Rollin 50's Brims (RFB). Within a short period of time the Rollin 50's Brims strikes an alliance with a set of the Denver Lane Bloods and changes its gang name to the 50s Lanes.

This name change is short lived as the 50s Lanes change their name again, back to the Rollin 50s Brims but still aligned with the Denver Lane Blood gang and their parent VNG. This change added to the mix of gang rivalry as the primary enemy of the RFB becomes the Rollin 40's and Rollin 60's Crip gangs. This is a great example of how dynamic the street gang culture is and how street gangs can develop and disappear in short periods of time.

Much of the history of the Denver Lanes is passed down to younger generations of the gang by the word of mouth. Many bona fide older DLB gang members know about one of the gang's most violent members Al Dog (deceased), the palm trees along Figueroa to Vermont streets; these members may also talk about the wild green parrots that fly from palm tree to palm tree. Having this kind of knowledge can separate real original gang members from those who simply claim DLB gang membership.

Pasadena Denver Lanes

There were a number of different African-American street gangs in Pasadena in the late 1970s. Gangs like the Project Boys, El Sereno Raw Dogs (at the time the second largest Black gang in Pasadena), the Bunarus and the Original Ghetto Boys were all active in Pasadena at the time. The Pasadena Devil Bloods (PLB) gang formed around 1979 in the New West area of Pasadena as a sibling gang of the Ghetto Boys (Mac, 2008 and Pasadena Police Department, 2009).

One version of the PDL history suggests that during the 1980's the Denver Lane Bloods were actively recruiting new members from surrounding cities and gangs. This included the city of Pasadena. In 1981, a DLB member named Vick Rock recruited the Pasadena Devil Lane gang to become affiliated with the Denver Lane Bloods (Mac, 2008). This affiliation and alliance instantly increased the size of both gangs and added to their street reputations.

An alternate version proposes that a 108th Denver Lane Blood gang member named Jerome Smallwood from Los Angeles moved from Los Angeles to the city of Pasadena in 1979. He is credited with founding the Devil Lane Blood gang in Pasadena and changing the Devil Lane Blood gang name to the Pasadena Denver Lane gang in 1981 (Love, 2009, Mac, 2008 and Pasadena Police Department, 2009). The original territory claimed by the Pasadena Devil Lane gang was Summit Ave between Washington and Painter streets. The area of the city at the time was known as the "Snake Pit."

Within the short period of time it takes for the Pasadena Devil Lane gang to form, the El Sereno Raw Dogs gang and the Raw Dogs gang becomes defunct as so many of their members are drawn into the PDL gang. In the early 1980s, the Pasadena Devil Lane gang changes its name to the Pasadena Denver Lanes and formally aligns with Denver Lane Blood gang. Around 1981, the Pasadena Denver Lanes adopt the hand sign of the letter "L" as one of the gang's symbols to represent the "Lanes." It is believed that by the end of 1982 the PDL gang was one of the largest Blood gang in California, probably making all Lane Blood gangs and affiliates one of the largest African-American Blood gangs in the L.A. area at the time (Mac, 2008 and Pasadena Police, 2009). There is some law enforcement anecdotal evidence that suggests the largest Blood gang during this time were the Bounty Hunters based in the Nickerson Gardens, Los Angeles County (Ross, 2009).

By the mid to late 1980s, there was a lot reported and non-reported PDL violence in the form of infighting. Some PDL gang sets tended to fight over drug trafficking issues. The Pasadena Denver Lane gang also started to fraction into smaller independent sets, some turned against the parent PDL gang. For example, in the 1990s a sibling gang known as the Parke Street Nine Lives (P-9s) broke away and realigned itself with the Crip gangs forever becoming a formal PDL and Blood gang rival. The original five members of the P-9s were later involved in a mistaken revenge gang related murder; they were arrested and convicted of the murder which occurred on October 31st. The incident became known as the "Halloween Massacre" (Pasadena Police Department, 2009).

The Pasadena Denver Lane Blood gang is a generational gang. The PDL gang is in its third and fourth generation (Love, 2009). Children of the original members of the Pasadena Devil Lanes are currently active in the Pasadena Denver Lanes and in a few cases, children of first generation gang members are now involved in the PDL gang life (Mac, 2008). As one original member of the Pasadena Devil Lanes and later Pasadena Denver Lane member told me, he is now a grandfather and has three generations of family members that are PDL gang members (Love, 2009).

Sets

The PDL gang can be divided up into smaller sub groups called sets. The set name tends to be derived from the location of the group. The name could be taken from a street or apartment complex name. In Pasadena at one time the PDL gang had three main sets; Project Gangsters, the Summit Street Hustlers (Russ, 1995) and the Young Gangsterz (YGs) (Clawson, 1995). The Young Gangsterz sometimes refer to themselves as the Summit Street Gangsters (SSG) or the "Low End Summit" (Low Endz) (Clawson, 1995). Other reported gang sets are Carlton Street and the Fairoaks Street Gangster Bloods (FSGB) and the Tip Top Bloods (TTP) (Pasadena Police Department, 2009).

Outside California the PDL gang tends to operate in a similar fashion. For example in Baltimore, Maryland law enforcement anecdotal evidence suggests the presence of the major sets and subsets of the PDL gang. Sets that have been identified include the "L-Gang," "754" and "187" or are called the "Lanes". Several subsets like the "Low End Lanes," "Devil Lanes," and the "East Side PDL" are all part of the Pasadena Denver Lane gang in Baltimore.

Indicia

Members of the PDL gang identify with the red color whether they are based in the west or east coasts. The color can be displayed in clothing, hats, bandanas, professional sports gear and even in contact lenses. PDL members can also use tattoos to identify themselves. Many gang members also have a nickname or moniker. It is common for peer gang members to know each other only by their gang moniker and not know a member's legal name. Sometimes a PDL gang member can have more than one moniker. The gang can also use graffiti to identify turf and presence in a community. The most common forms depict the gang set name and the letters PDL. Sometimes graffiti and writing will contain the letters CK, with the C crossed out to signify 'Crip Killer.'

DLB and PDL gang members will also use hand signs to show gang affiliation. The Most common hand sign is a form of the letter "L." This letter signifies the abbreviation for "lanes."

Membership

Like many gangs, the PDL has an informal leadership structure. Usually older members are "shot callers" and will direct the activity of other members. However, like many gangs the PDL has a formal social structure for its membership. This is a formal and well defined hierarchical membership status, where advancement is dependent on the amount of criminal activity attempted for the gang's benefit.

For example the highest level of membership is known as "Triple OG" or "OOOG." "OG" is a gang term that refers to original gangster, or one of the original members. The term implies that the member has been active with the gang for a long time; the member has acquired tenure. The next level would be identified as "Double OG" or "OOG;" these are seasoned gang members but do not have the tenure time of a Triple OG. Third in the social ladder are OG's (original gangster) and then G's (gangster). This nomenclature is used on both coasts (Love, 2009). New members are the lowest ranking social wise. A brand new member is called a "new booty or booty" (Love, 2009). On the west coast, the term "young gangster" (YG) or "baby gangster (BG) is used by PDL members to refer to those gang members who are generational and born into the gang (Love, 2009). On the east coast, the terms may be used to refer to new gang members. New gang members that have been active with the gang and have proven themselves are called "OYG" or "Original Young Gangsters." This social hierarchy is followed by the PDL gang on both coasts. OYG and YG status is considered as a junior rank as G, OG, OOG and OOOG are considered senior ranks.

Some PDL sets have set meetings where the regular membership is required to pay set dues. Usually, a shot caller orders the meeting where gang business is discussed. This could include talking about past acts of violence, other crimes committed by gang members, gang members that were arrested, police activity and discipline issues; which include the identification of police informants and witnesses. One other main reason why meetings are held is to plan, organize and discuss future PDL gang crimes which can include assaults, drug trafficking, money collection, burglaries, robberies and murder; and to talk about means to cover up these crimes and enforce gang membership rules.

Most new members tend to be sponsored by a PDL member or shot caller. New Pasadena Denver Lane blood gang members do not have to endure the common initiation ritual of being jumped in. This is a common behavior with many west coast Blood gangs. To join the PDL gang, a person has to contact someone in a set and put in work for the gang. This proves the worth of the potential member and insures gang membership. Females can join the gang in the same way. Females can also join the gang by being "fucked in" (sexed in). But according to one female Blood gang member females "who get fucked in don't have the same amount of respect as girls who go missions... these girls are used for gang pussy and head" (Nunn, 2009 and Love, 2009).

Once a person has put in work for the set, he or she is expected to continue to partake in activities that benefit the gang. Sometimes prospective members can be given a specific crime to commit for the gang this is another way one can earn gang membership (Nunn, 2009).

Summary

Sub groups of the Denver Lane Bloods are sometime called sets, cliques or blocks. For example these are a few sets of the Denver Lane Bloods; Figueroa Riders, Imperial Boys, 105, 106, 108, 108 112, 115 and 120 blocks. The Denver Lane Bloods are aligned with the Athen Park Boys, 50s Lanes, Pasadena Denver Lanes, Rollin 50 Boys and the Van Ness gangsters. The rivals can included the Hoover Criminal gang, the 92nd 107th and 112th Raymond Ave Crips and the 112 Broadway Gangsters (Mac, 2008). In a 2009 ad hoc survey DLB and PDL gangs have been reported in Washington, Utah, Ohio and Maryland (Valdez, 2009). In addition other PDL sets have been reported in Arkansas, Texas, Missouri, New York, Illinois, Maryland, Pennsylvania and Ohio (Love, 2009 and Nunn, 2009).

Bounty Hunter Bloods

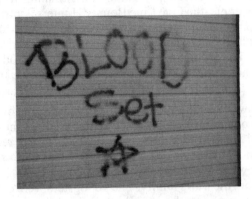

The Blood gangs are an organized and unorganized association of violent street gangs that have reported in at least 40 states with an estimated U.S. membership between 15,000 and 20,000. At least 6,000 Blood gang members were reported in the Los Angeles area in 2003 (NDIC, 2003). The Bounty Hunter Blood gang is part of this association. The Bounty Hunter shares many behaviors with street gangs but also has some unique characteristics that are not encountered in other street gangs. The Bounty Hunter gang is considered the largest Blood oriented gang in Los Angeles County (Ross, 2009).

History

The history of the Bounty Hunter (BH) varies and there are several stories on how the gang got its name. One of the most common histories suggests the Bounty Hunter gang name was derived from an old western movie (Ross, 2003). Another theory suggests the gang got its name because some of the older members were chased by legal bounty hunters (Schmidt, 2003). The gang allegedly started as a social group that eventually got involved in criminal activities.

The gang was formed in the Nickerson Gardens housing project during the mid to late 1970s (Ross, 2009). The first name of the gang was allegedly the "Lot Boys" as the early members hung around the parking lots of the housing complex and began to get involved in criminal activities (Schmidt, 2003). When that occurred the group adopted the now well known gang name, Bounty Hunters.

The gang has been and currently is concentrated in the Nickerson Gardens housing project in Watts, California and is located at 1590 East 114th Street. The Nickerson Gardens consists of 156 building with 1067 town house style public housing units. This makes the Nickerson Gardens the largest public housing development west of the Mississippi River (Flaherty, 2009). To give you an idea of the size of this housing complex it is estimated to cover 68 acres (Thompson, 2003).

The Bounty Hunters gang is known to rule the Nickerson Garden area through intimidation, force and fear. Many of the local residents are afraid of the gang and will attempt to avoid any contact with them. The Bounty Hunters in some cases have taken over apartments when residents move out and excluded the newly assigned tenants. As one resident said, "nobody in their right mind would live here, if they could live elsewhere" (Winton and Krikorian, 2004).

The Bounty Hunters have established a drug trafficking business in Nickerson Gardens. Most gang members do not qualify for housing, so they will rent kitchens, closets or take over an apartment to facilitate drug sales. Since many residents are considered low income it is difficult to refuse and extra $1000/ month to allow a gang members to use the kitchen and closet. Drug money unfortunately puts food on some house hold tables. The gang specifically targets single mothers and new families (Ross, 2003).

As the gang grew in size sets developed and took their names from the parking lots within Nickerson Gardens. For example, the Five Line Bounty Hunters control and hang out in the area of 115th Street; the Four Line Bounty Hunters control the area of 114th Street; the Ace Line Bounty Hunters control 111th Street and the Deuce Lane set controls and works the area of 112th Street (Ross, 2003). The 108th Street set is situated around 108th Street between Central and Compton Avenues (Thompson, 2003). Some sets names are derived differently.

The Folsom Lot set got its name because one the Bounty Hunter gang members spent time in Folsom prison. The Shaw Lot set derived its name because some of the Bounty Hunters used to show off their cars in a one parking lot. A gang slang word for show lot became 'shaw' and the gang set was eventually named Shaw Lot. The Brazy Brew set received its name from the fact that many of the Bounty Hunters is this set were heavy partiers and drinkers. The Hillbilly set originated from the new members (youngsters) having a habit of not wearing shoes. The youngsters were mainly from the Carrs family. The youngsters were called Hillbillies by the rest of the gang. The Blockhood set controls a small area in an adjoining neighborhood just east of Nickerson Gardens (Schmidt, 2003).

Gang sets do not always honor the geographical turfs, as sometimes one set will infringe and try and take control of another set's drug turf (Ross, 2003). This can and does lead to intra set violence within the Bounty Hunter gang. Bounty Hunter violence has also been documented against other Blood oriented gangs. This is a consistent gang behavior that has been encountered with Crip and Hispanic street gangs.

The gang sets are diversified in their criminal activity. Some sets are involved in robbery, extortion, burglary and assaults. Sometimes sets will attempt home invasion style robberies on peer and rival owned drug houses. Gun violence is often accompanies these crimes.

Within the Bounty Hunter gang a member may get more respect by assaulting or killing another Bounty Hunter member, rather than a rival gang member. Given the opportunity Bounty Hunters will rob and murder each other for a chance to move up the gang social ladder (Ross, 2003). This is cannibalistic behavior is common amongst many prison, street and outlaw motorcycle gangs.

The Bounty Hunter gang is a generational gang and second and third generation gang members have been contacted by the local police (Schmidt, 2003). Sadly, some gang members use the excuse of growing up in Nickerson Gardens as the reason they joined the gang. There was nowhere else to go.

Membership

The Bounty Hunter gang does not use the traditional 'jump in' initiation ritual (Schmidt, 2003). To become a Bounty Hunter a prospective member needs to be sponsored by another Bounty Hunter member. The member has to vouch for the prospective recruit. In return the prospective member is expected to do something for his sponsor. The new member must prove his worth to his sponsor before actually being allowed to join the gang.

The would-be gang member must be prepared to do anything his sponsor asks. This is much like what prospects have to endure for membership into an outlaw motorcycle gang. The more crime a would-be member is willing to be involved in (putting in work) the less chance that member would cooperate with police and reveal the gang's criminal endeavors. This makes him (or her) a better candidate for Bounty Hunter membership (Ross, 2003).

Other Bounty Hunter members suggest one can join the gang by living in the area or being related to someone that lives in Bounty Hunter turf. The prospective member has to prove their worth by committing crimes at the direction of bonefide members. Not everyone single Bounty

Hunter is required to prove themselves to the gang. Since the gang is generational in nature, some members simply hung out with the gang when they were young juveniles. Overtime these youths simply claim Bounty Hunter membership and then start to get involved in criminal activities (Schmidt, 2003).

Involvement in criminal activity is called 'putting in work' for the Bounty Hunters. Putting in work proves a new members worth to the gang and facilitates his recognition as a legitimate member. It is also a way to gain upward social mobility within the gang.

The more criminal activity a gang member is involved in the quicker that member can rise to the 'shot caller' level of the gang set. Having tenure in the gang does not automatically qualify a member to be a shot caller. Tenure and the type of criminal activity the member was involved might qualify a member for "OG" status in the Bounty Hunter gang. Because of this rule all OG's in the Bounty Hunter gang are not shot callers and all shot callers are not necessarily OGs (Ross, 2003).

Many Bounty Hunter gang members have a gang name or moniker. Like other street gangs sometimes the moniker is given based a personality or physical trait of the gang member. Sometimes the gang moniker is given to the member inadvertently as a child. Many parents give their children nicknames based on something the child did or based on the child's personality. For some Bounty Hunter members their gang moniker is taken from their childhood family nickname.

Bounty Hunter gang members can use hand signs and normally form the letters B and H. The same letters are often seen in tattoos and graffiti. Sometime set affiliation is shown by using a number in tattoos or graffiti (Schmidt, 2003). The Bounty Hunters also have a form of gang social hierarchy. Older members are referred to as OGs, Original Gangsters. OGs tend to be the older Bounty Hunter gang members and may not be involved in daily criminal activities. There is no clear age or tenure requirement for OG status. The gang members with less tenure are called YGs or younger gangsters (Schmidt, 2003).

Leadership is horizontal in nature. Sets are controlled by a shot caller. Shot callers usually tell the YG's what to do, who to assault or to commit robberies. Unlike other gangs if a member loses standing within the gang, sometimes nothing will happened to that member because he or she may be related to a powerful Bounty Hunter family. Even though by gang standards that member should be assaulted or killed nothing will be done for fear of the family retaliation (Schmidt, 2003).

Law enforcement anecdotal evidence suggests that some sets of the Bounty Hunter gang have regular mandatory meetings where gang business is discussed. The gang is deeply involved in the sales of drugs. During the meetings it is decided which gang members can traffic drugs and where they can. Gang discipline issues and criminal planning is also discussed (Ross, 2003).

Respect for the Bounty Hunter gang is important. The Bounty Hunter gang wants to be feared by the community and rivals. Like many gangs respect for the Bounty Bunters is based on fear. The more you fear me the more you respect me.

Indicia

Members usually wear any type of red colored clothing. Law enforcement anecdotal evidence suggests that members usually do not favor any particular type of college or professional sports team wear. The colors red and white are the predominate theme for clothing (Thompson, 2003).

Due to law enforcement suppression programs some Bounty Hunter gang members have been known to dress down. These gang members may only wear red colored shoelaces or have a red colored belt. Dressing down is thought to make the gang members less noticeable to law enforcement. A person wearing a red colored garment in Bounty Hunter turf will most likely be confronted and asked the gang hit up question, "Where are you from?" In gang parlance this in a very important question and can be the prelude to a violent encounter no matter how the question is answered.

Rivals

Being a Blood oriented gang the classic rival for the Bounty Hunters are the Crip gangs and any gangs that are affiliated with the Crips. There are several rival gangs near Nickerson Gardens; south of Imperial Highway are the Carver Park Crips, to the east of the Blue Line rail system are the PJ Crips, 110th Street Crips and the Jordan Downs housing project; to the north are the Franklin Squares and the Grape Street Crips; to the west are the Avalon Gangster Crips, Front Street Crips and the Back Street Crips. Being surrounded by rivals on all four sides prevents and limits the expansion of the Bounty Hunter gang (Ross. 2003). As with other street, prison and motorcycle gangs the Bounty Hunters will attack other Blood oriented gangs.

Drug Trafficking

The Bounty Hunters are divided up into sets within the Nickerson Gardens housing project. The sets tend to name themselves after the parking lot area they operate in (Flaherty, 2009). Each set then operates as an independent cell and traffics drugs to the buyers; yet is still part of the parent Bounty Hunter gang.

The most influential gang members are the ones that handle the largest quantities of drugs. These Bounty Hunters make their money by re-selling the drugs to other Bounty Hunters for retail sale (Ross, 2003). These high ranking Bounty Hunters are rarely seen in public, they are the behind the scene suppliers.

The mid level Bounty Hunter drug dealers in turn make their money by re-selling the drugs to the street dealer level gang member. These mid level dealers normally have a crew of low ranking gang members who do the actual hand to hand sale of drugs.

The drugs, cocaine, crack cocaine and marijuana are usually prepared for sales within an apartment. There are so many assigned parking lots to specific apartment units that the project tends to be literally divided up by the assigned parking lots for the gang. This becomes the basis for gang sets to claim turf and to operate their retail drug operations. Since the parking lots become the home gang turf for sales, many sales are completed from cars that are parked in and around Nickerson Gardens. It is almost like a drive through fast food operation. Buyers drive up and park next to a car that is dealing; the purchase is made and the buyer drives away. This is a very simple, quick and effective method to traffic drugs. And like some fast food restaurants they are open 24 hours/day, seven days a week.

It is logical to conclude if vehicles are being used to sell drugs that the sellers may be armed and weapons could be hidden within the vehicles they operate from. If drugs are being sold from pedestrian gang sellers weapons are likely to be hidden nearby with easy access.

Bounty Hunter gang members will work together to facilitate drug trafficking operations. The gang uses "hooks," these are gang members who direct potential buyers to the dealers."Lookouts" are exactly that, these gang members look out for any approaching police and will warn the hooks and dealers by whistling, using a walkie-talkie or calling on a cell phone (Ross, 2003). Often the lookouts ride around the neighborhood as roving watch dogs. Occasionally non-gang members are allowed to sell drugs in and around the Nickerson Garden turf. The Bounty Hunters will give that individual a "pass" and they will be allowed to sell drugs. The gang will collect some type of rent from the dealer. A non Bounty Hunter gang member would never attempt to or sell drugs in Bounty Hunter territory without a pass because the cost could be death.

The drug trafficking operations of the Bounty Hunters is sophisticated and has an informal vertical leadership organization. There is no organizational chart or formal titles for positions within the gang, yet each gang member completely understands the informal social and leadership structure. Informal means there is no written leadership organizational chart with clearly defined roles for positions.

Summary

Some Bounty Hunter gang members will move out of the Nickerson Garden neighborhood, but will return to be with peer gang members during various times of the day. Bounty Hunter gang members have been known to be extremely brazen. It has been reported that sometimes Bounty Hunter gang members will urinate against the walls of people homes as police units are driving by. Bounty Hunter gang members have also been known to flash gang hand signs at police officers while they are driving by (Bodell, 2003). In January, 2004 three Bounty Hunter gang members shot at a Los Angeles Police patrol car after a traffic stop. According to the police it was the fourth time Bounty Hunter gang members shot at Los Angeles police officers between December, 2003 and January, 2004 (Winton and Krikorian, 2004).

The Bounty Hunter gang is a turf oriented generational gang that specializes in drug trafficking. An ad hoc survey in 2009 suggested the gang has been reported in 11 states including: Minnesota, New York, Colorado, Texas, New Jersey, Virginia, Missouri, Michigan, Utah, North Carolina, Ohio and Maryland (Valdez, 2009). The bounty Hunter gang is the "Bully" of the Blood gangs in southern California. The Bounty Hunter gang will attack peer members, members from other Bounty Hunter sets, other Blood oriented gangs as well as Crip oriented gangs (Ross, 2009).

Rollin 60 Neighborhood Crips

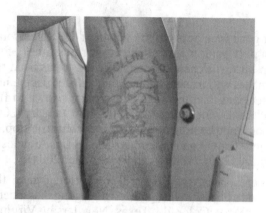

The Crips are most likely one of largest violent street gangs in the United States. The term "Crips" is used to describe a large association of gangs that unite under the name and are involved in criminal activities for profit. Some of these street gangs may have an organized vertical leadership structure and others can be totally unstructured. National membership is estimated to be 30,000 to 35,000 in over 800 sets (NDIC, 2002). Crip sets have been reported in 48 U.S. states. Consistent with the findings from the 2009 Gang Threat Assessment the primary source of income for most Crip gangs is the distribution and sale of cocaine, crack cocaine, marijuana and PCP. The Rollin 60 Neighborhood Crips (RSC), also known as the Rollin 60's gang is no different. This gang formed in Los Angeles and has spread nationally.

History

In 1976 the RSC gang formed as a sibling gang from the Westside Crips. The Westside Crips are considered the original Crip gang of Los Angeles. The split was apparently motivated by a female. Two gang members were dating the same girl. The girl named April, allegedly set up one of the gang members she was dating and he was killed. The two factions feuded and eventually split up. One faction later became the Slauson Boys and the other the Eight Treys. Later, the Slauson Boys became the Rollin 60 Neighborhood Crips gang and the Eight Treys used the name Gangster Crips (Martin, 2003). The two are still bitter rivals even though they are both Crip gangs.

There are several theories that suggest how the Rollin 60s got their name. During this time period many gangs were naming themselves after the streets within their neighborhood (Barrett, 2004). The most common history suggests that then gang got its name because 60th Street 'rolled' through the entire gang neighborhood. The neighborhood size current is approximately 27 blocks south from 48th Street to 75th Street (Barrett, 2004). Currently the Rollin 60 Crips celebrate their birth day on June 10, abbreviated as 6-10 or 6x10 because six times ten equals 60. This is a gang code (Martin, 2003). Every year on June 10 the gang will host some type of an event like a BBQ or as in the case in 2009 rented a Hollywood club for a large party. A few Rollin 60 Neighborhood Crips do not recognized the June 10th date and celebrate the gang's birth on October 31st (Martin, 2003).

Initially new members were recruited from two local high schools, Crenshaw and Westchester. The Rollin 60s had established a presence at Crenshaw High this probably why the gang recruited new members from this school. There was another smaller gang present at Crenshaw High School. This gang was known as the Van Ness Gangsters; which as Blood oriented. The presence of a Crip and Blood affiliated gang at the same high school resulted in conflict between the gangs. The Rollin 60s prevailed because they were much larger in membership size and were able to dominate the school even though it was outside their turf (Alonso, unknown year).

The Rollin 60's gang was highlighted and became nationally known on August 31, 1984. Two members, Horace Burns and Tiequin Cox were involved in the slayings of four people. The pair was burnt on a cocaine deal and they burst into the home of the suspected dealer. Unfortunately, they misidentified the residence and murdered four relatives of former professional football star Kermit Alexander. They had the right address, but were in the wrong block. The pair was arrested by the Los Angeles police in November of the same year. Both Burns and Cox were identified as Rollin 60's gang members (New York Times, 1984). After the shooting and arrests the Rollin 60's became well known and along with their growing conflicts with other Crip and Blood gangs developed a reputation of being one of the most violent gangs in Los Angeles.

The main strong hold of the gang is in the 77th Street Division of the LAPD. But factions of the gang have been reported country wide. There are three major sets of the Rollin 60's the Avenues, Front hood and Overhill. The gang at one time was considered the largest Black street in Los Angeles with over 1,600 members (Barrett, 2004). Another gang researcher estimates the gang's size to be closer to 2500 to 3000 members in the L.A. area (Martin, 2003).

Indicia

Besides wearing the obvious blur colored clothing some Rollin 60's gang members will wear Seattle Mariners baseball team gear. The team's trademarked logo is a stylized letter "S." The letter is used by the gang as an abbreviation for sixties. It is for the same reason that Chicago White Sox baseball team gear is also worn. The team gear for the University of North Carolina is also favored. The powder blue team color accents the Crip affiliation and the abbreviation for the college is NC. The gang favors this because the letters NC represent Neighborhood Crips. New York Yankee team clothing can also be used because the N for New York will represent part of the gang's name, Neighborhood (Barrett, 2004).

There are a number of Neighborhood Crip (NHC) gangs that use a street name to denote what set they represent. All are allied with each other and at one time used the name "O's" to identify gang affiliation. The different NHC gang sets tend to have a numerical set name, like the 40 or 90. So the gang abbreviates the alliances by simply using the O's (Barrett, 2004). The O's alliance may not be currently in place. The term O's may have been written as 'owes.' Other NHC allies include 67, 55 and 46 NHC gangs (Alonso, unknown year).

The gang will use graffiti like many street gangs. The graffiti may contain RSC (Rollin 60's Crips); RSNC (Rollin 60's Neighborhood Crips); R 60's (Rollin 60's); NHC (Neighborhood Crips) and the Rich Rollin 60's (Barrett, 2004). The same letters can be used as tattoos, personal drawings or logos to show gang membership and Crip affiliation (Barrett, 2004). Graffiti is used to show control of specific geographical areas that the RSC gang controls (Martin, 2003).

Other forms of indicia can include the use of tattoos. One tattoo "B3HK." The letters represent Blood (B) Eight Trey (3) Hoover (H) Killer (K). Other forms of tattoos or graffiti can be "6 x 10" which refers to the birth date of the gang. There is a tendency for youth children to see the R-60 graffiti as the gang tends to be territorial in nature. The graffiti makes off geographical turf and can act as a lure to new prospective members.

Tattoos and graffiti can include but are not limited to RSC (Rollin 60 Crips); RSCG (Rollin 60 Crip Gangsters); R60, 6 x10, Rollin Sixty's and 60 NHC. The gang tends to use tow handsigns. One is the 'neighborhood sign' which is made by having the thumb, index and middle fingers extended with the ring and pinkie finger closed. The letter N is formed and represents the word neighborhood. The second most common handsign used is the extending the index finger of one hand forming the number one and extending all the fingers on the second hand forming the number five. Collectively both hands form the number six for Rollin 60s.

R 60 gang members tend to wear a variety of clothing, sports wear and accessories to show their gang affiliation and membership. This can include but is not limited to baseball caps, beanies, shirts, sweatshirts, jackets, belt buckles, medallions, necklaces and rings. Traditionally many Rollin 60 Crips wear navy blue colored clothes to signify Crip affiliation. Currently powder blue colored clothes are popular and are also the same colors used by the University of North Carolina. The gang has identified with the university sports team because the logo for the school NC represents Neighborhood Crips to the gang.

The gang also favors the sportswear from the Seattle Mariners baseball team. The blue color is important but the letter S on the baseball cap represents sixty to the gang. The gang also wears sportswear from the New York Yankees baseball team. The NY on the clothing represents Neighborhood to the gang. Gang members will also wear designer gang shirts for special occasions (Martin, 2003).

Sets

The RSC gang controls a large area of the Los Angeles Police Department's 77th Division. Some of gang's borders are well defined and others are not. On the western border one street is literally cut in half and shared by the Eight Trey Gangster Crips and the RSC. The street Western Avenue is also the venue for RSC/ETC violence (Martin, 2003).

The Rollin 60 Crips are divided up into three major sets: Front Hood, Neighborhood and Overhill. These divisions are based on geography, but members of each set are considered different by members of other sets. Some Rollin 60 Crip members believe that members from the Overhill set are rich and comprise many of the sophisticated robbery rings within the gang. Many RSC members believe members of the Overhill set are "born with a silver spoon in their mouth." The geographical area where the Overhill set lies is also probably one of the cleanest neighborhoods where RSC gang members live (Martin, 2003).

Neighborhood set members are known for drug trafficking operations and are the largest set of the RSC gang. Some of the geographic turf lies within a social-economic impacted area. There are many apartment complexes which tend to draw a transient population and the people who live within these areas have very little pride of ownership. These apartment complexes tend to draw low income families.

The Front Hood set is most likely the smallest of all the sets and it lays on the gangs southern most border. The area where the gang set is located is also a cleaner neighborhood and does not attract low income families. Members of the Front Hood set are known for killing. The Front Hood set most likely earned this reputation because the gang's next door neighbor is their major rival the Eight Trey Gangsters (ETG) (Martin, 2003).

The Front Hood set is considered to be the area between Western Avenue (east side) and Arlington Avenue (west side) and Gage Avenue to the north and Florence Avenue on the south. The Neighborhood set generally occupies the area west of the Front Hood set out to West Boulevard. The Overhill set extends west from West Boulevard out (Martin, 2003). Rollin 60 Crips can claim a single set; but for some Rollin 60 Crips members they can claim membership to all three sets. This is an unusual behavior for many street gangs. Many of the gang members simply claim "R-60" an abbreviation for the Rollin 60 Crips gang.

Another unique characteristic for the RSC gang is that sub sets are sometimes formed with in a major set. These sub sets tend to derive their names from a street or neighborhood name. This implies that a RSC gang member may not only claim Rollin 60 Crips, but also 10th Avenue or "Dime Bloc." Sub sets are sometimes referred to as blocs (Martin, 2003). Other RSC gang members may simply claim "avenues" which refers to the number of streets that use the avenue name that run through the gang's turf.

Allies and Rivals

Since the RSC gang is part of the Neighborhood Crip gang, this implies that the RSC gang will align itself with other Neighborhood Crip gangs. This would include the Rollin 40 Crips (RFC), the Rollin 90 Crips (RNC), the 65 Menlos and the 55, 57 and 67 Neighborhood Crip gangs. Another ally is a sibling gang of the RSC known as the 58 Neighborhood Crips (58NHC). Allied gangs are also invited to the RSC annual birthday celebration. The RSC gang usually does not oppose or align themselves with Latino street gangs. However the Florencia 13 Latino street gang has a well established turf that is shared by the two gangs. Because of this situation occasionally violent attacks occur between the two gangs (Martin, 2003).

As expected thee RSC gang are bitter rivals with any Blood gang, the Gangster Crips or The Eight Trey Gangster Crips (ETG), the Inglewood Family Gangster Bloods (IFG) and the Van Ness Gangster Brims (VNG). These gangs tend to occupy areas which lay adjacent to RSC gang turf. Another rival that is well known are the Schoolyard Crips (Martin, 2003).

The Hoover Criminal Gangsters (HCG) was originally affiliated with the Crips. However, the gang as a whole dropped their affiliation with all Crip and Blood gang sets. The gang changed its name from Hoover Crip to the Hoover Criminal Gangsters and identify with the orange color (Barrett, 2004). Well known Hoover sets include the 52, 59, 74, 83, 92, 94, 107 and 122 sets (Martin, 2003).

One main crip gang rival for the Rollin 60's are the 83rd Gangster Crips. Some experts suggest that it was members of the 83rd Gangster Crips that initiated and fueled the L.A. riots in 1992 after the Rodney King verdicts (Barrett, 2004). There is law enforcement anecdotal evidence that suggests there is RSC gang violence within the RSC gang itself. Some set members fight with peer sets.

The most intense rivalry has reported to be between the Eight Tray Gangsters (ETG). This rivalry started in 1979 and few years after the Rollin 60's formed. Over 400 gang members from both gangs have died as a result of this rivalry (Alonso, unknown year). This rivalry is highlighted in Monster, a book written by Kody Scott. This is an autobiography of an Eight Tray Gangster (ETG).

Membership

Even though some gang members claim to have grown up with the gang the majority of members are "jumped in." A R-60 term that refers to this initiation ritual is "put on." During the initiation as many as 100 RSC gang members may be in attendance. The initiation is supposed to be a test of strength proving one's toughness and worth to the gang. Sometimes a prospective member may only fight one R-60 member and other times the assault can include two or three R-60 members. The fight can virtually take place anywhere, at a park, on school grounds or another gang hangout. In order to be considered for gang membership the person has to be known by other members of the gang and is considered worthy of the gang. New members are sometimes called a 'youngster' or 'new booty' (Martin, 2003).

Once jumped in or put on by the gang the new member is required to commit crimes for the gang. In R-60 terms this is known as "putting in work." Usually an OG (original gangster) member will tell a new member what crimes to partake in. This could include robbery, auto theft or the shooting of a rival gang member. In this way the new member earns his stripes or status in the gang. R-60 gang members are expected to remain criminally active while doing so they maintain their status within the gang (Martin, 2003).

Sadly, gang life can become an easy way out for youth at risk. Gang life for RSC gang members can include ditching school, disobeying parents and authority figures and a lack of traditional work ethic (Martin, 2003). The gang has some generational members where fathers and son's belong to the same set.

Like many other street gangs the Rollin 60 Crips does not have a formal vertical leadership structure. The gang has no known constitution or by-laws. There are no leadership titles like president or general. The gang sub sets operate like small squads and tend to be run by the oldest or most charismatic member. There is an informal hierarchy within the gang. As mentioned above new members are sometime called youngsters. Older members can be called 'ballers' those members who make money, usually through traffic narcotics which is sometimes called 'slinging.' Others may be called 'riders' and are the gang's shooters. These gang members tend to be armed or strapped where ever they travel. These gang members will go out 'hunting' or looking for rival gang members (Martin, 2003).

Some members are called 'OGs.' This term usually refers to an original gangster and tends to refer to tenured older members. The term 'G' can refer to a peer gang member. There is no steadfast rule, but normally OG and G refer to older (age wise) gang members. Sometimes the leader of sub sets is called a 'shot callers.' The term can refer to the member's status and reputation within the gang. Factors that can influence a member's status can include age, time in the gang, jail and/or prison sentences, financial means, history of putting in work for the gang and criminal activity.

There is no minimum number of shot callers. The number actually is a function of the gang's need. A shot caller can order meetings or give missions to youngsters. There is a general tendency for shot callers to be OG's, but not all OG's are shout callers (Martin, 2003).

The Rollin 60 Crips can have female members and they will use 'Lady' or 'Ms' with their gang moniker.

Trends

The gang is so large that inner feuds at one time were very common. This is because is divided up into many sets. So set rivalries can develop. Like other gangs, violence between sets or within a set can be due to gang discipline. Rollin 60 gang members can and will be assaulted if a gang rule is broken, especially if the member is suspected of cooperating with the police. Sometimes this is referred to as a 'calling out.'

Older gang members are also advising younger members not to use tattoos and dress down (traditional) to avoid police identification and contact. Members are being advised not to claim set affiliation or membership to law enforcement. Keeping gang membership confidential has become a priority for some sets.

It is common for individual gang members to have more than on moniker or to change monikers. This is not true with most other street gangs, especially traditional Latino gangs. RSC gang members have been known to change their moniker in an effort to shed a bad reputation.

Summary

A Rollin 60 Crip gang member reputation and respect by others is somewhat dependant on his criminal activity. A gang member who appears fearless and commits robberies and shootings for the gang is well respected. Any crime that benefits the gang in some way is welcomed. Members of the gang have also embraced the use of technology and regularly use cellular telephone technology, My Space and You-Tube. In an informal 2009 survey the gang was reported in 11 states: Minnesota, New York, Colorado, Texas, Oklahoma, New Jersey, Alaska, Virginia, Missouri, Washington and Oregon.

Jamaican Gangs

Jamaican gangs were originally formed in Jamaica and were linked to political groups. Since then Jamaican gangs have become transnational with their presence noted in England, the United States and Canada. So how did a local gang fro and island become transnational and why?

History

The presence of Jamaican gang members in the United States was noted as early as 1971 by law enforcement. Jamaican posses were identified in the eastern seaboard as early as 1976 (State of New Jersey, 1989). By the mid 1980s Jamaican posses were appearing in many U.S. cities (Potter, unknown year). The origin of these gangs can be traced back to the ghettos of Jamaica, where the gangs first appeared in the early 1970s. These gangs first appeared in the impoverished areas of Jamaica for many of the same reasons that contributed to the formation of American street gangs.

Jamaica is the third largest island in the Caribbean and was the world's largest producer of bauxite, the principle source of aluminum. A decline in the world demand for the chemical in the 1960s dealt the Jamaican economy a severe blow. This resulted in a mass migration of countryside workers and their families to the major cities, like the already crowded capital Kingston.

Many of the residents in Kingston were Rastafarians. This Jamaican group had achieved a considerable notoriety through the use and cultivation of marijuana. Ras Tafari was crowned Emperor of Ethiopia in 1930 and then adopted the name Haile Selassie. Rastafarians are a religious group with a Christian orientation with a considerable infusion of African culture. To Rastafarians, Haile Selassie became their leader and messiah. Many Rastafarians are easily recognizable because of their long stocks of hair that are braided that when washed are permitted to dry without combing. We know this style of hair as dreadlocks. Dreadlocks are a symbol of dedication and devotion to Ras Tafari to Rastafarians.

From the religious perspective, Rastafarians believe that Ras Tafari (Haile Selassie) was their living God. According to the religion, Ethiopia is the Black man's home and repatriation is a way of redemption for the Black man. Another belief that plays right into the religious philosophy is that the ways of the White man are evil and alcohol and gambling are forbidden. Marijuana (ganja) is a gift from God, who wants Rastafarians to smoke it. Ganja is considered a divine herb and when consumed gives a Rastafarian spiritual, physical and mental health. Rastafarians usually smoke ganja in five-inch long cone shaped rolls called "spiffs" made of paper or cornhusks. A special tea can also be made using marijuana.

Rastafarians are also associated with the "reggae" style of music that consists of a steady constant sound with two-beat riffs. Reggae musicians like Bob Marley who was famous in the United States and Jamaica wrote and sang songs praising and glorifying the use of marijuana (Potter, unknown year). The marijuana sub-culture in the United States and Jamaica still identifies with Bob Marley and his music.

Rastafarians and members of Jamaican posses represent two different and distinct groups. You can not stereotype all Rastafarians as members of Jamaican posses or drug dealers. The reverse is also true; all members of Jamaican posses are not Rastafarians. It is important to understand not all Rastafarians are criminals and not all Jamaicans are Rastafarians.

Jamaica during this time period was an environment of extreme poverty, rampant marijuana use and political corruption. The first Jamaican street gangs developed as a result. These gangs were formed on the basis of neighborhood boundaries and political affiliation.

There are a couple of theories that suggest how the first Jamaican gangs were formed. One suggests the gangs were first formed for the same reasons American street gangs were formed in the early 1800s; extreme poverty, overcrowded living conditions, unemployment and drug use. These are also known as quality of life issues or as marginalization (Vigil, 2001). The gangs may have formed as a result of the natural progression of life under those extreme living conditions. Add to this life formula polarization to a particular political party and the "us versus them" attitude can develop allowing the genesis of street gangs.

The second theory exposes a more direct intervention that facilitated the formation of Jamaican posses. This theory suggests a political component played a direct role in the genesis of posses. The same social conditions existed, except with this theory Jamaican urban gangs already existed. The political factor became a catalyst that caused the rapid formation of the posses that eventually became so well known. In this theory it is assumed that the street gangs already existed in Jamaica during the 1960s.

Natural Theory

Many young Jamaicans found that they could control an area by organizing and mobilizing their peers into criminal street gangs. Many of the original gangs were also named after the neighborhood they were formed in just like many American street gangs. The Jamaican gangs used the term "posse" to refer to their gang because of their fondness of American Western films and the word inferred the use of violence for neighborhood protection and enforcing a political will on others (New Jersey, 1989). The evolution from street gang to posse was gradual but was fueled by extreme social conditions in Jamaica (New Jersey, 1989).

One of the early survival techniques used by the Jamaican posses was based in politics. The island was under British colonial control and forced slavery. Although slavery was ended in 1833, the lasting impact of British colonialism and the economy made economic and political development difficult (Potter, unknown year). Jamaican posse affiliation can be traced back to the two major political parties in Jamaica, the Jamaican Labor Party (JLP) and the Peoples National Party (PNP).

Both parties fought for control of the government. The heads of both parties traded offices for thirty years. The posses would use drug money to financially support the political party they aligned with. In addition, many major posse figures claimed to have made their reputations by doing bidding for the party they aligned with.

In 1976, two large and violent posses emerged on the island of Jamaica: the Reatown Boys and the Dunkirk Boys. They had both geographical and political memberships and were rivals. The Reatown Boys consisted of persons from Reatown, Jamaica, most were loyal to the Peoples National Party. On the island, they soon became known as the Untouchables because of the number of homicides the posse committed. The Untouchables (Reatown Boys) later became known as the Shower Posse, the largest and most violent Jamaican posse.

The Dunkirk Boys later became known as the Magentas and were aligned with the Jamaican Labor Party. They later became the Spangler Posse. In return for their services, posse members would enjoy the favor of their chosen candidate. If elected to office, the politician would reward his supporters with public works projects and other items that would benefit the community.

Political Theory

According to the second theory Jamaican gangs formed in the late 1960s and early 1970s as the already existing urban gangs were recruited and armed by politicians. The theory suggests that members of both political parties; the Jamaican Labor Party (JLP) and the leftist People's National Party (PNP) created the posses These were the two major political parties in Jamaica at the time (Gunst, 1995). The theory also suggests this was done to organize local constituencies, distribute political favors, enforce party loyalty and to turn out votes (Moser and Holland, 1995 and National Committee on Political Tribalism, 1997).

The use of armed gangs and the promotion and use of violence as strategies to secure or retain political power became known as political tribalism (National Committee on Political Tribalism, 1997). The gangs eventually called themselves "posses" as the result of the gunslinger type characters presented American Western movies (Gunst, 1995).

Local "dons" who were in league with political party figures led the posses. Collectively they established political strongholds known as "garrison communities." Garrison communities were literally political fortresses completely controlled by one party or the other. These communities were literally states within a state, any person who oppose the controlling political party would be in danger of suffering from criminal activity at the hands of the posses (Gunst, 1995 and National Committee on Political Tribalism, 1997).

By the late 1970s PNP and JLP garrison communities were established throughout the capital of Kingston and in the adjacent northern parish of St. Andrew. Garrison communities were also established in the St. Catherine parish to the west, especially in Spanish Town (National Committee on Political Tribalism, 1997). During the 1980 elections running battles between the PNP and JPL posses resulted in an estimated 800 killings and almost 20,000 people burned out of their homes (World Bank, 1997).

By the early 1980s posses also became involved in the smuggling of cocaine and marijuana partly due because Jamaica was being used as a staging point for the drugs entry into the United States (Gunst, 19995 and World Bank, 1997). As a result of this new source of income posses and their dons became less reliant on their political party support. They began to operate more independently. Nevertheless, posses still maintained their relationships with the political parties in the 1980s and 1990s. Because of this overlap, boundaries between drug trafficking operations and politics were sometimes crossed (Moser and Holland, 1997 and Payne, 1998).

By the 1990s the level of posse violence decreased and political party leaders tried to disassociate themselves from the armed posses and garrison control of the early 1980s. Even though the politicians made this attempt, there is some evidence to suggest that garrison control of the communities is still achieved through posse intimidation (National Committee on Political Tribalism, 1997).

The leadership and relative strength of posses has changed. New dons emerged, some posses have split, reorganized or have established bases of operations in other countries. In some areas posses have also gotten involved in welfare fraud. With all these changes the communities are still aligned politically.

U.S. Jamaican Street Gangs

Jamaican posse members first appeared in the United States in the early 1970s. It is theorized by law enforcement that Jamaican posse members left Jamaica for three major reasons. First, many posse members immigrated to the United States to escape legal troubles in

Jamaica. Secondly, other posse members simply wanted a new gang territory to conquer and to make money. Third, some posse members fled to the U.S. because they feared assassination at the hands of the opposing political party. As the groups first appeared, most maintained their community and political ties in Jamaica. Do not forget many of these posse members left family members in Jamaica in order to come to the United States.

There is also another reported theory that attempted to explain the posse migration into the United States. The impetus may have been the need to generate funds to purchase semi-automatic and automatic weapons to be smuggled back to Jamaica to be used in the local gang wars (New Jersey, 1989).

After coming to the United States, Jamaican posse members tended to take over the already established marijuana trade of the U.S. based street gangs. Throughout the 1970s and 1980s the Jamaican street posses grew and expanded their operations across the United States. The posses tended to be very mobile just the Vietnamese gangs that appeared in California during the early 1980s. Many of the U.S. based posses were spin-off groups from the Shower or Spangler Posses. In many cities it was common for a Jamaican posse to take over the entire drug trade from the local street gangs. Often, the takeovers were very violent in nature. The escalating homicide rate in these cities was seen as a reflection of Jamaican posse takeovers of local drug operations.

Before the arrival of the Jamaican posse, the typical Jamaican drug dealer was seen as a Rastafarian. This stereotype was well-known, long dreadlocks, smoking and selling marijuana. The new Jamaican posse presented a different profile that changed law enforcement awareness of membership. Knowing what attracts law enforcement, many Jamaican posse members made every effort to blend in and to have attention diverted from them. As a result many Jamaican gang members wore conservative hairstyles, conservative clothing and avoided the excessive flashy jewelry and life style that was associated with posse membership. Remember the "low pro" behaviors of some Midwest and West Coast gangs during the late 1990s?

Unlike the Rastafarian dealers of the 1970s, who were content to make a little money and get high, second generation Jamaican posse members focused on one thing and one thing only, making money. It was this focus that drove and motivated the criminal activities of the gang. This is an attitude that is still shared by many American based gangs.

In the quest to make more money, the posses have expanded their drug businesses. Jamaican posses still import large qualities of marijuana and other illegal drugs. Over time, these posses learned about the profit margin associated with the sales of these illegal drugs. What the posses have done is effectively take out the middleman in the drug business, thereby maximizing profits. As a result, Jamaican posse drug trafficking has appeared in over 57 cities in 34 different states.

During the late 1980s there were at estimated 40 Jamaican posses predominately operating in the East Coast (www.emergency.com and Potter, unknown year and http: //beyondheros2. tripod.com). Anecdotal law enforcement evidence suggested that at one time the U.S. based posse membership was estimated at close to 13,000 (New Jersey, 1989). The Jamaican posses became so violent that it was reported between 1984 and 1987 there were an estimated 800 murders attributed to them (Potter, unknown year). The Spangler and Shower posses and their sibling gangs still remain bitter rivals.

Drug Sales

As part of their drug sale activity, Jamaican gangs would commonly operate networks of gatehouses. Gatehouses were normally heavily fortified structures used specifically for drug sales. These structures had the same function as the 1990s crack houses. Gatehouses could be found anywhere including, residences, apartments or small businesses. Some Jamaican gangs would operate several gatehouses at once. Weekly drug sales could run into millions of dollars.

There are also two other types of safe houses that Jamaican posses use. One is the money house. It is usually located near the gatehouses and is used to store the cash that is generated in drug sales. Of course, this house is guarded. The third type of house is some type of building that is used for housing undocumented immigrants that are smuggled into the country. Jamaican posses are involved in human smuggling like some Asian and Hispanic gangs (New Jersey, 1989.

Jamaican gangs sell a variety of illegal drugs and are involved in all aspects of the drug business. This includes importation, wholesale distribution and retail sales. Drugs normally sold by these groups include, but are not limited to cocaine, crack, marijuana, hashish oil, heroin and PCP. Another characteristic that makes Jamaican gangs competitive in narcotics trafficking is their flexibility and mobility. The Jamaican posses can move into a community and establish a sales turf quickly.

Some Jamaican posses can specialize in certain aspects of drug trafficking. One Posse may only be involved in the importation of the drug. Another may only take care of the shipping of the drug within the United States. Another posse may be responsible for the local retail sales of the drug at the gatehouse. From an economic stand point these Jamaican gangs attempt to control the entire drug trafficking operation to be able to maximize their profits.

By the late 1980s Jamaican street gangs evolved from the political enforcers in the ghettos of Jamaica into the drug kingpins now well known within the United States. As a result of this evolution, Jamaican street gangs were responsible for thousands of drug and gang related homicides, billions of dollars in illegal drug sales, the importation of thousands of illegal Jamaican immigrants, and a countless number of weapons that were illegally purchased within the United States and smuggled out of the country.

Gang Violence

Jamaican street gangs have made violence one of their most important trademarks. The 1980s Indo-Chinese gangs in southern California also used violence as a tool. Without a doubt during the 1980s and 1990s the Jamaican gangs established themselves as one of the most violent street gangs to operate in the United States. There is absolutely no hesitation on the part of Jamaican posse members to commit acts of violence on police officers and innocent citizens. For example, in Chicago, Illinois, on February 16, 1992 two members of a New York City Posse were arrested and charged with the shooting of two Chicago police officers during a botched robbery. One suspect was arrested in New York City; the second was arrested in New Jersey hiding amongst Jamaican posse members (www.emergency.com).

The Shower Posse, one of the largest Jamaican gangs in the 1980s, took its name from the fact that posse members showered their victims with bullets from automatic weapons (www.emergency.com).

In addition, Jamaican possess earned their reputation for being ruthless and violent. Gunshots to the ankles and knees and boiling people alive have used as forms of torture. It is suspected that many people have died at the hands of Jamaican posse members for little or no reason. A non-gang member could accidentally brush up against a posse member and be killed. Automatic weapons fire has also killed and injured many innocent bystanders.

Some Posse members have also been known to dismember their victims and scatter the body parts around the area. This procedure is known as jointing. One such incident was reported in the August, 1992, Financial Crimes Enforcement Network report on Jamaican gangs; "... several men were found playing soccer with the head of someone who fell prey to a Jamaican gang. After severing the head, the gang had wrapped it in tape and left it in a dumpster where the men presumably found it." It has become apparent that the Jamaican street gangs can use violence as a calling card, a signature to their activities. Other posse members would send the body parts back to family members in Jamaica to make a public statement.

Posse members have had access to explosives and explosive devices like many street gangs. In late 1987, during a national sweep MK-II military grenades were recovered from posse members. However, a common posse M.O. reportedly includes multiple shots with multiple weapons in a crowded public place. The Jamaicans are known to frequently use 9mm caliber large magazine semiautomatic handguns and sub-machine guns. Weapons have included, but are not limited to the Uzi, Mac-10, Mac-11, Intra-Tec, MP-5, Browning High-Power, Berreta F-92, Smith and Wesson 9mm pistols, Glock 9mm pistols and Colt 45 caliber semiautomatic pistols. If you will note these types of weapons are commonly used by military forces for war (www.emergency.com).

Jamaican posses throughout the country have been extremely violent. According to federal authorities between 1985 and 1992 there were more than 4900 homicides attributed to Jamaican narcotics trafficking (California, 1997). Jamaican posses have been identified as far west as California and in Toronto, Canada (California, 1997 and http: //toronto.cbc.ca.).

Leadership Structure

When the Jamaican gangs first appeared within the United States posse members were easily identified by law enforcement. Posse members made themselves high profile in the way they dressed, walked and talked. Posse members made no effort to hide or disguise their gang affiliation and membership.

Because of their high profile, Jamaican gang members were easy to pick out and identify, especially for law enforcement. In the 1980s law enforcement took advantage of this and high profile gang members were targeted in suppression programs. As a result, a large number of Jamaican gang members went to prison. The remaining posses members responded by changing their gang life style. This is an example of the flexibility and adaptability of Jamaican posses.

Jamaican gang members became much more cognizant of their profile. In an effort to be low profile, posses developed into much smaller and closer knit groups. Leaders would often go to great lengths to insulate themselves from the rest of the posse membership. By the mid to late 1990s many Jamaican posses operated using a three tier organizational structure. Imagine a triangle type leadership and organizational structure.

The upper level is the gang leadership and is often isolated and therefore protected from street level activity such as daily drug sales. The leaders also received the bulk of the profit from posse business. It was common to find the leaders were second-generation Jamaican gang members. Some members even had legal foreign national status, while others were second generation and born in the United States making them U.S. citizens.

The mid-level gang leaders were lieutenants, who over saw and ran the day-to-day operations of the gang. This included the operation of the posse gatehouse(s) and control over the lower ranking gang members. Some law enforcement experts theorized that the majority of the lower ranking gang members were undocumented aliens smuggled into the United States for the sole purpose of working in the gatehouses.

Criminal Associations

Jamaican posse narcotic trafficking has developed a certain sophistication and complexity. Gone are the flamboyant days of the highly stylized gang attire and crude violence. The posse image has changed in the 1990s. Because of the interest to make money criminal activity Posses also became more organized and this in turn caused the posses to develop some unique working relationships. Law enforcement anecdotal evidence has suggested that the Jamaican gangs will work together with themselves and other ethnic gangs. The non-Jamaican gangs probably supply drugs to the posses or benefit the posse in some fashion. For example, some Jamaican posses have also formed working alliances with other organized crime groups to launder drug money.

Another example, in the Northeastern portion of the United States, especially in New York, Jamaican posses have purchased cocaine and crack from the Dominican groups. The Dominicans seem to act as drug suppliers for the Jamaicans in this part of the country.

Since Jamaican posses import drugs into the United States an association with Colombian drug traffickers and Hispanic gangs should also be expected. These business ties can be at any level of drug trafficking operations. During the 1990s Jamaica was being used on a frequent basis as a staging point for Colombian cocaine smuggling operations. The country of Mexico also serves some Columbian cartels in the same manner.

Some Jamaican gangs have even become involved with the Nigerian heroin smuggling operations. There has been speculation that Jamaican posses would attempt to expand their drug operations nationwide. If this theory is valid then developing business relationships with the Nigerian crime groups is logical.

Jamaican Posses have even made associations with West Coast street drug suppliers. This has also facilitated the growth and activity of Mexican drug trafficking organizations that in turn has impacted the growth and activities of street gangs in Mexico and America. For example, April 2004 in Elizabeth New Jersey the Drug Enforcement Agency and the Elizabeth Police Department seized 700 pounds of marijuana believed to be destined for distribution by local Jamaican posse street gangs in New York and New Jersey. A tractor-trailer owned by Commercial Renaissance of Sacramento, California was driven to New Jersey with the shipment. The marijuana was hidden in a load of lettuce and two California men were arrested. The street value of the seized drug was estimated at $1.35 million dollars. The investigation involved the Champagne Posse (www.njsp.org).

In August 2003 the New Jersey State Police stopped a tractor-trailer that had a load of garage doors destined for Bronx, New York. The police intercepted 21 boxes containing 1,575 pounds of marijuana. Two New York men were arrested. The same group is believed to be responsible for both shipments (www.njsp.org). It appears that even though Jamaican posse members never trust outsiders, they are inclined to do whatever is necessary to make their drug trafficking business profitable. Now there is evidence to suggest the some Jamaican drug operations have taken on a transnational aspect.

Money Laundering

Because of their involvement in the lucrative drug sales market Jamaican posses end up with large amounts of cash. After collection, this drug money somehow has to be laundered or washed to make it legal tender.

One such money laundering operation is to use a "higgler." A Jamaican street merchant comes to the United States. The posse would then give the higgler (merchant) money. The higgler in turn buys goods in the U.S. and ships them back to Jamaica. Once in Jamaica the higgler sells the merchandise and returns the money back to the gang. This is a simple but effective way to launder drug money.

The Jamaicans have also tried to smuggle cash out of the United States as well. One operation that was uncovered included packing cash into 55-gallon drums. A corrupt airline employee made sure the drums got on the airplane. Once in Jamaica a corrupt Jamaican official insured the drums would make it off the airplane and through customs without detection.

Other types of money laundering schemes have included the purchasing of a car in the United States and shipping the car to Jamaica where it is re-sold. The cash goes back to the posse. Airline employees have also been used to smuggle cash to Jamaica. Sometimes the cash money would be sent through legitimate shipping companies.

Another unique money laundering scheme used the racetracks. Some Jamaican gang members would use the automated machines at thoroughbred horse racing tracks to convert the drug money into larger bills. Many tracks have machines that allow the patrons to purchase betting chits. These machines accept bills of small denomination. The posse member would simply use the dirty money to buy the betting chits. After the race he would cash the chits out, receiving larger denomination bills, which was clean money.

Business Fronts

The Jamaican gangs have also invested drug money in legitimate businesses like restaurants, nightclubs, grocery stores, record stores, boutiques and garages. The businesses are normally located where there is a large Jamaican population. Many times the business actually provides the advertised service. Almost always they are used as a front to launder drug money.

Some Jamaican posse members have found that it easy to conceal their assets by using a "straw." This practice simply uses an unknown woman to purchase the asset for a posse member. Real ownership of the property is easily concealed from authorities. For example, apartment leases, utilities, telephone and car leases for Jamaican posse members are often listed in a woman's name.

Membership Indicia

Remember, the one characteristic that distinguished Jamaican posse members from other gang members was their propensity for violence. Jamaican posses have access to high-powered weapons, grenades and explosives. Posses have also been known to use counter surveillance against investigating law enforcement officers. There have been several documented cases where posse members have attacked and killed police officers and put out contracts for their deaths. It is not unusual for posse members to attempt to get home telephone numbers and addresses of their victims. Jamaican posse gang members have also been involved in witness intimidation (Financial Crimes Network, 1992).

The posse trends still include the use of high-powered weapons. When stopped by law enforcement posse members tend to resist arrest and have been quick to use their weapons. Law enforcement has encountered a large number of posse members with fake identification and forged immigration documents.

The Rastafarians and Jamaicans may speak a form of English that initially is hard to understand. This form of English also has an island dialect characteristic to it. The language reflects the Rastafarian and Jamaican religious beliefs and the unity they feel. For example, in the language the letter "I" is used to express unity. The plural form of I is normally we or us. Jamaican posse gang member and Rastafarians will say, "I n I." Myself then becomes I self and ourselves becomes I n I self.

For example, in a Rasta conversation:

> Dread, I-n-I check you out to step
> You no see?
> Manifest
> Bring I-self tool and machine
> Mash it up
> I-n-I juke a brother

Translated, the short conversation means:

> Greetings, you and I are going to meet someone in person, to move on something.
> Do you understand?
> Plan a score.
> Bring me a gun and a machine gun.
> Handle it!
> You and me rip off a fellow Jamaican.

It is easy to see how understanding gang slang can play a crucial role in working with gang members.

Beards and hair are enjoined on men. Therefore, it would be unthinkable for a Rastafarian to shave or cut this hair. Dreadlocks are still the preferred hairstyle for Rastafarians. Another unique characteristic often seen is the use of military style dating methods like day/month/year, written as 26.9.96. The European style of number seven is also commonly used. That is the number 7 with a horizontal line drawn through the center of the vertical part of the number.

Yardies

The term "Yardie" is used by Jamaicans themselves to describe recent Jamaican immigrant arrivals in the United Kingdom (www.gangland.net). The term is slang that describes the back yard or being from back home but really refers to Jamaican posse gang members in England. During post World War II 1950s immigration was encourage by the British government to help fill existing job vacancies. As a result many Afro-Caribbean immigrants, mainly Jamaicans in search of a better living migrated to England. Much like the major immigrants groups did in the Unites States during the 1800's.

Most of the immigrants only found unskilled employment. Because wages were low, immigrants tended to seek cheap affordable housing usually located in the run down inner city areas of England. When England's economy changed many immigrants in this new work force felt the impact of the recession first. Second generation immigrants found it extremely difficult to match achievements with aspirations. Living in poor quality crowded housing with high unemployment rates resulted in violence within the immigrant population. The violence was usually drug related and continually plagued the residents.

During the late 1970s a second influx of immigrants arrived in England. Many of these immigrants did not have to same work ethic as the first wave of immigrants did. Some of these second wave immigrants were fugitives fleeing the Jamaican police authorities, and others were convicted criminals, neither came to England seeking a better life. This group of immigrants came to England to become involved in criminal activities (www.gangland.net). England just like the United States receives immigrants from many parts of the world, but the majority of the second wave immigrants were from Jamaica.

In fact, these Yardies distinguished themselves from first wave immigrants with criminal behavior and very quickly. Yardies tended to be single males between 18 and 35 years old. Usually they were not employed, often by choice. However, many Yardies claimed to be involved in the music industry as record producers or promoters or disc jockeys. Many times Yardies assumed false identities and entered England as tourists, to visit relatives or as a student. When contacted by the police, these Yardies produced fraudulent and forged identification and some have also produced fraudulent British passports. Remember the use of fraudulent identification was also popular with Jamaican posse members in the United States in the 1980s.

With the immigration of convicted criminals and fugitives a criminal infrastructure developed within the Jamaican community. This infrastructure also became a haven and refuge for fugitives and fueled Yardie membership. Initial venues for criminal activities became local Jamaican clubs, bars and house parties.

The United States immigration policies have also made it increasingly difficult for Jamaican criminals to enter the country. This had not deterred Jamaican posse members from finding another route into America. The solution became enter the United States through Britain. For many posse members the United Kingdom became a staging area for re-entry into America using fraudulent British passports. However, this strategy did not stop Jamaican posse violence from growing and becoming more entrenched Britain.

As in the United States, once Yardies established themselves in Britain they became involved in narcotics trafficking and drug related crime. Early on the criminal activity tended to be ethically based. Yardies started to sell drugs and victimize members of their own community within their neighborhoods. Criminal activity then also spilled over into adjacent neighborhoods. Robberies and burglaries became the crime of choice. These tend to be crimes that are committed to support drug abuse and addiction habits (www.gangland.net).

The Jamaican posse narcotic trafficking behaviors in Britain emulated the American versions of the Posses. Fortified houses were used as gatehouses. In addition some locations had external security and Yardies used cellular telephones and pagers to facilitate drug sales. Yardies like their American counterparts also used firearms. This presented an issue for British law enforcement because for the most part, British police are unarmed. Prior to Yardies forming gangs, shootings were rare in England, as firearm possession by the general public is strictly monitored and controlled. Unfortunately, that is no longer true.

Jamaican Yardies tend to resort to gun violence to settle any dispute, which was at one time thought to be only an American gang tradition. For example, in the shooting of a Yardie in the streets of a busy London suburb over drug deal dispute eight shots were fired into the victim from three different guns. In certain areas Yardies would openly wear and display guns, much like American gang members. The difference is that unarmed British policemen would have to patrol these areas. In America all police forces are armed and if anyone openly displayed a weapon in public there would be an immediate overt armed response by police. Knowing that the local police were unarmed tended to fuel the Yardie bravado, which in turn tended to intimidate the local residents.

The Jamaican police estimated that in the early part of 2002 there were 500 suspected Jamaican criminals operating in Britain running a narcotics trafficking operation that imported approximately 200 pounds of cocaine into the country weekly (www.jamaica-gleaner.com). The Jamaica-Gleaner newspaper also reported that the flow of drugs into England has increased partly the result of tougher U.S. immigration controls. Jamaican gang members found it easier to enter Britain and make larger profits from drug sales once in the country.

Yardie violence can be extreme. In another Yardie drug deal that went bad one victim was gun down outside his home and the second victim was tied up, skinned and had his tongue cut out. Two months before this incident a notorious Yardie was jailed for 12 years for kidnapping two men in north London and torturing them with a hammer, electric iron and boiling water (Bennetto, 2003).

The gang-violence-drug-gun connection is established in Britain. In 2001 England and Wales reported a 9 percent rise in gun violence. Yardie gun violence accounted for a significant portion of the reported 4,019 gun incidents. Jamaican Yardie gangs have also established themselves throughout Britain. In 2002, Jamaican police estimated there were 30 Yardie gangs operating Britain (www.jamaica-gleaner.com). The British authorities report 25 Yardie gangs operating in Britain (Bennetto, 2003). Yardie leadership structure is not organized like La Cosa Nostra organized crime groups. The gangs tend to be small groups, as in the United States. In England it is not uncommon to find out that a Yardie member belongs to more than one gang (www.gangland.net).

Summary

Jamaican Posse members are usually well armed with high-powered weapons. Posse members will easily confront police, rival gang members or drug users that owe them money. Posse members can also use extensive counter-surveillance measures against anyone they believe is watching them. Typically, Posse members have total disregard for innocent bystanders caught in a shooting crossfire. Jamaican posse members will still continue to use extreme forms of violence to send public messages and to make a statement about their seriousness.

Jamaican criminals will continue to use false identities supported with fraudulent identification and passports. Posses have a unique ability to adapt to law enforcement investigation and suppression methods. Male members will use female associates to transport drugs and weapons, and to make straw purchases. Posses will also continue to make criminal associations with other street gangs and criminal organizations, including gangs from the West Coast and the Colombian Cartels. The transnational status of the gang could aid in transnational criminal activities.

Female Gangs

Females have been involved in American street gangs as associates and have formed their own gangs since the inception of the male first gangs. Female gangs have a developmental history that is very similar to male gangs but has been influenced by many factors. Some of the earliest accounts of female gang participation were reported in New York during the 1800s (Asbury, 1927). Female gang members have had their roles glorified and interpreted in the media, movie and music industries. Simply put females involved in street gangs have been stereotyped. Societal and law enforcement attitudes have shaped the stereotypical female gang member for many years. As a cohort the number of females involved in street gangs is actually very small.

History

The role of females in the street and prison gang sub-culture has also changed over time. Historically, females have been thought to hold very minor roles in the predominately male gang sub-culture. For example, various academic reports and studies have shown that female gang members were once thought to be used only for sex by the male gangsters (Spergel, 1964). These lady gang members were like gang groupies. There is also some law enforcement anecdotal evidence that suggest this is still true for some females who are associated with outlaw motorcycle, prison and some street gangs.

For a while it was believed that females only became involved with a gang to get a boyfriend. This was a gender typed role influenced by societal norms. Some female gang members may have assumed this role early on and as long as they were faithful to their boyfriends, reputations would not be tarnished. Historically, females had taken a back seat in the gang sub-culture, so these female gangs were once also believed only to have a support role in the gang sub- culture. Society stereotyped female gang members as sex objects or tomboys. Often female gang members were defined in terms of their relationships with male gang members (Moore and Hagedorn, 2001).

Some of the earliest historical information on female gang members is from journalists and social workers (Moore and Hagedorn, 2001). Female gangs that have emerged can be violent in nature, while others seem to be more interested in the party scene, with selling drugs, with recognition and, for some, a support role.

For example in a study of Chicago based gangs the researcher notes that even though the majority of the gang was comprised of male members, there were female members. The main activities the female members were involved in were mugging, illicit sex, petting and necking (Thrasher, 1927).

During the late 1940s female gangs were reported growing in New York (Benard, 1949). Probation reports during this time period described initiation rituals that required prospective female gang members to have intercourse with male gang members (Klein, Maxson and Moore, 1995). This is most likely the first formal reporting of "sexing in" rituals by street gangs. Female gang members still acted as support to their male counterparts. During World War II some female gang members would lure soldiers into an area, only to be robbed by male gang members.

During the 1950s female gang members were either sisters or friends of the male member. Girls were considered as sexual objects to be tricked, cajoled or forced into sexual intercourse. Female gang members were not respected by their male counterparts (Klein, Maxson and Moore, 1995).

By the early 1970s female gang members acquired an independence not seen before. Female gang members would associate with male gang members but would not freely dispense sexual favors to them. These female gang members would steal, drink alcohol and be truant from school, committed vandalism and assaults. In an attempt to gain favor from their male counterparts these female gang members emulated and abetted male gang members.

By the mid to late 1980s U.S. female gang membership was studied more vigorously by academia and a clearer picture was developed about female activity in street gangs. These studies identified that culture, poverty class and type of gang the female belonged to have a direct influence on female gang behaviors and attitudes (Klein, Maxson and Moore, 1995).

The research suggests female gang behaviors and mentalities are more complicated than previously proposed. The community, parent culture and social class the females lived in also factored in molding attitudes and mentality. As with males, some females sought gang membership as a solution to issues at home or life. Gang membership also may have been a way out of the social rung the female member was in.

Some females join or associate with a gang to leave an abusive home or personal relationship, others because it represents a lifestyle they like. For others, joining a gang is a matter of surviving. Some female gang members have become drug dependent and stay in this abusive environment to support their drug habit or addiction. For a few females they are compelled to join or help a gang under threats of violence against them or their families.

The literature supports a number of estimates of female gang members. Female gang membership was estimated at 10% of the total gang population in the mid 1970s (Miller, 1975). In 1992 female gang membership in the U.S. was estimated at only 3.7 percent (Spergel, 1995). In 1996 a nationwide survey estimated the population at 11 percent and in 1998 at 8 percent (Moore and Terret, 1998 and National Youth Gang Center, 2000).

Law enforcement anecdotal evidence suggests that female gang populations fluctuate and also depends on whether or not female gang members are tracked. Ad Hoc studies that I have been involved with suggest that female gang populations can vary from 5 to 10 percent taking into account regional characteristics. One mid 1990s law enforcement estimate indicated the female gang membership in the Chicago area maybe as high as 30 percent. This estimate may be the result of regional influences and is not consistent with published academic studies regarding national female gang populations. The actual number of female street gangs still remains relatively small when compared to the number of male gangs.

Females who are involved in street gangs desire the association and membership appears to be wanted, welcomed and encouraged. Age wise, females tend to be adolescents when they join a gang. However, it has been my experience to find adult female gang members in co-ed gangs. In southern California female gang members have been reported to be as young as 10 years old (Valdez, 2000).

Myths

There have been some myths about female gangs and about relationships between the females in a gang. One myth is that female gang delinquency is associated with promiscuity. Girls who become involved with street gangs sometimes face a dilemma. If they allow themselves to be used for sex by the male gang members, their image is tarnished with their peer female gang members. If they become rough and not have sex to save their image, the peer male gang members look at the female gang member as a tomboy. With either image, female gang members are in a no-win situation. Rejection from female or male peers who are the same people they want to be with (Klein, M.; Maxson, C. and Miller, J. (1995).

The myths are myths. It is now known that female promiscuity is not the standard to measure female gang membership or activity. We are all aware of the double standard in our American society. If a male has multiple sex partners he is considered as a stud, a macho kind of dude. Peer males congratulate him, as if he was very successful. If a female has multiple sex partners she is a whore or slut. Often, this kind of women is shunned by males and peer females in a street gang.

Another common myth is that female gang members cannot and do not form strong relationships between themselves. You would not expect to find the same kind of same bonding between females as you do with male gang members. However, female gang members can form very intense bonds between themselves. Sometimes, the relationships are stronger than male-to-male gang relationships (Klein, M.; Maxson, C. and Miller, J. 1995). Based on my observations, female gangs mimic male gangs in all aspects of gang sociology and activities, sometimes with the same or greater intensity.

Female street gangs have been reported by law enforcement wherever there have been male street gangs. This implies that female gangs can be present throughout the United States, in rural areas, small towns to major cities. According the literature there is a tendency for female gangs to form in smaller cities (Moore and Hagedorn, 2001). However, their presence is not dependent on the presence of male gangs. Female gang members will refer to themselves as "homegirls" or "sisters" and refer to their gang as family (Brown, 1977, Campbell, 1984, Harris, 1983 and Quicker 1983).

Gang Types

Females can be involved in street gangs in several different ways. Based on my observations and experience, females have been involved with independent female street gangs, as members of hybrid gangs (co-ed) and as female auxiliary gangs aligned to a specific male gang. Academic studies also confirm my observations (Moore and Hagedorn, 2001). Female gang members have been identified within the Hispanic, African-American, Southeast Asian and Caucasian, Tagger Crews, Party Crews, Clubs, and Skinhead street gangs. Females are also involved with motorcycle and prison gangs as well.

Females are not considered members in prison and motorcycle gangs. These two groups have historically considered the female in a limited support role. In the motorcycle gang sub-culture females are considered property and are routinely exploited. Females are routinely used as prostitutes to make money for their male partner. In the prison gang sub-culture women are a resource for the in custody member. Females have been involved in assisting the prison gangs with criminal activity on the outside. There is no evidence to support the existence of female prison gangs in the United States (Valdez, 2000).

Independent Gangs

Some female street gangs have developed independently and are not affiliated with a single male gang. Association with a male gang is not required and independent female gangs do not have a support role. Their activity is not pre-planned by male gang members and is not dependent on what a male gang requests or demands.

Examples of these types of gangs are the Southeast Asian female gangs that emerged during the 1980s in southern California. These gangs had their own agenda for their criminal and social activities. Surprisingly, their independence led some of the gang members to use traditional indicia to identify their gang association. It is not surprising to find some female gang members who sport gang type tattoos and/or have cigarette burns and wear stylized gang attire. Based on my experience, some female gang members do not use the traditional membership indicia (non profile gang member) law enforcement has associated with male gang membership. Anecdotal law enforcement evidence suggests this was a unique characteristic for some female gang members.

Most female gangs typically have no turf boundaries. Early on criminal activity tended to focus on assaulting rival gang members. Female gang member also tended to use the gang to help them settle personal issues and for socializing.

In early the1990s three La Habra, California, female gang members went on a night of drive-by shootings. The gang's membership was comprised of approximately 12-15 young Hispanic females. The gang was independent and when members associated with a male gang, it was usually with the predominate male gang within the city. The females who were responsible for shooting and killing on young male gang member were only 16 and 17 years old. They were arrested, tried and convicted of the murder. One was pregnant at the time and gave birth to her daughter in state prison. The gang member's grandparents raised her daughter.

This Latina gang like many other female gangs became inactive when members were arrested or incarcerated or became pregnant. Sometimes motherhood for female gang members can signify the termination of gang membership and activity. This was true during the 1970s and 1980s. However with changes in the social attitudes towards working mothers, some female gang members who became mothers still maintained their gang membership and activity.

For the most part, female gang members would fight with small knives and fists. As the rivalries intensified, the fights became more violent. Initially, the availability of guns seemed limited because the male gang members usually held them. However, Southeast Asian male gang members were not the sole source of weapons. By the early 1990s female gangsters started to obtain guns for themselves from other sources.

Because of a few charismatic members some female gangs have became independent. These female gang members were the first unofficial female gang leaders. They led their independent gangs and established their own rivalries and agendas. These female gang members were no longer forced to abide by cultural values forced on them from parents and from male gang members. These female gangs ran their own agenda.

Some of these female gang members carried guns, although not at the same frequency as male gang members. Some female gang members wore stylized gang clothing to show their gang affiliation. Many female gangs also required an initiation ritual called jumping-in. In this ceremony the potential new female gang member had to fight two or three female gang members to prove she was worthy to be a member.

These independent female gangs in southern California used names like South Side Scissors, Innocent Bitch Killers and Las Chiquitas. Independent female gangs are commonly seen in the Southeast Asian and Hispanic races. These female gangs are commonly involved in drive by shootings, robberies, carjacking, assaults, assaults with deadly weapons, shoplifting, drug trafficking and even homicide (Nye, 1992 and Valdez 2000).

Auxiliary Gangs

There are still some auxiliary female gangs today that play a supportive role to a particular male gang. These gangs typically use names that are derived from the name of the male gang they associate with. For example, the Lady Rascal Gang (LRG) was the female gang that associated and helped the all male Tiny Rascal Gang (TRG). The TRG gang was one of the largest, if not the largest Indo-Chinese street gang in America. LRG gang members would associate only with members from TRG. Wherever TRG gang members went, LRG gang members would follow.

Sometimes, these female gang members would help by hiding guns or drugs for their male counterparts and would engage in consensual sexual conduct. These female gang members would also attack each other, as well as rival female gang members. Sometimes, female gang members would instigate fights between their male associates and other rival gangs by spreading false rumors.

Occasionally, an auxiliary female gang is absorbed into the male gang that it associates with. The new gang that is formed is a co-ed or hybrid street gang. Typically the membership is predominately male. For example, in Long Beach, California in early 1996, the LRG was assimilated into TRG making the Tiny Rascal Gang a co-ed, multi-racial Hybrid gang in late 1996.

Historically, in southern California the first Vietnamese female gangs were not independent. These early female gangs were associated with a particular male gang. Culture played an important role that helped identify the role of early Indo- Chinese female gang members. Contrary to early stereotyping, their male counterparts did not consider these female gang members as sex objects. Often, they were referred to as a "little sister" (Frank, 1988).

From the cultural perspective, females in the Southeast Asian culture were to be proper. Normally, young females would obey their parents without question, be excellent students; even help support their household, sometimes comply pre-arranged marriages, be a good wife, a good mother and be subservient to the male members of her society. Sound familiar? Females have had this stereotyped character forced on them in many cultures.

As these young Indo-Chinese females were exposed to the American way of life, conflict arose between the traditional way of life and the fast-paced West Coast lifestyle. Young Southeast Asian females started to run away from what was perceived as an abusive home in an effort to gain their independence. Several southern California law enforcement agencies, while conducting runaway investigations determined the reason the young female ran away was because her marriage was pre-arranged and the young female was going to be forced into the relationship (Frank, 1988).

In the early part of 1993, I found a 16-year-old Southeast Asian runaway at a male gang member's house. In the process of taking the runaway home she told me that she ran away because she wants to fit in with the American youth at her school, but her parents want to raise her in the traditional old ways. She stated there could be no compromise with her father who was very strict. When we arrived at her home and I talked with her parents, she began to cry. Her father thanked me and told me this was embarrassing for him and the entire family. He also said his daughter was a rebel and had disgraced the entire family. He was very angry.

As I was leaving, I noticed that the young lady was in a kneeling position in front of her father. Her dad had what appeared to be a bamboo switch and he started to hit the girl on the back with it, yelling at her.

I immediately went back into the house and stopped the corporal punishment. We took the girl out of the home and lodged her at a safe house after advising the father that kind of punishment was not allowed in the United States. He was angry because he felt he had the right to discipline his daughter in traditional ways. He told me he had punished his children like that before without any interference from the police. Cultural attitudes can play an important role in female gang membership and the role of females in a gang.

Indo-Chinese females who runaway quickly discovered the Southeast male gangs offered an instant support system. Some male gang member also ran away for similar reasons. Initially female gangs tended to support a single male gang. Females find out they can associate with the gang because they shared similar needs and issues. The male gang became the source of food, clothing, shelter, protection, friendship and emotional support. For many female gang members, the male gang membership became like big brothers who cared for them. Many female and male gang members referred to their gang as family (Frank, 1988).

Male gang members did not have sex with the females unless it was consensual. There was no expectation to provide sex in return for the acceptance and support. This unconditional acceptance provided a safe environment for the female gang members. Female gang membership tended to be small for these types of gang. The entire membership could be between 6 to 10 females.

These female gang members were once again serving a support role to the male gang members. Sometimes they would be excluded from planning crime, helping with the commission of the crime or committing crime themselves. Even though the first Vietnamese female gang members had gained some freedoms, they where limited within the gang culture by the same cultural attitudes that limited them in traditional family life.

Soon, female gang members associated with one gang began to fight with female gang members from other gangs. Some gang experts believe the motive for the fighting was frustration because of the restrictions the male gang members had placed on the female associates. The male gang members were not bothered with the fighting believing it was a girl thing (Frank, 1988).

The West Coast is not the only home for auxiliary gangs. They also appeared in the Midwest and East Coast. The Vice Queens of Chicago studied between 1960 and 1963 are an example of an independent African-American female gang. Most of the members of the Vice Queens lived in a predominately lower income African-American community characterized by poverty, unemployment, and illegitimacy, juvenile and adult crime. Through gang participation these females learned survival skills that allowed them to function within their community (Klein and Moore, 1995).

The Vice Queens were a loosely knit gang of approximately 30 females between the ages of 13 and 19 years old. The Vice Queens had their own leaders, meetings and activities. The main interest of the Vice Queens was supporting Vice King's activities (Klein and Moore, 1995).

Hybrid Gangs

In some instances female gang members belonged to co-ed gangs that are part of the Hybrid gang phenomenon. These types of Hybrid gangs had broken the gender and/or the race barriers that once limited gang membership to only males of a specific race or ethnic origin. Unlike auxiliary gangs, females in these gangs could take active roles in planning and the execution of gang activities.

Female participation in co-ed gangs is also dependent on the gang makeup. There can be specific types of gender based street gangs: all male, male with minor female membership, gender equal, female with minor male membership and all female. The makeup of the co-ed gang can influence the activity of the females within the gang (Peterson, Miller and Esbensen, 2001). Girls can be so active in some gangs they are considered as equal partners, as one of the male members.

A good example of this type of gang would be the Hoover Folks gang, from Little Rock, Arkansas. This gang has a multi-racial membership and also has broken the gender barrier. Females in this gang have equal status as the male gang members. They are quoted, an East Coast gang term for being jumped-in. There are no pulled punches in this ritual beating. The potential female members have to hold their own, just as the males do. In this gang, female gang members also write the gang's graffiti and teach other members how to make the proper gang signs.

Female gang members in this type of gang also enjoy equal support from peer female and male gang members. There is no pressure for sexual favors from the male gang members. If a gang fight occurs, the female gang member will also help to the best of their ability. The female gang members also have the same blind loyalty to the gang as their male counterparts. This intense loyalty facilitates the formation of strong bonds between the female gang members and other female gang members as well as with the male gang members.

Typically, female gang members act just like their male counterparts. The females and males use the same name for their gang. Often, they refer to their gang as family. Female gang members in general tend to believe they receive love and acceptance from the gang, just as male gang members.

Female gang members in co-ed gangs have been documented with Skinhead, Hispanic, Tagger, Southeast Asian and Blood, Crip, Party Crews, Posses, Clubs, Folk and People Nation gangs.

Motherhood

One side effect of gang membership for some females is motherhood. Getting pregnant is no longer a valid reason to leave the gang. I have encountered a few female gang members who have small children and still are active members of a gang. Females who were gang members and became mothers traditionally have left the gang to care for their children. A trend noted with Skinhead, Black, Hispanic, Hybrid, Southeast Asian, Folk and People Nation female gang members is to stay active with the gang even after bearing a child. In the cases I have encountered almost all female gang mothers were single parents. Several were receiving public assistance and a few lived with their parents.

In a couple of the cases, the fathers of the children were incarcerated gang members. In a few cases, the female gang members were incarcerated and delivered their children in state prison. The parents of the female gang members are raising their grandchildren. There are a number of cases where female gang moms have gotten arrested and sent to jail or prison for gang related crimes or drug offenses. While incarcerated, family members usually grandparents raise the children. In cases where there are no known family members, the child or children have to be taken into protective custody.

The female gang moms try for the most part to be caring mothers, but often have limited parenting skills. Most of the time, offspring are cared for in a satisfactory manner. The gang life for the mother is so luring that moms take part in risky behaviors that could have catastrophic long-term effects on their children. I have spoken with three gang moms who claimed to have taken their child with them when cruising and when they were with their home girls, kicking back in the neighborhood. These moms admitted to drinking and using marijuana while with peer gang members with their children present. Promiscuity, a distorted sense of reality, lack of education, poor financial stability and a need for consistency in their lives have been factors associated with motherhood and female gang members.

Current Trends

During the late to mid 1990s the formation of Vietnamese female party crews at local high school levels was identified by law enforcement. These groups of females seem harmless and may not appear to fit the gang definition. The membership normally denies gang membership or affiliation. The members of the party crews are normally all friends and attend the same high school. The females are always in a small group where ever they go, just as male Southeast Asian gangs (Frank, 1999).

Examining the group a little closer reveals that each member of these party crews is likely to have a nickname or moniker. The party crew itself also will have a name. The party crew will use graffiti on clothes, schoolbooks, backpacks and other personal items. These female party crew members have been involved in assaults against rival female party crews. These female party crews have also attracted the attention of Vietnamese male gangs. This resulted in friction developing between female party crews and the female gang that associated with the male gang.

As female gang members expand their criminal behavior they will also become involved in crimes for profit. In a few cases, female gang members have been involved in prostitution, carjacking, drug sales, grand theft, assaults and murder. There is some law enforcement anecdotal evidence that suggests there may be female gang members that carry weapons for themselves and some that will commit more violent crimes. As one 16-year-old California Hispanic female gang member stated, *"We can do it just as good as the guys."*

Females have also been involved in white supremacist gangs. Female associates can help set up victims for home invasion robberies or drug burn operations. Females can also use sex as a ploy to distract victims. Female gang members in these types of gangs tend to be older. Ad hoc studies suggest that these female gang members to be between their mid 20s and early 30s in southern California. Many hold down full time employment in financial institutions.

Females have also been used as drug couriers using a variety of transportation mechanisms such as the main highways, personal vehicles, trains, busses and airplanes. Female gang members can also be used as a diversion to set up potential victims and to collect intelligence on potential targets.

You have to remember gang membership does not happen overnight. Research suggests that typically gang members will hang out with gang members for some time. Often potential gang members will hang around as much as a year before making the commitment to join (Decker and Van Winkle, 1996).

Some female gang members tend to join a street gang because of dysfunctional home life. Research has uncovered common themes that have contributed to gang membership. Drug addiction among primary caregivers and being physically and/or sexual abused by family members were the most mentioned. The research suggested that females tended to spend more time away from home as a result of the dangers and difficulties there. Consequently, these females sought to get away and to fill their psychological and social needs. Street gang membership can fill these needs and provide a safe haven (Miller, 2001).

A number of researchers also have suggested that the gang can serve as a surrogate extended family for youth who do not see their own families as meeting their needs for belonging, nurturing and acceptance (Huff, 1993, p. 6; Campbell, 1990; Decker and Van Winkle, 1996 and Valdez, 2000). This conclusion may also apply to male gang members, but it tends to be suggested as a model mechanism that influences female gang membership.

Summary

The vocabulary female gang members will use will depend on the type of gang they are in, or what type of gang they associate with. For example, Female Hispanic gang members will most likely use the same slang as their male counterparts and female Southeast Asian gang members will use the same street vocabulary as their male counterparts.

Females in street gangs can have multiple roles from a helper to leadership positions within co-ed gangs. Females who use drugs tend to get addicted to drugs with less use than their male counterparts. This will also be the case with female gang members. Females will continue to be involved in the gang sub-culture whether or not they are parents.

Native American Gangs

The gang problems have emerged as a significant problem for all Americans. This includes those who reside in large cities to rural country towns. Gang membership is not biased and will allow Asians, Blacks, Whites, Latinos and Native Americans into a gang. Within the United States there are 562 federally recognized Indian tribes and Alaska Native groups. Each tribe has its own historical background, culture and traditions. In 2000, the Native American population was approximately 2.4 million, relatively small when compared to the national population; but unique in a few ways. In 2000, about 39 percent of the Native American population was under 25 years of age with only 35 percent living on reservation lands and 65 percent living in the general population (Grant, 2004).

History

Our nation's heritage and history is deeply rooted in many cultures. One culture that has contributed to our country's formation and sometimes-painful growth is Native American. Native Americans are considered by many to be the first occupants of what is now known to be the United States. It was a culture and people that has endured countless attacks, stereotypical analysis and forced change. Somehow, Native Americans have managed to endure and survive the prejudices and class distinctions that have been directed toward them.

In 1492, when Christopher Columbus landed on the Caribbean island of Hispaniola, he believed he had reached the East Indies. As a result of that error he labeled the islands inhabitants Indians. This misnomer is still used today to describe the indigenous people of North, Central and South America. It is interesting to note that in 1735, it was the Swedish taxonomist, Carolus Linnaeus, who gave the original inhabitants of the new world the formal recognition of American or red race (www.nativeamerican.com).

Millions of people in 2000 or more different cultures became categorized together under totally inappropriate racial and cultural terms. These Native Americans were neither Indians nor Red and could not be classified under a single cultural group because of their great diversity.

It is believed that the ancestors of the Native American people entered America from Asia more than 20,000 years ago with some estimates going back as far as 40,000 years. Just before the new land was discovered, anthropologists estimate that between 8.4 and 112 million Native Americans lived in the new world.

In 20th century America, there is no single definition of who is precisely Native American. To be eligible for Federal Indian aid in the United States, a person must live on or near a federal reservation or be of Eskimo or Aleut descent. The U.S. government generally accepts persons who are listed on the rosters of state reservations or who can prove one-fourth or more Indian ancestry as being Native American. However, in the eastern part of the United States some groups with mixed ancestry have claimed Native American status but have not always been granted it by the federal government.

Statistics

The 2000 census report indicated that there were approximately 2.4 million Native Americans, including Eskimos and Aleut who were living in the United States. This represented a growth of over 100,000 since 1999. Most Native Americans live west of the Mississippi River primarily in the states of Oklahoma, California, Arizona, New Mexico and Washington (Grant, 2004).

At one time, it was estimated that nearly a million Native Americans lived on or near the 287 federally recognized reservations located within the continental United States. To many, it is a surprise to find out that when combined, all the reservations only account for 54.4 million acres of land. As of 2002, the United States recognized 562 Native American tribes. Ironically, 226 of the tribes are located in Alaska (Grant, 2004). Being recognized means the tribes have special relationship with the U.S. government and its agent, the Bureau of Indian Affairs (BIA).

The largest reservation is the Navajo, covering some 16 million acres in the states of Arizona, New Mexico and Utah. Most reservations are 1000 acres or smaller and many are under 100 acres in size. Native Americans are not required to live on reservation lands. They are United State citizens and are free move about just like you and I.

Each reservation, depending on size is divided up into districts. Each district has an elected representative that becomes a member of the tribal council. The tribal councils handle the tribal leadership responsibilities. The district representative position is a paid job. The salary allows for a very comfortable lifestyle. There can be a degree of motivation to keep the job and thus, politics come into play. Representatives can be highly motivated to keep members of the district happy, in order to keep the job.

Population distribution analysis for Native Americans results in the following ranking: (U.S. Census Report, 2002)

New York, New York 87,241

Los Angeles California 53,092

Phoenix, Arizona 35,093

Tulsa, Oklahoma 30,277

Oklahoma, Oklahoma 29,001

Anchorage, Alaska. 26,995

Albuquerque, New México 22,047

Chicago, Illinois. 20,898

San Diego, California 16,178

Houston, Texas 15,743

When comparing entire state populations Alaska is unique, as it is estimated that over 44,000 Eskimo and over 10,000 Aleut Indians live in the state as well as an estimated 16,500 Native Americans. Surprisingly, California and Washington also have a sizeable Eskimo and Aleut population. The Census Bureau predicts that the Native-American population will increase to approximately 4.6 million by the year 2050 (Grant, 2004).

The Native American populations have had to endure numerous changes in Federal law that took away compensation for lost lands. An example of one policy, which failed, occurred in the 1950s when Congress called for the termination of special federal programs and trust relationships with Native Americans. It was hoped that this policy change would hasten the assimilation of Native Americans into society. For a number of tribes, trust status was ended, especially the Menominee of Wisconsin and the Klamath of Oregon. For them, this policy proved to be economically disastrous. By the mid 1960s the policy was terminated following widespread opposition by Native Americans and Americans.

Today, on reservations, about 50 percent of the population does not graduate from high school. Nationally, unemployment rates continue to run at all time lows, while on reservation land, they commonly run between 40 and 80%. Birth and death rates pass national averages. Suicide rates continue to run twice the national average. Alcoholism and crime rates are major concerns for those who live on and off the reservation.

Social Issues

A California newspaper article quoted Janet Reno, U.S. Attorney General, as saying "Violence and crime in Indian country imposes a terrible toll on Native American citizens and interferes with the ability of Indian tribes to achieve meaningful self-governance, as well as peace and stability in their communities." For example, the nation's homicide rate declined by 22 percent between 1991 and 1997, while at the same time it has soared 87 percent within the Native American population (Register News Paper, 1997). A 1990 estimate indicated that approximately 500,000 Native Americans still live on reservation land. In 2000, approximately 65 percent of Native American lived off reservation lands (Grant, 2004).

Interestingly, according to the 2000 census report the median age of a Native American is 26 years old and 39% of the Native American population is under the age of 25. Nationally, that age group accounted for only 29 percent of the general population. Don't forget, criminally, the most criminally active group in our country is the 14-24 year old age bracket. Nationally, it is this same age group that also seems to be targeted as victims of violent crime.

A trend seen across the U.S., which is also seen within the Native American population, is the reporting of a younger perpetrator and a younger victim. It seems logical that the Native American 14-24 year-old age groups would experience the same rate of criminal activity and victimization as in the general population. Since there are more people in the Native American 14-24 year-old age group, you would expect the crime rates to be slightly higher than in the general population.

Research reports that gangs in Indian Country tend to be younger youth. In fact research suggests that the majority of Indian Country gang members tend to juveniles (Major, et al, 2004). In the general gang population the majority of members are adults and approximately 20-25 percent is juvenile (Valdez, 2000).

Another factor that can impact the amount of crime committed within the Native American population is the number of single parent households. Within the Native American population, 1990 studies have shown that women without the presence of a husband maintain 27 percent of the families. At the time, this was considerably higher than the national average of 17 percent. If trends continued the percentage of female single parent households is still higher in Indian country than the rest of the United States.

The number of single parent households in general throughout the country has increased since then. Mental health professionals have noted that children who are raised in single parent households have a greater chance to fail in school than children raised in the traditional two-parent home. Failing in school is a primary risk factor associated with juvenile delinquent behavior.

It appears that the Native American population is influenced by several factors that could play a role affecting crime rates and gang membership: the actual number of people in the 14-24-age bracket; the high number of school dropouts; the exceptionally high number of single parent households, lacking a male figure; an above average 51 percent poverty level; loss of cultural identity; influence of off-reservation social issues; alcohol and drug abuse and moving off the reservation.

In single parent homes where there is no male figure, 50 percent live below the national poverty level. Nationally, as income level rises, crime tends to decrease; so it is not surprising and also saddening to encounter such high crime rates on Native American lands. However research suggests that much of the gang behavior in Indian Country is unstructured and informal. Native-American gangs tend to be loose knit, small and autonomous (Grant, 2004). The number of reported gang members and gangs tends to parallel general Native American populations. Gangs started to appear in Indian Country in the early 1980s, about one half of survey respondents indicated gangs were first noticed after 1994 (Major et al, 2004).

Above average substance abuse problems that includes alcohol continues to have a profound effect on the quality of life for many Native Americans. There is also an extremely high incidence of Fetal Alcohol Syndrome (FAS) within this population. The social factors mentioned here are similar to the ones mentioned in Chapter One. As suggested earlier, research data suggests that they tend to be part of the root causes for gang formation. They also have the same affect on the formation of gangs in Indian Country. At the same time these same social factors can affect gang growth and activity in other parts of the world. Quality of life issues compel migration for many.

I think it is clearly evident that for some Native Americans, life is not getting better. To compound these issues, as in many other parts of our country, grandparents are raising many Native American children. Unfortunately, substance abuse and alcohol have taken their toll on many parents. Grandparents volunteer or are volunteered to care for the children. As seen within many communities, a cultural conflict occurs. The grandparents are trying to raise the children with an emphasis on the traditional customs while the children want to keep up with fads and current trends seen on TV, movies, music videos and what is heard on popular music. Some Native American children present contempt for authority, disrespect for elders and have a distorted view of reality. Sound familiar? This is also the case for many American families.

At one time many tribes were stuck without gang awareness and the ability to learn alternative parenting skills. I have found that many Native American grandparents who are raising their grand children literally have no control of their wards. Without the knowledge of gang behavior and pre-gang behavior patterns, the grandparents and guardians are limited in response options. Candidly, to compound the problem, life for many on reservations is difficult at best. Unfortunately, denial plays a key role here.

The Native American experiences conditions that seem to be present for many other ethnic groups. Bias, prejudice and class distinction appear to influence the formation of street gangs in Indian Country and within the Native American population. These same conditions were present in New York when the first Irish street gangs formed in the early 1800s. Poverty, violence, criminal victimization, murder and abuse were experienced by immigrants and refugees and this was a direct result these social stigmas. Add to the formula squalid living conditions and it is easy to see that one of the byproducts is the formation of street gangs.

Gang Presence

The gang sub-culture has been present in Indian Country for some time. Teachers, Native Americans, tribal police officers and a few council members have confided to me that they recognized the presence of gang activity on some reservation lands since late 1990 to early 1991. This is almost 10 years after the presence of gangs was reported academically.

Interviews during late 1990s with educators who work at Native American schools or at schools with Native American populations have confirmed an increase in gang dress, gang graffiti, gang crime and the gang mentality since 1997. Because Native American reservations are spread throughout the country, some can be somewhat isolated. I have found that in a few cases the gang culture can exert an unchecked influence on local youth. The young Native Americans who live on these reservations can become an ideal target group for gang recruitment.

There have been a limited number of formal academic studies that estimate gang populations on reservations. Ad hoc studies I have been involved suggest that gang membership size varies as a function of reservation population. From contacts I have made, gang sizes vary from 6 to 8 members to as large as 30-100 members. Albeit the sample base was small and there were only a limited number of respondents.

A 1997 study suggested that tribal populations on reservations at the time were 526,627, with 196 tribes represented, but only 95 tribes participating in the survey. According to the summary report, there were 5,500 Native American gang members. A staggering number considering that gang membership has more than tripled on reservations within the last four years. 310 different gangs were reported, making the average size of the gang approximately, 17 or 18 members (Bureau of Indian Affairs, 1997). The myths that reservation gangs are not real gangs only wannabes is just that, only a myth. Reservations gangs are present and share many characteristics with non-reservation gangs.

A study completed in 2005 suggested there were 577 Indian communities in the United States comprised of 561 recognized tribes. A little more than one half of the tribes responded to the survey, 52 percent. Only 23 percent of the responding tribes reported the presence of gangs in their jurisdiction. According to the respondents the reservation gang phenomenon started in the early 1980s (Major et al, 2004).

Females are also involved in Native American gangs. In early 1997 from limited personal observations it appeared that female gang membership was lower than reported in the general population. Native American female gang membership can be as high as 20 percent (Major et al, 2004). This suggests that female gang participation within the Native American population tends to be higher than in the general population, more than double based on some research findings. Female gang membership in the general population has been estimated at 6 percent (Egley, 2002) and 10 percent (Valdez, 2000). This also suggests that males comprise 80 percent of the Native American gang population (Major et al, 2004).

A number of Native American female gangs have also been identified. These gangs are unique, and still associate with the male gangs on the reservation. Female gangs have names similar to non-reservation gangs, such as Latin Queens, Black Rose, Bad Girls, Purple Passion and Piru. The female gang members I have spoken to told me they enjoy being part of their own gang. Some have stated they get equal status with their male counterparts when they are with them.

The brief encounters with female reservation gang members did not allow the development of enough evidence to support whether they could be classified into the auxiliary female gang category or independent female category. Most of the states that responded to the 1997 study, reported some type of female gang activity. Many reported a small number of female gangs. Most of the gang activity on the reservation occurs west of the Mississippi River, which is not surprising since the majority of Native Americans are located there (Bureau of Indian Affairs, 1997).

In the late 1990s I suspected that co-ed gangs would eventually be found on the reservation. This phenomenon was reported on many reservations by the early 2000s. One research finding suggested that 82 percent of the identified gangs in Indian Country included both males and females (Major et al, 2004). This would tend to suggest that co-ed hybrid gangs have been present in Indian country longer than previously suspected.

There are a number of different types of male reservation gangs. Native American gangs tend to adopt gang cultures depending on the geographical location of the reservation. Indian Country gangs near the west coast tend to adopt west coast based gang behaviors. Native American gangs located in the Mid West and East Coast as a cohort tend to adopt Mid West and East Coast gang traits.

Crip / Blood

Native American gangs seem to be heavily influenced by four types of street gangs. No one knows for sure and it is suspected that geography tends to be somehow involved. The Crip and Blood street gangs that originated in Southern California seem to have the major influence on some Native Americans who do become gang members. Throughout Indian Country where gang activity has been seen and documented Crip and Blood sets can be found.

One unique characteristic of Native American gangs that claim Blood or Crip affiliation is that most do not claim any particular set of the Bloods or Crip. For example, in the late 1990s there were no reports of Rollin 60s or Grape Street Crip gangs or Rollin 20 Bloods reported. I have encountered youth who just claim generic Crip or Blood street gang membership. I suspect that as Native American gangs continue to evolve that sooner or later specific Crip or Blood set affiliation will be found on Native American lands.

As you would anticipate, the appropriate Crip and Blood stylized clothing that is associated with membership throughout the U.S., is also found being worn by those Native American gang members. Much of the time, the Native American gang members who claim membership with the Crip or Blood gangs will also use the street slang that is associated with these groups. The same is true for the type of graffiti that is found on reservations, personal belongings, schoolbooks, street signs, homes and public buildings.

I have spoken to several Native American Crip and Blood gang members who have indicated that early on, they were influenced by what they saw on TV, in the movies, what they read in newspapers and magazines and what they heard in the music. Some of the youth I have spoken to told me they liked the characters that were portrayed in the videos and movies they have seen and that is what they aspired to be. The gang culture has a tremendous impact on youth. Combined with all the complex social factors present in Indian Country and for Native Americans, it is easy to conclude that some gang memberships are used as a vehicle to escape the harsh reality of reservation life. However, observations like this tend to become the anecdotal evidence that supports the theory that the gang culture has been exported and imported throughout the country.

Even though the Crip-Blood influence is greatest in the western half of the country, the influence is nationwide for Native Americans. Gangs have been identified with names such as the Crips, Bloods, Westside Crips, Crypts, Compton Raiders and Boys in the Hood (Bureau of Indian Affairs, 1997).

Folk Nation

As you travel towards the East Coast, a major Mid-western gang has also exerted an influenced on Native American gang affiliation especially in Indian Country. The term Folk Nation is an umbrella term for a number of independent street gangs that have aligned themselves together for a number of reasons. In the Chicago area, the rivals of Folk Nation gangs are those gangs that align themselves with the People Nation gangs.

Some experts believe that the largest street gang in America is the Black Gangster Disciples, a Folk Nation gang with an estimated 50,000 members. Black Gangster Disciple members have even been encountered in Southern California and the U.S. military. The gang has spread its reputation and influence throughout the country and tends to be highly organized.

On reservations where gang activity has been reported gang members will also claim affiliation and membership with the Folk, an abbreviated term for Folk Nation. I have spoken to Native American gang members who claim Folk Crip membership that suggests the presence of Hybrid gangs in Indian Country. In the mid 1990s some law enforcement experts believed there is no real connection between the Crip and Folk Nation gangs. It was believed that Native Americans used these gang names to create a greater or more ruthless reputation for the gang and its members. Other gangs have used this tactic. For example, some Asian Boys cliques refer to themselves as Asian Boy Crips and identify with the color blue.

However, in the late 1990s Black Gangster Disciple Native American gang members were identified, which makes them part of the Folk Nation. The most common People Nation gang claimed by Native American youth is the Vice Lords. However, a number of Latin King and Latin Disciple Native American gang members have also been identified. The easily identifiable clothing style, hand signs, right/left orientation and graffiti have also been found.

Hispanic Gangs

A minority of Native American gang members has adopted the traits of Hispanic gangs. The influence can be seen in the style of dress, graffiti, personal writings and mentality. A look at personal mementoes has also confirmed the Hispanic gang influence, especially in the Southwest. As with most gangs the individual member's reputation is critical. The Bloods, Crip and Folk and People Nation gangs have a national reputation for being strong, ruthless and violent. In the late 1990s Hispanic street gangs did not enjoy the same national notoriety. However with the rapid growth of the 18th Street, Sureno and Mara Salvatrucha gangs, Hispanic gang affiliation and association can bring the same enhanced reputation.

As you would expect, the Hispanic street gang influence appears to be the greatest in the West and Southwest. Identified Native American gangs have included Westside Surenos and 18th Street. The Sureno gang influence from California has been identified on several reservations in the Southwest.

Tagging Crews

It is now known that Native American tagger crews exist on reservations. The presence of tagger type graffiti on a reservation is probably the first clue to alert for the presence of taggers. I suspect the formation of Native American taggers resulted for the same reasons the tagger crews grew in the rest of the country. I would compare the current status to the independent taggers that were present in late 1980s and early 1990s. With time, if left unchecked, these Native American tagger crews could evolve into tag banger gangs. Rivalries can develop between other tagger crews and the same explosion of tagging we experienced between 1990 and 1995 could be seen on Native American lands.

Tagger crews represent a small proportion of the total Native American gang population. Some gangs have used the name SSK that is often associated with a west coast tag banger gang known as the South Side Killers. For the Native American reservation, gangs it could also refer to the South Side Krips. There was a West Coast tagger crew known as Society's Sick Killers as well.

As Native American taggers compete with each other another trend might occur. Native American tagger crews could start to compete with the local off reservation tagger crews. This would force the Native American gang members to come off the reservation, tag up local areas and then return to the safety of the reservation. As rivalries intensify, hypothetically Native American taggers or gang members could be involved as suspects or victims of gang motivated violence, including murder.

Native American Gangs

A small number of Native American gangs have developed their own style. With reservation gangs such as American Indian Movement (not affiliated with the AIM political group), Ponca Boys, Native American Boys, Native American Mafia, Central Indian Village, Indian Pride, Crow Indian Gangsters (CIG), American Indian Clan (AIC) and the Menominee Imperial Warriors it is clear that the Native American culture influences the gang life.

These types of gangs will share a number of the common profile characteristics of non-reservation gangs. This includes, stylized clothing, hand signs, graffiti, weapon possession, drug use, and violent behaviors. General customs and practices of non-reservation gangs will also be commonly used, including the use of gang generic and specific tattoos. For example I have seen a few male Native American gang members use a tattoo that says "Red Power." Native American gang members will also form prison gangs when in custody (Grant, 2008).

Crime

Unfortunately, Native American gang members have adopted the same type of criminal behaviors as their general population counterparts. Gang related crimes have included vandalism, petty thefts, graffiti, drug possession, drug use, drunkenness and battery. More serious crimes which have been documented include drug possession for sales, sales of drugs, weapon possession, aggravated assaults, attempted murder, murder, and drive by shootings, robbery, home invasion style robberies and in a few cases, sexual assaults. A tribal council member was even attacked and had his arm broken in a gang related assault. However, research suggests that the majority of gang related crime is related to alcohol abuse and vandalism (Major et al, 2004).

This does exclude the fact that Native American gang members are capable of the same types of gang motivated violent attacks encountered with general population street gangs. Of all the crimes committed, drug sales and use seems to be on the rise. With below poverty living conditions, lack of parent or guardian awareness, drug sales offers and easy way to make money. Nationally, drug sales tend to be the primary source of income for street gangs (www.usdoj.gov).

Turf wars can be anticipated as drug sales competition increases between Native American gangs. This cycle has been seen and documented within general population street gangs. Money can give power, control and recognition within the gang sub culture. Having this perceived power and authority can become addictive and be highly motivating to continue to transport, supply, manufacture and sell drugs. Gang members who sell drugs tend to arm themselves. Drug trafficking can also have a secondary impact on the reservation. Someone or some group has to supply the drugs to the Native American dealers. Drug importation by non-Native American gangs and non-Native Americans can have a profound impact on the gang dynamics within the reservation.

By late the 1990s Native American gangs have been located in at least 18 states. Native American reservations can been found in no less than 33 states. One could conclude that the Native American gang population is probably higher than reported because all the tribes did not participate in the 1997 study. Of those who participated in the Major et al research project, only 23 percent of the tribes reported the presence of gangs on the reservation (Major, et al, 2004).

There are probably several reasons why Native American youth become involved in the gang life. Certainly the loss of the Native American culture and traditions has had a crucial impact. Juveniles and young adults residing on reservations have reached out to grasp a replacement culture and found as many other young people have, gangs can be a surrogate family. Gang membership might offer to fulfill everything they were looking for and could not find in their traditional lifestyle. However, there is a cost to everything. The cost here is the willingness to be violent and offer your life if necessary for the gang.

The onset of Native American gang membership is associated with a variety of social factors. Findings from a field study on gangs in the Navajo Nation suggest that the importation and spread of youth gangs are facilitated by specific structural factors in the community (Armstrong et al, 2002). These factors include the frequency with which families move off and onto the reservation, poverty, substance abuse, family dysfunction, the development of cluster housing instead of traditional single family housing, the waning connection to the Native American culture and traditional kinship ties among cousins (Major et al, 2004). These findings reflect a process of "multiple marginalization" whereby depressed "social and economic conditions result in powerlessness" among community members (Vigil, 2002). These changes in structural forces weaken families, schools and other institutions that are traditionally associated with social control (Major et al, 2004).

Education

It appears that gang populations are increasing on the reservation. Gang related crimes have become more violent and the drug culture continues to grow. There are some possible solutions. One of the most successful programs for young Native Americans at risk is located in Pierre, South Dakota. The Pierre Indian Learning Center has a proven intervention program and a very high success rate. This boarding school draws at risk students from 3 different states, which includes 15 different tribes. At risk students are admitted upon application to this comprehensive school program. Because of its size the school has to limit the number of students who attend.

This is not a psychiatric facility or a juvenile detention center. This is an alternative school for children with limited educational opportunities. These may be the result of social and/or family problems, language differences, undiagnosed learning disabilities, truancy and other factors, have not been successful in reservation schools or in their home environment.

The school is located on 193 acres of land and is complete with a sophisticated counseling center. The campus is well equipped for recreational, athletic and educational activities.

What makes the school unique is the staff. From the dorm-parents, teachers, counselors, school administrative staff and school director only one thing is focused on, the students. A co-ed learning environment has proven to be well accepted. The programs not only focus on traditional learning values, but emphasis skills needed to handle social issues on the reservation as well in society in general. Surprisingly, most of the students function well in this environment. The school offers a variety of educational and athletic programs for all types of at risk students.

Grades 1 to 8 are taught and the student population is around 300. The school only operates 9 months a year. During the summer months, students return back home. In many cases this causes a set-back because many of the students return to an unhealthy environment, in a few cases, the student literally returns back to a reservation gang. The school plans to expand in the future to allow for additional students and more activities. Of all the programs for Native American children at risk, this seems to be one of the more successful. Many of the graduates have continued their education at major universities and have become very successful. The key to the schools success is the focus on the student and the collaborative approach by the teachers and staff.

To contact the school:

Pierre Indian Learning Center
Box 148
Pierre, South Dakota 57501-9408
605-224-8661

There are similar types of schools in other states and all offer similar programs and have the same focus, to educate Native Americans and prepare them for a successful life.

Summary

The U.S. Census Bureau predicts the Native American population will increase to over 4.5 million by 2050 (Grant, 2004). As the population increase so will gang activity. A significant number of Native Americans will continue to live off the native lands. Native youth and young adults who join and affiliate with U.S. based street gangs will form unique relationships in an effort to generate income. Native American gang activity will continue to occur on and off Native lands. Native American gangs may also become more organized as illegal activities such as narcotic trafficking increases.

Chapter 3

Activity Based Gangs

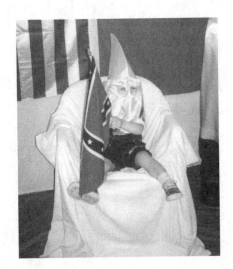

This chapter will discuss how some street gangs based their behaviors on the activity they are involved in. There are some unique behaviors based on political, religious and sociological attitudes and beliefs.

Skinhead Gangs

Skinheads are a type of street gang that is associated with the white supremacists movement. More contemporary words are used by white supremacists such as white pride, white separatism to describe white superiority. The street appearance of the movement is made by racist skinhead gangs. Most operate as independent cells with no direct connection between the gangs. However, the Internet and cellar telephony has made contact between individual members and gangs easier.

History

To understand the skinhead gang mentality you have to understand how and when the white supremacist ideology started. The white supremacist movement in the United States has been active since the Civil War. This movement has been referred to as the White Separatist movement (Leyden, 2004). Other terms may be used but they still refer to racists' attitudes and philosophies. This extremist movement seems to be composed of three distinct sub-groups. Law enforcement runs into highly visible skinhead groups who are easy to identify because of their distinctive hairstyle, tattoos, clothing, and criminal activity.

The second group seems to attract working, middle-class Americans. Organizations like the Aryan Resistance Movement (ARM), Aryan Youth Movement (AYM) or White Aryan Resistance (WAR) hold meetings and rallies that espouse supremacist ideas and philosophies. Some members of these organizations are part of a silent movement. A few experts might consider these groups or individuals as White sympathizers. If a catalytic event were to occur a number of these supporters would make themselves known. For some white supremacist the racist attitudes have been passed down through several generations within a family. This can be an employed strategy to assist white supremacists in infiltrating legitimate businesses, the military and the criminal justice profession. Sort of like sleeper cells of white supremacists.

The third level in the white supremacy movement is comprised of highly organized groups like the Ku Klux Klan (KKK) or militias. The Klan was originally founded in 1866 and has been active in the United States for over 150 years. Levels of activity have risen and fallen over the years, but the Klan has survived and membership is increasing again.

The Klan has also been recruiting new members from the ranks of skinhead gangs and is trying to change the image of the Klan from a white supremacist group to a White Pride organization. This is being attempted to try and change the public's image of the group. What distinguished these types of groups from skinhead street gangs is usually age. Skinhead gang members tend to be younger, early teens to mid twenties; while members in these types of groups tend to be older men and women.

Philosophies

White supremacist ideologies were actually developed during the 19th century with the propagation of a spurious and completely fabricated document entitled: The Protocols of the Elders of Zion, which purported to expose an international Jewish conspiracy. This anti-Semitic myth resurfaced in the United States during the 1920s. Automobile tycoon, Henry Ford, was one of the early and most influential promoters of the international Jewish conspiracy concept, which was adopted by the Ku Klux Klan. The Ku Klux Klan maintained Jews were not White and added this philosophy to their agenda of anti-Black and anti-Catholic ideologies (Ridgeway, 1990).

Jewish Conspiracy theory is based on the false premise that the Jews have taken control of the banks, entertainment industry, and precious metal and jewelry business. In short, the Jews are taking over the world's financial base and were or are held responsible for the problems the nations of the world have had and are currently experiencing. In essence, the Jewish people had become scapegoats.

The acceptance of this myth was increased with the development of the Christian Identity doctrine, which is another fundamental philosophy used to support White supremacist ideologies.

Christian Identity centers on the belief that Anglo-Saxons were really the lost tribe of Israel and that the Jews and all other non-whites are inferior. The philosophy also includes a belief that non-Anglo-Saxons were sent to earth as the scourge of God. When the apocalypse comes, these groups believe the earth will be rid of the inferior people and reserved only for the true Israelite people, the White Aryans. One alleged sign of true racial purity would depend on ones the ability to blush.

Skinhead Origins

The United States has a long historical background of racial purity movements that led to the development of such organizations as the John Birch Society, the United Klans of America, Aryan Nation, Posse Comitatus, and the Church of Jesus Christ Christian. Other groups include the American Nazi Party, Minutemen, the Populist Party, Knights of the Ku Klux Klan, White Aryan Resistance, California Knights, Church of the Creator and the Nazi Skinheads.

The skinhead movement was started in England during the mid 1960s. A portion of the English White working-class banded together in opposition to the rising number of immigrants that were competing for the available jobs. The Mod movement was active at the same time and had revolted against the standard trends and the values of the English community. The Mods developed their own style of dress, values and musical tastes. In the mid 1960s there was a split in the Mod movement and the first skinhead groups became known in England.

The Mods kept using the same stylized dress and were multi-racial in membership. The skinhead membership continued to be comprised only of all-white-working-class people. The skinhead movement continued stressing the development of White Pride. In protest against the long hair youth, skinheads shave their hair off.

Around 1978 a new band named Screwdriver formed and was led by Ian Stuart. This band became the catalyst for the development of the Neo-Nazi racist skinhead groups in America that we see today. The Neo-Nazi skinheads in the Unites States popularized the wearing of bomber or tanker jackets, and were heavily influenced by racist music and the white pride philosophy.

Sometime between the late 1970s and early 1980s the same time the punk movement arrived in the United States. Some of the punk bands in the United States continued to write and play music that contained racial overtones. As the punk movement grew in the U.S. it led to the development of skinhead gangs we see today. Two types of skinhead gangs emerged. They were racist and non-racist skinhead gangs.

The first racist skinhead gangs were observed in Los Angeles and New York in the early 1980s. In 1983, the then popular racist band Screwdriver toured the United States. The band was featured in underground nightclubs and played at Ku Klux Klan rallies. The band aided in popularizing the skinhead movement and the growth of the Neo-Nazi skinhead groups through its music and song lyrics. During the 1980s white power bands in Europe and the United States played racist Oi, a racist hardcore punk rock type of music that sometimes was called racist metal music or hate core (Bridgeman, 2000).

Like all youth street gangs skinheads place a very value on conforming to the group's consensus. Therefore, a specific street uniform was developed and certain behaviors and attitudes are expected of the membership (Ridgeway, 1990).

Classification

In 1989, the Anti-Defamation League (ADL) released a series of reports that indicated there were approximately 3,000 skinheads in 31 different states (Ridgeway, 1990). Today, there are three types of skinhead gangs in the United States and they comprise approximately 3 to 5 percent of the total U.S. gang population. The three major classifications are Neo-Nazi racist, non-racist skinheads (SHARP) and independents. At one time members of all three gangs dressed alike and only their different belief systems separated them. There is a second classification method used to categorize the skinhead groups. Some law enforcement experts classify the gangs as non-racist, independent, and white supremacist skinhead gangs (Miller, 1990).

Membership

All three gangs share general membership characteristics and behaviors. While some skinhead groups require a formal membership application, dues, and force the members to follow rules and regulations, other skinhead gangs are less formal. Distinctive stylized dress characterizes many skinhead groups. Generally, racist and independent skinheads are militant and aggressive. Frequently, they are involved in criminal activity, specifically targeting minorities and gays.

By 2000, Skinhead gangs have been reported in Arizona, Nevada, California, Colorado, Oregon, Washington, Illinois, Michigan, Missouri, Ohio, Wisconsin, Alabama, Georgia, Florida, Louisiana, Oklahoma, Texas, Tennessee, Maryland, New Jersey, and Pennsylvania and all over Europe. Skinhead activity has even been reported in Australia. During 2000, skinhead gangs were also actively involved in racially motivated incidents in Europe and responsible for several fire bombings.

Skinhead membership was thought to traditionally drawn from dysfunctional working-class families. Law enforcement anecdotal evidence suggests that many skinheads come from what appears to be normal homes in middle and upper middle class America. At one time, typical Skinhead gang members could be as young as 13 and as old as 25. Many skinheads are of average intelligence, but are often poorly educated high school dropouts. Most members are recruited at the junior or high school level. When skinhead gang members work, often the job is menial and pays only the minimum wage. Many skinhead gang members are unemployed (Miller, 1990).

However, there may have been a paradigm shift in skinhead membership demographics. There is some law enforcement anecdotal evidence that suggests the majority of skinheads are currently between 20 and 40 years old. It was once thought that skinhead ranks were filled only with teenage youth. Criminal activity supports the law enforcement theory that there is an active older skinhead sub-group working on the streets and recruiting new members.

Some skinhead gang members do not think they are completely racist or racist at all because they may work with or live in the same neighborhood with minority families. The Down Irish Brotherhood (Huntington Beach, California) is a good example of this type of gang. Many of the members hold down full time jobs, working out regularly, live in diverse neighborhoods; work with minorities and stay fit. However, on the weekend nights they like to get drunk and fight gang members, especially Hispanic gang members. Some members sport a green colored cloverleaf tattoo to show membership, as well as other common skinhead type tattoos. Individually, while not drinking, the members are well like by their peers, co-workers and neighbors. It is almost like these skinhead gang members led a double life and appear to be weekend skinheads.

Clothing

As with other gangs, the skinheads have acquired a special clothing style. A distinct part of clothing that is easily noticed is the work-style boots that many skinheads wear. These boots are known as Docs, short for Doctor Martin. These leather boots come in a variety of colors. They have 10, 12 or 14 holes for the laces. They can also be purchased with a steel toe. These boots were the popular and inexpensive work boot of the blue-collar factory workers that were used in England. Sometimes, any style of military boot is worn, especially if the Doctor Martin brand cannot be afforded. However, not all skinheads wear boots, other types of footwear can be worn.

Many Skinheads worldwide have adopted wearing boots as part of the skinhead uniform and a symbol of their belief system. At one time Skinhead gang members also wore tailored pants, tee shirts and suspenders or braces as they call them. The color of the braces can be important to the skinhead. Some racists Skinheads preferred braces and red bootlaces. The color red indicates that the wearer is ready to fight or spill blood for the cause. Black colored braces indicate the wearer is neutral. White colored braces indicate the wearer has a high sense of white pride. A nylon flight or bomber jacket is also a commonly worn outer garment. The clothing style exemplifies a working class attitude based in the philosophies of white supremacy.

The jackets and tee shirts may have symbols or phrases that are associated with the white supremacy movement such as Celtic crosses, the American flag, swastikas, the Confederate flag, or references to popular white supremacist bands.

To the non-racist skinhead, color has only an aesthetic value. White clothing makes up the essential skinhead uniform. The clothing has become an integral part of this sub-culture. Some skinhead gangs use a white colored railroad bandanna as a symbol for white power just as Blood and Crip gang members wear red and blue bandannas to show their gang affiliation.

Some skinheads still sport a shaven head style haircut. However, a trend that developed allows for many skinheads to let their hair grow out a little, but the hairstyles are still worn short. Initially skinhead gang members shaved their head so that hair could not be pulled during a fight. Currently, many Latino, Black, Taggers, prison and party crew gang members as well as non-gang members shave their heads. The shaven head style of haircut has become a popular haircut style nationwide.

Graffiti

Skinhead graffiti makes a general statement about anti-Semitic, racial or political attitudes using a variety of symbols, abbreviations and the names of hate music bands. It is also generally used to announce the presence of the gang in a certain area. Traditionally, skinhead gangs have not claimed turf.

Skinhead graffiti may also indicate current alliances with other gangs, and can include the use of swastikas, lightning bolts, racial slurs, and the abbreviations for Supreme White Power (SWP), White Aryan Resistance (WAR), White Power (WP) and the Ku Klux Klan (KKK).

Skinhead graffiti may also mimic other street gangs and show the name of the gang and can include member's nicknames along with a racial slur. Sometimes, skinhead graffiti will denote the county that a particular group is from. Skinhead graffiti could also be considered an extension of skinhead type tattoos or vice versa. However, graffiti does not have to be used by skinhead gangs. Older members of skinhead gangs tend not to use graffiti.

Mentality

What binds skinheads together is a philosophy or belief in white supremacy. This belief motivates membership and activity. As one 17-year-old skinhead said about another skinhead he had just met, "He is my brother because of belief and cause." Skinhead gang membership tends to be based on this belief and cause. Part of the belief and cause is the position that minorities and gays cause most if not all the problems in America and there is a plot to systematically destroy the White race. Skinheads must unite to save the country.

The white supremacist philosophy allows for skinheads who have never met to act in concert, because they have a common belief system and goal. This tends to act as a strong cohesive force that can bind skinheads who meet for the first time together.

Skinhead violent crime can appear to be spontaneous or haphazard and without apparent provocation. Many skinhead attacks are the result of a chance encounter like much of the violent gang crime. Because of the unique mentality and belief system, Skinheads involved in the same crime may not live in the same city. Do not forget one of the unifying factors for all skinhead members is the white pride (supremacy) philosophy. This allows Skinheads from different parts of a city, county or state to meet for the first time and commit crime together as if it was planned and rehearsed.

Another factor that will act as a cohesive force for skinhead gang members is the desire to make money. This desire has become a primary motive for skinhead and other gang members to become involved in identity theft, fraudulent check manufacture and mail theft. Many skinheads augment their drug trafficking operations with these non-violent financial crimes.

Violent attacks by skinheads can be initiated in a peculiar way. White pride statements can be made before the attack. A challenge to the victim's patriotism is also commonly used. The victim tends to react to a threat, as the inquiry becomes heated. Then the Skinheads attack, often as a group. This is a specific street tactic used by skinhead and fighting gangs. It becomes a perceived mechanism to enhance the gang's reputation and respect.

The verbal statements are often used as a precursor and signal to attack. Female members and associates may be involved in the verbal confrontation and may be involved in the ensuing assault. It has also been a common practice to for all present members to take part of the verbal confrontation and then part or the entire membership to commit the following physical assault. It appears almost as if there was an informal agreement or understanding that this is one way to start and complete an assault.

I have also interviewed skinheads who confided that their idea of having fun is to get drunk and fight. Often, skinheads from many parts of a county will gather at a popular location. This place could be a local beach, park or fun center.

As one 19-year-old skinhead candidly said, "We like to get drunk and fight the Mexican gang bangers." Getting drunk and fighting is a common practice for many skinheads." Based on law enforcement anecdotal evidence it appears that fighting or challenging to fight has become a common behavior for many skinhead gangs.

The victims are usually chosen at random and can be minorities, other whites, gang members, or military personal. During these confrontations a common triggering comment used has been asking this question. "What are you looking at?" This question is the form of a call out and has the same function as the question 'where are you from or who do you claim?' In gang parlance this questions are really gang challenges. Remember in the gang culture no challenge ever goes unanswered. The skinheads normally attack in small groups. Most fight for fun. It appears that fighting in groups is the skinhead version of kicking back.

Skinheads can also commit hate crimes. The victims are chosen based on race, religion and/or sexual orientation. In these types of crimes sometimes there is a plan to find a particular type of victim, and then make the assault.

An 18-year-old skinhead told me, "All skinheads are brothers no matter where they are because they share a common belief in white supremacy." It seems that the turf for skinheads is mental in nature and based on a philosophy rather than a geographical location. It is this shared belief that unites skinheads from all over the United States even though there are hundreds of different skinhead groups located through the country.

There is some speculation that this method of operation conforms to the white supremacist strategy of leaderless resistance. Small leaderless groups are involved in random, unplanned attacks that operate independently but are part of the whole white supremacist movement. This is sort of a calculated chaos, fueled by skinhead violence that benefits the white supremacist movement.

Intra Gang Violence

As with all gangs, violence between members of the same skinhead gang can occur. This may happen for a number of reasons such as jealously over a girl, a personal insult or an insult to peer gang members or to the gang itself. The attacks may be planned or be opportunistic in nature ranging from simple assaults to stabbing and shootings.

As with other types of street gangs Skinhead gang members want respect. In the gang sub-culture no insult ever goes unanswered no matter how small. Not to answer an insult would mean to lose respect. Therefore, skinhead gang members will attack another skinhead to get back lost respect. Doing so enhances the personal respect of the attacking gang member and protects the gang's respect. Violence between skinhead gangs or within skinhead gangs can be done for the benefit of the gang because the action enhances the gang's reputation to commit violent acts, even among themselves. The end result of these types of attacks is that the gang's reputation is saved and/or enhanced.

Hand Signs

Raising the right arm at 45 degree forming the Nazi salute was one of the original gestures used by skinhead gangs. That gesture is still used today and is often made as peer skinheads are arrested, during public rallies and toward incarceration facilities that house peer skinhead gang members. This is a form of salute to a comrade who is in custody for the white supremacist cause. Skinhead gangs also use more traditional hand signs that are formed by making letters of the alphabet. These types of hand signs might include a W, P, for White Power or the initials for their gang name. Skinhead street gangs can also use the hand signs as a form of challenge or insult to rival gangs as well as intimidation aimed at non-gang members.

Tattoos

Tattoos have always played a role in skinhead gang subculture. The most common skinhead tattoos are really an extension of skinhead graffiti (Miller, 1990).

Some of the most common tattoos seen on skinhead gang members include, but are not limited to: the swastika, lightning bolts, American, Confederate or Nazi flags, crossed hammers, S.W.P. (Supreme White Power), W.P. (White Power), W.A.R. (White Aryan Resistance), K.K.K. (Ku Klux Klan), Boot Power, Skins, Christian Crosses, OI (the name refers to skinhead music or a skinhead greeting), White Power, hooded figures, Viking figures, clover leafs, 88/14 and other numbers like 23 and Sieg Heil. The tattoos are located on the hands, arms, stomach, back, neck, and face and inside of the lips. Tattoos are a personal reminder to the wearer of his or her commitment to the group.

The presence of other street gangs has also influenced the type of tattoos worn by skinheads. It is not uncommon to find skinheads with tattoos of three dots or the happy and sad theatrical faces. Latino gang members initially wore these types of tattoos, but today they are seen on gang members from all types of street gangs. These are great examples of generic gang tattoos. They are encountered with those are somehow affiliated with the gang culture. Yet they do not indicate membership to a particular gang.

Some skinhead gang members may also claim allegiance to Southern California just like many Latino gang members. Tattoos that reflect this may be observed as "So Cal." It is not reference to the Sureno gang life style that southern California Latino gang members operate by. It a reference to a coalition of southern California skinhead gangs that wanted to adopt standards for their membership in the mid 1990s. It is unlikely that a skinhead would wear a Sureno or Sur-13 tattoo because that would denote an allegiance to Hispanic street gangs which is contrary to their belief system.

Attitude

Skinheads often use the acronym ZOG. To a skinhead, this is an abbreviation for the Zionist Occupational Government. It is another referral to the supposed efforts by Jews to control the United States and the rest of the world. Radical skinheads often avoid wearing Levis because they falsely believe the Levi Strauss Company is owned by members of the Jewish community and therefore is part of ZOG.

Any authority figure represents a member of ZOG to the skinhead. This would include all criminal justice professionals. Many skinheads feel it is their duty to save and purify the white race. This attitude justifies any action taken by skinhead gang members because it is done for this cause. It is logical to conclude that this can include assaults against law enforcement officers and other criminal justice professionals.

The racist attitude of a skinhead does not have to be espoused all the time. Some skinheads will get along with certain minorities. They may work and live with a racial diverse population. For example, a racist skinhead may live within a predominately Hispanic neighborhood and have no problems with his neighbors. The same skinhead may also have frequent contacts by the police for assaulting Hispanic gang members. Even though the same skinhead hates all African-Americans, he may have full time employment that requires him to work with Hispanics and African-Americans. He accomplishes this without incident.

Some hardcore skinheads will die in support of their racist beliefs. These are deep-seated beliefs that can take over the life style and behavior of a committed skinhead. Many skinheads also believe a myth. The myth is all whites are racist and skinheads are a just a little braver because they publicly exhibit their philosophy (Christensen, 1994).

Music

During the 1980s skinhead music was often called OI music and reflected its English working-class origin. The lyrics are racist and violent and play an important part in the skinhead lifestyle. Originally, the word Oi was used as a form of greeting. The founder of White Aryan Resistance, Tom Metzger said that music is one of the greatest propaganda tools around. You can influence more people with music than you can with a speech.

Skinhead music promotes not only racism, but a violent expression of that particular outlook against non-whites and Jews. It also reflects the skinhead attitude towards race mixing, inter-racial marriages and race traitors: they are not tolerated. One of the first bands to play this style of music was called Screwdriver. The band's leader, Ian Stewart is now dead, but the band's music is still popular with many skinheads. The band's name can also appear as a tattoo.

Sometimes this type of music is referred to as hate music. Hate music has three functions for the white supremacist movement. First, it is one of main ways neo-Nazis attempt to recruit youth into the white supremacist movement. Secondly, this music industry has become an important source of income for white supremacists. Lastly, the music plays an important role in the spread of the white supremacist culture (www.adl.org).

Hate music is also referred to as Racist Oi or Rock Against Communism (RAC). This is the oldest genre of hate music and was derived from punk rock music. Hate Core music is a subgenre racist version of hardcore punk music. The music lyrics can also take on several themes that promote and expose the philosophies and beliefs of the white supremacist. For example there are skinhead, confrontation, white racial, Viking-Norse and racial martyr themes in the music.

Band names can openly express their racist nature such as "Jew Slaughter" from Oregon; "Angry Aryans" from Detroit and the "SS Bootboys" from California. Of the number of producers of hate music probably the best known is Panzerfuast Records based in Minneapolis. In September 2004 the company announced "Project Schoolyard, USA." It was an attempt to target elementary and junior high school age children for recruitment. Panzerfuast Records created a special compilation of hate music in CD format. The CD was offered for sale for pennies in a hope that white supremacist groups would buy it in large quantities and distribute them to children at schools, concerts and other venues (www.adl.org).

Hate music genres will continue to change. However, the themes of the music will distinguish it as hate music.

Substance Abuse

Skinhead gang members, like other gang members use drugs and alcohol. Drugs such as cocaine and heroin are used with less frequency. Skinhead gang members seem to favor the use of alcohol, especially beer. However, there also appears an increasing use of marijuana and LSD by some skinhead gangs.

In the late 1980s and early 1990 one would not expect skinhead gangs to be involved drug trafficking. However, that is not the case today. Skinhead gangs are actively involved in the sales and distribution of methamphetamine. Methamphetamine has become the poor man's version of cocaine. Methamphetamine use seems to be concentrated in the working middle class population.

Some skinhead gangs have become semi-organized using older male and female members and associates to distribute this drug. It is not uncommon to encounter 20-30 year old skinheads involved in the trafficking of methamphetamine and other drugs.

When involved in drug tracking and other illegal activities the racist part of the skinhead lifestyle may not be the primary motivation for behaviors. In fact, even though many skinheads claim to be racists, they do not act in that manner. Doing so would hurt business.

Occult Religions

Some skinhead gang members have aligned their white supremacist beliefs with those of the occult underground, allegedly as Satan worshipers or practitioners of Witchcraft. For these skinheads, the occult belief system becomes a part of their political and racist ideologies. Additional anti-social behavior other than violence directed toward minorities also comes with this hybrid belief system.

Animal mutilations, church desecrations, grave-site disturbances, animal sacrifice, drug usage, secret rituals or ceremonies honoring Satan and self-mutilation are reportedly a few of the additional activities one could expect members of this hybrid gang practice. In addition, a few skinhead gang members have also joined the Goth Movement. All Goths are NOT skinheads.

An interest in occult religions and practices dates back to the Third Reich during World War II. There was a genuine interest because it was believed that occult practices might enhance the power of the Germanic people.

There are also modern day Christian based religions that cater to the skinhead. The Church of the Creator is a Christian based church that caters to the philosophies and beliefs of the white supremacist. The number of churches is increasing nationally and membership from the skinhead ranks seems to be increasing. All skinheads do not espouse occult beliefs.

Female Gang Members

Women are not excluded from membership status in skinhead gangs. At one time there were no reports of all female skinhead gangs. Women usually and many still associate with male gang and are members in a co-ed skinhead gang. Female associates and members are also often present at gatherings and social functions.

A small all female skinhead gang has developed and are known as the Featherwoods. The Featherwoods have not developed into a major gang, but are an example of how the dynamic the street gang population has become. The members usually tattoo a small feather or the word featherwood to identify them.

Female skinhead gang members may also use other tattoos, use the same hand signs, and wear similar clothing as their male counterparts. Female skinheads do not generally shave their heads. Hair length and style are optional. Many female skinhead gang members believe their role in the movement is to have as many White babies as they can in order to help re-constitute the Aryan race.

Crime

Hate crimes are committed based on race, ethnicity, religion or sexual orientation. The commission of these crimes is an outgrowth of racist skinhead philosophies and belief systems. The types of crimes range from misdemeanor malicious mischief to murder. Surprisingly, the most common first arrest for a skinhead is assault with a deadly weapon (Miller, 1990). However it is possible for an African-American, Latino or Asian gang member to commit a hate crime and the victim can be homosexual, a skinhead or another person. The commission of hate crimes is not limited to skinheads alone.

Skinheads have been known to arm themselves with shotguns, semi-automatic pistols and assault rifles. At one time the most commonly used weapons were the baseball bat, knife and the boots. However, an increasing number of skinheads are arming themselves with guns. A gun has become the weapon of choice for many gang members.

Some skinhead crime targets minorities and race traitors that pose a perceived threat to the White race. However, some skinheads have also been involved in drive-by shootings and home invasion style robberies, as well as non-violent financial crimes like identity theft.

A boot party refers to the boot stomping of a victim. The boots are normally steel-toed Doc Marten or work style boots.

Skinhead racist crime does not have to be violent. For example, a cross burning in the front yard of a residence owned by a minority family has no direct physical effect on the victim. The injury, in reality, is much more severe and is felt for a long time. The pain is emotional and psychological in nature and affects the entire minority population. These types of hate crimes can tear apart entire communities and disrupt the general well being of the entire victim family.

Other non-violent crimes could be in the form of racial epithets, both verbal and written or the marking of swastikas all over a church. During recruitment periods high schools, junior colleges, colleges and school libraries may be blanketed with racist flyers advocating for the White race to unite. The flyers are often degrading to minorities, full of racial cartoons and racial epithets. The flyers also blame many of today's current social issues on minorities, Jews and homosexuals.

The race traitor is an Anglo or Northern European who does not prescribe to the skinhead philosophy, or a skinhead who has changed his or her view of the supremacy movement. This would include a skinhead who leaves the gang and no longer believes in the gang's philosophies.

The number of organized White supremacist groups in the United States has changed. At one time the more well known ones included, The Order, Aryan Nations, Ku Klux Klan, The American Nazi Party and in Southern California the Aryan Youth Movement, White Student Union and the White Aryan Resistance. During the 1980s and 1990s, David Duke and Tom Metzger were the focus of many media inquires. David Duke was a Republican political candidate until his past membership and leadership status with the Ku Klux Klan was examined and he lost his mainstream conservative support.

Tom Metzger and his son John are most noted for their cable television program Race and Reason. Their television show explored white supremacy philosophies and at one time was reported to be carried by 45 different cable companies. Based in Fallbrook, California, the Metzger's also established and ran the operations for the White Aryan Resistance since its inception in 1982.

Tom Metzger had aligned himself with far-right political groups, including the John Birch Society, Knights of the Ku Klux Klan, the KKK Border Patrol in San Diego, California, The New Christian Crusade Church, and the White American Political Association.

The Metzger's have been involved in the White supremacist movement for a number of years and were the best known father and son team in America at one time. Several skinhead gangs have aligned themselves with Metzger's ideas and philosophies regarding race purity. A few criminal justice experts believed there was an attempt to organize the skinhead groups more formally through white supremacy organizations such as White Aryan Resistance (George and Wilcox, 1992).

The Civil Suit

On November 12, 1988, members of East Side White Pride, a skinhead gang in Portland, Oregon, beat Mulegata Seraw, an Ethiopian immigrant, to death with a baseball bat. Three gang members were convicted of the crime and were sent to prison. The Southern Poverty Law Center and the Anti-Defamation League, on behalf of Seraw's family, brought a civil law suit against two of the skinheads who were convicted of the murder. Tom and John Metzger of White Aryan Resistance were alleged to have inspired the fatal attack and thus were implicated as defendants.

The lawsuit uncovered ties between the East Side White Pride skinhead gang and Tom Metzger. Through their organization, the Metzger's were alleged to have promoted skinhead violence throughout the country. The suit alleged the Metzger's sent their representatives to Portland to contact members of the East Side White Pride gang to encourage them to physically attack minorities.

The lawsuit also alleged the Metzger's were vicariously liable for Seraw's death. In 1990 a civil jury adjudicated the case in favor of Seraw's estate and found the Metzger's guilty of inciting the violence. The jury authorized a financial award to Seraw's estate. The Metzger's lost their Fallbrook, California, home and television repair business. Unfortunately, this is not the first case where skinhead violence has led to the death or serious injury of a non-Aryan and it will not the last (George and Wilcox, 1992).

Recent attempts at unifying different skinhead gangs have included developing closer ties with some organized White supremacist groups. Certain factions of the Klu Klux Klan have targeted skinhead gang members for recruitment.

Skinhead gangs are constantly under a state of change. Some gangs are around for a short period of time, while others become well established. There are a number of skinhead gangs around the globe that communicate through an informal social network based on the white pride philosophy, hate music, racist literature and celebrating skinhead holidays.

Trends

Some skinhead gang members believe that the biblical end of the world is near. For some skinhead gangs, the year 2,000 marked the beginning of Armageddon, for other groups the year 2024 will start the great race war. Even though none of their predictions have come to past, many skinheads still feel the White race is still in danger and a major conflict will develop in the near future.

This particular belief motivates some skinheads and White supremacists to be prepared. Some believers of this prophecy started to stock pile survival supplies, including food, weapons and ammunition. It is believed that a war will signal the end of the world and that true Aryans will be responsible to rid the world of all the sub-humans, mud people, homosexuals, race traitors and Jews.

One just has to examine the Los Angeles, California, White supremacy conspiracy case broken by the FBI in 1993. The group included several skinheads who were going to try to start the race war by blowing up the First AME Church in Los Angeles, California, and by assassinating Rodney King. These actions were planned in order to precipitate a race war.

One skinhead gang in particular has shown some limited organizational structure. The Peckerwoods are usually composed of white males from 16 years old to middle age. In the late 1990s estimates suggested the group membership to be as large as 1,500 to 2,000 just within the state of California. Most Peckerwoods hate Black, Asian and Jewish races but seem to be able to tolerate Hispanics.

This is probably due to the fact that Hispanic inmates provide protection for the Peckerwoods while they are incarcerated. Even though there is no formal leadership for these gangs, there is some informal organizing starting.

The term peckerwood was originally used within the California state prison system. It was a term referring to white inmates. The term referred to, "any white boy who was down for his race, is against race mixing and believes in the white world." Members are usually tattooed, often with lightning bolts, rifle cross hairs, the words white pride, white power or the letters WP, peckerwood, wood or 100% wood, pure wood, swastikas and SWP (Supreme White Power).

Sometimes members are required to earn their lightning bolt tattoos referred to as bolts. To qualify, a Peckerwood would have to commit a felony type assault on a non-White individual. This group is involved in all types of criminal activity, from drug sales to assaults on police officers.

A specific phrase that is commonly used by some Peckerwoods is "in the car" or "riding the car." These phrases are gang slang, meaning the gang is from a particular geographical area. You could potentially have hundreds of members belonging to a single car. There is another possible meaning for this gang slang. Some prison gangs use the same term and it refers to as being with the gang or following the gang's bidding.

Summary

Skinhead gangs can also fight amongst themselves and between individual members. Inter and intra gang violence is common. Some conflicts can be over girlfriends or for disrespecting another skinhead or skinhead gang. Assaults against skinheads by skinheads can include attempted murder and murder. Some skinhead gangs have now diversified and are involved in identity theft, counterfeit checks and credit frauds. Some skinhead gang members have bee found working in financial institutions.

Skinhead gangs tend to operate in single cells with no direct local or national connections with other skinheads gangs. Yet these gangs are connected through a philosophical network that is facilitated with the use of the Internet, the video and written media.

There may be an attempt to unite several skinhead gangs. The western hammer Skins is a well known skinhead gang in the West and North West regions of the country. Some of the gang's actions appear to indicate that a formal vertical leadership structure may be developing and long with national organization.

The Hammerskin Nation

Introduction

In the following sections we are going to examine three different types of white supremacist gangs. The Hammerskin Nation is a group of skinhead street gangs that have united under one name and are known worldwide. The Hammerskin Nation started as a street gang in Texas, spread nationally and internationally. The Public Enemy Number One (PENI) skins started as a street gang that also operates in state and federal prisons. The Nazi Low Rider (NLR) gang is a gang that formed inside a California juvenile facility that now operates on the street, within county, state and federal correction faculties. All three gangs can have direct and indirect connections to the Aryan Brotherhood prison gang that now operates nationwide in state and federal correction centers.

History

The history of the first Hammerskin gang started in Dallas, Texas. The Confederate Hammerskins formed in the late 1980s (www.adl.org). Since the gang's inception the Eastern Hammerskins, the Northern Hammerskins, Western Hammerskins and the Arizona Hammerskins formed and all fall under the umbrella of the Hammerskin Nation. Other regional and international chapters have formed and align themselves under the Hammerskin Nation flag. This is very similar to how some 200 different street gangs align themselves under the Folk or People Nation umbrella. All are directly connected to a single gang, yet operate independently as a chapter of the gang.

Surprisingly, the name and symbol of the Hammerskins originated from the Pink Floyd album 'The Wall' that was released in 1979.The album's lyrics tell the story of a rock singer named Pink; who becomes a drug addict and losing his sense of reality. While doing so Pink turns to and accepts fascism. The lyrics of some songs indirectly refer to the Holocaust and refer to the "Jews" and "coons" in the audience. The Nazi swastika symbol is replaced by Pink with a pair of crossed hammers which will be used to batter down the doors of homes where minorities are hiding. In 1980 an animated movie based on the album was released and solidified the music connection with racism.

Pink Floyd is not a racist and the album was a venture in art for the musician, however the Hammerskin gangs have adopted the fantasy and have tried to make it a reality. The Hammerskins use two red, white and black colored crossed hammers as their symbol and fancy racist music and racist motivated violent crimes (www.adl.org).

One source suggests the Hammerskins formally got involved in the racist music scene in 1998 with the Panzerfaust Records label in Minnesota. The group started to market racist music in the U.S. under the record label (www.tolerance.org). Music and the Internet are cohesive forces that tend to bind national and international chapters together as well as the white supremacist philosophy. These globalizing mechanisms can unite Hammerskin members through the world. The Transnational Gangs chapter explains this phenomenon in more detail.

As of early 2000 the Hammerskin Nation web site listed 19 Hammerskin chapters across the country and 10 chapters located in other parts of the world. These included Hammerskin chapters in England, Spain, France, Canada, Switzerland, the Netherlands, Austria, New Zealand and two chapters in Germany (www.adl.org). In 2008 a Polish Chapter was added and a chapter in Slovakia, Czech Republic, Serbia and Russia was noted (www.tolernace.org and www.splcenter.org). This gang is a good example of a transnational gang; therefore the multinational membership should not be a surprise. Technology has facilitated the contact between members of international chapters as well as between members of national chapters.

To give you an example of how powerful the music mechanism can be, in four domestic venues Hammerskin nation contact points are maintained by hate rock bands. The Brawlers in Wichita, Kansas; Max Resist in Rochester, Michigan; Intimidation One, Clackamas, Oregon; and the H8Machine (formally the Dying Breed)in Harrison, New Jersey. Ed Wolbank, the leader of the Bound for Glory hate rock band based in St. Paul, Minnesota was quoted as saying, "Music is number one. It's the best way to reach people. Through music people can start getting into the scene. Then you can start educating them. Politics through music" (www.adl.org). Music can be a powerful and inspirational recruitment tool that can be used by any gang. After the now well known 'Aryan Fest' concern of 1988, the Springfield, Missouri chapter of the Hammerskins was formed (www.hammerskins.net).

Membership

The exact number of Hammerskin members is not known. A goal of the numerous chapters is to recruit from the ranks of unhappy disillusioned youth and to feed on the growing animosity towards a multi-cultural America. The Hammerskins like some other gangs appear to be selective on who they admit as members. Prospective members have to prove their worth to the local gang before formal membership is granted. Many skinhead gangs simply have the prospective member fill out an application.

There are some reports that suggest Hammerskin chapters can be found in 15 different states including: Arizona, California, Delaware, Florida, Georgia, Kansas, Michigan, Minnesota, Nevada, New Jersey, Oregon, Pennsylvania, Texas and Wash- ington (www.unitesdstatesaction.com).

At one time it was believed that all Hammerskins were violent racists. This may have been true for some, but not all. In the late 1990s a few Hammerskin members ventured into music promotion. A source of money for the gang had been through the sales of hate rock music and the promotion of hate rock concerts. These members planned and helped the gang sponsor hate rock concerts for profit.

Not all has been well with the Hammerskin Nation. In 2000 a group of Northern Hammerskins kicked out five members of the chapter for "not living up to their oath." When this occurred eight other members left and the 13 formed the Outlaw Hammerskins; which now claims to have chapters in four Midwestern cities. This has cause the Hammerskin nation to indicate they will not formally recognize the Outlaw Hammerskins as part of the Hammerskin Nation (www.adl.org).

According to one report Arizona is home to the Arizona Hammerskins; the Confederate Hammerskins can be found in Alabama, Georgia, Kentucky, North Carolina, Florida, Tennessee and Texas; the Hammerskin Nation is in Oklahoma; the midland Hammerskins are located in Colorado, Kansas, Missouri and Nebraska; the Northern Hammerskins are in Illinois,

Michigan, Minnesota and Wisconsin; the Northwest Hammerskins are in Idaho, Oregon and Washington; the Outlaw Hammerskins are in Illinois and the Western Hammerskins are located in California (www.adl.org).

Criminal Activity

The Hammerskin Nation is comprised of racist skinheads. The members are involved in racially motivated crimes which have included assaults against minorities, vandalism of Jewish synagogues, fire bombings and attempted murders. The racist philosophy has fueled the commission of hate crimes where a Hammerskin Nation chapter has established itself.

There is some anecdotal law enforcement data that suggests at the venues of a Hammerskin Nation sponsored hate rock concerts there are reports of racially motivated assaults and attacks. It appears that the music lyrics may incite this behavior as skinheads become enthralled with the music. Don't forget almost twenty five years before Ed Wolbank's statement about another well known white supremacist made a similar remark. Tom Metzger the founder of the White Aryan Resistance (WAR), Fall Brook, California is credited with suggesting that music was the greatest propaganda tool to reach youth. The power of music has been known for a long time and the white supremacist movement has capitalized on this for years.

Internet

The white supremacists were some of the first groups to utilize the Internet as a medium for communication, recruitment and advertising. Since then many street gangs have followed suit; this includes the skinheads. Of all the street gangs the skinheads most likely use the Internet the effectively for recruitment and communication.

This behavior includes the Hammerskins. Not only have they developed a web site; www.hammerskin.net, but are probably one of a few gangs that use mass emailing lists and electronic bulletin boards to communicate with the membership and recruit new members (www.adl.org). Using mass emailing the gang can advertise concerts and special events for the skinhead community. In addition some sites have special links that only members can enter. These are private areas where trusted members can communicate, socialize and plan criminal activities. The use of the Internet allows for worldwide communication between chapter members. A good example would be the online bulletin board hosted by the British Hammerskins where all Hammerskins can communicate, recruit potential new members. In the private areas for members only tactics can be discussed.

Summary

Loyalty to the Hammerskin Nation is very important. Hammerskins can join other racist groups like the Aryan Nations or the Aryan Brotherhood prison gang; but they are Hammerskins first. The Hammerskins have a saying "HFFH! Hammerskins Forever and Forever Hammerskins." Hammerskin members in prison also have a lot of influence on those members on the streets. Racist bands that have been affiliated with the Hammerskins have been Max Resist, Midtown Boot Boys, Dying Breed and Bound for Glory.

Public Enemy Number One

As we continue to examine white street gangs, no discussion can be complete without a look at the Public Enemy Number One (PENI) street gang or the PENI Death Squad (PDS). This acronym is not to be confused with another gang that uses the letters PDS "Pimp Dat Shit" (www.bebo.com/Pimp-dis-shit). Public Enemy Number One shares many characteristics with another older white supremacist gang known as the Nazi Low Rider (NLR) gang, yet is unique in many ways. The PENI gang is a good example of gang evolution in the United States and how quickly a street gang can evolve and change. The PENI gang as with many other gangs has now focused on making money. The gang's true color is not white, red or blue but green, the color of money.

Origin

PENI was initially formed by a small number of punk rock fans from Long Beach, California during the early 1980s. The youth would frequent venues where their favorite punk rock bands would play. The venues also attracted a number of racist skinheads because a few racist rock bands would also play at the same venue. The interest in music pulled both groups together. The white youths from Long Beach also became interested in the white supremacist philosophy and way of thinking. By the middle 1980s the group had grown in number and embraced the philosophies and beliefs of the skinhead movement.

The group took its name from a once popular hardcore punk rock band named Rudimentary Peni. By the early part of 1986 PENI members started to move from Long beach into the Orange County, California area. Orange County is still home to the majority of PENI membership. The gang does not claim a specific turf as traditional Hispanic gangs. Yet, the gang can appear to act territorially because often their criminal activity tends to be based in the area where members live.

Others believe the gang was formed and operated from and out of Orange County, California; and the gang modeled its behaviors after hard-line Nazi Skinheads of Europe (www.gangorus.com).

By 1988 PENI was recognized by law enforcement as a skinhead type street gang. In less than ten years a small number of youth evolved from a group of white youth who listened to punk rock music and abused alcohol to a violent street gang involved with the abuse of illegal drugs and criminal activity to support drug habits and use.

By the early 1990's PENI gang members were involved in major assaults and even residential robbery as well attempted murder. As the NLR gained a power structure within the general population within the corrections system, CDC again responded by placing NLR members into special housing units. This action effectively broke the NLR influence within the general prison population. This also created an opportunity for the PENI gang to take the place of NLR in the yard.

By the middle 1990s PENI had a defined relationship with the NLR and Aryan Brotherhood. This Orange County California based street gang now had prison gang connections and affiliations statewide. Remember the baseball analogy? The PENI gang quickly became a major farm team. What this did was to allow the PENI gang to develop contacts and recruit from the ranks of the local skinheads. This also allowed an opportunity for NLR and PENI parolees and local skinheads to work together with out of custody PENI gang members. All this occurred within 15 years of the birth of the PENI gang. By any standard this is a very quick maturation for a street gang.

Once the connection to the NLR was established the PENI gang became known for their involvement in methamphetamine trafficking, drug dealer shakedowns, robbery, home invasion robbery and murder.

This may have been happened and motivated by another factor. Early on PENI gang members were motivated by bigotry and the white supremacist philosophy. Even though many PENI members accepted the white supremacist philosophy and wore racist tattoos associated with the skinhead movement by 2000 they tended not to be involved in racially motivated crime. The racist aspect of the gang life style took second seat to the gang's focus to make money. The violent nature of the gang may have put it on the radar for the Aryan Brotherhood and Nazi Low Rider gangs.

Another peculiar characteristic was observed by California law enforcement. Many, if not most of the PENI gang members were adults between the ages of 18 and 40 years old. As you remember there is a gang myth that many still believe is accurate and true. The majority of gang members in the country are juveniles. This not true, however for the PENI gang almost all the membership was comprised of jail savvy young adults. This is unusual for a skinhead street gang. Usually these types of gangs tend to have a sizeable juvenile and early teenage membership.

Criminal Activity

As mentioned the PENI gang was involved traditional gang related violent crime. There is nothing new or surprising about this. In fact, the gang followed some academic models that described gang criminal activity. Between the middle and late 1990s the PENI gang made a paradigm shift in behaviors.

Still rooted in the white supremacist philosophies the gang tended to shy away from traditional violent gang related crime and move into economic crimes. However, the gang would resort to traditional gang related violent criminal activity as needed.

This behavior did not preclude the gang from continuing to commit murders and be involved in witness intimidation. It was that these criminal actions were no longer the primary activities of the gang. In fact, the white pride philosophy that is part of gang life style also became secondary to the gang.

"...Violence is a very central theme within PENI. The willingness to use violence is really the measure of a man within PENI. They tend to focus on violence, fantasize about it, talk about it quite a bit and they use it as a tool... They use it (violence) obviously to number one keep control within their own ranks and to keep control of other people around them, to intimidate witnesses, to discourage people from even reporting crimes. They use violence to showcase their commitment to the gang." (Epperson, 2003).

This philosophy may have the foundation for a PENI hit list that contained the names of an Orange County prosecutor and five police officers. The Anaheim Police, Orange County, California was able to finish a 10 month long investigation that culminated on December 14,

2006 with arrest of 67 alleged members of the PENI gang. Over 300 law enforcement officers from more than two dozen local and federal agencies started the sweep at 75 different locations in southern California (www.adl.org). The gang has also been involved in murder and drug trafficking investigations.

All gangs can be violent like PENI, but gangs like PENI appear to diversify in an effort to expand the ability to generate money. The PENI gang has become involved in mail theft, identity theft, and theft of credit profiles, credit fraud, counterfeit identification, counterfeit checks and currency. A semi-formal hierarchy or chain of command also developed. This seems logical as the gang expands its criminal activity. This behavior may also be motivated by PENI ideology. "…On the street, the expectation is that you are going to link up with others (PENI gang members) on the street and do something beneficial for the gang…you are to go out and do missions identified for you by the people above you" (Epperson, 2003). The missions do not necessarily have to be violent assaults. Anything that benefits the gang financially or reputation wise is welcomed.

Male and female PENI members, parolees, associated NLR and skinhead gang members became employed within the financial industry. Gang members and parolees were encountered working as loan officers for mortgage institutions. This infiltration allowed PENI gang members and associates access to credit profiles and confidential credit information. This information could be used and/or sold aiding in identity theft and credit fraud operations.

Some PENI gang members will also use a counterfeit checks and drivers licenses to purchase merchandise, then return it a few days later for cash. Other PENI gang members will produce counterfeit identification using pictures of other PENI gang members to impersonate the victims of stolen checks. Probably the boldest act occurred on July 17, 2002. A PENI gang member was arrested for attempted murder in 1999 and was housed in an Orange County, California jail. He was released after a friend using fraudulent identification posted the $500,000 bail using two counterfeit checks. 18 days passed before the banks notified the local authorities about the checks. The PENI gang member was re-arrested a short time later. I cite this only as an example of how brazen non-violent gang related crime can be.

Indicia

The first thing you may notice with PENI gang members is the name of the gang. It has been abbreviated in many ways. For example, PEN1, PENI, PENI Skins, PENI Death Squad, PDS all refer to the same gang. All abbreviations are frequently used by the PENI membership.

Some PENI gang members will use the code 737 to refer to the gang. Look at the telephone dial pad and the numbers 737 refer to PDS, PENI Death Squad. Other acronyms that are used are Peni 1 and Pen9; both refer to the PENI gang (www.adl.org).

Some writings or drawings may have the author's gang moniker, 737 or PDS with lightning bolts between the letters. You may also see more traditional racist skinhead type designs and symbols. For example, the number "23" which is the 23rd letter of the alphabet, the letter "W" for PENI gang members and other white supremacist the letter refers to being "white" (www.adl.org).

Tattoos

Like many other gangs PENI uses tattoos as a form of communication that shows gang's membership. Some common tattoos will reflect the member's belief in white supremacy and include swastikas, lightning bolts, Celtic crosses, German iron cross, the numbers "88" or "14", another skinhead gang's abbreviation or name, so cal, the number 23 or XXIII. It is important reminder to note that all tattoos are not gang related. This implies that gang members can sport non-gang related tattoos along with gang related ones. This is also true of some PENI gang members.

Membership

I should mention a unique characteristic about the PENI gang while in prison. Remember PENI functions both as a prison disruptive group (not officially classified as a prison gang by California Department of Corrections and Rehabilitations) and a street gang. While incarcerated skinheads from other racist gangs are allowed to join PENI. This expands the power base for PENI while in-custody. However, when the new PENI members are paroled, they return back to their community and re-associate themselves with their original racist gang. The PENI gang benefits again because it increases its power base out of custody.

This may help explain why PENI gang members have been reportedly arrested in 27 of California's 58 counties (a total of 101 different cities) and in Oregon, Washington, Arizona, Florida, Louisiana, Georgia, Maryland, Minnesota, New Jersey, Nevada, New York, North Carolina, Pennsylvania, Utah, Texas and South Dakota (California Department of Justice, 2002). This becomes anecdotal evidence to support the theory that the PENI gang has grown to national status.

The PENI gang has continually grown in size since the 2000s. For example, in 2003 the gang's membership was estimated to be around 200. By 2005 there were an estimated 350-400 members documented by California Department of Corrections and d Rehabilitation officials. Don't forget this gang, like many other gangs each member of PENI may have a number of associates and contacts who sympathize with PENI ideology.

The methamphetamine trafficking along with the production of counterfeit identification, checks and money may also facilitate PENI migration across the United States. There are a number of PENI gang members who are sentenced and housed in Federal correction centers across the country. Some family members and peer members and friends will sometimes relocate to those venues to be close to the incarcerated gang member. This may spread the PENI gang culture indirectly.

Of all the street gangs PENI tends to have a slighter higher component of female members. While across the country female gang membership in general runs between 6 and 10 percent, female members account for approximately 13 percent of the reported total PENI membership (California Department of Justice, 2002). Females can be used to maintain a source of income for their male counterparts. It is common for female PENI members to be legitimately employed. Although not officially accepted as members of the PENI gang females are sometimes referred to the "worker bees" of the gang (www.adl.org).

Females can be given monikers and in some cases are preferred to attempt criminal activity as they are usually not suspected of gang association. In the PENI gang women are expected to provide income for the gang. Some female associates have acted as drug couriers while others have been employed at jobs that would benefit the gang. Female PENI associates have also been known to facilitate three-way telephone calls between incarcerated PENI members and third parties. Sometimes female associates will add money in the accounts of incarcerated PENI members. Female associates can also help deliver messages from incarcerated members to third parties through personal visits or via the U.S. mail (www.adl.org).

In California at one time the entire documented PENI membership has been arrested at least once and many more than once. This may suggest that PENI gang members tend to be habitual offenders. The average age of PENI gang members tend to be around 30 years old. With continual gang involvement a generational membership may develop as siblings are exposed to the gang life.

Summary

Anecdotal law enforcement evidence suggests that PENI gang members will continue to be involved in white collar crime as well as violent gang related crimes. An alliance with the Aryan Brotherhood (AB) and Nazi Low Riders (NLR) may allow the PENI gang to evolve very quickly into one of the most powerful white racist gangs in the country. PENI can capitalize on the experiences and knowledge of the AB and NLR.

The PENI gang will continue to maintain a power base within state and Federal correction systems and will most likely continue to expand street membership. This gang demonstrates willingness to contact and work with other skinhead gang members.

Female members will continue to play an important role in PENI activity. Some male and female PENI gang members will continue to be gainfully employed to provide a source of income and to infiltrate businesses to aid in white-collar crime. Females can be considered indirect members of the gang.

There is also a type of social hierarchy within the California state prison system. The Aryan Brotherhood is the oldest white supremacist prison gang in California. Although small in numbers it is one of the most feared prison gangs. The Nazi Low Riders formed within the California corrections system and became the predominate force within the California corrections system when the leaders and most active members of the Aryan Brotherhood were transferred and lodged at maximum security prisons. In essence the NLR spoke for the AB in the prison yards.

As NLR criminal activity increased, correction responded and transferred many NLR members to maximum security prison. PENI gang members in prison then took up carrying the Aryan Brotherhood flag. There is relationship between the Aryan Brotherhood and the NLR and PENI gangs. Remember the power base for the Mexican Mafia prison gang is the Sureno gang members. PENI members become the power base for both the AB and NLR.

Nazi Low Riders

The Nazi Low Rider (NLR) gang formed within the California State Corrections system and because of the type of criminal activity qualified to be classified as a prison gang. Because of this, the gang parolees who return to the street have some status amongst skinhead gangs. Skinhead gang members have become the power base for the NLR and will follow orders given my NLR members. The gang has also become an ally with the well known Aryan Brotherhood prison gang.

History

Some ethnic based gangs enjoy a national reputation. One has just to look at the Gangster Disciples based in Chicago or the Blood and Crip gangs from the west coast. Many street gangs consider themselves as well known, but ultimately all aspire to be nationally known. For many reasons, most of the street gangs never organize under one name. They remain independent cells, often in conflict with each other or rival street gangs. But, don't forget there can be exceptions. Remember what happened in Albuquerque, New Mexico in the mid 1990s. Members from rival southern California Hispanic street gangs formed a new gang called Sureno-13 in order to import and sell crack cocaine more effectively.

What mechanism(s) made the Gangster Disciples, Bloods or Crips nationally recognized? Certainly, it appears that narcotic trafficking, violence and the lust for power became factors that were paramount in the formation of a national reputation. Another factor has to include media coverage that is associated with the gang activity.

There are many experts who believe the more a gang sees its name in the paper, or on the local and national news, the more the gang's street reputation is enhanced. Possibly, the media coverage was heavy because the gangs were extremely violent. Gangs use violence as one tool to get what they want.

The point is there are several factors that tend to unify a street gang that has several sets or cliques into one larger gang. From a sociological perspective these factors act as a cohesive force. Many gangs are formed based on ethnic backgrounds, geography, and criminal specialty or can be based on certain political philosophies. Could a political philosophy be the cohesive force needed to form a street gang with a national reputation?

The circumstances may have been right to see such a national reputation develop for the normally unorganized skinhead street gangs. In the early 1990s California law enforcement observed a gang growing in numbers and gaining strength through the lucrative methamphetamine trade. Considered both a prison and street gang, the Nazi Low Riders have developed a reputation for being cold blooded and ruthless.

Some criminal justice professionals are amused at first when they hear the name. Don't be fooled, NLR members have been linked to murders, home invasion robberies, witness intimidation, drug sales, assaults on police officers, narcotics trafficking, fraudulent identification, credit fraud and identity theft.

Gang activity can change as the membership becomes older. This includes skinhead gang members. As this maturation process continues the gang as a whole may take on a totally different look, develop new behaviors and/or allow females to take an active role in criminal activity. You may encounter older gang members whose primary focus may be on criminal activity rather than the gang's philosophy.

The origins of the NLR can be traced back to the California Youth Authority (state prison for juveniles in California). It is reported that the NLR formed initially for protection against the other ethnic based gangs between the late 1970s and early 1980s. Debriefings of NLR gang members suggested when the gang was formed most of the members were white, but there were many mixed race white members. The membership was comprised of male youth in their late teens and early twenties.

There some law enforcement anecdotal evidence that suggested Aryan Brotherhood leader John Stinson recruited skinheads at the Preston Youth correctional Facility in Ione, California and the Youth Training School in Chino, California to help act as middlemen for Aryan Brotherhood operations. The NLR gang formed from these recruits and used the "lowrider" name to show they were better than the Hispanics (www.adl.org). The gang's membership was small.

During this time period, the well-established white prison gang, Aryan Brotherhood (AB) was under attack from the California Department of Corrections and Rehabilitation (CDC). The CDC validated Aryan Brotherhood gang members were separated from the general population and housed in the Administrative Segregation Units or Secured Housing Units. This action effectively curtailed the Aryan Brotherhood activity within the prison system. The AB needed to maintain contact with the general population in order to maintain control of their illegal activities.

The timing was right. Quickly word spread that youth within the state corrections system wanted to form another gang the leader of the Aryan Brotherhood approved the action. With his blessing, NLR membership quickly grew. The NLR filled the void within the prison system for a white-based gang that was in the general population.

If the Aryan Brotherhood were to maintain control of illegal activities within the prison system, it would need allies to continue operations. NLR gang members also began to fill this need as they were sentenced to adult prison. The NLR offered another opportunity for the AB to further extend its influence on the streets and local jails. There is anecdotal law enforcement evidence that suggested the Nazi Low Rider and gangs like it, have impacted the methamphetamine trafficking market partly due to their relationship with the Aryan Brotherhood prison gang.

Ideology

The NLR is a white supremacist gang; therefore one would automatically think all the members had to be white. In the gang's early development, NLR rules allowed mix-race youth to join. Any mixed race youth could join, except those of African-American ancestry. Law enforcement officials encountered white supremacist gang members with Hispanic and other ethnic based surnames. Debriefings of NLR gang members confirmed at that time, that pure white heritage was not a critical factor for membership. Since the formation of NLR, other skinhead gangs have also followed this membership rule.

This phenomenon was new for white supremacist gangs, but not new behavior for other street gangs. Mixed race membership has been previously encountered with the tagger crews, the 18th Street, MS-13 and Tiny Rascal gangs.

You should not be surprised to encounter some skinhead or NLR gang members with Hispanic or other ethnicities. A former NLR member summed up the concept as, "you must have at least half white blood, but no black blood." The traditional race membership barrier for some skinhead gangs was now broken.

However, the white supremacist philosophy still acted the cohesive factor that bound these gang members together and can also bind members from different skinhead gangs together. Examining the customs and practices of the NLR will reveal that the gang and individual members share many common behaviors of other ethnic based street gangs. It is safe to say that the gang's activity is now profit motivated, even though it was original based in the white supremacist philosophy.

Membership

In 1996 California criminal justice professionals were able to identify only 28 NLR members. During the late 1990s, the NLR gang went on a major recruitment drive. Membership size has increased dramatically; by 2000 in California there were over 1,000 members and associates (California Department of Justice, 2000). By the early to mid 2000s the FBI suggested there were up to 1500 NLR members in prison with as many as 400 members in the county of San Bernardino, California. Some estimates suggested between members and associates the number could be as high as 3000. By 2001 NLR gang members were reported in Colorado, New Mexico, Florida, Illinois and Indiana (www.adl.org).

In fact, the NLR has actively recruited new members from the ranks of skinhead gangs and a few skinhead gangs have also aligned themselves with the NLR. It is this type of alignment that might facilitate the building of a national reputation for the NLR gang. A national alliance of skinhead gangs with the NLR or an NLR type gang would most likely be based on the white supremacist philosophy and methamphetamine trafficking. Both currently have a national impact and the focus on money making operations may be a stronger cohesive force than originally predicted.

The NLR gang is unique in a few ways. The NLR has an active street component, a juvenile prison component, a state and federal prison component. The NLR gang is also unique because of the nexus between all the different working sub-groups in and out of federal, state and local jails. This activity has produced a demographic shift within the NLR gang population. Currently, NLR gang members are usually between 21-35 years of age. Unlike the major prison gangs the NLR gang has established a presence in local, county, state and federal detention and correction facilities.

Theoretically, skinhead groups could align themselves with the NLR gang in two ways. First, an association can be formed with some type of direct formal support, pledge of support or business relationship. Secondly, an indirect type of association can be formed with the NLR. This informal association may not have a direct connection with, or recognition by the NLR gang. This type of association would tend to be by name only and may be used to enhance a street gang's own reputation.

Tattoos

Like some other gang members, many NLR members will sport tattoos such as; swastikas, lightning bolts, Viking warriors, and Adolph Hitler, NLR or Nazi Low Rider are commonly seen. At one time some gang members had NLR tattooed above an eyebrow, across the neck, above the back and some members had NLR tattooed across the neck above the chest. Depictions of Adolph Hitler or Nazi Storm troopers may also be seen as tattoos. Don't be surprised if you also find the traditional skinhead type tattoos on a NLR gang member.

A few NLR members have been contacted with no NLR or skinhead type tattoos. Conversely, a person who has white supremacist tattoos is not automatically a NLR gang member. This suggests and implies that all skinheads are not necessarily affiliated with the NLR. However, the skinhead gang population has become an ideal recruitment pool for the NLR gang.

Philosophy

The gang's philosophy revolves around racial pride. The members see themselves as warriors in the war against the Blacks, Jews and anyone they perceive to be non-white. Sound familiar? This philosophy mimics ideals and philosophies of the KKK and racist skinhead groups. Therefore, the NLR gang claims their natural enemies are Blacks, Jews, Hispanics, Asians and gays. Currently, the NLR gang considers all other white gangs subordinate to them, with the exception of the Aryan Brotherhood.

At one time a few NLR gang factions believed the Aryan Brotherhood was subordinate to them. Obviously, that made those NLR factions rivals of and in competition with the Aryan Brotherhood. Some gang members even sported a tattoo of "FTB" which meant "fuck the Brand." The "Brand" was another name for the Aryan Brotherhood. This faction did not last long. Currently, all NLR gang members are currently aligned with the Aryan Brotherhood prison gang.

To understand the gang hierarchy for the NLR I will use this analogy. If the Aryan Brotherhood were a professional baseball team, the NLR would be a major farm team and the Public Enemy Number One gang (PENI), college level players; and the skinhead street gangs would be high school level players. Baseball is not a white supremacist sport. But think about it, very few athletes make it in the professional arena with the majority being on farm teams.

Compared to the street gang sub-culture, only a few street gang members make it into a prison gang (professional gang-Aryan Brotherhood). Many more gang members are hard-core, career criminals (farm team- the NLR), and still more are street gang members (college and high school-skinhead gangs). Using this analogy helps understand the social hierarchy for these gangs within the gang sub-culture. The philosophy that binds are the levels together is white supremacy (the game of baseball).

Since the NLR is both a prison and operates with street gangs, it became the logical ally for the Aryan Brotherhood prison gang. The NLR gang could operate on the street for the AB and become a type of middleman. However, if we stay with the baseball sports analogy, with enough resources the NLR could become a formidable new franchise very quickly. It could establish itself become a major disruptive group or prison gang which may or may not be aligned with the Aryan Brotherhood. The NLR became so active that in 1999 the CDC qualified the NLR as a prison gang, which is the same status as the Aryan Brotherhood.

NLR gang members can even be found in the Federal correction system. NLR members were implicated in a 1997 murder within a federal institution. Many NLR gang members consider their group as a prison gang. Law enforcement considers the NLR as a prison and street gang. For the first time on the West Coast there is a gang that operates as both a prison and street gang. Like other gangs the NLR has become involved in criminal activity within the prison system and out on the streets. This could present some unique issues when you are trying to classify members when incarcerated at local jails.

Drug Trade

One of the major goals for the NLR membership in California was to increase the size of the gang and to become more organized. This was based on a two part operating philosophy. Part one is the white supremacist philosophy and the second part is based in methamphetamine (meth) trafficking operations. Many NLR gang members view themselves as meth tax collectors, meth vendors and meth users. In the prison system, it appeared that the NLR was attempting to control the drug trade and criminal activity within the white prison population. On the streets it appeared that NLR members were trying to take control of some of the methamphetamine trade.

After NLR members get paroled, they re-enter the street gang community. They were violent, arrogant and unashamed of their racist attitude. Quickly many NLR gang members got involved in the sales and manufacture of methamphetamine. The high demand for the drug also produces the need for many manufacturing facilities. Because of the cold manufacturing techniques and ease of set up, meth labs can surface in just about any type of location. Motel or hotel rooms, homes, car trunks and storage facilities are frequent locations. Don't be surprised if the cook has white supremacist ties and/or children are present.

People who use and abuse methamphetamine (speed) are also usually involved in other types of criminal activity. These consumers can become prime NLR targets for home invasion style robberies, especially if they are dealers of the drug. The victims may even know the suspects. Sometimes, NLR members use female associates to gather intelligence on potential victims. This is a similar practice which many Asian gangs use to set up their victims.

NLR members count on fear and intimidation to keep witnesses from cooperating with prosecutions, or even reporting the crime to the police. NLR members have been involved in witness intimidation, in-custody assaults and even the murder of an infant. Because of connections with NLR street gang members, in-custody members can ask for hits on witnesses or for intelligence.

Hierarchy

The NLR gang has developed an internal social hierarchy for the membership. Although the gang allows mix race members only all white members can become gang leaders. Because of this a three tier membership hierarchy developed. A NLR unit is lead by a 'senior' member. This is usually someone who has been associated with the gang for five years or more or was associated with the gang since its inception. To attain senior status tenure combined with a vote of three other senior members qualifies the candidate.

Juniors cannot grant new memberships and are considered just below the senior status level. However, junior level members can solicit new members. New members are called kids. Usually the senior member who inducts a kid becomes a mentor and disciplinarian to the new member (www.adl.org).

Attitude

As the unknown author from the Nazi Low Rider gang states in his version of white supremacy:

N L R

Our color, we will always hold true
White rags on our heads
Whites are laces too
Elite soldiers are what we are
Born to represent NLR
The battles we've fought
Were won with White Power
The brothers we lost
Are buried with a signal white flower
The rage we carry in our heart
Is racial hatred from the very start
From the streets or behind the wall
The Nazi Low Rider will always stand tall

Strength and courage of what we are made
This we will carry to our fuckin grave
Our hands we raise to preserve the White race
Masters of deception to hold our rightful place
Time has come to take a final stand
To rightfully claim our Aryan land
Our color you can always tell
If we are crossed, the Nazi Low Rider will send you strait to hell

The poem represents the basic philosophy and belief that binds white supremacist NLR gang members together. It is this philosophy that tends to bind any racist group together with other racist groups and gangs.

Even though NLR gang members share a common belief system rivalries can develop within the gang. Sometimes an NLR gang member will think a peer NLR member disrespected him. The insulted member is compelled to attack in order to save face. Sometimes if a NLR gang member fails to follow a gang order, that member may be punished in the form of a physical attack. The NLR is a prison based white supremacist gang. When paroled, NLR gang members tend to act alone or in very small groups. NLR gang members tend to affiliate with the NLR on a consistent basis and do not tend to change gangs. However, members of other skinhead gangs tend to associate with NLR parolee gang members. It is not uncommon to find that NLR gang members work with skinhead gang members in criminal operations.

The NLR or an NLR type gang could be the catalyst that unites the country's skinhead gangs into one nationally known gang. The normally small numbered white supremacist street gangs that continue to operate independently could be united through a national methamphetamine trafficking trade that is controlled by these types of gangs. The gang could also gain strength by increasing its membership and by having members on the street and inside juvenile and adult detention facilities and prisons.

Females

NLR female associates are not your run-of-the-mill type gang groupie or female gang members. These females can be just as ruthless and violent as their male counter parts. These women have been known to sleep with different gang members to collect intelligence and will run interference for their male counterparts. Sometimes a rivalry can develop between some of these female gang associates.

NLR female gang members have also been involved in witness intimidation. Some law enforcement officials have been able to use this rivalry to their advantage. Pitting rival females against each other in separate interviews proved to be pivotal in one of their cases (Doyle and Belt, 1998).

NLR female associates can also sport a variety of white supremacist type tattoos. One NLR female associate proudly displayed, "101 percent Nazi bitch" tattoo on her stomach. Like the PENI gang, females associated with the NLR gang are expected to provide personal and financial support (www.adl.org).

Summary

The NLR gang is yet another example of how some gangs can break the membership race barrier rule. It was done with some restraint for this gang. A partial break in the barrier is a more appropriate way to explain it. Nevertheless, because of the modification, NLR membership has been able to grow at a phenomenal rate. Because of its rapid growth, NLR has also been able to expand throughout California quickly. The NLR gang has been reported in the California Youth Authority, county jails, the state prison system, and in Federal correction centers.

The NLR mentality is common amongst many white supremacist groups. Getting involved in the drug trade is also a common trend within the gang sub-culture. The use of female gang members is not new; it has only expanded to this type of gang. The gang's involvement in the methamphetamine trade will potentially make this type of gang member prone to violence. The NLR gang and NLR types of gangs are also examples of the Hybrid gangs that may be increasingly more popular in the future.

Straight Edge

The music scene has heavily influenced many of today's "youth groups". Of all the movements, one group in particular still maintains strong ties with the music world. This group is known as the Straight Edge. A careful examination of the group's activities will indicate that it is a gang. At one time it was believed that certain Straight Edge groups were part of the skinhead movement (Miller, 1990). As it turns out some members of Straight Edge gangs (Edgers) are members and or affiliates with other extremist groups and gangs. Edgers and the movement have developed a reputation for violent attacks on non-believers and some members have been involved in acts of domestic terrorism. What makes this group so unique is that it is gang that does not engage in any type of substance abuse, including the use of alcohol and nicotine. In fact by any standard they led a very healthy life except for their group use of violence.

Origin

In the early 1980s the punk rock movement was thriving. This rock culture was entrenched in a self-destructive life style. The ideologies of the culture were communicated through the music. Remember this is the music movement where hate music originated. In the Washington D.C. area circa 1981 a counter movement was started against the wild life style of the punk rockers. Another punk rock band, Minor Threat lead by Ian MacKaye started the Straight Edge movement with a song by the same name (Arciaga, 1998).

The literature also provides a few more versions of how the Straight Edge movement began. John Quinones from the television news show 20/20 reported in March, 1999 that the Straight Edge movement began in the New York area in the 1980s by youth who were old enough to get into local nightclubs but not old enough to be served alcohol. These youth were marked with an "X" on their hands to identify them as not old enough the purchase alcoholic drinks (2020sxe.html at members.tripod.com.). These youth started to band together and very quickly the mark became a symbol of not using alcohol or drugs and not engaging in premarital sex. Initially the "X" was a symbol of clean healthy living.

The third version is really a combination of the first two. It suggests that the Straight Edge movement began in the early 1980s and the first followers were teenagers fed up the apathy and decadence that surrounded them. These youth rejected all activities that they believed could pollute their lives. They included the use of alcohol, nicotine, narcotics and promiscuous sex. Many of these youth were also into the hardcore punk rock scene as well. Within a short period there was a mixture of the unique life style and music.

The band Minor Threat, led by Ian MacKaye was formed by youth within this group. It is suggested that MacKaye coined the phrase Straight Edge in a song by the same name. A few people will argue that the movement really began before the song was written and released. Minor Threat's songs promoted the life style and movement, especially the songs "Out of Step" and "Straight Edge."

In this version of history MacKaye is also responsible for creating the Straight Edge "X" that is commonly used by members. Apparently, while on tour with his band MacKaye noticed that bouncers and club owners would place an "X" on the hands of minors so that could not be served alcoholic drinks. MacKaye adopted the practice as a symbol to show others of his abstinence from alcohol, narcotics, smoking or promiscuous sex. MacKaye would mark the tops of his hands while performing. Within a short period followers of Minor Threat began to mark their hands and clothing with X's to indicate they had the same life style and beliefs (Nelson, 2004).

The Straight Edge culture preached a life style against drugs, alcohol, tobacco, pre-marital sex and avoided issues such as racism, sexism and fascism. This particular style of punk rock music was used to spread the word of the new movement. As you would anticipate the culture spread across the country quickly and its popularity increased. At the time, the Straight Edge movement professed that not taking drugs or alcohol was a "cool" thing to do. This may have been the philosophy early on, something happened that motivated and compelled Edgers to become violent.

"The Straight Edge subculture developed as a subset of the punk movement, maintaining the high energy and aggression of the punk without the drunken and drugged brawls" (Arciaga, 1998).

There is some controversy on whether or not Straight Edge groups should be classified as a gang. A lawyer from Georgia questioned the label of gang. She asked in a public online information-sharing forum on gangs. "… do we label an entire movement for change as a gang based on the acts of a few mislead people…" (Jefferson, 2004). This is a great question. Remember the definition of a street presented earlier? Let's examine the Straight Edge movement and determine if the group qualifies as a gang.

Hardline

In the mid 1980s the movement began to take on a different persona. The East Coast was center for change. Bands like the Gorilla Biscuits, Bold and Wide Awake helped increase the popularity of the movement, but also help develop an "us versus them" attitude. The Straight Edge movement was quickly becoming intolerant of non-members. In 1986, another facet to the Straight Edge movement developed. The vegetarian and vegan ideology surfaced. Vegan means abstaining from all animal derived products.

In the summer of 1987 a band named Vegan Reich was formed. All five members were entrenched in the Straight Edge movement. The band's leader Sean Penn (not the actor) and the other members added a radical characteristic to the Straight Edge subculture. The members of Vegan Reich were all avid animal liberation activists. They used the band to promote their agenda of militant veganism and radical environmentalism (Arciaga, 1998). The new group caused an immediate controversy within the subculture. Veganism was unheard-of at the time. Don't forget until this time many of the movement's members were basically peaceful vegetarians soon this became rare.

Penn's moniker was "Hardline". The group still maintained the drug free lifestyle but also adopted expanded to include class war politics, social ethics as well as animal liberation and environmental issues.

In 1989, Vegan Reich developed the Hardline movement, a separate but related movement to the Straight Edge subculture. The band released a new album in 1990 called Hardline. It outlined the new ideology and declared war on all animal exploiters, earth rapers and drug users. Surprisingly, this version of Straight Edge movement gained popularity all over the United States almost overnight (Hardline Straight Edge).

The Hardline label was an "X" superimposed with two machine guns. It also became a popular tattoo and symbol of the movement. The music was hard-core punk, so it appealed to many Straight Edge members. Often, the music would motivate some to embrace the Hardline beliefs.

By the early 1990s the Hardline movement had gained sufficient momentum to become a problem for those who believed in the original Straight Edge philosophies. Many new Straight Edge members adopted the Hardline ideology. These members did not understand that Hardline was not part of the original Straight Edge movement.

By the mid 1990s separatism and violence entered the Straight Edge concert scene. Straight Edge members began to force their beliefs on non-Straight Edge advocates. Fights and stabbings became more common at concerts. The music lyrics were filled with rage and anger. By 1994 violence became increasingly linked to the Straight Edge movement, especially at concert locations.

Animal Liberation Front

Something unique also happened during this time. Straight Edgers, and Hardline Straight Edgers were exposed to animal rights information at concerts and on the Internet. The Animal Liberation Front (ALF) started to recruit new members for its organization from the ranks of the Straight Edge movement. Hardline Straight Edge members were particularly joining ALF. In fact some Hardline Straight Edgers began to create their own local ALF groups.

These groups would be small cells comprised of 3 to 10 members acting independently on "behalf of the animals." These ALF cells with no central leadership or structure also began to commit "direct action" terrorist acts against businesses that sold animal products. The connection between the Hardline Straight Edge and the ALF may have acted as a catalyst that aided in the increased ALF activity during the late 1980s.

ALF is a leftist organization that began in the 1970s. It is interesting to note that ALF is a radical off shoot of the group known as People for the Ethical Treatment of Animals (PETA). Based on the brag-list of direct actions posted on the AFL Web site it is easy to conclude that there are numerous AFL cells around the country and they are linked together based on their beliefs and the Internet. Therefore if one cell becomes inactive due to law enforcement suppression, its loss does not affect the movement (Arciaga, 1998). AFL action increased so much that in 1999 they average one per day.

Most AFL activity is targeted toward businesses and has included the use of pipe bombs, Molotov cocktails, graffiti and other forms of vandalism.

Earth Liberation Front

Another group that recruited Hardline Straight Edge members was the Earth Liberation Front (ELF). This is a splinter group of the Earth First organization. ELF has tried to link eco issues with animal rights. The common ties between ALF, ELF and Straight Edge hardliners are these philosophies, the use of violence to further their cause. In 1994 ELF and ALF joined forces. As you would expect, action by ELF increased during the later part of the 1990s. In 1998 ELF activists bombed a ski lift in Vail, Colorado causing an estimated 12 million dollars worth of damage.

One of more recent attacks occurred on August 22, 2003 when fires destroyed dozens of SUVs and a warehouse at a West Covina, California auto dealership. Three other dealerships were sprayed painted with slogans like "Fat Lazy Americans." An unsigned e-mail was sent calling the incidents "ELF actions."

Earlier in August 2003 a multimillion dollar fire that destroyed a five story apartment building in San Diego. ELF was suspected of this activity as well (www.foxnews.com).

Skinhead Straight Edge

Most Straight Edge members are non-racist. However, the Straight Edge movement has attracted members from other extremists groups besides the ALF and ELF. It is not surprising to find out that white power based groups have also successfully been recruited into the Straight Edge movement. Because of this mechanism Straight Edge racist skinheads have made their appearance. The World Church of the Creator also attempted to recruit these Edgers into their church. *"The Straight Edge White Power Skins web site is linked to the World Church of the Creator's wed site, but specifically targets members of the Straight Edge culture"* (Arciaga, 1998). The web site featured Straight Edge graphics and encouraged a white power philosophy linking up with the pure body concept and racial purity. The Web site is no longer in existence (Arciaga, 1998).

Membership Indicia

Straight Edge members are typically male Caucasians between 12-21 years of age. Often, members are from middle and upper middle class families. However, membership is not exclusively male. Members also tend to be more educated, more computer literate and able to access more modern technology than the average street gang member (Immoos, 1998).

Clothing styles vary with Straight Edge members. This might include close-cropped haircuts or shaved heads. Long side burns are common. Often, T-shirts with a large black "X", "XXX", "sXe" or the words "Drug Free" are worn (Immoos, 1998). Sometimes, members wear baggie style punk rock or skater style clothing. Some Edge members may use body piercing or wear heavy silver chains as a necklace or have them dangling from the waist area. These chains could be used as a weapon. Sometimes combat fatigues are worn, along with Doc Marten style boots. Sometimes personal items and bodies are marked with an "X" or "sXe" to signify membership. Straight Edge members often travel in groups.

Racist Straight Edge skinheads may wear Doc Marten boots, combat fatigues and shave heads. Some of these Straight Edgers may even using body piercing to accent their attire. Some Straight Edge members may tattoo themselves with sXe, X, or XXX. The word "hardline" may also be used. Skinheads who were part of the Straight Edge movement may also have racists white power type tattoos.

Generally Straight Edge members throughout the United States tend to share common appearances, attitudes, philosophies, beliefs and activity. Straight Edgers also tend to regularly group together at locally and meet and communicate nationally using the Internet and the latest communication technologies. Straight Edge members usually recruit new members by portraying themselves as positive alternatives for today's youth who are exposed to the gang and drug cultures (Arciaga, 1998). Recruitment seems to occur nationally and the Straight Edge movement has been seen in England and Germany, making the Straight Edge movement international.

Like many street gangs Straight Edge members will use the Internet to communicate and to spread their philosophies. Popular Straight Edge Internet sites have included, but are not limited to:

www.straight-edge.com

www.vegan-straight-edge.org.uk

www.starightedge.com

http://member.aol.com/vegedge/sxe.htm

www.geocities.com/SouthBeach/1794/

Vegan Straight Edge members or Hardliners who align themselves with extremist groups like the Skinheads, ALF or ELF may be involved in violent crimes, such as bombings or arsons. Straight Edge gangs may group together at the local level and can communicate at a national level using the Internet.

The heart of the Straight Edge movement appears to be based in four tenets. Living the Straight Edge life style means that a member will not smoke because nicotine is very addictive. This is in addition to the harmful effects that smoking and secondary smoke have. Straight Edge followers cannot become addicted to any substance.

Followers also will not drink alcohol because it is unhealthy and can be addictive. Straight Edge members are not casual drinkers they do not drink at all.

Straight Edge followers will also abstain from using any kind of narcotics. This will include legal and illegal drugs. The reasoning behind this tenet sounds logical. Any substance that impairs you is bad. However, this could cause medical complications in the event of a serious illness or injury.

The fourth life style tenet is that Straight Edge members do not engage in casual or uncommitted sex. Followers of this life style feel that sexual intercourse can be just as addictive and damaging as drug abuse. As a result most Straight Edge followers limit their sexual activity as they feel is necessary (Nelson, 2004).

Music

By the early 2000s there were over 150 Straight Edge bands in the United States. Music still continues to be a powerful recruitment and motivating tool. Victory Record label specializes in Straight Edge and Hardline music produces music. The Straight Edge movement seems to be entrenched in violence even though it did not start off that way.

There are three areas of the country where Straight Edgers tend to concentrate; Syracuse, New York, Salt Lake City, Utah and Seattle, Washington. Some of the popular music bands include Earth Crisis, Thrive, Youth of Today, Unbroken, Shelter, Function and Uniform Choice, Integrity and Snapcase (Arciaga, 1998).

At the concert venues literature about vegans, animal rights and drug abuse is available. Many youth who get involved in Straight Edge move on to Hardline, AFL or ELF.

Criminal Activity

At many concert venues concertgoers will dance in the mosh pit. This is where youth beat, kick and hit each other in a chaotic brawl. Often there are disagreements during this dancing frenzy and fights erupt in the pit area. All too often the violence spills over into the surrounding crowd and a riot situation develops very quickly. In one reported incident a concertgoer was attacked and beaten by Straight Edge members after the victim blew marijuana smoke into their faces. During the attack the victim was beaten severely and the attackers used a broken bottle to carve an "X" into the victim's back. This type of concert Straight Edge violence has been reported in California, Utah, Tennessee, New York, Texas and Utah (Arciaga, 1998).

Even though Straight Edge violence has been reported in many states there are a few places where it appears to be concentrated. Salt Lake City, Utah has been one of the centers of Straight Edge criminal activity. Salt Lake City area Straight Edgers have raided local mink farms in 1996 and were involved in the bombing of a fur breeder cooperative in 1997. Through the early 1990s Utah police investigated bombing and arson attacks that targeted animal-product stores that included leather furriers, fast food restaurants, assaults and stabbings at rock concerts (L.A. Times, 1998).

Then Straight Edge mantra is "True Til Death" and is shown through the use of force by using brass knuckles, baseball bats, pipe bombs, Molotov cocktails and knives. By 1998, there were an estimated 1000 Straight Edgers in the state and at least 40 cases of arson, vandalism and serious assaults were traced to them. In the late 1990s the Straight Edge gang was the fastest growing gang in Utah. Yes, I used the term gang here. I believe the lawyer's question has been answered.

A Salt Lake City psychologist, who is a gang expert, was trying to identify the reason why Utah's Straight Edge gang members' appeared to be more violent than (Straight Edge) members in other states and referred to this gang as "Utah's home-grown-upper-class gang" (L.A. Times, 1998). During the late 1990s the Straight Edge gang was reported to be the fastest growing gang in Utah. What caused this phenomenon during this rapid gang growth period in Utah?

The Salt Lake City psychologist, Terie Weiderhold explained a possible theory this way, *"Perhaps our Straight Edgers are different because in the Mormon culture, kids are told from Day One, Don't do drugs, alcohol, tobacco or premarital sex. What is not emphasized however is, don't fight. Of course that's not to say that Mormons are violent. But since they (Straight Edgers) don't participate in things that other gangs are involved in, our Straight Edgers may be finding an escape from boredom and a source of identification in violence"* (L.A. Times, 1998). The psychologist adds another excellent point that qualifies Straight Edgers as gang members, the use of violence as a source of identification.

Some Straight Edge gang members insist that they only resort to violence when peers give them flak about their life style and views or deliberately blow cigarette or marijuana smoke in their faces at school or at concerts. This could be considered a form of challenge or disrespect in the gang culture. No challenge or insult ever goes unanswered in the gang culture. For Straight Edge gang members the answer is usually in the form of violence. This is another behavior that qualifies the Straight Edge member as a gang member and the group as a gang.

How about this issue: some Straight Edge members are sometimes afraid to cooperate with law enforcement out of fear of retaliation to themselves or family members by peer members of their gang. Another attitude and belief that is consistent with all street gangs.

Slang

EDGER Member of the Straight Edge movement.

EMO-CORE A musical genre associated with Straight Edge.

GUAGING Stretching the pierce ear holes with larger items, like straws, film canisters or PVC pipe.

HARDCORE A nickname for another musical genre, generally punk rock style that is associated with Straight Edge.

HARD EDGER Member of a militant Straight Edge gang.

HARDLINE A term that refers to the militant Straight Edge movement can also be used as a tattoo.

HARDLINER A militant Straight Edger who does not like non-Straight Edge people.

MEAT IS MURDER Slogan for the vegan Straight Edgers.

STRAIGHT To have some or all the beliefs of the Straight Edge movement, but not intensely involved.

STRAIGHT EDGER Member of the Straight Edge movement.

sXe A Straight Edge symbol, often worn as a tattoo.

X Symbol of the Straight Edge movement.

Xer Member of the Straight Edge movement.

XXX   Symbol of the Hard-line movement.

X-ing Up   To write "X's" across the hands as a sign of membership

Summary

There also appears to be a couple of types of Straight Edge members, Straight Edge, Vegan Straight Edgers (Hard Edgers) and militant off shoots of these two groups called Hardline Straight Edge. Members from all three groups can be recruited into other extremist groups (Nelson, 2004).

Straight Edge members usually are small groups of friends who are known as crews. This is another gang slang term for clique or set. Straight Edge is a general term that describes the followers of this life style, sometimes referred to as a movement. The followers of the movement are known as Straight Edgers.

Tagger Crews

Tagging is now a worldwide phenomenon. Historically one could suggest that tagging has been part of the human culture since the caveman; citing cave drawings as man's earliest forms of tagging. However, the modern day tagging probably began in the late 1960s in the city of brotherly love, Philadelphia. Today taggers use written media, movies and the Internet to advertise their 'street art.'

History

Tagger crews or graffiti artists are another type of street gang. Compared to other gangs, tagging crews are one of the most recent arrivals in street gang sub-culture. Unfortunately, we have all seen the work of these gangs on the freeways, overpasses, and walls and on sides of buildings. In fact, taggers will now put their art on anything including large trucks, train cars, buses, vans; freeway over passes and signs; and even police and military vehicles.

Tagging graffiti may take the form of unreadable writing or initials, often made with spray paint in large rounded bubble-style letters. To the general public the letters and writings seem to have no meaning.

Tagging has been seen in urban settings for a number of years. Cities like New York are undeservedly famous for subway and train art during the early 1980s. Today, tagging or the street art phenomenon appears to be worldwide. Tagging crews now operate in Australia, Canada, Mexico, Europe, England and China.

Tagging incidents in the southwest part of the United States were a major issue during the 1990s and early 2000s. During the mid 1990s it was estimated that there are more than 35,000 taggers just in Los Angeles County. There are no known estimates for tagging population nationally. During the 1990s anecdotal law enforcement evidence suggested that at one time there were over 100,000 taggers in the United States. Taggers or art vandals are the individual members of a crew and sometimes they will choose unique monikers. They will use spray paint, broad tip markers, paint sticks and etching tools to mark their tag anywhere they can. The tag will most often include the name of their crew and their moniker. The color of the paint usually has no significance for the tagging crew. Remember some gangs identify with specific colors.

Crews

Groups of taggers are called crews. The life style of the tagger includes a theme of anti-authority or anti-establishment. This can be shown through the crew names, such as LOD, Legend of Doom, CMA, Criminal Minded Artist, EK, Enemy Killer or Evil Kids, SSK, Society

Sick Killers, UTAK, Untouchable Street Artist Kings or CBS, Can't Be Stopped. The crew names also send out a message to those who are swayed towards this street sub-culture.

Crew names are usually represented by three or four letters and may include numbers, which may have several meanings and may even change meanings. Sometimes a number will be used to represent a word. For example, B2K is a tagging crew name; translated, it is an acronym for Born to Kill. Another example, 2FK; the number 2 stands for word too. This crews name is Too Fucking Krazy.

Small or large, most crews have an informal association with other tagging crews. When these street artists first appeared they were thought of as vandals, not gang members. The street artists themselves started to sign their works and adopted the use of a moniker. For taggers it is a street name, pen name or tag. Probably the one of the most famous street artist of the 1990s was known as Chaka. He was finally arrested in Los Angeles, California, and was responsible for tens of thousands of dollars worth of graffiti damage. Chaka became an instant folk hero to the tagging crews in Southern California.

Some taggers will only use one moniker, while others will have several names or change monikers frequently. Unlike many street gangs, taggers can belong to several different crews and may use a different moniker for each crew. For some taggers there is no crew loyalty. If two taggers of the same crew want to use the same name, they will usually battle for the use of the name. A battle is a tagging term that refers to a tagging contest. Sometimes instead of using a moniker taggers will identify themselves with a number in the way to baseball or football players are assigned a jersey number.

Female Taggers

Like street gangs, tagging crews have taken on certain membership characteristics. One is the presence of all-female tagging crews, who are just as active as their male counterparts. Since the tagging phenomenon began females have been taggers. However they were certainly the minority. During the middle to late 1990s female taggers became better known especially in the New York area. For example, in Brooklyn, New York, "DONA", "DIVA" and Hope of the VIC (Vandals In Control) crew produced many murals (www.at149st.com). Female taggers can be involved in all types of graffiti from moving trains to tagging in the streets.

The male tagging crews sometimes use the letter K. The letter may be placed as the last letter on the crew name. The letter can be an abbreviation for the word King. Within the tagging sub-culture this is an announcement that your crew is number one or King. Remember graffiti can be used to communicate challenges, announce the presence of a group or be a form of intimidation.

Sometimes female tagging crews use the letter Q at the end of their crew name, an abbreviation for the word Queen. The female crews normally associate with a male crew, but do not have to. A few tagging crews have a co-ed membership.

Battles

Tagging crews regularly have contests or battles between crews. The battles are normally limited by a certain geographical area and time. The goal for the individual crews is to place the crew name and individual tag up as many times as possible within a specific area of the city and time period. This is a team effort because the crew's reputation is at stake. Anything in the specified area could be tagged, including building, buses, public buildings and private businesses.

As with any contest, there is a prize for the winner. The crews can play for a cache of spray paint. They can battle for take-outs. A take out means the losing crew has to give up their crew name. Crews also play for jump-ins. This means the members of the losing crew have to become members of the winning tagging crew.

The graffiti vandals can work in small teams, late at night to the early morning hours. However, many individual taggers place their tag up during all hours of the day. Crew members range from early to late teens; some have dropped out of school, and do not work. Others might work part time and go to school. Although there are a number of adult members, most taggers are under 18 years of age. This forces them to use public transportation to travel.

There seem to be no ethnic barriers for crew membership. The majority of the groups are predominately male, but there are a number of all female crews, especially along the East Coast. Tagger Crews also continue to use non- traditional gang graffiti locations to tag. The more unique the location the more respect the tagger receives from his peers and rivals.

The battles were initially non-violent. Many youth joined tagging crews to get away from the violent street gang sub-culture. Some taggers were gang members before joining the crew. Some tagging crews even operate within a gang territory and have a formal association with the gang. Because rivalries became so intense between some tagging crews some crews also became involved in violence.

Gang Influence

For the traditional street gang, graffiti is a form of communication. It gives a written warning, a greeting, marks turf, it can be an insult, and identifies the gang and the members. In short, gang graffiti is a form of advertisement.

Some tagging crews will put their street art and tags in locations that have been historically used by street gangs for their graffiti. This behavior is viewed as a turf invasion by turf oriented Latino and African-American gangs. These are areas where you would normally only find Latino or African-American gang graffiti. When taggers start to mark over the existing gang graffiti, something happens. Street gang members take offense at this action. The writing over or crossing out of their graffiti (plac) is taken as a challenge and insult. The street gang feels like they have been disrespected. This insult compels the gang to respond in an escalated manner. This is done so because the gang wants to reclaim respect that was lost and maintain control of their neighborhood. Sometimes the gang will mark out the tagging graffiti and replace it with theirs.

As tagging crews continued to infringe on the street gang turf, confrontations can escalate. In response to the gang attacks some tagging crews organized and banded together to protect themselves. There was anecdotal law enforcement evidence that documented instances where street gangs victimized individual taggers and crews. It was only natural to bond together when the common interest was survival.

Some tagger crews had affiliated themselves with street gangs. In fact, some tagger crews even joined violent street gangs. The end result was that many taggers armed themselves in preparation for violent confrontations with street gangs and other tagger crews. The reason for this behavior was to enhance the crew's street reputation and respect.

I have noticed several other recent changes with tag crew graffiti that suggest a gang influence. Tagging graffiti, which normally would only contain the name of the crew, now contains the names of the group's members, just like traditional African-American or Latino street gang graffiti. This may have been the result of ex or current gang members joining tagging crews.

I have photographed the number 13 next to tagging graffiti. For Latino street gangs the number 13 refers to the thirteenth letter of the alphabet, the letter M. It also refers to a Southern California heritage and an allegiance to the Mexican Mafia. When crews use this number in their graffiti it probably means they are claiming Southern California origin, like many traditional Latino street gangs.

Another changing characteristic encountered with tagging crews is clothing style. Some taggers have adopted a form of gangster chic, incorporating professional sports emblems and names, as well as the basic baggy black-and-white color clothing combination.

Membership Levels

Taggers in a crew sometimes observe a certain pecking order or hierarchy based on artistic ability. Taggers can be writers and/or piecers. Piecers draw the large cartoon-style characters or murals that are often seen. In Southern California a walk near the Huntington Beach sea wall in the 1990s showcased this type of street art. The goal of many taggers is to become a piecer. In reality, very few attain this status.

Another group of tagging specialist may work in the "heavens", writing on the overhead freeway signs. These taggers find it exciting to climb and "get up" (tag) in these high places. Other taggers run across freeway lanes to get up on the freeway sound walls or freeway dividers. The dodging of oncoming vehicles has not always been successful, as at least three taggers in Southern California have lost their lives doing this. Currently, freeway walls and center dividers are being "killed" a tagger term for being vandalized. Taggers have caused severe traffic hazards by running across freeway lanes to write. As one 17-year-old California tagger said, *"... that's the way I want to die... with a can in my hand."*

Taggers who work with slow moving trains or trains that are temporarily stopped place a style of tagging graffiti that is called "motions." Many taggers and crews take photographs or videotape their creations. The video media becomes proof of their work and is also used for bragging rights.

Activity

In cities all over the U.S. tagging crews go out on tagging missions called "bombing runs." One type of mission is called "bus mobbing," attacking a public transportation bus. Sometimes a tagger will hold open the rear exit door to prevent the bus from moving. While this is being done, other taggers will run around the bus and write crew and tag graffiti all over the exterior. Other taggers might even etch crew and tag name on the bus's windows with an etching tool. Some taggers will even stand on the rear bumper of a moving bus to spray paint their crew name on the back of the bus.

Sometimes a tagger crew will enter a store in a large group and collectively steal paint or other needed items. The large group is difficult to watch and the theft is committed as a team effort. This type of group shoplifting is known as "racking."

Other types of tagging have been done with etching tools. The most common glass targets have been bus windows. Many taggers are not old enough to get a driver's license, so they ride public transportation. While riding the bus they will etch their tag on the window.

Etching tag graffiti has also been placed on mirrors, display windows in malls, smooth painted surfaces in all types of locations. These could include the public restrooms in courthouses, schools, malls and even police stations. The cost to repaint is cheap when compared to the $5000.00 to $10,000 dollar estimate to replace a single large store display window.

The cost to remove this type of graffiti is surprising high. During the mid 1990s, the city of Los Angeles alone spent more than 4 million dollars a year to remove graffiti. The Los Angeles Rapid Transit System spent approximately 1 million dollars a year to remove the graffiti during the same time period. Overall, the California Department of Justice estimated a staggering cost of 200 million dollars a year to remove graffiti. And guess who pays for that?

Tag Bangers

The West Coast has also seen the evolution of some tagging crews into street gangs. The motivation to band together for protection was so strong that it promoted typical gang behaviors. This motivation was based in the same attitudes that helped form the first street gangs in the country. The assaults on tagging crews acted as a catalyst that promoted the payback or retaliatory attitude. This in turn facilitated the development of the violent street gang mentality within tagging crews. This included the gang philosophy that no insult goes unanswered no matter how small. With influence from the local street gangs and the victimization by street gangs and other tagger crews in was only a matter of time before some tag crews evolved into tag banging crews.

Coupled with an increasing growth in membership during the late 1990s, tagger crews developed a need for additional tagging space. Other street-based criminal sub-cultures saw taggers as lightweight she wolfs. Intense rivalries developed between some tagging crews, street gangs and even between other tagging crews.

Some ex-gang member taggers indirectly influenced the crew mentality. Even though they may have formally left the gang, it is difficult at best to leave the gang mentality behind. Some tagging crews tended to adopt many street gang behaviors and placed their tagging activity right in the middle of a known gang turf. The transition process started and evolved the tagging crew into another form of violent street gang.

Within these new tagging crews members call themselves "tag bangers." They carried guns, claimed turf, tattooed themselves and were involved in shootings and stabbings over tagging rivalries. In some parts of the country several tagging crews were reclassified as street gangs. In Southern California, a few tagging crews have even met the criteria to be classified as violent criminal street gangs under the gang enhancement law.

Trends

Some taggers have indicated they have joined a crew in an effort to avoid joining the local gang. Many taggers go to school and come from diverse social and economic backgrounds. Crew membership today can be composed of Latino, Anglo and African-American teenage youths; the race barrier does not exist for these gangs. Taggers ages can range from 11 to 28 years old.

Some tag crews claim no turf and are just interested in writing graffiti. These crews remain traditional taggers. Tagging crews have sprung up across the nation and are an international phenomenon. Most tagging crews have no formal lines of networking; however, they are aware of each other's activities through the informal street intelligence network. I have spoken to several traditional taggers who indicate they carry small handguns for protection. Some claim they have used the guns only in self-defense and would never use them in an aggressive fashion. When asked why, the reply was, "Why not? Everyone out there has one."

The Internet has become a popular form to advertise to show off and recruit new members into tagging crews. There are many Internet sites that sell tagging paraphernalia, recommend tagging magazines and clothing.

There are currently several publications that advertise and feature this type of street art, including the popular Southern California magazine Can Control that showcases piecer and writer art. Advertisements are for specialized stores that cater to the needs of the taggers, selling tagger-style clothing, tagger music (Hip Hop) and special plastic nozzle tips that vary the spray width of spray paint.

Street artists maintain their graffiti is a form of self-expression. While some taggers profess a formal rejection of gang life, many claim that only gang life; drug sales or tagging is worthy of involvement. As one tagger put it, "... there is nowhere else to go." For some taggers there is little mention of school or work because the act of spray painting graffiti can give these taggers an emotional high. Some taggers have reported they feel almost addicted to writing graffiti, and that no place is inaccessible. Just try putting a blank piece of paper and a pencil in front of a tagger and leave him or her alone for a few minutes.

A few taggers have stated they had to go through an initiation to formally join their group. There was no ritual or ceremony but they were dared to put their tag on a certain location and if they got it up, they were in. For others, there was a formal jumping-in ritual, similar to traditional street gangs.

In the late 1990s a new form of tagging appeared. It is called "daredevil tagging" a term coined by a Fox News investigative reporter in Los Angeles (Blatchford, 1999). Some taggers are specializing in putting their tag and crew names up in normally inaccessible places. These taggers sometimes literally hang on with one hand and write with the other. Bridges over freeways and outdoor billboard signs are very popular.

These taggers say they use these areas because the writing stays up longer since it is harder to remove (buffing). The taggers say they get more recognition this way. They appear to be challenging city and county workers who have to remove the graffiti.

Summary

Tagging crews can be as small as five or six members and as large as 1,000. Some U.S. tagging crews are so large that sub-sets or cliques were identified by local telephone area codes. Certainly, as tagging crews increase in membership size, the ability to tag anywhere increases. Tagging is now an international phenomenon with tagger graffiti being found virtually in every country. This has led to the development of international tagging magazines, videos and even Internet sites.

Party Crews, Posses and Clubs

There are a number of groups that refer to themselves as "posses, clubs, crews, cliques or party crews.' All will also claim they are not a gang. This belief allows the members to participate in low level gang activity and for the most part avoid the violence that is associated with street gangs. The sociological definition used in this book would suggest otherwise. These groups fit the social definition of a gang, but may not qualify to fit a penal code definition of a violent street gang. What qualifies these groups as gangs is behavior.

History

Street gangs have had a profound effect on the nation. The violence that accompanies that lifestyle has forced many people to change the way they live, where they go and how they dress. In fact, the gang violence has caused some gang members and young people to try to change their own street lifestyles.

In early the 1990s, law enforcement in Southern California began to notice the appearance of several new types of new youth groups. The groups of young males and females emulated traditional street gangs in several ways and yet were unique in their own special ways.

The first of these groups called themselves party crews. Party crews could contain both female and male members or could be composed of just one gender. The flexible or fluid turf they all claimed was the party scene. Although many of the crews had no certain dress style, often the crew members dressed in the stylized clothing that was worn by many street gangs. This included the use of baseball caps and oversized baggy clothing.

Membership Indicia

Some party crew members sported tattoos and used hand signs to communicate. Many party crews developed rivalries between other party crews. Party crews use a special verbal slang to communicate with each other. This mimicked the use of gang slang by gang members. Substance abuse was common and expected from party crew members. These behaviors also mimicked gang behaviors.

Some party crews have used deadly violence to settle disputes. These deadly encounters were also the result of gang like behaviors the same types of behaviors committed by street gangs and the results are the same, injury and death.

Party crew members also have some unique membership indicia that law enforcement did not associate with street gangs. The use of colorful flyers announcing parties is one. For most crews there is an attempt to avoid gang type violence.

The police do not contact some party crew members. Some crew members wear the traditional attire that is normally associated with street gangs others do not. Some party crews may appear to be transitionally similar to gangs in appearance, response action, and behavior. Even though many crew members activity state their crew is not a gang members react to real or perceived insults and disrespect as if they were bonefide gang members. Party crews have three basic philosophies that help shape the party crew mentality.

The first and one of the most powerful motivators that shape behavior is the party scene. Party crews can sponsor parties just about anywhere. The rivalries began between the crews by determining which crew sponsors the biggest party, who has the best DJ, who has the best music, which party has drawn the most women or which crew has the best dancers. Many times the rivalries are settled in a non-lethal manner, like a fistfight or verbal insults. All party crew members consider the party life a viable and safe alternative to the violent street gang life. In the later part of 2004 violence broke out at several L.A. party crew scenes. One party ended when a partygoer produced a gun and fired at a police officer. This armed party crew member and partygoer was killed and the officer wounded.

Not a Gang

This brings us to the second part of the party crew philosophy. All party crew members deny gang membership or affiliation. All party crew members maintain they are not part of a street gang because they sponsor parties and normally are not involved in violent acts. Some party crews make an earnest effort and attempt not to use gang style violence to settle disputes. Unfortunately, most party crew members maintain the attitude, we don't go looking for trouble, "…but if it comes our way we'll deal with it," as one 17-year-old party crew member explained.

That attitude in reality signifies that if a member or the crew is insulted or threatened in some manner, the crew membership is ready to retaliate. This is the same behavior that is encountered with a street gang as they retaliate when insulted or attacked. Party crew members also believe that they are not a gang because they claim no turf and they are called a crew. But party crew behaviors in general suggest the opposite. Here is a good time to apply our working definition of a gang that was presented earlier.

The desire not to use violence quickly disappears in conflict situations whether real or perceived. The party crew responds in the same manner street gangs do: with acts of deadly violence. Inter-crew violence is minimal. However, crew-gang violence is seen which much more frequency.

This style of conflict resolution has been seen before, with the tagging crews. Inter-tagging crew violence is rare, however tagging crew-gang violence is often seen. Remember, initially all tagging crew members also claimed they were not gang members and their crews were not a gang.

In the mid 1990s a split occurred in the tagging crew world. There was a division over the use of guns. Today, a few tagging crews still focus only on graffiti art. The second group kept the original tagging philosophy, but added street gang customs, behaviors and the use of guns. These crew members called themselves tag bangers.

Some of these tagging crews started to claim turf like the traditional turf gangs. Many of these crews have joined with traditional turf oriented Latino street gangs. On several occasions, tag-banging groups have assaulted police officers with guns. As expected, many of these gangs assaulted each other over gang rivalries.

Many party crews share behaviors with the tagging crews and tag banging crews. Once considered as safe alternatives to street gangs, many party and tagging crews just became another form of a street gang. Both share many of the traditional street gang membership indicia and behaviors. These can include: stylized clothing, hand signs, tattoos, substance abuse, slang and gang mentality and behaviors. Both claim and make attempts not to use gang-style violence, but both are involved in gang styled violence.

While tag crews concentrate on graffiti art, party crews concentrate on the party scene. Both groups find nothing wrong with their philosophies because there is no formal incorporation of gang style violence, unless your crew or a member of the crew is threatened or insulted.

The party crew scene is easily accessible and the parties inevitably attract can and do members from local street gangs. Street gang members tend to use any opportunity to justify exposing their violent nature. Even though the party crew attempts to stop gang violence, often either members of the crew or a party attendees become victims of gang violence. Then the party crew retaliates by using the same style of violence. Although rare, party crew members may attack each other over a personal or crew insult.

Substance Abuse and Sex

The third part of the party crew philosophy is centered on the party itself. The use of alcohol, marijuana, nitrous oxide (laughing gas), sex and music are a critical part of the party crew lifestyle. Nitrous Oxide is also known as "NOS."

Since the majority of the crew membership falls in the 14-24 year-old age group there tends to be underage drinking, drug abuse and teen sexual activity at parties. A common drug of choice is inhaling laughing gas to get high. The gas is sold in balloons and then inhaled. The inhalation of laughing gas in a non-medical environment is foolhardy at best, especially when combed with alcohol and/or marijuana usage. The most common form of alcohol that is consumed is beer. Many of the party crew members refer to this type of activity as fun and have commented that it is safer and better than gang banging.

I have spoken to several police officers that have responded to party crew-sponsored parties and found teenage nitrous oxide dealers working out of their cars. There would be hundreds of empty rubber balloons on the ground and the round metal cylinders of gas in or around their cars. These officers would observe teenagers lined up ready to purchase a hit, a balloon full of the gas for 5 or 10 dollars. In one incident there was a large gas cylinder was in the back seat along with wads of money, empty balloons and happy partiers all around the car. These officers have estimated that 200 to 300 hits of the gas were illegally sold at some of the parties.

Street Gang Defined

Remember the social definition of a street gang used in this book: a group with a common identifier, with three or more members in association and involved in criminal activity. You can easily see that party crews fit this definition. Also remember, gangs are not required to claim a geographical turf to fit within the definition. There is also no qualification demanding that the crime committed by the group be of felony status. Street gangs commit all types of crimes including felonies, misdemeanors and infractions. The media because of their propensity for senseless violent acts often notes Violent street gangs. The media rarely reports gang activity at the misdemeanor or infraction level or gangs that use violence on part-time or infrequent bases.

By using a standard gang definition you can note that even though the majority of party crew members do not commit felony crimes, that fact does not exempt them from the gang status. Some party crew members will attempt to avoid gang behaviors including violence. However, party crews still qualify as a street gang. Party crew members also qualify as gang members.

Party Types

Male party crews use names like Flash or Madness and all female party crews use names like Felines, Second Generation or Fusion. The crew size could be as small as six to eight or as large as 300 members. The focus of the crew is to have a good time at the party, dance, get high and get lucky. Very few party crews host parties where alcohol and marijuana were not available. NOS tends to be available at many party crew sponsored events. An alcoholic drink called jungle juice could be shared by using a straw. A partier could also smoke a primo, a mixture of marijuana and cocaine and /or purchase and use ecstasy.

The drug dealers pay to get in the party because they are normally not part of the sponsor's crew. At promoter and party crew parties, several sponsors have confided to me that while they do request or encourage drug usage or sales at their party, they know drugs are sold and used. One drug to make its debut into the scene (party crew party) is ecstasy. Sold for $20-25 a hit, E or X has become very popular in the party crew and rave scene. Party crew members have confided that other drugs are available at parties. They have witnessed heroin, crank (methamphetamine) and cocaine being sold and used at party crew parties.

The parties are categorized depending on the type of party. For example, a ditch party is usually started around 9:00 AM on a school day. These parties could have hundreds of participants, all ditching from school. If a crew hosts a part in the open like a front yard or parking lot, it would be called a street party. The partygoers would literally take over an entire street to have the party.

If the crew hosts a party at a home, you would attend a house party. Sometimes house parties are hosted at an apartment complex. This can cause problems for the tenants since hundreds of students attend. Sometimes a party crew will break into an abandoned warehouse to host a break-in party. Warehouses can also be legitimately rented to host a party.

There are a few legal party clubs where teenagers can go. A small cover charge is paid for attendance into this controlled environment. Many partygoers feel a bit easier in the club setting because gang members are normally not allowed in. Sometimes a dress code is enforced and attendees are checked for weapons. At some of these venues professional security has been provided to insure a safe social and pleasant atmosphere. Sadly though drug suppliers also attend these parties and still sell ecstasy, methamphetamine and NOS.

Party crew "flyer parties" are classified by the time they end, according to several southern California promoters and party crew members. These classifications may not be accurate for party crews that operate in other parts of the country. Hip Hop parties have break dancing and are characterized by having an open mike. The party can end between midnight and 3:00 am. Club parties are normally held at a warehouse or large rented hall. This allows more partiers to attend. Typically these parties will end sometime between 3:00 and 4:00 am.

The third type of party is called a rave party. Rave parties go on all night and usually end when the sun rises. The parties can be held in special after hour clubs. The drug ecstasy has become very popular at these parties.

Promoters have also told me about a special party called a pimp-n-ho party. This kind of party is especially popular with the younger yuppie jet set type Caucasians. They are normally held at a rented mansion or very large house. The promoter comes with the typical party crew type music and high-end special effects. There is an expensive pay-at-the-door fee. At these parties the people dress to impress. For this type of party, the men dress as "pimps" and the ladies dress as "hos" (prostitutes). As one DJ told me he loves to work these parties for several reasons. First, there are absolutely no problems because the people who attend are young white-collar professionals. Secondly, the promoter gets paid well and third and I quote, "...the women are scandalous and friendly."

Advertisement

Party advertisement is usually done through word of mouth and by passing out small party flyers. The flyers give the name of the hosting party crew, time, date and location. Hundreds of these flyers are printed and passed out at parties and locations where party scene youth congregate. Sometimes, at house parties the attendees would also have to pay a small cover charge to get in. Some party crew promoters that I have spoken to stated they will have their crew sponsor a party in order to make a profit. A small cover charge is collected at entry into the party. These party crews were able to sponsor a party and turn a profit at the same time.

If the police come and shut the party down, many times flyers would be passed out to the "after hours" party. The party scene would simply be transferred to different location and the festivities would continue, until the police shut down that party. Then the partygoers would go a different after hours party location until the arrival of daylight, signaling the new day. A large party can easily net the sponsor(s) $5000 to $10,000 dollars.

Party crew members in the late 1990s could subscribe to a sub-culture magazine catering to the party crew scene. The magazine was called Street Beat and was specially designed and printed for the party crews. It could be considered sort of a trade magazine. Party crew activity died down and stabilized between1993-1995. The party crew scene was very quiet in the late 1990s and early 2000s. An unexpected surge of party crew growth and activity was observed between 2000 and 2004. This was accompanied with a spike in party crew related violence and death especially in the Los Angeles County area.

In the middle part of 1995, law enforcement again noticed the emergence of party crew type groups. These groups called themselves crews or party crews. Again, the membership actively espouses a non-violent, non-gang attitude. The focus of these groups was centered on the party life. Alcohol, drugs, sex and the music seemed to control the member's behavior. These groups tended to be an extension of the1990s party crews and mimicked behaviors and attitudes.

These gangs identified with names such as Operation X, Rescue 911, the Wanderers, Qteez, Street Desire and Ladies of Mischief. The group's name referred back to the lifestyle of the 1990s party crew member. There is some anecdotal evidence that the party crew activity is cyclic. In southern California historically there was a surge of party crew activity in the early 1990s, again in the mid to later part of 1995 and again the in the later part of 2004. Obviously, there are other factors that influence this activity. The potential for serious violence at party crew sponsored parties is always present. The street gang sub-culture exerts a never-ending gang influence on the behaviors of the partygoers as well as the party sponsors. By 1997 this surge of party crew activity decreased.

Promoter Party

There are several kinds of flyer parties that crews attend and sponsor. There are legitimate flyer parties sponsored by a promoter or a small group of promoters. These parties can draw from several hundred to several thousand people with a nominal cover charge to get in and the promoters often hiring off duty police officers or armed security personnel to watch over the crowd. Commonly, $20.00 is the entrance fee.

The parties are held in the true spirit of a party, often having dress codes enforced to prevent the gangster look and to try and prevent gang members from attending. This is done to because as one promoter told me, "… if the cholos (gang members) get in there are always problems." Cholos and Gs are party crew terms used to describe gang members. Party promoters and party crew members understand and comprehend the gangster mentality and are aware of the potential for violence that often accompanies a gang presence. That is why many promoters do not want gang members to attend a flyer party they sponsor.

These parties are sometimes held at a rented hall, with appropriate paid fees and city permits. This type of party is a moneymaking operation for the promoter and the party is advertised by handing out small preprinted flyers. Many promoters take pride in their advertising, because of this attitude is common to spend $7,000 to $8,000 in printing costs. The flyers are handed out by friends of the promoters or by members of the crew that the promoter belongs to. This process is sometimes referred to as slamming or to slam. There are some independent promoters who do not belong to a particular party crew who just organize parties and are very good at doing that.

Sometimes, the promoter will even sell water and soft drinks at the party. The music and special effects, which can include lasers, enhance the atmosphere. There are usually no problems with violence or street gangs at this high end party crew parties. A promoter can easily spend $20,000 to $30,000 to purchase equipment or he may borrow the equipment from friends.

The promoters, are often ex-members of a party crew who have learned the in and outs of the party crew scene and are able to finance and plan parties. There may be battles (dance contests) in the mosh pit (circle of dancers, slam dancing) or a go-go battle (dance contest between girls) while the DJ (disc jockey) spins (plays) and mixes (getting a record ready to play a set (set of music) of house (a type of music with bass and vocals). These parties often have a DJ booth set up and a number of large speakers, operating lasers, very cool light shows. The lighting and smoke make these parties fun to attend. Close friends of the DJ can get hooked up (let in for free). A well-planned party can net the promoter $10,000 to $20,000 if the party is well attended.

The Party Crew Party

Party crews sponsor most parties. The crew will help set up the party, just like a promoter would, except at a smaller scale. The main purpose is to have fun and make a little money. These parties are usually held at smaller venues and draw smaller crowds. Often, these parties are referred to as Hip-Hop parties. This simply means there is an open mike and music is played. Hip Hop music is popular as well as techno (music made electronically).

The same kind of music is played but most likely there are not many special effects. The party crews focus is to have fun. Many times, there are no armed guards and usually there is no dress code. Just about anybody can attend. If there is a cover charge it will be minimal.

Unfortunately, gang related violence could easily erupt at these parties. Gang members can crash the party or may have been invited by a member of the sponsoring party crew. Don't forget, gang members who attend these parties will not be there alone. Often, these gang members are accompanied by many peers, some of who are strapped (carrying guns). Sometimes, several party crews will get together to sponsor a party. The locations for these kinds of parties can be small halls or private homes. Often, the police respond to loud party calls from angry neighbors who are annoyed at the noise and the number of people that invade the neighborhood.

Gang Party Crews

In the mid to late 1990s some party crews evolved into tagging crews and after a few years into street gangs. There are many factors that might cause this. Commonly, it is pressure from existing neighborhood street gangs on the party crew that is present in the same part of the city. The gang pressure can be exerted on the streets or in the custodial arena. For example, in-custody gang members pressure in-custody party crew members to become part of the gang or the gang will tax them. Taxed is a term that means the party crew will have to pay tribute or protection money to the gang in order not to be victimized by them. Since party crews are part of the street culture and members live within gang-controlled neighborhoods, it is logical to find the influence of street gangs.

Some gang members will occasionally act like a party crew member, even though they claim gang membership to and are active in a street gang. More often than not, it is a clique within the gang that sponsors a flyer party. In essence, the gang sponsors a flyer party. This gang party crew party draws a limited number of people, most being peer gang members and associates. There are no academic studies that reflect the incidence of violence at these parties. However, street experience as a gang investigator tells me that the potential for violence at these types of parties is high. There have been homicide or serious assault investigations that have begun at these locations, but there is no way to tell if the party was at the center of the violence or attendees. Also there are only estimates that indicate how many crimes have gone unreported.

At gang sponsored flyer parties there are no enforced dress codes or efforts to exclude weapons. At some party crew sponsored parties hand held metal detectors are used to screen the people who attend. If a gang sponsors the party there may be an overt effort to exclude weapons. The sponsoring gang will sometimes have internal security. This simply means that one or more members of the sponsoring gang will assume security duties and will be armed with handguns. The sponsoring gang members are prepared in case something happens. It has been my experience that at these parties, alcohol, marijuana and beer are commonly available. After a couple of hours of drinking and blazing (smoking marijuana) often fistfights erupt. When the boxing (fights) continues or increases in intensity eventually the handguns come out in an effort to control the situation. The result is a gang related shooting.

Another phenomenon encountered is that some party crews have a very close relationship with a street gang. The party crew members are not part of the street gang. However, they will associate and socialize with the gang and members of the gang. This can occur when a party crew forms within a gang turf or is operating gang turf. When the party crew sponsors a party gang members from the associate gang usually attend.

Rebels, Clicks, Posses and Clubs

The Rebels, Clicks, Posse and Club members all share a certain perspective. Even though they represent that they are against gang style violence, all maintain a certain gang attitude. As one Rebel claimed, *"... we wont take no shit from anyone... we are down for anything."* Like the 1990 style party crews, these groups will be involved in gang style violence if compelled or forced. There is one characteristic that distinguishes these groups from street gangs. Street gangs tend to use violence as a first choice to handle disputes. Party Crews, Rebels, Posses and Clicks for the most part tend to use violence as a last resort to settle disputes.

Another unique characteristic these groups share is that they do not formally claim any geographical turf. This allows them to feely travel throughout the city or county of origin. The ability to travel through gang turfs allows for members of these groups to attend many parties. Often, street gang members attend the same parties because of similar interests, to pick up girls, to have a good time and they are member of the hosting party crew or because of an invitation by a party crew member or someone who is going to the party.

Wherever the party goes, there tends to be strong street gang influence from within the crew membership, the party attendees or from the local street gang membership. Of all the types of parties hosted by the party crews the house party seems to be the most dangerous. The house can be physically located within a gang turf and local gang members have a tendency to crash the party. Either way street gangs exert an often-unwanted influence because of their presence. At the party you will find party crew members, posses, Click, Club members, gang members and youth. In these situations the ingredients for a violent conflict is present. The results are almost always a violent confrontation between the attending groups.

The Posses, Rebels, Clicks and Clubs claim they are active social groups much like the party crews. However, it is easy to conclude they another type of street gang. For example, members can be jumped-in using a modified ritual modeled after a gang jump-in. The ceremony can include a ritual cigarette burning or a good-natured jostling. Sex, drugs and rock and roll are still priorities for these gangs. Members of these groups would more likely be attending a party rather than sponsor one.

Members of these groups also present many of the traditional gang membership indicia that can are observed in traditional street gangs except for graffiti. Since these groups do not claim turf it is not necessary to use graffiti for turf marking. Club, Rebel, Posses or Click graffiti is unusual, if found. Behaviorally these gangs act similar to party crews as a group.

Some of the groups like the Rebels identify with the teenage rebels of the 50s and 60s like James Dean, Elvis and Jim Morrison of the rock band the Doors. The crew membership has taken what they believe is a non-gang and non-violent rebel stance against traditional society.

Another well-known Hollywood figure that heavily influences this group's activities is Marilyn Monroe. She is considered a sex symbol and the Rebels have adopted her as one their role models.

One southern California Rebel crew called themselves the Wanderers. They wear stylized clothing such as leather jackets, Harley Davidson boots and belt buckles, blue jeans and tee shirts with the cuffs rolled up. Almost all the members sport the Elvis style pompadour hair cut.

This crew also had an initiation ceremony for new members. They called it the "burn in." This was a cigarette burning ritual where the new member receives a large cigarette burn on the arm near the shoulder. The entire membership is present for this gala event and members burn the new member in the same place with cigarettes. The shoulder is usually the place where the large burn is placed. Don't forget cigarette burning is not a new phenomenon. Vietnamese gang members where placing self-inflicted cigarette burns on their arms, hands, legs and ankles in the 1980s.

Girls seem to make the party exciting and complete. Females can be involved in dance contests. Cash money is normally the prize and some of the young ladies will even strip during the dance in order to win, but this action also teases the male attendees. Dancing in this fashion is known as "strippin." The monikers used by females often refer back to the attitude toward sex, for example Scrumptious and Cuddles. Not all female party crew members are promiscuous and dance in this fashion. However, there is a general attitude towards sex that promotes frequent sexual encounters between partygoers.

Terms like Breakers, Go-Gos, Groovers and Snappin all refer to specific styles of dancing. The dance style may also require the dancer to wear a certain type of clothing. This could include wearing painter style paper masks, gloves or go-go style shorts and tops.

Summary

Party crews like other street gangs are affected by changing trends, law enforcement suppression programs, new members, older members leaving, gangs and technology. Admittedly, many party crew members do not seek the violence that is found on the street in fact, many party crews attempt to avoid it. However, as street gangs continue to be an influencing factor in the street sub-culture party crews will continue to gang-like behaviorally and continue to be involved in violent confrontations.

The Occult and Gangs

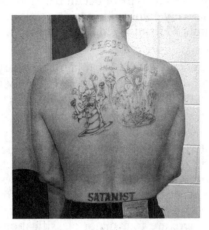

As you find out in this section the word 'occult' simply refers to a hidden knowledge. Some youth who dabble in occult religions claim to fully understand the hidden religion and their actions that violate the law help stereotype the true practitioners. Exploring the following occult religions helps us to remember the fact that all religions share equal protection under the law. There are several perspectives to review this material by; legally, media, religious and mental health.

History

Recently, there appears to be an increased interest in the revival of occult religious practices. Fringe religions have been around for hundreds of years, some for thousands of years. This section is not a course on religious history, but occult belief systems have had, and will continue to have, an impact on some street-gang activity. However I believe this activity will probably be limited and may be episodic in nature.

There are two reasons to present this section, one as an introduction to four occult belief systems and to note that the true practitioners of these religions are law-abiding citizens. Secondly, to provide a basic foundation to you understanding that some youth get involved in self-styled versions of these religions. These youth can become involved in ritualistic criminal behavior and be part of a street gang or as members of small gang.

The occult belief systems presented here are not illegal. The First Amendment of the United States Constitution guarantees freedom of religion. Granted, for the majority of Americans these belief systems are not what would be considered mainstream. Nevertheless, a significant percentage of the population in the United States believes in and is actively involved with these religions and they do not account for any more crime than any other sub-group of the population.

For many, an occult religion is a true way of life, harming no one. For others, it is an experiment to find out if this belief system is for them. For some teenagers an occult religion becomes blending of several characteristics from many belief systems forming a customized religion that is often called, Witchcraft or Satanism. Youth groups are quick to pick up the ideas that quickly become a fad. The so-called occult belief system is further changed by word of mouth. Some parents of youth who are involved in an occult belief system sometimes quickly conclude their child is in involved in a cult. There are distinct differences between a cult and an occult belief system. They are not the same.

A number of gang members accept the philosophies of occult belief systems. Individual gang members or small groups or gang members can practice personalized forms of these religions. In fact, there is law enforcement anecdotal evidence that suggests the activity of some gangs is based partly or solely on some type of occult belief system. A few white supremacist gangs have members that are actively involved in occult rituals and ceremonies. History tells us that some of Hitler's special units were involved in occult practices and research during World War II.

Teenage members of these occult gangs have told me that they joined for different reasons, including curiosity, free booze, drugs and sex. Others sincerely believe they can receive real supernatural power over others through the rituals they perform. Some youth become intoxicated with alcohol and/or drugs having the belief they have magical power over others.

Sometimes a public assumption is made that stereotypes all people who are involved with these religions. This tends to stereotypes all practitioners allowing the general public to believe they are involved in some form of bizarre ritualistic criminal activity. The reality is quite the opposite. Most adults who are involved in these religions are law-abiding citizens. Remember, criminal and deviant behavior can be committed by anyone and from any religious background, not just those who believe in occult religions. Let's take a look at where some youth might get ideas about occult practices. There are four major classifications of occult religions that are frequently encountered in the street and are sometimes confused with each other by the public.

Paganism

Paganism is a term used to describe one of mankind's earliest earth-based religions. It was an attempt to understand what was occurring in nature. While there are many denominations of the Pagan religion, there is no single Pagan religion. Generally, the religion involves the worship of many and various deities, which are the personification of natural forces. The word Pagan is actually derived from the Latin word *paganus* and means country dweller. Pagan holidays are centered on the changing of the seasons, the solstices and equinoxes.

Pagan religions hold that everything on earth has a life force to it. The water, mountains, flowers, trees and the smallest creature all have a life force. This life force must be respected, and if you can become one with the life force you yourself can be God-like. The small practicing religious groups are small and are usually led by a priestess or priest.

Ceremonies may include wearing special robes and forming a magic circle. In modern Pagan rituals there are no animal or human sacrifices. Offerings can be fruit or bread. Remember practitioners value the sanctity of life. Candles, a sacred knife, salt or bells may be used in the ceremony.

Like Wicca the main deity in the Pagan religion is a female. Often referred to as the Great Earth Mother, she has a male counter part. For the first practitioners the religion was a fertility-based religion. The ceremonies were design to influence nature to help the crops grow.

Witchcraft

Wicca or Witchcraft is also a nature religion, but utilizes magic to try to control or change reality. Witches are also known as practitioners of the Craft. Most are women, but there are also male witches. Most people automatically think of a witch as being evil, having a pact with the devil and practicing sorcery, an evil form of magic. However, several categories of witches can be found in both contemporary and historic literature about witchcraft. For example, the white witch practices the craft for the good of all. Magic is practiced to help relationships or to heal someone.

Black Witches allegedly practiced magic for malevolent reasons, and were accused of working with evil for their own purposes. Witches sometimes wear ceremonial robes and talismans. Candles are used in rituals and sometimes the colors are important. Practitioners of

Wicca today also may use ceremonial daggers, chalices, ropes and herbs just as did their ancestors. Witches come together in either formal or informal meetings of their covens or traditional circles. The rituals or ceremonies can be practiced almost anywhere, from the privacy of a home, converted garage to an open field. There can be an initiation to enter the coven, a group of witches.

The initiation ceremony for some Wiccan practitioners can be in the form of testing the belief of the initiate that uses symbols for earth, wind, water, air and fire.

The witches I have spoken to do not use black cauldrons or black cats in their rituals. Some use black colored robes and all do not sacrifice animals, small children or adults. All the witches I have spoken to practice their religion privately or in small groups. The reason is because they anticipate a stereotyped reaction by the majority of the public. Adult practitioners of Wicca come from all walks of life and from all professional backgrounds.

The locations of Wicca worship can be converted rooms or garages were ceremonies could be performed in small groups privately. Some witches practice ritual nudity, often called sky clad. The ritual nudity is practices in an effort to become closer to the life forces. For some practitioners cloths can act as a barrier and hinder contact with the gods and goddesses.

A priestess, again representing the female deity, the Great Earth Mother, leads most of these religious groups. Relying on its roots in early Paganism, Wiccan covens may include a male counterpart. Often the male witch may represent the male Horned God. The female and male genders are needed to promote fertility. It is not surprising to find that most believers and practitioners of this faith are law abiding citizens and do not attempt to harm anyone or anything.

Wiccan holidays like those in Paganism seem to follow the summer and winter solstices and the equinoxes. Some covens are composed of females only and a few are lead by male witches, called warlocks.

Satanism

True Satanists worship Satan as a good responsive deity. The Satanic religion is protected like all the occult belief systems, under the First Amendment of the Constitution, Freedom of Religion. This religion is not considered a mainstream religion and anecdotal law enforcement evidence suggests that Satanism attracts a following of approximately 5000 nationally. I have encountered religious and law enforcement trackers of the satanic religion who estimate the membership in satanic churches exceeds 100,000 nationally. This is probably an inflated estimate based on perspective rather than factual bases.

The Satanic religion bases its rituals and belief on the carnal needs of man. The symbols associated with this religion include snakes, candles, chalices, swords, daggers, black colored robes, the inverted pentagram, the numbers 666, triangles, the goat's head and naked females as altars. Most practitioners conduct satanic ceremonies in small groups.

The religion of Satanism can incorporate a symbolic form of human sacrifice. Practitioners have told me the ritual parallels the sacrament of Communion in the Catholic religion. Here the ritual symbolizes the eating and drinking of Christ's body and blood. In the Satanism, the ritual incorporates the same metaphor. The religion does not promote the actual sacrifice of a human in the literal sense.

For purposes of categorization, some law enforcement has classified Satanists into four loosely defined groups; first is the dabblers, people who are experimenting with the religion. This includes youth who say they are Satanists as an act of rebellion against family and society. Dabblers come from all walks of life, from the economically deprived to the financially well to-do. Most members share a common denominator, a feeling of disenchantment with life. They see Satanism as a way to receive gratification and fulfillment.

Dabblers may include street-gang members who have identified with or encountered philosophies of Satanism, in books such as Anton LaVey's The Satanic Bible, The Satanic Rituals, or The Satanic Witch. All three books have been used by people who self-describe themselves as Satanists. This same group may also have books on witchcraft and call themselves Black Witches. Sometimes they refer to their groups as covens. This is the same term used to describe a small group of Wiccans or Pagans.

Male members usually lead covens among Satanists. Skinheads, Latino, Stoner, prison gangsters and some motorcycle gang members have practiced various forms of these religions. Animal sacrifices and self-mutilation have been popular with some members of these groups. They are not normally part of any ritual or ceremony that is performed by true practitioners of the Pagan, Wicca or Satanic religions.

There is law enforcement anecdotal evidence from Central America that suggests some MS-13 gang members are involved in occult practices. This would include the use of occult symbols in graffiti and tattoos and unusual mutilations on their murder victims. A part of MS-13 history in Los Angeles suggests that early members of MS were Stoners who were a type of heavy metal occult gang. The Stoner focus was occult religious practices and the heavy use of drugs.

Heavy use of alcohol and narcotics as well as identification with Heavy Metal music has been reported to be important to some dabblers. The lyrics to this music often refer to anarchy, worshiping the Devil, murder, suicide, vampirism, cannibalism, torture, sex, the murder of babies and human sacrifice. There may be an emotional or psychological impact on a small percentage of the listeners to this type of music. Just what this could be has not been determined with any accuracy. Some feel that anyone who listens to this type of music will be affected by it.

The second type of practitioner is the religious Satanists. These believers belong to churches like the Temple of Set, founded by Michael Aquino, a former Army officer, or the Church of Satan, founded by Anton LaVey. Both are in the San Francisco Bay area. The Temple of Set enjoys Federal and State tax-exempt status.

Religious Satanists worship Satan as modern-day Christians worship the Christian God, with formal ceremonies and rituals. In the Church of Satan, sometimes-naked female members may be used as live altars. The founder of the Church of Satan once stated for an on camera interview, "The religion is a selfish one centered on the lusts and greed of men" (LaVey, 1969). If you want to worship Satan, he will give you the power to do whatever you want with no consequences. This narcissistic ideal can have great appeal to a gang member and is a central theme in all four sub-groups of this religion.

Self-styled Satanists are individuals who often mix philosophies and themes from Wicca, Paganism, Cultural-Spiritual religions and Satanism to develop their own self-formed version of Satanism. The Night Stalker, Richard Ramirez, and Charlie Manson have been cited as examples of self-styled Satanists. Many dabblers, as they gain experience, also self-style their belief systems.

The fourth classification includes generational Satanists. They distinguish themselves from the three previous groups by having been raised in a family that practices Satanism. As with many religions, devote followers may center family life on the belief system. The religious philosophies and way of life are passed on from generation to generation (Valdez, 2000).

Spiritual-Cultural Religions

The last general classification of occult religions is referred to as the Spiritual-Cultural Religions. These belief systems are formed as the result of non-Christian religions merging with Catholicism. This includes the Santeria religion, a synthesized religion that formed from the melding of two religions. Santeria was formed by the Yorubans who were captured and sold as slaves in the Caribbean, where Catholic missionaries converted them to Catholicism. Historically, the Yoruban people were the first African-American slaves.

The Yoruban people continued to worship their multi-deity religion but with a strong Catholic influence. The Santeria (Way of the Saints) religion gradually formed as the two religions blended together. Catholic Saints were chosen at first to camouflage or to represent the different deities of the Yoruba religion.

A black cauldron, sea shells, wood, iron (in certain shapes), egg shells, candles, altars for the saints, animal or fowl blood sacrifices are used in worship. Sometimes these are also incorrectly associated with the practice of Wicca and Pagan ceremonies. Santeria ceremonies and rituals are usually performed by a Santero (priest). The religious rituals practiced are for the Good of the Faithful.

A malevolent form of this religion is known as Palo Mayombe, where the ceremonies and rituals are performed for evil reasons. Another common term is Palo.

Ceremonies can also include the use of cigar smoke, tortoise shells, chicken or bird blood, special wooden or ceramic bowls, special wood and metal in the form of farming tools. Santeria ceremonies can include the sacrifice of a chicken, small bird and in rare occasions a goat. Practitioners of this religion do not sacrifice dogs, cats or people (Gonzalez-Wippler, 1992).

With a very brief exposure to these four occult belief systems, it may be easier to now understand that what is seen on the street is a syncratic or blended belief system based on a combination of several of two or more of these major occult belief systems (Valdez, 2000).

Street Activity

Satanic cult is a media generated term that has been used to describe groups involved in bizarre ritualistic crimes. Practitioners of mainstream Christian based religions also use this term. Satanic cults are purported to be interested in total chaos, disharmony and earthly power. Some of these cult members claim to have the power to control events at will and through the use of black magic. The rivals for many of these practitioners are the practitioners of mainstream Christian religions, traditional institutions, and societal values.

Street gang members can become involved with these self-styled religions that are more often than not belief systems based blended characteristics of all of the previously mentioned occult religions. I have spoken to self-styled teenage witches who claim to practice Satanism and use Pagan type rituals, involving blood. This is not consistent with the true follower of the occult religion.

Practitioners of this self-styled Satanism will sometimes use commonly accepted ways of doing things and invert them. For example, they will write redrum, which is murder spelled backwards. One 17-year-old practitioner I spoke to called himself "Legna", angel spelled backwards. Modern Christian religions use the crucifix as a symbol in the church. Practitioners also will use the Christian crucifix and place it upside down or inverted during rituals.

These groups will also use the ancient rune or witch's alphabet to write. Often, personal writings or graffiti will be seen with the numbers 666, a pentagram or an inverted pentagram. These occult symbols have been associated with the Son of Sam murders, the McMartin Pre-school case and the Night Stalker murders.

When members of these self-styled religious groups commit crime and are apprehended, the media labels them as members of "satanic cults" and infers the crime was committed as part of legitimate ceremony of an occult religion. Members of these groups will now refer to their group as a satanic cult and often call themselves satanic witches.

The entertainment industry has also played an important part in the resurgence of occult practices for some youth. Occult literature and music sells briskly at bookstores. The movie industry has also contributed to the revival of the occult with films such as Rosemary's Baby, The Believers, Exorcist movies, and the Craft.

During the 1990s the country experienced an apparent explosion the media reporting ritualized abuses of children and adults, often with occult overtones. Criminals such as sadists, masochists and pedophiles (adults who have an affinity to non-sexually mature males or females) can use occult religions to justify, mask or even enhance their criminal actions.

Some white supremacists will use Satanist philosophies to help enhance their philosophical position. A great deal of confusion surrounds some of these ad hoc beliefs. I have interviewed members of a Latino gang who claim to practice Witchcraft but call themselves Satanists. They perform Wicca style rituals but use animal sacrifice to honor the Devil to obtain protection from rival gangs and the police (Valdez, 2000).

Some young people who do not want to be gang members but are interested in a fringe lifestyle look to an occult belief systems to fulfill their emotional and psychological needs. As these youth get more involved criminal activity escalates. These occult gang members have been linked to vandalism and arson and the desecration of churches and cemeteries. Many of these youth that I have interviewed candidly indicated they like the sex, drugs, music and rituals associated with their belief system.

In San Luis Obispo, California, on March 14, 1996, three young men 15, 16 and 17 years old were arrested and four days later charged with the murder of a 15-year-old girl. Prosecutors in the case were quoted as saying, " ... *three high-school boys who formed a music group to glorify Satan drugged, raped, tortured and murdered a 15-year-old girl in hope a virgin sacrifice would earn them a ticket to hell.*"

The victim was missing for eight months before her remains were found a short distance from her home. One of the teenagers came forward and showed the police where the victim was. Apparently the three selected and stalked the victim believing that the blonde, blue-eyed girl was a virgin and her sacrifice would guarantee their entrance to hell.

Bias

Belief systems can motivate and control behavior especially if the person is a zealous believer. This can be good in many respects but can also lead to criminal activity if the belief system is distorted or changed. This personalization, or customizing and blending, of belief systems has become a bases for some criminal behavior.

In discreet interviews true practitioners or those who legitimately believe in occult religions stated to me they practice in complete secrecy. Since the general population rejects the occult religious beliefs a large majority of occult practitioners remain underground to protect their reputations, jobs and families. The occult belief systems are not accepted well by the vast majority of Americans probably over confusion, especially with terms like satanic cults and satanic witches and the stereotyped behaviors that accompany those perspectives.

People who involve themselves in the occult come from all walks of life. The preconception that all occult believers and practitioners are all evil, perverts, baby killers, or heavy metal music fans is totally false. The majority of believers and practitioners of these religions are very much like the rest the majority of Americans, law-abiding citizens.

Profile

There are some notable characteristics associated with membership in some of these occult groups. However, these indicators can also be a result of many different life changes. A change in clothing and friends is sometimes noticed. For youths, a drop in school grades and withdrawal from their family. A young person may have the preoccupation with death or suicide. There may be the presence of occult type graffiti on notebooks, abandoned houses, schools, churches and personal papers. Drug abuse and collecting occult literature, music and movies are also common.

Remember a single occult graffiti or symbol may have many different meanings. Many of the symbols and terms frequently encountered with young self-styled occult practitioners have only recently surfaced. There is no way to determine the origin of these words and symbols or to authenticate their meanings.

One other type of activity that is often associated with self-styled Satanism is animal sacrifice or mutilation. There have been a number of documented incidents across the country. When the scenes are examined it is appears obvious that the animal was killed by human hand. In some instances animal control and predator experts disagree on whether or not the site evidence shows a predator kill. However, I have examined scenes that do not fit the predator kill classification. At these locations the animals have been severed cleanly in half. There are no teeth marks, no signs of struggle, no displaced fur and no blood. By visual examination the animal appears to have been cleanly cut in half with a very sharp instrument.

I have also spoken to individuals who have confided that while belonging to a satanic cult have witnessed ritual animal sacrifice. During the ritual, members of the group consume the blood of the sacrificed animal usually a cat.

This type of self-styled occult activity is not seen often and the number of street gang members involved is relatively small when compared to the entire gang population. Some parents who have noticed something was wrong with their child's behavior may have concluded their child was associated with a street gang. Occasionally, the parent's find out their child had joined a small group called a coven, cult or satanic cult. The youth may have begun to practice their version of witchcraft, Satanism or self-styled occult religion. As individuals and as a group these self-styled practitioners demonstrate many of the same membership characteristics and behaviors of street gangs.

From a legal perspective, youth experience risk only when they are involved in criminal behavior while exploring these belief systems. Do not forget anyone can modify any of the four major occult religions to fit their particular needs or desires.

Law enforcement officers may encounter other crimes with possible occult religious overtones such as gravesite desecration, fraud, graffiti and, as previously mentioned, murder. One other area where occult belief systems might influence a criminal investigation is commonly referred to as ritual abuse. In these cases, victims are alleged victims of sexual, physical and psychological abuse over a certain period of time.

Ritual Abuse

Most often the victims describe the perpetrators of ritual abuse as members of organized satanic cults. The stories the victims tell are very compelling and unsettling. The victims are mostly women or small children, but I have interviewed a few male victims.

Cannibalism, human sacrifice, physical torture and sexual abuse are common themes discussed. All victims link their encounters through some type of satanic cult in which they are forced to participate to honor Satan.

Of the numerous cases I have investigated, there has been no physical evidence to prove criminal allegations in court. However, in a 1992 California civil case, in which 2 daughters sued their mother, the jury found the allegations of ritual abuse to be true. These cases are difficult to investigate and prove in many respects. There is a lack of physical evidence to prove the allegations, the crime occurred twenty or thirty years before it is reported and maybe in another jurisdiction and/or the victims or witnesses are too young to testify in court.

Summary

Youth who practice occult religions sometimes mix their beliefs with the street gang culture and could branch out and form a unique social gang themselves. When this does occur often symbols and ceremonies are borrowed and sometimes modified from the true religion. This may include the use of certain terms that are commonly used among the true practitioners. From a law enforcement perspective these gangs are the least problematic, but when crime does occur it could include and not limited to murder, grave desecration, drug trafficking, to vandalism.

The Goth Scene

You drive to the local mall for some shopping. As you are enjoying yourself in the mall, you see some strangely dressed youth and people all around are staring them. They are a small mixed group of male and female teenagers. The girls have red dyed hair, black lip stick, black fingernail polish, some kind of white colored makeup that makes them look real pale. The guys look the same. In fact, you mistook one of the males for a female because he was wearing a black colored dress. The young people seemed oblivious of the attention they are getting from all the other shoppers and mall security. You are a little taken a side by the style of clothing and extreme use of makeup and the blue and red hair. When I share this scenario with parents the most often cited question is "Are these youth some type of devil worshippers?"

History

OK, what is really going on here? Youth dressed like those mentioned above are frequently mistaken for Satan worshipers or the people who sacrifice animals or sometimes even witches. These youth are actually involved in a particular lifestyle and music scene. You have just encountered some young people who were involved in the Gothic scene, sometimes referred to as the Marilyn Manson movement. The youth are known as Goths. Among high school teenagers, this unique style of dress is increasing in popularity and can be found almost anywhere in the country.

The Gothic scene really is based in music this particular style has its roots in the heavy metal music scene that has been around since 1985. Between 1990 and 1997, the Gothic scene became extremely popular with the 14-24 year-old age group. There are a few Goths who are in there 30s and 40s. The Goth lifestyle focuses on the concepts of death, sex and the darker side of life. The followers of the scene can be of any race. The vast majority are Caucasians with only a few African-American, Latino and Asian Goths.

Gender wise, the scene is about 50 percent male and female. Contrary to a popular myth, the vast majority of Goths are not a criminal justice concern. Police get requests to respond when frighten citizens are concerned about these "devil kids, as one outraged elderly woman reported to me. Remember the different perspectives used to examine occult religions; legal, religious, media and mental health. Maybe from a religious point of view this youth may appear to be "devil kids," from the legal perspective most likely not. From a mental health point of view, some might conclude these youth have "issues." From the media perspective, wow lets sell some papers or have a nightly news special on "suspected devil worshipping youth." All are referring to members of the Goth scene. Has any penal code sections been violated by dressing in this fashion?

Malls, amusement parks, and Gothic nightclubs are popular hangouts for many Goths. The Goth scene had lost some popularity in the late 1990s, but there appears to be another resurgence of the movement in the early to mid 2000s.

As you probably guessed by now, high schools have become popular venues to show off Gothic attire. In a few schools, the student Goths were causing problems because they started casting spells on other students. Some school administrators also felt the special clothing and makeup were too distracting in school. A few high schools have dress codes that prohibit Goth styled clothing and makeup along with gang style clothing.

Music

There are a number of Goth bands that are popular. Probably, the most well known Gothic artist is Marilyn Manson. With a number of videos and albums Manson has set the tone for dress style, make up and trends for the music. A small splinter group of Gothic bands adds a racist overtone to the music. This type of music represents the influence of the white supremacist movement within the scene. A limited number of Goth publications also focus on the white supremacist movement. Therefore, it is possible that some Goths are racists and are connected to the skinhead movement.

There were a wide variety of bands that play in underground Gothic oriented nightclubs. The number of official Gothic nightclubs has diminished, but you can still find some that open once a month or once a week in many areas of the country. The nightclub scene attracts Goths and other youth to the venue. There is some anecdotal law enforcement evidence that suggests at some night clubs Goths have assaulted each other and non-Goths. This may also suggest that a particular type of Goth may be involved and not the general membership (Valdez, 2000).

Dress

Probably the first clue used to identify a Goth is the dress style. Black is the main color of choice and the clothes come in a variety of medieval styles. Some Gothic clothing may be designed from velvet fabric and will have a dark sexual flavor to them. The Gothic clothing may even be a dark blue or red color.

Some Goths prefer the PVC look. Their clothing is made of a Polyvinyl Chloride material and will have a shiny plastic appearance. Some Goths refer to this particular style of dress as "fetish wear." Some of the designs reveal much of the body. The material does not breathe well, so the clothes may become uncomfortable in warm weather. Some Goths also tend to wear long black colored PVC gloves.

This unique style of clothing can also be androgynous for the male Goth. Cross dressing is frequently encountered and readily accepted by male and female Goths. The cross dressing demonstrates a freedom of expression, which is important to many Goths. A few male Goths will cross-dress but the practice has not been that popular.

Some people will simply make a fashion statement by wearing Goth style clothing for a particular party or special occasions. Sometimes the eye-catching dress style can also show what mode the wearer is in. Goth fashion can be expensive with tee shirts running as high as $30.00 to $50.00 each. Considering that many of the Goths are unemployed and high school age, hello mom and dad. Some high school age Goths that I have spoken to have part time jobs and do well in school, but spend much of their money on Gothic style, music, icons, clothes and jewelry.

Goths can sometimes wear a special style of shoe or boot as well. Commonly the shoes have a thick heel and come in many colors. Black colored boots with buckles and pointed toes are also very popular with many Goths. A few Goths have explained that Goths who are also vampires tend to wear this particular style of boot.

Accessories

Besides the clothes, no Goth can be a Goth without the proper accessories. This might include a variety of silver colored rings, necklaces and icons. The five pointed star also known as the pentagram may be worn with a necklace. Other figures or icons can be displayed as tattoos, on tee shirts or as drawings might include dragons, medieval style crosses, skulls, skeletons, inverted crosses and crystals. Sometimes, Goths can also wear jewelry that is associated with the self-styled occult movement. This does not necessarily make the Goth wearer a practitioner of an occult religion or a self-styled occult religion. This becomes anecdotal evidence that suggests that gang behaviors are shared by all types of gangs and youth groups.

Most hardcore Goths will have their room decorated in dark colors, with black colored candles, maybe a silver chalice, skull shaped boxes, simulated skulls, or with bats and gargoyles. Some Gothic music artists will decorate their entire house this way, including bathtubs and bathrooms. The Gothic scene becomes a life style for these Goths.

The personal look of a Goth is just as important as the clothes. Therefore, many Goths dye their hair black or red. Both male and female Goths will paint their fingernails black and will wear black colored lipstick and some Goths will apply a white colored make up to make them appear dead. Facial makeup can be extreme, but for some Goths, even that isn't enough.

Body Modification

Many Goths will display some form of body art. For most of us, the thought of piercing ourselves is just something we would never really do. For some Goths, the tongue, lips, ears, eyebrows, nose, nipples, back and belly button are common body piercing locations. A few Goths have even had their genitals pierced. Other forms of body modification have included brands, scarring and inserting objects under the skin, like sterile marbles or shaped pieces. I met one Goth who had horns implanted in his forehead. This Goth told me the horns were a part of his self-expression. These types of body modifications will separate the hard core Goth from the high school age student who is experimenting with the scene.

You cannot forget the tattoos. Many Goths will tattoo themselves with primal types of designs. The tattoos can be placed anywhere on the body. Goths will also use common designs for tattoos. One female Goth proudly showed my partner and me a cute little butterfly on the top part of one of her breasts. I responded by saying, that's cool now, but by the time your sixty that will be a giant pterodactyl. She responded, Oh! I didn't think about that! Not all Goths go to an extreme with tattoos and body piercing.

Goth Subtypes and Behaviors

Fashion Goths

The fashion Goths tend to wear the stylized clothing only. These Goths wish to make a certain statement about themselves and express it through the style of clothes they wear. These Goths will go to a special party, a nightclub or dressed as a Goth. They will not wear the Gothic style of clothing until the next outing. They leave their Gothic interests at home. Many of these Goths function quite well in society and work. These Goths also tend to be a between 18-24 years old.

Younger Goths

There is a younger set of Goths, mostly found in the 12-20 year-old age group. These people are exploring the Gothic scene and may wear Goth style clothes and many dye their hair a red, black or blue color. The Gothic style of music will be an important part of their life. The lyrics talk about death, suicide, sex and the dark conflicts of life. There are a number of popular music videos as well. A lot of high school age Goths are in this category. For many of the youth, this will be a transitional experience. A few may live the lifestyle and take it with them on to college and for some the Gothic life style will follow them well into there 30s and 40s.

Hard-core Goths

A third group of Goths are the hard-core followers. All aspects of their life evolve around the Gothic scene. "One might get married in a cemetery, because of the peace and tranquility," as one 20 year-old female Goth explained to me. The hardcore Goths will also spend a lot of time in specialty shops that cater to the Gothic needs. These Goths live the scene with Gothic band members and band followers being found within this group. Some hardcore Goths tend to use extreme forms of body modification including scarifications and piercing.

Sex

A darker sexuality is explored in the Goth movement. For example, several Gothic magazines routinely examine bondage scenarios and some contain nudity and sexually explicit photos. Although the material may be suitable for adults, it may not be appropriate for minors to examine.

One of the more popular magazines is called, Blue Blood. The first time I looked at a copy, a 14 year-old male Goth gave it to me. There was a pictorial essay covering the pubic hair shaving of a female and subsequent sexual intercourse she had with her male friend at a beauty salon. I was surprised to find out that the kid's mom bought the magazine for him, without question.

I asked the mom if she knew what the magazine was about and she told me it was about the Marilyn Manson movement her son was in and that she did not find anything wrong with the magazine. I assumed she had looked at it since she was so defensive. I did not argue with her, I was just curious if she really knew what was in the magazine she provided to her son. As it turns out she had no idea the magazine was sexually explicit.

Occult Practices

A few Goths, I repeat, a few Goths are also self-proclaimed witches. Yes, it is true, a few Goths practice witchcraft. There is nothing illegal about that. If you are a Goth you are not automatically a witch. However, some witches and Pagans are Goths. Don't forget, Wicca is a nature based religion and protected under the First Amendment of the Constitution. I think the young people use the Goth scene to enhance their perception of what they think Wicca should be.

Most high school age self-proclaimed witches are just that. I find that very few really know what the belief system is all about and are not true practitioners of Wicca. However, based on their limited knowledge of the occult and Gothic style of dress the public often assumes these Goths are Satanists or Black Witches and they belong to a satanic cult. Unfortunately, this behavior just aids in stereotyping of Goths and true practitioners of Wicca.

Vampires

There are even a few Goths who claim to be Vampires. If you are a Goth you are not automatically a vampire, but some vampires are Goths. The vampire movement has gained nation-wide popularity in the mid to late 1990s, especially within the 14 to 24 year-old age group. This is probably due to a couple of factors. There was a game called, Vampire, the Masquerade. A Dayton, Ohio, Police Department sergeant said, "It is Dungeons and Dragons on steroids" (Williams, 1992). The game is centered on participant's role-playing being a vampire. In Vampire folklore, there are several klans of vampires, each having special powers.

For a few, the game becomes reality and the players believe they become the character they are playing. You might see people in costume playing the game. The goal is to become the strongest vampire and get rid of all your enemies using a variety of supernatural tools and powers. Well, it is easy to see that if a person already has a distorted sense of reality, this game will do wonders to enhance that distortion and might justify criminal actions. Remember, this fantasy world can become their reality.

The movement also caters to a certain group of people who are interested in the folklore and lifestyle of vampires.

Vampirism can also be used to explain some illness. There is a sub-category of vampires called psychic vampires. Physic vampires do not drink blood; instead they consume the life energies of their victim. A believer in the movement, when ill, justifies the illness by assuming they were victimized by one of these psychic vampires.

If you look at the dictionary definition of vampire, you will find a couple of meanings. Obviously, the first and most common, is a dead, blood sucking person who can turn into a bat and control your mind (Webster's Dictionary, 1996). Thanks in part to the movie industry, myth and folklore we have stereotyped an entity that we call a vampire. Don't forget that a darker form of sexuality is also explored here according the public stereotype of vampirism.

The secondary dictionary meanings refer to a predator or a seductive female who ruins men's lives (Webster's Dictionary, 1996). That is probably why the term "vamp" has been applied to unscrupulous women. It is the second set of meanings that might cause law enforcement to get involved. Vampires believe they get a type of energy and power from the blood they drink from their victims. The general rule is the more powerful the victim the more power is received by the vampire.

This mind set can have the potential to fuel criminal activity because the vampire believes that he or she is a powerful being, a predator and that humans are weak and are prey. Across the country there have been a few criminal cases that fit this scenario. Typically, a murder is committed by a small group of young people. The perpetrators may consume the victim's blood. Sometimes it is believed that the suspect(s) are involved in the Goth scene, quite often they are more involved in some obscure self-styled form of an occult religion or vampirism and dress like Goths. They may not really be involved in the Gothic scene.

Some Goths who are vampires will consume each other's blood. That is probably not a good idea because of the current health risks associated with human fluids. Some of these vampire Goths will keep blood vials that may contain a mixture of several people's blood. One 15 year-old vampire Goth boasted about drinking blood directly from a fresh wound on her boy friend. She even spoke of an over whelming feeling of relaxation as she drank his blood. She started her involvement in the Goth movement at age 11.

From a safety standpoint, you should be aware that some vampires will sport fangs. Although mainly worn for the look, a bite is a bite. Human bites are the most dangerous because of all the bacteria in the mouth. A person wearing fangs may be able to puncture the skin a little easier.

Summary

Most Goths will see how much they can get away with. Extreme make up designs, body modifications, extreme dress and hair color are just a few examples. A few Goths might be involved in delinquent or criminal behavior. Most will not be a law enforcement problem. In the late 1990s the Goth scene increased in popularity and in number partly due to the end of the world scenarios. Specialty shops catering to the scene can now be found in major malls. This may be a sign of the increased interest and size of the movement.

There are a number of Gothic Web sites. The Internet has become a useful tool to help recruit new members, announce venues for upcoming events and to communicate with peers. There are also so special slang words used by the Goths.

Juggalos

The Juggalos present a unique dilemma for law enforcement. Although considered a fan base for a music group by some, others feel the group qualifies to be defined as a street gang. As this text suggests it is ultimately the behaviors that qualify a group as a gang. Also as you are well aware by now, there are two definitions of a gang; sociological and penal code versions. Using the sociological definition some of the Juggalos are a gang; however behaviors by small number Juggalos qualify their cliques as a gang under a penal code definition.

History

In the early 1990s two Detroit, Michigan residents Joseph Bruce and Joseph Utsler started a street gang called the Inner City Posse. These two individuals were part of trio gangster rap group that used the same name. The Inner City Posse produced an album titled "Dog Beats." The gang was eventually overcome by the existing Detroit street gangs (Lefavor, 2009).

By 1991, Joseph Bruce claimed to have had a unique experience. Bruce believed he was visited by mysterious spirits that he called the "Dark Carnival" and the spirits advised him to spread the message of the "Dark Carnival" to anyone who would listen. The two decided to spread the "Dark carnival" message through music they would design. Shortly afterwards the two changed the name of their now duet rap group to the 'Insane clown Posse', also known as ICP. ICP produce six albums that are referred to as the "Joker Cards." The "Joker Cards" contain the messages from the "Dark Carnival" spirit messengers (Lefavor, 2009). The rapper names were 'Violent J' and 'Shaggy 2 Dope' (Beruman, 2008).

The first album was released in 1991-1992 and was titled the "Carnival of Carnage." This album refers to the Carnival that comes to drag you to heaven or hell. The second album, 'The Ringmaster" promotes a type of gang harmony and features a set of claws that represent rival gang signs of forks up and fork facing down as a symbol that all can have clown love. The third album is titled "the Riddle Box" and represents the vision many see when they die. When you turn the crank of the music box what pops out determines whether you go to heaven or hell. The fourth album is titled "the Great Milenko" and refers to Milenko as the master of illusion and who has the ability to allow people to see who they truly are. According to the lyrics the result is a hideous reflection of the evil soul.

The fifth album is called "the Amazing Jeckel Brothers: Jake and Jack" and refers to the war between good and evil. Jake is good and cares for the well being of people while Jack is sinister and evil. According to the storyline of this album when a person dies Jack and Jake juggle your sins that are in the form of balls. The more sins a person has the more balls have to be juggled. If a ball is dropped the person goes to hell. If they are able to juggle the balls without dropping one the person goes to heaven called Shangri-La. To complicate matters Jack is constantly trying to mess Jake up. The sixth album is titled "The Wraith" and refers to death, the entity that comes for a person at death (grim reaper). This is 'card' is represented in two albums: "Shangri-La and Hell's Pit." Each album aligns itself with the rewards one would get for leading a good and evil life (Beruman, 2008). The last album was released in 2004 (McDevitt, 2008).

The lyrics to the Joker Cards are vial by some standards. They refer to extreme forms of violence, including the murder of police officers. Many followers of the music identify with the theory that those people in higher, upper class look down upon those who live in the inner city, a form of class distinction. Many followers believe the government does not do enough to help those who are poor and in need. One essential belief is that the carnage and horror experienced in the inner cities should be taken to those who have turned their backs on the conditions in the inner cities.

Other followers believe the Joker Cards show the different sides of a person that can be improved upon. The Joker Cards help show the follower their own evils and weaknesses. The male followers of the "Dark Carnival" are called themselves Juggalos and the females Juggalettes. There is some anecdotal evidence to suggest the name Juggalo was given to the fan base by ICP and means the followers of the cark carnival (Beruman, 2008) ICP also been referred to as a rap horror group (McCoy, 2008).

Members

Juggalo membership appears to be drawn from the 13-30 year old age group. There is a small but significant female membership however; the majority of the members are male. Juggalos consider themselves family with a common origin; they are the outcasts of society (Beruman, 2008). One of the oldest mechanisms that facilitate gang formation begins with an excluded group who is affected by a bias real or perceived. The Juggalo mentality certainly fits here.

U.S. membership is estimated in the low thousands (McCoy, 2008 and Beruman, 2008). Exact membership population is difficult to estimate due to the gang definition issue. What started out as a group of music fans may have evolved into a gang that is associated with acts of violence, vandalism, arson, assault and murder. These are typical and well known gang behaviors.

The Juggalos sometimes refer to themselves as family and members will deny any type of gang affiliation. Juggalos can wear a distinct style and color of clothes; colors tend to be black, green, gray and red. Juggalos tend to like to wear a specific name brand of clothing called 'Hatchet Gear." ICP style and Hatchet Gear clothing can be purchased online and at specialty stores.

Some Juggalos will sport special tattoos. Many which appear to look like the clowns similar to those on the cover of the six Joker Cards or albums. A special Juggalo slang can also be used. On unique characteristic not seen with other street gangs is the use of stickers. The universal symbol for Juggalos is the silhouette picture of a man running with a hatchet. The stickers are usually bright colored and easy to see and they have the 'hatchet man' symbol. The stickers are placed on cars, notebooks, bedroom walls etc. Some tattoos are in the form of the running hatchet man.

One reason the hatchet man symbol might be so popular with the Juggalos is that it is the logo for the record label which produces the ICP music. The record label is known as Psychopathic Records.

Juggalo members often refer to themselves as homies, ninjas or family. While listening to music they will sometimes chant 'whoop, whoop, whoop, Juggalo.' The saying is in Juggalo music lyrics. There is another unique characteristic about the Juggalos. As a cohort they tend to favor a particular soda brand. Faygo soda is very popular with the Juggalos and has become an informal symbol of association or membership. Some Juggalos are known to carry hatchets and knives (McDevitt, 2008). Most Juggalos do have an issue with drug use or promiscuous sexual activity (Lefavor, 2009).

There is an annual event for all Juggalos called 'The Gathering.' It is sort of like a Woodstock gathering where all types of dark-rap bands play.

Criminal Activity

Some Juggalos have been involved in criminal activity. Some of the more notable media reported events have been in New Bedford, Massachusetts on February 2, 2006. A Juggalo entered a bar, ordered a drink and ask the bar tender if he was gay. The bar tender replied 'yes' and the Juggalo pulled out a hatchet and struck a patron in the head with it. Several other patrons in the bar tackled the male Juggalo to take the hatchet away. The Juggalo produced a handgun and shot indiscriminately injuring three people. He then fled the state and started a nationwide manhunt for Jacob Robido.

On February 4, 2006 in Gainesville, Arkansas a Gainesville Police Officer stopped a car. When the car pulled over Robido suddenly opened fire killing the officer and fled again.

In Norfolk, Arkansas on February 4, 2006 while being pursued by the police for the murder of the Gainesville officer Robido kills the female passenger in his car and then shoots himself in the head. He dies from his self inflicted gunshot wounds a short time later (McCoy, 2008). A subsequent search of his home revealed his connection and alliance to the Juggalo life style. The question here is what were the motives for his crimes? Did he do all this in the name of the Juggalos for further enhance the Juggalo reputation, or because Juggalos don't like gays, or the police are the enemies of the Juggalos? Or is this a case where a person committed a crime that was also a member of the Juggalos?

There is a difference and that is why I suggested it is the behaviors in totality that suggest whether or not this group is a social or penal code gang.

In Tacoma, Washington from June 18 to June 20, 2006 a group of Juggalos wearing clown makeup attacked and robbed nearly two dozen people using a machete while chanting "whoop, whoop, whoop Juggalo." The Juggalos threaten the victims with decapitation at Fort Steilacoom Park where the incident took place. The investigation resulted in seven arrests (McCoy, 2008). This case is a bit clearer as far as the gang motive. The chanting during the robberies suggests that the Juggalos are the perpetrators, announcing who is doing the crime. Announcing what group is doing a crime before, during or after is a consistent behavior associated with street gangs that qualify for the penal code definition of a violent street gang.

On February 4, 2007 in Lafayette, Colorado a 17 year old male who described himself as a Juggalo stabbed his girl friend's mother 18 times and attempted to dismember the victim. His girl friend a 15 year old Juggalo member and two of her friends were arrested for the murder (McCoy, 2008). Without knowing more about the circumstances surrounding the attack it is difficult at best to analysis this case. Each Juggalos case, as with each gang case should be analyzed individually.

The last case we'll examine occurred in Sacramento, California between September and December 1, 2007. More than 20 fires were started by four teenagers who claimed to be Juggalos. The fired caused over one million dollars in damage (McCoy, 2008). Here is a group behavior but without knowing the reason why the youth started the fires one cannot say with certainty if this group of Juggalos acted as street gang per the social or penal code definition.

Hybrid Gangs

He gang culture is constantly changing in some way. Sometimes there paradigm or small shifts if behaviors. These changes could include allowing members into a gang that traditionally would not have been granted access, changing a color or identifier for the gang. Changes may be more profound like not requiring gang tattoos and completely changing clothing styles. Other changes might be the existence of co-ed gangs where females are leaders or co-leaders. Finally changes may include forming alliances between gangs that re normally rivals. These types of changes cause the gang to change and in some instances become a hybrid gang.

History

Don't forget that gangs can form for a variety of reasons: protection, profit through criminal enterprises, and even based on certain political or religious philosophies. The two of the most common reasons have been for protection and criminal profit. Until the late 1980s gangs tended to follow similar genesis mechanisms and followed pre-established patterns of behavior. For example, following traditional membership rules that dictate all male membership or drawing membership from one particular ethnic group.

Understanding that the gang sub-culture is dynamic allows for recognition and identification of paradigm shifts in behaviors or trends. For example, the southwest Hispanic turf model for turf-oriented gangs has been followed for years and has been used to identify many street gangs and develop strategies to address gang issues. Today the traditional gang turf model may not accurately reflect turf trends for all Hispanic street gangs. This fact may also impact intervention, prevention and suppression programs. There is no one-size fits all remedy to the complex issues surrounding gangs. The biggest factor may be a community's demographics and dynamics.

For example, just look at how the entertainment industry has influenced and continues to influence our movie and music interests. In 1989, a year after the movie Colors was released, something happened to few traditional all-male Latino street gangs in Southern California. The gang membership structure and social dynamics changed. Non-Latinos were allowed into gangs that traditionally only allowed Latino members. The movie may have increased the popularity of the concept of Hybrid gangs. In essence the movie may have made the idea more in vogue with street gangs; Hybrid gangs were encountered shortly thereafter. The unique characteristics of these gangs caused law enforcement to label these groups Hybrid or Mutant street gangs. Are these the gangs of the future?

Membership

Some gangs once were only composed of males of the same ethnicity. Hybrid gangs tend to cross two membership barriers in 1989 and the early 1990s. The gangs started to accept and admit females and members of other races into their gangs. A once traditional all male Latino street gang could have Asian American, African-American, and White, mix race or female members. Females of any race could become gang members and may be actively involved in gang activities, including leadership. For traditional Latino gangs in southern California this was not traditional behavior.

However novel this was in 1989, the literature suggests that Hybrid gangs had been identified in the United States at least since the 1920s (Thrasher, 1927). In fact early Hybrid gangs were described mainly as mixed-race or mixed ethnicity (Starbuck, Howell and Lindquist, 2001).

I am not suggesting the movie "Colors" was the direct cause for the emergence of Hybrid gang in southern California or the nation. In the movie a Latino gang had White, Black and female members. Part of the story line focused on the rivalry against an African-American gang and the gang's battle against the police. A Hybrid gang played a central role in the movie. What the movie did was popularize the Hybrid gang that was already a phenomenon in the gang sub-culture. Focusing on this type of gang in the movie only aided in the recognition of this particular type of gang. It appeared that the Hybrid gang phenomenon became more popular throughout the country after the movie was released.

Law enforcement reported many types of Hybrid gangs that had formed in the between 1989 and 1999. As one gang member in Silver City, New Mexico, told me, "it was like a membership rule was removed." An L.A. based Latino gang member told me, "after the movie everyone was doing it... the movie kind of made it OK to allow anyone into your gang." More likely was the fact that a younger gang population identified with the already existing phenomenon and made it more popular. But the demographics within many gang neighborhoods had also changed. Most likely many social factors aided in re-establishing the Hybrid gang in the 1990s.

Changes

The Hybrid gangs of the 1990s led to the appearance of African-American street gangs with White or Latino female members or Latino street gangs with Asian-American members or Asian gangs with White, Latino and female members. Race and ethnic membership trends changed as well as rules concerning female membership and activity.

Another change that was observed was that many gangs that would formally claim association to Blood, Crip, Folk or People Nation street gangs. These hybrid gangs would demonstrate this allegiance by sporting the appropriate gang colors and using the appropriate graffiti and tattoos. This was probably done to enhance the gang's reputation more often than not there is no direct connection or formal association to the Blood, Crip, Folk or People gangs. The association seems to be in name only. For example, some sets of the Asian Boys gang claimed Crip affiliation and will identified with the color blue.

Some gangs that were normally rivals with each other formed associations that aided their money making operations or benefited the gang in some other manner. For example some West Coast based Crip gangs have formal associations with some Folk Nation gangs like the Black Gangster Disciples.

Another behavior change that was recognized was that some gang members started associating with several gangs. This was a behavior that prior to 1989 was rarely if ever encountered. In the 1990s many individual gang members changed gangs and loyalties for several reasons. Indo-Chinese gang members, especially Vietnamese gang members had no problem leaving one gang and join or working with another one. Some tagger and party crew gang members belonged to different crews simultaneously.

Profiles

In Orange County, California, Hybrid gangs first appeared between the later part of 1989 and early 1990. The majority of Orange County's street gangs are Latino because Orange County by history and demographics has a large population of Latinos.

These Hybrid Latino street gangs seem less territorial than their traditional counterparts. Some members did not even reside within the same area or even in the same city where the gang claims turf or hangs out. Gang members would wear some type of blue or black colored clothing if they claimed allegiance with the Crip street gangs. Red or green colored clothing could be worn if there is affiliation with the Blood street gang. At one time this Hispanic gang first aligned itself with the L.A. based Blood gangs; then switched to align with the L.A. based Crip gangs.

Some law enforcement anecdotal evidence suggests that some Hybrid gangs associate themselves with nationally well-known gangs and they tend to do so to enhance their street reputation. The Bloods, Crips, Folks and People are all well established street gangs that are known for their ruthlessness and violent tendencies. Their gang's reputation has instilled fear and awe within the sub-culture. The Hybrid gangs in an effort to establish themselves have associated with these groups to enhance their own reputation. This can give them instant credibility in the street, which is necessary for survival of the gang.

In other parts of the United States, Hybrid gangs formed alliances with the Folk or People Nations. This is especially seen in the Midwest and the East Coast. These hybrid gangs can also wear certain color of clothing and/or stylized clothing. Do not forget there is also a Crip and Blood gang influence in the Midwest and east coast. By the mid to late 1990s West Coast based Crip gangs had aligned themselves with the Folk Nation gangs and the west coast Blood gangs aligned themselves with the People Nation gangs furthering Hybrid gang growth in the early 2000s.

Also remember a Sureno gang formed in New Mexico during the middle part of the 1990s? This Sureno gang is another example of the Hybrid gang phenomenon. Rival Los Angeles based Latino gang members formed a new gang in New Mexico in order to facilitate drug trafficking efforts. In L.A. these gang members would fight each other and out of state they are working together. Criminal activity may also fuel the growth of hybrid gangs.

Since the emergence of Hybrid gangs, many types of hybrid gangs have been identified. For example, law enforcement has encountered white Crip and Blood gang members. The gender barrier has also been broken with these types of gangs. The Hoover Folk gang from Little Rock, Arkansas is a great example of female gang involvement in a multi-ethnic Crip Hybrid gang.

Another of Hybrid gang became known as the SHARPs, others were straight edge skinhead gangs. The acronym SHARP stands for Skinheads Against Racial Prejudice and does not maintain a racist attitude like traditional skinheads. In fact, the SHARPS are bitter rivals with the Neo-Nazi skinheads and do not follow the white supremacist movement.

The SHARPS are often waging war against the traditional skinhead groups. SHARP membership can include African-American, Asian, Hispanic and Jews who are normally not permitted to join skinhead gangs. The SHARPS and Skinheads share the same style of clothing, but SHARPs do not use swastikas, lightning bolts, etc., in their tattoos and graffiti, tattoos, clothing and writings. No racist's symbols are used in SHARP graffiti and tattoos.

Some Straight edge gangs have a skinhead membership who do not use drugs, alcohol or engage in promiscuous sex. Yet will maintain a racist attitude consistent with the white supremacist movement. As the name implies, the membership is clean in regard to substance abuse. Edgers may wear stylized clothing associated with traditional skinhead groups.

Some Latino based gangs have co-ed leadership and female members that participate in criminal activities. Other Latino gangs have given up identifying with the traditional turf concept that was developed in the 1930s and 1940s in southern California. Across the country some Latino based gangs will claim the entire city they are located in as their turf rather than a small geographic location within a specific area of the city. For many gangs the concept of turf has taken on a fluid nature and when the gang travels their temporary turf is where ever they stop.

Some Hybrid gangs in the Midwest and East Coast may adopt and use a gang name that suggests the gang is from the southern California. For example, Sur-13, Sureno-13, MS-13 and 18th Street gangs are well established in the Midwest and along the eastern seaboard. Even though the name implies the gang is from Los Angeles and it is assumed that the gang has connections to their LA based counterparts, they do not. More often than not the gang is not related to southern California based gangs with the same name.

Lastly, some gangs have combined to form alliances and will follow a specific leader and are called Nations. The numbers of gangs that align themselves with the Folk, People, Vice Lord and Almighty Latin King Nations are examples of this type of consolidation. These gangs have been referred to as Super Gangs because of their size, organization, and business like attitude toward criminal money making enterprises (Savelli, 2000). Super Gangs also tend to be more highly organized with leadership flow charts, specific codified rules and punishments for rule violations (Starbuck, Howell and Lindquist, 2001).

Examples of these behaviors changes can be noted with west coast Crip gangs aligning with Folk Nation gangs. In the past these gangs had been rivals. The same change can be encountered with west coast Blood gangs that have aligned themselves with the People Nation gangs.

Membership

Membership in this particular type of street gang seems to include the younger and trendier youth population. Hybrid gang membership can start at any age, but tends to be in the early teens on the West Coast. The total size of a hybrid gang also tends to be smaller or the same size as many medium sized African-American or Latino street gangs. However the ability and potential for Hybrid gangs to commit acts of violence is just the same.

In parts of the country where there are very small minority populations, it should not be surprising to find all white gangs sharing indicia of membership of Hispanic, Asian, Black, Folk or People street gangs. Some gangs could also be of mixed race. Remember the Nazi Low Rider gang or the Tiny Rascal Gang from California? The membership in these gangs becomes part of the evidence that supports this theory.

Asymptomatic Gang Members

A unique type of gang member has been found in some Hybrid street gangs. They are referred to as non-profiled gang members. Even though they are gang members in good standing, they share none of the traditional membership indicia normally associated with gang membership. Typically these gang members have never been or have had very few police contacts. Their names may not be found in any gang intelligence database. Many of these gang members tend to be gainfully employed and often do well at school. Some have even been honor roll students in high school or college. Non-profile gang members may not sport any gang style tattoos or wear any of the traditional stylized gang clothing. Many do not associate with their gang on a regular basis but rather on a part time basis.

These gang members from all outward appearances appear not to be associated with any street gangs. Unfortunately, that is far from the truth. Non-profile gang members have successfully shielded their membership from their family, school, work and church. It is not uncommon to be prosecuting a person for a gang related homicide that has never been arrested and has no prior documented gang contacts nevertheless the defendant is a part time active gang member or even a gang leader.

Part time membership may be due to the fact that the non-profile gang member lives out of the normal gang neighborhood. He or she may come back to the neighborhood or the area where the gang associates once a month to visit family and friends. It might even be while sharing a weekend with a divorced or separated parent. While present the non-profile gang member will take part of gang related activities, including criminal acts.

The number of hybrid street gangs continues to grow. In an ever-changing environment this type of street gang may become more prevalent in the future. During the late 1990s and early 2000s the impact of these street gangs on the overall gang population is continuing to change. This type of gang membership may become the model for future gangs. Actually, this membership model has helped develop the multi-racial street gangs we find today.

Indicium

Clothing

Like many street gang members, the hybrid gang member may choose to wear basic white, tan and black clothing. These colors, for the most part, indicate gang membership status, but no outward or obvious specific gang affiliation. This color combination is sort of a neutral gang uniform. The pants may also be worn low in the manner of traditional Latino street gang member. Baseball caps and athletic shoes are also commonly worn. If gang attire is worn these gang members also favor traditional gang style clothing and color combinations. Sometimes these gang members do not wear any type of gang attire.

Tattoos

Tattoos when displayed are shown with the same zeal that most gang members share. The tattoos may indicate the gang name and/or the names of the gang members. Hybrid gang members can wear or display a variety of tattoos, depending on which gang they affiliate with. For the most part these gang members will use all the same type of tattoos that most street gangs use however they may be concealable with certain types of clothes or located in a place that is normally not seen in public.

Graffiti

Hybrid gang graffiti generally follows the graffiti patterns of other gangs. Since turf may not be as important as it is for traditional street gangs, hybrid gang graffiti can be seen in a number of different locations. It may be used to announce their transient presence and not necessarily as a territory marker. For hybrid gangs that claim turf graffiti would become more important.

Criminal Activity

The age or the size of the hybrid gang unfortunately does not affect the type of criminal activity the gang is involved in. This implies that hybrid gangs can be involved in auto thefts, assaults, drug sales and homicides.

At one time the consistent motivation for the hybrid gang activity seemed to be money, a good time and to party. However, hybrid gangs currently exist for protection, status, and turf, and for profit, and a few based on a certain belief system.

The use of all types of drugs and alcohol can facilitate a gang philosophy to go out and be crazy. The propensity for violence for hybrid gangs is substantial. The violence is usually unpredictable and indiscriminate for the most part and may be the result of a chance encounter with a rival gang. Some hybrid gangs have maintained a traditional street gang personality and will react to a real or perceived act of disrespect or insult.

Recent Trends

The strange relationships between Los Angeles-based Crip and Blood sets and the Folk and People Nation gangs will continue to develop. A few Folk Nation-based gangs have associations Crip sets most likely for financial benefit. These hybrid relationships can sometimes be detected in gang graffiti. Some non-African-American street gangs will continue to associate themselves with the Crips or Bloods to enhance reputations.

Since the race barrier has been broken in some African-American gangs White membership in these gangs will continue, but will be limited. Some law enforcement officers theorize the White gang members may be used in drug sales or transportation operations in predominately White neighborhoods.

Law enforcement anecdotal evidence suggests that some Hispanic gangs no longer claim a particular turf. The concept of turf has become fluid for some Hybrid and traditional gangs. Some members of Hybrid gangs can also live in different cities or counties and will visit the gang on a part time basis.

Summary

In general street gangs tend to share certain generic behaviors and tend to follow general trends. However, gang trends and behaviors can and do change. They may be influenced by the media, entertainment industry or by youth movements, law enforcement suppression programs, criminal activity, gang rivalries or other factors. Hybrid gangs usually use the same terminology as the group they affiliate with. For example, if the group claimed allegiance to the Bloods, verbal gang slang will most likely be Blood gang related. The same holds true if Latino, Black or Skinhead gangs influence the Hybrid gang heavily.

The majority of Hybrid gang activity is believed to be prevalent in the Midwest region of the country (Starbuck, Howell and Lindquist, 2001). But Hybrid gangs can be found throughout the United States.

Midwest and East Coast Gangs

The genesis of street gangs along the East Coast and in the Midwest started well before the 1900s. Don't forget about the Irish street gangs of the 1800s. Some street gang in this region of the country started in prison; then spread to the streets. Some gangs started on the streets and later became membership power basis for existing prison gangs. All were interested in money and control of turf just as their west coast counterparts.

History

Examining the history of gangs in the Midwest and East Coast you conclude that the street gang phenomenon started in the late 1890 to early 1900s. Like Los Angeles, California, Chicago, Illinois has been the home to street gangs for over 100 years.

By 1899, the Five Points gang of New York was major recruitment pool for the young Sicilian Mafia. Leading the Five Points gang were immigrants Paolo Vaccarelli (aka: Paul Kelly) and his second in command Johnny Torrio. Torrio later became a member of the Mafia. The Mafia became established in New York and Chicago. A well-known gangster of the 1930s was also born in Brooklyn in 1899, Alphonse Capone. Capone joined the James Street gang and became known on the streets as "Scarface." The James Street gang was under the wing of the Five Points gang. One of Al Capone's childhood friends and member of the Five Points gang was Lucky Luciano (Savelli, 2000).

In 1919, Scarface moved to Chicago when he was called by Johnny Torrio to help control mob activities and was motivated to move quickly because the local authorities were looking for him over a mob related murder. Al Capone eventually became the most violent gangster in Chicago (Savelli, 2000). The reason this little bite of history is important is because the Al Capone style of gansterism molded the American gang experience and continues to influence America's street gangs (Savelli, 2000). This has been especially true in Chicago and the East Coast.

As the "gangsters" flourished in the 1920s and 1930s gangs became a symbol of lower income level life and the ethnic ghettos in Chicago. As Mexican street gangs were developing in the west coast between 1940 and 1950 gangs like the Latin Kings and the Vice Lords formed in Chicago. During the mid 1960s the 18th Street gang formed inn Los Angeles. In Chicago gangs the Savage Skulls, La Familia, Rampers and Savage Nomads formed in New York. One Ramper's gang member that became nationally known was Sammy "The Bull" Gravano (Savelli, 2000).

The local criminal justice system responded as they did in the West Coast. Gang and mob members were prosecuted for their crimes and sent to jail and prison. As the gang activity increased the more gang members were arrested, convicted and sent away. Some of the modern Midwest and east coast gangs had their genesis in prison.

Prison gangs started to form within the Illinois state prison system during the 1920s. These gangs were introduced onto the Chicago streets when the prisoners were paroled or released from prison. These early Chicago street gang members were mostly White career criminals.

As the Chicago defense industry slowed down at the end of World War II, many people who had moved to city for employment found themselves without a job. Within a short period, the prisons began to fill up with the unemployed workers, many who happened to be Black or Hispanic. During the 1950s and 1960s, these inmates formed additional prison gangs. These prison gang members when paroled would return to the streets and often return to neighborhood they called home. The constant influx gang members resulted in a growth in street gang activity.

Black Gangster Disciples

Between 1963 and 1964 two gangs emerged from the south side of Chicago. The Black Disciples and the Blackstone Rangers would eventually become two of the most powerful street gangs in Chicago. The Black Disciples were also known as the Black Disciple Nation. The largest gang to emerge during this growth period was the Blackstone Rangers. Jeff Fort and Eugene Harrison founded the Blackstone rangers.

The Blackstone Rangers believed the most organized gang attained national recognition and had support from prominent businessmen, politicians and entertainers. The gang had the support of W. Clement Stone a self-made millionaire and claimed to have entered into business ventures with Sammy Davis Jr. However the highlight of political influence came when Jeff Fort was invited to President Richard Nixon's inauguration. The Blackstone Rangers later became known as the "El Rukns" (Emery, unknown year).

During this time David Barksdale was the leader of the Black Disciple Nation. Barksdale was well respected and known; eventually he became the moist revered street gang organizer in Chicago.

A third street gang was growing and gaining strength in the Chicago area during this time. Known as the Gangsters, they were led by a young man named Larry Hoover. In order to try and maintain control of the street leaders of the Blackstone Rangers and the Black Disciples nation began courting Hoover in an effort to assimilate his gang. Jeff Fort leader of Blackstone Rangers made an offer to Hoover, but it only gave Hoover the position of ambassador within the gang. This was not satisfactory with Hoover and the proposed merger never developed.

In January, 1969 David Barksdale, leader of the Disciple Nations developed a broader vision about the mission of his gang. Barksdale was apparently tired of all senseless gang related violence that was disrupting the African-American community. He made a unique and tempting offer to Larry Hoover. Barksdale proposed merging the two gangs together and sharing equal power with Hoover. Hoover accepted ending forever ending the bloodshed between the gangs and the Black Gangster Disciple Nation (BGD Nation) was formed (Emery, unknown year).

This merger also made the Blackstone Rangers rivals of Black Gangster Disciples. Surprisingly, Larry Hoover was not a Chicago native. Hoover was born in Jackson, Missouri on November 30, 1950. In 1954 his family moved to Chicago and by 1973 he was sent to prison for a gang related murder. In 1997 Hoover was transferred to the Colorado State Penitentiary where he still controls the gang.

Larry Hoover also known as "King Hoover" while incarcerated led the BGD gang and developed the gang into a sophisticated retail drug network worth approximately 100 million dollars a year. Some experts consider the BGD the one of, if not the largest and most successful gang in the history of the country partly because the members are well disciplined and trained (Tyson, 1996).

The BGD gang is so organized the there are two different board of directors. One board controls street activities and the second to monitor and control the gang's prison population that is estimated between 5000 and 10,000. The chairman of the board is Hoover. Under each director there are approximately 15 governors that control drug trafficking operations within specific geographical areas. Typically each governor controls four regents.

Areas are normally sub-divided regents who supply illegal drugs and oversee drug trafficking locations within their assigned area. On the streets area coordinators collect revenues from drug sales from specific locations and transfer the money hourly to their regent. In prison, the area coordinator has hands on control of each location and its assigned security squad.

Enforcers handed out fines and punishments for violations of gang rules. Violations can include drug use and abuse, stealing from another member, showing disrespect to another member or engaging in homosexual rape, for being a bad sport, for not keeping in shape or being clean. When a member is violated (punished) it can include probation, a beating or death.

Shorties are new or young members who staff the drug dealing locations and sell drugs. The gang lures young recruits from the poor and jobless communities and promises easy cash usually 50 to 200 dollars a day (Tyson, 1996 and Newsweek, 1996).

Besides being organized in narcotic trafficking there is a semi-religious and discipline component to gang membership. The Folk's prayer is commonly recited: When I die show no pity. Bury me in deep in gangsta city. Lay two pitchforks across my chest. Tell my brothers and sisters I did my best.

Yummy

Gang rules are for discipline and often are memorized and strictly adhered to, but not always. Eleven year-old Robert "Yummy" Sandifer was murdered by two teenage BGD gang members a few days after Yummy shot two youths, killing one. Robert was shot twice in the back of his head and he was also a member of the BGD gang.

This 1994 Chicago incident sparked outrage and many asked the question, how could this have happened? Robert was well known by the Chicago authorities. He was a product of less than ideal home. As a baby he was burned and beaten. As a student he missed more school days than he attended. He was shuttled between homes, detention centers and gang safe houses. The police arrested Robert many times, but under Illinois law he could only be sentenced to probation. Robert was too young to be lodged at a juvenile home and his neighbors considered him a thug. Robert was involved in car theft, extortion, assault and list goes on. He was a young out of control gang member.

The public guardian assigned to Robert's case felt that he was a sociopath by the time he was three years old. Ironically, Robert's mother called him "an average 11 year old." Robert's mother was the third of 10 children from four fathers and she never knew her own father. She had her first child at fifteen, then another, Robert was her third child, eventually Robert's mother had five more children. She dropped out of 10th grade, found an apartment while nursing a crack habit. Robert's mother tried living with his father for a while. He was later convicted on drug and weapons charges and had a rather hot temper. Their living arraignment did not work out.

Robert's mom was arrested 41 times by the time she was 29 years old. She commented that Robert should have never died. The system could have saved Robert according to her. She insists that the court should have placed Robert in therapy and saved him. In 1986, a court psychiatrist warned there was no reason to believe that Robert's mom will be able to adequately meet her own needs, let alone meet the needs of her growing family. Robert was three years old then (Grace and Hull, 1994).

Youth killing youth is not a formal gang law. Police theorize that Robert was hit (killed) on order from one of the gang's leader and the two juveniles who were ultimately arrested for Robert's murder were under orders. For whatever reason, someone thought Robert was a liability to the gang. There was no evidence that suggested that Robert was following a BGD order. Robert was a young criminal, experienced on the street and a member of the BGD. His gang membership was partly the cause of his death, along with other factors. Ultimately, Robert died because peer gang members were following an order. Unfortunately, Robert wasn't only victim, there have been and will be more. Gangs required loyalty and obedience. Some gang members tend to be well disciplined and trained.

During the 1980s, the prison gang membership grew again. This time the prison gangs formed two factions, which fought for control of the prison rackets. These gangs aligned themselves with either the Folks or People Nation. One group composed of former Blackstone Rangers allegedly spoke for the disadvantaged people. They became known as the People Nation. The second group known as the Disciples wanted to build a nation for all folks. This group became known as the Folk Nation and can trace its history back over 30 years. The Folk and People names are used to show alliances for hundreds of street and prison gangs that operate in the Midwest, East Coast, South and, in a few instances, the West. The BGD align themselves with the Folk Nations and the El Rukns align themselves with the People Nations.

Vice Lord Nation

The Vice Lord Nation (VLN), originally called the Conservative Vice Lords, is one of the largest and most violent associations of street gangs in the country. The Voce Lord Nation is really a collection of structured gangs located in 28 states. In fact the FBI reports the Vice Lord Nation is a violent African-American street gang even though there are reported incidences of Caucasian and Latino members. The FBI also states that the Vice Lord Nation gang is the oldest gang in Chicago (FBI, 1994).

There are a couple of versions that explain the genesis of this gang. The FBI reports unidentified juveniles formed the gang in the 1958 at the Illinois State Training School for Boys at St. Charles. Once the juveniles were released they formed the gang in the Lawndale area of Illinois in order to defend themselves against other existing street gangs.

In the second version of history the CVL were formed in 1958 in the south side of Chicago by a group of juveniles who had met at Illinois State Training School for Boys at St. Charles. The gang was formed for protection against other gangs and for profit. The gang was initially only had 10 to 20 African-American members.

Both versions of history are very similar. After the gang was formed the membership grew. Recruitment was brisk and CVL also started to assimilate smaller gangs. During the 1960s CVL developed an informal structure, continued to increase membership in an effort to control the neighborhood and for protection against rival gangs. Leaders were recognized even though there was no formal structure. The gang was involved in organized criminal activity that became a money-generating vehicle.

By the early 1970s the CVL gang became involved in the distribution of methamphetamine and marijuana. Drug trafficking became a major money generator. By 1971 the gang was so large it was no longer a single gang but rather a formal association of a many gangs. The CVL became the Vice Lord Nation (VLN). Some of the larger gangs within the nation were the Four Corner Hustlers, Traveling Vice Lords, Unknown Vice Lords and the Mafia Insane Vice Lords.

By the mid 1970s the VLN gangs were heavily involved in the distribution of cocaine in the west side of Chicago. By then late 1970s the VNL narcotics trafficking and violent crimes landed many leaders in prison or killed them. This weakened the gang's activity and slowed growth.

By the middle 1980s the VLN gangs again had become a dominant distributor of cocaine and heroin on Chicago's West Side and were moving into the North Side and South Side. During this time VNL members started to migrate into other areas of Illinois and into neighboring states. The gang was very efficient and organized. By 1989 it was trafficking cocaine, heroin, crack and marijuana in eight states.

By the 1990s VLN members grew so much that law enforcement estimated the VLN members between 30,000 and 35,000. The gang continued to grow and operated in many states. By the early 2000 the gang's leadership was restructuring to consolidate power under a board of directors. Narcotics trafficking levels allowed VNL gang members to deal directly with Nigerian and Mexican drug cartels.

The VLN is a People Nation affiliate and allied with the Almighty Latin Kings, Black P Stone Nation, Blackstone Rangers, Cobra Stones, El Runs, Gaylords, Insane Deuces, Insane Unknowns, Bloods, Latin Brothers, Latin Pachucos, Spanish Lords, Villa Lobos and other gangs including the Latin Kings in and out of prison.

Following this alignment rivals of the VLN would include Folk Nation aligned gangs including, but not limited to Black Gangster disciple Nation, La Raza, Ashland Vikings, Latin Disciples, Insane Popes, Maniac Latin Disciples, Spanish Gangster Disciples, Spanish Cobras, Black Souls, Crips, International Posse and the Supreme Gangsters (FBI, 1994).

Latin Kings

The literature provides a variety of histories describing the genesis of the Latin Kings (LK). The original gang has been reported to have formed in Chicago as early as the 1940s (Savelli, 2000), during the mid 1960s (FBI, 2004) and in the mid 1970s (Daily, 2000). Early membership was primarily Hispanic and the gang also became known as the Almighty Latin Kings (ALK). However it is also reported that the gang formed in South Chicago and the Humboldt Park area during the mid 1970's and later developed factions in almost every Hispanic Chicago community (Daily, 2000).

By the 1970s the Latin Kings were one of the largest and violent Hispanic gangs in Chicago. The group may have spread to the east Coast through the prison system during the 1980s. Two inmates in a Connecticut state prison started the Almighty Latin King Nation of Connecticut during this time. These gang members fine tuned the Chicago version of the Latin Kings and wrote the King Manifesto. This was a formal gang produced document that incorporated beliefs and prayers. The ALK nation of Connecticut gang spread within the Connecticut penal system and quickly became the largest gang in Connecticut (Savelli, 2000).

In 1986 the King Manifesto was introduced in the New York prison system and a new gang the Almighty Latin Kings were formed at Collins Correctional Institution. Within a few years the ALK gang spread throughout the New York penal system and then onto the streets as the incarcerated ALK members were released. By the early 1990s New York State had hundreds of ALK gang members. By the late 1990s the ALK gang membership had grown into the thousands (Savelli, 2000).

According to the FBI in the 1980s after a lengthy power struggle with members of the Chicago based LK, the Connecticut and New York based LK gangs broke away and formed the Almighty Latin King Charter Nation (ALKCN) and the Almighty Latin King and Queen Nation (ALKQN) and both factions operated independently from the Chicago based LK (FBI, 2004). This implies that the New York and Connecticut based LK gangs were already formed and functioning.

In another perspective, the Almighty Latin King Nation was formed at Rikers Island prison, New York (unknown date). The Latin King Nation, Almighty Latin King Nation and the Almighty Latin King and Queen Nation are based on the east coast but still maintain connections with the Chicago based Latin King street gang. The terms ALKN and LK are both used interchangeably by the Almighty Latin king Nation (Daily, 2000).

The majority of ALKN and Chicago based LK gang membership is predominately Puerto Rican males, however a number of Spanish, Portuguese, Italian and South Americans have been allowed to join the gang (FBI, 2004). There was a reported trend that the LK were trying to recruit Caucasians into the gang. A predominately Caucasian faction of the LK gang reportedly formed in the Southwest Side of Chicago. In the New York City area Latin Kings recruit children as young as eight years old into the gang (Daily, 2000).

The national estimated ALKN gang membership varies. ALKN gangs have been reported in Connecticut, New Jersey, New York, Illinois, Iowa, Wisconsin, Indiana and Florida (Daily, 2000). However the FBI reports that the Latin Kings are now in 34 states with an estimated membership between 25,000 and 50,000. There are estimated 20,000 Latin King gang members in the Chicago area alone (FBI, 2004).

Like many of the larger Midwest and East Coast gangs, the leadership structure of the Latin Kings is formal and organized. Like the Vice Lords and Gangster Disciples, Latin King gang leadership takes on local, regional and national roles. By late 2004 the heaviest presence of the Latin Kings was in New York, Illinois, New Jersey, Florida and Texas.

Criminal activity by the Latin Kings is not limited to murder and attempted murder. Other primary criminal activities include but are not limited to narcotics and weapon trafficking, armed robbery, assault, kidnapping, auto theft, money laundering, extortion, racketeering, public corruption and human trafficking. In addition like some more organized gangs LK gang members have opened legitimate businesses. The narcotic trafficking has gotten so large that some LK factions have developed relationships with gang in Texas to supply drugs.

Several of the larger Midwest based gangs have a religious component to gang membership. The Folk Nation aligned gangs use the Folk's prayer. The Latin Kings also have a prayer: "Almighty father, King of Kings, hear us as we come before you, one body, mind and soul, true wisdom, knowledge and understanding. Give us strong brown wisdom, for we realize you are the best and wisest of all seeing eyes."

In addition to a gang prayer the ALK gang also has unique customs and practices not observed with West Coast based street or prison gangs. For example, if a male member marries his wife is called a Queen by ALK law. If they have a child, he or she automatically becomes a prince or princess of the ALKN (Daily, 2000).

In late 2004, the leader of the ALKN in the state of New York was Antonio Fernandez, known on the streets as "King Tone." He publicly espouses a Puerto Rican nationalism and at least publicly is trying to change the focus of the gang to a group that tries to improve the lives of the impoverished. In 2004 a HBO America Undercover special focused on the King Tone's efforts.

Membership Characteristics

The Chicago based Folk and People Nation gangs have strict dress codes and use body language as part of their non-verbal forms of communication. A simple act of crossing the arms is a form of announcing your gang association. All Chicago area Folk and People Nation gangs rely heavily on using subtle body-English as forms of communication as well as traditional verbal and written methods.

Numbers are also part of the communication process. For example, the gangs that ally themselves with the Folks Nation identify with the number 6. The gangs that associate themselves with the People Nation identify with the numeral 5. Combinations of numbers can also be used to show gang affiliation. Numbers can also be used as part of coded writings and in graffiti.

Colors play an important part in this gang sub-culture. Folk street gangs often use the colors blue and black. The People street gangs tend to use the colors red and black. The colors can be worn in clothing or hats and even fingernail polish. For example, a specific color of railroad bandanna may be worn to show gang affiliation.

Many Chicago- based street gang members are only wearing clothing that is colored black and white in an attempt to hide their gang affiliation. These gang members have realized the distinctive stylized clothing they wore not only gave them instant recognition amongst their peers and rivals, but with law enforcement as well.

These neutral colors announce that the wearer identifies with the gang sub-culture but does not identify a particular gang affiliation. The Blood and Crip gang members on the West Coast are using the same strategy because stylized clothing is easy for the police to identify. In the West Coast this strategy is sometimes called, "low pro," referring to keeping a low profile from the police.

Gang graffiti may be written using a certain color that would indicate gang alignment.

Right- Left Orientation

The Folk and People street gangs identify with opposite sides of the body. The Folk gangs place importance on the right side, and the People gangs place importance on the left side. This is the type of body English I was previously referring to. This orientation becomes so significant that it impacts the way a person wears a baseball cap. The side the brim is tilted to the right or left announcing a particular gang affiliation. The body side orientation is even important when crossing your arms, this can announce gang affiliation.

This right-left side importance can even dictate on which ear an earring is worn or what hand a glove will cover. The right-left side rule also applies to belt buckles, colored bandannas worn tied around a leg, and even whether or not a gym shoe is fully laced up on the right or left foot. The rule even indicates which pant leg partially rolled up.

During the early 2000s this right/left orientation became popular with some West Coast youth, a few gang members and some music entertainers.

Symbols

Symbols also have a special significance for the Folk and People Nation gangs. Specific symbols often represent gang affiliation and are used for the same purposes as their west coast counterparts. Whether in writings, tattoos or in graffiti the symbols can mark off turf boundaries, announce gang presence or declare gang affiliation. Graffiti marked over or displayed inappropriately is taken as an insult or challenge. As with any street gang, all insults and challenges must be responded to.

A six-point Star of David represents affiliation with the Folk Nation while the five-pointed star represents affiliation with the People Nation. The points of the stars have special quasi-religious meanings to the gang members. For example, on the six-pointed star each of the points stands for (clockwise) Life, Loyalty, Knowledge, Wisdom, Understanding and Love. These definitions are called the six principles of King David.

Other symbols that have significance for the Folk Nation gangs are pitchforks that represent the Nations power to overcome suppression. The sword represents the life and death struggle within the Nation and the struggle to survive. Devil's horns are used to represent the determination to overcome all obstacles. The devil's tail is used to symbolize the oppression that all non-white people suffer. The heart symbolizes the love the individual member has for the Nation. The numbers 7 and 8 are used to represent the year the Sons and Daughters were founded.

These symbols can all be incorporated into a single symbol using the six-pointed star as the base. Anyone can use these symbols to show affiliation with the Folk Nation gangs. Sometimes a symbol of a rounded crown is also used to show Folk Nation affiliation (Gang Prevention Incorporated, 1997).

There are specific symbols that People Nation gangs identify with. A circle can be used to symbolize the 360 degrees of knowledge that African-Americans used to rule the world and will again. Fire represents the Nations knowledge of being suppressed and the inability to reach that knowledge because of the heat caused by the fire. Darkness represents the African-American majority worldwide. Crescent moons are used to show that the Black Nation is divided into east and west. The five-pointed star represents the eye of Allah watching over his people.

A pyramid is sometimes used to symbolize physical, mental and spiritual knowledge. A sun can be used to represent the rising of truth. The top hat represents shelter. The cane and gloves are used to symbolize strength and purity to the majority membership of these two groups, who are composed of African-Americans.

Two of the larger gangs that identify with the Folk and People Nations are the Black Gangster Disciples and the Vice Lords. These street gangs exchange insults and challenge each other by displaying their rival's symbols upside down or by displaying a five or six- pointed star being blown apart. This is the equivalent to west coast gangs crossing out their rival's graffiti. According to a Youth Officer of the Chicago Police Department, the Chicago area gangs have already started to cross out rival gang graffiti, once just a west coast gang characteristic. Folk or People Nation gang members can be White, African-American or Latino descent, however at times the membership is ethnically based (Simandle, 1992).

Gang members can also communicate by simple code. Each letter of the alphabet has been given a number. It is not uncommon for gang members to speak in code when in public. Sometimes the codes can be a little more complicated and the gang will use symbols to represent the letters of the alphabet.

Membership

The leadership structure of many Folk and People Nation gangs normally consists of the original founder and core of members who started the gang. Membership can have four levels depending on the gang member's commitment to the gang. Hard-core members are considered to be unwavering in their loyalty to the gang. While associate members believe in unity and loyalty to the gang however, they will leave their loyalty behind when self-preservation becomes an issue. Marginal or fringe members allow outside activities to influence their loyalty to the gang. These members always have their loyalty tested. The outsider is a term that refers to a person who usually joins the gang to make money and they tend to be in their late teens or early twenties (Simandle, 1992).

Like other American street gangs the Folk and People Nations gangs use hand signs are also commonly used to show affiliation with a particular Nation gang. The handsign can also be a form of greeting or challenge or intimidation. East Coast street gangs can sometimes tell a story of their gang by using hand signs in series along with music. These gangs refer to this as stacking and music does not always have to be used.

Representing is the gang term that describes the act of identifying yourself as a gang member and showing your affiliation to a particular gang. The common West Coast gang term that refers to this is claiming. Representing can be done by verbal acknowledgment, by using hand signs, by wearing clothing in certain way or using body orientation such as crossing of the arms. Most of the Midwest and East Coast female gangs have held auxiliary positions supporting the male gang counterpart. Female gang members at one time tended not to be leaders or plan criminal activity in Midwest and East Coast based gangs. This is not true for their West Coast counterparts where female gang members can be co-leaders of co-ed gangs and leaders in all female gangs.

Crime

Folk and People Nation gang members are involved in all types of criminal activity, from car thefts to drug sales. Narcotic trafficking networks can be large and complex, and involve the use of extortion, intimidation and retaliation. Some trafficking networks involve multi-state jurisdictions. Some gang members have organized themselves into daytime burglary teams working in small groups or cliques in order to have the manpower to commit these crimes safely and avoid police apprehension (Simandle, 1997).

During the mid to late 1990s some West Coast law enforcement officials contacted subjects who claimed to be Folk and People Nation gang members from the Chicago area in the southern California area. Some of the contacted gang members claimed that more and more Folk and People gang members are going to attempt to travel west for the same reasons the settlers of the 1800s came; to make a better living. Unfortunately, there is anecdotal law enforcement evidence that suggests the better living part is really expanding narcotics trafficking operations and establishing business relationships with West Coast gangs. Especially southern California based gangs.

Writings

As with all street gang membership, personal writings and drawings can show gang affiliation. Many Folk affiliated street gangs use a written code to send messages. A Brother of Struggle member wrote the alphabet code included in this text, a Folk Nation affiliated street gang. The gang member was in custody was quick to add that there are many forms of this alphabet. He also added that gang tattoos could also include some of these cryptic letters.

As practiced by some street gangs, lists of peer gang members often appear in personal telephone books or membership rosters. As seen in the list below, peer gang members legal names appear on the left. The last names have been marked out to insure privacy. On the right side, written in the unique alphabet, are the gang monikers. The alphabet code has been broken down and the monikers can be read easily.

Clothing

Street gang members sometimes wear brand name shoes or clothes, as well as professional sports clothing. A particular brand name of clothing or collegiate/ professional sports team is chosen to represent the gang. Sometimes it is the team's colors or name abbreviation that identifies a particular gang. A professional sports team may be chosen to enhance the reputation of the street gang. Clearly the manufacturers of these clothing items and the sports teams do not endorse the gang lifestyle. Nevertheless, their products take on a second meaning to some street gangs. These are a few examples, as provided by one Black Gangster Disciple member:

REEBOK Remember Each and Every Bit of Knowledge

RAIDERS Ruthless Ass Insane Disciples Ever Ruling Satan

K-SWISS Kill Satan When I See Satan

HOYAS Hoover On Your Ass Slob; Hoover On Your Ass Satan

PUMA Problems You Maintain Accountable

KINGS Killing Innocent Niggers Gangster Style

49ers 4 Kings, 9 Disciples Eliminating Red Slobs

NIKE Niggers In Killing Effect

WHITE SOX When Hoover Insisted To Eliminate Slobs On Execution

KARL Killing A Red Lord

KANI Killing Another Nigga Instantly

It should be noted here that none of the manufactures or school manufacture or endorse the gang use or significance of their team wear, colors or logos. It is the street gang that seems to adopt the sportswear to fit a particular meaning to the gang not the sports team. The acronym meaning can also change as gang membership changes.

Mentality

Using special clothing and writings can be one way of showing gang affiliation and mentality. However, a person's level of commitment to the gang lifestyle may be seen in another subtle way. Personal notes and the use of gang slang can also help identify the gang mentality. Don't forget sometimes numbers are used as an alphabet code. For example the number code 2-15-4. The number 2 is the second letter of the alphabet, B; 15 represents the letter O, and 4 the letter C. The number 5 is usually written upside down because it is a number used by People Nation Gangs. 2-15-4 is the numeric code for BOD, which is translated to Brothers of Disciples.

Since the majority of Folk Nation gang members are African-American, the term "black" takes on a new meaning. It can represent Brothers Live As Crip Killers or Brothers Live As Cop Killers. The term Crip can mean Cousin Rest In Peace.

Many of these terms are used as derogatory slang towards rival gangs. Examples are the words PIRU and BLOOD. PIRU can mean Pussys In Red Uniforms. The word BLOODS can stand for Bloods Live Off Of Disciple Sorrow.

Acronyms are commonly used as an abbreviated form of speaking and writing. A few examples are:

BGD Black Gangster Disciple

BGDN Black Gangster Disciple Nation

GD Gangster Disciple

IGD Insane Gangster Disciple

DQ Disciple Queen

GQ Gangster Queen

L.L.L Love, Live, Loyalty or Look, Listen, Learn

MMM Money, Mack (sex), Murder

FOLK Follow Our Lord and King

FOLKS Follow Our Lord King and Savior or For Our Love of Killing Slobs

DDD Discipline, Dedicated Disciple

Wearing certain colors can also be symptomatic of gang status and mentality. For many gangs color is a significant indicator of particular affiliation. The set of colors used by a particular gang can also be known as flags. Examples for Folk-affiliated gangs are:

Blue Original color of the Nation

Black Color used for doing dirt

Green Money

Gold Wealth, used by higher ranks and kings

Purple Mourning, when a member dies

White   Peace and Purity

Leadership Structure

Following the organized leadership model, Folk Nation affiliated gangs have a formal chain of command. King Larry Hoover is considered to be the highest-ranking Folk Nation gang member, even though he is a BGD.

There are many Folk Nation affiliated gangs that follow a similar organized leadership model. The following is a typical chain of command, starting with the lowest ranking position:

- Soldier
- Foot Soldier
- Low Knight
- High Knight
- Chief of Security (3-15-19) The 5 is upside down
- Chief of Violations (COV)
- Righteous Endeavors
- Chief of Staff (COS)
- First Lieutenant Gladiator (FLG or 6-12-7)
- General
- 2nd Seer
- 1st Seer
- Regional
- Knight of the Round Table
- Honorable Chairman
- Set King

As with any gang, rank depends on the membership tenure and activity. The organizational structure resembles the U.S. Military, where promotions and rank are based on performance, time and grade.

There are also some law enforcement references to the Los Angeles-based Bloods and Crip gangs working with Folk and People Nation gangs and that the Chicago based gangs have been identified in California, Oregon and Washington.

Summary

The Folks and People Nation gangs each developed unique membership characteristics that make them easy to identify. They became bitter rivals in and out of prison. There are literally hundreds of different gangs in the Midwest and East Coast that align themselves either to the People or the Folks Nation gangs. For example, in the Chicago, Illinois, area during the late 1990 there were some 160 different street gangs (Simandle, 1997). The Folk and People gang members refer to their gangs as Nations. Individual members do not refer to themselves gang bangers, which appears to be a west coast term. Don't forget gangs like the United Blood Nation. These modern-day Nation gangs will continue to grow and form.

The Bloods, Crips, and Skinheads, along with the various Asian-American street gangs, have also made their appearance in the Midwestern and Eastern parts of the United States. However, often even though the gang will have a well-known west coast gang name that does not automatically infer the gang members are from the west coast or that the gang has a formal west coast connection.

Motorcycle Gangs

Among the most dynamic gangs worldwide are motorcycle gangs. Though relatively small in total member number when compared to general U.S. gang population, some motorcycle gangs have become so criminally sophisticated that their criminal operations are compared to those of traditional organized crime families. Some law enforcement experts consider outlaw motorcycle gangs as a form of organized crime (Tretheway and Katz, 1998). Some of these gangs can now be considered transnational gangs because they have established themselves throughout Europe, Canada, England and Australia.

History of Outlaw Motorcycle Gangs

Eventually the riding, drinking, fist-fighting, rebel image changed as the motorcycle gang members became involved in a wide range of criminal activities, including murder, prostitution, international white slavery, massage parlors, kidnapping, burglary, gun running, insurance frauds, truck hi-jacking, arson, loan-sharking, motorcycle and auto theft, bombings, gambling, assaults, interstate transportation of stolen property, forgery of State and Federal documents, theft of interstate shipments, theft from U.S. military installations, robbery, rape, bank robbery, extortion, blackmail and the manufacture, importation, manufacture and distribution of narcotics.

U.S. based outlaw motorcycle gangs can range in size from a single chapter with five or six members to hundreds of chapters and thousands of members worldwide. Because of their international scope some motorcycle gangs are able to coordinate drug smuggling operations in partnership with major international drug trafficking organizations. These relationships allow outlaw motorcycle gangs to traffic all types of drugs including methamphetamine, marijuana, powdered cocaine, heroin, crack, pharmaceuticals, MDMA and other dangerous drugs.

As motorcycle gangs matured into sophisticated criminal organizations, the American Motorcycle Association tried to maintain the image that most motorcycle enthusiasts were law-abiding citizens. In an attempt to distance itself from the outlaw motorcycle gangs the American Motorcycle Association formed an opinion and publicly stated it by saying that 99 percent of the motorcycle riders were okay. Outlaw motorcycle gangs immediately identified with this concept and began to refer to themselves the "one percenters." They were the one percent the American Motorcycle Association referenced (Lavigne, 1990).

It is suggested that two movies glamorized the outlaw biker lifestyle, The Wild Ones in 1954 and Easy Rider in 1969. A single incident allowed the Hell's Angels to gain broader exposure to the public. That is when the Hell's Angels were hired as security for a Rolling Stones concert at the Altamont Speedway in California in 1969. Sometime during the show some members of the Hell's Angels allegedly turned on the audience, which resulted in the death of a fan (Tretheway and Katz, 2004).

In the 1970s there were an estimated 900 outlaw motorcycle gangs in the country (Tretheway and Katz, 1998) another estimate suggested there are about one thousand motorcycle gangs in the United States and Canada (Lavigne, 1990). Outlaw motorcycle gangs have been reported active in 47 states (BATF, 2004). In California, there are approximately 55 gangs with a membership of around 3,000 (Williams and Vaughn, 2004).

Clearly, many of today's motorcycle gangs share little in resemblance to the early gangs that formed in the 1950s and 1960s. Today some motorcycle gangs have international chapters and membership can be in the thousands. As a group, like street gangs motorcycle gangs share some membership indicia and gang behaviors.

Gang Colors

To the outlaw motorcycle gang member his colors are his life. The gang's colors (patches) are worn with pride usually on a cut off Levi or leather jacket. Special patches are also worn to indicate a variety of accomplishments and rank of the gang member.

Some of the common patches that are seen, the number 13, this refers to the thirteenth letter of the alphabet, the letter M, which stands for marijuana for motorcycle gangs. The M.F. patch stands for "Mother Fucker" and the F.T.W. patch signifies "Fuck the World." The number 69 patch signifies joint oral copulation. The A.F.F.L. patch means acid (or alcohol) forever, forever loaded. The Hells Angels have another patch just for their club, A.F.F.A., which means Angels Forever, Forever Angels. The D.F.F.L. patch stands for Dope Forever, Forever Loaded. The "Deguillo" patch is also seen. The Hells Angels usually wear this patch as a badge of courage. It is worn by any HA member who has violently resisted arrest and dates back to the 1960's (Lavigne, 1990).

The Filthy Few patch signifies a special group within the Hells Angels and other outlaw motorcycle gangs. It represents members who have killed for the gang. Sometimes a swastika is worn for the shock value. A law enforcement patch displayed upside down means it was taken from a law enforcement officer. The gang's name-patch is worn on the top back portion of the jacket and is known as the Top Rocker. In the middle back of the jacket is the gang emblem and on the bottom back is the city or state patch showing where the gang is from. This is the Bottom Rocker.

Membership

Full membership in a motorcycle gang is limited to males only. They must have a license or some other form of identification to show that they are 21 years old. They must own or be able to obtain a motorcycle. Some motorcycle gangs require the ownership of a specific type of motorcycle, for example, a Harley-Davidson. Membership is only granted after 100 percent of the membership approves after a prospect period.

Potential members to motorcycle gangs are subject to a membership ritual. First, the person gets to associate with gang members. If the person demonstrates the right attitude and behaviors he is usually sponsored by a member and becomes a prospect. The prospect is am official "gopher" for the motorcycle gang and is a kind of probationary member. The prospect will complete any task ask of him. This builds his trust within the gang. Sometime between a six-month and a year probationary period the entire membership votes on whether or not to accept the prospect as regular member. The vote for membership has to 100 percent otherwise the prospect remains a prospect.

At this time the gang members receives his colors. Each gang has its own initiation ritual that can vary from disgusting college type pranks or outrages and shocking acts. Initiation rituals can range from sexual relations with a willing or unwilling female to having a prospect lie on the ground face down while fellow gang members urinate, defecate or vomit on the colors the member is wearing. Other outlaw motorcycle gangs pour grease and oil on the new member. Frequently the night ends with a huge drug and alcohol party (Williams and Vaughn, 2004).

The initiations are normally held at the clubhouse or an isolated location with all club members present. One reported ritual included that a female was undressed and was placed upon the new member's colors. Any and all male gang members who desire to have sex with the female did so. The newest member was last man to have sex with the female. All body fluids were allowed to run onto the new colors. Then members could urinate, defecate, vomit, pour beer, or do anything on the colors. On this night the new member is at the mercy of the club (Lavigne, 1990). This has been the accepted way of being jumped-in, biker style.

Many gangs have a rule that prohibits the members from ever washing his colors. The worst the colors look, the classier the gang member appears. This type of ritual still goes on within many outlaw motorcycle gangs, however a few gangs, like the Hell's Angels no longer require this particular ritual. It is felt that a thorough background including credit checks is enough. This philosophy change for the Hell's Angels means that you will not see a HA gang member with dirty colors (Williams and Vaughn, 2004).

It is safe to say there is plenty of anecdotal evidence to suggest that outlaw motorcycle gangs are ritualistic groups. It is these rituals that become the bases for building probate loyalty and group cohesion (Williams, 2004). It is a ritualized behavior that builds a group identity and reputation, as well as individual status within the group. Outlaw motorcycle gang rituals have the same effect as street gang rituals. Being an older group as whole allows the motorcycle gang rituals to be more formalized and more extreme.

Outlaw motorcycle gangs have created an unfavorable public image of themselves by choice. Their gangs are referred to as "clubs" by the membership. Non- members are normal "citizens." These gang members did not want to be like or dress like normal citizens. Their desire is to create fear within the public and to be a constant threat to law enforcement. Outlaw motorcycle gang members refer to their group as a club, the public and law enforcement call them gangs.

Tattoos

Almost all outlaw motorcycle gang members and associates will tattoo themselves. Tattoos can have a similar function as club patches that are worn on the colors. Common tattoos can include the motorcycle gang-name, white supremacist type tattoos, or the Filthy Few tattoo. Hells Angels motorcycle gang members who are the gang's hit men also have a set of lightning bolts tattooed beneath the words Filthy Few. Some outlaw motorcycle gang members will also sport the "FTW" tattoo or wear the patch on their jacket. The letters stand for "Fuck the World." Motorcycle gang tattoos exhibit the typical outlaw biker attitude and philosophies.

Of all the gangs, some outlaw motorcycle gang members tended to use a remarkable number of tattoos both as body art and for gang affiliation. At one time this was a common behavior. However this may not be true anymore as some members are trying to tone down the "biker tats" as to not draw so much attention to themselves (Dobyns, 2009).

Leadership Model

Motorcycle gangs tend to be organized by local chapters and have a vertical organizational structure. There are codified chapter rules and by-laws. Officers such as President, Secretary, Sergeant at Arms, Security and Intelligence officers are the leadership within a chapter. For some motorcycle gangs there are national and international officers. Almost all the gangs have other recognized positions within the leadership structure. For example, the Road Captain has certain responsibilities. The Road Captain is in charge of mapping out the travel route the club will take and making meeting arrangements for other clubs that may join them. It is the Road Captains responsibility to make sure all the motorcycles are legal incase of police contact.

There is also a security position that is assigned within each gang. Sometimes the member in that position is referred to as the Enforcer or Sergeant at Arms. This position will also take on the job of issuing discipline for those members who fail to carry out club orders. In a few clubs the enforcer is also tasked with obtaining illegal firearms for the club. He may also gather intelligence on rival motorcycle clubs and law enforcement.

Fully fledged and probationary members are required to attend meetings and follow a written set of rules. Outlaw motorcycle gangs have formalized written by-laws and rules like a few of the larger more organized street and prison gangs. On the bottom of the list are the associates or "hang arounds". These people may be allowed to attain certain runs and are not members of the club and cannot attend any meetings.

Most outlaw motorcycle gangs meet at a certain location. Normally the location is a building or home called a clubhouse. Only members are allowed to go to the clubhouse. It is the location for meetings, planning criminal activities and some socializing. Many clubhouses have external security to monitor people who approach the location. Clubhouses can have hidden compartments to conceal all types of contraband. Some areas of the clubhouse can also be booby-trapped.

Bike Runs

There is one important social event for all motorcycle gangs and is their annual run. The run is an event that takes the motorcycle gang anywhere. Some of the runs will incorporate checkpoints and video surveillance. The gang usually rides two abreast in a specific order.

The front of the group will always have the chapter president and road captain. The club president usually rides on the right side, nearest the curb and the road captain will ride on the left side (Grascia, 2004). The two officers have also been seen in reverse positions with the president near the center of the road (Williams and Vaughn, 2004). The main body of the club rides directly behind these two. Following the full fledged members are the probationary members.

Hang arounds and honorary members will ride in the next section. The last row of riders will have the enforcers or the Sergeants at Arms. About a mile behind or ahead of the group will be van or large truck that carries supplies for the club. This vehicle is usually in contact with the membership via a cellular telephone. The vehicle is also used to carry weapons for the club.

These are formal club sanction events that can be held on Memorial Day, Labor Day or the Fourth of July. They usually are planned around the warmer weather and can last from a few days to a couple of weeks. If rival gangs end up at the same location violence can result.

Criminal Activity

Some law enforcement specialists estimate that for every motorcycle gang member there are 10 associates. The term associate is used here not to designate prospective gang member but as an associate in the true sense of the word. Outlaw motorcycle gangs have developed a sophisticated network of contacts or associates, often including women in all levels of government and all types of businesses. The amount and type of intelligence collected by these gangs can be staggering. Some motorcycle clubs have even infiltrated law enforcement and the judicial system. Fraudulent driver's licenses, birth certificates, identification papers can be purchased with ease from these gang members.

Outlaw motorcycle gangs control a multi-million dollar methamphetamine market in the United States. Their sophistication and efficient method of operation rivals that of a modern-day organized crime syndicate. As with any major drug-trafficking business, there is a need for protection of the drugs and illegal gains. This implies that motorcycle gang members to be armed and ready to use violence.

This need has caused motorcycle gangs to develop a variety of methods to produce, transport and distribute methamphetamine. Methamphetamine is also known in the streets as speed, meth or crank. All outlaw motorcycle gang methamphetamine is hand-made or cooked by a cooker. A cooker can be someone who has a good chemical background or one experienced in the clandestine manufacture of the drug. The actual processes can be lengthy but not complicated and requires the use of several dangerous chemicals. The clandestine manufacture of crank also releases toxic gases and residue. Therefore, the production can be dangerous. Clandestine lab residue can harm the environment and is considered a toxic waste.

Sadly, cookers sometimes are also addicted to the drug and will have small children or infants present in the same areas they are cooking. This places the children at great danger because of the toxic chemicals and gases and the explosive nature of some of the manufacturing processes.

Biker gangs along with Mexican nationals have become adept in the manufacturing of crank in clandestine laboratories in isolated areas. Some of the labs can be mobile and are often moved around. The cooker is usually compensated very well. However, there are some simplified methods of methamphetamine manufacture and the drug can now be produced in motel rooms, cars, apartments and storage facilities.

In addition to drug manufacturing, outlaw motorcycle gangs are involved in the sale of the drug and debt collection. As with any drug business, when profits are missing or not received bill collectors are sent to collect the owed money.

Often, customers are motivated to pay up or die. Mishandled money can result in death. These strict rules lead to an efficient, profitable, no-nonsense business. The drug business has been so good that the entire image for some motorcycle gang members has changed to that of successful businessmen.

For some outlaw motorcycle gang members luxury cars have replaced motorcycles; suits have replaced the colors, and nice homes have replaced old clubhouses. Trips by boat and airplane have replaced the runs for some of these gang members. A few motorcycle gangs have matured. Along with this new sophistication came sophisticated weapons, innovative transportation techniques, increased narcotics trafficking, and national and international contacts.

Today's large motorcycle gangs have unique characteristics. For example, the Hells Angels use the Harley-Davidson motorcycle repair manual in place of the Bible. This manual is used for the Hells Angels weddings. A divorce is obtained by tearing up the book. Many other clubs have similar practices (LaVigne, 1990).

Do not forget that outlaw motorcycle gangs can also be involved in a variety of criminal activities, including extortion, witness intimidation, threats on public and criminal justice professionals. Some of the gangs have also aligned themselves with white supremacist ideologies.

As a group outlaw motorcycle gangs share many street gang characteristics and differ in many ways. For example, in outlaw motorcycle gangs only males can be members and they have to be adults. Many outlaw motorcycle gangs require the new member to be at least 21 years old. Although, there are no written rules about ethnicity the majority of biker gang membership tends to be Caucasian. However in the late 1990s and early 2000s the California based Mongol motorcycle gang recruited heavily from the ranks of the 18th Street gang.

Unlike Hybrid gangs, females are never allowed to be members of an outlaw motorcycle gangs. Females can be associates and girlfriends and wives of gang members. One other uniqueness about these gangs is the requirement of owning a motorcycle as a prerequisite for membership. Most street gangs do not run credit histories or thorough backgrounds on potential members however many outlaw motorcycle gangs do.

Some outlaw motorcycle gangs will use smoke screens to deceive the general public. Charity events like collecting and giving toys to homeless orphan children or collecting funds for the Statue of Liberty restoration program have changed the public's image of some outlaw motorcycle gangs. This strategy has been successful because many consider outlaw motorcycle gang members fashionable rebels.

Gang trends have blended into RUBs (Rich Urban Bikers). Larger gangs recognize this and have attempted to insulate their operations with puppet clubs and associates who believe the motorcycle gangs are nothing more than fun loving motorcycle riders. However the gang's mottos tell a different story. "Three people will keep a secret if two are dead" for the Hells Angels. "God forgives, Outlaws don't" for the Outlaws motorcycle gang. The Banditos motorcycle gang uses the phrase, "we are the people that our parents warned us about" (Tretheway and Katz, 1998). The Pagan motorcycle gang has a unique club motto, "Do unto others and split" (Grascia, 2004).

There are four major motorcycle gangs in the United States, and over 1000 smaller motorcycle gangs operating in Canada, Europe, Australia, New Zealand and the United States. The smaller gangs seemed to have aligned themselves with one of the four major outlaw motorcycle groups.

Hells Angels

The most infamous and famous motorcycle gang in the world started in San Bernardino, California. The first chapter of the Hells Angels was established on March 17, 1948 (Lavigne, 1990). While the prototype for motorcycle gangs had been around years before, their union and activity was not classified as such until the formation of the Hell's Angels.

The Hells Angels started with a group of rowdy discharged veterans who found themselves together in Southern California after World War II. The initial members were ex-military pilots, bombardiers, navigators and gunners who were having trouble adjusting to civilian life. These men were a rebellious group in the military, and they brought that attitude and lifestyle back to their civilian lives. They created what they believed was the final frontier, a fast, hard-drinking, nomadic life on a motorcycle (Lavigne, 1990).

The Hells Angels motorcycle club (HAMC) has become internationally known. The gang has grown from a small group of men to an organization with over 200 chapters and 1300 members worldwide. This makes a basis for an intelligence network and a reliable pipeline for the international transport of contraband. In the United States the Hells Angels have chapters all over the West, Midwest, Northeast, and East Coasts. By late 2003 the Hell's Angels chapters had increased to 229 worldwide. The United States is home to approximately 70 chapters, 19 located in California.

With approximately 1300 members throughout the world the HAMC operates so efficiently they might well claim 10 times that number in membership. Some law enforcement agencies have classified the motorcycle gangs as an organized crime group rather than street gangs (Lavigne, 1990, Williams, 2004).

Motorcycle gangs usually control the areas where they work, but may not claim it as a geographical turf like many traditional Hispanic street gangs. Some chapters of the HAMC have been able to corrupt the police and public officials that can helps insulate the gang from prosecution. The HAMC may also use their associates to operate storefronts, to help laundering money and influence people. This is another fundamental difference between outlaw motorcycle gangs and street gangs. Street gangs usually do not exert a corruption influence on public officials and criminal justice professionals.

Millions of dollars are at stake because of the types of illegal and legal businesses owned and operated by HAMC chapters. Therefore, life is cheap. The illegal drug sale profits have been invested in a number of real estate projects, bars, clubs, auto salvage yards, entertainment companies, catering businesses, restaurants, construction firms, motorcycle shops, tattoo parlors, massage parlors, and trucking firms, just to name a few. In the world of motorcycle gangs, the Hells Angels are feared as the toughest, most sophisticated and wealthiest.

It is generally believed that the Hell's Angels formed in San Bernardino County, California after World War II. A small group of veterans in 1945 formed a social club in the Bloomington/Fontana, California area. They called themselves the Pissed Off Bastards of Bloomington (POBOB). The purpose of the club was to raise hell and make society dislike the members.

The July 4, 1947 Hollister, California incident probably marked the public image of outlaw motorcycle gangs forever. Hollister is located south of Oakland and the American Motor Cycle Association sanctioned weekend of racing and hill climbing went bad. Over 4,000 motorcycles tore up the small town protected by seven policemen. Most gang members went to the town and ended up partaking in a 40 hour drunken party. The POBOB and the Booze Fighters motorcycle gangs took over San Benito Street, the main street in Hollister. They drank, fought and urinated in public. The motorcycle gang members drove their motorcycles into restaurants, ran red lights and held drag races in the middle of the street. They threw thousands of beer bottles onto the sidewalks and streets from hotel rooms.

A POBOB gang member was arrested and the other POBOB demanded his release. The police refused and the POBOB went on a rampage. The town's seven policemen were helpless and had to call for assistance. Forty California Highway Patrol officers responded. The Highway Patrol threatened to use tear gas and the outlaw motorcycle gang members left the town, but not before almost 100 gang members were jailed, over 50 people injured. The rampage ended three days later on July 7th. This incident helped establish the annual July 4th runs and affirm the one-percenter status of the outlaw motorcycle gang member.

The Hell's Angels motorcycle club was formed by Otto Friedli and some disgruntled members of the POBOB. The "Berdoo" chapter is the first Hell's Angel club and Otto Friedli is credited with its formation on March 17, 1948 in San Bernardino, California. The gang adopted a name favored by World War II fighter pilots, but the name was used a lot earlier when Howard Hughes purchased 87 airplanes and filmed his war epic, Hell's Angels in 1927 (Lavigne, 1990). The now copyrighted symbol for the gang is the famous smiling winged death head. It has undergone some changes because the first death head had a leather fighter pilot's helmet on it.

Unlike street gangs, the member's colors are owned by the HAMC and the member has to give them back when he retires or is dismissed in bad terms. In 1958, Ralph "Sonny" Barger took over leadership of the HAMC and moved the headquarters to Oakland, California.

Of all the incidents the Hell's Angels have been involved in between the late 1990s to early 2000s one clearly stands out. On April 27, 2002 at the 20th Annual Laughlin River Run, Laughlin, Nevada a shooting occurred between several Hells Angels and Mongols motorcycle gang members. In the early morning hours in Harrah's Casino a heated discussion between gang members started. Mongol motorcycle gang members surrounded a Hell's Angel. The Hell's Angel kicked the International President of the Mongols in the chest and a massive fight started. This resulted in the death of two Hell's Angles and one Mongol and the left nine other outlaw motorcycle gang members injured.

The Hells Angels motorcycle gang also uses the Internet to advertise the gang's activities and chapter locations.

The Outlaws

The HAMC has been at war with the Outlaw motorcycle gang since 1974. The Hells Angels and Outlaws have demonstrated a propensity to kill each other wherever possible. The Outlaws motorcycle gang is the second largest motorcycle gang in the United States. The Outlaws are also called the American Outlaw Association. Criminal activity includes white slavery; prostitution and drug trafficking provide most the membership income.

The Outlaws, like other motorcycle gangs tend to physically abuse the women that associate with the gang. Besides beatings, torture and mutilations, it is not uncommon for a woman to have sex with the majority of the gang members in one night at a club party. These women hold no status within the gang and are sometimes allowed to wear only a Property of Outlaws rocker on their jackets. The women seldom, if ever, go to the police or complain about their treatment.

Females in this motorcycle gang are treated as property. Females in street gangs can be full fledge members, co-leaders or assume an auxiliary position and never treated like females who associate with outlaw motorcycle gangs.

It is generally believed the Outlaws were established in Joliet, Illinois around 1959 (Grascia, 2004 and Lavigne, 1990). However the literature also suggests that the club really began as the McCook Outlaws in 1935 in McCook, Illinois, which is near Chicago. The club remained intact during World War II. After the war, in the late 1940s the club allegedly requested a Hells Angels charter, but the request was never answered. This became the genesis of the hatred between the two motorcycle gangs that currently exists.

The motorcycle gang grew and by 1950 had moved its headquarters to Chicago. This is when the gang changed its logo from a winged motorcycle to a white colored skull. During this time period another unrelated motorcycle gang formed by Johnny Davis in Joliet, Illinois. The Johnny Davis Outlaws used a logo similar to the one actor Marlon Brando wore in the movie, The Wild Ones. The gang placed pistons behind a skull instead of bones.

In 1954 a faction of the Johnny Davis Outlaws moved into Chicago and challenged the McCook Outlaws for control of the city. After several violent incidents and by the early 1960s the McCook Outlaws had prevailed. They adopted the skull and piston logo as theirs and called it "charlie." By 1963 the outlaw motorcycle club had started to develop the antisocial and antiauthority philosophy of the HAMC. At midnight on January 1, 1965 the McCook Outlaws officially renamed itself the American Outlaws Association (U.S. Department of Justice, 2002).

In the early 1990s the club had one chapter in Australia and 34 different chapters in United States and Canada (Lavigne, 1990). Between 1992 and 2002 it is believed that the Outlaw motorcycle gang established 27 new chapters in the United States (Grascia, 2004) and 45 chapters in Europe (U.S. Department of Justice, 2002). There are more than 900 members who follow a strict chain of command, with elected officers who report to a directorship.

The regional governing body for the gang is known as the Mother Club. It is sort of an executive board that runs the gang. The emblem for this gang is a white skull with a pair of pistons crossed in the background. The Outlaws motorcycle gang also has a hit squad known as the SS. Outlaw gang members usually work in pairs and must own at least one firearm. Among motorcycle gangs, the Outlaw gang members are considered exceptionally violent.

The drug trafficking includes prescription pharmaceuticals such as Diazepam (Valium), which is illegally manufactured in Canada and smuggled into the United States. The Outlaw motorcycle gang also distributes methamphetamine and cocaine imported from the Colombians.

For the Outlaws, their old ladies show their love for their man by being involved in prostitution and giving all the money they earned back to the gang member. Most of these women range in age from 16 to their early 20s. Many are addicted to drugs, and many remain with the gang out of fear (Lavigne, 1990).

By the early 1990s the Outlaws motorcycle gang had established chapters in Wisconsin, Indiana, Illinois, Pennsylvania, New York, Ohio, Tennessee, Georgia, South Carolina, Florida, Oklahoma, Arizona and Canada. The gang had also forged an alliance with the Bandidos motorcycle gang for the purpose of protection against Hells Angels attacks (Lavigne, 1990).

Sometimes Outlaw motorcycle gang members will tattoo themselves with the colors of their gang. Just like other motorcycle gang members. The Outlaws refer to their colors as Charlie. The Outlaws motorcycle gang has three goals: money, power and territory. To assist in reaching these goals the Outlaw motorcycle gang also uses the Internet to advertise, recruit and show chapter location.

Pagans

Third in line among the big four motorcycle gangs in the U. S. are the Pagans. The Pagans motorcycle gang was originally founded in Price George County, Maryland, in 1959. As of 2002 this is the only motorcycle club of the four major ones that has no international charters (Grascia, 2004). By the early 1990s the Pagan motorcycle gang had established 44 chapters with a total membership of approximately 900 (Lavigne, 1990 and http://courses.smsu.edu).

Almost all of the gang's chapters are located in New Jersey, Pennsylvania, Delaware, Maryland, Florida, and Louisiana. Unlike the other three major gangs, the Pagans are far more nomadic and tend not to have formal clubhouses.

The Pagans governing body is composed of the 13 to 20 ex- local chapter presidents. These members wear a black colored number 13 on the back of their colors that signifies their position as a governing body member. This group comprises the leadership structure for the motorcycle gang; also known as the mother club. Gang meetings are held in different locations because there are no chapter clubhouses. Pagan gang members often will meet at each other's homes or other pre-arranged locations.

Mother club members are each responsible for the chapters in their areas. The local chapter presidents are under the direction of the mother club member who oversees the area. The Pagan motorcycle gang's primary source of income is from the sales of narcotics and prostitution. For a Pagan motorcycle gang member, a mistake with the business is the same as death.

The Pagans also have an excellent intelligence network. In one instance the outlaw motorcycle gang found a federally protected witness. Fear and corruption of public officials are the Pagans greatest weapons against prosecution. This is common strategy with many outlaw motorcycle gangs.

Law enforcement anecdotal evidence suggests that the Pagans motorcycle gang manufactures and distributes most of the methamphetamine and PCP sold in the northeastern part of the country. It has been estimated that this can account for approximately 15 million dollars a year in sales. Some Pagan chapters have formed their own drug manufacturing groups including experienced chemists, as well as distributors of cocaine, marijuana and parsley sprinkled with PCP.

Even though the Pagan drug network is well organized, it remains unsophisticated and lacks a business ethic. It appears the greed for profits has led the motorcycle gang to sell their product with little or no quality control (Lavigne, 1990).

Pagans have access to all types of weapons and explosives as do all outlaw motorcycle gangs. The club, like other gangs, launders illegal profits through legitimate businesses. The Pagans have a hit squad like many other motorcycle gangs. It is made up of 13 members who wear black T-shirts and are known as the Black Shirts. The Pagan motorcycle gang also uses the Internet.

Of the big Four it appears that the Pagan outlaw motorcycle gang has the best connections and ties with Italian organized crime groups. Pagan gang members have acted as drug couriers, enforcers, bodyguards and hit men for the mob, especially in the Pennsylvania and New Jersey areas (http://courses.smsu.edu).

The gang's president and vice-president are figurehead positions because they do not really run the club. The president can set the selling prices for drugs. The president also receives an honorary salary; it was the same as the President of the United States, approximately 200,000 dollars a year (http://courses.smsu.edu).

Bandidos

The fourth major group is the Bandidos motorcycle gang, also known as the Bandido Nation. The Bandido Nation was formed in Houston, Texas in 1966. Donald Chambers is credited with the gang's formation and was the first president. The Bandidio motorcycle gang is the youngest motorcycle gang of the Big Four. However, it appears to be one of the fastest-growing outlaw motorcycle gangs in the United States with about 30 chapters and 500 members (U.S. Department of Justice, 2002).

The Bandidos first international chapter was established in Australia, 1983. Other chapters have been established in Asia, Europe and Canada. The club has several chapters in Texas with the main chapter located in Corpus Christie. In the early 1990s there were chapters in Louisiana, Mississippi, Arkansas, New Mexico, Colorado, South Dakota, and Washington. Usually, members will meet at their homes, which are used as clubhouses and are fortified.

Like other motorcycle gang members the Bandidos tend to be stopped by the police. Some Bandido gang members carry small tape recorders. They record the ensuing dialog and attempt to bait the unsuspecting officer in an effort to record statements that can be used in court. This is a well-known strategy that is used by many motorcycle gang members.

Like the members of the Big Four, the Bandidos motorcycle gang has a vertical leadership structure. Elected and appointed officials at the international, national and local levels govern the gang. The leaders establish and enforce rules, settle disputes, appoint new officers and coordinate Bandido activities, including criminal actions.

As with other motorcycle gangs the Bandidos have a security squad known as the Nomads. This group made up of members who have been with the club for more than five years; they handle security, intelligence work, and disciplining of gang members. True to their moniker, they are nomadic, moving constantly collecting information on law enforcement and rival motorcycle gangs. Being as violent as any other motorcycle gang, Bandidos gang members can chose to kill if they are unsuccessful at corrupting a targeted individual.

The attempted murder of a United States Attorney and the murder of a Federal Judge are good examples of how bold and brazen the Bandidos gang can be (Lavigne, 1990).

As a group, the Bandidos can be involved in welfare fraud, gun running, arson, prostitution, extortion, narcotics trafficking, white slavery, bank fraud, and contract murder. The majority of illegal profits come from the sale of methamphetamine. One goal of this outlaw motorcycle gang has been to increase drug sales. The Bandidos have formed an alliance with the Outlaw and Mongols motorcycle gangs. This was done to help combat the influence of the Hells Angels. This formalized the rivalry between the groups. The Outlaws become the source of cocaine for the Bandidos (Lavigne, 1990).

As with other gangs, rivalries exist between motorcycle gangs. These rivalries, some based on narcotics territory wars, have resulted in the brutal deaths of hundreds of people in the last fifty years. Homicides have been committed as contract murders, because of gang rivalry, lack of payment for narcotics and for no reason at all.

In 2009 law enforcement anecdotal evidence suggested that in the south eastern region of Texas this outlaw motorcycle gang may have a few members that direct connections with a Mexican drug cartel. This connection would be source of wholesale priced illegal drugs which could be distributed and re-cut for retail sale.

Canada

A discussion of outlaw motorcycle gangs cannot be complete without examining motorcycle gang activity in Canada. Since the Big Four motorcycle gangs have established international chapters of their gangs, international relationships between the gangs can impact national and local gang business.

Outlaw motorcycle gangs first appeared in Ontario and Quebec in the early 1950s. The motorcycle gangs focused on the manufacture of methamphetamines. The largest two motorcycle gangs during this time period were the Satan's Choice based in Ontario, which also had a Montreal chapter, and the Popeyes, a Montreal based gang with chapters in Quebec (Gazette, 2002).

The Outlaws motorcycle gang entered Ontario in March 1977 and absorbed about half of the Satan's Choice gang by taking advantage of an internal Satan's Choice dispute. In December 1977 the Hells Angels expanded its operations in the Montreal area by absorbing the Popeyes motorcycle gang. Since the Hells Angels and Outlaws were rivals their presence in Canada only continued the intense hatred for each other. A bloody motorcycle gang war started as the Hells Angels attempted to take control away from the Outlaws motorcycle gang.

By the mid 1980s the Hells Angels motorcycle gang had taken control of away from the Outlaws in Quebec. Throughout the 1980s and 1990s the Hells Angels motorcycle gang expanded in Canada. As of 2002 there were 26 outlaw motorcycle gangs in Canada. Surprisingly, the Hells Angels had influence over all the gangs but one, the Outlaws motorcycle gang.

By 2002 the Hells Angels had established 34 chapters of their gang in Canada with close to 600 members. In 2002 Canadian authorities reported that there were 10 Outlaw and four Bandido motorcycle gang chapters operating in Canada.

Like their U.S. counterparts outlaw motorcycle gangs in Canada are involved in murder, murder for hire, fraud, theft, money laundering, counterfeiting, extortion, loan sharking, prostitution, escort agencies, selling alcohol illegally, illegal weapons trafficking and possession. The motorcycle gangs also continue to be involved in the importation and trafficking of cocaine and the exportation of high-grade marijuana. Since the gangs make drug trafficking their primary revenue source, ecstasy, methamphetamine and other synthetic drugs are manufactured or imported and sold.

Motorcycle gangs in Canada also utilize fortified clubhouses. Some of the clubhouses can contain boardrooms, gym equipment and garages. Many have extensive and complex security systems. The gang members also use the same patches and tattoos as gangs based in the United States (Gazette, 2002).

Female Associates

Females are always associate or auxiliary gang members, never full members. There can be three different associate levels for the females in outlaw motorcycle gangs. These female associates are referred to as Mamas, Old Ladies, and Mothers. The Mamas are available to any member of the gang for whatever purpose they desire. An Old Lady belongs to one particular member and could be his legal wife, girlfriend or live-in girlfriend. A mother is usually an ex-mama who may supply false identification, stolen credit cards or a place to hide for members who are wanted by the police (Lavigne, 1990).

If female associates wear colors it will most likely be some type of jacket showing only a "Property of (male member's name)" patch on the back. That is normally the only patch a female associate is allowed to wear in public. Females are used to help make money for the club they are associated with. Some female motorcycle gang associates will work as prostitutes, other will sell drugs. Females are considered public and private property within the outlaw motorcycle gang culture.

When the gang holds a meeting it is called going to Church. Only full fledged club members are allowed to attend. Female associates and prospective members are not allowed to attend and club business will never be talked about outside the meeting. The meetings are normally held at the Clubhouse, or chapter headquarters. A code-of-silence is always in effect.

Graffiti

Motorcycle gang graffiti tends to be a private affair if it occurs at all. Outlaw motorcycle gang graffiti is never seen in public. This may be due to the fact that most motorcycle gang members are at least 21 when they join. Graffiti as the written language used by street gangs is a form of advertisement for the gang. It can define turf, announce the presence of a gang, or be a form of challenge or insult. Outlaw motorcycle gangs do have a need to claim turf the way street gangs do. Outlaw motorcycle gang members do not as a rule use gang handsigns to show gang affiliation, membership status or to issue challenges like street gangs. Clothing, especially the colors a motorcycle gang member wears can be used instead of graffiti.

Summary

Although there are many different motorcycle gangs in the world the type of criminal activity they can be involved in has been unchanged. Some motorcycle gangs have become aware of their antisocial image and have attempted to soften it up collecting toys and /or money for orphan children or public projects. Gang rivalries still exist between outlaw motorcycle gangs worldwide. Some rivalries are based on narcotics territory wars and have resulted in the brutal deaths of hundreds of people in the last fifty years. Outlaw motorcycle gang related homicides have been committed as contract murders, because of gang rivalry, lack of payment for narcotics and for no reason at all.

What can be expected is the continuance of violent attacks between rival gangs. Some outlaw motorcycle gangs will also continue to use explosives and high power, high caliber weapons. Motorcycle gangs have been involved in home invasion or home take style robberies for some time. The Southeast Asian street gangs made this particular style of robbery popular with the street gangs in the early 1980s. Outlaw motorcycle gang home invasion robberies have always been very violent and brutal and predated the Asian gang use.

One of the purposes of the violence is to send a message to the rest of the people who conduct business with the gang members. Sometimes these extreme actions can be done to a motorcycle gang associate and / or his family because of a serious transgression that was made against the club. Violent home invasion robberies could also occur because someone is skimming money off an operation or failing to complete an assigned task.

Chapter 4

Prison Gangs

This chapter is broken down into two parts; California and Texas based prison gangs. There are a number of prison gangs in U.S. correction institutions. This two sections cover the prison gangs that are the most active on the southern border.

Prison Gangs in California

This chapter will discuss the origins of several prison gangs. Prison gang membership is a serious commitment in becoming a lifelong gang member. Many street gang members aspire to join a prison gang. The power bases for all prison gangs lies within the street gang population. Street gangs have become the recruitment pool for all prison gangs. Prison gang members, whether in custody or on parole, can influence the criminal activities of the street gangs they are associated with.

History

Prison gangs have developed and evolved in the country's state prison systems for a number of reasons. Probably the two most common reasons are for protection and control. Prison gangs tend to initially form to protect members from another prison-based gang or group. At first the strategy works, but in order to maintain the protection the gang has to resort to protecting its reputation, which compels it to become violent. The gang that initially formed to protect, now protects the members by becoming another predator in the system. In turn, prison gangs also exert an influence on street gang activity and activities at the county jail level.

State prison gang members carry a lot of power, respect and influence to the street-level gang member. Most street-gang members will honor and pay homage to a prison gang member. To the street level gang member the prison-gang members are *"the bad of the bad,"* as one 18-year-old Latino street gang member said. Prison gang members are professional gang members and are held in high regard, at least by younger street gang members. The more violent a prison gang member is the more respect he has with his peers.

There is another social factor that plays an important role for street gang members. There was once a bad social stigma associated with going to jail or prison. For many gang members there is an opposite effect, going to jail and prison elevates a member's status within his or her gang. In fact, incarcerated gang members earn more respect by spending time in custody (Valdemar, 1999).

Once out of prison, the prison gang member will continue to conduct business and follow directions for the prison gang. For many gang members, the ultimate commitment to the gang lifestyle is to join a prison gang. You join a prison gang for life (Duarte, 1999). The saying, "... *blood in and blood out*." is really true for most prison gangs.

There are many major prison gangs established within the country's penal systems and a number of smaller affiliate and independent gangs. The major prison gangs control the life of the inmate once inside a state correctional institution. Most prison gangs are ethnic based. The gangs can flourish inside a prison because the system is a totally enclosed community, isolated from the rest of society. The legal rights for inmates are very limited once in the prison. As a result prison gang members have developed and formalized their own set of rules, ethics, and way of life. If there are rules to follow there is punishment for rule violations.

The prison gang population is usually composed of a significant number of street gang members who have committed violent crimes. Therefore, street gangs tend to become the recruitment pool for prison gang membership. The everyday gang rules that are followed on the street do not always apply in prison or jail. For example, gang members who once were bitter rivals on the street may now become allies based on their ethnicity. Once inside prison, protection and safety comes in numbers. For example, Hispanic gangs tend to group together; it then appears that inmates of specific ethnicities group together. Because of this inmate populations tend to be polarized by race.

Ethnic groups become a power base for prison gangs because of this behavior. Hispanics, Whites and African-Americans tend to group together for protection. This includes both non-gang affiliated inmates and gang member inmates. Rival gang members are normally not housed together for safety reasons. This also polarizes gang members.

There is one other uniqueness about prison gangs. In the country there are many definitions that qualify disruptive groups as a prison gangs. There is correction based anecdotal evidence that suggests the standards that qualify a group as a prison gang tend to vary with jurisdiction. In some correctional institutions if an incoming inmate was a street gang member, he qualifies as a prison gang member from the same gang. This tends to assign prison gang status to street gang members when they are incarcerated at the state level even though they might not have a history within the institution. Other definitions qualify the group as disruptive or a security threat group before the group can be reclassified as a prison gang. Another definition only classifies a group as a prison gang if it formed within the correctional setting.

So a familiar issue develops with regards to prison gangs. There is no nationally accepted definition of a prison gang. The same issue is present when trying to ascertain accurate data on street gang demographics. Without a standard definition it is almost impossible to correctly triage the problem. If the problem can't be defined it cannot be treated effectively.

Mexican Mafia

History

During the early to mid 1950s there was a power struggle between the inmates within the California prison system. In the mid 1950s, 13 California Youth Authority (CYA) wards were sent to the Duel Vocational Institute located in Tracy, California. Since the wards were juveniles, they were housed in a special section of the adult corrections facility.

These wards were violent and had a defiant attitude. They were the worst of the worst, as far as in-custody street gang members went. Eventually they were transferred to San Quentin prison. While at the Duel Vocational Institute between 1956 and 1957, they formed the gang of gangs. The gang became known as the Mexican Mafia or La Eme. Eme is the Spanish word for the letter M in the alphabet which is also the thirteenth letter of the alphabet. La Eme became the nickname for the Mexican Mafia. When street gang members use the number 13 in a tattoo or graffiti it implies that the gang is from southern California and if a member goes to prison he will align himself with the Mexican Mafia while incarcerated. The number 13 also states in the gang world that the gang member is a sureno, a southern California gang member.

The formation of the gang is credited to a L.A. County gang member Luis "Huero" Flores from Hawaiian Gardens, a Mexican street gang. The nucleus of the gang was comprised with "Snuffy" Sanchez from Florencia 13; Jose "Sluggo" Pineda from El Hoyo Maravilla; Rudy

"Cheyenne" Cadena from Primera Flats; Eddie Loera from Geraghty Loma and "Lito" Pedroza also from Primera Flats. Ironically, all the original members of the gang were U.S. citizens, not Mexican nationals. All primarily spoke English and Calo, and only a few spoke Spanish. Curiously, these gang members who were rivals on the street had become allies while incarcerated (Bauer, 1997).

By 1960 this cadre of street-toughen gang members created the rules of conduct for new members. One of the rules of membership required a prospective member to be sponsored by four bonefide Mexican Mafia members. In addition, by a new member was also asked to take a blood oath for life. This was done to confirm complete unquestioned allegiance to the gang. This oath help create a bond for life that made membership more important than anything, including the member's family. The oath required a new member to do whatever the gang asked, without question or comment. Any violation of this oath was punished with death. Because of this philosophy, the gangs rally cry became, Blood in, Blood out.

1960s

By the early 1960s, the Mexican Mafia had gained such a reputation, that many street gang members aspired to join the prison gang. These young gang members would be willing to do just about anything to show their loyalty to the prison gang. Because of this attitude Mexican Mafia membership grew rapidly and its influence spread throughout the California prison system and onto the streets, especially in southern California.

There is some law enforcement anecdotal evidence that suggests the Mexican Mafia was the first gang to break racial membership rules because the original gang had African-American and Asian members. The Mexican Mafia chose and still chooses its members based on their practice of the Mexican gang culture. This allowed growth for the Mexican Mafia to be based on quality.

By 1967, an informal rivalry developed between Mexicans from Northern California and those from Southern California. One Eme member named Rudy Cheyenne Cadena was trying to unite all Mexican inmates under the Mexican Mafia. This union was an attempt to establish control of the prison drug, extortion and prostitution trades. This attempt to link the north with the south was disrupted by a strange set of events that occurred in 1968 at the San Quentin prison.

As detailed in the Sureno chapter, a stolen pair of shoes, a gift, an insult to an Eme gang member and subsequent stabbing of a Mexican inmate from northern California prompted formal negotiations to stop. The northern Mexicans would forever be rivals of the southern Mexicans because of this incident. The northern California Mexican inmates formed a prison gang of their own; the Nuestra Familia (Our Family). This prison gang was initially formed to protect the northern California Mexican inmates from the Mexican Mafia.

This north south prison gang split also caused street rivalries between gangs to be set aside while in prison. The split acted as a bonding agent for Mexican gang members while incarcerated because now they had a common enemy. By the late 1960s, a gang ethic had been formed and there were certain rules that were followed by the prison gang membership. Standard gang practices, customs and behaviors had been developed and were followed in and out of prison. The Mexican street gang members also became the power bases for the prison gangs.

1970s

In 1970, the now well-known Mexican Mafia member, Joe "Pegleg" Morgan was recruited into the gang. Morgan was highly respected and feared in and out of the correction system. One reason for this was because he was a member of a Mexican street gang, even though he was of Slavic decent. Morgan spoke, read and wrote Spanish fluently. He could speak Spanish better than some Mexican gang members. He took pride in the Mexican culture and was raised in Los Angeles. He earned a street reputation for being a violent, ruthless and cunning inmate through his association with the Maravilla street gang. Morgan had also established strong ties to other L.A. based street gangs, the Italian Mafia and with the drug traffickers from Mexico (Valdemar, 1996).

By 1972, Joe Morgan had become the figurehead leader of the Mexican Mafia. However, there are no formalized leadership positions in this prison gang. Morgan was a charismatic person and that gave him a special influence over the gang's membership. Because of his abilities to negotiate Morgan was able to solidify the alignment between the Mexican Mafia and the Aryan Brotherhood. This was done in order to strengthen the Eme power base in prison. The Black Guerrilla Family prison gang had also formed by this time. It appeared that the Mexican Mafia was preparing for a war.

La Eme flourished in the 1970s and started to exert its influence on the streets. Eme parolees were honored and treated with respect by street gang members. These parolees would routinely carry out Mexican Mafia business including assigned hits. Between 1976 and 1977 there were more than thirty Eme executions on the streets in California. One victim was a California State Senator's aid, who was assassinated in Los Angeles (Valdemar, 1996).

By 1975, La Eme started to infiltrate federally funded community organizations. One such organization was Project Get Going. The grant writer for the project was murdered while traveling to Sacramento to testify against the Mexican Mafia. The project director was the grant writer's husband and also member of the Mexican Mafia.

The common enemies of the Mexican Mafia were the remaining two prison gangs, the Black Guerrilla Family (BGF) and Nuestra Familia (NF). The BGF and NF also made a pact that aligned themselves against the Aryan Brotherhood and the Mexican Mafia. These formalized rivalries within the prison system resulted in an escalation of violence between the prison gangs. The gangs were heading toward a major conflict.

The Mexican Mafia prepared for the upcoming battles by purging its own ranks of members who were weak or not following the rules. Mexican Mafia members would shave their heads when they went to war. The shaved head became a silent signal to other Mexican Mafia prison gang members and inmates of an on coming attack. Today street gang members commonly shave their heads, especially when they are battling with rival gangs. The shaved head hairstyle has also become a very popular hairstyle for many younger Americans.

In the late 1970s, the Mexican Mafia's influence was weakened and damaged because a couple of the gang's members became police informants. The cooperating prison gang members helped initiate major criminal investigations against the gang. In May 1978, Morgan was sent to Federal prison for five years, after pleading guilty to felony charges. However, this did not stop the Mexican Mafia from continuing business nor did it take away the gang's influence. It just introduced the Mexican Mafia into the Federal corrections system.

1980s

Even though major criminal investigations had been started against the Mexican Mafia its members continued their illegal activities. The prison gang expanded its control in heroin trafficking, gambling, debt collection, extortion, prostitution and other illegal inmate activity into the community. Mexican Mafia members refer to themselves as "carnales," a term for blood brother.

By this time, the Mexican Mafia had established control of the Hispanic inmate population in Southern California. Hispanic inmates who were not members of the Mexican Mafia were called Surenos. La Eme had also established a great degree of control over the Hispanic drug dealers operating in Los Angeles County. When a Hispanic gang member went to state prison he was not forced into joining the Mexican Mafia, however the inmate was expected to back up the Hispanic race and would be expected to join in a fight against a rival prison gang.

The late 1980s brought further changes for the Mexican Mafia. The gang started to consolidate its power base. It also appeared that the north-south dividing line of Bakersfield, California had been moved north to the city of San Jose. By 1987, Joe Morgan's influence was so great, that he helped establish the so-called Folsom Truce between the Mexican Mafia and the Black Guerrilla Family. As it turns out, it is really a set of battle rules to help avoid detection by the prison staff (Bauer, 1997).

1990s

The 18th Street gang formed in 1966 and broke the race membership barrier for different reasons. The 18th Street gang allowed anyone to join. In essence the 18th Street gang admitted people who could not qualify for membership in other Mexican street gangs. The non-race based membership philosophy also allowed 18th Street to grow quickly, but the growth was based on quantity.

More importantly, 18th Street established itself in the drug market very quickly. Due to its size 18th Street had established cliques in many southern California neighborhoods and even out of the state. The Mexican Mafia took notice of this growth. By the early 1990s, the Mexican Mafia put pressure on certain 18th Street cliques to conform to more traditional Mexican street gang culture and weed out the non-Hispanic members, especially those who were not entrenched in the Mexican street gang philosophy. This happened because 18th Street was claiming Sureno status (Valdemar, 1996). Remember there are several meanings applied to the term Sureno. In this instance I am referring to the Southern California style of Hispanic gang life.

The Mexican Mafia exerted a strong influence and control over Southern California Hispanic street gangs in the early 1990s. Between 1992 and 1993, the Mexican Mafia orchestrated a series of mandatory meetings for the street gangs. The meetings were used to notify the street of the Eme Edict. Basically, this was an order issued by the Mexican Mafia directing the Hispanic street gangs to stop all the drive-by shootings and end the brown on brown gang violence.

Publicity wise, the general media jumped on the wagon. The word that a prison gang was trying to stop the street gang violence quickly spread. What was not commonly known at the time was that there were additional non-public directives. Hispanic street gangs were also being required to pay a tax. The tribute was allegedly going to be paid for Mexican Mafia protection. The tax was based a surcharge per gang member and a percent of the drug profit money. If a gang did not pay the tax or disobeyed the directive it was met with the threat of assault or death on the streets or in prison (Valdemar, 1996).

The Mexican Mafia gang had so much influence that drive-by shootings stopped in an area of east L.A. between April and September 1993. The reality of the situation set in and it was quickly determined that the killings were not going to stop; only the method in which they were done. According to the Mexican Mafia directive, the drive-by shootings were to be stopped instead walk-up style shootings could to be used (Guzman, 1992).

Non-tax paying street gangs and disobedient gang members were placed on a green light list. This gave compliant street gangs permission to kill the non-compliant gang members with the blessing of the Mexican Mafia. Ironically, this was the same gang that publicly denounced the gang violence. At the same time some 18th Street and Maravilla cliques refused to pay the tax. The Mexican Mafia had developed a method to use street gang members for their dirty work and maintain their public image.

In November 1993, Joe Pegleg Morgan died of liver cancer while in prison. No one knew who will take over the figurehead leadership, but Morgan's style of leadership established the Mexican Mafia as one of the most influential prison gangs in the country.

By late 1999, the Mexican Mafia had suffered through two Federal RICO prosecutions in California and one in Texas. The leadership structure was essentially dismantled. Gang operations were temporarily slowed. Some Mexican Mafia members were trying to collect taxes, but had to endure many embarrassing events. Mexican Mafia impersonators collected the tribute tax and stole it. Some Mexican Mafia members shot up wrong houses in assassination attempts. Other Mafia parolees were shot at and chased out of gang controlled neighborhoods. There was also a fair amount of infighting between Mexican Mafia cliques. The internal and external wars only weakened the influence and power the Mexican Mafia had on the streets and in prison.

2000's

The Mexican Mafia is now a transnational gang because it can be found in at least 13 states and Eme parolees have been contacted and arrested in Mexico. This makes the Mexican Mafia the largest prison gang in the United States, as well as an international prison gang.

What the Mexican Mafia lacks in sophistication is made up with strength. Gang members develop a warrior cult type attitude. The gang is efficient at generating fear, but lack business skills. This places them in curious position of having power, but no money. When out of prison it is common for Mexican Mafia members to live in cheap motel rooms or apartments. Surprisingly, most members consider themselves at the top of the world with, pressed pants, a crisp white T-shirt and $300 in their pocket. Not the glamour image you would expect for an organized crime figure.

Mexican Mafia membership is estimated to be between 300 and 1,000 members and associates. When law enforcement and correctional experts are asked just how many murders has the prison gang been responsible for in its 45 year plus history, the number of 1,000 plus is frequently given. A symbol that is often affiliated with the Mexican Mafia is a tattoo of black colored hand with the letter M in the middle. The leadership structure is loosely structured, but follows strict rules. Mexican Mafia members have always shown a willingness to murder any gang member or person who does not follow orders. As one Eme prison gang associate said, "... *its like a murder, incorporated.*"

Nuestra Familia

Northern California Mexican inmates formed the Nuestra Familia (NF) gang at Soledad prison in the late 1960s (Bauer, 1997). Further literature review suggests that the gang may have been formed in 1966 at the Duel Vocational Institute in Tracy, California by Mexican national inmates. By 1967 members were added at Soledad and Folsom Prisons, California (U.S. Department of Justice, 2003). Another theory expresses that the Nuestra Familia was formed as a result of the stabbing and killing of northern California inmate at the hands of two Mexican Mafia gang members in 1968 (Valdez, 2000). The Nuestra Familia was the second Hispanic prison gang to form in the California correction system.

The motive for the formation regardless of the exact date was conflict between Mexican Mafia gang members and Mexican inmates from northern California.

Initially the gang was formed for protection against further Mexican Mafia attacks and to protect younger Latino inmates from older experienced inmates.

Competition developed between these two prison gangs to control criminal activity, especially the drug trade within the penal system. This only increased the violence between the two gangs. The majority of the membership for the Nuestra Familia gang came from Mexican streets gangs in Northern California. They also form a power base for the Nuestra Familia and are called Nortenos (northerners).

Like the street gang members from the south, northern California gang members that ordinary would be rivals on the street became allies in prison. The conflicts increased because both the Mexican Mafia and Nuestra Familia each tried to control the distribution of heroin and marijuana within the prison system. And after the stabbing of a northern California inmate by Mexican Mafia gang members on September 16, 1968 open hostilities were formalized. Each gang vowed to kill on sight and the now infamous "Shoe Wars" started.

NF tattoos picture a sombrero and bloody dagger with the words Nuestra Familia. Also seen are the letters NF or a picture of a sword. The leadership structure in the Nuestra Familia is considered highly structured and formalized. A written constitution was prepared and defines the gang structure along military lines. There are official positions like general, captains, lieutenants, sergeants and soldiers. Gang members also follow a chain of command and strict written rules. For example, each member is required to uphold standards of dress, hygiene and behavior. With harsh discipline imposed for any infraction.

When the Nuestra Familia and Mexican Mafia gangs would come into contact there was always violence. Both gangs will attack each other wherever and whenever the opportunity presents itself. The Nuestra Family has an estimated membership of 250-300 in the California correction system and is supported with more than 1000 Nortenos.

The primary source of income for the Nuestra Familia is the distribution of cocaine, heroin, marijuana and methamphetamine within the jail and prison systems and in communities in Northern California. Nuestra Familia parolees have also been involved in robberies, murder and the extortion of drug dealers on the street. Nuestra Familia gang members have also been involved in home invasion robbery crimes.

The first Nuestra Familia street presence was established in Fresno, California and was initially referred to as the "Car." Quickly it became known on the streets as the "Fresno Car." The Fresno Car distributed marijuana, heroin and extorted drug dealers within its barrio. The Fresno Car sent illegal drugs back to the prison and 25 percent of the extorted and drug money was also sent back as a tribute back to members of NF who were incarcerated (U.S. Department of Justice, 2003).

By the late 1970s, Hispanic inmates entering prison became formally known as either Surenos or Nortenos depending on where they lived or where they were arrested. This label also fueled the development of new rivalries on the street. They became between Nortenos and Surenos. These groups became the power bases for the Nuestra Familia and the Mexican Mafia.

Northern Structure

Because of the involvement in criminal activities the Nuestra Familia was targeted for investigation and prosecutions by state corrections, local and federal law enforcement. As a result the Nuestra Familia formed a sibling gang in 1983 at Folsom State Prison, California. The Northern Structure prison gang was formed as a means of distracting law enforcement attention away from the activities of the Nuestra Familia. The Nuestra Familia wanted to conduct its business clandestinely through the Northern Structure without incurring blame. The Northern Structure became the front organization for the Nuestra Familia prison gang.

The Northern Structure has also been called Northern Raza (NR). Peer members refer to each other as "brothers" or "bros." The Nuestra Familia also wrote the XIV (14) Bonds of the Nuestra Raza Movement as bylaws for newly formed Nuestra Raza prison gang between 1983 and 1984. Even though the NR appears to be defunct, gang members who wish to become NF members must learn and adhere to the 14 Bonds now known as the 14 Bonds of the Nortenos Movement. The organizational structure of NF was three tiered. There were categories that separated new members from the more experienced members from those who were heavily involved in the prison gang (U.S. Department of Justice, 2003).

The Northern Structure is a criminal enterprise just like any other prison gang. The primary operations include the control of drug trafficking within and outside the prison. The Nuestra Familia has had and maintains control over the Northern Structure in order to prevent it from becoming a rival gang.

One unique characteristic of the Northern Structure is that members are free to leave the gang when they want to. All other prison gangs have mandatory lifetime membership. Most Northern Structure members are unaware that the Nuestra Familia leadership approves the orders and directives they receive and follow.

Conflicts

By the 1980s, the conflicts between La Eme and the NF grew to such a level that the California Department of Corrections began to separate gang members from these two prison gangs by placing them at specific institutions. As a result of the ongoing conflict between the Mexican Mafia and La Nuestra Familia, two separate alliances were formed. These alliances involved the two other major California prison gangs; the Black Guerrilla Family (African American), which became allies of La Nuestra Familia and the Aryan Brotherhood (Caucasian), which allied itself with the Mexican Mafia.

California Youth Authority (CYA) is the equivalent of state prison for minors. In the late 1960s, the CYA began to house its wards on a north and south regional basis with the idea in mind that matriculation back into general society would be easier for the minor. The program instead further polarized the young gang members and intensified prison gang rivalry. Some experts think this separation may have been part of the mechanism that transported the state prison level rivalries into the youth institutions.

Within a short period of time after the state order separation the Nuestra Familia rivalry spread into the California Youth Authority. As the rivalry expanded, it also helped in turning Northern California street gangs against Southern California street gangs. Each began fighting for the control of drug sales in and outside the prison systems, for power, for protection and for respect.

Mexican Mafia prison gang members also identify with the term Sur, the Spanish word for south. Sureno or Southerner was also used meaning the inmate was from Southern California. The Latino street gangs also started to band together under Sur-13 once in prison. The number 13 was used to indicate a general alignment with the Mexican Mafia.

Northern Latino prison gangs reacted by adopting the number 14, representing the fourteenth letter of the alphabet, N. This indicated a general alignment with the Nuestra Familia. The number corresponded to the letter "N" which is the first letter in the Spanish word Norteno, meaning northerner or from the north. The symbol can be written or tattooed as 14/NF. By the 1980s some Latino gang members from the North sometimes referred to themselves as Chicanos while those from Southern California called themselves Mexicanos. Peace between these two rivals is infrequent. Don't forget in the late 1960s Mexican street gangs in southern California also used the term and it referred to the gang's pure Mexican heritage.

Fresno Bulldogs

During the early 1970s Hispanic juveniles from northern California who were incarcerated and from the same area started to band together for protection against the more savvy Sureno gang members. These wards of the court identified with the number 14 because it represented the fourteenth letter of the alphabet, the letter N. N is the first letter in the word norteno. Because of the big split between northern and southern California Hispanic gangs, Nortenos also identified with the color red. By 1973 these gang members also started to identify themselves as

F-14, which represented the city they were from, Fresno. This symbol became the parent logo for gangs that formed later.

Although other Hispanic gangs formed in the Fresno area, they tended to use the F-14 as a precursor to their gang name or clique. Gangs like F-14 East Side, F-14 Park Side, F-14 Sunset and F-14 Pinedale appeared in the mid 1970s. Don't forget Sureno gangs had been active since the early 1900s. Prior to the 1970s, Hispanic street activity in Northern California had been virtually unheard of (Castro, 1998).

As more new gangs appeared criminal activity increased and more F-14 gang members went to jail and prison. Between 1975 and 1979 some F-14 gang members had a significant impact on the California Youth Authority. As F-14 gang members attempted to make a name for themselves some joined the Nuestra Familia prison gang. By 1976, a NF regiment was established at Preston School of Industry, in Northern California. It appeared that the F-14 street gang members would follow the unwritten rule and affiliated with and or supported the Nuestra Familia prison gang.

In October 1976 a young 15 year-old California Youth Authority ward was released from the Preston School of Industry. He was just a couple days shy of his 16th birthday. He was ultimately suspected of murdering three subjects for the Nuestra Familia. In a twelve-month period between 1976 and 1977 a total of 23-prison gang related homicides occurred in the Fresno area. The majority related to Nuestra Familia activities and drug trafficking. This resulted in a law enforcement response that focused on gangs in Fresno and the Nuestra Familia. By the 1980s much of the NF/ F-14 activity had been stopped. Some F-14 gang members dropped out and or stopped associating of the Nuestra Familia prison gang (Castro, 1998).

Between 1980 and 1982 Nuestra Familia ranks began to dwindle and there were internal conflicts with the NF leadership. The Federal government also started its RICO investigation. The subsequent RICO prosecution and mass defection of NF members left the Nuestra Familia in disarray.

Between the fall of 1984 and summer of 1985 the Nuestra Familia and Northern Structure attempted to bring F-14 gang members under the 14 Bonds at San Quentin Prison. Many F-14 gang members resisted. This resulted with a number of violent confrontations between N-14, Nuestra Familia and Northern Structure gang members. The Nuestra Familia and Northern Structure became enemies of F-14 gang members.

The F-14 gangs also started to refer to themselves as the Fresno Car and by 1986 changed their name to the Fresno Bulldogs or BDS. The gang adopted the Fresno State University bulldog logo as a gang symbol and the school color (red) as their gang color. The Bulldog gang started a two-year series of confrontations with Nuestra Familia, Northern Structure and Sureno based gangs. By 1989 the Bulldog gang had established itself as a violent street gang.

Criminal activity included rape, commercial take over robberies, narcotics trafficking, carjacking and murder. By the 1990s the Bulldogs had grown into one of the most violent Hispanic street gangs in California. Membership continued to grow in the mid-1990s and membership on the streets was estimated at over 1,500. It is not surprising to find a number of Bulldogs in state prison. The Bulldogs continued their rivalries and criminal activities even while in local jails and state prisons.

Although not officially recognized as a California prison gang at this time, the Bulldog gang might as well be because criminal activities gang members committed on the outside were also committed while in prison. The Bulldog gang is known for their brazenness and violence in and out of prison. The number of Bulldog gang members sent to prison has also increased their strength as well as reputation. By the mid 1990s there were a number of Bulldog cliques in and surrounding Fresno, California.

During 1993 and 1994 a concerted effort was made by the gang to unite all Bulldog factions. This successful endeavor led to renaming the gang, F-14 Bulldogs. The Fresno

Bulldogs have isolated themselves from the traditional north-south alliance and have become an independent street and prison gang, just like the United Blood Nation gang on the East Coast (Castro, 1998).

Aryan Brotherhood

As Latino prison inmate populations grouped together to survive, so did the White and African American inmates. The Aryan Brotherhood (AB) was founded in 1957 at the Duel Vocational Institute, Tracy, California (Bauer, 1997). Further literature review also suggests the Aryan Brotherhood prison gang was formed in the mid 1960s by White inmates at San Quentin Prison (Valdemar, 1998). These inmates incorporated white supremacist philosophies by 1968 (Bauer, 1997). Another source indicates the prison gang was formed in 1967 at San Quentin Prison (www.knowgangs.com). The gang was also reported to have formed initially for protection against the other ethnic based prison gangs (Valdemar, 1998). However, this prison gang went through a number of name changes before getting to be known as the Aryan Brotherhood.

At one time this gang was known as the Diamond Tooth Gang because each member had a piece of glass embedded in a tooth. Then the gang changed the name to the Blue Bird Gang because each member had a tattoo of a blue bird on his neck (Bauer, 1997, Valdemar, 1998 and Valdez, 2000).

Most Aryan Brotherhood prison gang members are housed at San Quentin and Folsom prisons in California and they have formed a loose alliance with the Mexican Mafia. Each gang supports each other with contract hits within the prison system and armed robberies, narcotics trafficking and murder out on the streets.

The Aryan Brotherhood even reportedly established an association with the infamous Manson family. This relationship allegedly started when the Manson girls solicited help from the Aryan Brotherhood to assist Charles Manson in an escape attempt when he was facing trial. The Manson girls joined the Aryan Brotherhood in an auxiliary position and became outside drug contacts. Manson's escape attempt never materialized (Valdemar, 1998).

The Aryan Brotherhood is now well organized with leadership positions and delegated responsibilities. Initially, the gang would have been considered loosely structure that had a governing counsel. Even though the gang is loosely structured, it is organized enough so there is an accounting for all activities both within and outside the prison system. Like most prison gangs, Aryan Brotherhood membership is a lifetime commitment. There are a few membership characteristics that are specific only to this gang.

For example, Aryan Brotherhood tattoos are somewhat unique. The cloverleaf, swastika, lightning bolts, the number 666 and the letters AB are commonly seen together. The words or abbreviations of Supreme White Power, White Power, Supreme White Pride or White Pride may also be seen. The number 666 is also used by some 18th Street gang members. Three times six equals 18.

As indicated by the tattoos AB membership is limited to White inmates only. Some law enforcement experts feel that a few members of the AB believe in and practice occult rituals, as evidenced by numbers 666 which have a definite meaning for those people who practice occult beliefs.

The main source of income for this gang tends to come from narcotic sales within the prison and out on the streets. This involves the distribution of cocaine, heroin, marijuana and methamphetamine (U.S. Department of Justice, 2003).

Members of this gang also use the American Sign Language used by the deaf to communicate with each other in a non-verbal fashion. Communication in this manner allows for some privacy between those who may not want the prison guards in on the conversation.

In the summer of 2006 the U.S. attorney's office was successful in prosecuting several leaders of the Aryan Brotherhood who issued orders to start a race riot in an east coast prison. Even though the death penalty was sought, it was not given by the jury. The case involved over 30 defendants all in custody.

Black Guerrilla Family

The Black Guerrilla Family (BGF) is the most politically oriented of all the prison gangs. The gang initially followed and espoused the Marxist-Leninist-Maoist revolutionary philosophies. George Lester Jackson, a Black Panther leader while incarcerated in San Quentin prison, around 1966, established the Black Guerrilla Family (Bauer, 1997). Jackson established this group believing the Black Panther Party was not responding to the needs of the African-American prison inmates. Jackson first called this gang the Black Family. Prospective members were solicited into the gang by telling them their crimes were a result of the White oppression. This was a recruitment great tool because it made disgruntled minority inmates feel as if they were the victims.

Jackson soon changed the name to the Black Vanguard after a sizeable membership was established. This name remained with the gang until 1971, when Jackson was killed in an escape attempt. Since Jackson's death the gang's membership continued to grow. A literature review also suggests that the gang adopted the name "Black Guerilla Family" or BGF in 1977 (Bauer, 1997).

The BGF has a very close relationship with a splinter group of quasi-criminal revolutionaries the Black Liberation Army or BLA. Some prison gang experts believe the Black Guerrilla Family is just an extension of the Black Liberation Army. Some of the gang's goals were the eradication of racism, to continue the struggle to maintain dignity in prison and in a "racist" society and to overthrow the U.S. government and end capitalism (Bauer, 1997).

There are two tattoos commonly associated with the Black Guerrilla Family. They are a prison guard tower with a dragon surrounding it. The dragon has a quarter moon depicted in the body. The second tattoo shows the silhouette of a rifle with a sword lying over it to form an X. The initials BGF are placed between the spaces that form the X.

Membership into the gang has to be sponsored and it open to heterosexual African-American males. Usually a verbal and written background is completed on prospective members. Like other prison gangs the BGF considers membership status permanent. New members can be drawn from the ranks of the Blood and Crip street gangs. BGF members call each other comrade or rade. The BGF also uses a code to reference the gang. The numbers 276 are used because they represent the second, seventh and sixth letters of the alphabet, BGF.

The BGF maintains close ties to street gangs, most likely in an effort to facilitate drug trafficking operations. As far as prison gang politics, the BGF allies itself with the Nuestra Familia gang. The BGF rivals are the Mexican Mafia and Aryan Brotherhood gang.

Texas Syndicate

The Texas Syndicate was introduced into the California state prison system in the early 1970s at Folsom Prison however the roots of the gang were from Texas (Valdez, 2000). As with much of the prison gang history the literature review sometimes suggests different origins for the same gang. It is also reported that the gang formed in 1973 at the San Quentin Prison, California (Bauer, 1997).

The establishment of the west coast faction of the gang was probably the result of migrating parolees or street gang members from the El Paso area. The west coast gang's membership is comprised of Mexican/ Hispanic male inmates, no White or African-American members are allowed. Coincidently the west coast TS gang initially was formed for protection against the other existing prison gangs, just as their Texas counterparts.

In the late 1990s TS membership grew because of a national recruitment effort. The Texas Syndicate in the California Department of Corrections (CDC) started accepting members from Columbia, Cuba and Mexico. A small group of TS members are referred to as "carnales", while the term carnal refers to a single member. New recruits are often called cardinals. The institutional leader is known as the chairman. Of the prison gangs, the TS gang is one of the youngest and does not appear to have a formal constitution or vertical leadership structure.

The gang's tattoos contain the letters TS and are sometimes hidden in a design. Sometimes, the figure of a woman or a face is used to hide the tattoo. More often, the letters TS are made by a dragon figure, ribbons or flowers. The right forearm area seems to be the most popular location used for tattoos, but remember tattoos can be placed anywhere.

The Texas Syndicate has also developed associations with a smaller gang called the Texas Mafia. The rival gangs of the Texas Syndicate have been the Mexican Mafia, Mexikanemi, Mandingo Warriors, La Nuestra Familia and the Aryan Brotherhood. Outside prison, gang members are involved in drug trafficking, transportation of illegal aliens and contract murders. Inside prison, the gang focuses on drug trafficking, extortion, pressure rackets and internal discipline. The same focus as many other prison gangs. Currently, there are a small number of TS members in the CDC and the gang is based in the Texas Department of Corrections.

Blood/Crip Gangs

The Crips and Bloods also have founded their own groups. While on the street, Crip sets may war with each other. Inside the prison system, however, there seems to be a truce and alliance between these groups, probably for protection from the existing prison gangs.

In prison, some Crip gang members formed the Consolidated Crip Organization, (CCO) and Blood gang members founded the United Blood Nation (UBN). As new Crip or Blood gang members were being incarcerated, members from either of the two groups would be joined, ensuring protection and guidance. This began in 1993. The CCO created a constitution and code of ethics based on the acronym CRIPS: Community Revolutionary International Party Structure. On the west coast neither of the two groups has been impacted by prison gang politics.

On Riker's Island African-American inmates who were being victimized by the existing gang formed a gang within the prison for protection. They called their gang the United Blood Nation and at first was not associated with the UBN on the west coast which was started by west coast Blood gang members. During an interview with an UBN gang member from the east coast it was revealed that some east coast UBN members feel that any Blood gang member is an ally and part of the UBN (Grizzard, 2005). This attitude may facilitate the planning and commission of criminal activity between west and east coast based Blood sets. It also may be the precursor of a paradigm shift in the unification of Blood sets across the country.

Other Prison Gangs

NETA

The Neta is one of the larger prison gangs found in the northeast part of the country. However, the original gang was formed in the Puerto Rican prison system and was then imported into the United States. This all male prison gang was established in 1970 in the Rio Pedras Prison, Puerto Rico and initially was formed to stop the violence between the prison inmates. Membership can include Hispanic and Puerto Rican inmates.

The main activities and primary source of income for the Neta prison gang includes drug trafficking, extortion and gang related violence. Some Neta prison gang members have developed specialty roles within the eastern prison systems. Neta gang members will often keep a low profile while other Hispanic groups attract attention. Neta gang members use this tactic to cover a drug or gang related prison hits. The gang is always recruiting and usually members are required to procure 20 perspective members. This prison gang operates under the facade that they are a cultural organization.

The Neta, like many other prison gangs has established ties with street gangs. Some Neta gang members appear to be patriotic while other members have associated themselves with a Puerto Rican revolutionary group called Los Macheteros. The philosophy of Los Macheteros is independence for the island of Puerto Rico. As with many prison and street gangs, any disrespect shown to an individual Neta member is received by the entire gang. Extreme violence often follows the insult. The Neta rivals are considered to be the Latin Kings (People Nation) and Los Solidos.

Neta members are secretive and will not freely admit their membership. The gang identifies with the colors red, white and blue. Florida prison gang experts have also noted that sometimes the black color is substituted for blue (www.dc.state.fl.us). Members wear clothes, including bandanas and beads of these colors. Probationary gang members will wear a necklace of all white beads to show their status. Gang members that are considered loyal may wear black colored beads with the white ones, plus a single red bead. Some members will display the Puerto Rican flag and will carry a membership card.

The gang uses a hand sign where the middle and index finger of the right hand are crossed forming the letter N in sign language. If this signal is placed over the heart, it becomes a salute. The emblem of the gang is the symbol of a shackled hand over two crossing Puerto Rican flags, placed within a heart.

Outside prison, Neta gang members have been known to carry automatic weapons. Neta gang members usually are not deterred by police presence and have had a history of attacking field officers. The Neta prison and street gang presence seems to be confined to the eastern part of the United States.

Cuban

The Mariel Boatlift officially began April 15, 1980 and ended October 31, 1980, with the arrival of over 125,000 Cubans to Southern Florida from Port of Mariel, Cuba. Some of the immigrants who arrived in the United States were criminals. The Cuban government swept its prison system of its worst criminals and allowed these criminals to enter the US under the guise of being a Cuban refugee. The end result: thousands of violent and hardened ex-prisoners were freed in the United States.

Cuban criminals possessed two unique characteristics. First, all inmates had been military-trained, due to Cuba's mandatory three-year military obligation. Secondly, in Cuba's prisons, inmates were often subjected to physical and psychological torture.

For the first time law enforcement in the United States had to deal with a group of criminals who not only possessed a criminal mentality, but were also trained military fighters, familiar with all types of weapons and tactics. This presented a whole new set of problems for law enforcement and the prison systems here in the United States.

These Cuban criminals became known as the Marielitos and had their own set of identifying characteristics. The Marielitos could be in their late teens to late fifties. Most were in good physical shape but many had poor personal hygiene. Almost all had some type of body scaring, either self-inflicted or due to physical torture. Skin color varied from black to white. Not all Cuban refugees who came over in the Mariel boatlift were criminals. The majority of Cuban immigrants were, and still are, law-abiding citizens. This is most likely true with all immigrant groups.

Marielito tattoos were almost a secret code or language. Most of the tattoos are found on the hand and between the first finger and thumb. The tattoos indicate the type of crime(s) the individual was involved in. Five dots forming an X represented a habitual criminal; while four dots forming a box indicated homicide. Three dots, which form a triangle, show a crime of theft while three dots in a straight line indicate a crime of robbery.

Symbols are sometimes used to represent specialty trades. A heart with an arrow pointing to it with the word Tutu is the symbol of an executioner. A Christian cross on its side indicates that the person wearing it can supply weapons, cars or equipment. Three descending and diverging lines with two horizontal lines indicates a narcotics trafficker.

Asian

Due to the ever-increasing population of Asian-American street gang members in the prison system one might expect to see the development of Asian prison gangs. The primary factor for the formation of these groups would be the same as for other prison gangs, protection. However, in prison the Asian gang members tend to become model prisoners. Asian inmates seem to adapt well to the rigid rules of prison life. It is not uncommon to find Asian inmates on parole who indicate prison life was not a problem for them.

For many Asian inmates, prison life is reported to be a good life. While incarcerated Asian gang members take advantage of the system benefits and are able to complete school, work, eat three meals a day and a place to stay. Granted, individual rights are compromised, but for many Asian gang member inmates, prison life can be better than their street gang life. Many paroled Asian gang members have confided to me that prison also provides security and safety for them. Apparently some Asian gang members feel it is somewhat safer in prison because all outside street rivalries are dropped in prison. "*You hang with your people and just watch your back,*" stated Kiet, a 23-year-old parolee.

Trends

Some street gang members feel going to prison and joining a prison gang is a natural goal. It can be equated to going to graduate school or getting that Fortune 500 company job after college. Unfortunately, the prison system is where many young gang members learn the secrets of becoming a professional criminal. Remember, in the gang sub-culture a veteran of prison receives the respect and admiration of the street-level gang members.

As of the mid 2000s there were over 2 million inmates in U.S. prisons and jails. The cost of incarceration is also increasing. It is estimated that it costs between $28,000 and $30,000 per year to house a sentenced prisoner. Public schools spend approximately $3,000 per year for the formal education of each student. This is a sad reality of today's world.

According to the California Department of Corrections at least one MS-13 gang members has been accepted into the ranks of the Mexican Mafia. Some reports suggest as many as three MS-13 gang members. Needless to say, some cliques and members of MS-13 have transnational connections. This could help the Mexican mafia become a transnational prison gang and also confirms and insures the dominance of the Mexican Mafia over all sureno based gangs including those that may be involved in transnational gang activity. These contacts could help the Mexican Mafia diversify and become more organized.

Summary

Prison gangs in the United States have two basic genesis mechanisms. First, the gang forms within a prison. Secondly, the gang forms in the street and recruits additional members while incarcerated. The gang's activities while in prison qualify it as a prison gang. This is really a corrections definition issue. Some corrections departments require that the gang form in prison for it to qualify it as a prison gang. Other departments base the requirement on the group's activities.

As the gang membership becomes larger the gang develops as a force within the corrections institution. While in prison the gang competes with other prison gangs for control and power.

Most prison gangs are involved in drug sales and control issues. Some gangs have a formal leadership structure and other do not. Many prison gang members follow a routine of physical exercise and academic study. Almost all consider themselves as gang warriors ready to do anything they are asked.

Once a prison gang member is released on parole he does the gang's bidding. This may include murder, extortion and drug sales. Some parolees have left the country and established working relationships with Mexican drug trafficking organizations. The prison gang establishes its reputation based on how much it is feared within the prison gang community. The fear is created through violent and brutal acts.

In the west coast paroled prison gang members do not recruit other members to form a street version of the prison gang. In the Midwest this is not true. Released prison gang members have formed street versions of their gangs. A good example of this phenomenon is the Black Gangster Disciple gang from Chicago. This gang has become so organized that is has what some experts consider a board that over sees prison and street gang activity. Board members report to a gang CEO. There are no reports of female prison gangs forming within the United States. Female gang members have not yet exhibited this behavior. Many female gang members tolerate each other while in prison.

Prison Gangs in Texas

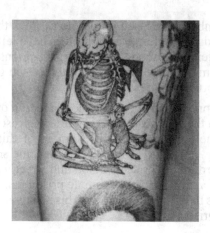

There are a number of prison gangs based in the Texas Department of Corrections that have a direct influence in Texas and other parts of the country and even in Mexico. Like prison gangs in California Texas based prison gangs draw new recruits from the ranks of local street gangs.

Barrio Azteca

Like several other prison gangs Barrio Azteca can be considered a transnational gang, because of the illegal activities some members are involved in. The gang is active within the Federal Bureau of Prisons, the Texas Department of Corrections and county correctional facilities throughout Texas and in the southwest and northwest regions of the United States. Like many other prison gangs barrio Azteca operates both in and out of prison. In 2007, the gang's presence was noted in 20 states and in Mexico (JICC, 2007).

Barrio Azteca is a Texas based prison gang that originally formed in 1986. The Barrio Azteca gang was originally founded by five incarcerated Hispanic street gang members who banded together for protection from rival gangs (HIDTA, 2007). This is the same onus that inspired and acted as a catalyst for the formation of other prison gangs like the Black Guerilla Family, Mexican Mafia, Aryan Brotherhood, the Tango Blast and many street gangs.

In 2004, the gang's population was estimated to be around 2,000. By the mid 1990s Barrio Azteca was the third largest prison gang in the Texas Department of Corrections (NDIC, 2004). However in 2007, the gang population was estimated to be between 3,000 and 3,500 members (JICC, 2007; FBI, 2007). The largest faction is noted to be based in the El Paso (Ibid). This is supported by the FBI who suggests there are approximately 600 barrio Azteca members in the El Paso area (FBI, 2007).

The Texas Department of Corrections estimates there are approximately 800 Barrio Azteca members in custody. The Federal Bureau of Prisons notes that approximately 375 Barrio Azteca members have been identified within their prison system. Barrio Azteca gang members have been reported in Arkansas, Alabama, California, Colorado, Florida, Georgia, Hawaii, Kansas, Kentucky, Louisiana, North Carolina, New Jersey, New York, Ohio, Oklahoma, Pennsylvania, South Carolina, Tennessee, Texas, Virginia and West Virginia (JICC, 2007).

Law enforcement anecdotal evidence based on criminal investigations reveals that Barrio Azteca members were involved in the sales and distribution of drugs within the Texas Department of Corrections by late 1986; less than a year after the gang was formed. The gang's membership was also increasing during this time and as a result a formal constitution was developed. The constitution outlined leadership positions and membership responsibilities and suggested a vertical command structure for the gang.

Barrio Azteca uses a para-military type leadership structure. The gang has a single leader known as the Supreme Commander; whose job is to make all the major decisions that affect the gang. Another report suggests this position is called the 'Capo-Mayor' (JICC, 2007). Captains (Capos) assist the Supreme Commander in making decisions, ensure the decisions are implanted and discipline members for serious rule infractions. Lieutenants (Tirilon/Teniente) are responsible for regional activities and are assisted by the Sergeants. Sergeants (Sangron/ Sergento) collect the taxes; oversee the discipline of all members and are responsible for recruiting and sponsoring of new members. Soldiers (Soldado/Carnal) usually carry out the criminal activities for the gang (NDIC, 2004; JICC, 2007). Members are also sometimes referred to as "Indios" (HIDTA, 2007).

It should be noted that this type of vertical command structure and organization only facilitates national and international criminal operations. Using this type of highly networked and centralized authority, along with current cellular and Internet technology allows for clear communication and non-disrupted criminal operations.

Before the 1990s sometimes leaders will use colored feather tattoos to indicate rank. For example four gold colored feathers indicate the rank of Supreme Commander. Three gold feathers would be a Captain, two silver colored feathers would suggest the rank of Lieutenant and one bronze colored feather shows the rank of Sergeant. However, this practice was discontinued in the early 1990s.

The gang recruits new members from the Hispanic population within the Texas Department of Corrections and from El Paso area Hispanic street gangs like Varrio Northwest, Barrio Canutos Rifan and the Kernal Street Locos. Sergeants will sponsor a new recruit and membership has to be approved by a Captain. In correctional facilities a member in good standing can act as a sponsor and acts as a godfather (padrino) and is responsible for the education and initiation of the new member (JICC,2007).

Tattoos are not required for membership (HIDTA, 2007). Barrio Azteca members who do use tattoos will use the number 21 or XXI for the letters B and A. Gang specific tattoos can include a BA, 21-4-life (Barrio Azteca for life), 915 (area code for El Paso)or EPT for El Paso. Sometimes a member may sport the tattoo of a plumed Aztec warrior or an Aztec Chieftain carrying an Indian woman superimposed on an eagle with upswept wings, the word Azteca or simple a form of the letter A (for Azteca).

By the late 1980s the Barrio Azteca gang was well established in the streets of El Paso and deeply entrenched in drug trafficking operations in the El Paso area. Heroin, cocaine and marijuana were the drugs of choice. A few short years later law enforcement anecdotal evidence suggested the gang was obtaining drugs from the Carillo-Fuentes drug trafficking organization based in Mexico (NDIC, 2004). In fact criminal investigations suggested Barrio Azteca members were smuggling drugs into the United States for the cartel. Having this 'direct connection' to a major supplier only facilitated the expansion of the drug market for Barrio Azteca throughout Texas.

As a result Barrio Azteca has been known to also traffic methamphetamine and MDMA (ecstasy). One of the favorite routes has been the El Paso-Juarez corridor. Multi-kilograms quantities of heroin, cocaine and marijuana and thousands of tablets of ecstasy have been smuggled from Mexico into the U.S. using private vehicles and couriers on foot. You cannot underscore how females play a role in drug trafficking. Law enforcement anecdotal evidence suggests minivans driven by females are frequently used to transport drugs across the U.S.-Mexico border (JICC, 2007). This can happen because single female drivers of mini-vans do not fit the typical profile of a drug trafficker.

This kind of diversification also affords opportunities for Barrio Azteca to forge business relationships with other street and prison gangs, as well as other Mexican drug trafficking organizations when it becomes profitable. Having multiple sources of product and distribution networks allows for a continual non-disrupted money making operation. Coupled with strict and brutal enforcement of gang rules it becomes easy to conclude that Barrio Azteca operates as a criminal enterprise and how the gang is capable of street and prison drug trafficking.

The Barrio Azteca tends to enforce its rules through violence and intimidation and will order 'green lights' on individuals they believe betrayed the gang. Barrio Azteca members are not allowed to claim membership to any other gang, except when they are questioned or interrogated by law enforcement (JICC, 2007). This means if detained by Customs Border Patrol, ICE or other Federal or local agencies Barrio Azteca members will not be truthful about gang affiliation or membership. If a members is 'X out' he has fallen out of favor of the gang and is no longer allowed to associate with Barrio Azteca, mostly he is also marked with a green light.

For example, in Juarez, Mexico some members of the Juarez Municipal Police work with Barrio Azteca in drug trafficking operations. This type of relationship assists Barrio Azteca because it protects the gang from police operations in Mexico. This also helps ensure that Barrio Azteca maintains control of drug operations in Juarez as it prevents other gangs from gaining a part of the business (JICC, 2007). In Mexico the gang is referred to as 'Los Aztecas." In the Ciudad Juarez Social Rehabilitation Center, Chihuahua, Mexico there are more than 800 Azteca members in custody (Ibid). Members who are not in custody tend to stay in the area of Ciudad Juarez. This gives the gang international communications and business opportunities. This also clearly supports the fact that some factions of the Barrio Azteca gang are transnational.

The gang's growth in the drug trafficking industry also allowed it to develop a growing presence throughout the U.S. By2007 Barrio Azteca presence was noted by law enforcement in no less than 19 states and in Chihuahua, Mexico (JICC, 2007). This expansion allowed Barrio Azteca to form alliances with other gangs including the Chicago based Latin King gang, the Surenos and the Mexikanemi prison gang to facilitate drug trafficking operations. Like most modern day gangs Barrio Azteca has also been known to cooperate with rival gangs in criminal endeavors if it is financially beneficial for the gang (NDIC, 2007).

Like many gangs Barrio Azteca its menu of criminal activities. This gang is also involved in human smuggling, kidnapping, robbery, murder, arson, extortion, auto theft, assault, burglary and weapon violations. This includes assaults against other Barrio Azteca members. It has been documented that often leaders will use violence against lower ranking members for breaking gang rules, associating with rival gangs without permission and for cooperating with law enforcement (NDIC, 2004). In addition, a few barrio Azteca members own and operate legitimate businesses, while others are gainfully employed.

Because of this diversification Barrio Azteca activity has been reported in Arizona, Arkansas, California, Colorado, Florida, Idaho, Illinois, Indiana, Kansas, Missouri, New Mexico, New York, New jersey, Nevada, North Carolina, Tennessee, Texas, Utah and Washington. FBI, DEA and local law enforcement anecdotal evidence based on criminal investigations supports this (JICC, 2007).

Rivals of Barrio Azteca include the Texas Syndicate, Aryan Brotherhood of Texas, Partido Revolucionario Mexicano (PRM), Texas Chicano Brotherhood, Raza Unida, Black Guerilla Family, Mexicles, La Nuestra Familia and the New Mexico Syndicate prison gangs. Barrio Azteca also maintains rivalries with several street gangs including, but not limited to Del Sol, Folk Nation gangs, the El Paso area Latin Kings and the Nasty Boys (NDIC, 2004).

Of all the gangs operating in the United States the Barrio Azteca gang has done something unique. Members and associates outside prison sometimes use codes to communicate using public radio. Gang members will use coded messages in the form of dedications aired by announcers on public radio. Unwittingly, radio hosts would read the dedications over the air, unknowing that they were really sending orders and messages for Barrio Azteca (JICC, 2007). This is very similar to the 'carnival talk' the California based Mexican Mafia has used during visits. What on the face appears to be normal conversation is really a verbal code to issue orders, collect intelligence and conduct criminal activities.

Barrio Azteca also uses a written code to communicate. Many other street and prison gang use various codes to communicate in writing, but the codes that Barrio Azteca uses are somewhat unique. The use of codes by gangs offers a form of operational security. The Barrio Azteca gang has been known to use a code called 'Sufamelico." The word comes from the Aztec Nahuatl language. It should be noted that other Latino prison gangs also speak and write in Nahuatl. The Sufamelico code uses a series of paired letters that are substituted for a single letter and are used to form words (FBI, 2007).

Barrio Azteca members have also been involved in arms trafficking. Law enforcement criminal investigations have shown that Barrio Azteca has maintained stash house for weapons in Texas and Juarez, Mexico. As with other gangs that traffic arms Barrio Azteca members obtain firearms from members of other street gangs, organized firearm traffickers, organized narcotic traffickers, straw purchases and through residential, vehicle and commercial burglaries. Barrio Azteca members have been known to carry weapons for protection against rival gangs.

Barrio Azteca members have been involved in the kidnapping of X-out members and others who are smuggled into Mexico where they have beaten, tortured and killed. Barrio Azteca members have also been involved in the transportation of victims murdered in the United States for body disposal in Mexico (JICC, 2007).

Of potential concern is the fact that Barrio Azteca like other prison and street gangs in involved in smuggling aliens across the U.S.-Mexican border. Like all gangs background checks are not conducted on this individual seeking illegal entry into the United States. This can pose a potential danger to U.S. security because often people other than Mexican utilize this mechanism for entry. For example, law enforcement anecdotal evidence has shown that illegal entry into the U.S. has been made Chinese, Middle Eastern and European immigrants through the U.S –Mexican border. On the other side of the border Mexican officials have detained and subsequently deported Middle Eastern immigrants posing as Mexicans with Greek passports (Sandoval, 2009).

Like many other street and prison gangs Barrio Azteca operates to make a profit. With that in mind understanding trends in drug trafficking can become an important factor in suppression operations. For example, in late 2007, there is some anecdotal evidence that suggested an alliance had been formed between the Carlos Fuentes, leader of the Juarez Cartel and Joaquin "el Chapo" Guzman of the Sinaloa Cartel. Both leaders are part of the Federation, which is an alliance with leaders of Mexican Drug trafficking organizations from the Mexican state of Durango. Some evidence suggests the reason the leaders of three different cartels formed this alliance was to help take control of lucrative drug trafficking routes in Sinaloa, Durango and Chihuahua assuring easy access to Ciudad Juarez, El Paso, Interstate 10 to Texas and Californian and Interstate 25 north to Albuquerque. This alliance would also insure that the Juarez Cartel could control drug trafficking into Texas (HIDTA, 2007).

In order to complete the equation here, Mexican Drug Trafficking Organizations enlist the help of U.S. based prison gangs like Barrio Azteca and street gangs that are located in California and Texas. The proceeds of drug distribution and retails sales would most likely follow the same route back to Mexico and also could be laundered through legitimate businesses own by Barrio Azteca members.

Hermanos De Pistoleros Latinos (HPL)

Hermanos de Pistoleros is a Texas based prison gangs that originally formed in the Texas Department of Corrections during the mid 1980s. Since its formation the gang has spread in and beyond the state prison system. Currently, the HPL gang has been reported throughout Texas and Laredo is considered the main power base (FBI, 2007). Prison transfers and migration has helped spread the gang out of Texas and now can be located throughout the United States and Mexico.

HPL members have been reported on Minnesota, Tennessee, Georgia, Wisconsin, Michigan, Montana, New York, North Carolina, North Dakota, Iowa, Illinois and California. Anecdotal law enforcement evidence suggests that the HPL presence may not be strong in some states. The Federal Bureau of prisons reports HPL members in custody in Alabama, Arkansas, Florida, Georgia, Illinois, Indiana, Kansas, Kentucky, Maryland, Michigan, Mississippi, New York, North Carolina, Ohio, Oklahoma, Oregon, Pennsylvania, South Carolina, Tennessee, Texas, Virginia and West Virginia (FBI, 2007).

According to one report more than 1, 300 HPL members have been documented in the U.S. There is no current estimate that provides the HPL population in Mexico. A 2007 estimate suggests there were a little over 100 HOP (BOP, 2007). In late 2006 the Texas Department of Corrections reported 440 HPL members in custody (TDCJ, 2006).

Currently, with the globalization of some American based gangs including street, prison and outlaw motorcycle gangs there is plenty of anecdotal evidence to suggest cross border connections between the United States and Mexico and Canada. Based on law enforcement experience there also seems to be a large contingent of HPL members in the country of Mexico. It is logical to conclude the Mexican based HPL members maintain contact with HPL members in the U.S.

It is also logical to surmise the Mexican based HPL members can and do have contact with Mexican drug trafficking organizations. It is clear to determine the distinct possibility that this prison based gang is well entrenched in the drug trafficking and distribution business. The HPL street gang connection provides a natural U.S. based retail distribution network that the prison gang can control. For example, there is a reported HPL faction operating in Laredo, Texas and also directly across the border in Nuevo Laredo, the venue of much Mexican drug cartel violence.

This can present border control and safety issues for several reasons. Hermanos de Pistoleros Latinos is a prison based gang that operates on the street and has developed strong connections between local street gangs and Mexican based drug trafficking groups. Like all prison gangs HPL speaks with a language that is universally understood. That is the language of violence. Law enforcement investigations suggest that HPL members are often armed. Many tattoo a life size 45 caliber semi-automatic handgun on the waist area of the body so it appears that they are armed (TDCJ, 2007).

HPL members have been reported to be involved in home invasion robbery, drug trafficking, assaults human and arms trafficking and murder. There is some evidence to suggest that HPL members have also been involved in arms trafficking into Mexico. When HPL members traffic drugs the drugs of choice have been cocaine, marijuana, ecstasy and ice.

HPL has a vertical command structure and a written set of rules governing its members and even a formula that details procedures for members to advance in rank. The rank structure for this gang from lowest to highest: Encagardo which is in charge of a particular area but holds no rank with HPL; Soldiers, which are the rank and file HPL members, Sergeants, which are members that assist Lieutenants; Lieutenants, which are in charge of a unit of HPL members within the Texas department of Corrections; Captains are in charge of a specific city or town; Majors are in charge of several cities or towns within a specific geographical region; A general will be charge of a specific geographical region of a state. The highest ranking HPL members are known as Llavero (key holder). This small group of HPL members will make all executive decisions which can affect the gang. There are three members and any decision takes a majority (two out of three) vote. Llaveros are voted in by the general membership. This military style management allows for a small number of HPL members to be efficient and prosperous.

This prison based gang is well organized and has a set of written regulations and rules and procedures that explain what is to be done to a prospect and new member. The executive rules of the HPL state that "Pistoleros shall be of any Latin origin; Chicanos, Mexicans, Puerto Ricans, Venezuelans, and all persons that speak Latino or are descendants of Latin families." Law enforcement has also identified females as HPL members, which is unique among Hispanic prison gangs that traditionally have not allowed women to gain membership into their organizations (Texas Department of Public Safety, 2007).

In May 2008 the Federal government was able to get arrest warrants for 24 HPL members alleging a conspiracy and laundering millions of dollars generated by the sale of contraband in the United States. On May 30, 2008 21 of the 24 wanted HPL gang members were arrested in Laredo, Beeville and Houston, Texas. The indicted HPL members were allegedly involved in the importation and distribution of multi-kilogram quantities of cocaine. The cocaine was smuggled across the U.S. Mexico border.

Those members who sport tattoos tend to wear a tattoo of the letters HPL. The letters can be hidden within a large tattoo mural. Some tattoos incorporate the numbers "16" and "12," which represent the letters "P" and "L;" or the number "45," which represents the caliber of a .45 handgun. The HPL rules suggest that anyone of Latino decent can be a member of the gang. Law enforcement has also identified female HPL members which is highly unusual for a prison gang that traditionally never allows female members (TDCJ, 2007).

The HPL prison gang has operated drug and arms trafficking between Nuevo Laredo, Laredo and Houston, Texas. The HL gang has operated under the law enforcement radar because like most prison gangs they tend to operate in a low profile mode. They can be considered a transnational organization due to their international business connections.

Texas Syndicate

The El Paso Tip was a prison gang that formed in the 1920s in the Texas state prison at Huntsville. Members would ask each other if they were "tipped" or "tipped up." This was prison slang that really was asking if you were from the El Paso area. The gang continued to grow well into the 1950s and originally was formed by Mexican street gang members for protection within the prison. During this time the number of Mexican street gangs continued to grow in California as well and Mexican form Texas and other states were being incarcerated as well.

The Texas Syndicate (TS) or Syndicato Tejano was introduced into the California state prison system in the early 1970s at Folsom Prison; however initially the roots of the gang were from Texas (Valdez, 2000, NDIC, 2005). Other research suggests the gang was formed in the late 1960s by Francisco 'Panchito' Gonzales within the California Department of Corrections (NDIC, 2005). As with much of the prison gang history the literature review also suggests different origins for the TS gang. It also has been reported that the gang formed in 1973 at the San Quentin Prison, California (Bauer, 1997).

As with all prison gangs the initial onus for formation is protection. This is also true to the Texas Syndicate. It was formed to primarily protect Texas born Mexican inmates from the violence associated within prison (NDIC, 2005). As a result Texas Syndicate gang members are extremely loyal to each other and hence the gang. There is also a faction of Texas Syndicate in the Federal corrections system.

The establishment of the West Coast faction of the gang was probably the result of migrating parolees or street gang members from the El Paso area. At one time the West Coast gang's membership was comprised of Mexican/ Hispanic male inmates, no White or African-American members are allowed. However, by the mid 2000s the gang was for all practical purposes non-functional within the California Department of Corrections (CDC). As of 2005 there were only two documented members in the CDC and they affiliated themselves with the Mexican Mafia (NDIC, 2005).

During the mid 1970s the TS gang was introduced into the Texas Department of Corrections and Justice (TDCJ) by resettled California TS members who were released from the

California Department of Corrections and continued their criminal activities. The gang was established within the TDCJ but remained under the radar until 1977 when the first murder occurred that was linked to the TS. While the TS gang was growing within TDCJ it did not have any rivalries with other groups from the 1970s to 1977 (NDIC, 2007).

In the mid 1990s some conflict within the TS was reported. The older members known as 'veteranos' considered newer members (those who joined after 1995) as ill trained, less disciplined individuals who violence indiscriminately rather than using it to control criminal activities (NDIC, 2005).

In the late 1990s TS membership grew because of a national recruitment effort. The Texas Syndicate started accepting members from Columbia, Cuba and Mexico. A small group of TS members are referred to as "carnales", while the term carnal refers to a single member. New recruits are often called cardinals. The institutional leader is known as the chairman. Of the prison gangs, the TS gang is one of the youngest and did not appear to have a formal constitution or vertical leadership structure early on.

This is not true now. Texas Syndicate is now highly organized prison gang that has a constitution which directs member behavior in and out of prison. Each prison or custodial facility has a leader called a 'chairman.' Outside prison the TS member who directs out of custody activity is also called the chairman. Although not as complex as other prison gangs the Texas Syndicate still has a vertical command structure. The chairman (silla or sillon for chair) is an elected position. Duties include running the TS at a facility or defined geographical area outside of prison. This can include managing drug trafficking operations, solving problems or ordering hits after a membership vote (NDIC, 2005).

The Cableman position is next in line and is selected and reports to the chairman. His duties include writing letters (kites) and to communicate between facilities. The lowest ranking members of TS are known as soldiers. Members are elected into the gang and report to the chairman, recruit and educate new members and carry out TS orders. A literature review also suggests the TS gang operates under a para military structure; where the oldest, most experienced member serves as the chairperson called the 'sillon' (TDCJ, 2007). Lieutenants and sergeants are selected by the sillon. Texas Syndicate also appears to be one of lager prison gangs in the U.S. with a reported estimated membership of 1300.

The gang's tattoos contain the letters TS and are sometimes hidden in a design. Sometimes, the figure of a woman or a face is used to hide the tattoo. More often, the letters TS are made by a dragon figure, ribbons or flowers. The right forearm area seems to be the most popular location used for tattoos, but remember tattoos can be placed anywhere. Some TS members have a tattoo that depicts a set of horns (cuernos) with words containing the letters T and S. Other common tattoos are objects shaped in the form of the letters T and S.

Texas Syndicate gang members have been reported as inmates Federal Correction facilities and state prisons in the following states: California, Colorado, Oklahoma, Texas, Missouri, Arkansas, Minnesota, Wisconsin, Michigan, Indiana, Kentucky, West Virginia, New York, Pennsylvania, North Carolina, Georgia and Florida and even in San Juan, Puerto Rico (NDIC, 2005). This is a testament of how prison gang members can travel. In the federal correction system TS also has a rivalry with the Surenos and the Paisas.

The Texas Syndicate has an alliance with the Gulf Cartel that was once run by Osiel Cardenas. Since his arrest and subsequent extradition to the United States the cartel's interests have be maintained by Los Zetas, a para military gang hired by Cardenas. By 2004 federal and state law enforcement anecdotal evidence suggested that Zetas members were working closely with the Texas Syndicate. TS have had working alliances with the Aryan Brotherhood and the Dirty White Boys. The Texas Syndicate has also developed associations with a smaller gang called the Texas Mafia.

Like many prison gangs Texas Syndicate has contact with several street gangs and even the Bandido motorcycle gang in Corpus Christi, Texas (NDIC, 2005).. Inside prison, the gang focuses on drug trafficking, extortion, pressure rackets and internal discipline (NDIC, 2005). The same focus as many other prison gangs. The Texas syndicate is considered one of the most violent gangs in TDCJ.

The rival gangs of the Texas Syndicate have been the Mexican Mafia, Mexikanemi (EMI), Mandingo Warriors, La Nuestra Familia, Tangos and sometimes the Aryan Brotherhood. There are intermittent conflicts with Barrio Azteca, Hermanos de Pistoleros Latina (HPL), Partido Revolucionario Mexicano (PRM). Outside prison, the gang is involved in drug trafficking, transportation of illegal aliens and contract murders. To be more specific the members of the Texas Syndicate have been involved in the smuggling of multi-kilogram quantities of powered cocaine, heroin and methamphetamine. The gang has also been involved in the trafficking of multi ton quantities of marijuana. All drug trafficking routes are across the U.S.-Mexican border. The gang is well established in at least 37 Texas cities from the El Paso to Houston and from Austin in the north to Brownsville in the south. The Texas Syndicate is concentrated along the southern Texas border cities (NDIC, 2005).

Chapter 5

Military Gangs

This chapter will exam how some street gangs have infiltrated the U.S. military system. Gang members will join the military for many reasons and all are not nefarious. The American military has demonstrated over and over that it is major institution that protects the citizens of this country and there are many dedicated men and women who answer the call. Since the military draws its ranks from the general population, issues that affect the civilian world like gangs will also affect the military.

Gangs in the Military

Members of nearly every major street gangs, some prison gangs and outlaw motorcycle gangs have been identified on both domestic and international military installations (U.S. Department of Justice, 2009). Deployments, transfers have helped facilitate the spread of gang activity within the ranks of the military. Gangs have not taken over the ranks of the military, but they have had an impact. The United States military continues to be a source of tradition, values, and continues to turn young boys into men. Our military continues to enjoy the status of being the best-trained and equipped fighting force in the world. We all owe our freedoms and lifestyle to the countless men and women who have served in our military and given the ultimate sacrifice for our nation... for you and me.

History

The United States military has become the world's mightiest fighting force. The U.S. Army, Air Force, Navy, Marine Corps, National Guard and Coast Guard have become synonymous with tradition, success and untold stories of dedication and heroism. Our military history is filled with example after example of young boys becoming men. The basic and specialized training has provided the needed fundamentals for military personnel to become career oriented or to be successful in the private sector.

The ranks of all branches of the military have traditionally been filled from the general population. Historically, the military has been able to isolate most of its members from societal issues, such as drugs and gangs. However, since the mid 1980s it has become apparent that what affects society can and does affect the ranks of the military. The draft required many men to give service to Uncle Sam. Family tradition also motivated many to serve for our country. For some time, kids at risk were given the opportunity to join the military instead of serving time in jail. In addition there are countless stories of young men running to the military to escape life on the streets, which offered little or no chance for survival.

Unfortunately, the military's immunity to societal woes has proven to be limited, at best. Frankly, whatever affects society can, and affects the military but probably to a less degree. As the white supremacist movement influences the general population it will affect the military. As drug problems are dealt with in civilian life they must also be dealt with within the military. The same also holds true for domestic violence, child abuse and of course gangs.

For example, the media has reported the discovery of the White Supremacist movement within the military. As far back as 1980 there have been documented incidents where enlisted ranks have come forth and shared their membership in the Ku Klux Klan and skinhead gangs. A Times magazine article detailed how two Army soldiers stationed at Fort Carson, just outside

Colorado Springs, organized a KKK den in 1978. The two claimed by the end of 1978 they were able to recruit more than 100 members into the newly established den, most of them fellow soldiers from Fort Carson, an infantry post (Wedekind, 1980).

In a 1989 case, an Air Force sergeant stationed at the Yokota Air Force Base, near Tokyo was arrested for selling guns to the local Yakuza gangsters. The local police believed the guns were purchased on the base then sold illegally to the Yakuza gang members. There seems to be some conflicting stories about whether or not the airman knew what he was doing was wrong. Apparently, he was legally buying the weapons on the air base and then reselling them in town.

In December 1992, at Fort Lewis, Washington, Army investigators were called to a small house located on post. They made a grisly discovery. A father and his three small children were all hacked and stabbed to death. Seven weeks after the murders, investigators believe Los Angeles based street gang members killed the family. Law enforcement officials arrested five people in the deaths, including two active Fort Lewis soldiers and a recently discharged soldier.

On March 1, 1993, the Air Force Times reported, *"the back gate area of Oceanside, California, is one of the worst areas in the city for gangs. Drive-by shootings and other violence are not uncommon."* This area of violence is right outside the Camp Pendleton military base. It was determined that about 50 percent of the population in Oceanside was military and that most gang members who are military dependents live off base. An interesting observation was made in the article: *"to assume that a child is immune from gangs because he or she lives on base is a wrong assumption."* Being a member of a gang is not illegal therefore by law the military has to allow gang members to enter.

Gang killings have become too common in major cities across America. Military bases, long believed to be sanctuaries from the worst of urban problems, have been experiencing the same problems, of course not at the same frequency. It certainly difficult to accept the idea that the drugs and violence associated with street gangs has penetrated the military's world of discipline and order. There is anecdotal evidence that suggests that the drugs and gang related violence has infected all ranks of the U.S. military.

Crime does not have to be felony status or violent to qualify as being gang related. In November 1991, a juvenile dependent and gang member at Luke Air Force Base, Arizona helped spray paint graffiti on a perimeter block wall. He and his family were promptly moved off the base and there was unspecified disciplinary action taken against the military member. This was a gang related crime, even though no drive by shooting or felony assault was involved. It was misdemeanor gang crime.

The Army's image of racial harmony isn't all that it can be either. Newsweek magazine reported that three white soldiers from the 82nd Airborne Division murdered two African-Americans in Fayetteville, North Carolina. The Fayetteville police classified the homicide as a hate crime. The suspects in the murder appeared to be members of a local white supremacist group known as the Special Forces Underground (Newsweek, 1995).

The Army has also found the existence of white supremacist and Neo-Nazi groups within the ranks. For example, white enlisted men in Wildflecken, Germany formed a hate group called, Fuck the Niggers. At Fort Carson, Colorado active duty soldiers have joined skinhead gangs and were suspected of selling stolen military weapons to local extremists. Two white soldiers stationed in Orlando, Florida, have been linked to the Florida Corps Skins, a Neo-Nazi gang.

In July 1996, the U.S. Army offered a $10,000 reward for information leading to the arrest and conviction of the vandals who painted Nazi swastikas on the bedroom doors of Black soldiers living at Fort Bragg, North Carolina. Someone painted red colored swastikas on the doors to eight barracks. Six of the rooms belonged to Black members of the U.S. Army Special Forces; the two other rooms were empty.

There can be no denial that gangs have affected all branches of the military. In 1978, gang related crime on military bases could have been classified as isolated incidents. By 1996, gang crime within the military had become more common. Gang activity within the military can increase and can take on many forms.

For the longest time military regulations have not prohibited service members from belonging to extremist groups such as Neo-Nazi organizations. The regulations prohibit members from promulgating the group's beliefs. But what about cases like T.J. Leyden Jr., a self admitted skinhead. While in the Marine Corps, Leyden said that while off duty he would walk around in a tank top so that everyone could see his skinhead tattoos. Leyden admits to wearing his Doctor Marten boots, keeping his hair as short as possible and blousing his pants the way the Nazis did. Leyden said he had a third Reich battle flag in his locker and the Confederate Stars and Bars flag on his wall. All were clear indicators of skinhead membership and a belief in white supremacy.

These indicators were a clear symbol of what was happening inside Leyden. They were symptomatic his gang mentality. He had developed into a sophisticated Neo-Nazi activist. According to Leyden he was contacted by Tom Metzger, founder of the White Aryan Resistance (WAR) based in California. Leyden told a Time magazine writer that Metzger wanted more military recruiters and Metzger's organization started to send him literature. Leyden said he was able to solicit and recruit four other Marines, who in turn went to different bases to continue recruitment.

In 1990, the Marine Corps reacted when Leyden had Nazi-storm trooper style lightning bolt tattoos put on his neck. The same year in an evaluation, Leyden's superior officer wrote, "Loyalty is questionable, as he willingly admits belonging to a radical group called skinheads." Leyden received an "other than honorable discharge" for what the military called alcohol-related misbehavior (Leyden, 2004).

Gang Activity

All types of gang related crime has occurred on national and international military bases. The presence of gang graffiti can be found on board naval ships, on many national and international military bases. Graffiti is one of the first indicators of gang activity and usually is suggestive of the presence of gang members. This is commonly found to be true whether the gang is operating on or off a military base. Graffiti is used when a gang wants to make its presence known.

Military gang crimes have included murder, attempted murder, drive-by shootings, hate crimes, vandalism, assault with a deadly weapon, simple assault, rape, robbery, burglary, weapons violations and vehicle theft. There have been gang fights between enlisted ranks and dishonorable discharges for placing gang graffiti on military uniforms. After Desert Storm and Desert Shield, photographs of enlisted military personnel in uniform were seen flashing gang handsigns. I have also seen advance military training videos where the enlisted trainees are flashing gang handsigns. The videos were produced by the military as a memento for the trainee. The military does not produce gang videos using enlisted personnel.

There was a reported take-over style robbery of a fast food restaurant located on a naval base by members of a Southeast Asian street gang. The suspects in this case were not military personnel, but local street gangsters who victimized the base. In some instances, response to the gang violence has been to build walls to protect the dependent families from stray bullets from drive-by shootings. Many military police departments hold awareness briefings for their officers. Command staff has become involved and focused on maintaining base security and integrity.

Several military bases have tried to implement special programs for dependent children. The extent of military gang activity varies from base to base as well as the extent of military dependent children involved in gangs. Every military instillation does not have a gang problem.

Gang membership within the ranks of the military can be encountered in four basic areas; enlisted ranks, dependents, civilian employees and from the ranks of officers.

Enlisted Personnel

Let's examine how gangs could affect a military instillation. One of the easiest influences can come from those who enlist into the military. There are a number of reasons why young adults join the military one is to escape the violence on the street. There are many instances where ex-gang members, gang members and gang associates join the armed forces to get ahead in life. For the most part, almost all succeed in adapting to the discipline and military way of life. This is a compliment to the basic and advanced training programs and military instructors.

For others though, the street gang mentality is still part of the enlisted person. These military men and women continue with their gang activities, sometimes on limited bases. Understanding that if caught they will lose their enlistment or rank these gang members have successfully been able to shield themselves from discovery. For example, although most military bases have little or no drug problems, drug sales continue and drug arrests are still be made. Military police routinely still find gang graffiti on base and the theft of military hardware still continues.

It is almost like these gang members work undercover while they are enlisted and they can recruit new members while on base. There can be many reasons for this. Some can be maybe perceived and some are valid. Even ethnic gangs form on racial boundaries. Being part of a racially diverse unit does not mean that racism is not practiced all or part of the time. This could be a catalytic factor to help group alliances to form, especially for protection against the insulting person or group. The gang may not form immediately, but the group does. A single charismatic person or series of events could gel the group into a gang. There could be a single precipitating incident that catalyzes the gang genesis since all the necessary ingredients are present.

Because of the excellent training programs gang members can become involved with the military police, intelligence operations or logistics. Also because of the DREAM Act, better known as the Development, Relief and Education for Alien Minors act U.S. citizenship can be granted to undocumented immigrants in exchange for military service. This provides access to a new recruitment pool for the military. It is also the very same recruitment pool for many street gangs, including 18th Street and Mara Salvatrucha. It is logical to conclude that some military recruits from this pool may have gang connections.

The other unique factor now observed within the enlisted ranks is that post Vietnam gang members who entered the military no longer give up their gang life style. Before and during the Vietnam conflict gang members who entered the military tended to abandon their gang life style and develop a more traditional model for living. Gang members have serving in the military for many years; this is not a new phenomenon.

Civilian Employees

Besides active military personnel, civilian employees can also bring a gang influence onto a military installation. I was surprised to recognize an active Hispanic gang member working at a southern California Marine Corps Air Base in the early 1990s. I was happy to see the young man at work, but it made me recall incidents on military bases such as a commercial robbery of high tech computer hardware, where it was later determined that full and part time civilian employees were actually part of the robbery team. Their job was to collect intelligence for the robbery team. The employees were gang members, gang associates and gang sympathizers.

In one civilian theft, millions of dollars of computer hardware was simply picked up at the business by gang members in a rented truck. A fellow gang member had gotten an assignment in shipping and receiving. He was considered an "ideal hard working employee" according to his immediate supervisor. It was this sleeper gang member who master minded the theft. It would be crazy to think that this could not happen on military bases. Money is a powerful and key motivator for gang members. Pay scales for enlisted personnel are not the best, even in light of some recent raises and civilian employee wages are not better. Unfortunately, in some cases civilian employees were drug contacts and suppliers on military bases.

Civilian employees can also the conduits to local street gangs that operate outside the military installation. Military gang members when off post can make contact with local gang members with the assistance of civilian employees.

Military Dependents

A third gang influence can come from military dependents. These children can be influence by the gang sub-culture whether or not they live on a military installation. The youth can have a greater degree of exposure if they attend school off base, which is very common.

When these children become involved in gangs a couple of things could happen. First, these new members want to prove themselves to their gang family. This may result in an increase of juvenile crime on the military installation. You would expect to see increased reports of theft, assaults, and graffiti. With time, as the gang grows and matures it may become more active and more violent crimes will occur on base.

The second thing that frequently happens is these juvenile military dependent gang members often sponsor their fellow civilian gang members on base. Military police will have their hands full as this starts to happen. Gang member vehicle and pedestrian traffic will increase on base, especially in the housing areas. Gang fights are likely to occur in base housing and recreation areas as the gang attempts to establish its street reputation. The presence of gang graffiti in the housing area can be a sure sign of dependent involvement with street gangs.

There also can be a safety issue here. Anyone entering a military installation has the ability to smuggle contraband like drugs or weapons on or off the base. If a gang has established itself on base, sponsored visitors, especially armed civilian gang members have the chance to bring weapons onto the base. The advent of drive-by shootings on military bases becomes the anecdotal evidence that tends to suggest this mechanism is used. The weapons used in the shootings have come from off base.

Some military bases have sponsored functions like dances and invited the local non-military residents as well as those assigned to the base. In one instance a naval air base located in central California hosted a dance for the teenage dependents that lived on base. The base also extended a welcome to the local teenage population and word of the dance spread quickly to the surrounding cities.

The general welcome proved to be disastrous. Rival gang members from different parts of the county arrived to attend the party. They also brought their intense hatred for each other with them. The dance was hosted to help the dependent teenagers on base and as well as a good will gesture to the surrounding cities.

A fight broke out between rival gang members at the dance. The fight escalated to a gang shooting on the base. The shooting ended with a vehicle pursuit that started on the base and ended off base. It is clear how civilian gang members can impact gang activity on a military installation.

Officers

Although rare, it still can happen. The instance that brought this to light was a fellow police officer friend of mine who was also in the Navy Reserve. He told me while on a training weekend he was the roommate of another naval officer. As they struck up conversation the roommate started to change clothes. While tee-shirtless the police officer immediately notices at tattoo on the lower neck area of the subject. The tattoo was "NLR."

The other officer was also in the reserves and the tattoo suggested membership in the California Nazi Low Rider prison gang. In the gang sub culture a person cannot wear a gang membership tattoo without being a bonafide member. To do so otherwise would most likely result in a severe assault or death.

OK, only one incident reported here. There are a few more and this by no means suggests there is a trend of officer involved gang members. I mention it here to suggest this is another possible mechanism that could result in gang members who are officers.

Stolen Property

There is also a flip side to increased civilian gang traffic onto military installations. Military property that has been legally or illegally obtained on base can be smuggled off base and sold. There have been numerous documented instances where active military personnel have been involved in gang related crime off base. Some of these enlisted gang members have access to all types of military munitions. In the mid to late 1990s the military experience and documented an increase in theft of these items.

In May 1993, the General Accounting Office released a report concluding there was widespread theft of military small arms by defense personnel. The same month, the Washington Post reported that street gangs, white supremacist groups and other criminal organizations are stockpiling stolen Department of Defense issue machine guns, grenades and other equipment.

The newspaper also reported that two former Michigan National Guardsmen stole military parts for years without being caught. One stole small arms parts for at least five years. Some of the stolen gun parts were sold to a national gun dealer who was connected to sales of such equipment to the Branch Davidian sect in Waco, Texas.

The losses were still continuing. In September, 1996, an Orange County, California, law enforcement intelligence bulletin advised that a Southern California Southeast Asian street gang called the Tiny Rascal Gang, TRG, had issued contracts to kill two local policemen. The bulletin advised that the gang had access to stolen military C-4 explosive, grenades and a LAWS rocket.

As the civilian population encountered a variety of types of street gangs so has the military. Military gang members, whether enlisted or juvenile dependents, have been members of Hispanic, Black, Skinhead, Hybrid, Folk and People Nation street gangs. White supremacist groups seem to recruit from adult enlisted ranks only.

There is some substantial anecdotal evidence to suggest that military hardware isn't the only thing being stolen. Many extremist groups have modeled their training exercises after the military. Field strategies, knowledge of munitions storage, use and disposal and training strategies have been taken from military, some of it illegally, some of it legally. You can consider it a type of intellectual property form the military. Just go into a military surplus store and you will be surprised to find a number of outdated and current military manuals for sale. Also check Internet libraries and it will become clear how easy it is to obtain military training and knowledge.

A Fayetteville, North Carolina detective noted "There is evidence that suggests some gang members are actually sent into the military to learn about military tactics" (Glass, 2005). If you examine the released security video of the 2005 shooting of two Ceres, California police officers you can easily see suppressive firepower aimed at the police officers. The Fayetteville, North Carolina detective noted it was a style of shooting learned in the Marine Corps. The shooter was a Hispanic gang member who was a Marine who has just returned home from the Middle East.

For the most part, gang activity and criminal investigation is handled internally by the military at the local level. Gang activity and criminal behavior may be sporadic and will differ from base to base. It occurs nationally and internationally, on board ships, and on land bases.

Because of the natural rivalry between the branches of the armed forces, it would be difficult at best to even estimate the amount of military gang crime. It would even be harder to estimate how the gang phenomenon has impacted the military in general. Even though the picture may not be totally clear, it is evident that the drug and violence associated with the street gang sub-culture has and continues to impact all branches our military forces.

If this was not true, a superior officer aboard one aircraft carrier would not be advising that gang members have claimed certain parts of the ship as their territory by marking it with graffiti and that the sailors should educate themselves about these locations to avoid problems by recognizing the graffiti symbols. He advised these areas of the ship are off limits to non-gang members; sailors should abide by these boundaries to avoid potentially fatal confrontations.

In an intercepted letter written to an in-custody gang member in state prison, a marine writes to his friend El Wino, the gang member's moniker. He talks about enlisted life in the Marine Corps. The letter stated, "we are kicking back here…here are a couple photos of the homeboys… the Raza has to stick together our here… got this new girl in yesterday, homeboys told me she's a surena…I checked her out and she's got SURENA tattooed on the back of her neck." The letter is signed TURTLE. There was an enclosed photo that showed three marines flashing gang hand signs.

It is a sad commentary on what has happened in some of our military units. Awareness, zero tolerance and re-writing some federal laws have helped. Military police investigators need to be given tools and training to handle gang intelligence, juvenile arrests and the investigation of gang related crime. Networking with other military investigators and local law enforcement can be a great resource for the military.

Military Victims

In a number of cases, enlisted military personnel, officers and dependants have become victims of gang violence or gang related crime. Sometimes, bonafide gang members make a mistake when they incorrectly identify a military enlisted person as a gang member. Some crimes have been the result of random attacks on and off military installations where military personnel and dependants reside.

In areas of the country where military bases are located sometimes segments of the local community do not appreciate the military presence. The military personnel will not only bring added business to the city but, in some cases military personnel become rivals of the local street gangs without even knowing it. Remember, to a local gang member military personnel are outsiders and some street gangs purposely target service men and women.

If an active duty enlisted person, officer or dependant is a member of a gang distinctive clothing may be worn and gang related tattoos might be displayed when off duty. In an effort to fit in sometimes young service men and women wear popular civilian clothing styles, including gang style clothing. Civilian street gang members consider certain clothing styles and colors gang indicia of membership to a gang. To the local gang member these unique clothing styles can mean something, often symbolizing or representing gangs that are rivals of or unknown to the local gang members. These clothing styles therefore can mark the service men and women as targets. You should also consider the fact that gang violence can be random.

Three of my sons have served the military, two in the Army and one in the Marine Corps. They all felt a sense of duty to serve our country. As any parent I worried about their safety, in battle or where they were stationed. Remember I said gang violence could be random.

On March 9, 1998 at 2:33 am, the telephone rang at my home. When I answered, the person said; "Mr. Valdez, I am First Sergeant Cline, 43rd Engineers, Fort Carson. I'm sorry to inform you that your son Joshua has been seriously injured and is in intensive care at a local hospital." The natural response was how bad is he? To my horror, the First Sergeant told me my son had been shot in the head and was not expected to survive. At the time my son Joshua was active duty enlisted with the 43rd Engineers, United States Army at Fort Carson, Colorado Springs, Colorado.

All at once, many thoughts started to run through my head and I got a very sick feeling in my stomach. I was in shock and stumbled down stairs to use my office telephone to continue the conversation and attempt to get more information. Some gang members in the Colorado Springs area had attacked my son while he was off duty. He was on life support and been given his last rites. First Sergeant Cline talked me out of panicking and gave me all the information he had. I immediately made plane reservations and flew to Colorado Springs later that afternoon with my father. The First Sergeant tried to comfort me as much as he could and assured me that members of the 43rd Engineers would be helping my family through this.

All I could think about was getting to my son. My father offered to go with me to the hospital and frankly, I did not know if I would ever see my son alive again. The plane ride was long and not much was said between my dad and me. I remembered talking to Josh on the telephone, just a few days before this happened. He had just re-enlisted and was planning to make the Army his professional career. He had just qualified for and was accepted into the Army Ranger and Jump schools. I was very proud of his accomplishments.

When we landed, my son's Platoon Sergeant was waiting at the airport to escort us directly to the hospital. The ride was made easy by Sergeant Sarracino's demeanor and courtesy. You cannot imagine the anxiety that had built up in me during the six and half hours it took to travel there. To my surprise the Army had arraigned for my father and I to stay at the hospital. The Army had reserved a quiet comfortable room in a small house on hospital property. Sergeant Sarracino helped us drop our luggage off and led us to my son's room, about a five-minute walk away.

I saw Josh and his status was given to us - the reality of the situation set in. Josh had been shot twice in the head with 9mm rounds, which blew up on impact. The bullet fragments had done terrible damage to his brain. Josh was unconscious and placed on a respirator. Any hopes of my son surviving had quickly disappeared. Like many in law enforcement, I had seen this scenario many times before during my investigations. Few victims, if any, wounded this seriously, ever survived. Those few that did were terminally comatose, bed-ridden or permanently disabled. No matter how much you prepare yourself for what you will see and experience sometimes you are still unprepared.

Sergeant Sarracino remained with us. The decision was made to remove the breathing tube to make my son more comfortable. There was a good chance we would lose him when this was done. We prepared by saying our goodbyes to Josh. This is probably the most un-natural act a parent can do for his child. It's almost like something dies inside you. There are no words that can possibly describe those feelings. The only thing I can relay to you is that the intensity of those feelings changes you forever and they are never forgotten.

When the tube was removed, a miracle occurred; to everyone's surprise Josh continued to breathe on his own. No one slept that night.

Josh was still in extremely critical condition. His vital signs fluctuated with every labored breath. He was unconscious most of the time but after the first few days he would occasionally have short periods of semi- consciousness. It was apparent he was in excruciating pain. Plastic tubes were in every body orifice. The sight was really overwhelming. As family members began to arrive, the members of the 43rd Engineers, from the Squad Leader, Platoon Sergeant, Platoon Leader and Platoon Commander continued to come to the hospital and gave their support to me and my family. Little things like bringing us something to drink, reminding us to eat, staying with my son while we ate, being there ready to help at a moment's notice was done without request or question.

As the miracle of my son's life continued to shock everyone, including the doctors, another miracle occurred, he began to stabilize and get stronger. His periods of consciousness would last longer as the first few days went by. He would mumble for water. He had to be restrained because it is common for people with head wounds to become combative. At one point he began screaming; "Dad please, please cut me out of this, dad, dad please help me." I could do nothing because he could hurt himself. I will never forget those words.

It is an awful feeling to listen to your own child scream for help and beg you to help, especially when you can do nothing. Again, the Army was there to assist. The sergeants would take turns watching Josh during these periods, so we could have a break. I probably was a mental basket case. I was so upset, I cried until there were no more tears. I was so frustrated that I could do nothing but be there and listen to my son suffer. Every hour or so a member of my son's unit would check on us, just to make sure we were all right. I will never forget that Army support.

During the first week we were literally escorted everyday by members of the 43rd Engineers and the rest of soldiers at Fort Carson. Enlisted personnel would come by to check on Josh and us. We were greeted and treated with the utmost respect and courtesy. It was so comforting to know that so many people cared about my son and his family. I felt bad because I never had the honor of meeting any of these people before and they were now helping me and my family. I didn't even get to thank them all when I left.

The young men and women in my sons unit even took up a collection and gave us a cash gift to help pay for expenses. As this miracle continued, my son got stronger and stronger and began to regain the use of his mind. He gradually became fully conscious and remembered his family. He knew who I was and he wanted to eat pizza. Josh told me the first thing he could remember was waking up and seeing his mother's face.

By the end of the fourth day, Josh could actually talk using small sentences. He was still disoriented, but at least he was attempting to talk. There is a cost to everything and the cost for my son's survival was his diagnosis. I learned a terrible word at the hospital that week, tri-pelagic. Basically, my son only had partial use of his right arm. He could not sit up by himself. He was held up in a sitting position with a restraint.

As soon as he was stable enough for the long and difficult recovery, the Army transported Josh to Walter Reed Hospital in Washington, DC. The Army has taken my son under its protective cover. The members of his unit never gave up on him. They expected a full recovery. Their positive attitude and faith in Josh's ability strengthen our hope for a good recovery. More importantly, they helped give Josh the courage and strength he used not to give up. My son was devastated when we described the extent of his injuries to him. No one knew if his injuries were temporary or permanent. All we could do was take one day at a time.

The Colorado Springs Police Department started investigating the case immediately and thoroughly. As a family member, I have been given case up dates in a timely manner. The case was solved rather quickly. The alleged shooter was arrested and prosecuted. This fact demonstrates the high solvability rate of the Colorado Springs Police Department's Major Crimes unit. Being on this side of the fence now, I clearly understand the frustration of the victim's family members, which is caused by not knowing information. I appreciated the candor of the detective assigned to my son's case.

I was told that my son drove a van to a popular under-21 nightclub, which was a hangout for young people from the Army post and the city. Josh and three soldiers got caught in the middle of a gang fight as he was parking the van he rented. He and one soldier never got out of the van before the shooting started. Josh was shot as he was trying to drive the rented van out of the area. He was shot, twice in the head. Two of the four soldiers he was with managed to get out.

The gunshot wounds to his head caused a nerve reaction and his foot slammed on the accelerator. The van drove off with him and another soldier inside at a high rate of speed. The van crashed into a concrete embankment and flipped twice. It landed, inverted on the front end. It took the paramedics twenty minutes to rescue my son and his fellow soldier. As a parent I felt I had a right and need to know what happened. This information as horrifying as it was, helped me cope with the situation and understand what happened. It was given to me in a truthful, but gentle manner by the lead detective. I will continue to treat victims and the families of victims, as I would like to be treated.

Albert Einstein was quoted as saying, "In the middle of difficulty lies opportunity." As tragic and ugly as this incident was, some things can be learned here. This becomes another painful reminder that gang violence can happen anywhere and anytime, even to service men and women. Gang violence can be random. We must now use cautions we never used before, in order to better insure safety.

I have always had a tremendous amount of respect for the families that continue to go on, after losing a loved one. Like many law enforcement professionals, I too have been at the crime scenes or hospital rooms where another person dies from gang violence. I have seen the pain family members go through when the shock of losing a loved one sets in. I have always tried to be as gentle and empathetic as possible in these situations. I never imagined how hard this lost could be on the family members physically and emotionally. It is hard to imagine how difficult it is to continue on with life during these times. I can't even think of words that could describe the intensity and diverse emotions that overwhelm you.

My family, which includes Josh's four younger brothers, took the news of this incident very hard. I work in this field and we all had developed a sense of security-this would never happen to us. As a family we were totally unprepared to deal with terrible news. We had bad days, but now they are fewer and far between. Josh's youngest brothers, ages 5 and 8 at the time, were never told the truth until they were 10 and 13 years old. They believed Josh was in a car accident. How do you tell young children about gun shot wounds to their brother's head?

I suggest that compassion and empathy will go a long way for a victim and the family of a victim. Enough can never be said or written about the compassionate and empathetic response made by the soldiers stationed at Fort Carson. Their actions became a major reason for my sons and family's survival during this ordeal. The kindness and gentle support offered by all the soldiers and especially, Sergeants Cole and Sarracino, First Sergeant Cline, Lieutenant Stinnett and Captain Benson, will never be forgotten or unappreciated. Without the help of the United States Army, my son's incident would have become just another statistic. I never realized that my family grew by about 5,000, when my son joined the Army. Thank you to the United States Army. Josh was doing OK and discharged from the Army in the fall of 2000.

Remember miracles do and can happen. One afternoon while I was at the hospital I came in to check on Josh. I found a young female soldier sitting at Josh's bedside. She introduced herself to me and I was glad to meet Lourdes. She told me she was a friend and met Josh when they were stationed in Korea. However, I saw something in her eyes and the way she looked at my son. I left and immediately called my bride and told her I just met Josh's future wife. She laughed a little, asked about the young lady and ordered me to collect more intelligence.

Josh and Lourdes were honorably discharged and eventually got married. They both finished college. Without Lourdes I think my son would have been lost. Here is anecdotal evidence to suggest behind every successful man there is a wonderful loving strong woman. Josh is still disabled and walks with a cane, but now works as a full time chemical engineer and Lourdes is a successful registered nurse and have a son. They both consider part of their continued success is due to the military training and discipline they learned while in the Army. Whoooah!

Military Response

An Army Times article did a great job of outlining the military response to gang crime committed by enlisted service men and women. The story highlighted the Army's prosecution of a Fort Hood Specialist and two soldiers. As the prosecutor, Major Michael Mulligan said: "Within our Army, we have GD (Gangster Disciples), a criminal street gang. They rob, assault and they murder. [They] took soldiers and turned them into criminals." The specialist, a female seven-year Army veteran, was the leader of a Gangster Disciple group operating out of Fort

Hood. She was convicted of two counts of assault and one count of conspiracy for her role in a July, 1997 double homicide and a subsequent robbery in Killeen, Texas (Army Times, 1999).

The specialist was also charged with premeditated murder for ordering three gang members to kill a Killeen bar owner. Being part of the Folk Nation, the Gangster Disciples have formal titles and ranks for gang members. The specialist was a local leader and also held the rank of governor. Unfortunately, the prosecution was unable to prove the charge of premeditated murder. However, she was sentenced to 27 years at the U.S. Disciplinary Barracks at Fort Leavenworth, Kansas.

The prosecutors presented a clear picture of gang discipline and rules issued by the governor. She applied a military type order to the gang. The specialist even required after-action reports on member activities according to the witness testimony.

The motive for the double homicide was apparently an insult. Remember, no insult ever goes unanswered in the gang world. The specialist was kicked out of bar located in the outskirts of Killeen. She then sent three gang members, two soldiers and one civilian, to kill the owner because of the prior incident. The three gang-members instead killed two of the owner's friends by mistake.

This only underscores the fact that gang activity within the military can be extreme, just as extreme as in the civilian world. Obviously, this type of gang activity is not commonplace, but it still does occur. Legal strategies commonly used in civilian gang trials were also used in this one. For example, tight court room security. Spectators needed special passes to get into the courtroom. After the sentencing the defendant was immediately removed from the area. These types of actions are essential to maintain safety for both the defendant and those working in the courtroom. Just like in major civilian gang trials, a gang expert was used.

A Chicago Police Department Detective Division investigator, and gang expert, Sergeant Robert Stasch was quoted as saying, *"Major national gangs are trying to get their members to join the military."* Sergeant Stasch testified as the prosecution's gang expert in the specialist's court martial. For some gangs, joining a branch of the military can be a replacement to the traditional initiation, like a jump or crime in.

After a tour in the military gang member-soldiers can return home and teach younger gang members the skills they learned in the service. Unfortunately, those some of those skills are welcomed by the gang just as much as a civilian employer would. The military can offer tremendous training in leadership skills, discipline and small unit field tactics. Servicemen and women also learn how to use and have access to all kinds of equipment and weapons. They can share this knowledge with their civilian gang counterparts. The court martial was only one example of the aggressive response to gang crime by our U.S. military.

The Truth

The head of any military recruitment command will correctly tell you that being a gang member is not a crime and itself cannot necessarily exclude the gang member from military service. The First Amendment of the Constitution allows for freedom of association. This would include being a member of the KKK or a street gang or the Church of Satan. Therefore, as mentioned before gang membership is not illegal.

What could disqualify a gang member from military service is a felony arrest and conviction record. Some gang members have even used false identities to get into our nation's military. All branches of the service are now looking very closely at this issue. An attempt to rid the ranks of illegal activity and unprofessional conduct is currently being made in all branches of the service. The Army's Criminal Investigation Command (CID) has been following gang activities for over 20 years. Military and civilian law enforcement routinely educated commanders and the military communities about the customs and practices of street gangs and exchange information.

One possible solution might be some type of service contract, signed when entering any branch of the military notifying the service person that it would be a federal offense to engage in criminal activities, gang related criminal activities and the selling or trading of certain military training or equipment. It might also forbid the display of gang related tattoos on base, whether on or off duty and offer an in-service program for their removal.

With the advent of gang members serving honorably in the military there have been reported cases that while on active duty these gang member servicemen did well, extremely well in some cases. They may have been in combat during the Middle East conflict during the early to mid 2000s. However, upon returning back to the neighborhood where their gang is sometimes these veterans return to active duty gang membership. Unfortunately, some have used guns in assaults against rival gang members and law enforcement.

Military combat tactics then can become part of the armed response. This potentially becomes an issue because it can certainly increase the levels of violence. Anecdotal evidence with gang members from Central America tends to suggest this because of the impact of military experience has had with MS-13 levels of violence seen in Central America and the United States. Don't forget many MS-13 gang members had prior military experience.

Street Gang Connection

So what is the impact of military trained gang members returning back to civilian life? I would suggest one thing and one thing only. People tend to react the way they are trained. I would suggest that a few gang members join the military for the wrong reasons. But for those gang members who do join no matter what the reason they receive some of the best training in the world. Small arms tactics, hand to hand fighting, ambush techniques, cover operations and the list goes on.

When a military gang member retires or is dishonorable discharged that training stays with him. There is law enforcement anecdotal evidence that suggests some military trained gang members share their training with civilian counter parts. This in theory could pose a problem for local law enforcement. In 2007 the FBI's report on gangs in the military cited this very issue and a potential problem (FBI, 2007).

Then research also suggested that some gangs were found to have military trained members; which implies that the gang members had to be able to enlist and be trained in the military. Street gangs that reported this were: 18th Street, Asian Boyz, Bloods, Crips, Florencia 13, Gangster Disciples, Latin Kings, MS-13, Nortenos, Surenos and the Vice Lords. Outlaw motorcycle gangs that reported this fact were: the Bandidos, Hells Angels, Mongols, Outlaw Motorcycle Club and the Vagos. Prison gangs that reported this finding were: the Aryan Brotherhood and the Mexican Mafia. There are probably more, but this partial list illustrates the fact that military trained gang members can pose a potential safety problem for criminal justice professionals (FBI, 2007.

Summary

The actual number of gang members in the military is small when compared to the total military population. It has been estimated as one percent or less. Not surprisingly this is the same percentage that has been suggested for the general civilian population (Glass, 2007). If this is close that would suggest between 10,000 and 14,000 gang members within the U.S. military.

With the growing influence of the Mexican drug cartel drug trafficking market within the country new connections for cross border shipment of contraband is needed. Between 2005 and 2009 a number of drug investigations have revealed the assistance of military personnel from all branches assisting in drug and human trafficking operations. The key factor here is money. The Mexican drug cartels do not have a budget. Compromising military personnel becomes the cost of doing business in the United States. Police officers, [parole officers, Department of Motor Vehicle officers and even a few Federal agents have been comprised.

As we continue to deploy our men and women of the U.S. armed forces we acknowledge that 99 percent are law abiding hard working citizens. Prudence also requires acknowledging the other one percent. The last point, if less than one percent of the general population (gang members) accounts for a disproportional amount of the violent gang related crime; why wouldn't this be also true for the military gang population?

Chapter 6

Transnational Gangs

This chapter will discuss controversial issues regarding immigration and illegal immigrant gang members. Although is believed by many that U.S. deportation policies are the primary cause for the explosive gang growth in Mexico and Central America research data suggests otherwise. Although there is no hard research yet, anecdotal evidence suggests that less than five percent of the total immigrantpopulation gets involved in street activity.

Mexico Drug Trafficking Organizations

There is a lot of controversy about legal and illegal immigration and effects it has on the United States. Before a discussing of the gang activity in Mexico I want to caution the reader that the information in this chapter does not define the country of Mexico or all Mexicans, just as the street gang activity in the U.S. does not define the country or all Americans. However, due to the Mexican drug cartel activity, the violence along the southern border and the intrusion of Mexican drug cartel activity into the United States candid remarks are necessary in order to fully understand the connection between Mexican drug cartels, U.S. based prison and street gangs.

Immigrants

In a speech given by Steven Sample, President of the University of Southern California in 2008 for the World Affairs Council in Los Angeles he cited how diverse the city of Los Angeles was. President Sample stated that Los Angeles has nearly 1200 miles of freeways and they are important arteries to the rest of the country and Canada. The Los Angeles International Airport is the number one airport for origin and destination in the United States. In 2007, the airport handled 62 million passengers and almost two million tons of cargo (Sample, 2008).

President Sample further stated that Los Angeles is an international economic infrastructure with 10.4 million people from over 120 different cultures, 96 cradle languages, 600 different religious groups and 49 foreign language publications. L.A. has more people of Mexican decent than any city outside of Mexico, the largest Korean population outside Seoul, Korea; the largest Japanese population outside Japan and the largest Asian-American population in the country (Sample, 2008).

President Sample cited Jim Clifton, the CEO of the Gallup Organization, the world's leading pollster. According to Clifton researchers have proposed that it just took 1000 individuals, inventors, scientists who contributed to the United States to get this country far, far ahead of Japan and Germany. This is why America is the world leader in technology, medicine, business, telephony and science. What is particular noteworthy is that of these individual American pioneers more than half migrated from another country... they were in fact immigrants (Sample, 2008).

Mexico

I cite these facts here because of all the controversy surrounding the immigrant issue. Immigrant populations can be stereotyped. The actions of few can be used to describe entire populations. As of July, 2008 the CIA reported the population of Mexico to be a little less than

110 million people (CIA, 2008). Los Angles is a major business hub with an infrastructure that is ideal for transport and travel for both legal and illegal business.

With those thoughts in mind consider the issue of America's drug appetite. We will discover that this hunger drives the business for the trafficking of illegal drugs and also provides business opportunities for those who get involved. The Drug Enforcement Agency (DEA) has suggested that approximately 90 percent of the illegal drugs that enter America come through the southern U.S.-Mexico border. The Mexican drug cartels supply contraband to the American public by camouflaging their use by piggy backing transport on the same routes that immigrants take. Sadly, the cartels fight each other for control of these routes.

Cartels

There a number of drug cartels operating in Mexico. We will examine those that tend to impact the U.S. –Mexican border. They include The Arellano-Felix Organization, known as the Tijuana Cartel, the Carrillo-Fuentes Organization, known as the Juarez Cartel, the Osiel Cardenas-Guillen Organization, known as the Gulf cartel, and the Guzman-Loera Organization, also known as the Sinaloa Cartel. Los Zetas have developed into a drug cartel and there is a separate chapter that will examine their impact on the U.S. (Refer to Los Zetas).

These cartels have geographically divided up turf in Mexico in order to control drug trafficking routes through Mexico and into the United States. What is at stake here? The answer is a consumer driven market that is estimated to have an annual profit worth of 13.6 to 48.4 billion dollars (Cook, 2007). Of course this much of this money is sent outside of the United States to be laundered through foreign banking systems. So much money is at stake here that Joaquin "El Chapo" Guzman leader of the Sinaloa cartel was named by Forbes Magazine on the World's Billionaires list, March 11, 2009 as one of the world's richest men (Forbes, 2009).

The Mexican government suggests there are seven major cartels working in Mexico. Three of the larger cartels operate throughout much of Mexico. They are the Gulf, Sinaloa and Juarez cartels. Law enforcement anecdotal evidence indicates the Juarez cartel operate in 21 Mexican states with principal basis in Culiacan, Sinaloa; Monterrey, Nuevo Leon and the cities of Ciudad Juarez and Ojinaga, Chihuahua; Mexico City; Guadalajara, Jalisco; Cuernavaca, Morelos and Cancun in Quintana Roo. The Sinaloa cartel has been reported in 17 Mexican states and important centers are located in Mexico City; Tepic, Nayarit; Toluca and Cuautitlan, Mexico State and most of Sinaloa (Cook, 2007). However the city of Nuevo Laredo across from Laredo, Texas has been a traditional hot spot for cartel fighting between Los Zetas and the Sinaloa cartel.

The Gulf cartel operates in 13 Mexican states with important operation centers in the cities of Nuevo Laredo, Miguel Aleman, Reynosa and Matamoros, Tamaulipas. The Gulf cartel although smaller size still operates in a number of venues; they have reported in Nuevo Leon, Monterrey and Morelia, Michoacan. The Tijuana cartel has been reported in 15 states and important operations centers located in Tijuana, Mexicali, Tecate and Ensenada in Baja California and in parts of Sinaloa (Cook, 2007).

There was a catalyst that most likely allowed the Mexican cartels to come to power. It probably was the demise of Cali and Medellin cartel leadership in Columbia during the 1990s. In physics there is a saying "that for every action there is a reaction." When the Columbian cartel leadership fell that open an opportunity for the trafficking of illegal drugs to other groups. A logical direct route would be through Central America and Mexico. This gave the somewhat "smalltime" Mexican cartels an opportunity to expand their operations.

As the Mexican cartels gained power American and Mexican law enforcement responded and a number of key cartel leaders were taken into custody. When this was happened rival cartels attempted to move in and take over the lucrative smuggling routes. Mid level leaders became cartel leaders. It was this action that most likely caused the spike in violence along the U.S.-Mexican border and throughout the country of Mexico that has resulted in the death of over 5,400 people in 2008 (CNN, 2009). Sadly, in 2008 alone more people have been murdered in Mexican drug war than all the American military casualties in the entire Iraq war; 4260 casualties (icasualties.org).

Collateral Issues

In addition to the brutal cartel drug battles there are a couple of other factors to consider that may contribute to the instability and violence in the country. Corruption continues to be a thorny issue for the Mexican government. Even though the current administration has made gainful strides in trying to combat the corruption, the Mexican drug cartels have an unlimited budget. No matter how much military or government officials' wages are raised the cartels have the ability to counter the effort. Corruption issues have lead to arrest and investigations of top level federal law enforcement agents, military officials to local law enforcement. This only demonstrates that everyone has a price under the right conditions. Corruption also undermines the confidence of the citizens in the government, judicial system and law enforcement.

Secondly, an often overlooked issue is the fact that street gangs exist in Mexico as well as the cartels. Street gang membership can become a recruitment pool for new cartel membership. So there are two issues to deal with. Ignoring street gang activity while focusing on the violence caused by the cartels could potentially lead to the formation of other "junior cartels" that will work with or against the existing cartels or against themselves. This could only end up with increasing the violence within the region. As street gangs evolve they also tend to become more violent as gang populations increase in size and as rivalries develop between gangs.

There some anecdotal evidence that suggests street gangs operate in throughout most of Mexico. They appear to operate like many U.S. based traditional Latino street gangs. No vertical leadership structure. They tend to operate in specific geographical areas within a city or town. The gang will use graffiti and hand signs to communicate. These gangs tend to be involved in robberies, extortions, drug sales and even home invasion type robberies. The money that is earned is often used to purchase and use drugs. There is no data that can estimate the number of street gangs or the membership is Mexico. There is some anecdotal evidence that suggests for some street gang members there is a developing relationship between Mexican prison gangs and the drug cartels. This seems logical since the same types of relationships exist between their U.S. counterparts.

Another issue to consider is the growing population of drug users and addiction in Mexico. Again there is no data or academic research that can provide an estimate on the number of adults and juveniles in this population. Anecdotal evidence suggests that the drug use is increasing throughout Mexico especially along the U.S. - Mexico border. A growing population of addicts can only tax an already overloaded public resource system. This population will also cause the demand for illegal drugs in Mexico to increase. There are an estimated 200,000 addicts in Tijuana, Mexico. In Tijuana there are over 20,000 little 'tienditas' or little shops where anyone can purchase drugs (San Pedro, 2009).

Cartels also take advantage of arms trafficking. The military grade weapons that are being used by some cartels may have two points of entry into Mexico. The obvious and most cited in the media and by law enforcement is the United States. Straw purchases, stolen and illegally sold weapons are smuggled into Mexico. These weapons can include automatic assault rifles and high capacity handguns and according to U.S. law enforcement approximately 90 percent of the weapons seized from Mexican drug cartels come from the United States (Ellingwood and Wilkinson, 2009). It has been suggested that astonishingly up to 2,000 weapons per day are smuggled from the United States into Mexico. A November 2008 weapons seizure in Mexico and subsequent analysts revealed that 90 percent of the arms originated from 11 American states (Johnson, 2009).

But there is a second portal arms travel through to enter Mexico. In the overall picture it is seldom mentioned. Military grade arms, including grenades, grenade launchers, anti-tank weapons, amour piercing rounds, bazookas, rocket propelled grenades (RPGs) and 50 caliber sniper rifles can enter Mexico through the Central American country of Guatemala. These weapons could be stolen and /or left over arms from the civil wars in that region (Ellingwood and Wilkinson, 2009). Anecdotal evidence has also suggested that a wide sampling of the enhanced weapons have come from the international arms bazaar, with grenades and launchers produced by U.S., South Korean, Israeli, Spanish or former Soviet bloc manufacturers (Ellingwood and Wilkinson, 2009).

Concurrent with the arms race are the expansion of the drug armies that were initially formed to protect the cartels. These private mercenary armies can employ military deserters, ex-state and federal police and private citizens working for them. The two most known are Los Zetas and Negros and they are rivalries. There is no accurate estimate for the size of these security groups. It well understood that they are responsible for much of the violence in Mexico and they outgun local and federal police. To further compound the issue even though there more than 40,000 troops deployed throughout Mexico there have been 150,000 desertions from the military in Mexico during the past six years. Their departure has affected military operations in the states of Chihuahua, Guerrero, Sinaloa and Michoacan, all considered hot stops for cartel activity. Soldier's loyalty can be bought especially when they earn $196-$229 per month (Rodriguez, 2009).

As noted with Los Zetas, drug armies can also evolve and become more sophisticated. Los Zetas initially was formed to be the enforcement arm of the Gulf cartel. In 2003 after the leader of the cartel, Osiel Cardenas was arrested and extradited to the U.S.; Los Zetas continued to watch over interests of the cartel. However by 2009, Los Zetas has evolved into a drug cartel itself; still maintaining its connection with the Gulf cartel and expanding its recruitment pool. Estimates place the membership between 100 and 200. That does not include members joining the cartel from U.S. based street and prison gangs. Or the Mexican street gang members who join or the Mexican citizens who assist the cartel or the ex-military members from the Guatemalan Special Forces.

Although drug cartel violence is encountered throughout Mexico the main battle grounds appear to be the northern border cities of Tijuana, Nuevo Laredo and Ciudad Juarez. Add to this formula the presence of more than 3,200 maquiladora plants with approximately one million employees. These are factories that are able to use duty free materials and components from foreign suppliers to manufacture finished products like electronics, car parts and soft goods like textiles (NDIC, 2004). These products are then returned duty-free back to the suppliers. Most of these plants are located close to the U.S. –Mexican border; where much of the cartel violence is occurring. For example, in 2003 the Ciudad Juarez, across from El Paso, Texas there were nearly 200,000 employees working in over 300 maquiladoras. The two largest maquiladoras in Mexico are located in Ciudad Juarez and Tijuana (NDIC, 2004). Much of the drug cartel violence has also occurred in these two cities where it is common to find decapitated bodies.

In response to the violence Mexico sent more than 7.500 troops to the Ciudad Juarez in early March, 2009. Preliminary reports suggest that violence has decreased. But now the city is virtually under martial law. This may have been a necessary remedy because the violence was extreme and involved cartel attacks against federal military troops. For example in February, 2009 a cartel cash with the army troops ended with the death of 21 people after cartel members abducted local police. By the early part of 2009, President Calderon had committed 45,000 troops throughout Mexico to fight the drugs. With a total Army population of roughly 200,000 this is a sizeable resource allocation (Cardona, 2009).

Transnational Characteristics

Let's examine the transnational nature of some Mexican drug cartels. The violence is not only in Mexico, some of it has spilled over into the United States. Reports suggest that Mexican drug cartels operate in at least 230 U.S. cities (Associated Press, 2009; CNN, 2009). The FBI confirms that at 60 American citizens have been kidnapped into Mexico. Many were taken directly from U.S. soil and smuggled across the border. As the violence expands it even hits U.S. Federal agents. For example, the Washington times reported in 2008 that a U.S. Border Patrol Agent was held at gun point by people dressed as members of the Mexican military who had crossed the border in Arizona. The so called 'Mexican soldiers' fled across the border as back up arrived for the Border Patrol agent (Seper, 2009).

CNN reported that the city of Atlanta, Georgia has become a hub for the distribution and the collection of drug monies for the Mexican cartels (Mungin, 2009). The same article also reported how a victim was found chained to a wall by his hands and feet in the basement of his Atlanta home. The victim was gagged and beaten because he owed the cartels money. He was a dealer operating in the Atlanta area (Mungin, 2009). Another news article reported that the Federation, Gulf and Juarez cartels operate in Illinois and an estimated 10 to 24 million drug proceed dollars are sent back to Mexico each month (Meyer, 2009).

Phoenix, Arizona has become the 'kidnap capital' for the United States. Most of the kidnaps are a result of groups connected to the cartels that simply cross the border and kidnap the victim then retreat south. These groups are known as 'bajadores' or take down crews that usually operate in groups of five. In 2008, there were a reported 386 kidnappings in Arizona. This is more than any other U.S. city the vast majority were drug cartel related. It is suspected that some kidnappings never get reported to the police. Often the victims are drug dealers who don't want the police attention (CNN, 2009).

Some bajadores work directly for the cartels collecting money or acting as enforcers. Other groups act as freelance mercenaries stealing drug or human trafficking shipments from traffickers making them responsible for the loss. The Phoenix Police Department also has reported that cartels will levy a tax on Mexican drug dealers utilizing their trafficking routes. This tax (el piso) can be up to $2,000 per week and $10,000 per week for Chinese and Middle Eastern dealers (Conant and Camp-Flores, 2009). Other cartels have followed the lead.

The Tijuana cartel has been reported operating in 26 U.S. states; Alabama, Arizona, California, Connecticut, Delaware, Florida, Georgia, Hawaii, Illinois, Kansas, Louisiana, Massachusetts, Michigan, Nebraska, Nevada, New Jersey, New York, North Carolina, Ohio, Oklahoma, Oregon, Pennsylvania, Tennessee, Texas, Washington and Wisconsin (NDIC, 2004).

The Juarez cartel has been reported operating in 27 U.S. states: Arkansas, California, Colorado, Florida, Georgia, Illinois, Indiana, Iowa, Kansas, Kentucky, Massachusetts, Michigan, Minnesota, Missouri, Nebraska, Nevada, New Jersey, New Mexico, New York, North Carolina, Ohio, Oklahoma, Pennsylvania, South Carolina, Tennessee and Wisconsin (NDIC, 2004).

The Gulf cartel has been reported operating in 10 U.S. states: Alabama, Florida, Georgia, Illinois, New Jersey, New York, North Carolina, Pennsylvania, Tennessee and Texas (NDIC, 2004). Los Zetas one of the newest cartels has been reported operating in three states, Arizona, New Mexico and Texas.

The cartel expansion is not limited just to the United States. It is logical to conclude that the cartels will also enter into Central America and Canada as their drug business expands, if they are not already present. The operation of U.S. street and prison gangs has already been cited in both regions. Drugs and arms are smuggled into Canada from the United States by outlaw motorcycle and street gangs.

The relationships are somewhat complicated between the Mexican drug trafficking organizations and U.S. based outlaw motorcycle, prison and street gangs. Some Mexican cartels have direct connections between U.S. based street and prison gangs. Some U.S. based prison gangs also have drug contacts with street and outlaw motorcycle gangs. Some prison gangs also have multiple connections between different Mexican drug cartels. A few street gangs become recruitment pools for the Mexican drug cartels. The overlapping umbrella that connects all these groups is drugs, contraband and ultimately money. These groups form business relationship to make money.

Money provides the most effective weapon any gang can use, that is corruption. The Mexican drug cartels use this weapon efficiently and with purpose. For example, in November, 2008 Noe Ramirez who was the prosecutor in charge of the Organized Crime unit of the Mexican Federal Attorney General's office was charged with taking a monthly bribe of $450,000 to pass information to the Sinaloa drug cartel. Six other members of his unit face similar charges. The comments in this chapter do not define Mexico or all of the people who live there. This country is the world's twelfth largest economy and the United States second biggest trading partner and an important oil supplier (Economist, 2009). The stakes in this country are enormous for both Mexico and the United States.

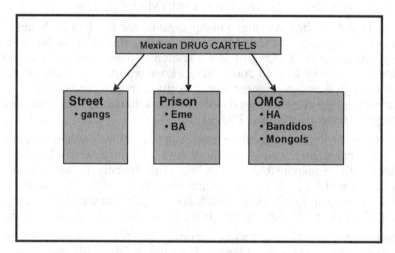

Mexican drug cartels are drug traffickers and U.S. based gangs become the major distributors.

However, the instability in several regions in Mexico caused by the drug cartels can have a lasting effect on the country and its citizens. For example, in a 2007 survey the data suggested that 70 percent of the crime goes unreported to the police. Mexico is a country of 32 states each operating independently from the government, not totally cooperative with the government or between each other. State governors are often reluctant to comply with national requests. The local police departments are designed to keep political peace not solve crimes and there are over 1600 municipal police forces in the country. The courts and police do not do their jobs properly; and Mexican society and the police do not work together (Economist, 2009).

Solutions?

There is hope and President Calderon's government is making some progress. In June, 2008 a constitutional reform reorganized the courts and police. A new law signed in January 2009 set up a new national public security system. This law requires all national, state and municipal police force to adopt uniform procedures for recruitment, vetting, training, operations and promotions. Every policeman in the country is supposed to be completely vetted. The federal police force has been expanded from 9,000 (2006) to 26,000 officers. The government has made extra funds available to local police forces. Another proposed law is designed to update the judicial system and allow oral evidence and move toward adversarial trials (Economists, 2009).

This is a start, but it will take time, national effort and money to compete with the cartel's most effective weapon.

Suggested border security ideas have included talk about using the U.S. military to secure the border. In effect this would shut down the border. If that is done a couple of things could happen. There could be a domino effect on the people who travel across the border for legitimate work. Without the opportunity for U.S. employment the opportunity for employment by the drug cartels could become more viable. Look at the case of Santiago Meza in Tijuana. His nickname was the "El Pozelero" (the soup maker). When Mr. Meza was caught by the police he confessed to dissolving the bodies of over 300 people in acid since 2000 on orders from drug cartels (The Economist, 2009). Mr. Meza was a civilian employed by the cartels. There is already anecdotal evidence that suggests cartels employ civilians and Mexican and U.S. street gang members.

Possible solutions for border security can include completely shutting down the border. This is not a long term solution. There are a number of immigrants who are gainfully employed in the United States. Immigrants send home remittances. In 2007 over 60 million dollars of remittances were sent back to Latin America including Mexico (Mac Harg, 2007). In 2008 the amount of remittances worldwide was estimated at 240 billion dollars. The remittances seem to be decreasing in 2008 due to the economic woes and less money is sent home. This worries the Mexican government that matches the remittances 3 to 1 if used for community projects (Time, 2008). Shutting down the border would effectively stop the remittance flow back to Mexico.

With the prospect of no work in America job seeking Mexicans could eventually be employed by the cartels. Not because they want to but because in order to survive they have to. As cartels gain more and more of an economic base they could become major if not the largest employers in Mexico.

The U.S. –Mexican border should be kept open. It will good for commerce for both countries. May a more controlled approach to border security can work. For example to more effectively monitor cross border traffic why not double the amount of entry points on both sides of the border. This could provide much employment for citizens of both countries. More portals means faster transit times between countries.

To further expedite movement between countries why can't some form of biometric identification be used and shared with vetted Mexican counterparts. This would make legitimate travel across borders easy and more easily monitored. Use U.S. Border patrol and ICE agents collaboratively at the formal points of entry, concentrating their efforts.

To prevent unauthorized or re-entry into the United States use a combination one to one Border Patrol-U.S. Army border interdiction task force to guard the border areas between the formal points of entry. Often local law enforcement can be cross designated to Federal law enforcement task forces. Use the same procedure to cross designate U.S. military to assist another Federal law enforcement agency. By doing so resources like vehicles, technology and aircraft can be shared between the military and Customs and Border Patrol agents. These teams could focus on guarding the areas between the formal entry points between Mexico and the U.S.

The caveat here is that on the opposite side of the border these Border Patrol team would have a vetted Mexican counterpart engaged in the same activity. Both sides of the border guarded vigorously forcing travel between countries to well controlled funneling points of entry. To make this work travel through entry points should be coordinated between countries so that there are no long lines with hours of waiting. This is where biometric identification of individuals who regularly travel between countries can be facilitated.

Also vehicle inspections could be performed on both side of the border. This could be a double check system and again technology can used to help prevent illegal crossings of humans and contraband. With more border agents on both sides of the border more vehicles can be inspected expeditiously. Traditional visual inspections and the use of canines can further complement this process. More formal entry points means less vehicles at each entry points.

With increased personnel presence that could include military-Federal agent teams more vehicles can be inspected.

At the World Trade Bridge located between Laredo, Texas and Nuevo Laredo, Chihuahua, Mexico something similar could be done in order to physically inspect more trucks entering and leaving the United States. This in theory also could limit the amount of drugs entering the country and limit the amount of drug cash and weapons smuggled back into Mexico. Vehicles should be inspected coming to and leaving the United States.

Another enforcement activity should be implemented. Roving teams of ICE agents should be patrolling the areas adjacent to the formal points of entry. They could be the secondary net that randomly checks vehicles and individuals leaving the border area. Sort of like airline travelers randomly selected to participate in secondary random screening before boarding the aircraft. Why not have random secondary inspections of vehicles going to and from border points of entry.

Collectively these interventions could help decrease the amount of illegal drugs entering the United States; thus helping decrease the flow of drugs through Mexico and ultimately decrease revenue going to the drug cartels. Limiting the revenue cartels can earn will eventually decrease cartel influence in Mexico by decreasing the amount of corruption. Remember the cartels most powerful weapon is money. These programs could also limit the amount of weapons travelling across the borders assisting the Mexican government in deescalating the arms race between cartels.

To fully impact the illicit drug and arms trade similar programs should be implemented along the southern Mexican-Guatemalan –Belize borders. Working internationally between countries, a coordinated effort is need to insure total stability in Mexico. Don't forget I mentioned the physics principal earlier that for every action there is a reaction. We should anticipate a reaction by the drug cartels and street gangs in Mexico. Violence may initially increase or become present in areas where cartels have not previously been established. We should anticipate that cartels will attempt to develop alternate drug trafficking routes. Logically this means there could be an increase in maritime smuggling between countries. Also we should exclude activity on the Canadian-U.S. border area. Mexican cartels could attempt to establish operational centers in Canada in order to continue operations in the United States.

One other intervention may be helpful in the united fight against Mexican drug cartel actively. It has been well documented that drug cartels are diversifying into other types of criminal activity like kidnapping and extortions. The U.S. and Mexico should be prepared to monitor and investigate these types of crimes with specially trained law enforcement-prosecution teams. There are also collateral crimes that assist in arms and human smuggling and cartel criminal activity in both countries; namely the false identification business. More resources are needed to monitor, investigate and prosecute this type of criminal activity.

I think there are enough laws in the Penal Code. However, the countries of Canada, the United States and Mexico should collectively enact new laws that are specifically designed for smugglers; aimed at any type of smuggling between countries. This would include but not limited to pharmaceuticals, illegal drugs, weapons, ammunition, human beings, pirated soft goods, music CDs and movie DVDs, software and the transport of large sums of cash, $4000 or more. The caveat here is smuggling and it does not have to be associated with any type of gang or cartel activity. Enforcement and punishment of violators could deter further such activity. The law should be written and adopted to that any prosecutor's office could charge the crime. That would empower federal, state and local prosecutors giving a tri-level approach to smuggling.

Zetas

One of the most prominent and most violent gangs in Mexico is Los Zetas. They are known for the military style training and their calling card, extreme violence. The gang and their activities have to be included in this book because of the transnational nature of their migration, ties to U.S. prison and street gangs and the types of crime the group is involved in.

History

Los Zetas presence south of the U.S.-Mexico border is just as important as their presence north of it. The best way to describe the gang is to say they started as a rogue group of Mexican Army Special Forces type soldiers that are responsible for hundreds of drug related murders, drug and arms trafficking and corruption along the southern U.S. border.

The gang 's activity were highlighted in 2005 when a 56 year-old father of three took the oath of office and became the police chief in the city of Nuevo Laredo, Mexico. The town is located across the Rio Grande River from Laredo, Texas. Within six hours he was dead; he was shot with more than 30 bullets and was killed. The hit men were believed to be members of Los Zetas (Grayson, 2008).

It is believed that Los Zetas (Spanish for the letter Z) was formed in 1995. Thirty one Mexican Army Special Forces soldiers deserted their units to become enforcers for Osiel Cardenas, the leader of the Gulf Cartel. The Zetas were originally members the Grupo Aeromovil de Fuerzas Especiales (GAFE). Translated the name is Air Mobil Group and was the 350 member elite paratrooper and intelligence battalion of GAFE. The unit was deployed in the state of Tamaulipas, México to fight drug traffickers along the Texas-Mexican border in 1995 (DOJ, 2005). Another source suggests the gang was formed in 1998 (Charlton, 2007). The title of Los Zetas was taken from the radio code used by the Mexican Federal Police in Tamaulipas. It referred to the highest ranking commanders (DOJ, 2005).

The Mexican soldiers who formed the original group of Los Zetas were highly trained in small arms tactics, as well as collecting intelligence. Members of GAFE also received advanced training from the U.S. Army Special Forces. At least one third of the original members of Los Zetas received training at the School of Americas in Fort Benning, Georgia. GAFE soldiers even received advanced training from military special operation units from Cuba and Brazil (DOJ, 2005; Grayson, 2008; Maldon Institute, 2009).

Currently, Los Zetas recruits from the pool of Mexican State Police, criminals, street gang members and civilian population. Los Zetas is known for its superior firepower, weapons handling, assault tactics, intelligence gathering expertise and brutality. Los Zetas have reported to operate through Mexico, but especially in the states of Nuevo Leon, Tamaulipas, Sonora, Guerrero and Veracruz (Charlton, 2007). In Tamaulipas los Zetas presence has noted in Matamoros, Reynosa and Nuevo Laredo. They are active throughout the gulf region of the country and the states of Tabasco, Yucatan, Quintana Roo, Chiapas, Oaxaca, Michoacan and Mexico City (Grayson, 2008).

Los Zetas are known for their common use of military tactics, automatic weapons, including grenades and explosives. Los Zetas are responsible for shoot outs with Mexican local and Federal police the Army. The gang is highly organized and disciplined and criminal investigations have revealed the gang's presence in Texas, Oklahoma, Arizona, and California (DOJ, 2005). Between the para-military groups operating in Mexico there is almost an arms race going on. Gangs like Los Zetas have armed themselves with weapons of war including rocket propelled grenades, 50 caliber sniper rifles and grenades (Maldon Institute, 2009; Ellingwood and Wilkinson, 2009).

Unlike traditional law enforcement and military Los Zetas virtually has an unlimited budget. This means the gang has the purchasing power for the most current weapon systems and the ability to pay handsomely for intelligence. This translates to the fact that often Mexican law enforcement is outgunned and outmanned when confronting a unit of Los Zetas. Law enforcement anecdotal evidence suggests that a large percentage of the weapons used by Los Zetas originate from the United States. This confirms the concept of arms trafficking from the U.S. into Mexico.

At one time members of Los Zetas were known to wear military style uniforms. This can include military grade body armor. The members can be armed with AK and AR series automatic assault rifles, hand grenades, rocket propelled grenades (RPG) and global positioning equipment. Los Zetas are also known to drive armored vehicles such as Lincoln Navigators, and SUV type trucks, including 'Hummers.'. Law enforcement anecdotal evidence also suggests that Los Zetas may have access to helicopters (DOJ, 2005). There is a vertical command leadership structure to this gang.

The lowest ranking members of Los Zetas can be referred to as 'Hawks' (halcones). These members function as intelligence gathers who watch assigned area. Based on the comments from a former Zeta member, "there is nowhere to hide in Mexico because Los Zetas have bought off officers in the municipal police, state police, ministerial police, soldiers, federal preventative policy and military on the border." This same former Zeta member also suggested that some Zeta units have specific ties with the Mara Salvatrucha gang. He claims that some current Los Zetas members were former members of the MS-13 gang (News Channel 5, 2006).

Other members are in charge of stores or locations where drugs and other contraband are processed. Los Cobras or Los L's provide armed security to the Los Zetas members working in these areas. There is another level of Zeta memberships called Nuevo Zetas and are also called Kaibiles. These members are former Guatemalan Special forces soldiers who have deserted and now work with Los Zetas. During operations the Nuevo Zetas appear to give orders to Los Cobras when to shoot or when to handcuff kidnap victims (Maldon Institute, 2009).

There are relatively few original Los Zetas members left. Many are dead or in custody. Of those who remain they are the highest ranking members within Los Zetas. They are often referred to as 'university graduates' or 'teachers' or 'lawyers' or 'engineers.' These are code names that are used in public or when talking on telephones in order not to be identified in case the conversation is monitored (Maldon Institute, 2009).

Each Zeta unit has an accountant assigned to it. These positions tend to be held by the most trusted members of Los Zetas because they distribute payroll and bribes. The highest ranking accountant for the entire Zeta organization is known as Comandante Sol. The accountants also have a list of the payroll listing the name of public officials being paid money by the gang. The gang also has informants and security details that guard the homes of unit commanders. The informants are like assistants to the commander. The informants have no legal issues; can move around the city with no difficulty and have connections that the gang uses (Maldon Institute, 2009).

The Zetas have also been known to operate in platoon size units between 10 and 15 members using military style tactic in their operations. Due to the extreme levels of poverty in many parts of Mexico new member s can be easily drawn to the gang because they will pay approximately 3000 peso per week; the equivalent of about $300 U.S. dollars per week (Charlton, 2007). A Mexican soldier might make that pay per month. Other law enforcement anecdotal evidence has suggested Los Zetas can operate in smaller groups with three to four members in a vehicle.

In 2003, the head of the Gulf Cartel, Osiel Cardenas was arrested by Mexican law enforcement. Los Zetas continued to protect his interests in the cartel. The main rival for Los Zetas is the Sinaloa cartel headed by Joaquin 'el Chapo' Guzman and battle ground for control of the I-35 corridor drug trafficking route through Texas was and still is the city of Nuevo Laredo, Mexico. This is the sister city of Laredo, Texas and is where the world Trade bridge is located. The Sinaloa Carte was and is the main rival of the Gulf Cartel. Subsequent to his arrest Osiel Cardenas was extradited to the United States pending trial for drug trafficking and other charges (Maldon Institute, 2009).

Since the arrest of Cardenas there is some law enforcement anecdotal evidence which suggests Los Zetas have evolved into its own drug trafficking organization. "The Zetas don't ask the Gulf cartel for permission for anything anymore. They simply inform them of their activities whenever they feel like it" (Grayson, 2008). As a result there is fierce and brutal fighting between the gangs which includes the murder of police officers and innocent bystanders. It appears that Los Zetas are involved in the trafficking of the crystal form of methamphetamine commonly known as 'Ice.'

Diversification

Los Zetas are also involved in human smuggling of Central Americans and Mexicans into the United States. There is some evidence that also suggests Los Zetas are involved in smuggling Middle Easterners from Mexico into the U.S. (DOJ, 2005). During the mid to late 1990's law enforcement anecdotal evidence suggested Los Zeta s had specifically targeted U.S. Border Patrol Agents other law enforcement officers. The gang reportedly placed a bounty on the agents ranging from $30,000 to $50,000 for each death (DOJ, 2005). In one case Los Zetas members allegedly kidnapped and executed several Mexican police officers form the city of Matamoros, Mexico.

Kidnappings traced back to Los Zetas have increased over the years. Between 2004 and 2005 the FBI reported 35 abductions of U.S. citizens within regions controlled by Los Zetas. From January to August, 2005 there were 202 kidnappings reported in the Mexican state of Tamaulipas. Tamaulipas is the Gulf Cartel's and a Los Zeta's operational center. Many kidnappings go unreported by the family for fear of retaliation by Los Zetas (Swecker, 2005).

Here is another fact that supports the transnational nature of Los Zetas. The gang has established an auxiliary gang composed of the children and nephews of Los Zetas. This gang is called 'Los Zetillas.' Los Zetillas also recruits from the ranks of U.S. based Latino street gangs in Texas. It has been reported that for U.S. Latino street gang members to be initiated into Los Zetillas they have to commit a murder (History Channel, 2009). Los Zetas have set up training camps for 15 to 18 year-old recruits. Los Zetas have also recruited members of the Kaibiles; these are specially trained Guatemalan jungle warfare fighters (Grayson, 2008).

The internal training program for new members usually includes weapons use, explosives, personal defense and physical fitness (History Channel, 2009). The training camps have been reported in locations south of Matamoros, Mexico across the border from Brownsville, Texas and a second venue just north of Nuevo Laredo airport, near the town of Abasolo, Mexico (Grayson, 2008).

To fully understand the impact Los Zetas can have you have to understand the changing dynamics of the drug cartels and the growing rivalries between them. For example, law enforcement anecdotal evidence suggested in 2004 the Gulf Cartel formed an alliance with the Tijuana Cartel. This alliance impacted rival cartels (Sinaloa and Jalisco). The cartels were fighting over drug distribution routes and territory. This conflict led the Sinaloa and Jalisco Cartels to recruit their own paramilitary forces to protect themselves from Los Zetas who were the enforcement arm of the Gulf Cartel. The Sinaloa and Jalisco Cartels established the 'Los Negros' (Los Lobos) and 'Los Chachos' mercenary gangs in an effort to defeat Los Zetas. In 2005, the alliance between the Gulf and Tijuana cartels dissolved over a dispute, but the conflicts between the four cartels still remains (DOJ, 2005; NDIC, 2007).

Los Zetas have evolved into a drug trafficking organization that in truly have transnational connections with the United States, but also with Central America. The L.A. Times newspaper reported that much of the military grade weapons that Los Zetas use are purchased from contacts in Central America. The gang is taking advantage of the porous borders between Guatemala and Mexico. It has been suggested that the weapons are left over from the Central American civil wars. For example, military grade grenades have been found in 10 Mexican states.

According to the L.A. Times "The Mexican government said it has seized 2,239 grenades in the last two years, in contrast to 59 seized over the previous two years" (Ellingwood and Wilkinson, 2009). Los Zetas have now become involved in the International arms Black Market. Anecdotal evidence suggests that a wide sampling of the enhanced weapons have come from the international arms bazaar, with grenades and launchers produced by U.S., South Korean, Israeli, Spanish or former Soviet bloc manufacturers (Ellingwood and Wilkinson, 2009.

Transnational Activities

Anecdotal evidence law enforcement evidence also suggests that members of Los Zetas have been active in the United States. It is suspected that los Zetas were responsible for the death of a Jamaican drug trafficker in Phoenix, Arizona when they dressed as Phoenix Police SWAT officers in June, 2008. In Birmingham, Alabama, Los Zetas were suspected in the death of a number of Mexican men in August, 2008. The victims' throats were slashed and the money and drugs in the apartment were not touched (Maldon Institute, 2009).

It is now very clear that the gang's criminal activities have now moved north into the United States in a couple of ways. First, even though Los Zetas is based within the Gulf Cartel turf their transnational operations have lead to development of alliances and the recruiting of U.S. based gang members. Law enforcement anecdotal evidence suggests that Los Zetas has been involved in multiple assaults in the United States and have attempted to hire the services of the Mexican Mafia prison gangs for contract killings.

There is some law enforcement evidence that also suggests Los Zetas use members of Barrio Azteca (BA) and Texas Syndicate (TS) and Hermanos de Pistoleros Latinos (HPL) as operatives in the United States (Maldon Institute, 2009; Grayson, 2008). Reaching out for U.S. based allies does not prevent Los Zetas members from entering the country and conducting criminal activities themselves. That is the second way the gang can impact U.S. based gangs and criminal activity. According to the L.A. Times Los Zetas are suspected to be active throughout Arizona and at least 22 different U.S. states and the District of Columbia (Meyer, 2009).

Transnational Gangs

Gangs are now clearly an international phenomenon. Street gangs have been observed in Australia, Africa, Canada, England, Europe, Jamaica, Mexico and Spain, in many other countries, as well as the United States. Some researchers feel that American street gang behaviors appear be the standard for gang behaviors worldwide. In effect, American gang behaviors have become globalized, as have a few street gangs. There is some evidence that suggests some gangs are transnational (Manwaring, 2007; Breve, 2007, Seelke, 2008). Although the discussion has been on street gangs, transnational gangs may include Outlaw motorcycle gangs, some Asian gangs, Jamaican posses, Bloods, Crips, Black Gangster Disciples, Latin Kings, tagger crews, some Hispanic gangs and even some prison gangs.

Globalization

Europeans, like many other nations, deny the existence of street gangs because the gangs they see do not fit the stereotypical depictions of leader-dominated, well organized, violent and cohesive groups found in American media and films. There is a tendency for governments not to recognize the existence of gangs even when they are present. This is sometimes referred to as the "Euro-paradox" (Klein, 2001). This is an academic way of describing denial. It is denial that prevents a full and universally global understanding of the gang phenomenon. The "Euro-paradox" might be more aptly named the "global-paradox." One fundamental issue is a common set of terms that can be used to describe aspects gang culture.

That need leads us to a discussion on gang globalization and begins with defining the term "globalization." The term is defined as the *"increased mobility of goods, services, labor, technology and capital throughout the world"* by the Economic Concepts, Government of Canada. Globalization is really the description of a process. To fully understand this process we also have to consider the impact of technology, especially the advances in the telecommunications infrastructure and the use of the Internet.

Technology facilitates and enhances globalization. However, Investors Worlds also describes globalization as 'the name for a process of increasing connectivity and interdependence of the world's markets and business". For the purpose of this discussion, let us consider some of the activities of street and prison gangs as a business, albeit a criminal business.

So how and why does this term apply to a social and criminal justice issue like gangs? Some gang sets or cliques have established themselves and their criminal enterprises in other countries. They have shown to have an increased mobility of their goods, services and transfer money throughout the world. In essence some U.S. and non-U.S. based gangs have become transnational. Such gang cliques have become pioneers within the gang culture and have resources not normally available to other street gangs. A question that comes to mind is why did some gangs become transnational? Was it an intentional execution of a business plan or an accident? Or was it the result of opportunities to visit family or look for employment?

Another factor to consider is whether the reports of globalized gangs are really part of the gang's activity or an act of a single or few gang members using the gang's association to help operate independently in a venture. This would clearly be an issue exemplifying both types of involvement and activities of globalized street gangs. In other countries, for example Central America some feel their gang problem is a direct result of U.S. policies.

Central America

> *The violence unleashed by thousands of youth gangs, or 'maras' in Central America is a result of globalization and the poverty and marginalization that grip this region, say social scientists, who note that many of Central America's maras are branches of gangs in the United States.*

— José Luis Rocha

According to Nicaraguan philosophy professor José Luis Rocha, *"Gangs in the region are part of transnational organizations." In Central America the largest and most active gangs are in El Salvador, Honduras, Guatemala and Nicaragua. Central American researchers propose the gangs are highly organized and heavily armed (Manwaring, 2007). Research indicates members of these gangs are both victims and victimizers, just as they are in the United States. The Central American street gang phenomenon is also believed to have been largely imported from Los Angeles, California (Rocha, 2000).*

The complex gang issues from the Central American perspective may be viewed by some and the media as a direct result of American deportation policies. Imported 18th Street and Mara Salvatrucha (MS-13) gang members, mainly from southern California seem to be the focus of such arguments. This implies the gangs were transplanted from the United States. Professor Rocha believes that MS-13 and the 18th Street gangs are a linked to migration, stemming from poor youth who have returned from or have been deported from the United States. Interestingly, Professor Rocha concludes that *"this is simply one clear illustration of the globalization process."*

Even though Central American street gangs present a serious social problem, Professor Rocha makes a unique observation; the Central American street gang members are not common criminals. "Instead, they steal or attack out of hunger or to be someone. The gang members wanted respect; to be taken seriously by a society that has excluded them" (Rocha, 2000). This conclusion is supported by other researchers (MacHarg, 2007 and Cruz, 2007). MacHarg and Cruz suggest poverty alone is not the cause of gang violence and growth. The researchers advise it is the effects of poverty along with social stigma and being ostracized that fuels gang membership and the growth of street gangs.

Central American Poverty

Nearly one billion people of the world population live on one dollar a day or less. Latin America's population amounts to 525 million people to which approximately one third live in poverty. The average per capita income is only $3,600. Astonishingly, 32 of every 1,000 children die before the age of one (MacHarg, 2007). This clearly reflects in the quality of life and opportunities available in this region of the world. For example, in Honduras approximately 65% of the population lives on less than $2.00 a day and in 2005 the unemployment rate was 25% (Seelke, 2008). Like many other Central American countries, the Honduran youth have very limited opportunities. In Honduras 30% of the population is 15-24 years old (Seelke, 2008). Curiously, research according to the U.S. Department of Justice indicates the 14-24 year old age-group in the United States is where most of the violent crime and victims of violent crime occur. This may be true in Central America too.

This observation is supported by the fact at least 50% of Central America's 36 million people live in poverty; and the fact that non-governmental organizations have concluded society's hostility towards the gangs has merely fuelled the violence. Because of this, the youth are marginalized, giving way to the imported American gang culture proliferating in Central America (MacHarg, 2007).

Latin America has stereotypically been portrayed as a region of extreme poverty and inequality. These terms accurately describe the plight of 224 million people who live in dire poverty, struggling to feed their families and to stay healthy (MacHarg, 2007). The effects of poverty have become a destabilizing force in Latin America, especially in Central America. A direct impact of economic poverty tears away at the fabric that binds family and society. For example, a lack of a steady income and available employment can separate families as the breadwinner must move to another city or country to earn money while the spouse or eldest child stays home to care for children (MacHarg, 2007).

This dramatically amplifies the number of single parent households. Single parent households have been shown to be a significant risk factor multiplying the likelihood of youths joining street gangs (Hill, Lui, Hawkins, 2001). This turn suggests that the homebound spouse and/or siblings must supplement their survival income with some type of local employment. If the homebound adult parent works, this leaves the children alone without parental control.

UNICEF reports of the 200 million teenagers and children in Latin America and Caribbean, half are considered to be living in poverty and ten percent are working (MacHarg, 2007). For example, in El Salvador human rights groups estimate that at least 800 underage girls work in brothels. About seventy-five percent of the street children have some family links, but spend most of their time on the streets. Most youth never go beyond the fourth grade. The remaining twenty-five percent live on the streets often with groups of older children and sleep in abandon buildings, under bridges or public parks (MacHarg, 2007).

Violence may be the primary reason why children seek shelter in the streets. Six million children and adolescents are subjected to physical violence each year in Latin America. Violence is also part of street life in the form of physical and sexual assaults. Some are purportedly done by local law enforcement. Prostitution and sexual abuse are common among street children (MacHarg, 2007).

Many areas of Central America are underdeveloped. To exacerbate the situation, rural areas often lack sewers, running water and electricity. Many of the roads in these areas are undeveloped or poorly maintained. Living conditions are primitive and the ability to communicate and commute is compromised. Consequences beyond the meager living conditions are poor state and municipal government management and the perception of this population. These factors can create instability and societal fragmentation in the region

Geoff Thale, from the Washington Office on Latin America, in a January 2008 presentation made at the University of Southern California (USC) correctly stated there are push factors in Central America leading legal and illegal immigration from this region to America and other countries (Thale, 2008). Thale classified the push factors can be the direct result of poverty, lack of employment opportunities, failure to complete high school level education, a lack access to personal and public health resources and a lack of confidence in local municipal and state government entities, but not poverty alone.

In addition to the "Thale push factors," Central America gang members are stigmatized and treated as societal lepers. Gang members are further excluded from the already limited resources available; including employment, health care, education and they often targeted by local law enforcement (Cruz, 2007). Economic poverty can also tear apart the fabric of society and families further marginalizing those who are currently are struggling to survive. Conditions, if not changed will also affect future generations.

The "Thale push factors" can also lead to living under conditions of cultural and economic disenfranchisement, causing many youth to seek refuge in street gangs, which provide a sense of belonging, identity, support and respect (Vigil, 2001: Cruz 2007). The "Thale push factors" that affect inter and intra state migrations in Central America are actually identical to the Hill, Lui and Hawkins (2001) risk factors that heighten the risk of joining a street in the United States.

Some estimates suggest there are 63,700 gang members in El Salvador, Guatemala, Honduras and Nicaragua (Manwaring, 2007). The U.S. Southern Command placed the figure around 70,000, which is also the figure cited by the United Nations (Seelke, 2008). The Salvadoran National Council on Public Security estimates that El Salvador has 39,000 gang members. The figure breakdown is 22,000 are in MS-13. 12,000 in 18th Street and 5,000 gang members in smaller gangs (Manwaring, 2007). Interestingly, if one uses the 39,000 figure as a good estimate and compare it to the total population of El Salvador 6,672,218 people (Internet Worlds Stats) reported street gangs are only 0.58% of the total population; less than one percent. Comparatively, street gang populations in the United States have been estimated at less than one percent (Valdez, 2005).

Hispanic street gangs have been present in the region since the late 1950s (Cruz, 2007). 18th Street and MS-13 were noted to be present in Central America in the early 1990's (Manwaring, 2007 and Cruz, 2007). One author suggested that the MS -13 gang was present in Honduras as early as 1989 (Breve, 2007).

General Bantz J. Craddock, Commander, U.S. Southern Command in 2005 reported the gang problem is most severe in El Salvador, Honduras and Guatemala (Seelke 2008). Gang populations were reported to be approximately 10,500 in El Salvador; 36,000 in Honduras and 14,000 in Guatemala (Craddock, 2005). This amounts to 60,500 gang members in the three countries alone. The issue of the number of gangs and gang members is nebulous at best, because the involved Central American countries tend not to keep records of the number and type of street gangs. Further literature analysis and media reports indicate as many as 80,000 to 100,000 gang members in the region.

It is then with significant interest to note in 1996, U.S. immigration law changed and criminal aliens were actively deported back to their countries of origin. But deportation of criminal aliens by the U.S. began before 1996. A number of illegal and criminal deportees ended up in Central America before 1996. The post 1996 deportation mechanism is often cited as the primary reason why Central America has experienced an explosion in activity and membership in the 18th Street and MS-13 gangs. However, it is clear that both gangs were present and operating in the region prior to that period (Cruz, 2007; Breve, 2007). It is possible the "Thale push factors" may contribute more to the growth of Central American street gangs rather than the deportation mechanism alone.

In fact, gangs in Central America, like those in other parts of the world, including the United States are an outcome of a construction process that was and is affected by historical events, social conditions, political decisions and circumstantial events (Cruz, 2007; Valdez, 2005)). Add to this equation the variables of social stigmatism, a non-empathic upper class and the huge illegal American drug appetite. The result is both internal and external migration and the fragmentation of society. It is then, not so surprising to observe the formation and development of violent street gangs. Gangs in Central America as in other parts of the world began with an excluded group, whether the exclusion is real or perceived (Valdez, 2005). This process was occurring in this region of the world well before 1996.

Gangs quickly became a perceived escape route out of dire social conditions for many youths. As a result gangs in Central America grew in size. Being a gang member can give a sense of special rank in their community, a sense of belonging and respect, albeit a respect based on fear (Breve, 2007). The truism holds; the more you fear me, the more you respect me. Sadly, in Central America, as in other parts of the world including the United States gang membership and association can become a survival mechanism. Gang membership becomes a way to eat, get protection, to receive a type of social status and to be important because you are feared.

Gang Development

Researchers Sullivan and Bunker in 2003 described a model for gang development which may be used to help understand why internationally and in Central America there has been such large growth in the number of street gangs and gang related violence. Summarily, the researchers theorize there are three distinct levels of gangs develop from locally based street gangs and classify the levels as generations. This is not to be confused with traditional generational gang where the son is in the same gang as his father and grandfather. The Sullivan and Bunker model refers to a Darwinist type evolution of a gang, not individual gang members.

First Generation Gangs

These are traditional street gangs that are primarily turf oriented. They have a loose and unsophisticated leadership focusing on gang loyalty and turf protection to gain cash. These gangs will most likely claim a geographical area as their neighborhood (turf). If the gang is engaged in criminal money making activities, it tends to be individualistic and opportunistic in scope. These criminal money making activities also tend to be localized and in the lower end of the violence scale. Many street gangs stay within this developmental cycle, but some evolve (Sullivan and Bunker, 2003).These gang will use violence to protect reputation or perceived turf ownership. There is no distinct separation between generational levels in this model. There is some overlap between generational levels, a sort of gray area.

Second Generation

These are gangs or cliques of gangs that continue to change and expand their criminal business. These gangs or gang cliques tend to organize for business and commercial gain. They have a more centralized leadership that focuses on drug trafficking and market protection. These gangs may also operate in a larger geographical area, including neighboring cities and countries. Second generation gangs use the level of violence necessary to protect their markets and control their competition. These gangs can use violence as a political interference, to negate and minimize enforcement efforts targeted against them by local or national law enforcement. These gangs can attempt to obtain control or incapacitate state security institutions and dominate vulnerable community life with in certain areas of their country (Sullivan and Bunker, 2003).

Operating within the second generation level infers there likely must be a link with other groups to provide or to buy mercenary services. This connection provides a direct link to transnational criminal organizations and insurgents. If these gangs develop broader market focuses and political agendas to improve their market share and revenues, they may overtly challenge state security and sovereignty (Manwaring, 2007). In 2004, El Salvadoran Vice Minister of Justice Silva Aguilar confirmed Manwaring's observation by stating "Domestic crime and its associated destabilization are now Latin America's most serious security threat" (Aguilar, 2004).

Third Generation Gangs

Sometimes, part of a gang's membership continues to develop and expand their geographical turf, and commercial and political objectives. As these gangs continue to develop they tend to become a more seasoned gang with broader markets and a variety of allies. As second and third generation gangs develop, they will tend to expand their activities to intimidation, money laundering, home invasion robberies, trafficking and smuggling people, weapons, cars, intellectual property, and kidnapping and robbery, and murder. As a result of this diversification, these gangs can develop into sophisticated transnational gangs or other types of criminal organizations (drug trafficking organizations) with their own economic and political agendas.

At this level, third generation gangs begin to control rural or ungoverned territory within a nation or state and/or begin to acquire political power in poorly governed space (Sullivan and Bunker, 2003 and Manwaring, 2007).

Manwaring (2007) argues that some gangs in Central America fit this model and are currently operating within these countries and contributing to regional instability and destabilization. For some gangs, Manwaring's observation may be correct based on the Sullivan and Bunker gang development model. However, many of Central American's street gangs are in the "first generation" stage.

For those gangs that are in the advanced second and the third generation, involvement in criminal activities becomes the source of income that finances further development and expansion into the criminal markets. For those few gangs, criminal sophistication and organization follows; as well as alliances with other criminal organizations (Manwaring, 2007).

What the Sullivan and Bunker provides is an understanding of how some gang and/or gang cliques can evolve as their criminal endeavors increase. Three distinct things happen as this process occurs. The gang will become more globalized (expand geographically), the gang will become more sophisticated (develop a vertical leadership structure) and the gang will become in local politics (directly or indirectly through support of their politician). As these three factors increase a gang will become transnational. It is important to note that this process in not under a time schedule. It is a process that is affected by many other outside factors such as law enforcement suppression programs, military interventions and government interdictions. The purpose of the gang's increased operations is to make money. As more and more money becomes at stake there will be a tendency for violence to increase.

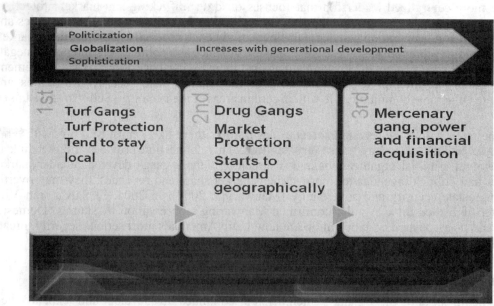

This simple chart illustrates how a gang can evolve as a function of politicization, globalization and sophistication.

Gang Movement

Street gangs and the American gang culture are apparently proliferating around the world. According to some media reports, the United States has unwittingly spurred this phenomenon by deporting thousands of undocumented immigrants with criminal records each year. No one can estimate the actual number and type of gang member deportees returned to their countries. The United States deports illegal immigrants to many countries around the world, not just Central America.

A number of deportees were sent back to El Salvador, Honduras and Guatemala. The table below shows the breakdown according to year. The total number of deportees in 2007 figure was obtain through ICE and is their official number of subjects deported back to the three countries in Table A.

Table A

Year	2005	2006	2007
Non-criminal	27,634	42,868	62,981
Criminal	7,055	12,919	14,347
Total	34,689	55,787	77,328
Data obtained from (Seelke 2008 and ICE, 2009)			

We can see the numbers each year in every category are substantially higher. During this three year period, a total of 167,804 deportees were sent back home; and of that figure 34,321 were classified as criminal, representing 20.45 percent of the deportees (Seelke, 2008). The criminal category includes all types of crimes including traffic citations, drunk driving, petty thefts and homicide.

There is very little evidence to calculate the number of gang members that deported because allegedly that data is not tracked. It is difficult to estimate or calculate the number of gang members deported by or who have left the United States, as gang members may be deported in either category or voluntarily transport themselves back to their countries of origin. This is one reason why the deportation argument may not be as valid as some believe.

It appears that some U.S. based street gangs and the American gang culture is proliferating around the world. According to some media reports the United States has unwittingly spurred this phenomenon by deporting thousands of undocumented immigrants with criminal records each year and that deportation is the primary cause for global gang growth, especially in Latin America.

Caution should be used here. The data does not support this as a valid argument. No one can estimate the actual number and type of gang member deportees that have been returned to their countries. The United States deports illegal criminal and non-criminal immigrants to many countries around the world, not just Central America or Mexico (Vaughan and Feere, 2008).

In 2005, a total of 34,854 deportees were sent back to El Salvador, Honduras and Guatemala; 28,333 non-criminal and 7521 criminal subjects. In 2006, the numbers are higher, 13,621 criminal and 44,559 non criminal for a total of 58,180 subjects. Through June 18, 2007, 9402 criminal and 37,590 non criminal subjects were deported to the region for a total of 49,992 people. During this two and a half year period a total of 144,026 deportees were sent back home, of that figure 30,544 were classified as criminal; that represents 21.20 percent of the deportees (Seelke, 2008).

Compare the criminal deportee figure (30,544) with the number of deported gang members from the Center for Immigration Studies (1168) for those same countries during the same time period (1168/30,544) and the percentage of deported gang members is only 5.46% of the criminal deported immigrants. This suggests that 5.44% of the deported criminal aliens are gang members. The number is significantly lower when compared to the total deported population. This can only be an estimate because it is hard to track those gang members who voluntarily returned home or fled the U.S. to avoid criminal prosecution, or who deny gang membership. But the data tends to suggest that the number of illegal immigrant gang members is small when compared to the entire immigrant population. How could such a small number of deported gang members be responsible for the prolific growth of gangs in Latin America?

I suspect the actual number of globalized gangs may be small when compared to the overall gang population. But for those gangs who become transnational technology can facilitate the process. The use of the Internet and wireless telecommunication systems have facilitated gang globalization, even though most gang members do not have a clue of the globalization process, many can use technology intuitively (Papachristos, 2005).

One issue becomes the ability to distinguish cliques or sets of the same gang operating like street gangs and those that operate like organized criminal groups. Another question begs asking here. Could the transnational gang phenomenon be the result of individual gang members who join or start criminal organizations which simply use the gang name and thus, have no real formal contact with foreign based gang?

There are several types of gang movement that may contribute to the globalization process. Rarely a few gangs will migrate solely to increase business opportunities. This is sometimes referred to as the mafia theory. This occurs when street gangs evolve into sophisticated organized criminal groups seeking out new markets for new members or drug trafficking operations. These gangs are examples of the advanced second and third generation gangs (Sullivan and Bunker 2006). In the United States this may be exemplified by a few Crip and Blood sets which have evolved into more sophisticated gangs to increase drug trafficking operations. Law enforcement reports suggest that Crip and Blood sets are in no less than 45 U.S. cities (Vittori, 2006). And do not forget Crip and Blood sets have been found in other countries. The Gangster Disciples gang from Chicago may be another example of a globalized gang.

Because of the ease and ability to travel gang members can relocate to another city, state or country. Often, a family move is motivated by better employment opportunities or to increase the quality of life (Maxson, 1998). The "Thale push factors" also play a critical role in this type of national or international migration. The push factors can explain much of the gang migration within the United States. However, there are three other mechanisms which help explain gang movement within and outside the country. One cannot conclude a discussion on the gang globalization process without a short examination of deportation.

Country	Year 2003
El Salvador	2, 121
Honduras	2, 041
Guatemala	1, 739
Total of Criminal Aliens deported to El Salvador, Guatemala and Honduras	5, 901
Total of Criminal Aliens deported from the U.S.	156, 599
Table B: Data obtained from Office of Immigration Customs Enforcement, Laguna Niguel, CA, 2009)	

For example, in 2003, the department of Homeland Security (DHS) Office of Immigration Statistics breakdowns the total of 156,599 criminal aliens were deported from the United States (see Table B above). The reported number of criminal immigrants deported to El Salvador, Honduras and Guatemala was 5,901 subjects. This represents only 3.77 percent of the total deported population for that year. Vittori (2006) reports a finding of 39 percent U.S. criminal deportees to these countries during the same time period.

Nevertheless, deporting U.S. trained gang members back to their countries of origin can facilitate the transplant of the U.S. gang culture in other countries. The deportees carry the American gang culture with them. These deportees influence the local population and form a new clique or set of the gang. The new gang may or may not be linked to the old one. This is sometimes known as the symbolic association theory (Vittori, 2006). This is where the new gang simple adopts the brand of the parent gang, often there is no direct link back to the parent gang. For lack of a better metaphor, the new gang is a bastard child of the original gang.

More recent data indicates that in FY2006 Latin America and Caribbean countries accounted for 95 percent of the almost 197,000 immigrants deported. The Central American counties of Honduras, Guatemala and El Salvador are now the countries with the highest amount of U.S. deportees after Mexico. In FY 2006, more than 30,000 Hondurans, 26,000 Guatemalans and 20,000 Salvadorans were deported from the United States. Between 2000 and 2004 an estimated 20,000 criminals were deported back to Central American; many who had served time in American prisons for drug and/or gang related offenses (Seelke, 2008 and ICE, 2009).

During the 1990s transplanted American MS-13 and 18th Street gang members were considered a novelty and quickly learned they were looked up to by indigenous Central American gang members. The deported gang members became street mentors. They introduced and taught American street gang behaviors and customs to local gangs. That is not true today. Many deported U.S. MS-13 and 18th Street gang members are ostracized by Central American street gangs. They are often targeted for physical attacks and sometimes death by the local gangs, vigilante groups and the police. Local rival gangs and even members from the same clique have been reported to target deportee gang members from the United States (Sanchez, 2008; Jones, 2007).

One issue are extrajudicial killings and they community's belief in the existence of groups known as the "Sombre Negra" (black shadow). Many of the general population believe these groups exist and are responsible for many reported and unreported deaths of local and U.S. deported gang members. This is a contentious issue and it is often cited in deportation hearings for those requesting asylum. Personal interviews at Projecto Victoria, Tegucigalpa, Honduras with gang members on December 2, 2007 confirm the belief that local vigilante groups are targeting gang members. The gang members also indicated the cost to have someone murdered was $300 to $500 dollars.

It should be noted the local governments officially formally deny the existence of such groups and do not condone the operation or support of such groups. Yet reports continue to surface by human rights groups that deaths do and continue to occur (U.S. Committee for Refugees and Immigrants).

Another type of gang movement can be by inadvertent. A gang member may visit a family member or friend in another city, county, state or country. Once in the new venue the U.S. based gang member can establish a clique or set of the gang he or she belonged to. Often the new clique may not have formal connections to the American based gang, but may have informal connections to the American clique through peer members or family of the relocated gang member.

The symbolic association model prevails here, except that the relocated gang member may maintain contact with other members of his clique. For example, a member of the Chicago based Gangster Disciples moved to a small Arkansas town to live with his non-gang member brother and got a legitimate job. The gang member brother found that his status as a gang member from Chicago gave him a formidable street reputation in the small town. Soon thereafter, he started a sibling chapter of the Gangster Disciples with fifteen members, although the gang did not have any direct ties with the parent Chicago based chapter (Papachristos, 2005).

In 1995, a Los Angeles based Hispanic gang member went to visit his relatives in Albuquerque, New Mexico. He quickly found out the local gang and African-American dealers were fumbling crack sales. This gang member went back to Los Angeles and returned back to New Mexico to start the traffic of crack cocaine. However, several gang members from rival L.A. Hispanic gangs also returned. The rival gang members worked together to traffic crack and take the business away from the local gang members and drug dealers. The new gang used the name Surenos to identify themselves. The gang's leader even used his Caucasian girlfriend to transport drugs from L.A. to New Mexico because she did not fit the police profile for drug traffickers (Blatchford, 1996).

The third type of movement is when a gang member is wanted by the police for suspected criminal activity. The family members of the wanted subject (usually the parents) facilitate the transport of that person back to their country of origin; effectively hiding the family member from the police. The symbolic association model works in this scenario as well. The relocated gang member can establish a clique of his gang and most likely does not have a direct connection to the parent gang. Because of his wanted status this gang member may depend on visits from peer gang members or cellular telephone communications (Papachristos, 2005).

In the scenarios the relocated gang member can return to the United States or travel back and forth. For example, when a gang member from the Chicago based Latin Kings got into legal trouble his family sent him to live with his aunt in Mexico. This gang member quickly became the go between for U.S. gang members looking to avoid police detection and for Mexican immigrants looking for employment in America. The Latin Kings turned these connections into a lucrative business by manufacturing fraudulent identification. During a 1999 criminal investigation involving several Latin King gang members law enforcement authorities recovered 31,000 fraudulent identifications and travel documents (Papachristos, 2005).

There is another possible mechanism that could facilitate the spread of gangs within Central America. It has been reported that some gang members have joined the local military (Breve, 2007). Of course this may be a legitimate attempt to leave the gang lifestyle. The American military has been used by youth at risk and gang members for the same reason (Valdez, 2005). However, as in the U.S., some gang members in Latin America may not have such a noble cause. These gang members may use military service to further their criminal activities and recruit new members. This has been noted in Mexico with the formation of Los Zetas (ex-Mexican Special Forces) and some members of the Kiables (Guatemalan Special Forces) who are mercenaries for Mexican drug cartels. It has been suggested that as many as 100,000 soldiers have deserted from the Mexican Army.

Internet

Of all the communication mediums, the Internet offers a virtual international way of exchanging information 24 hours/day from a single geographical location. It has been estimated that 85 percent of American youth between the ages of 12 and 24 use the Internet regularly (NDIC, 2001). The Internet has revolutionized global com- munications and it also has revolutionized communications between gang members.

The Internet indirectly has been used to globalize the American gang culture. The Internet acts as a conduit for other mechanisms aiding in the globalization of American gang culture. These can include the media, entertainment and music industry. It can be a venue to recruit new gang members, challenge rivals and electronically spread gang culture. Communications over the Internet are difficult to monitor and Internet telephone use cannot be monitored. Because of the built in security features, the Internet becomes a logical venue to conduct clandestine activities with virtual anonymity. Latest estimates as of December 31, 2008 placed over 1.5 billion people using the Internet world-wide (Internet World Stats).

The Internet offers the perfect means to privately discuss criminal activity in public forum using written codes. There are Web sites that offer free encrypted telephone calls and other sites that offer encrypted e-mails. These sites can be used to facilitate drug sales and coordinate illegal activities. Do not be surprised to note that major drug traffickers have been known to use the Blackberry telecommunications device to aid in their business (Maltz, 2006). An example of this can been seen with the Hammerskin Nation who utilizes mass emailing and electronic bulletin boards to help advertize hate rock concerts, communicate and recruit new members. Refer to chapter 23 for more details. The use of the Internet can facilitate gang movement.

Transnational Gang Economy

A literature review suggests there are at least five areas where transnational gangs operate globally. These include, but not limited to drugs, arms, intellectual property, people and money trades. If you think about it there is a legal legitimate version of these markets fueling international trade, so let us flip the coin and examine the illegal markets for these commodities (Naim, 2003).

Drug Trafficking

With America's drug appetite it is no surprise to determine that some street and prison gangs are involved in drug trafficking. The 2005 National Association of Gang Investigator Associations (NAGIA), in conjunction with the FBI, National Drug Intelligence Center and the Bureau of Alcohol Tobacco and Firearms issued a report on gang activity in the United States. The executive summary based on current data concludes the primary source of income for street gangs is generated from drug trafficking (NAGIA, 2005). Further research indicates most gang members who sell drugs, do so independently and are not directly connected to large organized national and transnational gangs involved in drug sales.

For example, a look at Hector, the son of Mexican immigrants who is a Latin King gang member in Chicago. He is 19 years old. He wears the uniform of his gang and has never traveled outside the city. Hector stands on the corner near his apartment complex and sells ten dollar bags of crack.

By the time the crack that Hector sells hits the streets of Chicago; it has most likely been touched by more than a dozen people in three countries. Hector has no interest in the global supply chain of the drug he sells. His daily concerns and priorities center around the few blocks around his home like sleeping, talking to girls, hanging out with friends , standing on the street corners laughing and selling drugs for a few hours every day. Hector's drug selling business is indirectly connected to the global drug market even though it only generates about 50 dollars of profit per day; a little more than he would make at McDonalds (Papachristos, 2005).

Hector's profile is typical of many U.S. gang members who engage in drug trafficking. Some law enforcement anecdotal evidence proposes this is the same way many gang members in other countries traffic drugs. It has been reported that in some areas of Central America, street gangs are used by narcotic trafficking organizations to help with street muscle or security. These gang members are then paid in drugs rather than money (Manwaring, 2007). While many Central American street gangs are part of the global drug market, they like Hector can't see their role in the larger picture.

Drug trafficking in the United States is dependent on the importation of the drugs that are consumed. This is a very complicated issue because some drugs are manufactured and grown within America. DEA research discloses the majority of drugs sold and consumed illegally in the country are imported from foreign countries via our neighbors to the north and south. Canada and Mexico have been portals for illegal drugs for many years. New observations reveal that now some street and prison gang members are involved in this international business (Manwaring, 2007). In years past, it was only the non-gang member drug dealer and foreign drug cartels who were involved.

Street, prison and outlaw motorcycle gang members have to establish themselves in foreign countries to facilitate the supplier connections and importation routes. This requires some gangs to have members in other countries or to have connections with contraband suppliers in other countries. The drug market compels some gangs to globalize and get more organized in order to continue and expand their drug business.

If Hector becomes the sales model of drug dealing gang members, then very few gangs are actually involved in the globalized drug connection process. This is consistent with research data collected by NAGIA, 2005. Most gangs involved in drug trafficking operate like the "Hector model" or in small groups with individual "Hectors" trafficking.

Anecdotal law enforcement evidence also informs that gangs like MS-13 have established cliques in Canada, El Salvador, Guatemala, Honduras, Mexico and Spain. 18th Street is reported to have cliques in Australia, Canada, El Salvador, England, France, Germany, Guatemala, Honduras, Lebanon, Mexico, Italy and Peru. The Latin Kings have been reported in Canada, El Salvador, France and Mexico. The Black P Stone gang has been reported as far north as Canada. Blood sets have been encountered in Bermuda England, Haiti and Honduras. Crip sets have been reported in Bermuda, Canada, England and the Netherlands. The Gangster Disciples have been reported in Canada, Panama and South Korea. Jamaican gangs have established themselves in England and the United States (DeVelasco, 2006 and Valdez, 2006).

This is by no means a complete list; however, it does demonstrate the fact some gangs have established cliques in other countries and are in fact transnational. The issue here is how this data can be interpreted. The presence of cliques in other countries does not necessarily imply that an entire gang is involved in criminal activities, or that they maintain ties with their counterparts throughout the United States. Does this automatically qualify the gang as transnational?

Detecting a well known U.S. based gang presence in another country is often interpreted by the media and law enforcement as all members and cliques of the gang are involved. This is simply not accurate. A few members of the gang or no members of the parent gang are actually involved. The identification or detection alone should not qualify the gang as transnational.

The deployed gang members and cliques can and sometimes do facilitate drug trafficking operations. Often these gang members speak a second language and are familiar with the geographic area. These gangs are unhindered by local rules and international trade regulations that legitimate businesses have. Gangs that have established themselves in the drug trade also have unlimited financial resources. It therefore becomes very easy to expand operations and draw in more gang members to work the business (Manwaring, 2007).

In any business, communication is essential. This is also true for the gangs whose businesses operate as transnational criminal networks. Cellular telephones, faxes and the Internet fulfill those criteria. In 1999, the United Nations' *Human Development Report* calculated the annual trade in illicit drugs between 341 and 400 billion dollars. That is roughly the size of Spain's economy and accounts for approximately eight percent of the world's trade (Naim, 2003).

The global supply chain uses everything from passenger jets carrying up to 500 million dollars worth of cocaine in a single trip to custom built submarines that use the waters between Columbia and Puerto Rico to human mules that carry small amounts of drugs on or in their person. Drug smugglers can also use satellite cellular telephones, broadband radios and the Internet to help coordinate transport and delivery. Gangs may get involved in smuggling drugs into the United States and later moving into transporting, manufacturing and distributing drugs within the country. Then the drugs end up in the hands of the Hector type street dealers. Street dealers become the last in the chain before retail consumption. The National Youth Gang Center (NYGC) estimates that at least 34 percent of all U.S. street gangs are actively involved in organized drug trafficking (Naim, 2005).

It has been concluded gangs which sell drugs essentially fill a void in the post-industrial urban economy, replacing the manufacturing and unskilled labor jobs that traditionally served as means for social mobility (Naim, 2005). Unwittingly, the Hector style drug dealers are part of the global drug economy making their gangs part of the globalization process and indirectly and intentionally transnational.

There should be a distinction made between drug traffickers and drug distribution. The drug trafficking organizations move large quantities of drugs to boarder areas. These large quantities then are broken down in to smaller loads that can be smuggled across the border. Distribution begins here. These smaller quantities of drugs are then moved within the target country and then divided up again for retail sale. Trafficking is the movement of large quantity of drugs; distribution is the movement and retail sales of smaller quantities of illegal drugs.

Arms

Unfortunately drugs and guns go together. According to the United Nations, only 18 million of the 550 million small arms and light weapons in circulation today are used by government, military, or police forces. That is only about three percent of all the small arms. Illicit transport and sale of arms amounts for almost 20 percent of the total small arms trade and generates more than $1 billion a year. Small arms helped fuel 46 of the 49 largest conflicts of the last decade and in 2001 were estimated to be responsible for 1,000 deaths a day; more than 80 percent of those victims were women and children (Naim, 2003).

A gun can give a person instant control and power. According to the FBI guns have become the weapon of choice for gang members in the United States and guns are involved in almost 90 percent of all gang related homicides. MS-13 and 18th Street gang members have been involved in the illegal trafficking of small arms (Manwaring, 2007). Based on anecdotal law enforcement evidence, members of these gangs have been reportedly caught trying to smuggle arms out of the United States into Canada and Mexico. In the past some gangs in Central America used home-made weapons called "chimbas" and have now graduated to automatic firearms like AK-47's (Manwaring, 2007). Gang members using guns in Central America are likely to have had their weapons illegally imported into their country from America.

Law enforcement anecdotal evidence also suggests members of these gangs have been involved in export of weapons from the United States into Mexico. Members of same gang were in turn involved in the transport and subsequent sale of the weapons to other gang members and drug dealers in Central America. No one knows how many weapons have been smuggles or sold worldwide. Illegal arm trafficking is another way transnational gangs can make money. Involvement in this criminal activity becomes part of the globalization process.

By the mid 1970s homicides in El Salvador, Nicaragua and Guatemala surpassed 20 deaths per 100,000; more than double the rate in Latin America at the time (Cruz, 2007). Currently, Latin America has one of the highest homicide rates in the world. Over the entire region the average homicide rate is now 27.5 deaths per 100,000 people. In 2005, one estimate suggested the homicide rate in El Salvador was approximately 56 deaths per 100,000 people, 41 deaths per 100,000 in Honduras and 38 per 100,000 in Guatemala. The average worldwide is reported as 8.8 deaths per 100,000 people (Seelke, 2008).

Human Trafficking

Human trafficking generates billions of dollars a year and is becoming one of the fastest growing criminal activities. Some experts assess human trafficking operates at the same level of arms and drug trafficking. There is a difference between human trafficking and human smuggling. A key distinction between trafficking and smuggling is the individual's freedom of choice. A person may choose and arrange to be smuggled into a country. When that person is then forced into a situation of exploitation where their freedom is taken away, they become a victim of human trafficking. In most cases the global conditions of extreme poverty and political turmoil (Thale push factors) leave people who are seeking to improve their lives vulnerable to false promises and the manipulation of traffickers (IACP, 2006).

Human trafficking is not voluntary and entails the use of force, fraud or fear to exploit the victim for labor or services. Human trafficking can occur within a country and does not have to be international. Human smuggling is voluntary and the person contracts a smuggler to take them across a border. The relationship normally ends after the border crossing. A fee is usually paid in advance or upon arrival and the smuggling is always international in nature.

The trafficking of humans (including smuggling) has become a business that some gang members have entered into. The connections, understanding of the local culture and language and contacts in the U.S. or other country helps establish communication, transfer routes and contacts to facilitate business.

Anecdotal law enforcement evidence suggests along the southern border, members of 18th Street and MS-13 gangs and a few Mexican drug trafficking organizations are involved in human smuggling. Cases have been investigated where members of these gangs were involved in the smuggling operations in Central America and along the southern border of Mexico (Breve, 2007). Members from these gangs have also been involved in transporting the immigrants once they were in the United States. It is uncertain just how many gang members are involved or how intimately they are part of the trafficking group; but definitely plausible as smuggling is often a precursor to trafficking. It also not clear if the gang itself is involved or rouge members who claim to gang's name and affiliation to facilitate their operations.

The anecdotal evidence also suggests this is not the case in other countries. In the southern Mexican state of Chiapas members from both gangs have been reported to be heavily involved in human smuggling operations. It will be hard to confirm these observations, without a proper academic or law enforcement study. However, there is a limited validity to these conclusions. Breve (2007) suggests illicit human smuggling has become a lucrative market for gangs. If you consider the price of $3,000 to $5,000 per person that "coyotes" charge, then multiply that by approximately 5,000 illegal immigrants per month (totaling between fifteen to twenty-five million a month); you can get a feel for the magnitude of the problem (Breve, 2007; Pickard, 2005).

In these countries social economic conditions are ripe for gang members to get involved in criminal money making activities. Lack of employment and education opportunities cause people want to leave their country to look for a better living and employment (Thale push factors). This in turn can become motivation and provide opportunity for some gang members to get involved in illegal activity. Some gang members will engage in human trafficking and smuggling operations to make money.

Human trafficking is a seven billion dollar a year business according to the United Nations and appears to be the fastest growing organized crime specialty business. Approximately 500,000 immigrants enter the United States illegally each year from around the world. About the same number illegally enter the European Union, collectively, they are part of the 150 million people who live outside their countries of origin (Naim, 2003).

The issue is much larger and complicated than many people believe because it is a worldwide illegal business. For example, some of these undocumented immigrants are voluntary migrants who pay smugglers up to $35,000, the top-dollar fee for passage from China to New York. Others, instead are trafficked, bought and sold internationally just like commodities. The U.S. Congressional Research Service reckons that each year between one and two million people are trafficked across borders. The majority are women and children.

Fraudulent promises are made as traffickers initially tempt victims with job offers. With children they make offers of adoption in wealthier countries. The traffickers then keep the victims in subservience through physical violence, debt bondage and passport confiscation, threats of arrest and deportation or violence against their families back home (Naim, 2003). It is easy to observe that this market can provide money making opportunities for gang members that have transnational connections through family, the gang or business associates.

Intellectual Property

Piracy of movies, music and software is an illicit trade that cost the United States at least 9.4 billion dollars in 2001. Piracy in other countries is tremendous. In Germany and England it is reported to be 30 percent. In Japan and France it is reported to be 40 percent; in Greece and South Korea it is estimated at 60 percent (Naim, 2003).

So how do transnational gangs play a role in pirated products? First let us briefly discuss a few of the drivers of this illegal market. Technology is boosting both the supply and demand of illegally copied products. The internet allows for free exchange of music and video files. For example, it is estimated that 500,000 film files are traded daily through file sharing programs like Kazaa and Morpheus. In late 2002 approximately 900 million music files could be downloaded for free on the Internet (Naim, 2003).

Global marketing and branding also play a part as more people are attracted to name brand products like Prada or Coach or Gucci. Gang members who peddle knock-off imitations will probably fit the "Hector model" for drug sales. Few gang members are directly involved in the importation of pirated products, but most likely involved in the retail sale or manufacture of pirated products.

For example, Indo-Chinese street gang members were involved in pirating Disney movies, Microsoft software and Spanish music CD's, Karaoke music and pornographic DVD's in Orange County, California (Valdez, 2004). In this case, the pirated products were being manufactured by a legitimate company but Asian street gang members were working in the plant as manufacturing managers. The products were being "run" (made) during the manufacture of legitimate CD and DVD orders. The illegal copies which cost under a dollar to manufacture were then sold in the United States and other countries. The replicator machines used to make the CD/DVD's cost about one million dollars each. This manufacture had seven machines.

The counterfeit software, DVD and CDs are sold worldwide costing the legitimate owners of the products millions of dollars. That does not include the taxes and royalties that are lost. Law enforcement anecdotal evidence suggests gang members have been involved in the manufacture, transport and sales of these counterfeit products.

In addition counterfeit cigarettes are sold with counterfeit tax stamps on them. These cigarettes are sold locally in mom and pop stores. Street gang members have been involved in the whole sale and transport operations. Street gang members are "Hector type" salesmen. Unwittingly, like gang member street dealers they are part of a transnational criminal activity.

To answer the first question, gangs get involved in the manufacture, distribution and sales of pirated software, movies, music and soft goods because money can be made. Millions of dollars are stake in this illegal market.

Money Laundering

This is not normally a crime associated with gang globalization; but it can be. The cash money generated through illegal drug, arms, intellectual property, human smuggling and trafficking has to be cleaned. Dirty money is laundered through legitimate business. For example, several street gangs have created their own record labels to produce and sell gang music CD's. Such businesses have been notoriously involved as a front business that has been used to launder drug proceeds.

No one can say for sure just how much money is being laundered. Naim (2005) in his research notes that the Cayman Islands only have a population of 36,000 people. Uniquely it is home to 2,200 mutual funds, 500 insurance companies, 60,000 businesses and at least 600 banks and trust companies with almost 800 billion dollars in assets. The volume of global money laundering ranges from two to five percent of the world's annual gross national product, the equivalent being between 800 million and 2 trillion dollars (Naim, 2005).

Of course all this money does not all come from globalizing street gangs. The laundered funds most likely come from a variety of illegal enterprises. Street gangs account for a certain percentage, but regardless of the amount being involved in money laundering operations is further evidence of the globalization process and transnational status. Uncontrollable national and international market forces control profits. As long as illegal businesses continue, they will involve organized criminal groups, prison and street gangs. It becomes very easy to hide assets from law enforcement agencies.

The Terrorist Connection

Gangs can also become global by dealing with terrorist organizations. There have only been a few reported incidents where this has occurred. This is not a standard gang globalizing behavior, nevertheless these few incidents require prudent people to recognize the fact that this type of globalization can occur.

For example, in 1986, members of the Chicago based El Rukns street gang conspired to commit terrorist acts on the United States on behalf of the Libyan government for 2.5 million dollars.

The El Rukns represent the worst of what gangs can become. Originally known as the Blackstone Rangers, the gang emerged in the late 1950s on Chicago's South Side. Their leader, Jeff Fort, eventually consolidated the Blackstone Rangers with 21 smaller gangs, creating a powerful organization. In 1968, Fort was convicted in federal court of embezzling $1.4 million dollars in anti-poverty grants from churches and community organizations. Rather than create jobs, as the grants were intended, Fort used the funds to purchase guns, cars, and drugs. Released from Leavenworth prison in 1976, Fort joined the Moorish Science Temple of America and converted to Islam. The Blackstone Rangers then assumed the new identity of the El Rukns. The gang's name is Arabic for "the foundation of knowledge" (Papachristos, 2005).

Three high-ranking members of the El Rukns traveled to Libya in March 1986 to broker a deal with military officials in which the gang would commit "terrorist acts on U.S. soil" in exchange for $2.5 million. Again, the gang was apparently motivated by a desire for cash and notoriety. In May, a second meeting between the El Rukns and Libyan officials occurred in Panama. Upon their return, customs officials searched the luggage of two of the gang members and turned up documents that contained the vague outlines to several terrorist plots. Their plans, concocted in Chicago, included destroying federal buildings, blowing up an airplane, assassinating a Milwaukee alderman, and simply committing a "killing here or there."

Two months later, the El Rukns purchased a light anti-tank weapon for $1,800—from an undercover FBI agent. The purchase, as well as the testimony of informants and conversations recorded on wiretaps, convinced a federal judge to issue search warrants. Authorities ultimately uncovered the anti-tank weapon, as well as 32 firearms, including a MAC-10 machine gun, a fully automatic .45-caliber pistol, and several rounds of armor-piercing bullets. Five senior members of the gang, including Jeff Fort, were convicted of conspiracy to commit terrorist acts and remain in prison today (Papachristos, 2005). This story shows how seemingly ordinary street gang can become transnational through business dealings with terrorist organizations.

In the 1990s members of the Latin King gang funneled money to the FALN, a militant group based in Puerto Rico through contacts made inside the U.S. prison system. The FALN was a Puerto Rican clandestine paramilitary organization that advocated complete independence for Puerto Rico. At the time of its dissolution, the FALN was responsible for more than 120 bomb attacks on United States targets between 1974 and 1983. The FBI classifies the FALN as a terrorist organization.

No one can forget the June, 2002 incident where Jose Padilla was arrested at Chicago O'Hare International Airport. It was alleged that Padilla, a gang member was en route to detonate a "dirty bomb" in a U.S. city (Papachristos, 2005).

There were reports in the early 2000s that an al Qaeda leader was seen meeting with a leader from the MS-13 street gang these were shown to be inaccurate. The research suggests that likely the meeting never occurred. Although there is no evidence corroborating the reported connection between the MS-13 gang and al Qaeda, prudence requires everyone to consider the connection as possible. Street gangs tend to make unique alliances and business relations in order to expand markets and increase profits (Manwaring, 2007). For the right price such a connection is possible.

It has been clearly demonstrated that some gang members will do just about anything for the right amount of money. When the gang's focus is on making money, a connection between street gangs and al Qaeda is plausible. The point here is that gangs can become transnational by building business partnerships for money with terrorist groups. U.S. officials have acknowledged at least one subject who was connected with al Qaeda used false identification; Mohmoud Youssef Kourani was smuggled into the United States and later imprisoned for providing support to Hezbollah (Bowers, 2006). Research and law enforcement anecdotal evidence supports the fact that analysts do not find any link between Central American gangs and al Qaeda or other terrorist groups (Seelke, 2008, Swecker, 2005).

Summary

A common myth used to explain global proliferation of gangs is they "migrate" in search of new members, turf, or criminal opportunities. Although this might be true in a few cases like the Latin Kings and MS-13, very little evidence suggests gang proliferation is mainly associated with calculated entrepreneurial ambitions. A more plausible explanation is that when people move, they take their culture with them (Maxson, 1998). If a gang clique is formed by the relocated gang member, it most likely does not have any connection with the parent gang.

Globalization and street gangs exist in a paradox: Gangs are a global phenomenon not because the groups themselves have become transnational organizations (although a few have), but because of the recent hyper-mobility of gang members and their culture. At the same time globalization isolates neighborhoods heavily populated by gangs; it also helps spread gang activity and culture. Some gang cliques have gone global generating the belief that he entire gang is transnational.

Criminal activity that appears to be a result of globalization include the drug trade, arms and human trafficking, the manufacture and sales of pirated intellectual property and international money laundering operations. Modern communication technology plays a role in the globalization of the American gang culture. The end result of the globalization process is the formation of transnational gangs. Transnational gang members have no restrictions and if involved in criminal activity such as drug or arms dealing or the trafficking of humans or stolen and pirated intellectual property potentially have unlimited funds.

A transnational gang might be defined as a group of three or more, with a common identifier, associated with other and involved in transnational criminal activity. This is a sociological definition and could be used to separate local gangs with those who are identified as transnational.

Chapter 7

Responses

This chapter will exam reactions and responses by the criminal justice, family, school and correction communities. It will also cover some of the most common drugs of abuse that are trafficked by street gangs.

Drugs and Gangs

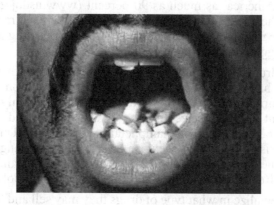

Previous chapters have discussed histories, genesis, behaviors, customs and practices of various types of gangs and basic indicia that can help identify gangs, gang members and gang activity. The use of drugs or alcohol by gang members and associates has been mentioned in these discussions. Certainly, the use of drugs is not limited to gang members; but gangs do sell, transport, manufacture and use legal and illegal drugs. The use of these drugs is a serious issue and has international and national effects. The illegal drug industry in the United States accounts for billions of dollars in profits, while billions more are spent on the arrest and prosecution of drug dealers, incarceration of convicted drug offenders, and diversion and treatment programs.

History

It was reported that drug usage doubled between 1993 and 1997 amongst America's teenagers. Studies have also suggested that drug usage increased amongst high school age young people. All kinds of drugs are being used at an alarming rate. Some drugs that are used today are more powerful than they were 25 or 30 years ago. For example, marijuana, sometimes called chronic or bud can be 10 to 30 times more powerful than the marijuana available in the late 1960s. The same can be said for the purity of heroin and cocaine available on the street today.

Reports currently suggest that drug use is down in the country. This is measured by reported use. If this fact was true the American drug appetite should have also decreased. This is not the fact. The American drug market has grown, Drugs are easier to get and according to some estimates the American drug market is worth roughly one half of the world's drug market.

You might be thinking about now, why is he writing a chapter on drugs and substance abuse? The illegal trafficking of drugs is very important because there is movement of large quantities of methamphetamine, heroin, cocaine, marijuana and other dangerous drugs into the United States. Some research has suggested that street gangs, outlaw motorcycle gangs and prison gangs are the primary distributors of illegal drugs on the street of the United States. Drug distribution has also become a primary source of income for those gangs. As gangs attempt to control and expand their drug transportation and distribution operations the threat of high levels of violence is magnified (www.usdoj.gov /ndic).

Criminal justice professionals throughout the country report that gangs are responsible for most of the serious violent crime in the major cities of the country. Gangs now conduct criminal activity in all 50 states. Although there are many gangs in major cities, gangs are also proliferating in rural and suburban areas of the country. This may be the result of gang members fleeing increasing law enforcement pressure and attempting to seek more lucrative drug markets.

Mexican drug trafficking organizations and gangs are responsible for smuggling in the majority of drugs into America; as much as 90 percent (www.usdoj.gov /ndic). Many street gangs are involved in the street level sale of drugs and a few have made contact with major suppliers, cutting out the middleman. American has a tremendous drug appetite so illegal drugs will continue to be smuggled in and sold.

This underground drug sales economy is driven by street sales of drugs. Unfortunately it appears that California has become one of several major distribution hubs for illegal drugs. Even though the California portion of the Southwest border is only 7 percent, in 1999 it accounted for 18 percent of all the seized drugs (www.usdoj.gov /ndic). For example, it was estimated that about 80 percent of the methamphetamine used in the United States comes from Mexican drug gangs. It is believed that Mexican drug trafficking gangs control a third of the cocaine distribution in the United States and 20 percent of the heroin and most of the marijuana (U.S. News and World Report, 1998). The gang-drug connection is solid.

Some gangs can specialize in what type of drugs they may sell and the level of sales. There is plenty of anecdotal evidence that suggests gangs can sell any type of drug. Some gangs are responsible for the manufacture and transport of specific types of illegal drugs. Other gangs may specialize in drug conversion and sales of the drug. Sometimes gang members themselves become abusers of the drug they sell.

Historically, there is little mention of gang drug use and trafficking in published gang studies before the 1960s and 1970s Even in the 1970s, drug use did not appear to be the dominate form of illegal activity among gang members. During the 1960's studies suggest that some gang members drove drug dealers out of their neighborhood (Howell and Decker, 1999).

Some research finding also suggest that there are increasing numbers of females involved in gang drug trafficking and violent crime. However, the consensus is that female involvement in these behaviors has not increased commensurately with the increase among male gang members (Howell and Decker, 1999).

Drugs seriously affect the human body. When dealing with anyone under the influence of drugs, parents, teachers, mental health and law enforcement professionals need to be aware of the observable and unique physical symptoms of being under the influence or being high as most kids say.

Definition and Classifications

Our working definition of drug is: Any chemical substance synthetic or natural, that when taken into the human body can effect perception, motor reflexes, body functions and coordination (California Department of Justice, 1990).

Drugs are classified into seven major categories. Each acts differently in a human being and each has specific and unique observable characteristics. The seven categories are:

1. Central Nervous System Stimulants

2. Central Nervous System Depressants

3. Hallucinogens

4. Phencyclidine (PCP)

5. Narcotic Analgesics

6. Inhalants

7. Cannabis

These are the seven categories main categories of substances that are commonly manufactured, distributed and used by street, motorcycle and prison gangs. Don't forget drugs are also legally obtained through a doctor's prescription. Several drugs that belong to the seven classifications mentioned above can also be legally obtained with a doctor's prescription. So let's examine how drugs are taken, their effects and some of the drugs within these categories.

Ingestion

There are a number of ways drugs can enter the body. The four most common are through ingestion or swallowing, snorting, smoking and injecting. The speed by which a drug can affect the body is governed by the method of use. The slowest body response comes from ingesting (swallowing or eating) the drug(s). This is because the drug is absorbed through the small intestines into the circulatory system and then to the various organs and body systems. This process can take up to 45 minutes for the drug to pass through the stomach into the small intestine and then affect the body.

The key for abusers is to get the drug into the bloodstream fast. Snorting is the next fastest method. The effects begin within a few minutes and peak within 15 to 20 minutes. When a drug user snorts (inhales powder through the nose) the substance, it is absorbed through the blood vessels and the mucus membranes of the nose, then into the blood stream. Drugs can be applied wherever there are mucus membranes, like the eyelids and certain areas around the genitalia.

Smoking drugs gives the user an almost instantaneous rush. If smoked, the drug is in a vapor form, and it is readily absorbed into the blood through the lungs.

The quickest way to get a drug into the body is through injection. The drug is placed directly into the blood stream through the use of a syringe via a blood vessel. The effects are felt instantly.

Physical Effects

Drugs affect the body in a physical way. Heart rate can increase, decrease, or show no change when using a drug. The pupils of the eyes may dilate, constrict or show very little if any change at all. The eyes may appear to be bloodshot or the eyelid may droop. Breathing can be slowed or increased. Blood pressure can be increased or lowered. Body temperature may increase or stay the same.

Drugs can affect the perception of the user as well. Often, memory can be severely affected. Motor skills, such as the ability to drive a car, walk, talk or shoot a gun and the ability to feel pain may also be affected.

Drugs can also have a combined effect on the body if several types are taken within short period. Some drugs, when taken in combination, have an enhancing effect on the body. Some drugs when taken in combination may mask certain observable physical symptoms. There are seven major drug categories each with observable physical symptoms.

Stimulants

Cocaine

Cocaine and amphetamines are the two most commonly used stimulants. The smokeable forms are knows by the names crack, freebase and ice. Cocaine is extracted from the coca plant, which is grown in South America. Cocaine has several different forms:

- Cocaine hydrochloride (refined white powder form, water soluble)

- Coca Paste (semi-refined form of cocaine powder)

- Free Base (smokeable non-water soluble form)

* Crack (smokeable cocaine)

Coca paste is smoked in South America and is a crude or raw form of Cocaine hydrochloride. Cocaine hydrochloride is the powered form of cocaine that is sold on the street. This powdered form is water-soluble. Large chunks of cocaine are called rock. Thousands upon thousands of kilos or keys of cocaine hydrochloride are seized by law enforcement every year. Sadly, many thousands more are successfully smuggled into the United States.

This is the form of cocaine that is often snorted or dissolved in water and injected by the user. The author, while working as an undercover narcotic investigator, saw users put this form of cocaine on their gums and on the inside portion of the eyelids.

Freebase is the chemical alteration of cocaine hydrochloride to convert it into the smokeable form. The freebase is a pure form of cocaine. Smoking freebase is very dangerous because it involves the use of highly flammable solvents to help in the preparation of the cocaine. It is not one of the more popular forms of cocaine used today.

Cocaine hydrochloride physically appears as a white powder, similar in consistency to powered sugar, but with a flaky or crystalline texture. Freebase Cocaine is an opaque colored crystal and, when freshly made will usually have a solvent odor.

Crack cocaine has an appearance of a thick pancake batter just before drying. Once dried it is in a brittle cake form. The color can vary depending on the liquid used in the process. If the crack is not dried completely it can be molded into small balls, and if colored can be mistaken for something other than crack cocaine.

Crack is the most widely used form of cocaine today. Crack is also a smokeable form of cocaine. Selling crack offers a high profit margin to the dealer by doubling or tripling the initial investment. The formula is really simple. Mix one part of cocaine to two parts inexpensive cutting agent. Starting with one ounce of cocaine, two ounces of cutting agents are added, creating three ounces of relatively inexpensive crack. The process does not use flammable solvents and is quick. Crack can be manufactured in a kitchen. The actual price of a rock can be as little as five dollars.

Crack is the most addictive form of cocaine. It is very easy to become addicted and very hard to stop using. Dealers will sometimes give out free samples of the drug to children to get them hooked. That is one way of building a steady customer base. Some gangs specialize in selling crack to make money. The crack business can be deadly. Gangs often fight over sales turf and the ensuing battle becomes costly as far as death and injuries are concerned.

Amphetamines

Amphetamines are the second most commonly used major central nervous system stimulant. This group also includes three closely related drugs; Phetamine, Dextroamphetamine and Methamphetamine. In the pure form they are yellow crystals that are packaged into capsules or tablets. Abusers of the drug will snort it or liquefy it for injection.

Both Cocaine and Amphetamines have legitimate medical uses. Cocaine is an effective anesthetic and vasoconstrictor (constricts blood vessels) and therefore helps control bleeding. Cocaine can be used as an anesthetic where medical procedures to the face and nose could cause hemorrhage. Today, however, most doctors use other effective local anesthetics and cocaine is almost never used.

Amphetamines are also legally prescribed to treat narcolepsy, a sleep disorder, and for short-term treatment of obesity (diet pills).

Amphetamine, when manufactured illegally will have a distinctive chemical odor, and will be white to a dingy yellow color. Its chemical form is methamphetamine. The color variation comes from the cookers chemical manufacturing techniques. If the methamphetamine is needed quickly, the final washing or cleansing of the unfinished product may not be completed.

Medical quality amphetamine has an opaque crystalline appearance with no chemical odor. Methamphetamine is also called speed, crank or tweek. A user may be known on the street as a tweeker. Being under the influence is called tweeked. Methamphetamine has become very popular with high school age kids and is commonly used and sold by many street gang members. It is inexpensive and can be snorted, smoked or injected.

A popular derivative form of methamphetamine is called MDMA. It is also known as Ecstasy. It is a chemical cousin to the stimulant and is very popular at nightclubs. It is very powerful stimulant and is now believed that use can cause brain damage after prolong or repeated use.

Ecstasy

Other names for this particular kind of stimulant are MDMA, Ecstasy, Adam, XTC, hug, beans, and love drug. In 2002, an estimated 676,000 people in the U.S. age 12 and older used MDMA (www.nida.nih.gov). The drug is popular because it affects the body as if you were taking two different types of drugs. Ecstasy acts as a stimulant but also acts as a hallucinogen. Ecstasy is really a psychoactive-stimulant.

MDMA has probably become so popular because it goes well with dance parties, where the demand for the drug usually exceeds supply. Users have confided this happens almost all the time at rave parties. Since the demand is so high at raves there are suppliers who regularly sell the drug and unscrupulous dealers that sell virtually anything as 'ecstasy'. Raves are all night dance parties. Sometimes they are held in large venues like deserts, or abandon warehouses. Large parties can attract thousands of dancers.

While 'ecstasy' is the popular name for MDMA, a more functional definition of ecstasy is any pill represented as MDMA on the street. This means that Ecstasy pills are notoriously unreliable in content. The drug can be mixed with caffeine, ephedrine, amphetamines, MDA (3,4-Methylenedioxyamphetamine), MDE (3,4-methylenedioxy- N-ethylamphetamine) or DXM (dextromethorphan). Ecstasy pills can be so contaminated that users can now buy special testing kits to insure that the drug is safe to use (www.erowid.org).

The drug use and popularity increased rapidly in the mid to late 1990s and has now become the drug of choice for those who attend "rave "parties and late hour nightclubs. It is usually sold in tablet form and will cost between 10 and 60 dollars per tablet. Most of the Ecstasy is manufactured in European countries then smuggled into the United States. At wholesale prices and in bulk quantities the tablets can cost as little and 2 to 5 dollars each.

Since the drug is taken orally its effects will depend on how much the user has recently eaten. So the initial effects of the drug can take be felt in as little as 20-30 minutes to a couple of hours. The primary effects of MDMA can last for 3 to 4 hours when taken orally. For many users there are post effects that can last for 2 to 6 hours, which can include difficulty in sleeping and a noticeable difference in perceiving everyday reality. The users claim the effect is not strong enough to be considered "tripping." Many users also can experience a noticeable mood shift for a couple of days after use. For some this is a period of depression and others experience a lifted mood.

The drug can be ingested by swallowing it as a tablet or powder. It can also be snorted, smoked or injected. Ecstasy is the most popular designer drug. Changing the molecular structure of an existing drug to create a new substance creates a designer drug. Ecstasy has been reported to cause brain damage in animals (Caruso, 2001).

When the full effects of the drug manifest the user will feel an emotional openness, euphoria, feel energized (stimulation), and have a reduction of critical and cynical thoughts and a decrease of inhibitions. Along with effects users tend to have feelings of love and empathy, forgiveness, an increased awareness of the senses, especially taste, hearing, seeing and smelling. Colors are intensified, the music can be perceived as a feeling. Some users will wear painter's mask with Vick's Vapor Rub smeared on the inside. The smell is intensified while under the influence of the drug. Under the influence of the drug users tend to develop an intense urge to hug and kiss people. This is why some users refer to MDMA as the "hug drug."

The drug can have several side effects that are easily recognizable. Users can experience nystagmus (rapid eye jittering) increased heart rates and blood pressure. Physically the user may feel restlessness, nervousness or shivering. With higher doses or frequent use an abuser may feel inappropriate and/or unintentional emotional bonding. There is also a tendency to say things that might make you feel uncomfortable later. You can experience mild to extreme trisma (jaw clenching and bruxia (grinding of the teeth). This is why you see many users of MDMA with baby pacifiers in their mouths (www.erowid.org).

Other automatic body responses can include hyperthermia and dehydration due to the body's inability to control body temperature. As a result many users drink water, sometimes lots of it. Without understanding how the body works the user does not realize there is also a lost of electrolytes. Drinking an excessive amount of water can also cause a fluid an imbalance occurs. Hyponatremia results when a person drinks too much water and become over hydrated. This can be a serious potentially fatal medical condition. This condition can happen without taking drugs. In the early 2005 a California college student accidentally died after drinking gallons of water for a fraternity prank.

Typically users will also have a hangover the next day. It can last for up to a few days to a week. The hangover can take the form of a harsh comedown from the intense high. Symptoms can include mild to moderate depression and feelings of fatigue. After heavy use, some users report bouts of dizziness or vertigo, which generally subside after cessation of drug use.

Some Ecstasy dealers have reported they can make up to one thousand dollars a night while selling the drug at rave parties. Party crews sponsor some raves. Underground parties, nightclubs and raves have become the primary venues for club drugs that can include Ecstasy, GHB, Special K and Rohypnol.

General Symptoms of Stimulant Use

Regardless of the type of stimulant taken, the physical symptoms are the same. Heart rate and blood pressure increase as well as the overall body metabolism. There can be a slight increase in body temperature. The user's pupils will be dilated even in daylight. Most peoples' pupils will constrict in response to the sunlight.

When a police officer is examining a person's eyes at night, he is looking for a pupillary response to light. Normally pupils will constrict in response to light stimulus. When they do not, that lack of response becomes a big indicator.

Restlessness can also be observed in people who are under the influence of a stimulant. Some subjects are unable to stop talking or to sit still. The mouth may be dry and a light sheen of perspiration may be present. The person may appear to be hyper.

Depending on the method of use, signs of ingestion may be present, especially if the ingestion method is through injection. Wherever the needle is inserted to administer the drug you will find a little injury to the skin. The wound will look very similar in size and appearance when a doctor or nurse gives you a sterile injection. Most of the illegal injections are not sterile. These types leave marks and have a tendency to heal slowly or become infected.

Law enforcement officers call these injection sites track marks. Once you have seen them, they are easy to locate. In an effort to hide the marks, I.V. drug abusers may try to use the same injection site more than once or try to cover them up with tattoos. These injections are made directly into a vein. With frequency of injection the wounds leave a trail of marks where ever the user shoots or slams.

While most commonly found on the inner elbow areas of the arms, track marks can be located on any part of the body, including the legs, neck, underneath finger nails, between toes, under the tongue and even the genitals.

Depressants

As the name suggests, this is the category of tranquilizers, sedatives or sleeping pills. These drugs will cause body functions to slow down. The legitimate medical use is to calm anxious people or to help them sleep. Barbiturates and benzodiazepine were the two most common types of depressants.

The most popular barbiturates are Seconal or Secobarbital, and Nembutal or Pentobarbital. Familiar names such as Valium, Librium, and Tranxene belong to the benzodiazepine family of drugs. Other drugs that fall into this category but do not belong to the two major classifications of depressants are Quaaludes or Methaqualone, Placidyl, Chloral Hydrate and Meprobamate.

Abuse of these drugs can lead to both physical and psychological addiction. As with most drugs, use over a long period of time can lead to tolerance and require higher and higher dosages to achieve the same effect or just to keep with drawl symptoms from appearing. After long periods of use, the person who stops will experience withdrawal symptoms, and even death.

The street name for this class of drugs is downers. These drugs, when used in combination with alcohol, can lead to death. The use of alcohol intensifies the effects of the depressants to the point where the heart stops working or the abuser simply stops breathing.

One of the most common drugs abused today is Valium. A legitimate prescription drug, Valium is easily obtainable on the streets and the drug is often used in combination with alcohol.

The most commonly abused drug, probably in the world of course, is alcohol. Alcohol acts like a depressant. We all know the results of long-term use of alcohol and the dependency that can develop. Almost every gang member claims that while socializing at a party they always use alcohol. Unfortunately, since alcohol is a legal drug, most people do not consider it a drug of abuse (California Department of Justice, 1990).

In California, and most other states, alcohol cannot be sold to any one under the age of 21. In some other states you have to be at least 18 years old to purchase it. Nevertheless, many teenage alcoholics have been identified. Alcoholism is a treatable disease and can affect school age youth, not just adults. Alcoholism is not gender specific.

A physician normally prescribes many of the depressants that are currently used. They are usually available in capsule or pill form and taken orally. When under the influence, one will appear to be drunk and have similar objective symptoms, but with no odor. A staggering walk and slurred speech are two of the more common symptoms seen. The person will look and act as if he or she is sleepy.

The most common method of ingestion is swallowing a tablet or capsule. Barbiturates are also sometimes snorted, where the contents of a capsule are removed. Do not forget the obvious, if you suspect alcohol abuse you may be able to detect an order of alcohol on the breath.

GHB

Gamma hydroxybutyric acid (GHB) is a drug that was initially used by body builders to stimulate muscle growth. During the late 1990s it became a popular recreational drug used among rave and club goers. GHB is synthesized from a chemical used to clean electrical circuit boards. GHB is available in liquid and powder forms. GHB is liquid form can be odorless and nearly tasteless. Users report that GHB induces a state of relaxation. It costs approximately ten dollars per dose and is often used in combination with Ecstasy. Poly drug use is common among drug abusers. The effects can be felt within 5 to 20 minutes after ingestion. The high from the drug lasts between one and half to three hours.

GHB is also known as a date rape drug. Because of the drugs odorless and tasteless qualities it can easily be slipped into someone's drink undetected. Because the drug may be unknowingly consumed in an alcoholic beverage it's depressant qualities may be enhanced. This drug has been primarily used to assist in sexual assaults but has also been abused by high school age youth.

In high doses the drug causes heartbeat and breathing to decrease. This could lead to potentially fatal respiratory failure or to a coma state. Other common reported symptoms can include memory loss, muscular fatigue and loss of consciousness.

In lower doses the drug produces a euphoric state and loss of inhibitions. Users have described the euphoric feelings similar to those of alcohol intoxication. GHB became illegal in the United States in 1990 after 57 cases of GHB induced illness were reported to poison control centers and emergency rooms. The drug has also been implicated in several deaths.

Rohypnol

Rohypnol is the brand name for a drug call Flunitrazepam. The drug is a sedative 10 times more powerful than Valium. Rohypnol is not legally available in the United States, but is legally sold in over 60 countries including Mexico for treatment of insomnia. During the late 1990s the drug became a popular in the South and Southwest and usually sells between 1 to 5 dollars a dose.

On the street the drug is often referred to as roofies, the forget pill, rophies, ruffies, rib, rope, pill and roofenal. Drug intoxication in low doses causes a sleepy, relaxed and drunken feeling that can last 2 to 8 hours. Like many recreational drugs Rohypnol is used with other drugs and alcohol. The drug has been used to enhance the heroin high or ease the experience coming down from cocaine or crack highs. When combined with alcohol Rohypnol produces inhibition loss and amnesia. The drug is normally purchased in Mexico then smuggled into the United States and resold.

This drug has another moniker. It has become known as the "date rape" drug because females around the country have reported being raped after involuntarily being sedated with the drug. The common mechanism used has been when the drug has been slipped into a drink by the attacker. The tablet has no taste or odor when dissolved in a drink so the victims have no idea what is happening.

Within about 10 minutes the victim will feel dizzy and disoriented; simultaneously she may feel too hot or too cold. She may experience trouble speaking or moving and then pass out. Such a victim typically will have no memories of what happened under the drug intoxication. The drug's effects can peak in one to two hours. Depending on the dose size the drug's effects can last up to 12 hours.

The drug can be ingested as a pill, snorted or dissolved in a liquid, like a soda, tea or alcoholic beverage. In high doses the drug can produce blackouts, complete loss of memory, slowed breathing, hallucinations. Prolong use can cause addiction. It is manufactured in one or two-milligram tablets, some tablets have a single or double score. The manufacture is Roche. A drug overdose can cause death.

Rohypnol and GHB have been suspected in many date rape crimes. Typically the victims realize they have had sexual relations but have no memory of them. The victims felt as a chunk of time in their life was missing or unaccounted for.

In November 1996, five people collapsed at a Los Angeles, California, nightclub after they took the drug GHB. Often, this drug is taken voluntarily and mixed with alcohol or other drugs. Poly drug use can enhance and quicken the effect of GHB or Rohypnol. This can also occur especially if taken unknowingly.

Hallucinogens

This group of drugs includes both organic and synthetic compounds. Hallucinogens cause a shift in the brains perceptual capacities creating a state of altered consciousness. Hallucinogens can induce states of excitement in the central nervous system, accompanied by changes in mood. These can sometimes be euphoric in nature, but at other times severely depressive. While under the influence of a hallucinogen, the senses of direction, time and distance may become distorted. The classic example of being under the influence is when the user sees sounds or hears colors.

In large enough dosages, these drugs can produce delusions and visual hallucinations. There have been reported instances where the depression and depersonalization the user experiences have been so great that suicide has been attempted. The most dangerous aspect about hallucinogens is the impaired judgment that leads to accidents and making poor decisions. Other symptoms of hallucinogen intoxication may include acute anxiety, restlessness, sleeplessness, and self-destructive behavior.

Another unique characteristic of the hallucinogen influence is that on occasion after the drug has been eliminated from the body, the user may experience a flashback. These are the spontaneous and fragmentary recurrences of the psychedelic effects of the drug, like the movement of a fixed object or the intensification of color as seen by the user.

With regular use, a tolerance can be built up requiring increasingly higher dosages to achieve the same effects experienced after the first time use. However, there does not seem to be any evidence of physical addiction to hallucinogens when the drugs are withdrawn. Some experts feel a psychic dependency develops with use according to dose and frequency of use and, of course, the user.

Probably the most important fact about hallucinogen intoxication is the unpredictable effect the drug has on the individual user. The so- called bad trip is such a result. A bad experience does not have to be caused by some contaminate in the drug. Sometimes the psychological make-up of the user may cause the bad trip. Hallucinogens may even intensify existing fears or anxieties, depending upon dosage and tolerance levels.

In the Northern Hemisphere hallucinogens have two naturally occurring, origins. They are found in the form of the Peyote cactus and the Psilocybin mushroom. The active chemical ingredient in the cactus plant is Mescaline found in the fleshy part of the plants. Native Americans from Northern Mexico have employed the consumption of Mescaline as part of traditional religious practices for hundreds, if not thousands, of years. Mescaline can be consumed orally in the form of a capsulated ground powder.

Another natural source of a hallucinogen is the Psilocybin mushroom. The mushroom, like peyote, was used for centuries in traditional Indian religious ceremonies. The active ingredients are the chemicals Psilocin and Psilocybin. Chemically they are related to LSD and they affect mood and perception.

When eating peyote (shrooms) a bitter taste is encountered. Some users have indicated they become nauseated and have even thrown up after use.

There are a number of synthetic or chemically manufactured hallucinogens. Probably the most common is LSD. The initials are an abbreviation for Lysergic Acid Diethylamide. The base component for LSD is Lysergic Acid, which is derived from the ergot fungus that grows on rye grain or from Lysergic Acid Amide found in morning glory seeds.

First manufactured in 1938, the psychotomimetic effects (a fancy term for a trip) were not discovered until 1943, when a chemist accidentally took some LSD.

LSD is usually sold three ways: tablets, thin squares of gelatin (window panes), and impregnated on paper (blotter acid). The average dose can range from 30 to 50 micrograms. A tolerance can develop quickly and the effect of higher doses can last up to 10 to 12 hours. LSD has become a very popular drug of abuse with some Skinhead gangs (California Department of Justice, 1990).

Phencyclidine

Phencyclidine, or PCP, was experimented with during the 1950s, as a human anesthetic. Because of some serious side effects, work was discontinued for human use. In 1960, PCP became available for veterinary use under the brand name Sernylan. In 1978, PCP was outlawed, and commercial manufacture was stopped.

Today, all PCP is manufactured illegally in clandestine laboratories. PCP is known by many other street names that can include: Angel Dust, Supergrass, Killer Weed, and Crystal. When the liquid form is applied to a cigarette, it is known as a Sherm or Super Kool. The high occurs as the cigarette is being smoked along with the PCP. In powder form PCP can also be injected.

In a pure solid form, PCP will have the appearance of a white powder. Due to the lack of quality control in clandestine labs the color may range from tan to brown, depending on the contaminants. PCP can also be sold in tablets and capsules. The liquid form is probably one of the most popular. It can be applied to a cigarette, marijuana, parsley, mint leaves or oregano, which is then smoked.

PCP can affect the user in a variety of ways. The user may have a sense of detachment, distance or estrangement from his surroundings. Slurred speech or numbness can also be present. There may be a loss of coordination, accompanied by a feeling of superior strength. A blank stare and rapid involuntary eye movements are two of the most noticeable and common symptoms. The user may walk as if he or she is trying to walk up a flight of stairs. There have been reports of auditory hallucinations, image distortions and severe mood disorders. These can produce an anxiety and paranoia response in the user. PCP can create a psychotic state similar to schizophrenia with repeated use. Since PCP was initially designed as an anesthetic, the user may literally feel no physical pain while under the influence of the drug.

Today, there are a number of chemical analogues (related compounds) to PCP. Chemically, they will give the user similar effects as PCP would. Manufacturing PCP is a relatively easy process, despite the explosion hazard.

Liquid PCP can be readily absorbed through the skin and is fat-soluble. The liquid or powder forms may have the chemical odor of ether. Most of the chemicals that are needed to make PCP are not sold to the public. Law enforcement officials monitor the sales of those chemicals.

Special K

Special K is the street name for ketamine hydrochloride. The drug is widely used as an animal tranquilizer by veterinarians during pet surgery. The illicit form of the drug is prepared by drying the liquid medication over a heat source until it turns into a powder. When used Special K is a powerful hallucinogen.

Physical symptoms can include euphoria, quick burst of energy and the loss of inhibitions. In low doses some users have reported confusion, ringing in the ears, delirium and amnesia. In higher dosages users may experience tunnel vision, shortness of breath, loss of balance and no sense of time. Some users also report out of body experiences, body numbness and high tolerances to pain. Coma can be induced in very high doses.

A single dose of Special K usually costs between 20 to 40 dollars. The drug is normally snorted, but is also sometimes sprinkled on tobacco or marijuana cigarettes and smoked. As with many drugs, Special K is also sometimes used with other drugs like Ecstasy, heroin and cocaine.

The users sometimes call the Special K high the "K hole." The term describes the profound hallucinations that include visual distortions and a lost sense of time and identity. Special K highs can last up to two hours. This drug was first used recreationally in the 1970s and was known as "Vitamin K." The drug resurfaced again in the 1990s in the rave scene.

Narcotic Analgesics

Analgesic is a term that refers to pain relief medicine. The Asian Poppy, Papaver Somniferum, is the main source of naturally occurring narcotic analgesics (addicting pain killers). This type of poppy has been grown in the Mediterranean region since approximately 300 B.C. and has been cultivated in countries around the world. The un-ripened seedpod is slit and the milky colored fluid that oozes out is scraped off by hand. It is air dried to produce opium gum.

At least 25 alkaloids (chemically similar compounds) can be extracted from opium. There are two main types of alkaloids that are derived from opium; one class is used as pain relievers and cough suppressants and the other class is used as an intestinal relaxant and a cough suppressant. The second group has no effect on the central nervous system.

Morphine and Codeine are the two most common opium alkaloids. Morphine is the principal constituent of opium and is one of the most effective pain relievers known. Opium appears as dark brown colored chunks, or powder and is smoked or eaten.

Heroin, a morphine derivative, is normally a white or brownish colored powder and is usually dissolved in water and injected. Commonly, street preparations of heroin are cut with other powdered substances such as Quinine or sugar. Clandestine prepared heroin can also look like black roofing tar. It normally will have a vinegar type odor to it. On the streets this form of heroin is called "black tar or tar" heroin.

Opiates tend to relax the users. When injected, opiates give the user an immediate rush. Some users have described the rush as equivalent to a five-minute sexual climax. The only problem is the initial rush one receives from the first experience with an opiate is never achieved again. The intensity or duration is never the same. Abusers tend to use more and more of the drug as body tolerances increase.

To obtain the similar satisfaction similar to first time use requires the user to take more of the drug and/or increases the frequency of use. However, once the user stops taking an opiate, the body experiences withdrawal symptoms.

The symptoms are like a very severe flu. If one tries to stop using heroin suddenly, the sudden stop can become a life-threatening event. The abuser can suffer severe abdominal cramping, vomiting and diarrhea. These symptoms can be so severe that at times the abuser may wish for death. Gradually, the symptoms relieve themselves and with time the addiction can be kicked. However, the process is long and difficult. For that reason many ex-addicts give in to temptation and restart using the drug again.

At one time the most common method of taking heroin was through injection. Frequent and long-term use of heroin in this manner led to scarring at the injection sites (track marks). These sites can be anywhere on the body where a vein is close to the skin. Like people who abuse cocaine by injection, heroin track marks can be located between the toes, under the tongue, on the genitals, on top of the hands and fingers, the inner elbow area, the neck and the legs.

Because of the AIDS scare and IV (intravenous) drug abuse many abusers have stopped injecting heroin. As a result many people have chosen to smoke heroin instead of injecting it. The process is called "chasing the dragon." Heroin is placed on a piece of tin foil in a thin line. A cigarette lighter or other heat source is placed on the other side of the tin foil. The tin foil is heated by the cigarette lighter and the powdered form of the heroin is vaporized. The user inhales the vapors for an instant high.

Opiates also cause the users pupils to become constricted. For example, when the user is under the influence of heroin, the pupils may stay constricted even in the dark. This constriction and lack of response to light stimulus are two of the first physical symptoms that are easily noticed.

Heroin was first discovered in 1874 when the English chemist D.P. Wright manufactured it from morphine. The Bayer Company in Germany began to manufacture heroin as a commercial pain reliever in 1898. Heroin was widely accepted as a pain reliever until 1914, when the Harrison Narcotic Act made it a controlled substance. Heroin accounts for about 90 percent of the drug abuse for this class of drugs. The United States legally imports 400-500 tons of Morphine annually to be used medically.

There is a legitimate medical use for drugs in this category. Morphine, even though highly addictive, if administered properly is an excellent pain reliever. All medical forms of this drug class, if taken properly, limit the potential for abuse and addiction.

Inhalants

These drugs are breathable chemical vapors that when inhaled have psychoactive effects on the user. These chemical vapors are intentionally inhaled to get high. Most people do not think of some of these chemicals as inhalant type drugs because they were not designed to be used that way. They include solvents, aerosols, some anesthetics and other chemicals. Model airplane glue, nail polish remover, cleaning fluids and gasoline are a few examples.

Aerosols that are used as inhalants include paints, cookware coating agents, hair sprays, propane, and other spray type products. Medical anesthetics used to get high include nitrous oxide; also know as laughing gas, and Halothane. Nitrous oxide is commonly used for dental procedures. Amyl and butyl nitrite cardio-stimulants are also abused. Inhaling substances like these is also known as huffing.

Amyl Nitrite, with the nickname of snappers or poppers was first used in the 1960s. Amyl Nitrite is used for heart patients for diagnostic purposes. When inhaled, it dilates the blood vessels and makes the heart rate increase. Amyl Nitrite usually is in a cloth wrapped one-inch glass bulb. When used, the glass bulb is broken. That makes a popping or snapping sound. To curb the abuse, California law made Amyl Nitrite illegal to possess without a prescription. When this happened abusers then turned to Butyl Nitrite.

Butyl Nitrite is packaged in small bottles and sold under a variety of names such as, Locker Room or Rush. The high that it produces lasts from a few seconds to several minutes. When used, the immediate effects are lowered blood pressure, followed by increased heart rate, a flushed face and neck, dizziness and headache.

Inhaling the aerosol spray from spray paint cans has again become popular, especially among some Latino street gangs. The most popular colors of paint used are gold and silver because this color contains the highest concentration of toluene, the chemical solvent that makes a person high. The paint is readily available and inexpensive. The most use seems to occur with the younger gang members, according to a 1990 survey in Southern California. Toluol or Toluene also gives model airplane glue that distinctive odor.

Nitrous oxide use and sales are very popular at party crew sponsored parties. Laughing gas is known as NOS on the streets. Some gang members and non-gang members specialize in selling NOS hits at these parties. Most of the time sales are made from a car and the hits of gas are packaged in regular small rubber balloons. One gang dealer told the reported to me that he could make up to $500.00 at a party and he services three or four parties during a single weekend.

Some cities have enacted ordinances that prohibit the sale of spray paint to minors. Some stores have even attempted to place the can behind the counter or in secure cabinets.

Cannabis

Marijuana comes from the Cannabis plant. The dried leaves or dried flowery top portions of the plant are smoked. The resin from the leaves or flowery tops mixed with pollen is made into semi-dry cakes called Hashish. A strong concentrated liquid may be refined from hashish (as oil). All forms can be smoked in a rolled cigarette, pipe or water pipe known as a bong.

There are more than four hundred chemicals in the Cannabis plant. The main psychoactive chemical (chemical that makes the user high) is THC, which is an abbreviation for Delta-9 Tetrahydrocannabinol. The chemical name is pronounced: tetra-hydro-can-NAB-binol. It is the chemical generic name that all chemists use to describe the compound. THC is a lot easier to use.

Marijuana is probably one of the most popular recreational drugs of choice. Users come from all walks of life and from all social-economic backgrounds. Most users feel that smoking marijuana is just like drinking an alcoholic beverage. Many view marijuana as a harmless recreational drug.

When the dried leaves or buds are rolled up in a cigarette form and smoked, the THC is vaporized and inhaled. The strength or concentration of THC in the smoked plant depends on the producer and his growing techniques. The type of plant and climate will also influence the potency of the plant. Some types of marijuana are estimated to be 10 to 30 times stronger than the marijuana grown in the late 1960s, according to the California Department of Justice.

A person under the influence of marijuana can feel tranquilized. Physically, the heart beat initially increases. Often, alcohol is used in combination with marijuana. There is no scientific evidence that supports the rumor that smoking marijuana improves hearing, eyesight or skin sensitivity. Marijuana acts like alcohol and decreases ones inhibitions. Some users have reported enhanced sexual experiences while under the influence of the drug.

Scientific studies do show that marijuana use can impair or reduce short term memory, alter the sense of time and reduce the ability to complete tasks which require swift reactions and coordination; such as driving a car, operating a train, work with machinery or fly an airplane.

Long-term users may acquire a psychological dependence on marijuana; however, there is no strong evidence to support a physical addiction process. However, some medical professional suggest that some users make acquire a physical addiction. More and more of the drug has to be used to get the same euphoric effects, as if the body is building a tolerance to the drug's effects.

Some research evidence suggests marijuana use during adolescence can affect the balance of hormones relating to sexual development. Women may have irregular menstrual cycles and both men and women may experience a temporary loss of fertility. With new testing techniques and the fact that the active ingredient in marijuana, THC seems to collect in certain parts of the body, THC can be detected for up to 30 days after use.

Other limited research suggests that marijuana use during pregnancy may cause some damage on the chromosomal level. The research also shows there is a higher incidence of children suffering from learning disorders such as ADD and ADHD when parents have a history of long-term marijuana use. This research is not conclusive, but why takes the chance.

Use Warning Signs

No matter what type or combination of drug(s) one uses there are some physical detectable signs of use. These may include:

- Increased or decreased pulse rate
- Increased or decreased blood pressure
- Flushed face
- Abdominal pain
- Runny nose
- Bloody nose
- Sensitivity to light
- Dilated or constricted pupils
- Increased or decreased breathing rate
- Respiratory problems
- Odor of alcohol
- Fatigue or drowsiness
- Sudden increase or decrease in appetite
- Weight loss or gain
- Nausea or vomiting

- Dry mouth
- Perspiration or chills
- Seizures
- Muscular weakness or ache
- Accidents or medical emergencies
- Ataxia, inability to coordinate voluntary muscular movement
- With use ones mood may also change. The user may experience:
- Depression
- Feelings of worthlessness
- Tearfulness
- Diminished interest
- Agitation
- Talkativeness or rapid speech
- Insomnia

While under the influence of drugs thought processes can also be affected. The user may have trouble concentrating or may feel confused or distracted. The user may experience visual mis-perceptions and may even hallucinate. Some users have a preoccupation with death or suicide. Many engage in self-destructive behavior. Ultimately, the user may become verbally abusive or make physical threats. There may be talk of desires to hurt other people. Some abusers may have angry outbursts and typically have problems with authority or the police.

The parent or teacher may notice an isolation or withdrawal of the person. One may notice a change in personal habits including hygiene and self-care. The intoxication of some drugs may also cause nervousness and you may notice excessive talking.

As you can see there are many signs of substance abuse and addiction. If you think someone you care about has a problem with substance abuse talk to a knowledgeable person, there are plenty of reassuring, confidential sources to that are available and can help.

Attitudes

Some Americans feel we have lost the drug war in America. After spending billions of dollars every year, America still has a drug crisis. Drug use is increasing and drugs are just as easy to purchase as they have always been. For example, it is estimated that 35 million Americans smoke marijuana and that is approximately 15% of the population.

Since President Nixon's term in office, Americans have declared a war on drugs. Black market drug sales also account for billions of dollars of illegal unreported revenue. Drugs have an impact on crime and violence, AIDS, addiction, drug addicted babies, the judicial system, the medical systems, educational system, probation and prison over-crowding. The annual cost to society is staggering, an estimated 67 billion dollars. Presently, there are more than 300,000

Americans in jail for drug related offenses. Some are dangerous drug sellers and many are non-violent drug users. Drug violations represent almost one third of incarcerated subjects.

Some Americans are re-examining the issue of addiction. These people feel addiction is a socio-medical issue and not a legal problem. According to their suggestion based on experiments in Europe and Great Britain some sort of drug legalization is necessary to get a decrease in drug related violent crime.

According to followers of this philosophy the controlled disbursement of cocaine, heroin and marijuana would lead to harm reduction. The release of these drugs would be controlled through government packaging and sale centers. This would hopefully stop the black market sales of these drugs. There would be treatment program information on the packages being sold directly to the addicts.

According to the followers of this idea the community gets nothing in return when an addict goes to jail and spends somewhere between $28,000 and $33,000 year to house a prisoner. Allowing addicts to purchase the drugs legally should decrease the prison population and decrease drug related crime.

Legalizing drug usage and possession is a radical new approach to the issues regarding the drug abuse problems in America. Followers of this type of legalization come from all walks of life, including law enforcement officials, judges, lawyers, political office holders, academics and the general public.

The current strategies have enjoyed limited success in curbing drug importation, use and sales. With the recent increases of drug usage by the general population, the prospect of legalization brings forth a myriad of questions. As the great debate unfolds, experts will help shape future drug policies for America.

Canada began a 6.5 million dollar program in the Spring of 2005. It is a clinical trial that will provide 90 heroin addicts pharmaceutical grade heroin under controlled conditions. At the same time 90 addicts will receive methadone. The study will start in Vancouver then expand to Montreal and Toronto. The focus of the study is to try and help the most desperate addicts' dependence on prostitution and crime to pay for their drug habits. The director of the programs hypothesizes that the addicts can stabilize their lives and get "onto a better path" (Time Magazine, 2005)

Gang Drug Connection

It has been well established that drug use and sales are part of the gang sub-culture. Research has suggested more street gangs have become involved in drug trafficking (National Youth Gang Center, 1998 and 1999). This increase in drug transport and sales has lead to the development of unique relationships between a few gangs that are normally rivals with each other. These business relationships are based on the drug trafficking and based in the effort to make money.

A 1998 Department of Justice report indicated *"of the gangs involved in drug trafficking, 33% are involved in drug distribution for the purpose of generating profits for the gang."* There are several suggested reasons that help explain the involvement of street gangs in drug trafficking.

Some academic researchers believe that many youth gangs were transformed into drug trafficking operations during the crack cocaine epidemic during the late 1980s. Other academic researchers believe the extent of youth gang involvement in drug trafficking is unclear (Howell and Decker, 1999; Howell and Gleason, 1999).

A couple of factors may determine the impact of youth gangs and their involvement in drug sales. First, is the definition of a street gang that is used. This age-old definition problem becomes a paramount issue. What exactly is a youth gang? Do all the members have to be younger than 18 years old? What happens to definition where the majority of members are adults? Are they a composite gang or an adult gang? Some researchers define the term youth gang as a group with a membership of young adults or youths that is referred to as a gang.

Ad hoc law enforcement studies suggest that approximately 60 to 70 percent of the nation's gang members are between 14-24 years of age. U.S. Department of Justice research suggests the majority of gang members in the country are adults, not juveniles.

Why not just keep it simple? A street gang is three or more individuals, some type of common identifier and the group commits crime. Age, thus does not become a qualifier to define a gang. We are simply concerned with street gangs.

Secondly, drug sales and use have been part of the street gang sub-culture since the mid 1800s. Drugs have been traditionally sold to make money. Drugs are used for recreation, to escape reality, for sex, to increase a market base, for social interactions, for income and as currency within the street and prison gang sub-culture. Recent research suggests that drug trafficking has become the primary source of income for many gangs. Street experience and observations also suggest that many gangs traffic drugs in an unorganized manner (NDIC, 2003).

A popular misconception is that many street and prison gangs control certain drug markets. This is simply not true. Research by the National Drug Intelligence Center (NDIC) has shown that in reality a few street gangs have an organized control within specific drug sales turf. At one time a limited number of Blood and Crip street gangs demonstrated this level of organization and drug trafficking. Having an established national base seems to be a key factor in forming these types of street gang organizations. Some academic researchers have referred to these types of street gangs as drug gangs, gangs that specialize in drug trafficking (Howell and Decker, 1999).

During the late 1990s other street gangs established themselves on a national basis. Marasalva Trucha, Sinoloan Cowboys, the Border Brothers, 18th Street, Ghost Shadows, United Blood Nation, Gangster Disciples, Vice Lords and the Tiny Rascal Gang are just a few. If a national basis is a precursor for organized drug sales these street gangs may join the ranks of nationally based gangs that control drug markets within specific areas. For example, the Rolling 60s Crips were reported in 59 jurisdictions within 23 states, a nationally based street gang involved in organized drug sales (National Youth Gang Center, 1999).

By far, the majority of gang members who are involved in drug trafficking are independent and operate at street level distribution. They are not part of a formally organized drug gang or organized crime group. Research data suggests that at least 43 percent of gangs are involved in drug sales (Howell and Gleason, 1999). Street level gang drug dealers will hide the drugs they are selling and normally work within a well-defined sales turf. More importantly, the current trend is that more of these gang members are younger and are armed (National Youth Gang Center, 1999).

These individual gang members can amass a small fortune of money, specifically from drug sales. The large amount of money can offer the opportunity for the individual gang member to assume leadership of their gang. It can also allow for the purchase of larger quantities of drugs, expanding the market, employing other gang members and becoming a larger dealer. Does it happen? Today, there are a few 18th Street, Blood and Crip millionaires. The drug trafficking business can be lucrative.

A third factor has been the impact of prison and street gangs on street level drug distribution. Since more and more street gang members are getting involved in drug sales, this offers an opportunity for some street and prison gangs to try and collect a tax on these sales. Non-gang member drug dealers in some areas of the country are paying the local street gang a tax for the right to sell drugs in the street gang turf. Some 18th Street gang members are involved in this type of activity. In fact, some 18th Street cliques are known to even tax local prostitutes and street venders.

Prison gangs can also try and levy a tax on drug sales by street gang members. The Mexican Mafia, a well-known and nationally established prison gang, is currently collecting a tax from some Southern California Latino street gangs. The prison gang places individual gang members and street gangs that do not pay the tribute, on a green light list. This allows the taxpaying street gangs to assault or kill those on the green light list.

Fourth, during the late 1990s Mexican based drug cartels have been recruiting and employing street gang members from the southwestern part of the country. The Mexican drug cartels supply a large amount of the illegal drugs that come into the United States. As Mexican cartel drugs reach central, middle, northeast and southern states, street gang members can be recruited to help transport, guard and sell the drugs. Street gang members have also been used to collect drug monies and act as muscle for the drug cartels.

Fifth, drug traffickers can offer very lucrative rewards for law enforcement assistance. Sworn criminal justice professionals including prosecutors, police, and probation and corrections officials have been involved or implicated in drug trafficking operations. Often, the motivating factor is money. In foreign countries, this can become a major problem.

Academic research also indicates that on average, between 43 and 78 percent of street gang members are involved in drug trafficking. However, debriefings with street gang members indicate that at least occasional use of alcohol, marijuana, cocaine, crack, methamphetamine, heroin and LSD is common with the majority of gang membership. Some gang members indicate that 99 percent of their fellow gang members use drugs on an occasional basis. When gang members socialize, combinations of drugs are commonly used. Frequently, the most commonly used party drugs are alcohol, marijuana, marijuana laced with cocaine. PCP use has been reported with a few Latino street gangs in Southern California (Valdez, 2002).

There have been no formal studies to determine how frequently inhalants are used or how designer drugs, such as MDMA fit into the street gang drug trafficking profile. These kinds of drugs are also very popular among the general 14-24 year-old age group. A few street gangs are involved in the sale and distribution of ecstasy.

Academic research suggests that nationwide drug sales by street gangs are especially high in large cities and suburban counties. In 1997, street gangs were estimated to be involved in 33 percent of crack cocaine sales, 32 percent of marijuana sales, 16 percent of the powdered cocaine sales, 12 percent of the methamphetamine sales and 9 percent of the heroin sales nationwide.

Some gangs that have traditionally not been involved in drug trafficking have now started to get involved. For example, many of the country's skinhead gangs have historically not sold drugs. Within the last couple of years some skinhead gangs have ventured into the drug trafficking business at the local level. Methamphetamine and marijuana seem to be the commonly sold drugs, although a few gangs have been involved with LSD sales. The presences of groups like the Nazi Low Riders have also had an impact on the methamphetamine market.

Gang migration has also been reported as factor that affects street gang drug sales. A few gangs have attempted to start drug franchise business in rural parts of the country. It can no longer be considered an isolated incident when California based gang members relocate out of state to sell drugs. I am not suggesting this is happening at epidemic proportions, but rather more frequently. Inter and intra state migration will become increasing more influential in drug trafficking by street gangs.

But a nagging question still has to be asked. Why has youth gang involvement in drug trafficking increased during the past decade? The literature may provide some clue. One researcher suggested that there were two reasons that might help explain the increase: the dramatic expansion of the cocaine markets in the 1980s and the subsequent price reductions (Fagan, 1993). Socioeconomic changes in American society that disrupted traditional social controls may have also influenced the change (Curry and Spergel, 1998).

The decline in manufacturing jobs in the 1970s and the development of technological and service industries led to economic restructuring in many cities. New jobs were created, but many were in the suburbs. This left many unqualified minorities in the inner cities. This resulted in dramatic increases in unemployment for minority males in specific areas of the country. Drug markets provided "work" for displaced workers (Howell and Decker, 1999). The growing popularity of public drug consumption provided and still provides opportunities for youth to make money.

T.A.R.G.E.T.

T.A.R.G.E.T. is the acronym for the Tri Agency Gang Enforcement Team; it is a law enforcement suppression model. Originally the team's design was based on a collaborative framework between three distinct criminal justice agencies that normally worked independently of each other. The concept was to put representatives of each agency together in one office to investigate gang cases within a single city.

History

One gang custom that is followed religiously is: no insult goes unanswered, no matter how small. A look, an accidental bump, the answer to a hit up, or the presence of rival gang graffiti can lead to serious injury or death to many people. Many times the victims are innocent bystanders. Some might refer to their victimization as being in the wrong place at the wrong time. Gang members in an effort to follow this particular custom tend to commit all types of crime from simple assaults to carjacking. The gang members will steal a car to use in a retaliatory drive-by shooting.

Westminster, California, is one of the most culturally diverse cities in Orange County. With a population of approximately 85,000 people, this city has the county's largest Southeast Asian refugee and immigrant population. Westminster and the sister cities of Garden Grove and Santa Ana combined have the largest population of Southeast Asians in the United States. The city also has a strong Hispanic influence. Some Hispanic families have lived in Westminster for generations. The Westminster population also has a Caucasian middle class working majority. Demographics show a very small percentage of African-Americans within the population.

In all culturally diverse and growing cities in the United States, gangs have exerted an influence on the quality of life for many citizens. The city of Westminster was not immune and experienced the impact of Southeast Asian, Hispanic, Black and Skinhead gang activity.

On a warm evening in the summer of 1991, five Hispanic gang members from Westminster lay in wait for the next car to come down the street. The gang members had planned to carjack the next vehicle and then use it in a drive by shooting. They had found insulting graffiti from their rival gang in the turf they claimed. The drive by was going to be the payback for the insult. Many street gangs like to retaliate in an escalated manner commonly it is a shooting.

Just at that moment, Janet Bicknell, a 49-year-old teacher's aide stopped her car at the nearby intersection. The five gang members immediately swarmed the car. In the process of attempting to steal the car, one of the gang members put a gun to Janet's head and shot her. Janet died instantly. It was the first time that fatal gang violence had claimed the life of an innocent victim in the city. This senseless murder made everyone realize that no one in the city was safe from gang related violence.

As you would expect, this gang related murder caught the eye of the media. The public, to say the least, was outraged by the action of these Hispanic gang members. The Westminster police responded immediately with the gang homicide investigation. What many people did not know was that the Westminster Chief of Police, James I. Cook, responded to the gang's impact before Janet's murder took place.

Since late 1990, the Chief had been working on an idea to manage the growing issue of gang violence in the city. He and his staff were busy designing, writing, and applying for a California state grant. Grant writing is not easy and it is very competitive, since only a few of the hundreds of grants submitted are ultimately funded. The grant was unique and based on two concepts: First, it would put three distinct parts of the criminal justice system working together in one office. Secondly, in daily, face-to-face contact, the team would select certain Westminster gang members to monitor, providing intense probation supervision and vertical prosecution if necessary. Vertical prosecution allows the same prosecutor to stay with the case from beginning to end. This was not a gang task force concept.

Janet's murder as senseless as it was had a positive impact. It helped crystallize the Chief's novel idea and the state ultimately issued the grant to the city of Westminster in 1992. Members of the Westminster Police Department, the Orange County Probation Department and the Orange County District Attorney's office would work together, forming the Westminster Police Department's gang unit. The probation and district attorney personnel would be assigned to work at the police department, yet remain county employees.

Normally, these three agencies would work together, but from separate offices. The general public is unaware that sometimes information exchange is slow and seldom immediate. If a telephone call is made for assistance and the attorney, investigator or police officer is not there, a message is left. Often, the call is returned later the same day or the next day. These requests for assistance are left after normal working hours as well. With shift work, odd hours, rotating days off and different work schedules at each agency; it is easy to see how a message may not be answered for a day or two, or even up to a week.

Putting all the team members together allows for instant information exchange. As Chief Cook said, "placing the team members together had a synergistic (enhancing) effect on the unit." The Chief was right. The first team members, two Westminster police detectives, a police sergeant, a full time probation officer, a district attorney investigator (myself), a deputy district attorney and two police service officers (PSO) and a part time police intern quickly gelled into a team with focus and direction. From the chain of command perspective, a detective lieutenant was assigned to oversee the unit's direction, investigations and activity. The acronym, T.A.R.G.E.T. was chosen for the team name: Tri Agency Resource Gang Enforcement Team. Chief Cook's brainchild was finally formed and starting to work in the city of Westminster.

The second focus of the T.A.R.G.E.T. program was based on selection. Marvin Wolfgang, a professor from the University of Pennsylvania, had come to some unique conclusions from work he had been doing. Professor Wolfgang, after studying U.S. populations, was able to find some unique trends regarding criminal behavior. He noted that in any given population, a small segment, approximately 15 to18 percent was responsible for approximately 52 percent of all the crime.

This is simplistically stated. Professor Wolfgang's work was time consuming and complicated. Nevertheless, the 15 to 18 percent group is also commonly known as recidivists. A relatively small population segment will commit a disproportionate amount of the crime. This observation was part of the bases for the selection criteria used by the team. What if 15 to 18 percent of the gang members in the city of Westminster were responsible for 52 percent of the violent gang crime? In theory, if the T.A.R.G.E.T. team identified and targeted these gang members, violent gang crime should decrease in the city. This was Chief Cook's grant concept.

Working with the Michael Shumaucher, the Chief Probation Officer and Michael Cappizi, the District Attorney, a Memorandum of Understanding (MOU) was designed and written. The MOU was a document that outlined the team member's functions and who would supply logistical support. The document was needed to formalize the working agreement among the three agencies.

Gang Intelligence

Target selection was aimed at active gang leaders and the most active gang members. To maintain a current working knowledge of gang activity, an efficient gang intelligence and information collection and exchange system is a must. Gang intelligence was routinely exchanged with neighboring and distant police departments. Networking with gang investigators across the country was established because Westminster's Southeast Asian gang members would routinely leave California and commit crimes in other states. The city's Hispanic gang members could also flee the country.

At the time the team used the G.R.E.A.T. system developed by the Los Angeles County Sheriff's Department to track gang members. The information in this intelligence database was never used as probable cause, but rather as a source of gang intelligence used in active investigations. The information aids in tracking the size of a particular gang or confirming individual gang membership or association. The data system has changed names and by the early 2000s was called Cal-Gangs. In addition to intelligence files, gang intelligence is also obtained from field interviews, probation and police reports, and expert court testimony and from gang member debriefings. Intra-agency intelligence sharing is just as important as inter-agency communication.

Patrol personnel are a key source of information. These men and women are the eyes and ears of every police department. On several occasions, they were directly responsible for breaking a case because of a field interview report they completed or because of an observation arrest of the suspect for an unrelated crime.

Ultimately, individual state guidelines and department policies direct the gathering, saving, filing and purging of gang intelligence. This type of intelligence is strategic because its value will change with time and it has to be analyzed and interpreted.

Probation and parole officers are also a great source of information and intelligence. These professionals often have current addresses and telephone numbers of probationers or parolees. Their information has saved countless hours of research and investigation. No need to re-invent the wheel. These professionals are an excellent resource. For example, in one case in particular, I had obtained an arrest warrant for the mother of four gang members. The family had moved several times during the month and was no longer living at the last address I had. Because of the instant communication between team members, the assigned probation officer knew of the attempts to locate and arrest the gang mom.

He had one of the sons on his caseload. He simply called and left a message with a friend of his probationer to call him. Within the hour the probationer called the office and gave his new address and telephone number to his probation officer. I got the new address thanks to the help of the probation officer. The arrest was made without incident and the mom was ultimately convicted of witness bribery.

On several occasions the T.A.R.G.E.T. unit was fortunate to have the aid of federal law enforcement agencies. The Bureau of Alcohol, Tobacco and Firearms (ATF), Customs, Immigration, Internal Revenue Service, U.S. Postal Service, U.S. Department of Housing and Urban Development and the Federal Bureau of Investigation (FBI) have all offered and assisted with the units gang investigations as requested. The Federal agencies are another good resource to call on specific cases.

Of all the federal agencies that have been a part of T.A.R.G.E.T. operations, special thanks should be given to the special agents of the ATF office, Santa Ana, California. In the early to mid 1990s these Federal agents volunteered and assisted with search warrant services, surveillance, intelligence information exchange and advice on countless occasions.

T.A.R.G.E.T. Concept

By December 1993, the task of identifying the gang members within the city limits was complete. A total of 2,158 gang members had been identified. Of these gang members, only 647 met the criteria to be placed into the G.R.E.A.T. system. The targeting process was limited to these gang members, and by the end of 1993, 77 individual, verified, gang members were selected for the T.A.R.G.E.T. Program. This group was monitored for new criminal activity.

The team provided intense investigation for all crimes committed by the targeted subjects. When arrests were made of targeted gang members they, and any co-defendants, faced vertical prosecution, enhanced penalties aimed at street gang crime, and aggressive probation supervision. Many times the prosecutor was present in the field when T.A.R.G.E.T. arrests were made. For the first time, the prosecution team and probation officer were at the front end of the criminal justice system, next to the police officers. This provided them with valuable insight to the case, the defendants and the victims.

The focus of the team was to build strong criminal cases against the targeted gang members. Cases were built through surveillance and by investigating most of the gang crimes committed within the city limits; maintaining the gang intelligence files; performing probation searches, assisting other agencies, exchanging intelligence information with other agencies, executing search warrants, working with informants and identifying subjects to be targeted are all part of the surveillance and investigative process.

Often gang members would receive gang terms (special conditions) as part of their grant of probation. These terms provided one more tool for the team to use. Gang terms could be given to both adults and minors. Typically, gang terms are somewhat more restrictive than traditional probation conditions. For example, a curfew specific for minors is a typical condition. A non-association condition with peer gang members is another example of the probation gang terms. These special conditions help the gang member break away from his gang. All gang members do not want to leave the gang life. Therefore, these probation conditions become a valuable mechanism that can be used to compel compliance with probation terms.

Gang Injunctions

Another function of the T.A.R.G.E.T. team was to explore the use of other legal tools to help manage gang violence within the city. Los Angeles County had been successful with several Civil Abatement or Gang Injunction programs. After studying these programs, in the mid 1990s the T.A.R.G.E.T. team decided to use this innovative legal tool. The team felt a program of this type might be a helpful in stopping an ongoing Hispanic gang rivalry that had been growing in intensity in the early 1990s.

The city had two indigenous Hispanic gangs. They were the Orphans and West Trece. The Orphans had taken over a group of apartment complexes near the police department. An abatement program was started against members of the Orphan gang. The program was terminated shortly after it started because a large number of gang members were either arrested and in custody, evicted from the apartment complex, or simply moved away after finding out about the program. Intense enforcement, community involvement, focused probation supervision and vertical prosecution lead to the dismantling of the forty-member Orphan gang before the abatement process was completed. Starting the program helped fuel the efforts that ended up dismantling the gang. Many of the apartment complex residents told me they were no longer afraid of the gang members. Being asked to participate in the program empowered many residents of the apartment complex.

The well-established, generational West Trece gang (trece is a Spanish word for the number 13) was rivals with the Southside gang whose turf was located in the neighboring city of Huntington Beach. One gang would attack another and the all too familiar cycle of violence would start. There would be retaliation and another attack and retaliation. Weekly shootings were becoming common.

West Trece claimed approximately twenty-five square blocks in the city of Westminster as their turf. Many innocent non-gang members also lived within this area. These citizens were also affected by the gang violence between the West Trece and Southside gangs and were also being victimized by West Trece gang members who lived in the neighborhood. The quality of life for these people had deteriorated. Small children would no longer play in their front yards during certain times. When I would work the streets along with the other team members, almost no civilian foot traffic could be seen in this geographical area, except for West Trece gang members and associates.

West Trece with a membership of around 100 had taken over part of the city. Even though several hard-core West Trece gang members had been targeted, the gang continued to function, victimizing citizens and becoming victims themselves when Southside attacked. A new strategy had to be adopted. The team targeted the entire gang. Typically, West Trece gang members would roam the streets in small groups, seldom, if ever by themselves. It was when they were in groups of three or four or more that they either were attacked by their rivals or victimized the citizens who lived in or near their neighborhood. Several West Trece gang members, as well as several citizens, had been shot and wounded.

In the summer of 1993 the assigned prosecutor working with the city attorney's office started a gang injunction program. The injunction is a civil process where a restraining order is issued against individual gang members of the same gang. The order specifically prohibits certain behaviors and activities within a specified geographical location.

The orders have to be very specific and supported by declarations of the gang experts. Logistically, a complete and thorough background of the gang's history and activity had to be completed. Several months of preparation were required, including several drafts of the supporting documents for the injunction. The theory for the injunction was based on the fact that members of West Trece gang had become a public nuisance based on their gang behaviors and activities. If the order worked, gang related crime and activity should be reduced in the area, resulting in increased community safety and a better quality of life, even for the gang members.

The city was able to get an emergency temporary injunction in the summer of 1993. With the initial assistance of the entire police department, I began to serve the 49 gang members listed in the order. They were chosen because of their consistent activity in the gang. Serving the gang members was mechanically simple. Find the gang member and hand him the lawsuit paperwork. After serving the gang member with the documents, I simply filed out a pre-printed form documenting date, time and location of service.

The documents also indicated the next court date for the injunction hearing. Basically, the city of Westminster was civilly suing the West Trece gang for being a public nuisance, and until the court date a temporary restraining order was in place. Almost all the gang members were served with the notices.

The order prohibited the served gang members from being in public view in groups of more than two just within a specific area of the city. The order also prohibited gang behaviors such as congregating at corners and the local park within the specified area. The goal was to limit the gang behaviors that cause victimization of the citizens and victimization of the West Trece gang members from their rival gang. Every effort was made to make the order as specific as possible for the affected part of the city.

When the court date arrived for the hearing for the permanent injunction order the ACLU had decided to represent the gang members in the civil suit. Their theory was that the injunction was an infringement of the gang member's right of freedom of association, guaranteed by the

First Amendment of the Constitution. Apparently, the rights of the innocent citizens of the city, although important, were not as important as the rights of active gang members.

Surprisingly, the judge who heard the arguments for the case agreed with the ACLU. He removed the existing temporary restraining order, even though orders of this nature have been previously approved by other courts and had been found to be legal and binding in Los Angeles County and in other parts of California.

Something happened when the temporary restraining order was in place. I served the gang members with the order in late July 1993. Almost immediately the T.A.R.G.E.T. team noticed a marked decrease in West Trece gang activity. In fact, serious gang related crime went to zero during the short time the temporary restraining order was in place. You could drive by the area and see kids playing in their front yards. You could see neighbors on porches talking. You did not see West Trece gang members loitering on the streets or corners. It appeared that the citizens of Westminster had won back part of their community. The abatement tool had worked and worked well.

After the restraining order was lifted in late August 1993, gang crime and activity immediately picked up and stabilized at slightly lower rate than when the program started. During the limited time the restraining order was in effect, no West Trece gang members were injured in rival gang violence. The order was sort of like when a parent puts his kid on restriction. Limiting gang behaviors not only made the community safer for the citizens, but also helped prevent the gang members from being victimized whenever their rival gang would drive into the neighborhood.

The legal issues are important and any violation of rights guaranteed under the constitution, has serious ramifications. The issue, simply stated, do the rights of the majority outweigh the rights of few? This is a serious legal question. Only time and the appellate courts will decide. However, as the data shows, the injunction process works. It increases community safety for everyone, even the gang members. The program empowers community members and controls gang activity. As of the early 2000's gang injunctions have been used legally and successfully in Los Angeles County against African-American and Hispanic street gangs. Injunctions can be an effective tool to help manage gang violence.

Since this attempt the City of Los Angeles has used the injunction tool over 50 times. Some academics would suggest gang injunctions may only have a temporary relief effect in the impacted area. Gang injunctions are a tool that can be used to curb gang behaviors, but like any tool they have to be used to be effective. The key use of an injunction is enforcement. If the injunction is not enforced it will have little if any impact overtime.

Search Warrants

Another tool used by many gang units, including the T.A.R.G.E.T. team, is multiple dwelling search warrants. This type of warrant is more complicated to write than a standard search warrant. As many as 40 or 50 houses can be searched using a multiple dwelling search warrant. It is not the number of houses searched that is important. Officers search the number of houses as required by the individual cases being investigated. Multiple locations are searched based on the group nature of gang crime and gang customs and practices. These types of search warrants are only requested when necessary. Legal standards have to be met and the logistical support needed can easily deplete the resources of a medium sized police department.

In addition to search warrants, probation and parole searches are valuable tools. While they are limited in the scope as to the areas that can be searched, they can be initiated with little preparation. Don't forget many gang members on probation and parole have search and seizure status.

STEP Act

In addition to using the multiple dwelling search warrants, T.A.R.G.E.T. prosecution included charging the special gang enhancement known as STEP. The acronym stands for Street Terrorism Enforcement and Prevention Act and found in Section 186.22 of the California Penal Code. The law was enacted in an attempt to deal with the excessive violence committed by street gangs. Many states now have similar enhancement laws.

The law created specific and enhanced penalties for certain gang related crimes. The law spells out over twenty crimes that are routinely committed by violent criminal street gangs. A crime committed for the benefit of the gang qualifies for gang enhancement prosecution. Being a member of a criminal street gang is not a crime. However, being a member of a criminal street gang and participating in the commission of one or more of the listed crimes can qualify the gang member for heavier sentences if convicted.

The statute specifies that any person who actively participates in any criminal street gang with knowledge that its members engage in or have engaged in a pattern of criminal gang activity, and who willfully promotes, furthers, or assists in any felonious criminal conduct by members of that gang, shall be punished by imprisonment in the county jail for a period not to exceed one year, or by imprisonment in state prison for one, two or three years.

Subdivision (b) of the statute specifically allows for prison sentences for anyone convicted of a felony or misdemeanor crime committed for the benefit of, or in association with, any criminal street gang, or who acts with the specific intent to promote or assist in any criminal conduct by gang members (California Penal Code 186.22).

The law allows for more effective prosecution of gang related cases. As a result of using this law, many gang members have begun the practice of not admitting gang membership or association when contacted by the police. Remember, not all street gangs fit the legal definition of a criminal street gang under this particular section of the law.

Unit Results

In 1995, the National League of Cities recognized the T.A.R.G.E.T. program for its innovative approach to managing gang violence. It was one of three programs that were recognized nationally that year. The program was also adopted by Orange County, California. By the mid 200s there were 11 units based on the T.A.R.G.E.T. concept, operating with eight different law enforcement agencies. There is even a multi-agency TARGET unit working with 3 different police agencies.

Research analyst, Dr. Douglas Kent, collected and analyzed the initial Westminster T.A.R.G.E.T. team data. The individual team members in the monthly statistics that were compiled reported the data. Dr. Kent was hired by the Westminster Police department to continue the research on the impact that the T.A.R.G.E.T. team had on serious gang-related violence in the city.

The program does work. In four years after the start of the program the Westminster Police Department was able to document a 52 percent decrease in violent gang crime and a 70 percent decrease in overall gang crime. The conviction rate for tried cases was 99 percent. Since the start of the program, a total of 3,642 verified gang members have been contacted in the city. As of November 1996, there were 71 targeted gang members from 14 different street gangs. Gang members who are vertically prosecuted have received increased sentences. As of 1999, Orange County, California has enjoyed an unprecedented decrease in violent gang crime. This decrease in part has to be a direct result of the 12 functioning TARGET teams. Gang activity can be cyclic and without intervention and prevention programs may spike even though an aggressive suppression program is in place (Kent and Smith, 1995).

Soft Gear

Another factor that ended up playing a key role in the success of the unit was the use of soft uniforms. The T.A.R.G.E.T. team members routinely wore soft raid gear, consisting of a pull over blue colored collared golf shirt. The shirt had all the appropriate police markings on it, including a cloth badge. In addition, team members wore jeans, tennis shoes and web type police equipment belts. This became the unique uniform that the gang members on the street identified with. Many times gang members would tell me they knew they could not try to scam us, because the type of uniforms the team wore indicated they were specialists familiar with street gangs.

Over and over gang members have indicated the police are the enemy. They have identified the standard patrol uniform with this enemy concept. For the most part, gang members seemed to be a little more cooperative, less hostile and combative when contacted by officers wearing a soft uniform. Many police and sheriff departments allow this type of uniform to be worn during daily field operations. This is functional, distinctive and comfortable uniform that affords the wearer a little more status with the gangsters.

The success of any program really depends on the personnel who implement it. There would be no success to report about the T.A.R.G.E.T. program without the dedication and personal commitment of everyone involved and the cooperation between the Westminster Police Department, Orange County Probation Department and the Orange County District Attorney's office.

New Strategies

The original TARGET concept continued to be so effective, that by September 1998, a 12th TARGET gang unit was in operation within the county. This was the North County TARGET team. The first multi-city TARGET unit was established. The same team members were used, except the police component was comprised of one gang detective from three different cities. Officially, known as North County TARGET, the cities of Fullerton, La Habra and Buena Park were represented. The city of Placentia joined the team in June 1999 letting the team expand for assist 4 cities. By December 1999 plans were finalized to add a fifth city. Like the other TARGET units, the North County team explored possible suppression and intervention strategies that would help in gang investigations. The fifth and sixth cities were on board by February 2000.

A current popular investigative philosophy includes using a search warrant as part of the investigation, especially with gang murders. As the investigation unfolds a search warrant is prepared. Some investigators will try to serve the warrant within a couple of days; others can't serve the warrant for five-ten days because of preparation time. To complicate the issue a little further, some agencies prepare a multiple dwelling search warrant when investigating gang homicides. These warrants allow the search of several locations simultaneously. The number of locations to be searched does not matter, only the locations relevant to the investigation.

For example, you have three suspects in a gang related murder. Through solid investigation you can connect the three suspects with five other gang members from the same gang. You can show a very close relationship between these eight gangsters. They are contacted in the field together and interviewed, they all have claimed membership to the same gang, they have committed crime together, they have some of the traditional indicia of gang membership, you have intelligence linking the eight together as clique of the gang, or the most active gang members.

You may also have personal knowledge of the relationship between the eight and the gang. With enough probable cause you can obtain a search warrant to look in all eight houses for evidence of the murder. If your state has a gang enhancement law, similar to Georgia, Iowa or California you may also search for evidence of gang membership. Remember, this is gang related or a gang motivated crime. You have a couple of options here.

Compiling all the information needed to prepare a multiple dwelling search warrant takes time. In the affidavit you must link all eight members to the gang. Using field interview cards, police reports, gang intelligence can require additional extensive investigation. Some warrants have taken weeks to prepare. A general rule is, that the more locations you want to search the more time will needed to prepare the warrant. Not to mention the manpower required to serve it.

Multiple dwelling warrants are a great tool. You can literally hit an entire gang, or a major part of the gang. This philosophy is the basis of one possible strategy to investigate serious gang crimes. Understanding gang sociology can allow you to attack as much of the gang as legally possible. The cost however, is long preparation time and lots of manpower to serve the warrant. When applicable, this is the way to go and cases can be cracked open or solved. This is one option.

An alternative strategy to consider was pioneered by the North County Target team. Why not use the search warrant during the honeymoon period? Simply defined, it is the first 2 to 12 hours after the incident. For example, in gang related murders, where you develop good suspect(s) information and identification, why not try and serve the warrant as soon as possible just on the main suspect(s). There is always the option to piggyback another search warrant later, if required, on lesser-involved gang members. Sometimes, serving a warrant quickly prevents other members of the gang from obtaining and hiding evidence from the police.

It is a common practice for gang members to help each other out by hiding weapons and contraband so the police cannot seize them, especially after a major crime. Striking quickly with a honeymoon warrant may stop this action. Obtaining a warrant within this short period may also cancel the need for additional locations to be searched because the evidence may well be found in the initial search warrant service. If the weapon is not seized, evidence collected may confirm your opinion on who is and who is not involved with the crime you are investigating.

Honeymoon warrants can also offer the possibility of closing cases quickly, especially when you cut off the chance of evidence being destroyed or hidden. By concentrating on the main suspect(s) and making the case strong against them, you only increase your chances for a successful prosecution. There may also be some advantages here, especially for smaller departments. Closing a case rapidly releases your investigative resources. The ability to prepare the honeymoon warrant depends on the quality of your gang intelligence, assistance from other team members and your expertise. The North County TARGET team has successfully used the Honeymoon search on several investigations.

Another technique that may be useful in gang investigation is to understand the cooling off period. It is a common practice for gang members to conceal contraband from law enforcement in order to protect members from prosecution and to try and save a weapon or other contraband for later gang use.

If a weapon is used in an assault and is being sought by police, gang members will try to hide it. After a period of time, when they think the pressure is gone, the weapon will resurface for use by the gang. This is the cooling off phenomenon. If you can develop relevant current information that the weapon has resurfaced within the gang, it may be possible to obtain a search warrant for that weapon.

Summary

Some cities even have more than one TARGET unit assigned to them. Remember, for each unit there is a deputy prosecutor, DA investigator, deputy probation officer and one or two police officers. That is a lot of resource commitment by the Probation Department, District Attorney's Office and the individual police departments. The results however, far out weight the costs. The county has experience a major decrease in violent gang crime. The quality of life for many residents has increased.

The concept of the original TARGET unit has been expanded and changed, but the operating concept has remained the same. The idea of forming a collaborative gang enforcement unit that utilizes resources from various agencies working a selected gang or selected gang members has remained. This concept will work at the city, county, state and federal and international levels.

Gangs and Schools

Gang members have gone to school for many years. The old school rules, including no gang banging while on campus, have changed. Today those rules no longer exist. Gang related violence has made its presence too well known on school grounds and on routes taken by students travelling to and from school. School safety becomes an issue as academics at all educational levels struggle to cope with the issue.

Changing Times

Even though street gangs have been part of society for over 100 years, for a long time the concern and fear of their influence was not felt in schools, malls, movie theaters and churches. Unfortunately, times have changed, especially for students. According to the California Department of Education, the top seven discipline problems in public school around 1940 were:

1. Talking
2. Chewing gum
3. Making noise
4. Running in the halls
5. Getting out of turn in line
6. Wearing improper clothing
7. Not putting paper in waste baskets

Besides the normal everyday social hurdles and changes a young person goes through in getting through those teenage years, the school environment has also changed. Research by the California Department of Education and the Fullerton, California, Police Department suggested that during the late 1990s the top student issues were, in no particular order:

1. Drug abuse
2. Alcohol abuse
3. Teenage pregnancy
4. Gang violence
5. Suicide
6. Rape

7. Robbery

8. Assault

9. Bombings

10. Abortion

11. AIDS

12. Venereal disease

13. Extortion

14. Murder

15. Arson

16. Vandalism

17. Absenteeism

The impact of gang violence at private and public schools has unfortunately been felt for a number of years. The education of America's youth has become a difficult challenge with all the issues confronting students today. For example, the 1996 National Report on School Violence estimated one in five students were armed with some sort of lethal weapon at school. The report also stated that a crime on or near school grounds occurs every six seconds.

The focus of this chapter is not to lay blame on schools, teachers or school administrators, nor is aimed at the social conditions that students live in. The focus is to examine the impact that street gangs have on schools and students, some who could be members of local street gangs. Just as important is to learn how the fear of gang activity on and near a school impacts the learning and teaching processes.

Crime on or near school campuses not only affects students, but teachers as well. For example, in 1996 four Los Angeles County middle school students, two boys and two females tried to kill their sixth grade teacher by poisoning her. The students who were 11 and 12 years old were arrested for attempted murder. They had spiked the teachers Gatorade with rat poison (Orange County Register, 1996).

In 1995, a Fairfax County, Virginia Spanish teacher had to obtain a restraining order against an 18-year male student who was terrorizing her in class. The school initially responded with a 40-minute detention, sadly the teacher had to go to court to protect herself in class. A Washington Education Association spokesperson stated, "I think what you're seeing is a real frustration from a rising of violence"(Register, 1995).

The 1993 National Crime Prevention Council report shows that nationally, one out of eight student's fears being attacked going to or from school. The National Crime Prevention Council also reported that over half of all violent crimes against teenagers ages 12-19 occur in school buildings, on school property, or on the street. Crime in the street is three times more likely to involve the use of a weapon than crime in schools.

A significant factor contributing to the climate of fear and intimidation in schools is the presence of street gangs in the surrounding community and in school (Arnette and Walsleben, 1998). Since gangs exist in all 50 states it becomes logical to conclude that street gangs potentially can impact any school.

Statistically, the majority of gang members in the country are adults, not juveniles. Although this statistic is true, if an age analysis is done for gang members, you will find that at least 50 percent and in some cases as high as 70 percent of the general gang membership falls within the 14-24 year-old age category. This age category continues to be the most criminally active in the country. Students at junior high school, high school and community college and college level fall within this age category. Some of the youngest documented gang members have been as young as eight years old, second graders.

Just look at what occurred at a college in San Diego, California. A university honors graduate student lived a double life: a clean cut housing counselor by day that kept an arsenal of weapons and ran a violent street gang by night. He was convicted for four gang related murders and was sentenced to life in prison (L.A. Times, 2001).

Sadly, for many children, school is no longer a sanctuary from the issues affecting society. Gone and lost are those naive days where school was simply an academic institution, a safe place to learn and to have fun. It has to be understood that many factors affect the quality of education. The explosion of gang violence on or near schools is only part of the cause. Academic studies have suggested that it is hard for children who fear for their safety to learn (Arnette and Walsleben, 1998). The presence of gangs and/or the perception of gangs on a school campus can contribute to this state of mind.

Look at was reported at a Philadelphia middle school in February 2004. Girls at a middle school alleged that lesbian students were harassing them with gay remarks. The straight students claimed the lesbian students were bullying, grouping and harassing them in the gym. The lesbian girls formed a gang called "Dykes Taking Over" (DTO). The school administrators and district officials stepped in immediately and worked with parents. Think about this, 15 years ago a gang such as this would most likely not have formed at school (www.nbc10.com).

Before discussing gangs and school safety, there are a few social factors that can impact the quality of life for students especially where they attend school. The social factors and geographical location where a school is located, the types of programs, student demographics, over crowding and poverty levels can impact the quality of campus life for students. Local school administrators do not get to choose where a school might be built or what school they will be assigned to.

Growth

The State of California has approximately 7,500 schools and a student population of 4.5 million students. Every new school year approximately 120,000 to 150,000 students enter the school system. At this rate, 11 new classrooms have to be built every day just to keep up with the growth (California Department of Education, 1997). Unfortunately, like many states, there will not be enough money to build the necessary new schools to maintain the same level of educational service or keep the same student-teacher ratio. Classroom overcrowding is already an issue for many school districts.

With the growth in student population, we experienced a growth in classroom size and a greater demand on the most underpaid professional in the world, the classroom teacher. Increased class size and subsequent increased school population size have taken their toll on many teaching professionals. This ultimately has to impact the quality of education.

With student growth there is also going to be a greater demand for the already limited school resources from class room equipment to program money. The greater number of students with limited school resources puts yet another added pressure on the teacher and impacts the quality of education. Factor into this social equation overcrowding and a school can become at risk for violence.

Curriculum

The actual curriculum chosen for the students can have a profound impact on the parents as well as the students. Remember the uproar over sex education? There are school programs in New York that address issues of homosexuality and lesbianism. These programs pose difficult questions. Parents ask whether or not our children should be educated by the school system in these sensitive areas. The curriculum chosen is partly affected by the issues touching our children's daily lives and the community the school is in. You can clearly see there is a need to address some of these issues. The question is whose responsibility is it?

As the arguments for and against special school curriculums continue, schools recognized they also have a duty to protect their students. Education and exposure to problem solving techniques tend to arm students with abilities to analyze issues. These can become unique tools that can enhance student safety on and off campus. It seems logical that special curriculums can benefit today's student.

Language

A second major issue facing some schools is what language should be used to teach. There are Sheltered English programs, English as the Second Language (ESL) programs and Bilingual Education. All programs are aimed at aiding the student to become proficient enough to enter regular educational programs by teaching and enhancing English comprehension, reading and speaking abilities.

For some, these programs may hinder rather than help. Most surveys suggest that students want to learn English. Some of the programs can aid in the continued segregation of non-or limited English speaking students because it authenticates a "you are different" label. Sometimes, minority kids who speak English are entered into the programs because they have a minority surname. Once in a program it becomes very difficult to get out. Parents of these students have told me they have tried to get their children out of bilingual programs because they were born in America and speak fluent English. All too often, the answer has been, "go to another school."

Many parents believe schools receive extra funding for each limited English student. Logically, the more limited English-speaking students a school can claim the more money the school can get. These parents feel the language limitation, if present, again further segregates their children.

For example, many southern California high school and elementary minority students have confided to me that bilingual really means uni-lingual. In other words, the classes are taught in one language only, their native tongue. No English was spoken at all in the classroom. These kids have candidly admitted that little or no English is learned. They have told me that they feel further separated from the mainstream student because of this. So there seems to be an issue as to how bilingual is defined.

The language issues vary from state to state, but do not forget Chapter One, social issues. For example, in the 1990s the State of California had 40 percent of the nation's 3 million limited English speaking students. In Los Angeles County, California, 46 percent of the students had trouble speaking and understanding the English language. Language skills limit the pace that classes can be taught. The biggest complaint parents and students repeatedly relate to me is that the classes go too slow when a second language is spoken. Many of the students become bored and subsequently uninterested in school. Sadly, some students have frankly told me they have ditched school because their classes were too boring for them. Some subsequently joined the open arms of local street gangs. The language issue is also related to culture.

Culture

School programs can also be influenced culturally. The cultural impact can have a profound effect on the student's and parent's outlook on school curricula. If a single perspective is presented and focused on, students can become biased. Many minority parents do not understand what is expected of their student and of them. On a nationwide bases survey after survey indicates that most minority parents want their children to identify with a national culture, rather than one particular culture.

This is not to say forget minority cultural histories. Every minority group has a history rich in culture and each has a lot to offer to current lifestyles. Traditions are good and are considered by many to be fundamental building blocks to help shape good citizens. However, we must not forget we all are part of national culture that is changing as the nation's demographics continue to change. Each culture aids in forming a blended national culture.

Gangs

The end result of the impact of these variables can be an under performing and unhappy students. The American educational system is geared toward age, not necessarily ability. Immigrant students may not have the educational ability associated with a particular age. In additional, many immigrant families suffer a cultural shock and students may live a dysfunctional home environment. The issue is complicated because students who are academically troubled and have an unhappy home life are often greeted with open arms or victimized by a street gang.

Gangs offer instant acceptance to students who join or affiliate with them. As new members they become instantly recognized achievers in gang school. All too often, new students can also become new targets for gang members on and off campus. Victim students are often fearful of their family's resident status and tend not to report victimization. Instead of being a continual victim, sometimes these students join the gang.

To further compound the issue some parents also become less supportive of the educational system because they are disenchanted. As a result many things can happen under the radar to the student.

Believe or not other students also notice the presence of gang members. Between 28 and 37 percent of peer students report the presence of gangs in their schools (Howell and Lynch, 2000). It appears as the students get older the more gang presence is reported as 40 percent of 14 year-olds and 43 percent of the 15 year-olds reported the presence of gangs in a 1999 survey (Howell and Lynch, 2000).

Sometimes, schools have students who are members from a variety of local street gangs. Gang rivalries can be taken to school and are sometimes settled on school grounds. Other schools may have a student gang membership from one predominate street gang. Middle and elementary schools are not immune. The gang influence here can be a bit subtler. Students may have older brothers and sisters who are gang members. Sometimes, they will come to the school to settle the score for a little brother or sister. Unfortunately, denial sometimes prevents some educators to realize that gang members can be as young as eight years old.

Gang related crime can occur before, during and after school and can be near or on campus. As illustrated all too often by the media, the student gang crime occurs on the way to or on the way home from school. Even though crime happens off or near the campus students tend to associate it with the school. The gang crime does not have to be violent in nature to qualify as a gang crime. The presence of gang graffiti on school grounds, especially in the bathrooms, is a good example and possibly warning sign of impending gang violence. Research indicates the majority of gang crime on school campus involves drug sales, carrying a concealed weapon and violence (Howell and Lynch, 2000).

School Rules

How about the October 1996, Dayton, Ohio case when a 13-year-old girl who was found with Midol on campus? Because of a zero tolerance policy for prescription, over the counter medication or illegal drugs, the student was disciplined with suspension. The female student who gave her the medication was also suspended.

Do you remember the October 1996, Lexington, North Carolina incident where a 6-year-old Johnathan Prevette kissed a fellow 6-year-old girl on the cheek at school after the girl asked him to? He was accused of sexual harassment and was suspended for one day from his first grade class at Southwestern Elementary School. The action was confronted with a hailstorm of criticism and negative publicity from around the world. The school soon changed their mind about the incident. What has happened here?

Rules are important for many reasons. They help keep the peace, maintain public safety and provide general order to society. They also set limits for behavior and provide consequences for actions. These are all good. Law enforcement officials are trained to examine the spirit of the law as well as the letter of the law. Another term for that is common sense. How about using a little common sense when applying school rules to these types of situations?

Student's Perspective

The fear associated with gangs on schools can be identified through student-expressed concerns. Research based on student input suggests that gang presence at school impacts students in the following ways:

1. Fearing gang disruptions at school or in the neighborhood

2. Encountering gang members on the way to and from school

3. Anticipating violence from known gang members enrolled at school

4. Receiving specific threats or being harassed by gang members who stake out territory on school campuses or in neighborhoods

5. Facing peer pressure to join a gang.

6. Being mistaken as a gang member during school or in neighborhood skirmishes between rival gangs.

7. Feeling threaten by school/ neighborhood graffiti displaying gang territorial claims.

8. Perceiving an increased presence at school of firearms and other weapons related to gang activity.

9. Experiencing alarm due to escalating interracial/ethnic tensions between gangs at school and in the community. (Arnette and Walseben, 1998).

All of these factors can impact school safety and the learning process. For students, school safety is also a function perceived and real threats. Sometimes students are afraid to report school crime. For example, at a Southern California elementary school a fifth grade student reported to me that he and many other male fifth graders were being charged 25 cents to use the restroom. Three sixth grade gang members would attempt to charge male students to use the school restrooms at recess. The victim students were fearful of reporting this crime to their teachers because the gang member students made the victims think their families would be deported. The students were intimidated into victimization.

You may be thinking that would never happen at my school, but it can. In addition, the victim students were also bullied into not reporting the extortions to teachers because they were threaten with the safety of smaller brothers and sisters attending the same school. The staff was quick to respond once they were made aware of the situation and the three-gang members were dealt with. All gang related incidents at school do not have to be violent or use a weapon.

School Safety

As mandated in most states, schools are required to recognize that all students and staff have the right to attend safe campuses. In fact, the legal duty to provide safe schools has been recognized by the courts for many years. For schools, the failure to attempt to make a situation at school safe or safer could result in criminal or civil liability.

Developing a safe school for student and staff actually includes the right to be protected from foreseeable criminal activity. To be protected against student crime or violence that can be prevented by adequate supervision. To be protected from identifiable dangerous students. To be protected from dangerous individuals negligently admitted to school, allowed on school grounds or placed in school. To be protected from school administrators, teachers and staff negligently selected, retained or trained. School administrators have a tremendous responsibility to follow the law and design, implement and enforce school safety rules.

Liability

Recent court cases seem to hold the school liable for all aspects of safety. Under the scope of duty, cases have been lost on three grounds: because the school fails to provide any supervision, provide enough supervision or failure of the teachers to supervise adequately.

The courts have shown through their decisions they feel that teachers have a duty to act. The courts have made it clear that it is always the teacher's duty to prevent disorderly and dangerous practices. This duty includes calling on law enforcement. Many school officials consider calling law enforcement as a last resort. Clearly, there are no sanctuaries where any person, minor or adult, may indulge in crime without having to answer to the law. Every person is liable for punishment by the laws of the state, for a public offense committed by him or her. This includes school campuses. Students are not immune from the law while at school.

The decision whether an adult should be prosecuted is vested with the county or city prosecutor's office. The decision to prosecute a minor who has committed a crime lies with the probation department and the county prosecutor's office. Public or private school administrators have not been delegated this authority. They should use extreme caution in deciding whether to report a crime and/or withhold evidence of a crime from law enforcement. I recommend the practice of reporting all crime to the police as soon as possible.

Understandably protecting the school's image is important, but should it be used as motivation to break the law. I have spoken to many school administrators and teachers who have confided that in an effort to try and save a student after they have confiscated illegal soft and hard drugs, they have destroyed them and not called the police. This may aid the teacher or school administrator in building rapport with the students, but also sends out a clear message: the students do not have to be held legally accountable for their actions. In addition, this type of behavior exposes the teacher or school administrator to possible criminal and civil liability.

Non-reporting is unfortunate when it happens. Anecdotal evidence suggests it happens frequently. I have interviewed high school students who told me that teachers have discovered classmates in possession of marijuana in class and simply told the students to put it away. Some of the students think the teacher is cool, but what really is the message being sent to all the students?

There are five areas where school administrators and teachers have failed to report criminal offenses to law enforcement. In most states it is a criminal offense not to report when:

1. A pupil attacks or menaces a school employee,
2. When child abuse is detected
3. When a pupil commits an assault with a deadly weapon,
4. When a pupil possesses or sells drugs
5. When a pupil possesses a weapon on campus.

It is not ironic that the third, fourth and fifth violations are also the top three criminal activities that student gang members are involved in (Howell and Lynch, 2000).

School Risk Factors

The United States Department of Justice has discovered that a school has a greater potential for aggression and violence when these risk factors are present:

1. Large schools, secondary schools with over 1,500 students and elementary schools with student populations exceeding 800.
2. Schools that are overcrowded, exceeding capacity.
3. Schools that have little or no student involvement.
4. Schools where there is rapid enrollment increases.
5. Schools with a high number of students in transition.
6. Schools with a large number of students with a family history of violence.
7. Schools that are located in communities with a high crime rates.
8. Schools with a large number of students of low socioeconomic status.
9. Schools where there are homogeneous groupings.
10. Schools where people lack sensitivity to and understanding other groups.
11. Schools where the staff is not trained to deal with the issues of student aggression and violence.
12. Schools that are not communicating rules, expectations and consequences clearly.
13. Schools with policies, regulations and procedures that do not adequately manage aggression and violence.

The more risk factors present the greater potential for school violence. Schools cannot select their student cliental. The student populations are demographically determined and constantly changing as community demographics change.

Individual Risk Factors

The U.S. Department of Justice also reports there are risk factors that exist in the lives of individuals that are primers for violent or aggressive behavior. These are also applied to students of all ages.

1. Lack of bonding and connection to family, school or the community.
2. There is a family history of and favorable attitude toward violence.
3. Where the student has been poorly parented.
4. Where the individual has the lack of basic physical needs being met.
5. Where the individual associates with violent peers, gang members.
6. Where the individual has had poor social skills development and clearly defined social norms.
7. Where there is substance abuse including alcohol.
8. Where the individual has been over exposed to violence in the media.
9. Where the individual experiences academic failure and little commitment to school.
10. Where the individual experiences frequent school transitions and moves.
11. Where there is lack of clarity and/or understanding of school rules, expectations and consequences.

12. Where schools have the inability to effectively manage aggression and violence.

The more risk factors present in a student's life the greater potential for aggressive or violent behavior. The presences of both types of risk factors can be a formula for deadly school violence.

As many Americans have started to re-examine the virtues of classroom discipline, values based teaching and a core curriculum, private and parochial schools have come back into fashion. During the late 1990s in Cleveland, Ohio at Saint Adalbert's Catholic primary school, principal Lydia Harris made a funny, but shrewd observation, about why her well-ordered school works. We provide the same thing a gang provides: family, code, color, belonging and activity. Her gang is growing; the enrollment is increasing despite all the other issues surrounding the children's education.

Did Principal Harris find an answer to one of the most fundamental questions facing the nation's classrooms? What should teachers teach and how should they teach it? Beyond that has Principal Harris been able to minimize or neutralize the risk factors associated with individuals and schools at risk for aggressive or violent behavior? With this educational model, what are the factors that seem to decrease the risks of aggressive or violent behavior and aid in educating the children? At least for her school, the solution seems to answer a common question. What should a good working school safety formula contain? More importantly, understanding risk factors and gang customs and practices clearly demonstrates that school safety is a very complicated issue.

School Uniforms

At Saint Adalbert's Catholic primary school almost immediately one can notice the presence of school uniforms worn by the students. The stylized gang attire once only worn by gang members has become a popular dress fashion worn by many young people. What many parents, teachers and young people do not understand is fashionable clothing may also be unique gang attire. Gang clothing is a gang uniform to real gang members. This stylized dress sends out a particular message to the student gang member. That is based on the way you are dressed you have to be a gang member or associated with a gang. Some stylized clothing that is commonly worn by gang members if worn by students can make them targets for gang violence.

The student gang member is compelled to contact the student based on the way he or she dresses to determine whether or not that student is a threat or a friend to his gang. Understanding gang customs and practices becomes paramount when considering school safety issues.

In the gang sub-culture clothing can act as a form of greeting, challenge or intimidation to another gang member. Young people emulating this dress style silently advertise an affiliation to a gang whether or not they really are gang associates or members. Naturally and logically real gang members will respond to this silent signal. This can happen on and off campus and at school sponsored events.

There are many documented instances where non-gang member students inadvertently wearing a certain color or style of clothing have been targeted and attacked by gang members, sometimes, receiving fatal injuries. Gang members key on the style and the color of dress other people are wearing. Remember, stylized clothing can be gang signal, a recognizable gang uniform. Many innocent citizens have been killed because they were mistakenly identified as a gang member by other by gang members, based on clothing.

Many students and teachers become street savvy and understand the meanings of color and gang clothing. One way to minimize the impact of gang clothing has been the use of school uniforms. School uniforms can offer positive reinforcement to the students. Uniforms can help build greater self-esteem. When wearing school uniforms gang member students do not stand out in as being different. The gang attire can no longer function as a silent way of claiming gang membership, acting as a greeting, challenge or intimidation.

As outward appearances become less of a factor, self-consciousness decreases and self-confidence tends to increase. The students also simply look neater and tend to feel better about themselves. Remember, these changes may take some time. Anecdotal evidence that tends to support this comes from the military. What happens to young men and women in boot camp?

Secondly, it is well established that students do not learn well when scared. Gang clothing can cause fear, intimidation and uneasiness especially when recognized by the students. Uniforms can take away this gang signal. Uniforms can help take away the real or perceived intimidation and threats cause by gang style clothing. The classroom becomes and feels safer and the students can focus their attention on learning. Teachers tend to become more relaxed and can focus their attentions on teaching.

The school uniform also becomes representative of the school. Students who dress to learn will learn, youth that dress for play will play. The concept is simple, just like kids attitudes and behaviors change when wearing Cub Scout, Girl Scout, or sports uniforms. These uniforms send out clear and specific messages to those who wear them and are easily recognizable by those who are familiar with them.

The uniforms have a couple of additional effects. People who do not belong at school or on campus are easier to identify. These non-students will stand out in the school setting. Obviously, this would aid school administrators and staff to keep the campus safe by keeping unwanted non-students off campus.

The other unique benefit also happens within the classroom. I have spoken to a number of teachers who like the fact that all the students within their classrooms are equal. Gang members can no longer intimidate other students and teachers through dress style. Teachers have commented that it has become easier to teach because no particular student(s) stand out. If the teacher is more comfortable, the better job of teaching he or she can do.

It follows that if students feel better about themselves, they will feel better about attending school. The school can become a safe haven for the children and they will want to be there. When children are consistently in school they will be more likely to work. School attendance can and will increase and become constant.

Naturally, if students come to school on a regular basis, their grades are bound to improve. When students do not have to worry about school safety or about what they are wearing, it gives them more time to concentrate on their studies. Overall scholastic performance will tend to increase for the school.

It also follows that students who enjoy school will also tend to participate in extracurricular activities. They will stay busy and are less likely to get in trouble. There will no longer be any competition for designer sports logo clothing or brand name clothing. For the most part, youth who are busy are more likely able to stay out of trouble and less likely to join street gangs. This suggests that juvenile crime should decrease on and off campus and the impact of the gang can be decreased if not minimized.

With the breaking down of the stand out barrier a school tends to become more unified. The students and parents identify with the school. Education becomes a motivating partnership between the school, the student and parents. With this partnership comes greater school pride and better student behavior. Students can develop a sense of unity and identity with the school. The school becomes a supplemental and in some cases a primary source for that sense of belonging. Choosing styles and color of clothing used to be only a matter of fashion and taste. Unfortunately, today it can be a matter of life and death for students and teachers.

Dress Codes

Along the same line as school uniforms are school dress codes. There are those who feel school uniforms would be an infringement of the First Amendment right to freedom of expression. Remember students who dress to learn will learn, just like youth who dress in football uniforms play football, and those who dress to gang bang will gang bang. In today's world, gang style clothing can be a distraction to students, teachers and other gang members in and outside the classroom. Strict dress codes are yet another way to control the impact of gang attire and influence on campus.

Dress codes can take away the gangs silent advertisement of affiliation or membership on school campuses. The only focus is to make the school a safer place to learn, not to restrict the style of dress one wears out of school. School uniforms and strict dress codes are both effective ways of managing the gang presence at school. School uniforms and strict dress codes can help make the school campus a neutral zone for all. This neutral zone is for all students, teachers and staff. This implies that schools can become a safe zone for education. In most states, schools are authorized by law to control dress styles worn by students while at school.

Search and Seizure

The United States Supreme Court has provided definitions of reasonable suspicion and scope of a search. This high court of the land has set the standard for reasonable and legal searches.

The school district is also responsible for creating a climate in schools that insures the safety of all, besides education. Equipment such as lockers and desks belong to the school district, but may be used by the students for their convenience. Most school districts understand it is their responsibility to insist the equipment is properly cared for and not used to store contraband. In some states there are statues that permit the use of metal detectors and trained animals to conduct authorized searches.

Case law has provided that under certain conditions, school administrators and staff may legally search lockers and desks. Obviously and foremost, school officials must follow district policy. This discussion here is to make all concerned aware of an additional tool that can be used to manage violence on school campuses.

In addition to searches of school property there can be an issue of personal searches by school employees. Again, district policies should be strictly followed. Students have the right of privacy of person as well as freedom from unreasonable search and seizure of property as guaranteed by the Fourth Amendment of the Constitution.

In two legal cases Nelson v. State, 319 So. 2nd 154 (Fla 2d D.C.A. 1975) and New Jersey v. T.L.O., 469, U.S. 325, 105 S. Ct. 733 (1985) applicable law was determined. The individual right protected by the Fourth Amendment is balanced by the schools responsibility for protecting the health, safety and welfare of all its students. Search of a student may be conducted upon reasonable suspicion that the student is in possession of contraband or evidence that shows that he or she has violated a law or a school rule.

Any policies regarding searches of property or person should be clearly defined and explained to the students and their parents. Precise and clear boundaries are important to avoid any misunderstanding of what is happening. Strip searches are never allowed. If a search is conducted, it is advisable to have two adult staff members present. This helps because an adult witness is present to confirm whether or not the search went beyond the scope and to provide proof of how the search was conducted.

Random, unannounced metal detector searches can also be conducted within school buildings and on school grounds. Classrooms or hallways should be selected on a random basis. A random selection of students, for example every third student could be done, if students are to be searched. This procedure could be utilized after appropriate signs are posted in prominent locations advising that persons on the premise will be subject to search for weapons by metal detector. The signs may have to be posted in several languages depending on the student composition. This is a key to have a successful and legal program.

The purpose of a metal detection program is to deter students from bringing weapons, like guns, knives or any other items that might cause injury or harm to other students, to school. Under no circumstances should metal detectors solely be used for the purpose of checking students who might be suspected of violating other school rules.

The legal authority for property and personal searches by schools is present. This is a sensitive area, and to avoid any legal or criminal liability consult your school district legal counsel before starting or updating any school policy. Remember, this is one of many tools a school can used to effectively manage violence and make the campus safer.

A few suggested policies to use if searches are to be conducted might be as mentioned earlier. Always have an adult witness present. This is for your protection, because the witness can corroborate what happened during the search. If you ever have to testify, an attorney will not be able to ask you what happened to the students (his clients) $100.00 cash that was in the locker at the time of the search. The issue does not become he said she said issue.

Whenever a female student is being questioned or searched, have an adult female present. A male school employee should not leave himself open to accusations of making inappropriate comments or taking liberties with a female student. A witness is like having an insurance policy covering the incident.

Always conduct the searches in a manner that affords the least amount of embarrassment to the student. Use common sense and remember this is a safety issue. If searching a locker, have the student(s) who use the locker present. Have them stand away and have the witness watch them. The last thing you want to do is to let them have access to locker first, especially if you suspect it contains a weapon.

The best advice is to plan ahead. Have a procedure in place, train staff and follow it. Remember, your primary objective for conducting the search is to fulfill you legal duty to provide for the safety and welfare of all the students and staff in the school.

Remember, no person(s) should ever be selected for any kind of search based solely upon their gender, race, color, religion, ethnic or national origin, political beliefs, marital status, age, sexual orientation, social and family background, linguistic preference, disability, manner of dress, or association with any particular group.

As an alternative to the search issue, some schools have removed student lockers. All books and related materials are carried with the student throughout the day in a backpack. This has been a reported inconvenience to some students, but has been a necessary action to make the school safer for all.

Closed Campus

Many schools have increased safety by closing the campus during school hours. This prevents non-students from entering the campus during school hours. It also can provide an increased feeling of being safer for the students and staff, like closing and locking a door at home, security.

If a school is physically large this may be costly and some schools are simply physically too large to close the campus. If a school has an extremely large student population, closing the campus may also be logistically difficult as well.

Closing a campus if practical can increase school safety. A closed campus can provide a means to control who enters the school as well as those who leave. The frequency of school violence has changed within the past ten years. So have ways of monitoring, preventing, and deterring it.

Video Cameras

Some schools have installed security video cameras to monitor student activity. The cameras in a way act as a deterrent because the students do not want to be videotaped participating in violent or criminal acts. The cameras, at first may seem like an intrusion but have aided in campus security for some schools.

Practically speaking these systems can be expensive. The hardware needs to be purchased or donated, then installed. A monitoring station then needs to be set up, including some type of recording equipment. Then, someone has to watch the monitors. In high crime areas these systems offer the luxury of watching many locations at one time with one or two people. The initial cost may seem high, but the trade off is being able to monitor a large area with a limited number of people.

For other schools teachers have walked out to the student drop off and pick up areas and have video recorded the process. These areas in the past had been the locations of gang conflicts before school during student drop off and the after school during student pickup. A hand held video camera can also serve as a deterrent because nobody wants to be filmed committing a crime. This can be done on a random basis and is an inexpensive way to prevent and deter school crime. Volunteer parents can assist by donating their time and using their cameras.

Armed Security Personnel

Other schools have responded to the increase of student violence by providing armed plain clothes and uniformed school security throughout the campus. Some school districts have school police present. In other areas of the country local police officers or sheriff's deputies are used to assist with school safety.

Police officers are well-trained law enforcement professionals. They receive special training in the areas of search and seizure and the laws of arrest. All school security personnel should be trained in the same areas if they are not sworn police officers. The minimum training should comply with state and local regulations. This insures that qualified personnel who are armed will be able to prevent, respond to and handle school safety issues in an appropriate manner.

Day Curfew

In another attempt to manage, prevent and deter youth violence and the impact of street gangs, some cities have tried to enact daytime curfew ordinances. This type of law would allow local law enforcement to legally stop any school age child and determine why he or she is not in school, during normal school hours. This could be the enforcement tool cities could use to help keep kids motivated to stay in school and help fight the growing gang problem. Ordinances like these put teeth back into the truancy laws.

The penalties vary from calling parents and having their child picked up at the police department, to taking the student to school and letting the administrators handle the issue, fines, community service or arrest. For chronic truants, there may have to be stiffer penalties. The ordinances are aimed at those who are chronically not in school without a valid reason. Many times, these non-attending students are affiliated with street gangs or involved in other delinquent behavior.

Some parents are afraid ordinances such as this would put too much power in the hands of the police and could lead to flagrant violations of young people's civil rights. Opponents also fear the ordinances automatically make young people who may a legitimate right to be in public during school hours a suspect of a crime.

These types of ordinances are only valid during normal school hours. The ordinances allow for legal detention to determine the status of the minor. A legal detention is not an arrest; it is like being pulled over on a traffic stop. If the minor has a valid reason for not being in school, the encounter is brief after a few questions are asked. It would easy to verify if a minor was in a home schooling program or on a year-round schedule and not in school. Again, nothing would be done to the minor, a very small inconvenience to make a city safer for all.

With the current law enforcement workloads, police officers are not going to donate all of their morning and early afternoon hours looking for school truants. However, think of this scenario: a school administrator calls the police because there is a group of kids on his campus that are not students.

The police arrive and determine whether or not these youth are truants. The ordinance would give instant authority to allow the police to immediately place the youth into custody, get them off school grounds, and deal with them at the police department and call their parents if they were truant. It would allow for a quick and easy solution to a school safety issue.

Like all laws, common sense is needed when enforcing them. The mere detention by police is not a crime and is not recorded on an individual's criminal history. Remember a detention based on a truant ordinance is a simple legal stop and talk scenario, just like when the police pull you over in a traffic stop.

Keeping truant students in school during school hours helps keep crime down. As one 17-year-old student told me, *"I'd rather be embarrassed a little, being stopped by the police to check why I am not in school even though I might not have to be there... because I know the streets are safer, other school age kids who are criminals wouldn't be around... I wouldn't feel afraid as much as I use to."*

Zero Tolerance

Some schools have adopted a zero tolerance policy for weapons and drugs. This policy certainly sets limits for the students. Normally, suspension or expulsions are the common punishments for violations. Remember, law enforcement officers are trained in the enforcement of the spirit of the law as well as the letter of the law.

Workable solutions have to be made for the students who suffer from an occasional headache or monthly menstrual cramps. A waiver from the parent allowing the school nurse to give an aspirin or Midol, for example, might be a simple solution. The parents who know of minor medical problems can even provide the medication, saving a cost to the school.

Schools should not become free clinics. However, making a student feel physically better with over the counter medicine would certainly help enforce the zero tolerance policy, because there would be a way to provide limited treatment for very minor problems. Students would not have to sneak over the counter medications on campus, conceal and use them as if they were illegal addicting drugs. Of course, some type of signed waiver from the parents would eliminate liability issues and parents would provide the medication.

The second benefit is directed at the school. There would be no more bad publicity from the world for the suspension of a student for taking a Midol if the school provided a method to obtain the medication that falls within school policy. There would be no excuses and the schools will have acted in good faith. If there were a violation, schools would have a solid, well-understood policy to fall back upon. Remember, kids who feel good will stay in school. Maybe common sense should prevail as the guideline.

Staff Training

A candid staff-training program can also aid in preventing gang violence on campus. A clear understanding of gang practices and sociology can help staff become alert to potential violent situations. Being aware offers an opportunity to identify and prevent the incident.

The local law enforcement agency or probation department can provide gang training. Training should focus on the district policies, including those for searches, suspension and expulsion. Gang history, identifiers, graffiti, hand signs and substance abuse are a few of the topics that should be covered. Training like this would give the teachers another tool to help at risk students. Being able to recognize the early warning signs of gang involvement increases the chance of intervention programs working.

The gang presence can show up in the funniest places. For example, in student art work and writings. Gang symbols and colors can be found if you know what to look for. These subtle indicators may aid the teacher in dealing with a student at risk.

Project Yes

One training program that has aided teachers is Project Yes, sponsored by the Orange County, California, Department of Education. The program is intended to deter youths in grades 2 through 7 from involvement in drugs and gangs. The program will help any teacher understand the scope of youth violence and destructive behavior, learn to identify signs and symptoms of gang behavior and learn successful strategies that support community collaboration.

The lessons center on five themes: responsible citizenship, dynamics of cultural diversity, refusal skills, choices and consequences, success and achievement. There are five lessons for each grade and the lessons can be incorporated into current curricula.

S.T.A.R.

Another well-known program is sponsored by the Jefferson Center for Character Education, a nonprofit corporation located in Pasadena, California. The program's aim is to teach middle and junior high school students sound character values and personal responsibility. The curriculum, called S.T.A.R., spans three years and comes with 100 lessons, some of which can be covered in as little as ten minutes. S.T.A.R. is an acronym for STOP before taking action, THINK about alternatives, ACT, REVIEW and evaluate outcomes of actions.

There are many programs designed to aid teachers in educating and preparing students for life. The two mentioned here illustrate the types of programs currently available. Alert and aware staff is essential in the formula for a safe school.

School / Law Enforcement Programs

There are a number of successful programs that allow sworn law enforcement officials to teach in a local school. In California, two of the most popular police and school programs are the S.A.N.E./ GANG curriculum sponsored by the Los Angeles County Sheriff's Department, and the G.R.E.A.T. project sponsored by the United States Bureau of Alcohol, Tobacco and Firearms.

S.A.N.E./ Gang

The Substance Abuse and Narcotics Education Gang (S.A.N.E./GANG) curriculum is designed to be team taught by the teacher and deputy sheriff and is offered for grades 4, 5 and 6. The program contains an overview of the gang problem that highlights key points that are addressed in the gang prevention lessons. Lessons include addressing issues like developing a positive self-identity apart from the gang, counteracting violence, resolving conflicts, taking pride in ones heritage and contrasting materialism with traditional values.

The basic premise of this program is that learning should be interactive. Less emphasis is placed on lecture and films. More time is devoted to engaging the students in active discussions. The lessons are structured to address cognitive, emotional and behavior attitudes. The goal of instruction is to make the students aware that gang membership and violence are not necessary, fulfilling or inevitable by giving the students behavioral strategies for avoiding gangs.

G.R.E.A.T.

The second program is actually very popular throughout the United States. The U.S. Bureau of Alcohol, Tobacco and Firearms, the Federal Law Enforcement Training Center (FLETC) and the Phoenix Police Department sponsor the Gang Resistance Education and Training (G.R.E.A.T.) program. The G.R.E.A.T. Program trains police officers to conduct a comprehensive anti-gang education program for middle and elementary school children.

For example, the G.R.E.A.T. program for 7th graders involves eight one hour classroom sessions covering crime and the hurt it causes, conflict resolution, drugs and their effect on neighborhoods, civic responsibility, and goal settings. A separate curriculum of four lessons was designed for 3rd and 4th grade students.

These are just two examples of programs. The point is that if at risk students are identified maybe a program like these could help decrease the potential of gang related violence or incidents from happening on campus. In the early 2000s some research suggested that the G.R.E.A.T. program might not have long term effects on reducing gang violence. The implementation of the program does not focus on long term solutions. The program attempts to give middle and junior high school students mechanisms to deal with issues related to their particular age group. As young adults certainly some of the programs fundamentals may be applied, but young adults think and act differently than middle and junior high school age students. Young adults are also confronted with a myriad of different age related issues.

Student Training

The students of any school can be an excellent resource. Many students are looking to get involved in some other aspect of their education besides the academic part. Two student programs moderated by school staff have enjoyed a great deal of success. Being involved also tends to allow the student to develop a sense of ownership to the school. This in turn the student to feel more attached to the school.

Conflict resolution programs are an excellent way to demonstrate that violence is not needed to settle problems between the students. These programs use student moderators, who stay impartial and get the involved parties to talk about the issue rather than fight over it. The whole purpose is to guide the disputing parties into a peaceful settlement.

The arbitrations are usually successful and the outcomes normally are enough to leave all involved parties satisfied. The program is student oriented and operated by students.

A peer-counseling program may be another useful tool for students. In these types of programs volunteer students are trained to become active listeners. Sometimes, a student just needs to talk to an unbiased person to get a second opinion or to blow off some stream. The peer counselor is there to be that listening person. Sometimes peer counselors are used to discuss serious matters. The peer counselors are not mental health professionals and do not offer that kind of help.

However, peer counselors are fellow students who hold sessions with concerned students in total privacy. Peer counselors do not discuss these private issues with other students or teachers unless someone's life is in danger. If matters arise like suicide or a plan to hurt or kill another student, the peer counselors have a protocol to follow just as any mental health, medical or law enforcement professional does. Having a resource like a peer counseling program has benefited many students as well as the peer counselors themselves.

Cooperative Programs

One key to a successful education program has been to involve as much of the community as possible. Collaborative or cooperative programs are often the basis for a successful community-school relationship. These may include the participation of law enforcement, probation, prosecution and private business, all working together with the school. The purpose is to keep the student in school, to let the student know what is expected of him, and to let parents know what is expected of the student. The business partnership also allows student to discover and prepare for whatever opportunities are open for them.

CUFFS

One of the most successful programs I have seen in action was called CUFFS. This program involved the Fullerton, California, Unified School District, and Fullerton Police Department, Orange County District Attorneys office, the Orange County Probation Department, local private business and parents and worked to build a coordinated prevention, intervention, and suppression coalition. Expected and obtained outcomes were designed to provide a supportive educational environment, increase effective parental involvement in each students educational and social development, and use available community and school resources to reduce negative influences impacting the students.

The basic goal of the program was to keep kids in school. The teeth of the program are the law enforcement components. Working very closely with school officials, any student knows that if he or she is not in school there better be a valid reason. Sometimes parents are involved in the process by attending School Attendance Review Board (SARB) meetings at the school, to determine why the student is not attending class. It was not out of the program scope for the police to show up at the front door of student to escort him or her to school. If the student gets into to trouble criminally, the assigned prosecutor becomes involved.

Local business gets involved by explaining their business and providing intern programs for qualified students. Emphasis is also placed on succeeding as well as attendance. Parents also volunteer time at the school to assist with lunch hour monitoring and other important tasks. The Boys and Girls Club, Parks and Recreation, YMCA and YWCA are just a few of the available resources used in the program.

This successful program gets the community involved at a unique level. The school becomes the unifying force for the students, parents, probation department, prosecution office and private business. For a community grappling with the root causes of gang activity, these types of programs can help formulate a successful effort to counteract the gang influence. Partnerships with the school work because they tend to bring a community together. The community then can develop a sense of focus and commitment ... the welfare of the students that in turn improves the quality of life for the community. This can be a win-win scenario if everyone gives a little.

A school law enforcement partnership tends to promote a safe campus as well as let the students identify with the local police. In addition, these partnerships promote instant communication between the school and local law enforcement. This type of real time communication aids in keeping track of school incidents and can develop into direct, one to one partnerships between school officials and the police.

Schools can also sponsor training for parents and teachers on gang issues, youth violence and the warning signs of a student at risk and parent-student relationships. At many school-sponsored training sessions the participating police, prosecution and probation departments actually provide the training.

Schools have been very successful at starting and maintaining parent volunteer programs. Parents can be another major resource for the school. Parents can assists in many areas of daily school activities such as lunch hour monitoring, office attendance, tutoring, mentor programs, the monitoring of the campus, parking lots or bus stops. Parents also need to have the opportunity to be involved at school. This opportunity also helps parents identify with the school. It helps foster a sense of ownership to these students as well as making their sibling students feel better (I'm important because my mom or dad donates time to my school.) An elementary school student once said to me, *"I'm special because my mom comes to my school and helps in my class."*

Schools have also been able to impact the community by starting before and after school and weekend programs to give students a safe place to study, receive tutoring, and participate in social and recreational activities. These types of programs tend to keep kids motivated about school. They actually help maintain student attendance and are a type of a drop out prevention program.

Pre-violence Indicators

Violence is a learned behavior. On school campuses there are a few identifiable pre-violence behaviors that can be recognized. If violence can be predicated through the recognition of pre-violence behaviors then it can be prevented. What this means is that there are some pre-gang violence indicators that if identified and dealt with could stop the development of a serious gang related incident on campus. Teachers and school officials should watch for:

1. Students who are mad dogging.
2. Students who are displaying handsigns.
3. The presence of derogatory graffiti.
4. The presence of defaced graffiti.
5. Groups of students squaring off.
6. Increased show of colors by students.
7. The presence of non-students on campus.
8. Cars rolling by the campus.
9. Increased altercations on campus.
10. Heighten tensions amongst the students.
11. Increased number of weapons on campus.
12. Reports of student concern.

These are 12 of the most common pre violence indicators that have been reported before gang violence has erupted on campus. However, some gang violence can be spontaneous and the result of a chance encounter. Rivalries born off campus are brought to campus. These rivalries can cause major disturbances on campus, sometimes without any warning signals because of what has happen off campus.

When gang violence does erupt there can be some type of triggering event that played a direct role. Sometimes the event can be a traditional school activity such as a football game or dance. Sometimes the event happens off campus. This is why a good working relationship with your local police, probation and parole departments and knowing about the gangs that operate in your school jurisdiction is so important. Common event triggers can be:

1. Releases from state prison
2. Probation or parole relocations
3. An assault of an associate gang member
4. Acts of gang violence at the school
5. Acts of gang violence off campus
6. Acts of disrespect like defacing graffiti, mad dogging, showing handsigns
7. Intra-school events dances and sport events

8. The formation of new gangs on campus

9. Recent jump ins of new gang members

10. Enrollment of new students who are gang members

11. Picture day

12. Formation of new gang alliances

These are certainly not the only event triggers for gang violence. This partial list may help you determine where and when gang violence might erupt at your school. This also requires some awareness training for teachers to identify the pre-activity and activity that is associated with this type of gang behavior.

It is important to know what gangs are on campus and near the school grounds. In addition, it is helpful to know the gang members are who attend your school. Unfortunately, the gang mentality does not permit any insult to go unanswered. Gang members with the best of intentions could be forced into spontaneous violent confrontations to protect their honor, get respect or save face.

When talking to gang members a few guidelines should be followed, teachers and administrators might consider these safety tips:

1. Try not insult gang members

2. Do not call them by their gang moniker

3. Do not disrespect their gang or set

4. Never accuse without cause

5. Never put two rival gang members together

6. Never embarrass a gang member or put him/her on the spot in front of peer gang members

7. Never assume anything

8. Do not mimic handsigns

9. Do not mimic clothing styles

10. Do not use gang slang

When interviewing or talking to gang members, the location of the contact may also be important. Good body language is always helpful. Sometimes, there may not be time to choose a convenient location or the time. If the situation is critical, such as a classroom shooting or bomb explosion on campus, the stress may cause some feelings of panic to develop.

Many youth grow up with natural disasters such as floods, earthquakes, tornadoes and power outages. Parents and home life provide pre-conditioning for these events. Students are seldom prepared to deal with campus shootings, the loss of a teacher or classmate. It is unfortunate that some schools now have the students practice drive by shooting and intruder safety drills. These drills are a necessary prevention to insure student safety.

Some emergencies are truly accidents, for example a helicopter falling from the sky and crashes on campus, believe it or not, that has happened.

Despite all that can happen on campus a school should have a plan or procedure to follow in the event something catastrophic does happen. This should be in a written form and developed to insure the safety of all the students and staff during emergency situations. Hopefully, this will never happen at your school but the emergency procedures are needed to prevent panic and chaos in tense situations.

For Students

Although it may seem like common sense to an adult or a person who understands gang behaviors, sometimes students do not have the same perspective. Here are few common sense guidelines for students to consider.

Do not hang around gang locations because rival gang members will automatically associate you with the known gang members they see there. To a rival gang you are part of the gang because you were seen at a gang hangout.

Do not wear gang attire. Rival gang members also automatically judge a person by what they are wearing. Gang clothing is a recognizable uniform to gang members. They almost always assume anyone wearing this stylized clothing is a gang member or gang associate. To them this means you are a potential target.

Do not claim gang membership or association to anyone. You know how quickly information travels on campus. If you claim membership or association to a gang, the real members will come to you. A physical assault is the usual punishment for falsifying membership. More importantly, rival gangs can target you for a deadly assault because you claimed membership or association to a gang.

In the gang sub-culture there is a "hit up." This is a formal greeting to another person asking them to state their gang affiliation for the record. This is serious because the asking gang member(s) are waiting for a formal response back. Ignoring to answer the question sometimes is viewed as a form of disrespect. Answering incorrectly can also be a form of disrespect. The "hit up" is sometimes asked because the asking gang members already know the answer and they want to fight. This is like the slap in the face challenge that was done before a duel. There is a neutral answer that is sometimes accepted and deescalates the situation. The answer "I am from nowhere" is sometimes accepted. If you are not dressed like a gang member and have not been hanging out at known gang locations the neutral answer can work.

If you are wearing gang clothing and hang around a known gang location and a rival gang is asking the question the neutral answer may not work. Answering neutrally may still result in an assault.

There is one more thing to consider. Gang members often do not discern between socializing and gang socializing. If you have a boy or girl friend that belongs to a gang you may inadvertently place yourself in harm's way. Because rival gangs don't take the time to ask before assaulting being out on a legitimate date with a gang member can result in something bad happening. Not because of the gang member on the date, but because of assumptions made by rival gangs that cannot be controlled.

Summary

Schools alone cannot address all of the societal issues contributing to this national crisis. The family, community and school are an essential part of prevention strategies. Ultimately, a collaborative community effort is needed to keep our children safe at school. Educators should become informed and know the signs and symptoms of gang activity. Relevant in-service training for teachers and staff is a must. Students must understand that gang membership and association for many is a choice.

Schools have a critical role in many areas of a student's life. Because of societal changes, schools and the education professionals have been forced to adjust curriculums to address a myriad of problems affecting students. These can include school violence, pregnant students and students with little or no English speaking abilities and street gangs. If that was not enough, state laws now require schools to make an effort to maintain safety on campuses for the student and staff and hold them responsible for doing so.

Keeping school campuses safe is certainly a challenge and only part of the ultimate goal, education. That goal should also include a place where children can learn, feel comfortable, get a sense of belonging and identity. The schools have a major impact on a community and society. Teachers and school administrators have an opportunity to reach out and affect an entire community, not just the students.

We all have to understand that students also use a code of silence. This code of conduct requires them not to report weapons or violence on campus. This behavior is reinforced through intimidation and the fear of retaliation for cooperation. The pay back part of the gang mentality has motivated many students not to get involved. The same fear has motivated many adults not to get involved. For fear of being hurt themselves some students are forced in cases not to help, even though they may want to get involved. Often, this fear extends to the route to and from school and at home especially when gangs are involved. This is not the traditional bully syndrome.

These are a just some of the issues facing the nations educational system at any level. America's changing demographics and attitudes also add to the complexity of teaching. Teachers are heroes in the true sense of the word. Often, spending their own money and working on their own time, they are saddled with pay scales that are not commensurate with the work they perform. Teachers are some of the most unrecognized and dedicated professionals in our country. A "teacher" is commonly cited by gang members as mentors who helped them get out of the gang life and proved that they are worth something.

Gangs and Family

Some of the information presented in this book might be a little overwhelming and/or intimidating. That is understandable. Across the United States, from rural towns to large cities, the gang subculture has affected the way many of us live. For some families gangs have stolen children and taken lives away. Data suggests that 1 in 32 Americans are incarcerated (US Department of Justice, 2002). If you think about it, street gangs, in one form or other, have been around for hundreds of years in the United States. What makes their presence so influencing now? Don't forget these same issues face families worldwide.

The Family Unit

Many family experts believe the family unit in America has changed, and changed drastically. Think for a moment as you read this sentence of how your life was when you were growing up. What kinds of movies or television programs were available to you? What kinds of worries did you have? Were you weary of wearing any specific color or staring at someone for a while?

Times have obviously changed and today our children grow up (emotionally and psychologically) a lot faster than many of us want. There are a number of sociological reasons for this. In today's world, many parents are two-income families and have 50 or 60-hour workweeks. There seem to be a large number of single parent families resulting in an increased number of latch key kids.

By some estimates 27 percent or 18 million of America's children are raised in single parent homes. It appears that in the 1990s and 2000s parents have little or no time to spend with their children. Some studies suggest that parent(s) spend as little as three and a half minutes a day talking with their children. As parents, we all are tremendously busy with work and the remnants of a social life. But what did your children do today? Ask yourself what kind and color of clothes did your children wear today. Can you truthfully answer?

Today our youths have life pressures older generations never had. Take for example the use of drugs and gang violence in our schools. Young students are bringing weapons to school at an unprecedented rate. Guns, for some youth, equal power. A 14-year-old male student (non-gang member) who brought a loaded .45 caliber semi-automatic pistol to school told me, "When I have the gun I am in control... people are afraid of me because I have the ultimate power." The truth is that guns can bring instant control and power to some youth. The rash of school shootings across the country is a painful reminder that they can also bring long-lasting sadness.

Think for a moment of how complicated our world is today. Sex education, teenage pregnancies, teen suicides, and the feeling they have no control of their lives are just a few of the real issues our children have today.

Statistics

Ken Bell, Senior District Attorney Investigator in Los Angeles, California, presented some startling facts at a law enforcement gang seminar in Riverside, California, (April, 1992). If you compare statistics for juveniles committing homicides worldwide, the United States ranks fifth. The other countries in order were Guatemala, Thailand, Puerto Rico, and Brazil. This ranking represents kids killing other people.

Narrow the focus a little, and look only at the United States. California ranked fifth in the country as far as juveniles committing homicides. Alaska ranked surprisingly number one when this data was presented on a per capita basis.

In the late 1990s juvenile homicide rates by county in California suggested that youth violence was on the rise. As you would expect Los Angeles County ranked number one in the State. In order of ranking from number 2 to 10 are the following counties; Alameda, San Joaquin, San Bernardino, Orange, Contra Costa, San Francisco, Riverside, San Diego and Sacramento.

For the time period the data suggested that our youth were killing at record rates. There was anecdotal evidence that suggested gang related violence was responsible for a large percentage of this increase. Is this just another statistic or could societal factors influence youth violence? For example, murder is the largest cause of death for African-American males in the 14-24 year-old age range. That is the same age range where we find a large percentage of African-American gang members.

The latest FBI report suggests that one violent crime occurs every 21 seconds. One murder occurs every 31 minutes. One forcible rape occurs every 5 minutes. One robbery occurs every minute. One aggravated assault occurs every 32 seconds. One burglary occurs every 14 seconds. One theft occurs every 4 seconds. One motor vehicle theft occurs every 25 seconds (National Center for Victims of Crime, 2000).

This happens every hour, 24 hours a day, 365 days a year. Some experts would tell us we live in one of the most violent countries in the world. Yet, the victimization only touches a small percentage of the country's population. I believe a major portion of this crime can be attributed to street gang activity and youth violence. If you work out the numbers for the homicide rate per year in America it is equal to 16,955 murders each year. This is a sad commentary for the most advanced and powerful nation in the world.

Special Programs

The big question is: can anything be done to stop the gang killings and other gang related crimes? Right now there are three types of programs used to combat gang violence. They involve prevention, intervention and suppression strategies.

Prevention programs target at youth to give them the tools needed to prevent them from joining street gangs. Intervention programs are focused at helping those who want to leave gang life. Suppression programs are mainly used by law enforcement agencies and are aimed at using law enforcement techniques. All programs when used collectively can help lower and manage the levels of gang violence.

In theory, that's how it is supposed to work. However, real life implementation of these programs can be a nightmare. With the current lack of available funding at all levels of our government, these types of programs seldom, if ever, get the necessary monetary backing. Federal, state and private foundation grants are very limited.

All three types of programs are needed to help resolve gang violence. All three types of programs have one other thing in common. The training, education and guidance of the target youth group is done by someone other than the parent(s). These programs are all excellent and work under the right conditions.

Back to Basics

Look at who really raises our children today. How many hours a day is your child at school or day care or after school care? How many hours a week do you spend talking with your children? On a national average our children spend about six hours a day with their teachers and peers. This can be as high as eight to ten hours if the student is involved in extracurricular school activity. As a working parent, I know first-hand how difficult it is to find time to talk with, not at, my children. There is a big difference.

The family unit needs to become the strength of our nation, not its weakness. Parenting is a profession. The pressures and decisions a parent has to make are just as important as the ones any company president makes. Think for a moment of the hours of formal and informal training you have received for the job you do. How many training sessions have we attended to further our expertise as parents?

As parents we need to get back to being involved with our children's lives. We need to know what going on at school and with their personal lives. As parents we not only have the responsibility of providing all the physical needs of our children (home, food, clothes, etc.) but also a loving home environment. As parents, we need to provide consistent supervision and guidance to our children. The key here is being consistent. As parents, we need to hold our children accountable for their actions. That is easier said than done.

Denial

One of the greatest challenges we have as parents is confronting denial. As parents we must have the ability to RECOGNIZE and ACT appropriately when dealing with issues regarding our children, especially with street gangs. To do this we must be aware of what issues and who influences our children. How powerful can denial be?

During the Fall of 1994 I became involved in the investigation of a gang related witness intimidation case. A mother and father in Southern California had four sons. All the sons were heavily involved in street gangs. All were members of the same Latino street gang. One of the brothers was in state prison and another was on probation; both for gang-related violent crime.

In late 1993, one of the four brothers robbed a pizza deliveryman of $16 and the pizza. Three other peer gang members helped him. The only eyewitness to the robbery was an 18-year-old female who lived in the neighborhood, in the apartment complex next door.

She cooperated with the police and one of the brothers was arrested. She immediately started to receive threats from the brother's gang. The eyewitness was moved around and about a month before the trial she was contacted by the mother of the four-gang members. The mother eventually offered $500 to the witness to change her testimony.

The mother told the witness just to change her testimony enough not to identify her son. The mother actually told the witness she knew this was wrong to do but she wanted to save her son from going to jail.

Telephone conversations between the mother and eyewitness were monitored and audiotape recorded. During one conversation the mother mentioned how she had done this before for another son, and how she was never caught. Dad even had a short conversation with the witness and reminded her that as long as he was alive she would be physically OK. However, if he was gone, he could not guarantee her safety.

Checking the court files and histories of her four sons, I found the other case the mother was referring to. In late 1990, the son now in state prison robbed and fondled a lady who was waiting in a parked car in the apartment complex where they used to live. The victim immediately went to the police and reported the crime. The loss was jewelry and a guitar that was removed from the trunk. There were a total of four suspects in this crime. That night the police recovered the guitar from the first son and arrested him.

In this case file I found a hand written note start to the deputy prosecutor, dated the day the trial was supposed to start. The note, written by the victim, stated she had made a mistake in identifying the perpetrator and the case had to be dismissed by the prosecutor.

About a month later I found the victim in another state and flew there to interview her. Reluctantly, she admitted that she had taken money from the mother to change her statement. The victim said she was scared of what would happen if she did not take the money the mother offered. She admitted writing the note to the prosecutor saying she made a mistake on the identification and was leaving the state. The family even returned all the jewelry that had been taken. The mother had arranged it all, and even apologized for her son's actions.

What happened here? Is this a case where a mother would do anything to protect her sons, or is this a case of denial? The mother had committed felony crimes in an attempt to prevent her sons from going to jail for their crimes. The cases here did not involve any identification issues. The boys were involved in the criminal actions.

How about making your children accountable for their actions and providing constant supervision and guidance? Denial can cause the formation of a biased perspective on issues and can control behavior. That is what happened in this case. A parent's denial prevented recognition and action that led this mother going to jail. The gang issues in this case had been developing for several years. Both mother and father had many contacts with the local police and were notified of their son's gang membership and activity. The mother still maintains that her son's are noble men and the police are just out to get them. Surprisingly the local media portrayed the mother as a church going lady who volunteered and helped other people.

It is hard to be surprised any more about the responses from some parents when we notify them of the arrest of their son or daughter. Most parents' first question is, what did he do? What did he do now? Sometimes early in the conversation, the parents ask if their son or daughter is hurt or is anyone else hurt.

Often, law enforcement telephone calls are made late at night or in the early morning hours. Sometimes parents ask are you sure it is my child? She should be in her room asleep? Are you sure? She was spending the night at her girl friends house?

Many parents then ask what is going to happen next or what do you want from me? About 12:30 AM one particular Saturday morning I stopped a car for a traffic violation. A teenage boy drove the car and the passengers were another teenage boy and two teenage girls. No one had any identification. The car was "borrowed" from a friend.

The driver had several tattoos that police often find on gang members. The driver and male passenger talked the talk. They spoke with the street slang that some gang members use. They both claimed to be members of a street gang. Both said the girls were associate gang members.

The driver then told me he borrowed the car from his parents but forgot to ask or tell them. He told me his parents probably did not know he was out or that he had the car. All four juveniles were extremely nervous and began to tell conflicting stories as to where they were going and where they came from.

When asked for their identification the girls both replied they had none. The driver was arrested for driving without a license and as allowed by law, the car was searched for ownership paper work. The two girls were seated in the back seat together. In the back seat on the floor was a loaded handgun hidden in a white athletic sock.

No one knew where the gun came from and since the car was borrowed the gun probably belonged to the owner of the car. All four juveniles were taken to the police department. Checking the serial number of the gun on the computer indicated it was reported as a stolen weapon.

Protocol required a call to the parents to advise them of their child's situation. Sometimes the juveniles are released to the parents after arrest especially if the violations are misdemeanors. This was the case here, and the parents asked the usual questions. I called the mother of the girl whom I suspected had the gun. It was three in the morning. The call elicited this response:

"Why are you waking me up to tell me my daughter was arrested? ... You are supposed to wait until a decent hour to call me.... I don't care what you think happened, she is responsible for herself. ... Don't bother me anymore and I'm not coming down to pick her up." Then she hung up the telephone. The girl was only 13-years-old.

Don't let denial prevent you from recognizing and acting to help your children the right way. Too many parents say it will never happen to my son or daughter or it only happens to children in that part of the city. Today, anyone can become involved in street gangs. Remember, street gang members come from all economic, ethnic and social backgrounds.

Solutions

We all can do something to help stop the gang violence. If you witness a crime call the police, be a witness. Employers, give your employee help if he or she has to go to court on a criminal case. Pay for parking fees and don't dock wages for court appearances. This is a wise and sound business investment because gang crime is bad for business. The judicial system only works if we all are involved.

Parents also need to get involved with their children, especially those children at risk. Spend time talking with your children, not at them. Why can't we change role models for our children? What is wrong with being a teacher, a plumber, an artist, a coach or a nurse? Most males make their ideal role model a professional athlete. In reality, very few athletes make it into the pros when compared to the number who try (statistically only about one percent).

Why not start parental education programs aimed at the high school level before our children become parents? Increase the number of conflict resolution programs at the intermediate and high school levels. Let our children understand that violence is not needed to settle a problem. Start peer and become involved in peer counseling and mentor programs.

Baggy style clothing has become a controversial issue for many people. As we have seen in this book, baggy style clothing is an accepted way of dress for many street gang members. Baggy clothing is not used as indicia of gang membership because the style of dress is so popular with the younger generation as well as with gang members. Clothing style can have a significant role in the gang sub-culture. Clothing or stylized dress can act as a form of advertisement and uniform for gang members. Remember the greeting, challenge and intimidation functions of stylized clothing.

To a real gang member, another person dressed similarly represents a rival or associate gang member. This is an assumption that all gang members make based solely on clothing style. In gang sub-culture when a gang member encounters another perceived gang member he or she is required to hit that person up. In other words, the gang member is asking that person to identify his gang association or affiliation. The gang member does not ask if the person is only wearing the style of clothing to be cool.

Young people who wear this style of clothing, whether they are gang members or not, simply announce that they are part of gang sub-culture to the real gang member. These youths who wear this style of clothing and are not gang members have camouflaged themselves as associates or gang members. Stylized gang clothing will increase the chance of the wearer to become a victim of gang violence.

The Mall

Part of my job used to require me to be actively involved in witness and witness/victim liaison. I become a link for these people between the court system and police departments. A face is associated with a name and a real person helps guide them through all the legal processes. Witnesses do not have to listen to a recording and press a telephone pad key to get more information.

In July 1993, at 4:08 p.m., a 17-year-old Asian gang member opened fire with small caliber hand gun from the second floor of the enclosed Westminster, California, mall. The juvenile was aiming at a small group of Asian females standing below him.

After firing several rounds at four young girls, two found their mark. 13-year-old, Katie, was hit twice in the back, seriously damaging her liver. A bullet grazed one other girl and the remaining two were unharmed. Katie underwent emergency surgery to save her life. She struggled to survive and made it through the long recovery road.

Katie had just started to hang around with her friends who were members of a female Asian street gang. She told me that she was thinking of joining the gang. Katie was the middle child. Her older siblings had started to work and the youngest siblings were receiving most of the attention from mom and dad when they returned from work. Katie told me it was exciting for her to be with her "sisters" because they went around together as a group and had fun.

Katie told me on many occasions she never thought she would survive a shooting. She said, if I get shot, I die. It doesn't matter anyway because I won't live past 21. Katie shared the attitude of many young people, especially young gang members. She had a huge, grotesque scar extending from the bottom of her neck to the top of her pubic area as a result of the multiple life saving surgeries she endured. It looked like something from a science fiction horror movie. The scar was so shocking that the prosecutor used a photograph of the injury instead of having Katie show the jury her wound in person. This also prevented Katie from being traumatized about showing 12 strangers something that was very embarrassing and private to her.

The gang member who fired the shots was captured within eight hours of the crime and he confessed to the shooting. He was tried and convicted on four counts of attempted homicide and special California gang enhancements. In California, as in many other states, victims of violent crimes have the right to address the court before sentencing in an attempt to persuade the judge to sentence the defendant to the maximum sentence allowed by law.

Katie was given this opportunity. Katie confided in me and the victim/witness advocate that she was afraid to go to court and talk. The whole shooting incident and trial had a profound effect on Katie. I realized that she was not only frightened but also weakened from the entire ordeal. I could tell that Katie was not strong enough to return to court to address the judge. Instead Katie wrote a statement and it was read into the court record.

Read Katie's statement and realize, as she did, that there are consequences to actions. Katie and I shared a lot about life and what is important and what is not. She taught me that sometimes surviving is harder than dying. Katie's recovery was difficult, long, complicated and painful. One day Katie finally confided to me that she wished she had died, because that way she would not have to go through all the pain while healing. Katie was an average teenager as far as desires, fears and hopes.

Katie wrote this describing her feeling and thoughts.

After I got shot at the mall it seemed like my whole life changed. It affected my life a lot. I became very weak. My eating habits changed. I am unable to go to regular high school and every time I see a gun I get scared.

I also get scared going places where there are many people because I am afraid something might happen again.

The scar on my stomach bugs me. I can't wear a bikini or a short shirt. I really hate that scar, I want it removed.

My used-to-be-friends call me Katie Bang Bang. It hurts me a lot. Everywhere I go people know me as the one who got shot at the mall. I want to be known as Katie_____.

Sometimes I wished I had died at the mall because now my life is really missed up. I always have nightmares about someone trying to shoot me. I feel really sad when I think back what happened. I could have died.

Phong_____ ruined my life. So I want to teach him a lesson not to go shooting at everyone. I really want him to be sentenced to life for what he did to me.

The Superior Court judge listened to Katie's statement in April 1994, just before Phong's sentencing. The judge handed down the sentence that morning. Now 18 year-old Phong would have to spend at least 64 years in state prison before his first parole hearing date. That would make him 82 years old before he would be eligible for parole, if he survived.

Katie and her family relocated to another state after the trial. Katie was still in much discomfort, but relieved somewhat, because Phong, the man who shot her would spend a considerable amount of time behind bars. Phong was the leader, or shot caller of a local Asian street gang. He was an excellent student and had very few contacts with law enforcement before this incident and no prior arrests. He did not wear traditional gang clothing and did not have a single tattoo.

In February 1996, Katie died as a result of complications she developed from her original gunshot injuries. Her family was devastated, as you would expect. Thousands of miles away, years later, Phong reached out and still took Katie's life. Another statistic to be recorded in the files, except this time, it was a lot more difficult for me. Katie had become a friend, not just another victim, and a number.

You cannot imagine how many more Katie's are out there. Gang violence has changed many lives, whether the injuries are fatal or not. As a country we have a whole sub-population of children and teenagers that are veterans of extreme violent acts committed by other young people. That alone should be enough to make everyone else take a stand and get involved.

Summary

Sadly, as have mentioned before many youth do not have a strong family unit to support them. This may not be their fault and these youth usually find a way to survive. The survival mechanism for some becomes street life, the life of a gang member. Don't forget many gang members view their gang as family and form strong psychological and emotional bonds to the group. These bonds are difficult to break, but not impossible.

The gang issues can be confronted if we ALL get involved. Everyone has something to give or offer. You do not have to have children to help. The children should be our nation's greatest asset because the future is with our children. The future is now.

Gangs and Corrections

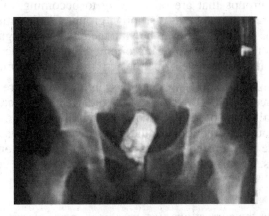

The growing incarcerated population has impacted the U.S. corrections system. Currently, this national population has increased, by some estimates, to over 2.2 million prisoners. It is well understood that disruptive and illegal activity is brought into correctional institutions from the streets. Adult and juvenile institutions are both affected. These criminal activities then return to the street with a highly educated offender. As a result prison gangs form within correctional institutions. These gangs attempt to control the criminal activity within the prison. At the same time prison becomes a college for young street gang members who aspire to become professional gang members.

History

It is a cycle that is well-known and yet very difficult to control. Working within the corrections system, parole and probation officers have become the monitoring group for those who are released back onto the streets. As the inmate population increases so does the parole and probation population. One impact of the growing custodial population has resulted in a case overload for probation and parole officers. It is estimated that by 2006, there will be over one-half million parolees on U.S. streets.

Since the mid 1960s, the Federal courts have scrutinized correction institutions. Today, nearly every prison system, Federal and State is under court order to correct inhumane conditions ranging from overcrowding to poor medical care. Without a doubt, court mandated changes have brought about a noticeable improvement in the correctional living environment. One focus of litigation has been how correctional institutions provide adequate protection for those who are incarcerated.

In several cases judicial intervention in the correctional process has stripped away some authority to handle problems within an institution. Along with these sweeping changes came a proliferation of gang members sentenced to State and Federal prisons. The increased in-custody gang population only strengthened the existing prison gangs and helped with the formation of new gangs. This forced the corrections system to develop an alternative way to handle problem inmates.

Strategic Threat Groups (STG) has become the current term that refers to the activity and subsequent problems associated with specific groups inside a prison. Everyone who is a validated member of a Strategic Threat Group is not necessarily a gang member or a prison gang member. The STG activities disrupt the normal prison operations and are directed at inmates and correctional employees, compromising institutional security. These activities can include assaults, murder, drug sales, sexual assaults and other criminal activity. Ultimately these activities tend to tear away at the security and safety of the institution and that is why the groups are monitored.

Some groups are formally recognized and validated by corrections officials and are known as prison gangs. Other groups that are on the way to becoming validated prison gangs or strategic threat groups are also known as disruptive groups. Their nature, level of activity and membership size has not qualified them to be validated as a prison gang. Sometimes, groups exist that are neither disruptive or prison gang oriented, but are a security problem. The term strategic threat group is also used to describe the activities of those inmates.

Strategic Threat Groups, Prison Gangs and Disruptive Groups are all dangerous. Many of the groups have influence in and out of prison. The corrections system is at a disadvantage because it has to house all types of street and prison gang members, many who are rivals with each other, in a closed housing situation. Candidly, where do you house everybody, keep a safe environment and provide the required services to the inmate population. Not an easy task. Yet, corrections professionals, day in and day out, attempt to provide a safe custodial environment.

Classification

As new inmates enter the corrections system, some type of classification process is needed to keep inmates safe. The classification process is sort of like a triage of the inmate. Special considerations are considered for medical, mental health reasons as well as gang affiliations.

Some correctional institutions in the country monitor gang activity and gang growth, but do not separate individual street gangs. Security measures and enforcement has worked well for these institutions. In other institutions, street rivalries are so intense that they are carried into the custodial environment. In some institutions separating gang members is part of procedure. Debriefing a new inmate should be done so that rival gang members are not put together. This helps insure inmate safety because rival gang members on the street could carry their gang rivalry with them into an institution.

The classification process can be as simple as asking gang affiliation or gang membership. Some classification processes are a little more detailed. These are done for institutional security purposes only. The inmate's safety and the overall safety of the institution may depend on these classifications. Gang inmate separations can and have prevented gang confrontations inside a jail or prison.

The classification process has been both an informal and formal part of the complete booking process. The information may be kept on a computer database or hard copy files. The information can be used to insure the safety of the inmate and staff by noting where rival gang members are, current status between rival gangs and the presence of new gangs.

Historically, disruptive activities in prisons were made by small groups of inmates. The number, type and nature of these disruptive activities have changed dramatically since the early 1960s. Many of these groups developed in response to geographical, ethnic, racial or ideological influences. As they grew in size, some of these groups formed institutional and community components. As gang members flooded the institution, gang related activity created an increasingly severe custodial management problem. The classification system was developed in an effort to try and control these problems.

Coincidently, law enforcement began to closely monitor these gang problems on the street in the late 1960s, about the same time correction administrators started to identify their disruptive influence.

Validation

There are several validation methods that are used by corrections officials. Validation is a process that confirms the existence of a particular group. The group can be classified as a disruptive group, prison gang or strategic threat group. The validation process can also identify particular inmates as members of that group. The nature of activity, size and type of group are a few of the distinguishing characteristics used for validation.

Some validation criteria will establish whether an inmate is member or associate of a particular group. The validation process will also give a census of the number of inmates involved, the size and types of groups that have formed. It can also serve as a database to track members of security threat groups within the U.S. prison systems.

Street Gangs

In the prison arena many gang members temporarily give up street rivalries. Most prison gangs are based on race. For example, many Hispanic street gang members would probably align themselves with the Mexican Mafia in California by becoming part of the Surenos. Outside the State of California Hispanic gang members in prison may align themselves with the same gang, the Surenos or a Hispanic based prison gang. Skinheads might align themselves with the Aryan Brotherhood or Nazi Low Rider prison gangs. It has been reported that some state correctional institutions do not house inmates based on racial separation. In some state correctional institution gang members from different gangs are house together.

Throughout the 1960s and 1970s, prison gangs focused primarily on uniting inmates for self-protection and monopolizing illegal prison gang activities to make money. The prison gangs combined the philosophies of street gangs and traditional organized crime families. At the same time, gang rivalries started to develop and fostered predatory and violent behaviors inside and outside of the institution. As the groups became larger and more organized, formal command and control structures were established. This organization was used to strengthen and groups ability to carry out its goals. Some prison based gangs established written rules and bylaws to operate their gang.

Most gangs recruit along racial and ethnic lines with membership being limited to males only. Female prison gangs may develop in the future, however, at the time of this writing there have been no reported female prison gangs within the United States. In a few instances females have claimed to be part of all male prison gangs, but this has never been seen as a growing trend.

In many cases, validated prison gang members are less of a management problem than individuals who are seeking formal gang membership. Sometimes referred to as wanna bes, these prison gang recruits are responsible for a large number of violent acts as they attempt to impress prison gang members with their ability to be ruthless and supportive of the group's activities.

By the 1980s, prison gangs had extended their influence beyond the prison walls. Many prison gangs established selective alliances with other prison gangs and street gangs in the community. These affiliations were motivated by the desire to expand illegal activities outside the prison, divide activities within the prison, to maximize drug profits and to avoid violent confrontations which might adversely affect a gang's power and profit margin. Interestingly enough, some groups may be rivals, but still conduct business together out of financial self-interest.

Juvenile Institutions

Juveniles who are incarcerated must have certain federally and state mandated benefits. Schooling, safety, security, dental, eye and medical care are just a few. Once in-custody, these wards of the Juvenile Court receive these benefits at no cost to them. The public, you and I must pay the costs. Therefore, budgets for juvenile detention facilities may seem proportionately higher than for other institutions. In reality, they are probably short of money.

Another factor about juveniles who are currently in-custody is that today is the belief that they are different than juveniles who were in-custody twenty years ago. The juvenile offenders of today are much more sophisticated, street wise and violent. Attacks on staff, once considered isolated incidents, are sadly much more common. Don't forget, we have a juvenile justice system that was founded on a rehabilitation philosophy. This was based on the assumption that most juveniles can be rehabilitated.

Probation departments still keep that goal in mind, however with the type of juvenile criminals the job is a lot harder. Because of serious over crowding issues, juveniles who committed minor offenses are rarely kept in custody. Alternative courts and sentencing seem to help. Deputy probation officers who carry active caseloads are still overwhelmed.

Some probation departments have specialty units, much like the police. Drug offender, sex offender and gang units can be found within these departments. This type of probation specialization will be more common in the future. Specialization and education will probably become pivotal for the future deputy probation officer. Probation departments, which have participated in collaborative efforts with local police, have also seen great success with police-prosecutor-probation combinations working extremely well together.

Because of safety issues, some deputy probation officers are now armed when on duty, particularly probation deputies assigned to gang units. Expertise in areas of gang customs and practices has allowed a few deputy probation officers to become co-affiants in search warrants and to testify as court experts.

There are three areas where the probation department plays a vital role in the correction system. First, the probation department is tasked with housing juveniles who are sentenced and are waiting court appearances or hearings. Secondly, the probation department also assists the juvenile court by preparing pre-sentencing and sentencing reports. These reports aid the magistrate in determining the appropriate sentence for a minor. Third, the probation department monitors grants of probation for juveniles who are out of custody. In certain jurisdictions, these probation grants include special gang terms. These terms might make it a probation violation for a convicted juvenile gang member to be around or socialize with other members of his gang, except of course, siblings or parents who might be members of the same gang.

The gang terms have been designed to prohibit certain behaviors that are related to gang membership. These special probation terms are imposed in an effort to help the probationer avoid violating the terms of his grant. Curfews, non-association, and the wearing of gang attire are frequently used.

Other areas where probations departments are heavily involved are research, house arrest programs, juvenile courts and alternative sentencing.

Juveniles Sentenced As Adults

Because of the degree of violence committed by the younger population, many juveniles are prosecuted as adults. When convicted of adult violations, these juveniles are sentenced to a state run institution. Most juveniles by law can be released by the time they are 21 or 24 years old. If they are not released, the young adults are then transferred to a state run prison for adults.

These institutions are operated in the same general manor as juvenile detention facilities. The same benefits are provided, but to an older juvenile population. Again, security of the inmates and staff is paramount and special precautions are taken not to mix rival gang members together. In these juvenile-adult institutions inmate populations often unite under ethnic or racial lines. Street rivalries between gangs are sometimes suspended because of this.

These types of institutions have also experienced a major population growth. The majority of new inmates being sentenced have been gang members and drug offenders. Street and prison gangs have also exerted their influence here. Often, young gang members sentenced to these types of institutions aspire to become career gang members. These wards are easily swayed and many times actively seek to join a custodial-based gang.

Like in some state prisons, juvenile wards have separated themselves by race or gang affiliation once inside a youth authority prison. On the outs, special parole officers will be assigned to monitor the young parolees. Gang member parolees, like their juvenile counterparts must adhere to strict rules and conditions of their parole. Many parole officers are armed. Both juvenile and adult parole offices may have specialty units to handle particular types of parolees. This may include sexual assault, substance abuse and gang caseloads.

Adults

The state prison system in any state is complicated and expensive to operate. Adult prison populations continue to grow. If this growth continues as the expected there is a predicted population explosion of 14 to 24 year olds that is expected to arrive and peak around 2006. With more adults in the judicial system you can expect adult corrections to be taxed. Don't forget that ad hoc studies suggest the majority of the country's gang population falls within this age group.

Gangs operate in the adult prison with reasonable freedom. They take advantage of legal loopholes to communicate and continue the illegal enterprises they are involved in. For example, if an inmate legally represents himself, it is called pro-per. Doing this allows the inmate to subpoena any other inmate as a witness for his court case. What happens is that a prison gang recruit will be asked to legally represent himself. This prison gang recruit will then subpoena other prison gang members from different correctional institutions as witnesses in his criminal case. The corrections system is then forced to transport the witnesses to the local county jail in the county where the criminal case is set. This way prison gang members are able to meet with each other to conduct gang business under the guise of being witnesses.

Even though subpoenaed witnesses are housed at different correctional institutions the state has to provide transport to court where the case is set. Sometimes prison gang members will attack another member for failing a task or not obeying the rules of conduct. In these cases, a pro-per inmate will subpoena a gang hit man or men as witnesses. The result will be an attack occurring in the local county jail.

Prison gang members can also be convicted of violating Federal laws, most commonly the RICO statues, weapons and drug violations. When this happens, they will serve time in Federal institutions. As a result some prison gangs have established themselves at the Federal corrections level in many states. A good example of this is the Mexican Mafia prison gang. The EME, as it is known has active members in Texas. In fact in March 1999 several members were tried and convicted for violating Federal RICO statues.

There are a few inter-state prisoner exchange programs that allow different states to share the custodial responsibilities of certain inmates. Inmates could possibly be transferred to other states to complete their sentence under this program. This transfer program can act as a migration mechanism for some prison gangs. For example, if a Mexican Mafia prison gang member were transferred from California to Montana, that gang member would attempt to start a faction of the Mexican Mafia in the Montana corrections system.

Community Influence

Prison gangs have formed and operated in the corrections system since the 1920s. Their nature or personality has changed with the growth in prison population. The impact of prison gangs on the community has also increased. Some experts believe that some prison gangs have attempted to control the activities of street gangs. By controlling the local street gangs, prison gangs can extend their drug markets, increase in size, strength and reputation.

There are many prison gangs with street gang counterparts. Larry Hoover, who is now in Federal prison, controls the Chicago area Black Gangster Disciples. The BGD street gang has a chain of command to follow, just like BGD prison gang. There are two distinct factions of the same gang, one operating on the streets, the other in the corrections system. Both are controlled by Hoover, who is like the CEO of then gang. There is even a board of directors for prison gang and street gang activities.

To help control the gang's community influence parole agents closely monitor gang member paroled inmates. These correction department officers play an essential role in this management model. Some parole offices have special units to monitor parolees who are street and/or prison gang members. Don't forget that a prison gang member is an at-will employee of the prison gang while out on parole. The prison gang member will continue to conduct prison gang business while on parole. Prison gang member parolees have been responsible for a number of attacks on witnesses, other prison gang members, rival prison gang members and street gang members. As one EME prison gang associate said of his gang, "It is like a murder incorporated."

Personal Safety

Personal safety issues for the corrections professional should not be over looked. On duty status includes, court, field and institutional work. Off duty status is defined by individual department regulations. Working with gang members within an institution presents some issues concerning staff or inmate safety and the security of the institution.

An assault can happen at any time. For example in January, 2005 a California State Prison guard working the Chino Institute for Men (CIM) was fatally stabbed by an East Coast Crip gang member while on duty. During the previous couple of years before the attack prison officials had been working a number of cases involving this gang where they had or planned to assault prison staff (Los Angeles Times, 2005).

In The Institution

Appropriate classification of inmates upon intake will certainly help decrease potential gang verses gang assaults within the facility. Knowledge of an incoming gang member's affiliation and housing area, along with the number and type of other gang members and their locations may assist in staff with inmate and staff protection. Inmates must adhere to institution procedures, policy and rules in order to keep the institution secure.

Doing your job professionally does not mean you cannot treat inmates with a little respect. This could have the same effect as treating out-of-custody gang members with a little respect. A rapport is sometimes built and that facilitates communications.

Communication with other staff members can also have an effect on over all security and safety. A shift briefing and debriefing is often used as a formal method of passing information from shift to shift. This way a review of shift activity and intelligence can be exchanged. Critiquing inmate and inmate-staff incidents may help prevent them from reoccurring.

Field Contacts

Contacting gang members in the field presents an entirely different set of safety issues for parole officers. Most if not all parole agents are armed however many deputy probation officers are not armed. Understanding that part of the focus of parole and probation is rehabilitation may allow a gang member to take advantage because they are master opportunists. If given a chance most gang members will take advantage of it. I am not advocating the arming of all probation deputies, just those who work with gang members.

I also advocate that parole agents and probation deputies never make house calls by themselves. I always recommend being backed-up by a uniformed police officer or sheriff's deputy. Family members and associates can present unexpected problems, not to mention the gang member being contacted.

When making house calls or working in the field, I also recommend that you only take what you need. Ladies do not take your purses unless they are kept with you. I would suggest not leaving personal valuables like case files, portable radios or other police equipment in the car. While you are busy making contact with your parolee or probationer peer gang members can burglarize your car. If you were not issued a department radio it would not hurt to have a cell phone turned on. I would suggest that it be pre-dialed with the local police dispatch number. In case of emergency, just press and send. It may not be a bad idea to call the local police dispatch to advise you will be making a home contact and give them the address. This implies that you will call them back when you leave to advise you are OK.

Off duty safety is just as important. Gang violence has a tendency to be random. So what exactly do you do if you are in a bank and a take over robbery happens? Would you act any different if you were with your child or spouse? What would you do with your criminal justice identification in a case like this?

Here is some food for thought. I am not saying be paranoid, just be safe. Know where you are at, pay attention to who is around you. Follow your instinct and use common sense and your head.

Summary

The corrections component of the criminal justice system is often forgotten. The reality is that the correction system experiences the same problems as society. The corrections system is part of an informal suppression model used to manage gang violence that includes law enforcement and the courts. Together, they comprise the criminal justice profession.

As prison overcrowding becomes more paramount, one suggested solution has been the early release of prisoners both at the county and state levels. The current national financial issue will have a trickle down affect. That affect will be funding. As funding sources dry up for corrections , so will inmate services, staffing and ultimately to the early release of inmates.

Bibliography

Aguirre, Alejandro (2001) Homicide Mortality in Latin America. College of Mexico. Presented at XXIV General Population Conference, Salvador, Brazil: August 2001

Aguilar, Silvia (2004) Statement made at a U.S. Army War College/ Florida International University (USAWC/FIU) conference entitled "New Security Threats in the Western Hemisphere" held in Washington, D.C.; The Center for Strategic and International Studies (CSIS) June 29, 2004

Alonso, Alex (unknown year) *Rollin 60s N-Hood Crip* also see: http://www.streetgangs.com/crips/rollin60s.html
Alonso, A (1999) Territoriality Among African American Street Gangs in Los Angeles. Unpublished Masters Thesis, Department of Geography, University of Southern California

Anti Defamation League (2009) Racist Skinhead Project. Also see: http://www.adl.org/racist_skinheads/states/california.asp

Anti Defamation League (2009)Racist Skinhead Project. Also see: http://www.adl.org/racist_skinheads/states/california.asp

Arciaga, M. (1998) Suburban Terrorists. The Animal Liberation Front and Straight Edge. 1998 Utah Gang Update Manual. Salt Lake City, Utah: Salt Lake Area Gang Project

Asbury, H. (1927) Gangs of New York. New York, New York: Capricorn

Associated Press (2009)Cartel Gangs Seep Into Houston March 8, 2009: http://www.chron.com/disp/story.mpl/ap/tx/6299933.html

Badley, James (1988) Dragons and Tigers. Loomis California: Palmer EnterprisesBenard, W. (1949) Jailbait. New York, New York: Greenberg

Barrett, Beth (2004) *Rollin 60s Give Unique Window Into Gang Culture.* Los Angeles Daly News. Thursday, September 30, 2004 also see: http://lang.dailynews.com/socal/gangs/articles/dnp5_culture.asp

Bennetto, J. (2003) Mobile, Lethal Caribbean Gangsters Swamp UK. The Independent Newspaper, November 3, 2003: http://www.rense.com/general44/swamp.htm

Beruman, Eric (2008).*The Juggalos*. Western States Information Network, Group of Interest Brief, June, 2008

Blatchford, C., (1996) FOX News investigative reporter, Los Angeles, personnel interview.

Blatchford, C.,(1999) FOX News investigative report on Daredevil Tagging.

Blatchford, Chris (2006) FOX News investigative report on Stanly "Tookie" Williams

Bing, Leon. (2005) Do or Die . New York, New York. Harper Collins Publishing

Bodell, Canaan (2003) *Declaration in Support of Plaintiffs Ex Parte Application For Order To Show Cause Re: Preliminary Injunction.* Los Angeles City Attorney's Office

Booth, Martin (1990) The Triads. New York, New York: St Martin Press

Bresler, Fenton (1981) Chinese Mafia. New York, New York: Stein and Day Publishing
Brown, W. (1980) Black Female Gangs in Philadelphia. International Journal of Offender Therapy and Comparative Criminology, 21, 221-228

Blatchford, Chris (1996) FOX News, Channel 11, Los Angeles investigative report on Sureno Gangs

Boser, Ulrich (2006) And Now Aryan Rap. U.S. News and World Report, January 23, 2006

Bowers, Faye (2006) "Why Mexico Helps U.S. Fight Terror" The Christian Science Monitor. January 26, 2006

Breve, Federico (2007) "The Maras- A Menace to the Americas" Military Review: pages 88-95: July-August 2007

Campbell, A. (1980) Friendships as a Factor in Male and Female Delinquency. Foot, H., Chapman, A. and Smith, J. (Eds) Friendships and Social Relations in Children. New York, New York: John Wiley

Bibliography

California Department of Justice (2002) PENI training seminar

California, State of (1997) Jamaican Criminal Groups in California. Sacramento, California: California Department of Justice

Campbell, A. (1990). Female Participation in Gangs. In Huff, C. (Ed.) Gangs in America: Diffusion, Diversity and Public Policy (pp. 163-182). Newbury Park, California: Sage Publications

Cantu, Jerry (2003) California Department of Health Services, Fraud Investigations, Memo on his debrief of Mr. Chino.

Cart, Julie (2006). Thieves and Vandals Put National Gem at Risk. Los Angeles Times Newspaper; August 28, 2006 Inland Empire Edition

Casa Aliancia (2006).

Cantu, Jerry (2003) California Department of Health Services, Fraud Investigations, Memo on his debrief of Mr. Chino.

Channel Five News(2006) Zeta Breaks Silence; June 6, 2006. www.informaworld.com/index/795362331.pdf

Charlton, Lee (2007) Militarization of the DTO's. Senior Intelligence /Research Specialist, DEA, San Diego: April 2007 debrief.

Christensen, L. (1994). Skinhead Street Gangs. Boulder, Colorado: Paladin Press

CIA (2009)World Factbook-Mexico. Population data also see: http://www.cia.gov/library/publications/world-factbook /geos /mx.html

Civilian Informant (2003), author interview, Norfolk, Virginia; October

Clawson, Jason (1995) Injunction *Declaration for PDL*. Los Angeles District Attorney's Office

CNN (2009) 20 Dead in Mexico Prison Riot, Official Says. March 5, 2009 www.cnn.com

CNN(2009) Senators Want To Fight Mexican Drug Cartels' Expanding Influence. CNN March 17, 2009

http://www.cnn.com/2009/POLITICS/03/17/mexican.drug.war/index.html

Coleman, Jennifer (2005) Report Forecasts Future of California's Population. Inland Valley Daily Bulletin. November 23, 2005

Cook, Colleen (2007) Mexico's Drug Cartels Congressional Research Service Report for Congress, October 16, 2007: RL34215

Conant, Eve and Campo-Flores, Arian (2009) The Enemy Within. Newsweek: March 23, 2009

Cooper, Anderson (2009) The War Next Door. 60 Minutes; March 3, 2009

Covarrubias, Amanda and Blankstein, Andrew (2006) Mom Drives, Sons Tag Police Say. Los Angels Times Newspaper, August 30, 2006 Inland Edition

Cardona, Julian (2009) Drug Gang Clash With Army Kills 21. Yahoo News; February 10, 2009

Cruz, Miguel (2007) Street Gangs in Central America, Centralamericana University, San Salvador, El Salvador

Cruz, Mike (2005) Handgun a Gang Member's Weapon of Choice. Inland Valley Daily Bulletin. December 3, 2005

Daily, W. (2000) Almighty Latin King Nation, National Alliance of Gang Investigators Association: http://www.nagia.org/Almighty_Latin_King_Nation.htm

Decker, S. and Van Winkle, B. (1996) Life in the Gangs: Family, Friends and Violence. Cambridge, UK and New York, New York: Cambridge University Press

Delgadillo, Angel (1994) Detective Sacramento Sheriffs Department, telephone interview.

Decker, S.H.(1996). Collective and Normative Features of Gang Violence. Justice Quarterly 13:243-264

Decker, S. and Van Winkle, B. (1996) Life in the Gangs: Family, Friends and Violence. Cambridge, UK and New York, New York: Cambridge University Press Dunn, William (2007) The Gangs of Los Angeles. Universe, Inc. Lincoln, Nebraska

Department of Justice. JICC Joint Intelligence Product, May 2007.

Department of Justice (2005) Los Zetas. U.S. Attorney's Office, Western District, Intelligence Bulletin: March 15, 2005.

DeVelasco, Edward and Valdez, Al (2006) collaborative unpublished analysis of law enforcement anecdotal evidence, Wichita, Kansas; July.

Doyle, G. and Belt, B. (1998) Upland Police Department (California) training

Dunn, Toby (2004) Phoenix, Arizona Police Officer, author interview; September

Economist, The (2006) Special Report: Criminal Gangs in America. January 7, 2006, p23

Economist, The (2009) On The Trail of Traffickers March 17-13, 2009, Volume 390,Issue8621

Ellingwood, Ken and Wilkinson, Tracy (2009) Drug Cartels' New Weaponry Means War. Mexico Under Siege, L.A. Times; March 15, 2009: http://www.latimes.com/news/nationworld/world/la-fg-mexico-arms-race15-2009mar15,0,229992.story

Emery, R. (unk. Year) From a Gangster Disciple to the Blue Print of Growth and Development, http://gangresearch.net/ChicagoGangs/BGD/bgdhistory.html

Epperson, C (2003) Sergeant Costa Mesa Police Department (California) expert testimony in a PENI criminal trial.

Escalante, Astor (2007) Vice Minister for Public Security and Justice. December 5, 2007 briefing to WOLA delegation; San Salvador, El Salvador

Federal Bureau of Investigation (2009) Crime in the United States -2006. Also see: http://www.fbi.gov/ucr/cius2006/data/table_01.html

Federal Bureau of Investigation (2007) El Paso members of the barrio Azteca Gang Using Encrypted Communications to Avoid Law Enforcement Detection. FBI El Paso Division; December 10, 2007

Federal Bureau of Investigation (1994) Vice Lord Nation Gang Profile, Washington D.C. Federal Bureau of Investigation (Freedom of Information request, redacted report)

Federal Bureau of Investigation (2004) The Latin Kings Gang Profile, Washington D.C. Federal Bureau of Investigation

Flaherty, Tim (2009) FBI agent telephone conversation June 4th, 2009

Forbes (2009) Joaquin Guzman-Loera- World's Billionaires. March 11, 2009: http://www.forbes.com/lists/2009/10/billionaires-2009-richest-people_Joaquin-Guzman-Loera_FSY.html

Fonce-Olivas, Tammy and Acosta, Gustavo (2006). (Teens Insist Party Crews Are Not Gangs). El Paso Times Newspaper, March 26, 2006 Edition

Frank, Marcus (1990) Sergeant Westminster Police Department, FOX News Interview, Los Angeles

Frank, Marcus (1988) Southeast Asian Gangs, California Asian Gang Investigator Conference, Anaheim, California; April

Franco, Celinda (2008) The MS-13 and 18th Street Gangs: "Emerging Transnational Gang Threats" CRS Report to Congress, January 30

Gangs Across America(2009) unknown author: also see www.gangsacrossamerica.com/profiles_bloods.php

George, J. and Wilcox, L. (1992). Nazis, Communists, Klansmen and Others on the Fringe, Buffalo, New York: Prometheus Books

Glazer, Andrew(2006) Black-Latino Gang Rivalries Send Summer Chill Through L.A. Inland Valley Daily Bulletin, San Bernardino County, California. August 13, 2006

Goldstein, A.P. and Huff, C.R. (Eds). (1993). The Gang Intervention Handbook. Research Press: Champaign, Illinois

Gonzalez-Wippler, M. (1992) Powers of the Orishas, Plainview, New York: Original Publications

Grace, J. and Hull, J. (1996) So Young to Kill, So Young to Die. Time Magazine, September 19, 1994

Bibliography

Grant, Christopher (2004)Native American Involvement in the Street Gang Subculture. Also see; http://www.knowgangs.com_resources/newsmenu/04mar/0304marnews_010.htm

Grizzard, M. (2004) Personal e-mail reference UBN gang member debriefing.

Gunst, L. (1995) Born Fi'Dead: A journey Through the Jamaican Posse Underworld. New York, New York: Henry Holt and Company

Guzman, Joseph, Sergeant Los Angeles County Sheriff Personal Interview, September 1995

Grayson, George (2008) Los Zetas: The Ruthless Army spawned By A Mexican Drug Cartel. Foreign Policy Research Institute. May 2008: www.fpri.org/enotes/200805.grayson.loszetas.html

Gregory, S. (1998). Black Corona: Race and the Politics of Place in a Urban Community. Princeton, New Jersey: Princeton University Press

Grossman, Dave.(1996) On Killing. New York, New York, Back Bay Books; Little Brown and Company

Guzman, Joseph (1992) Sergeant, Los Angeles County Sheriff, Hispanic Gang History, author Interview, Whittier, California; June

Harris, M. (1988) Culture, People, Nature: an Introduction to General Anthropology. (5th ed.) New York, New York: Harper and Row Publishing

Hatch, Sheila (2006) *Juggalos and Juggalettes*. King County Sheriff, King County, Washington Training Bulletin

Heim, Kelly (2003). 18th Street. MAGLOCLEN, Pennsylvania

HIDTA (2007) Barrio Azteca. Post Seizure Analysis Team (PSAT). Volume 6 Issue 8; August 2007

Hill, Karl G. Lui, Christina and Hawkins, David (2001). Early Precursors of Gang

Membership a Study of Seattle Youth. Bulletin. Washington, DC: U.S. Department of

Justice, Office of Justice Programs, Office of Juvenile Justice and Delinquency

Prevention.

History Channel(2009) Los Zetas. Towers Production, Gangland Series

http://www2.bc.edu/~brisk/korea.htm#Immigrants_in_the_United_States

http://asp.washingtontimes.com/printarticle.asp?action=print&articleID=20020824-58413998

http://www.americas.org/news/nir/20030801_flores_vows_action_on_gang_violence.asp

http://icasualties.org/Iraq/index.aspx

http://www.gripeforkids.org/BLhis.html

http://www.raddict.org/18th_Street

http://www.streetgangs.com/18thstreet.html

http://www.ispn.org/asg08107.html

http://en.wikipedia.org/wiki/Vietnam

http://davadnai.users.omniglobal.net/crips.html

http:www.streetgangs.com/history

http://en.wikipedia.org/Crips

http://en.wikipedia.org/Bloods

http://en.wikipedia.org/wiki/Skinheads

http://www.nizkor.org

http://www.splcenter.org/intel/news/item.jsp?sid=21

http://www.journals.apa.org/prevention/volume3/pre0030032a.html

http://www.dmusastore.com/Page.bok?template/=history

http://www.rainbownetwork.com

http://www.splcenter.org/intel/intelreport/article.jsp?aid=585

http://www.cgiaonline.org/gangs2000/white90s.html

http://skunklabel.com?english/200503skinhead.html

http://www.parapundit.com/archives/002648.html

http://www.adl.org/racist_skinheads/skinhead_groups.asp

http://www.adl.org/PresRele/NeoSK_82/4860_82.htm

http://www.at149st.com/glossary.html

http://en.wikipedia.org/wiki/Graffiti_terminolgy

http://www.theaustralian.news.com.au

http://at149st.com

http://en.wikipedia.org/wiki/Graffiti

http://en.wikipedia.org/wiki/Style_Wars

http://archives.cnn.com/2001/TECH/industry/04/19/ibm.guerilla.idg/index.html

http://www.casacolumbia.org/absolutenm/templates/ChairmanStatements.aspx?articleid=240&zoneid=
    31

http://thepioneer.com/international/jan19_youthgangs.htm

http://www.gangsorus.com/clothes1.html

http://www.hmdin.com/police/sdu/gangbook08.htm

http://www.expage.com/page/cripinfo

http://www.chmod-x.com/ccc/pubs/ganglist.html

http://gangsacrossamerica.com/profiles _tinyrascal.php

http://www.wikipedia.org/wiki/Tiny_Rascal_Gang

http://en.wikipedia.org/wiki/Skinheads

http://www.nizkor.org

http://www.splcenter.org/intel/news/item.jsp?sid=21

http://www.adl.org

http://www.dmusastore.com/Page.bok?template/=history

http://www.rainbownetwork.com

http://www.splcenter.org/intel/intelreport/article.jsp?aid=585

http://www.cgiaonline.org/gangs2000/white90s.html

http://skunklabel.com?english/200503skinhead.html

http://www.parapundit.com/archives/002648.html

http://www.adl.org/racist_skinheads/skinhead_groups.asp

http://www.adl.org/PresRele/NeoSK_82/4860_82.htm

http://www.gangsorus/prisongangs.html

http://www.brownpride.us/forum/forumdisplay.php?f=11

http://www.dc.state.fl.us/pub/gangs

http://www.tgia.net/Links/Information_Sites/Prison_Gangs/prison_gangs.html

http://www.chicagotribune.com/news/nationworld/chi-border_18mar18,0,1216683.story

http://www.en.wikipedia.org/wiki/Internet users

http://www.internetworldstats.com/stats.12.htm#central

http://thepioneer.com/international/jan19_youthgangs.htm

http://www.foreignpolicy.com/story/cms.php?story_id=2798

http://www.refugees.org/article.aspx?id=1933&subm=75&area=Participate&ssm=118

http://www.en.wikipedia.org/wiki/Federal_poverty_level

http://www.adl.org/hate_symbols/numbers 23.asp

http://www.americas.org/news/nir/20030801_flores_vows_action_on_gang_violence.asp

http://www.at149st.com

http://beyondheros2.tripod.com/jamaicanposse.htm

http://davadnai.users.omniglobal.net/crips.html

http://www.emergency.com/jamaica.htm

http://www.foxnews.com/story/0,2933,95447,00.html

http://www.homieunidos.or/newsandmedia/the%20tidings.htm

http://jamaica-gleaner.com/gleaner/20020225/lead/lead2.html

http://www.njsp.org/pro040804a.htm

http://www.washingtonpost.com/ac2/wp-dyn/A23901-2003Nov30

http://asp.washingtontimes.com/printarticle.asp?action=print&articleID=20020824-58413998

2020sxe.html at members.tripod.com

http:/www.usdoj.gov/usao/cac/pr2002/013.html

http://asp.washingtontimes.com/printarticle.asp?action=print&articleID=20020824-58413998

http://www.raddict.org/18th_Street

http://www.streetgangs.com/18thstreet.html

Huff, C. (1993) Gangs in the United States. In Goldstein, A. and Huff, C. (Eds.) The Gang Intervention Handbook. (pp. 310-317) Champaign, Illinois: Research Press

Immoos, H.(1998) Straight Edge unpublished manuscript

International Association of Chiefs of Police(2006) Human Trafficking Pamphlet: International Association of Chiefs of Police

ICE (2005) ICE Arrest 582 Violent Gang Members and Associates in Two Week Nationwide Enforcement Operation: August 1, 2005;see: www.ice.gov/pi/news/newsrelease/articles/050801washington.htm

Jankowski, M.(1991). Islands in the Street. University of California; Berkley

Jefferson, S. (2004) Ganginfo@lists.bigiron.com . December 15, 2004

Jensen, M.M. and Yerington, P.C. (1997). Gangs, Straight Talk, Straight Up. Longmont, Colorado: Sopris West Publishing

Johnson, Mary Helen (2006) "National Policies and Rise of Transnational Gangs" Migration Information Source, Migration Policy Institute: April 1 Johnson, Kevin (2009) ATF Takes Aim At Deep "Iron River" Arsenal. USA Today; March 19, 2009

Jones, Rick (2007) Catholic Relief Services, San Salvador, El Salvador Personal interview: December 4, 2007

Justice Intelligence Coordinating Council (2007) Barrio Azteca Gang: Evolution of a Criminal Enterprise. United States

Khalfani, Akil S. Batani (1996) Personal interview, San Diego, California

Kice, Virginia (2009) Removals By Country FY 2003-2008 (as of 11/10/2008) Immigration and Customs Enforcement, Laguna Nigel, California Office; March

Kim, Annie (2003)South Korea and Korean-Americans in the United States also see:

Kiser, Sheila (1999). STG Update. Georgia Parole Board

Klein, M.W. (1995) The American Street Gang. New York, New York: Oxford University Press.

Klein, M.W. (1971) Street Gangs and Street Workers. Englewood Cliffs, New Jersey: Prentice Hall

Klein, M.; Maxson, C. and Miller, J. (1995). Los Angeles, California: Roxbury Publishing Company

Lauritsen, J. (2003).How Families and Communities Influence Youth Victimization Bulletin.Washington, DC: U.S. Department of Justice, Office of Justice Programs, Office of Juvenile Justice and Delinquency Prevention.

LaVey, A.(1969) The Satanic Bible, New York, New York: Avon Books

Lefavor, John (2009) *Juggalos*. Paper presented at Mid Western Gang Investigator Association symposium, April 2, 2009.

Leyden, T.J. (2004) Know Gangs Conference presentation, Las Vegas, Nevada

Los Angeles Times (1998) The Twisted World of a "Straight Edge" Gang. January 7, 1998

Loftin, C. (1995). Assaultive Violence as a Contagious Social Process. Bulletin of the New York Academy of Medicine, 62:550-555

Logan, Sam (2007) Gangsters Without Borders. http://www.samuellogan.com/articles/US-gangsters-without-borders.html

Los Angeles County Probation Department and Youth Studies Center (1962) Study of Delinquent Gangs: Progress Report. Los Angeles, California. University of Southern California

Los Angeles Police Department (1961) Annual Report. Los Angeles, California

Love, Unknown (2009). Personal telephone call to 'Mr. Love' original member of the Devil Lane blood gang and subsequent member of the first generation of Pasadena Denver Lanes on June 24, 2009

MacHarg, Kenneth (2007) From Rio to the Rio Grande. Atlas Books, Ashland, Ohio ISBN: 978-958-8285-56-6

Major, Aline, Egley, Arlen, Howell, James, Mendenhall, Barbara and Armstrong, Troy (2004) Youth Gangs in Indian Country. U.S. department of Justice, OJJDP, Juvenile Justice Bulletin; March

Maldon Institute(2009) Los Zetas Structure. Memorandum to File, January 6, 2009. Washington, D.C.

Malinowski, Zachary (2008) Man Wounded in Providence Shooting. Rhode Island News, Providence Journal; February 7, 2008 also see www.projo.com/news/content/GANG_SHOOT_02-07-08_418TQ7L_V11.348721.HTM

Maltz, Derek (2006) Technology Obstacles for Law Enforcement. Special briefing to the Drugs and Dangerous Drugs Committee; International Association of Chiefs of Police: Boston, Massachusetts

Manzer, Tracy (2004) Gangs still Thriving in Neighborhoods. L.A. Daily News; September 26, 2004 also see http://lang.dailynews.com/socal/gangs/articles/Ibp1_gang1.asp

Manwaring, Max (2007). "A Contemporary Challenge to State Sovereignty: Gangs and Other Illicit Transnational Criminal Organizations in Central America, El Salvador, Mexico, Jamaica and Brazil" Strategic Studies Institute. U.S. Army War College, Carlisle, PA: December, 2007

Martin, Jeffrey (2003). *Declaration Rollin 60s Injunction*. Los Angeles County District Attorney's Office

Maxson, Cheryl (1998) Gangs on the Move. Office of Juvenile Justice and Delinquency Prevention, U.S. Department of Justice, Washington DC; Juvenile Justice Bulletin; October, 1998

McBride, Wes (1996) Personal interview, Los Angeles, California

McBride, W.(2000) Understanding Street Gangs. Incline Village: Copperhouse Publications

McBride, W.(2000) Understanding Street Gangs. Incline Village: Copperhouse Publications

McBride, Wes (2002), Author interview, Norfolk, Virginia, October

McCoy, Hank (2008) *Juggalo*. Fairfield Police Department, Fairfield, California: Training Bulletin

McDevitt, Katie (2008) *Fans or Gang: Meet the Juggalos*. East Valley Tribune, Scottsdale, Arizona ; July 27, 2008; also see http://license.icopyright.net/user/viewFreeUse.act?fuid+MzYxOTAzOA%3D%3D

Miller, R.K.(1990) Sergeant Huntington Beach Police Department, Training seminar.

Miller, J. (2001) One of the Guys: Girls, Gangs and Gender. New York, New York: Oxford University

Miller, Jody, Maxson, Cheryl and Klein, Malcolm (2001). The Modern Gang Reader(2nd Ed. Los Angeles, California. .) Roxbury Publishing

Mish, F. (ed.). (1996) Webster's Dictionary, Springfield, Massachusetts: Merriam-Webster, Inc.

Mohan, Geoffrey (2003) Tag This One Tough battle for Chief Bratton. Los Angeles

Bibliography

Times: April 14, 2003 Inland Empire Edition

Moser, C. and Holland, J. (1997) Urban Poverty and Violence in Jamaica, Washington, D.C.: World Bank, February

Moore, J. and Hagedorn, J. (2001). Female Gangs A Focus on Research. Bulletin. Washington, DC: U.S. Department of Justice, Office of Justice Programs, Office of Juvenile Justice and Delinquency Prevention.

Moore, J. and Terret, C. (1998) Highlights of the 1996 National Youth Gang Survey.

Tallahassee, Florida: National youth Gang Center

Moxley, Scott (2006) Baby Faced Hoodlums. OC Weekly: August 3, 2006 also see www.ocweekly.com/news/baby-faced-hoodlums/25593/

Mozingo, Joe (2006) Highland Park Trial Paints Landscape of Hate. Los Angeles Times, July 25, 2006

Murphy, Shelley (2006) Reputed Gang Members Arrested. Boston Globe September 7, 2006; also see www.boston.com/news/local/massachusetts/articles/2006/09/07/reputed_gang_members_arrested

Mungin, Lateef(2009) Mexican Drug Cartels Thrive in Suburban Atlanta. CNN March 19, 2009

http://www.cnn.com/2009/CRIME/03/19/atlanta.drug.cartels/index.html

Myer, Josh (2009) U.S., Mexico Blamed IN RISE of Drug Gangs. Chicago Tribune: March 18, 2009

Meyer, John (2009)730 in US Arrested in Cartel Probe. Los Angeles Times; February 26, 2009 L.A. Edition

Naim,Moises (2003) Five Wars of Globalization. Foreign Policy: January/February 2003. www.foriegnpolicy.com

National Drug Intelligence Center (2001) Drug Trafficking Organizations: California Northern and Eastern Districts Drug Threat Assessment: January, 2001 Unclassified Bulletin; also see www.usdoj.gov/ndic/pubs/653/meth.htm

National Drug Intelligence Center (2007) Drug Trafficking Organizations: New England High Intensity Drug Trafficking Areas (HIDTA): June, 2007 Unclassified Bulletin; also see www.usdoj/ndic/pubs23/23854/dtos.htm

National Drug Intelligence Center (2004) Barrio Azteca. Intelligence Bulletin, U.S. Department of Justice; October: Product number 2004-L0424-023

National Drug Intelligence Center (2005) Texas Syndicate Prison Gang. Intelligence Bulletin; September 2005 NDIC (2004) El Paso, Texas Port of Entry. Intelligence Bulletin, U.S. Department of Justice; May, 2004

National Drug Intelligence Center (2007) Drug Threat Overview. Houston High Intensity Drug Trafficking Area Drug Market Analysis: June 2007

National Drug Intelligence Center(2001) Drugs and the Internet. United States Department of Justice, Johnstown, Pennsylvania

National Alliance of Gang Investigators Associations (2005) "National Gang Threat Assessment" Bureau of Justice Assistance, U.S. Department of Justice; Washington, D.C.

National Youth Gang Center (2009) national youth Gang Survey Results also see: http://www.iir.com/nygc/nygsa/measuring_the _extent_of _gang_probelms.htm

National Committee on Political Tribalism (1997) Report on the National Committee of Political Tribalism. Kinston, Jamaica: Government of Jamaica

National Drug Intelligence Center, National Street Gang Survey Report-1998, NDIC, Johnstown: 1998

National Youth Gang Center (2000) National Youth Gang Survey. Washington D.C. U.S. Department of Justice, Office of Justice Programs, Office of Juvenile Justice and Delinquency Programs

Nelson, J. (2004) Straight Edge XXX. 2004, Utah Gang Update Manual. Salt Lake City, Utah: Salt Lake Area Gang Project

New Jersey, State of (1989) State of New Jersey Commission of Investigation 1989 Report. New Jersey: New Jersey Attorney General's Office

New York Times (1984) *Two Gang Members Arrested in Alexander Family Killings*. API News, Novembern5, 1984, also see:
http://nytimes.com/1984/us/1105/two-gang-members-arrested-in-alexander-killings.html

New York Times (2004) Shuttling Between Nations, Latino Gangs Confound the Law. September 26, 2004

Nguyen, Long, (2001) Orange County District Attorney Investigator, Author Interview; Santa Ana, California, June

Nguyen, Long, (2002) Orange County District Attorney Investigator, Personal Interview

Nguyen, Long, (2004) Orange County District Attorney Investigator, Personal Interview

Nunn, Sylvia (2009) personal telephone conversation June 23, 2009 on Denver Lane Bloods and Pasadena Denver Lane Blood gangs. Sylvia was a member and co-leader of Lueders Park Piru

Nye, Mark (1992) Sergeant Westminster Police Department, Personal Interview

Nye, Mark (2004) Smile Now, Cry Later. Utah Gang Conference paper

Office of Juvenile Justice and Delinquency Prevention (2006). Highlights of the 2004 National Youth Gang Survey. OJJDP Fact Sheet, April 2006. U.S. Department of Justice, Office of Justice Programs, Office of Juvenile Justice and Delinquency Prevention. Washington D.C.

Office of Juvenile Justice and Delinquency Prevention (2000). National Youth Gang Survey. U.S. Department of Justice, Office of Justice Programs, Office of Juvenile Justice and Delinquency Prevention. Washington D.C.

Orange County Register, October 9, 1993

Orange County District Attorney (2003) Annual Gang Report. Santa Ana: District Attorney Publications

Orange County District Attorney (2002). Annual Gang Report. Santa Ana: District Attorney Publications

Orange County District Attorney (2001). Annual Gang Report. Santa Ana: District Attorney Publications

Orange County District Attorney (2001). Annual Gang Report. Santa Ana: District Attorney Publications

Osman, K. (1992), Gangs, San Diego, California: Lucent Books

Papachristos, Andrew (2005) Gang World. Foreign Policy: March/April 2005. Also see:
www.foriegnpolicy.com

Payne, D. (1998) The 1997 Jamaica Elections: Post Election Report. Washington, D.C.: Center for Strategic and International Studies, January 21st

Perkins, U. (1987) Explosion of Chicago Street Gangs. Chicago, Illinois: Third World

Peterson, D., Miller, J. and Esbensen, F. (2001) The Impact of Sex Composition on Gangs and Gang Member Delinquency. Criminology 39(2), 411-439

Pickard, Miguel (2005) In the Crossfire: Mesoamerican Migrants Journey North, October 18, 2005, General Directorate of Migration of the Secretary of the Interior and Justice of Honduras.

Ponce, Carlos (2009) Conference on Central American Gangs, Indiana State University, Indiana; April 2.

Potter, G.W. (unknown year) Transnational Criminal Organizations. Criminal Justice and Police Studies, Eastern Kentucky University,
http://www.policestudies.eku.edu/POTTER/International?Jamaican.htm

Quicker, J.(1983) Homegirls: Characterizing Chicano Gangs. San Pedro, California: International University Press

Ribinson, C. (1997)Black Movements in America. New York, New York. Rutledge Press

Ridgeway, James (1990) Blood in the Face. Thundermouth Press, New York

Rodriguez, Rey (2009) Army Desertions Hurting Mexico's War on Drugs. CNN, March 13, 2009

Ross, Victor (2003) *Injunction Declaration for Bounty Hunters.* Los Angeles County District Attorney's Office

Ross, Victor (2009) Personal telephone conversation regarding Bounty Hunters and PDL gangs; June 22, 2009

Ruiz, Mona, Two Badges, The Lives of Mona Ruiz.(1997). Houston: Arte Publico Press

Russ, Christopher (1995) *Injunction Declaration for PDL.* Los Angeles County District Attorney's Office

Sample, Steven (2008) Los Angeles: The Capital of the Pacific Rim. Address to the World Affairs Council; November 10, 2008, Los Angeles, California

Sanchez, Alex (2008) Homies Unidos: Personal conversation February 8, 2008, University of California, Irvine, symposium on Youth and Transnational Policy

Sandoval, Edna (2009) Personal interview, Northern Baja, Mexico: January 31, 2009

San Pedro, Emilio (2009) Tijuana: In The Cartel's Shadow. BBC Radio 4's Crossing Continents: February 26, 2009   http://newsvote.bbc.co.uk

Savelli, L. (2000) Introduction to East Coast Gangs. National Alliance of gang Investigators Associations, http://www.nagia.org/east_coast_gangs.htm

Savelli, L. (2000) Introduction to East Coast Gangs. National Alliance of gang Investigators Associations, http://www.nagia.org/east_coast_gangs.htm

Schmidt, Ken (2003) *Injunction Declaration for Bounty Hunters.* Los Angeles County District Attorney's Office

Simandle, J (1992) Chicago Gangs, National Youth Task Force seminar, Washington D.C.

Seelke, Clair (2008) "CRS Report for Congress: Gangs In Central America" Congressional Research Service, Washington, D.C.: January 11, 2008

Seper, Jerry (2009) Soldiers Cross Into U.S., Hold guns To Agent. Washington Times Newspaper: August 6, 2008

Shakur, Sanyika. (1993) The Autobiography of an L.A. Gang Member. New York, New York. Penguin Books

Simpson, Colton. (2005) Inside the Crips . New York, New York. Saint Martins Press

Smith, Peggy and Kent, Douglass (1995) The Westminster Police Department TARGET Gang Unit Report. Westminster Police Department, Westminster, California

Spear, A. (1967) Black Chicago: The Making of Negro Ghetto (1890-1920). Chicago, Illinois: University of Chicago Press

Spergel, I. (1995). The Youth Gang Problem. New York, N.Y.: Oxford University Press

Stallworth, Ron, (1991) Sergeant, Salt Lake Area Gang Task Force, Salt Lake City Gangster Rap paper presentation.

Starbuck, D., Howell, J. and Lindquist, L. (2001). Hybrid and Other Modern Gangs. Bulletin. Washington, DC: U.S. Department of Justice, Office of Justice Programs, Office of Juvenile Justice and Delinquency Prevention.

Spergel, I. (1964) Racketvill, Slumtown, Haulberg. Chicago, Illinois: Oxford University Press

Sullivan, John P and Bunker, Robert (2006) Maras Morphing; Revisiting Third Generation Gang. Global Crime. Volume No. 7: August-November 2006 (pp 487-504)

Sullivan, J. P. and Bunker, R. J. (2003) "Drug Cartels, Street Gangs, and Warlords," in Robert J. Bunker, ed., Nonstate Threats and Future Wars, London: Frank Cass

Sully, Jim (1990) Filipino Street Gangs. Los Angeles County Sheriff Department

Teran, Sandra (2006) Canada Immigration Services, personal conversation

Texas Department of Corrections and Justice (2007) Texas Gangs: An Overview of Security Threat Groups and Other Major Gangs in Texas. Criminal Intelligence Service. July

Thale, Geoff (2008) Remarks made at the University of Southern California, January 23, 2008

Thrasher, F.M. (1927). The Gang, a Study of 1,313 Gangs in Chicago. Chicago, Illinois: University of Chicago Press

Thompson, Phillip (2003) *Injunction Declaration for Bounty Hunters.* Los Angeles County District Attorney's Office

Time Magazine (2008) Remittances. May 19,2008

Time Magazine, September 18, 1995

Time Magazine, October 9, 1995

Time Magazine, November 6, 1995

Thrasher, F.M.(1927). The Gang-A Study of 1,313 Gangs in Chicago. Chicago, Illinois: University of Chicago Press

Tita, George and Abrahamse (2004). Gang Homicides in L.A. 1981-2001. Sacramento, California. California Attorney General's Office. Crime and Violence Prevention Center

Tyson, A. (1996) How Nation's Largest Gang Runs Its Drug Enterprise Christian Science Monitor, July 15, 1996

U.S. Homeland Security (2006) Yearbook of Immigration Statistics:2004. Washington, D.C., U.S. Department of Homeland Security, Office of Immigration Statistics

U.S. Department of Justice (2009) Criminal Street Gangs in the United States. Gang Unit, also see: http://usdoj.gov/criminal/gangunit/about/usgangs.html

U.S .Department of Justice, Office of Justice Programs, Office of Juvenile Justice and Delinquency Prevention (October, 1998).

U.S. News and World Report, August 1, 1994

U.S. News and World Report, September 18, 1995

U.S. News World Report, November 13, 1995

U.S. News and World Report February 12, 1996

U.S. News and World Report, February 19, 1996

U.S. News and World Report, March 25, 1996

Valdez, Al (2007) Gangs, A Guide to Understanding Street Gangs.4th Edition Law Tech Publishing, San Clemente, California

Valdez, Al (2007) Gangs Across America. Law Tech Publishing, San Clemente, California

Valdez, Al (2007) Author Interviews with MS-13 and 18th Street gang members at Projecto Victoria, Tegucigalpa, Honduras: December 4, 2007

Valdez, Al (2000) Author Interview, Witness party crew murder trial, Santa Ana, California January

Valdez, Al (2005) HIDTA presentation, San Jose, California

Valdez, Al (2006) North Carolina Juvenile Officers Association presentation, Virginia Beach, North Carolina Valdez, A. (2000) Occult and Ritual Crimes, Santa Ana, California, Orange County Sheriff Department, Class manual 8 hour occult crime class

Valdez, A. (2002). A High Tech Spin on Counterfeiting. Police Magazine. December 2002. Bobit Publications: Torrance, California.

Valdez, A. (2003). Mara Salvatrucha History, Virginia Community Policing Institute Training, Virginia

Valdez, Al (2009) *Rollin 60 Crips, Denver Lane Blood, Pasadena Denver Lane and Bounty Hunter State Survey.* Unpublished manuscript based on an Internet informal survey for gang presence June, 2009.

Valdemar, Richard (1990). Sergeant Los Angeles County Sheriff (retired) author interview, Anaheim, California; June

Valdemar, R. (1996) Sergeant L.A. County Sheriff, Retired; Personal interview, Fullerton, California

Vaughan, Jessica and Feere, Jon (2008) Taking Back the Streets: ICE and Local Law Enforcement Target Immigrant Gangs. Center for Immigration Studies; Backgrounder: October, 2008

Bibliography

Vigil, Diego (1993). The Established Gangs. The Origins and Impact of Contemporary Gangs in the United States, ed. Scott Cummings and David J. Manti. Albany: State University of New York p.99-100

Vigil, James Diego (2001)Barrio Gangs: Street Life and Identity in Southern California In; Jody Miller et al The Modern Gang Reader: Los Angeles: Roxbury Publishing Company (pp22-31).

Vittori, Jodi (2006). The Gang is All Here; The Globalization of Gang Activity. University of Denver research paper, Department of the Air Force. C104-1748

Vogel, Chris (2007) Gang Lite. Houston Press. August 16, 2007; www.houatonpress.com/2007-08-16/news/ganglite

Williams, Stanley. (1998) Life in Prison, San Francisco, California. Sea Star Books

Wolcott, Holly (2002) Tough Graffiti Sentence May Send a Message. Los Angeles Times Newspaper; September 10, 2002, Inland Empire Edition

Williams, D. (1992) Occult Investigation, Mid-Western Gang Investigators Association

Training Conference, Cleveland, Ohio

Wisenbaler, Ed (2007) Tango Blast: Houstone. Texas Department of Corrections and Justice, Power point presentation

World Bank, Violence and Urban Poverty in Jamaica: Breaking the Cycle. Washington, D.C.: World Bank, January

Winton, Richard and Krikorian, Michael (2004) *41 Arrested in Police Sweep Through Nickerson Gardens*. Los Angeles Times, January 22, 2004 also see: http://www.streetgangs.com/topics/2004/012204bhraid.html

www.ispn.org/asg08107.html

www.wikipedia.or/wiki/List_of_California_street_gangs

www3.tky.3web.ne.jp/~edjacob/bloodbaths.htm

www.cgiaonline.org/gangs2000/asian90s.html

www.pbs.org/wnet/wideangel/shows/elsalvador/handbook.html